TRANSTOPIA IN THE SINOPHONE PACIFIC

Transtopia in the Sinophone Pacific

Howard Chiang

Columbia University Press

New York

Columbia University Press
Publishers Since 1893
New York   Chichester, West Sussex
cup.columbia.edu
Copyright © 2021 Columbia University Press
All rights reserved

Library of Congress Cataloging-in-Publication Data
Names: Chiang, Howard, 1983– author.
Title: Transtopia in the Sinophone Pacific / Howard Chiang.
Description: New York : Columbia University Press, [2021] |
Includes bibliographical references and index.
Identifiers: LCCN 2020032449 (print) | LCCN 2020032450 (ebook) |
ISBN 9780231190961 (hardback) | ISBN 9780231190978 (trade paperback) |
ISBN 9780231549172 (ebook)
Subjects: LCSH: Transsexuals—China—History. | Transgender people—
China—History. | Gender nonconformity—China—History. |
Gender identity—China—History. | Queer theory.
Classification: LCC HQ77.95.C6 C45 2021 (print) | LCC HQ77.95.C6 (ebook) |
DDC 305.30951—dc23
LC record available at https://lccn.loc.gov/2020032449
LC ebook record available at https://lccn.loc.gov/2020032450

For my parents and Hao-Te
And in memory of Yeh Yung-chih

Contents

Illustrations

Acknowledgments

Every book has an origin story, and this one is no exception. One of the earliest moments when I realized that my approach to history has been crippled by the available categories can be traced to the way *Transgender China* (New York: Palgrave Macmillan, 2012), the first book I edited, was received. Specifically, some Anglophone readers criticized the ways in which the term *transgender* was used to describe a range of phenomena in Chinese culture that they did not deem sufficiently genuine to the concept as it is understood in the West. Many of the examples discussed in *Transgender China* were simply not "trans enough" for these readers. For a field that was just beginning to acquire shape and foundation, I was surprised by the degree of boundary policing imposed by its interlocutors. Perhaps I should not have felt so dismayed, but those reactions pushed me to think harder about the promise and limitations of transgender discourse.

There was a subsequent episode that led me to rethink my approach to trans studies. In 2016, I was invited to talk about transgender issues at a workshop on marriage and the family in China. In a room full of (presumably straight) sociologists and demographers, my paper met an enthusiastic and supportive response from the group. There was one question that caught me off-guard, though, and has left a legacy on my thinking over the years. One senior participant asked me to provide a quantitative estimate of the number of trans people in the country. I could sympathize with the interest in such statistical measures in social science, especially in terms of their function as an aggregate indicator at the population level. But as a historian of sexology, I was deeply suspicious of such numerical measures and the practicality of acquiring them. Apart from the notorious difficulty with definition and sampling, Chinese academia remained—and remains—extremely hostile to lesbian and gay studies, let alone transgender research. More importantly, queer theory has taught me to challenge a purely minoritarian conceptualization of variance.

If the critical reception of *Transgender China* raised the question of what a non-Western perspective can bring to the study of "transgender," my experience at the workshop convinced me of the need to reorient the way transness and queerness are understood in the field of Asian studies. This book coins *transtopia* as a neologism in order to peel back the layers of cross-cultural politics in antitransphobic inquiry. In the journey of developing this new rubric, I have been blessed with the company of Hongwei Bao, Ari Heinrich, Benjy Kahan, Alvy K. Wong, Lily Wong, and Shana Ye. Hongwei and Benjy, in particular, read the entire manuscript and offered prescient suggestions on how to make it better. Like them, Ari, Alvy, Lily, and Shana responded to my multiple last-minute queries with plentiful patience and advice. I am also grateful for the rich dialogues and exchanges with Adam Dedman, John Erni, Jun Pow, E. K. Tan, Linh Vu, James Welker, and Alan Michael Williams. They engaged with various parts of the manuscript at different stages of the writing process.

Since graduate school never taught me how to write a second monograph, my appreciation of the friends and colleagues in my academic network has grown exponentially by day. My intellectual and spiritual debt accumulated over the years as I became increasingly reliant on that network for writing this book. In the course of researching and completing this study, I learned boundlessly through conversations with Shu-mei Shih on Sinophone theory, Susan Stryker on trans historicism, and Helen Hok-Sze Leung on queer Sinophone films. Observant readers will find the footprints of Shu-mei, Susan, and Helen throughout the book. The introduction of the book benefited enormously from the feedback of Gabrielle Bychowski, Angelina Chin, and Leah DeVun. Chapter 1 could not have been written without the meticulous input of Laura Doan, Alexa Huang, Ryan Jones, Leila J. Rupp, and Katie Sutton. I thank Ta-wei Chi, Hoching Jiang, and Mark McConaughy for their helpful comments on the early drafts of chapter 2. They pointed out blind spots and suggested useful ways to overcome the gaps in my conceptualization of queer Sino-phone studies. My thinking on queer archiving has been shaped by the scholarship and guidance of Anjali Arondekar, Kevin P. Murphy, Carolyn Steedman, and Zeb Tortorici. Chapter 4 is the product of a series of discussions on the theoretical advancement of Sinophone studies with Andrea Bachner, Brian Bernards, Yu-lin Lee, Jin Park, Carlos Rojas, Shuang Shen, Chien-hsin Tsai, and David Der-wei Wang since 2014. My approach in chapter 5 is inspired by the work of Celina Tzu-Hui Hung and John Smolenski, both of whom offered tireless counseling on the theory, history, and anthropology of creolization. Laura and Leila read and assisted with honing the conclusion at the eleventh hour.

Many friends and colleagues engaged with me and my ideas in different phases of this project. Appreciation is due to the following esteemed individuals: Hanadi Al-Samman, Bridie Andrews, Ien Ang, Tani Barlow, Emily Baum, Chiara Beccalossi, Chris Berry, Amy Brainer, Francesca Bray, Susan Burns, Peter Carroll, Shelly Chan, Antonia Chao, Hsiu-fen Chen, Mian Chen, Wei-Jhen Chen, Yi-Chien Chen, Hsiao-wen Cheng, Jih-Fei Cheng, Jens Damm, John DiMoia, Rebecca Ehrenwirth, Elisabeth Engebretsen, Marc Epprecht, Harriet Evans, Jennifer Evans, Sara Friedman, Veronika Fuechtner, Takashi Fujitani, Ting Guo, Marta Hanson, Douglas E. Haynes, Dan Healey, Wai-Siam Hee, Todd Henry, Dagmar Herzog, Derek Hird, Guo-Juin Hong, Yu-Ying Hu, Clara Iwasaki, Lucetta Kam, Dredge Kang, Ying-Chao Kao, Jane S. Kim, Travis Kong, Tong Lam, Joyman Lee, Victoria Lee, Sean Hsiang-lin Lei, Angela Ki Che Leung, Ping-hui Liao, Wes Xiaodong Lin, M. Antonio Lizada, Tamara Loos, Christopher Lupke, Nathan Madson, Jen Manion, Fran Martin, Keith McMahon, Leisa Meyer, Joanne Meyerowitz, Durba Mitra, Izumi Nakayama, Hoang Tan Nguyen, Hsiao-yen Peng, Ronald Po, Don Romesburg, Tze-lan Sang, Amy Sueyoshi, Margaret Schotte, William Schroeder, Kyle Shernuk, Emily Skidmore, Soyoung Suh, Eric Tagliacozzo, Denise Tang, Hsiu-ping Tseng, Jing Tsu, Charles Upchurch, Andy Chih-Ming Wang, Chun-yen Wang, Chunchi Wang, Hsiu-Yun Wang, Yin Wang, Chia-ling Wu, Chao-Jung Wu, Harry Wu, Weiting Wu, Yi-Li Wu, Dominic Meng-Hsuan Yang, Jonathan Te-hsuan Yeh, Audrey Yue, and Jamie Zhao.

Although I have presented fragments of this study at numerous venues and gatherings, a few of them served as a catalyst for what was to become *Transtopia in the Sinophone Pacific*. The first time I proposed the main idea behind this project occurred at "Sinophone Studies: An International Research Workshop" at New York University, Shanghai, in August 2016. I thank Celina Hung for organizing the event and inviting me to participate in it; I am also indebted to Yuting Huang's extensive feedback both during and after the workshop. I circulated an early draft of chapter 4 at the Toronto-based Critical China Studies Working Group in February 2018. I am grateful for the feedback of Joshua Fogel, Zhipeng Gao, Joan Judge, Noa Nahmias, Shana Ye, and other participants of the seminar. I delivered a preliminary version of chapter 1 at the Cross-Cultural Women's and Gender History Colloquium at the University of California, Davis (May 2018), and the History of Sexuality Seminar at the Institute of Historical Research, the School of Advanced Study in the University of London (May 2019). I thank Quinn Javers and Jana Funke for chairing my presentations and the thoughtful conversations that followed over coffee and dinner. Chapter 2 was first conceived as a Henry J. Leir Chair Lecture delivered at Clark University in September 2018. This was made possible through Robert Tobin's generous invitation, which encouraged me to develop an early draft of the chapter. I presented a more polished version of the same chapter at the landmark "Sinophone Studies: Interdisciplinary Perspectives and Critical Reflections" conference organized by Shu-mei at UCLA in April 2019. In that same year, I gave a systematic discussion of the concept of transtopia twice at Stanford University: the first time as part of the Feminist/Queer Colloquium at the Stanford Humanities Center and the second time as part of the Trans History Lecture Series in the Department of History. I thank Alexis Bard Johnson, Laura Stokes, and Matthew Sommer for their warm hospitality. My colleague Omnia El Shakry expressed enthusiastic support toward the theoretical underpinnings of my work when she attended the Stanford Humanities Center event. The Graduate Institute of Taiwan Literature and Transnational Cultural Studies at National Chung Hsing University has invited me to present my work related to this project on multiple occasions, and I am fortunate to have taught the full manuscript of this book for the first time there as part of the graduate seminar on Sinophone studies in December 2019. The colleagues there deserve special mentioning for their friendship in the last decade: Kuo-wei Chen, Huei-chu Chu, Kuei-fen Chiu, Chia-li Kao, Dominique Liao, and Min-xu Zhan. I thank the participants at all of these venues for their perceptive questions and suggestions.

My heartfelt thanks also go to the extraordinary group of colleagues at the University of Warwick, the University of Waterloo, and the University of California, Davis. Above all, I would like to thank Ali Anooshahr, Maxine Berg, Beverly Bossler, Blaine Chiasson, Corrie Decker, Edward Ross Dickinson, Rebecca Earle, Michael Foster, Sarah Hodges, Ari Kelman, Jennifer Liu, Omnia El Shakry, Ross Forman, Anne Gerritsen, Daniel Gorman, Anna Hájková, Geoffrey Hayes, Wendy Ho, Quinn Javers, Kyu Hyun Kim, Greta Kroeker, Heather MacDougall, Lisa Materson, José Juan Pérez Meléndez, Jane Nicholas, Giorgio Riello, Susan Roy, Marian Schlotterbeck, Karl Schoonover, Laura Schwartz, Xiaoling Shu, John Smolenski, Rachel St. John, Carolyn Steedman, Daniel Stolzenberg, Michiko Suzuki, Lynne Taylor, Mathew Thomson, Cecilia Tsu, Charles Walker, Charles Walton, Louis Warren, and Li Zhang. Without their steadfast support in the last few years, the completion of this monograph would be inconceivable. I have also learned vastly from the students in my graduate seminar, "Global Intimacies," taught at Waterloo and UC Davis.

I am especially grateful for the encouragement and professionalism of Caelyn Cobb, my editor at Columbia University Press. Caelyn's belief in the project and unwavering support along the way have made the writing of this book a pleasurable and meaningful experience. The assistance of Miriam Grossman and Monique Briones merits recognition for having shepherded the manuscript into print. The detailed reports of the two readers, at both the proposal and the full submission stages, were filled with keen insights and scrupulous recommendations for revision. I cannot thank all of these individuals enough for nourishing the book into what it has become. Any remaining flaws in this work are entirely of my own doing.

Over the years this project received generous funding from many sources: a Templeton "Science and Religion in East Asia" Project Visiting Fellowship at Seoul National University; research grants from the Centre for the History of Medicine, the Department of History, the Humanities Research Centre, and the Global History and Culture Centre at the University of Warwick; a Start Up Grant at the University of Waterloo; a Start Up Grant, two Small Grants in Aid of Research, and three Research Travel Grants at the University of California, Davis; and a Multicampus "Transgender Studies Working Group" Grant from the University of California Humanities Research Institute.

All translations from foreign sources are my own except where noted. East Asian names are given in the customary order, with family name preceding personal name. In general, the book follows the Pinyin system per scholarly convention in the United State, but I use other transcriptions if they are common, for example, in some names. In this study, I use LGBT (lesbian, gay, bisexual, and transgender) and LGBTQ (queer) interchangeably.

Earlier versions of parts of chapters 3, 4, and 5 originally appeared in "Archiving Peripheral Taiwan: The Prodigy of the Human and Historical Narration," *Radical History Review*, no. 120 (2014); "Sinoglossia Incarnate: The Entanglements of Castration Across the Pacific," in *East Asian Men: Masculinity, Sexuality, and Desire*, edited by Xiaodong Lin, Chris Haywood, and Mairtin Mac an Ghaill (New York: Palgrave Macmillan, 2016); and "Intimate Equality and Transparent Selves: Legalising Transgender Marriage in Hong Kong," *Culture, Theory and Critique* 58, no. 2 (2017).

Last but not least, gratitude is due to my family for their support. Writing a book is a selfish feat. I remain astonished by how my parents, Hui-Min Chiang and Mei-Fang Yang, put up with my radical departure from their traditional views and how my husband, Hao-Te Shih, tolerates my endless demands for solitary moments. I am lucky to share my life with someone who is willing to see me through this task yet again, after *After Eunuchs*.

At the same time, this acknowledgment would be incomplete without mentioning the tragedy of Yeh Yung-chih, whose death in April 2000 drew national attention in Taiwan and continues to serve as a reminder of how little we have accomplished and how much more we can do in the Sinophone world and beyond. The experience of Yeh, a teenage victim of a transphobic hate crime, and its historical significance are unpacked in greater depth in the last chapter of this book. Suffice it to say here that the core concept of this study, transtopia, is in many ways inspired by his story, because there is simply no existing category of gender and sexuality that best describes Yeh. This book is dedicated to others like him, like us, who struggle with different mechanisms of power and coercion, gendered and sexualized, threating and oppressive to the most quotidian way imaginable, but often brushed aside for their seemingly organic presence.

Introduction

Queering History from the Sinophone Pacific

A t the inaugural Queer History Conference (QHC19), held on June 16–19, 2019, at San Francisco State University, I found myself tuning out during gripping presentations.[1] My inability to concentrate arose in part from knowing that I chaired the only panel on Asia.[2] Yet something else drew my attention. Off and on, my mind was carried away by what was happening on the other side of the world: the antiextradition bill protests in Hong Kong, which began in March but persisted into the following year.[3] The protests were a series of demonstrations against the Fugitive Offenders and Mutual Legal Assistance in Criminal Matters Legislation (Amendment) Bill coercively imposed by the Hong Kong government. Prodemocracy activists and lawyers worried that its passing would subject anyone living in or passing through the city to de facto jurisdiction by courts controlled by the Chinese Communist Party. The Hong Kong legal system, consequently, would have no power to stop people from being extradited to China if they were charged for committing a crime against mainland Chinese laws. The measure would erode Hong Kong's civil liberty and autonomy, undercutting the "One Country, Two Systems" principle as stipulated in the Sino-British Joint Declaration of 1984.[4] Western-centrism, as it turned out, constituted only a partial cause of my struggle to focus at QHC19; my looming unease emanated from a concern with the tightening tentacles of the Chinese state.

At QHC19, keynote speaker Susan Stryker, a transgender activist and historian, recast the Stonewall riots as a transitional moment into the rise of queer neoliberalism.[5] During the Q & A, one person queried her about how Stonewall always seems to be "taken over" by different groups every time its history is retold—for instance, by gay advocates in 1989 but then trans activists in 2019. In this regard, I laud Stryker's effort to centralize the transgender liberation movement in Northern California for the purpose of reperiodizing the Stonewall narrative. This framing reflects the growth of the Committee on LGBT History (the host of QHC19) and its attention to the increasing importance of regional and transgender perspectives in queer history. Another member in the audience raised an intriguing point about how we might invest in thinking about political riots comparatively. He mentioned the classic work of E. P. Thompson on the moral economy of the English working class a century and a half before Stonewall.[6] My mind was immediately brought back to—indeed, "taken over" by—the events in Hong Kong.

On the evening of June 16, the number of people who participated in the antiextradition bill protest tipped over two million. That figure accounts for one in every four residents in Hong Kong who took to the streets to voice their frustration with the decision and action of the Carrie Lam administration. On June 21, Amnesty International verified the violation of international law and standards by the Hong Kong police force through the use of tear gas, rubber bullet guns, pepper spray, and baton charges in suppressing a largely peaceful protest.[7] The outpouring reports of police brutality continued to shock the international community. By July 1, the twenty-second anniversary of the handover in 1997, international demonstrations in solidarity with Hong Kong erupted all over the world: New York City, San Francisco, Los Angeles, Toronto, Vancouver, London, Paris, Berlin, Frankfurt, Tokyo, Sydney, and Taipei. Hong Kong is a small region (comprising 0.0002 percent of the world's surface area), but its political outcry had assumed a planetary salience.[8]

And there we were, celebrating the fiftieth anniversary of Stonewall on the other side of the Pacific in the middle of a sunny pride month. No one brought up the devastating developments in Hong Kong, let alone thinking about the relative scale of resistance across half a century. I myself was guilty in some ways of perpetuating this indifference when moderating the token panel on Asia. Making a case for why it is important to study LGBTQ history in East Asia today, I called attention to the fact that just in May, Taiwan underwent a constitutional revolution: it became the first country on the Earth's largest and most populous continent to legalize same-sex marriage.[9] This celebratory tone contradicts my long-standing belief in the value of "feeling backward" at the very moment that we revere pride and progress.[10] After all, Asia and Asian America share many contact zones where people, ideas, and commodities flow across rigidly defined borders on a daily basis.[11] When flexible citizens, such as myself, observe the Hong Kong protests from abroad, our mind can still be trapped by the time and place of the otherwise.[12] The larger point I wish to make here, and an underlying theme of this book, is to introduce the specter of the Chinese empire to the study of queer struggle.[13] To recognize the geopolitical tensions in Hong Kong in relation to other conditions of oppression begins to mark a long overdue transversal mode of thought.[14] Therein lies the possibility of a new historiographical practice.

Both Hong Kong and Taiwan, like sexual and gender variance, have occupied a peripheral space in mainstream historical inquiry. They are too small, too invisible, and thus too unimportant.[15] It is true that the histories of Hong Kong and Taiwan and the histories of homophobia and transphobia are not easily comparable, nor should they be. But their mutual refraction offers a valuable lesson: the interwoven fabrics of political hegemony demand a *multidirectional* battle for the recognition and visibility of marginal subjects. It is therefore imperative now more than ever to entertain the comparative bargain of political resistance. The celebration of pride builds on a shameful past; the promising progress Taiwan has made sits side by side with the gloomy uncertainty hanging over Hong Kong's future. When we begin to consider the ways in which geopolitical factors intersect with gender and sexual injustice, May 2019 (Taiwan's constitutional revolution) can be treated more as the inception, rather than the endpoint, of a new mode of coalition politics mandated by the contemporary world. Although the field of queer Asian studies has vigorously "decolonized" Western theoretical norms, this gaze must be turned upon itself in order to avoid reinstating an opposite set of biases: the scaffolding of Asia-nativism.[16]

So on the one hand, this book makes a very specific claim. The geopolitics of Chineseness provides one analytically useful prism to unpack the uneven history of LGBTQ experience around the world, especially when accounting for those communities that seemingly share a common "Chinese" linguistic or cultural descent. As the protests in Hong Kong make clear, putting the word *Chinese* in quotation marks is necessary for demarcating the geospatial diversity of Sinitic-language communities and cultures worldwide. On the other hand, I develop a theoretical framework far more ambitious in its reach. The identitarian-based arguments for achieving social justice that have accelerated since the 1970s are no longer sufficient for grasping how actors are transforming and transposing their agential self, whether through the crossing of gender, location, culture, or time. Temporal and spatial displacements—including the kind of heterogeneous dissonances between modes of be(long)ing that characterized my QHC19 experience—suggest the feasibility (indeed, the need) of a new type of historical thinking.

To advance such novel style of inquiry in the history of gender and sexuality, this book introduces what I call *transtopia*, a neologism that performs both ontologically and epistemologically oriented analytical work. In this book, I use transtopia to refer to different scales of gender transgression that are not always recognizable through the Western notion of transgender. To the extent that this usage captures specific *ways of being* in the world, it represents an ontological intervention. At the same time, transtopia enables different *ways of knowing* in which transness appears less as a fixed entity than as individual and structural gradations that fundamentally ground most, if not all, facets of human life. In this sense, it denotes a critical epistemology. I examine the ramification of this master concept in unlikely times and places and argue that the merging of *trans-* with *-topia* occasions a generative tool with which to disrupt the stability and coherence of knowledge about the past.[17]

The Trouble with Transgender

Writing about Hong Kong, author Dung Kai-cheung (董啟章) uses *transtopia* to designate "a place with transit itself as destination."[18] Dung's usage is akin to *utopia* (no place), its opposite variant *dystopia* (ill place), and Michel Foucault's *heterotopia* (another place), wherein the idea of *place* serves an indispensable definitional role.[19] I build on these formulations, especially their attention to structures of power, but my conceptualization of transtopia diverges from this genealogy in its insistence that, supplementing Eve Kosofsky Sedgwick, any aspect of human culture must be not merely incomplete but damaged in its central substance to the degree that it does not incorporate a *conjunctural* analysis of transphobia and homophobia.[20] This book presents transtopia as the antidote to transphobia, frames it in terms of a continuum model that accredits the diversity of queer experience, and situates the pertinence of this new vocabulary in relation to the practice of critical history.[21]

To amplify the queer durability of the *trans-* prefix, I conceive of transtopia as a method of historicizing gender mutability that exceeds the transphobic denial of the past and the transgender presumption of the present.[22] It signals the way different manifestations of transness take shape in relation to one another and through the simultaneous movements of time and space. To anticipate myself a bit, the specific histories of sex transformation, queer inhumanity, cinematic castration, and civic change enumerated in this book cannot be understood without tracking the coevolution of time and space. These idiosyncratic formations have been more or less catalyzed by, in the context of this study, the heterogenization of Sinitic cultures on the geopolitical margins of continental China. It is vital, especially for decolonial queer thought, that sensitivity to time-space transference includes resisting any preconceived criteria of being "properly trans." That is, a teleological overcoming of the alleged pre-transgender typologies must never be assumed a priori in these disparate trajectories.

My delineation of transtopia interprets the unfolding of transness beyond a monolithic trapping with a single point of historical lineage/closure. Transtopia deconstructs a stable and constant narrative template by which transness is validated. Expanding our vocabulary from *transgender* to *transtopia* turns long-standing fetishizations of a coherent, fixed "origin"—or destination—of experience upside down. On an individual basis, this is a determined move to *queer* transness so that its diverse manifestations can be readily acknowledged.[23] First articulated over thirty years ago, Sedgwick's axiom still serves as a useful reminder: "People are different from each other."[24] It is indeed surprising how few eloquent conceptual tools queer theorists have developed to unpack this mundane and self-evident fact of life. This book argues that transgender differences are best thought out as interconnected and relational, rather than discrete and stratified.

But transtopia also issues a mandate to rethink broader disciplinary concerns. As anthropologist David Valentine has shown, when a discipline came to be consolidated around the very category of "transgender" in the 1990s, the rubric was typically imagined to capture something more advanced than premodern, traditional, old-fashioned, or "local" non-Western understandings of gender, embodiment, and identity.[25] Recent efforts to revise trans historiography through the lens of race or class, however compelling, continue to circle back to the confines of the West, within which to locate the crucible of resistance and renarration.[26] Hence, to paraphrase Rey Chow, "whereas it would be acceptable for authors dealing with specific cultures such as those of . . . the United States . . . to sue generic titles such as [*Female Masculinity, Transgender History, True Sex: The Lives of Trans Men at the Turn of the Twentieth Century, Black on Both Sides: A Racial History of Trans Identity, Female Husbands: A Trans History*], and so on, authors dealing with non-Western cultures are often expected to mark their subject matter with words such as Chinese, Japanese, Indian . . . and their alike."[27] The ethnic supplementarity of the latter fixes their intellectual content by way of a locational realism. To this day, Americanists and Europeanists are still considered the proprietor of novel theoretical insights concerning transgender proper.

Individually or collectively, it is long overdue to question a one-sided hierarchy often embedded in the umbrella concept of transgender, where the criteria of determination is transness, or, to put it more precisely, different degrees of transness. In this normativizing scheme, one can be *more* trans, and another can be *less* trans, and transness effectively becomes evaluable, measurable, and quantifiable.[28] Transtopia seeks to unsettle the power structures that sustain the need to pose the question, as medievalist Gabrielle Bychowski once raised to problematize it on a *TSQ* roundtable, "Am I trans enough?"[29]

The politics of transness is nowhere more pronounced than in cross-cultural contexts. A transtopian pragmatics leaves behind the romanticization (or denigration, as the case may be) of non-Western gender dissidence as ontologically static and distinct from Western formations. Transtopia offers a middle ground between, on the one hand, the claim that certain native categories—such as *hijra* in India, *waria* in Indonesia, *kathoey* in Thailand, *muxe* in Oaxaca, *renyao* in Sinitic-language societies, and two-spirit people in Native American and First Nation cultures—have been homogenized through the historical forces of globalization and recast as modern "transgender" identities and, on the other, the argument that such a typological remaking renders local nonnormative gender configurations legible in a global context and thereby conditions the plausibility of a transnational movement for universal recognition, acceptance, and solidarity.[30] None of these categories is easily assimilable into a strictly "transgender" frame; the richness of historical and cultural nuance cannot be overdetermined by the complacency of Western presentism. Reformulating these categories as "transtopian" navigates a way out of the deadlock of minoritarian identity politics and brokers a commensurate platform for differential articulation.[31] The following chapters ground this postidentitarian approach in specific regional and cross-regional contexts—a constellation within China's globalizing influence.[32] The time has come to think about not just gender but transgender trouble.

This book shows that the conception of transgender, itself a mutating signifier, is not one with roots in Western history alone. A more globally dispersed and regionally inflected perspective helps to parse the differentiated layers of transgender existence and its historical sedimentation. A *continuum* model of transgender variability authorizes pluralistic coalitions not predetermined by an antagonism between a copy and an original. "Such engagements with difference," to quote historian James Hevia from a different context, "allow the possibility of other forms of critique." This is so that we "can see that there were other kinds of constraints, other limitations, other forms of power that shaped subjectivities quite different from our own."[33] Though as the author of this book, for example, I do not identify as transgender in the traditional sense of the term, I comfortably claim a transtopian standpoint. This is because my affinity with folks who self-identify as trans is now rerouted through the coordinates of a shared commitment to antitransphobic justice.[34] Similarly, even though I was born and grew up in Taiwan, I easily grasp the anxiety of Hong Kong residents over Beijing's political imposition. On the broadest metaphysical level, then, this study invites a more inclusive and transversal style of thinking on the politics and ethics of knowledge, empathy, and being in the history of our interconnected world, especially through an insistence on upending interleaving systems of objectification and marginalization.[35] To transgress boundaries is also to displace "an imaginary distance that we must cross," in the hope that "we might be able to grasp, however fleetingly, that there were other ways of doing things, other ways of being in the world."[36]

Timing as much constitutes the heart of the matter as the deterritorialization of cultural belonging. I began by sharing my experience at QHC19 because 2019 turned out to be a year of great significance. One might race to the conclusion that the half-century between Stonewall and the legalization of gay marriage in Taiwan delivers an indisputable proof of political progress. Yet as numerous critics have pointed out, the battle for marriage equality all too often symptomatizes a neoliberalist cause. A certain echelon of the gay and lesbian community, especially those with the means to accumulate material wealth and exchange other forms of capital, has been upheld as respectable, dignified citizens. However, this is predicated on the further marginalization of other members of the queer community for whom state-sanctioned monogamy comes nowhere close to their interest, sexually or politically. In fact, the state regulation of monogamous intimacy frequently fails to address many ongoing problems of social disparity.[37] Queer theorist Jasbir K. Puar coined the concept of *homonationalism* to illustrate how such a tenuous inclusion of some queer subjects ("properly homo") relies on the stigmatization of ethnic and religious minority groups, especially Sikhs, Muslims, and Arabs, in the context of the contemporary United States.[38]

Despite the persuasive rhetoric of pinkwashing and homonationalism, when scholars apply these concepts to Asia, they often reduce neoliberalism to a matter of class.[39] Rarely do transregional politics, for example, or other forces of social partition factor into debates about these otherwise powerful concepts in the Asian context in ways their intersection has been vital to the original formulation.[40] For instance, if empire-making is central to Puar's conceptualization of US homonationalism, studies of Asian homonationalism tend to sideline the discriminatory folding of minority subjects for *imperial* projection purposes. Alternatively put, are we ready to call postcolonial states such as Singapore or India "empires," or to collapse their processes of minoritization as simply mimicking the US model? Using nation-ness or nationalism as the barometer of analysis also falls short in understanding how regimes of sovereignty compete in *regions*, such as Taiwan and Hong Kong, for which the very construct of nation-state remains contested on a transhistorical and global scale.

Moreover, across the board, whether the spotlight is put on Israel, the United States, India, Singapore, Hong Kong, or Taiwan, critical discussions of pinkwashing and homonationalism routinely ignore the social challenges faced by transgender people (e.g., changing the legal status of gender or having the right to marry in self-identified gender, both issues taken up later in this book). It is somewhat ironic, then, that critiques of homonormativity end up being the most homonormative of all.[41] Part of the problem lies in the way that the concept of *transnationalism*, unlike homonationalism, has been deployed principally by straight, white, and male scholars since the 1990s.[42] If transnationalism is not to transgender the same way that homonationalism is to gay and lesbian, how might we think about the contrived (neo)liberal state in relation to a global reinstrumentalization of gender diversity? This book develops the rubric of transtopia to remedy the lack of a consistent vocabulary that enfolds geopolitics as an explanatory vector into antitransphobic inquiry. A disavowal of "properly trans" complements the repudiation of "properly homo" in homonationalist analyses. Methodologically, this study grounds queer theoretical critiques of politics, the state, and other agents of cultural authority in source-driven historical perspectives.

In contrast to a popular trend in queer Asian studies, this book does not try to offer an alternative model of queer theory to reinscribe the boundary between the West and the rest.[43] Instead, as I have been doing in my engagement with the concept of homonationalism, my proposal of transtopia as a new historiographical practice relies on building bridges, rather than walls, with the various strands of queer theory. Each chapter therefore immerses itself in at least one distinct theoretical turn or register in queer studies. Chapter 1 borrows from the continuum model in lesbian feminist theory to historicize the rise of an epistemological assemblage that adjoins gender variations. Chapter 2 brings queer indigenous analysis, postcolonial theory, and sound studies to bear on the study of Sinitic-language communities worldwide. Chapter 3 engages with critical discussions of queer inhumanism and archival practice to bring to light the liminality of Taiwan's metaphysical presence. Chapter 4 draws on the discussion of somatechnics to show why corporeal politics matters to the visual queering of Chinese history. And chapter 5 extends the antisocial thesis debate to rethink the comparative horizons of queer citizenry across the Asia Pacific. In deconstructing the stability of transgender, the conceptual refinement of transtopia leverages the productive tension between queerness and transness.[44] Throughout the book, transtopia is theorized from the Sinophone Pacific milieu, as opposed to seizing this milieu as an empirical litmus test for its epistemic cogency.

Sinophone Recalibrations of History

This brings me to the second major intervention of this book, which is to make a parallel disciplinary move from "China" to the "Sinophone." The classic definition of the Sinophone concept can be found in the pioneering work of literary scholar Shu-mei Shih: "a network of places of cultural production outside China and on the margins of China and Chineseness, where a historical process of heterogenizing and localizing of continental Chinese culture has been taking place for several centuries."[45] Both Hong Kong and Taiwan bear a historically embedded and politically contested relationship to the People's Republic of China (PRC). Since Mao's regime took over mainland China in 1949, these two "Chinese" societies have been shaped less directly by the economic and political turmoil driving China's transition from high socialism to market reform. Seventy years after the founding of the PRC, the antiextradition bill protest in Hong Kong and the legalization of gay marriage in Taiwan mark an unambiguous *différance* from the political regime of Beijing.[46] This study follows the footsteps of scholars such as Shih to distinguish Sinophone communities in Hong Kong and Taiwan from the Chinese communities in the PRC.[47] This is not the only operational value of the Sinophone, as we will see throughout the book, but here I merely wish to point out the analogy between the diffusion of transness by transtopia and the decentering of Chineseness by Sinophone analysis.

Once we bring queer theory and Sinophone studies into a conjunctive formulation, it opens up new vistas of cross-disciplinary encounter.[48] An underlying goal of the book is to engage queer Sinophone studies with medical humanities in light of their overlapping interdisciplinary concerns. One obvious point of entry hinges on the question of being human and the cognate materiality of queerness.[49] In the history of sex reassignment and forensic adjudication, for instance, modern medicine has played a decisive role in shaping queer subjects' understanding of gender and sexuality and the parameters of their embodiment (chapter 1). The influx of early-twentieth-century Western sexology humanized a native Chinese transgender concept called *renyao* (human prodigy), which grew out of its earlier lexical capacity to reference human-animal hybrids (chapter 3). By the late Cold War period (1947–1991), Sinophone cinema began to depict castrated characters as extremely powerful but also monstrous. Such visual queering of Chinese castration trafficked the body-as-signifier across history and between geopolitical regimes, such as the Ming dynasty (1368–1644), anti-Manchu nationalism, revolutionary Maoism, radical France, Asian America, and postcolonial Hong Kong (chapter 4). Last but not least, contemporary transgender activism continues to be haunted by the question of to what extent medical authorities ought to intervene in the legal decision-making process (chapter 5). Although Sinophone studies has been driven primarily by debates over linguistic governance and cultural resistance, the demand and recognition of full humanhood resonate with the goals of confronting gender-binary, heterosexist, racist, colonizing, and other forms of *bodily* violence.[50] In this sense, a medical humanities perspective broadens the purview of queer Sinophone studies to critique the interlocking apparatus of power and hegemony. Conversely, since the dehumanization of trans subjects is systematically interrogated in this book, it is my hope that medical practitioners will be inspired to probe more carefully the (post)humanistic underpinnings of gender and sexual health management.

Transtopia in the Sinophone Pacific is divided into two parts. Part 1 contains two manifestos that challenge the foundation of the disciplines that this study seeks to transform. Chapter 1 establishes the overall framework of the book by drawing on an international archive of sexual science. It charts the formation of a global episteme in which doctors, lawyers, journalists, educators, and gender and sexual minorities around the world articulated a nonhierarchical continuum of transgender subjectivity. Chapter 2 situates this study in the geocultural terms of postcolonial Sinophone sites. It argues that the Stonewall legacy needs to be put *aside* in order for queer scholars to take the contemporary rise of China seriously. If chapter 1 refocuses the terms of transgender studies from internal to structural coherence, chapter 2 raises the urgency of resisting both China-centrism and Western-centrism in queer theory. Whereas chapter 1 lays out the epistemological rubric of the book, transtopia, chapter 2 locates this study against the concrete backdrop of the Sinophone Pacific. Taken together, this pair of interventions underscores how the book is as much about drawing attention to the politics of transness in Sinophone studies as it is about highlighting the contested status of Chineseness in queer studies.

Part 2 integrates this dual paradigm to strike a farther-reaching move and, through a series of case studies, makes an overall contribution to the theory of history. It does so by scrutinizing the relationship between transgender formation and the various *rhetorical* strategies that history assumes. My thesis is that trans subjects cannot be presupposed to exist in historical time for recuperative purposes (as this "reality" is often rendered the subject of redemption in contemporary history writing); rather, transgender expressions and politics should be more accurately conceptualized on the basis of a continuum model.[51] This model offers a degree of elasticity with which to distinguish the stylistic, symbolic, and political tenor of interpretive readings into the past. As such, it highlights the kind of methodological rigor embedded in the new frontiers of transgender history. This is why I invoke the concept of rhetoric to denote something more encompassing than Hayden White's narrativity (which is also about rhetoric, but in the narrower sense of the language device of fiction: tropes, narratives, and so on).[52] Rhetoric is concerned with the full art of persuasion.[53] A crux of this study, rhetoric thus cannot be "deemed icing on the cake of history," but "it is mixed right in the batter."[54] Part 2 comprises thick deliberations on the rhetoric of history through a sustained focus on transtopian hermeneutics.

In order to think about the production of transness from the vantage of multiple sites without resorting to a traditional area studies approach, which would reduce the use of Sinophone sources to either illustrate or debunk Western models of queerness, I advance three methods whereby the category of *transgender* acquires historical potency: titrating, inscribing, and creolizing. These are uneven paths in which the meaning of transgender has metamorphosed across time and place, as well as heuristic procedures by which we can subject that very same category to systematic historical analysis. Chapter 3 troubles the rhetoric of linearity in historical narration by introducing the technique of *titration* to pivot the dispersed occurrence of bodily transgression against the historicization of geopolitics.[55] Historiographically, this chapter provides a long overdue analysis of the history of *renyao* in the twentieth century. Chapter 4 espouses the rhetoric of constructivism by attending to how history itself not only serves as a reservoir of facts and information for the present, but embodies pulses and rhythms often brought to life by the retrospective desire for its existence. Focusing on the conditions of *inscription* in mediated visual culture, this chapter reveals the lingering afterlife of a Chinese corporeal type—castration—in the supplementary logic of the Sinophone Pacific.[56] Chapter 5 eschews the rhetoric of uniformity in positivist history by tracking the competing political currency of transgender as it circulates across regions and settles across borders. Through the prism of comparative *creolization*, this chapter contrasts the limits of legal mobilization in Hong Kong against the radicalizing effects of LGBTQ activism in Taiwan.

To return to how my attention wandered at QHC19, we have come full circle to the significance of the year 2019 in Chinese history. It is after all the centennial anniversary of the May Fourth movement, the seventieth anniversary of the founding of the People's Republic, and the thirtieth anniversary of the Tiananmen Square suppression in Beijing. The marriage equality movement and the antiextradition bill protests seized the residual momentum from two episodes that captivated the world's attention in 2014: the Sunflower Movement in Taipei and the Umbrella Movement in Hong Kong. Considering these recent democracy protests in the Sinophone Pacific forces us to reflect on the evolving nature of student and mass protest in Chinese history, Sinophone cultures, and the resonances of their dispersion over the last century.[57] This tactic reorders the geopolitical and chronological grid with which we historicize queerness and transness beyond the terms dictated by the fault lines of heteronormativity.

Attributing significance to 2019 does not (and never has to) align with the premise of how that turning point comes to carry symbolic weight in Western queer historiography. The year also marks the centennial anniversary of the founding of the Institute of Sexual Science by the Jewish sexologist Magnus Hirschfeld (a pioneer homosexual activist), the fiftieth anniversary of the Stonewall rebellion, and, in the case of QHC19, the inaugural conference organized by the Committee on LGBT History. In coining transtopia, I provide a historical *recalibration* of all of these turning points through particular recursive themes: intercultural circulation and sexological modernity (1919), continental China and Sinophone alterity (1949), sexual liberation and political repression (1969 and 1989), and grassroots activism and legal change (2019). Transtopia enables us to redraw the violent outlines of transgender history that problematically include some subjects, flagrantly exclude others, and ostensibly predicate specific "regimes of authenticity."[58]

Finally, a few words on my choice of scientific metaphors throughout the book, whose argumentation is often routed through the models and concepts of quantitative science. Some readers might find the language of certain reigning idioms in this book foreign: surjection, injection, asymptote, titration, differentials, chimera, isomerism, and so forth. Admittedly, I have borrowed these terms from the scientific lingua franca to illustrate the historical phenomenon under inspection. By integrating them with postmodernist ideas such as genealogy, assemblage, deconstruction, hauntology, and supplementarity, my narrative strategy joins the work of a growing number of scholars to challenge the subsidiary role often assigned to the humanities in modern academe.[59] As someone who has been immersed in both worlds, I view the contrasting of the humanities disciplines in sharp opposition to the allegedly "more important" STEM subjects as a falsifiable arrangement.[60] The fact that all of the concepts listed aim to deduce certain underlying structures of a system—be they scientific, mathematical, natural, social, cultural, economic, or political—suggests that the animosity between the humanities and the sciences is as much constructed as the system these disciplines seek to understand. As White made clear over half a century ago, the positioning of the historical profession in the middle ground between the "two cultures" is a *product* of the nineteenth-century historical imagination.[61] Accordingly, history as half-baked science and semiartistic practice has long outlived its utility.

Transtopia in the Sinophone Pacific overcomes this impasse by making historicism relevant to the contemporary strife of transgender geopolitics and vice versa. To quote White, "*the burden of the historian* in our time is to reestablish the dignity of historical studies on a basis that will make them consonant with the aims and purposes of the intellectual community at large, that is, transform historical studies in such a way as to allow the historian to participate positively in the liberation of the present from *the burden of history*."[62] Whereas French philosopher Jacques Rancière would call into question the scientific status of history by aligning its tenets closer to the epistemological interventions of critical philosophy, this book seeks to level the field by using the art of scientific reasoning to deepen the rhetorical strategy of historical apprehension.[63] The interdisciplinary approach advanced in this book not only displaces the ahistorical universality commonly assumed in leading theorems of gender, such as performativity, but also adds transcultural texture to the variability of human experience.[64]

With respect to disciplinary crossing, my point is that both sides need to reach out more: scientists should feel comfortable with the rigorous vocabulary of critical theory and humanities scholars ought to appreciate the use value of scientific models. In this sense, structuralism provides one often overlooked clue to establishing such an equivalence. As is well known, both Foucault and Jacques Derrida, given their interest in discourse and the regularities of language, expressed skepticism toward the characterization of their work as "postmodern" or "poststructuralist."[65] In order to recast their ideas alongside mathematical abstractions and other scientific metaphors, our inquiry begins with the strategic deployment of structuralism.

PART ONE

Unsettling Origins

Two Manifestos

CHAPTER I

Transtopia

Epistemology of the Commensurate

T he instability of gender norms is a common feature of history. By virtue of their function as social scripts, we can expect exceptions and differences wherever we look. But this seemingly ordinary insight acquired urgency rather late and only as a recent development in human society. Foregrounding the interest of gender variant subjects, an activist agenda and an academic field cohered into a global movement only by the end of the last century. *Transgender* became a unifying concept that ties together a range of identities, inclinations, bodies, and behaviors that depart from conventional gender expressions.[1] However, the extent to which this broad rubric is useful for historicizing gender diversity has remained far from clear, especially with respect to the more distant past.[2] The difficulty lies in part in the pitfall of imposing later categories and taxonomies on earlier historical moments.[3] The cohesion of "transgender" further obfuscates the study of gender variance in places where that very concept carries a foreign status.

This chapter proposes a bold solution. It takes cues from the development of structuralism in interwar mathematics for the purpose of cross-cultural historical inquiry.[4] In doing so, it issues a challenge to think more carefully about how our categories, especially categories of identity, over-determine what we can know about the past.[5] In the social or the mathematical sphere, structuralism questions the significance of the internal nature of an object, be it a number, function, set, point, identity, or culture; rather, structuralist thinking gives foremost weight to how these objects *relate* to one another. By coining the notion of *strategic structuralism*, I argue that social categories, such as the category of transgender, have no intrinsic nature and carry no inherent value.[6] But if we provisionally accept the structuralist foundations for social cohesion as a strategy for collective representation, such emergent modes of solidarity—indeed, new means of relational existence—can be mobilized to pursue certain chosen political ends, especially coalitional ones.

This chapter focuses on one particular example of strategic structuralism that I call transtopia. Proposed here as a new paradigm of queering history, transtopia calls into question any essentialist understanding of transgenderism and its assumed coherence. There has been a steady commitment in queer studies to posit an overarching definition of "trans/gender." For example, queer theorist Jack Halberstam uses *trans** to "open the term up to unfolding categories of being organized around but not confined to forms of gender variance. . . . The asterisk modifies the meaning of transitivity by refusing to situate transition in relation to a destination, a final form, a specific shape, or an established configuration of desire and identity."[7] Historian Susan Stryker employs *transgender* to "refer to people who move away from the gender they were assigned at birth, people who cross over (*trans-*) the boundaries constructed by their culture to define and contain gender."[8] Instructive and inclusive, these two definitions share an emphasis on moving *away* from rather than *toward* fixed ideas of gender. Both hold bodily change, or "perpetual transition" in Halberstam's case, paramount.[9]

But what if we do not start from a coherent definition of trans/gender? By suspending the need for an all-encompassing definition, transtopian thinking reframes transgender as a social structure as opposed to a minoritarian identity. Working with archival materials, sociologist Clare Sears coins "trans-ing analysis" to draw attention to "the historical production and subsequent operations of the boundary between normative and nonnormative gender."[10] This mode of reading allows Sears to bring together examples of cross-gender phenomena not typically considered alongside one another. In this sense, trans-ing analysis yields a constructive angle to deploy transgender as a *continuous* category. Building on this insight but also pushing it further, the ethical predicament of transtopia is concerned less with who qualifies as transgender than with how different actors relate to one another *through* the category of transgender. Transtopia shifts the criteria of inclusion, especially in critical analysis, from whether one is trans enough to how broader patterns emerge from a web of historical relations in which transness gains intelligibility. If we temporarily accept that structures exist only in the system that exemplifies them, and that, by extension, transtopian analysis outlines a shared set of symbolic and material parameters, then the political currency of transgenderism can be broadened along a more inclusive, rather than alienating, line of collective action and representation. By inferring from mathematical logic, this chapter posits one measure of charting those parameters in which the transgender past becomes enlivened, that is, one method of bringing together seemingly disparate cases across time, space, and culture through the lens of transgender continuity.

My conceptualization of transtopia is critically inspired by Adrienne Rich's classic essay "Compulsory Heterosexuality and Lesbian Existence" (1980).[11] Even though, strictly speaking, transgender issues fall outside the core concerns of Rich's manifesto, the theoretical push for a more fluid conceptualization of gender and sexuality does not. Specifically, I borrow from Rich's formulation of the lesbian continuum a way of situating gender/sexual variation beyond the social periphery. As gender critics C. L. Cole and Shannon Cate have argued,

> Where Rich would have heterosexual feminists in the 1980s strategically claim a place on the "lesbian continuum," today, we might use her logic and her calls to challenge prescriptive sexuality to imagine a *transgender continuum* on which so-called male-born men and female-born women can find themselves building political connections with those whose gender is more obviously outside society's narrow frame of the "normal," ultimately challenging heteronormative and homonormative investments in binary genders altogether.[12]

This notion of a transgender continuum constitutes the kernel of my study. Within the framework of transtopia, specific types of transitioning or transitivity do not designate an ontological requirement for calibrating people's relation to trans subjectivity. Rather, transtopia pivots an infinite set of adjacent variations as the basis for grasping the underlying structure of transgender existence. More than a nominal label or descriptor, it can be understood as an epistemological tool, a mode of historical envisioning that maps gender fluidity onto the mutual transcending of place and time. This historiographical practice pinpoints the precipitation of specific transgender events, or the crystallization of certain trans phenomena, through the concurrent movements of chronology and geography. If the metaphors of home, destination, and becoming/arriving are central to the discrete narration of transgender experience, transtopia deprioritizes the individual rationale and parameters of a given iteration of transness and makes a collateral case for forging alliance on the ground of collective, intersecting, and globally circulatory paths. With a cross-cultural and intertemporal traffic, transtopia moves beyond fixating on *what transgender is* and pushes for the collaborative thinking of *what transgender can do across time and space.*

Since transphobia has historically taken on varying shapes and scales in disparate contexts, transtopia, as its antidote, recognizes the need to attend to the uneven breadths of injustice and, accordingly, the demand for different forms of political battle and ammunition. In defining transgender as a continuous category this way, transtopia exceeds the long-standing investment within a certain strand of queer studies that views trans★ as a zero-sum game of two, three, or more gender configurations.[13] In short, the transtopian spectrum turns the binary continuum that has long anchored normative understandings of gender inside out. I ask: What if "hypermasculine males" and "hyperfeminine females" are not idealized poles but constitute only one elusive point on a larger gradation of gender fictive possibilities? What if transgenderism is not the exception but the norm by which all embodied subjects can be measured and understood? What if we start to pay more, not less, attention to how the regulatory systems of gender shift contextually along the space-time axis?

This chapter establishes the theoretical framework of the book by mapping two genealogies of transtopia. First, it analyzes the centrality of continuum thinking to mid-twentieth-century sexual science. Whereas the Kinsey reports have dominated most critical studies of postwar sexology, I focus on the Sex Orientation Scale (SOS) developed by Harry Benjamin (1885–1986), a medical doctor, and situate it in a wider global context. Benjamin's work on the SOS consolidated an epistemology of transgender continuum with which individuals with different gender afflictions and of diverse cultural backgrounds came to identify and learn about themselves. Second, the chapter compares three lesbian murder cases across distinct historical junctures, paying particular attention to the role of forensic medical expertise. Widely reported and sensationalized, these three episodes spanned eight decades in the United States, China, and Iran. In foregrounding trans over homo historicity, my approach goes beyond a metaphoric borrowing of Rich's lesbian continuum theory. By supplanting it with transtopian insight, such critical inflection mobilizes the methodological rigor of a "border war" within queer studies: to reconceptualize subjects long considered by historians as lesbian in a transgender light.[14]

Though Benjamin's (net)work and the lesbian cases may seem unrelated at first, the overarching purpose of this chapter is a methodologically inventive one: to take a stab at broadening the histories of transness beyond a singular pedigree (as in descending from an individual, a location, or an event).[15] Stepping back in reach for a "bigger picture," I will conclude with two diagrams, inspired by quantitative science, to suture the parallel genealogies of sexual knowledge. This synthesis outlines the commensurability of the various case studies examined in this chapter with the models of *surjection* and *injection*—abstractions first introduced by a group of interwar structuralist mathematicians.[16] The use of mathematical models underlines the parallel between the conceptualization of natural occurrences and patterns in quantitative argumentation and structuralist thinking in social theory. By appealing to strategic structuralism as the modus operandi of transtopia, I present the global impact of the Benjamin scale and the three lesbian stories as two overlooked paths that have molded transness into a conceptual regime of indeterminacy. Such indeterminacy constitutes both a manifesto proclamation and a means as an end. What follows interweaves archival depth with theoretical propositions to envision a new program of doing transgender history cross-culturally.

Continuum Science

Making Rich's continuum theory central to our reframing of transgender studies is possible by adding context and texture to its intellectual purchase. Specifically, a valuable lesson can be drawn from the history of continuum thinking in sexual scientific research. This genealogy of continuum science runs through the work of notable twentieth-century sexologists, intersecting with disciplines as diverse as psychology, biochemistry, anthropology, sociology, and medicine. While all of the interlocutors sought to establish an empirical framework for understanding the relationship between gender norms and deviations, epistemic tensions have arisen between *discrete* and *spectrum* models in sexological taxonomic practices. The discrete model induces the biopolitical strategy of creating caesura that divide, classify, and specify surveilled heterogeneous populations (as examined in the work of Georges Canguilhem, Michel Foucault, and Ian Hacking);[17] the spectrum model is linked to (neo)liberal diversity models, emancipatory utopianisms that envision the overthrow of racialist, colonialist, capitalist, heteronormative, and patriarchal regimes (illuminated by Deleuzian-Guattarian assemblage theory)—all of which offer different ways of thinking transversally across scales and can be mobilized to resist the discrete model of biopolitical hierarchization.[18] As one exemplar of the spectrum model, rather than the root of the paradigm itself, Rich's notion of a lesbian continuum represented a significant cultural-political instance of imagining diversity in the context of the 1980s. It contested the homophobic marginalization of lesbianism within feminism and conceived of a nonhierarchical range of embodied personhoods.[19]

A telling example of the continuum paradigm in mid-twentieth-century sexology is the Sex Orientation Scale proposed by Harry Benjamin. A clinical endocrinologist, Benjamin came from a German background of sexual science. Having worked with Magnus Hirschfeld (1868–1935) and Eugen Steinach (1861–1944) in glandular biology, Benjamin coined and popularized the concept of "transsexualism" in the 1950s.[20] Benjamin fleshed out the definition and application of the SOS in his magnum opus, *The Transsexual Phenomenon*, published in 1966.[21] As figure 1.1 illustrates, his SOS taxonomy was intended to account for the intensity of gender role uncertainty and ambivalence. Formulated on the basis of consultation with other experts and his own patients, the SOS was also decisively influenced by the 0–6 Kinsey scale (0 referring to exclusive heterosexuality and 6 exclusive homosexuality).[22] Yet the reason that the Kinsey scale has overshadowed the Benjamin scale, I suggest, has to do with the absence of a critical vocabulary to contextualize the latter's cultural reach. The concept of transtopia provides a key to unpacking the significance of Benjamin's work. This and the next section will construe the Sex Orientation Scale as a *transtopian innovation* in modern sexology. Specifically, the revolutionary power of Benjamin's formulation lies in the way it comprehends gender nonconformity across historical time and space: the SOS marks a culminating episode, a moment of epistemic uncertainty, and a juncture of global convergence in the history of sexual science.

When Benjamin proposed the SOS, his primary objective was to define *transsexualism* as a medical condition distinct from *transvestism*. He credited

The Benjamin Sex Orientation Scale (S.O.S.):
Sex and Gender Disorientation and Indecision (Males)

TYPE O
Normal sex orientation and identification, heterosexual or homosexual.
The ideas of "dressing" or "sex change" are foreign and unpleasant.
Vast majority of all people.

PROFILE	TYPE I	TYPE II	TYPE III	TYPE IV	TYPE V	TYPE VI
	Transvestite Pseudo	Transvestite Fetishistic	Transvestite True	Transsexual Non-Surgical	True Transsexual Moderate Intensity	True Transsexual High Intensity
Gender "feeling"	Masculine	Masculine	Masculine (but with less conviction).	Uncertain. Wavering between TV & TS.	Feminine "trapped" in a male body.	Feminine. Total "psycho-sexual" inversion.
Dressing habits and social life	Normal male life. May get a "kick" from "dressing". Not truly TV.	Lives as man. "Dresses" period-ically or part-time. Dresses under male clothes.	"Dresses" constantly or as often as possible. May live and be accepted as a woman. May dress under male garb.	"Dresses" often as possible with insufficient relief of gender discomfort. May live as man or woman.	Lives and works as woman if possible. Insufficient relief from "dressing".	May live and work as woman. Insufficient relief from "dressing". Gender discomfort intense.
Sex object choices and sex life	Hetero-, bi, or homosexual. "Dressing" and sex change in masturbation fantasy mainly.	Heterosexual. Rarely bi. Masturbation with fetish. Feels guilt. "Purges" and relapses.	Heterosexual except when dressed. Dressing gives sex-ual satisfaction, relief of gender discomfort. May purge, relapse.	Libido low. Asexual or auto-erotic. Could be bisexual.	Low libido. Asexual, auto-erotic, or passive homosexual activity. May have been married and have children.	Intensively desires relations with normal male as "female". If young; later libido low. May have been married and have children.
Conversion operation	Not considered in reality.	Rejected.	Rejected but idea attractive.	Attractive but not requested.	Requested.	Urgently requested & usually attained.
Estrogen medication	Not interested. Not indicated.	Rarely interested. May help to reduce libido.	Attractive as an experiment. Can be helpful.	Needed for comfort and emotional balance.	Needed as substitute for or preliminary to operation.	Required for partial relief.
Psychotherapy	Not wanted. Unnecessary.	May be successful in favorable environment.	If attempted, not usually successful as to cure.	Only as guidance; otherwise refused or unsuccessful.	Rejected. Unless as to cure. Permissive psychological guidance.	Psychological guidance or psycho-therapy for symptomatic relief only.
Remarks	Only sporadic interest in "dressing".	May imitate M & F double personality with M and F names.	May assume a double personality. Trend toward TSism.	Social life dependant on circumstances.	Operation hoped for and worked for, often attained.	Despises his male sex organs; danger of suicide or self-mutilation if too long frustrated.

Fig. 1.1 The Benjamin Sex Orientation Scale.
Source: Courtesy of Sexual Minority Rights Archive.

Magnus Hirschfeld for coining the term *transvestism* to refer to people with the desire to cross-dress.[23] In this sense, Hirschfeld followed the nineteenth-century sexological tradition to label and give meaning to previously untapped terrains of clinical medicine. Both Richard von Krafft-Ebing (1840–1902) and Havelock Ellis (1859–1939) had included cases of cross-gender identification in their writings: the former called the most extreme form "metamorphosis sexualis paranoica" and the latter proposed the term "eonism" for similar conditions.[24] In positing a theory of what he called "sexual intermediaries," Hirschfeld advanced an understanding of transgenderism as benign, natural, and diverse in scope, while making a strong case for why transvestism must not be confounded with homosexuality, fetishism, or other forms of psychopathology. In *Die Transvestiten* (1910), Hirschfeld argued that "The number of actual and imaginable sexual varieties is almost unending; in each person there is a different mixture of manly and womanly substances, and as we cannot find two leaves alike on a tree, then it is highly unlikely that we will find two humans whose manly and womanly characteristics exactly match in kind and number."[25]

In the first half of the twentieth century, sexologists adopted various continuum frameworks for conceptualizing sex and sexual difference. Psychiatrist George Henry (1889–1964) led a team of researchers in New York to investigate the bodies and case histories of homosexual men and women under the rubric of "sex variant."[26] In the 1920s and 1930s, endocrinologists discovered the universal presence of both male and female sex hormones in the human body.[27] Joining the psychoanalytic chorus in upholding the theory of bisexuality, biochemists viewed everyone as an inherent mixture of both sexes.[28] Meanwhile, most renowned for his work on intelligence measurement, Stanford psychologist Lewis Terman (1877–1956), in collaboration with Catherin Cox Miles (1890–1984), devised a new scalar instrument for analyzing human sex psychology. They introduced the Masculinity and Femininity Test (also known as the "M-F test") and argued that all men and women could be situated on this seven-part diagnostic tool.[29] Anthropologists Ruth Benedict (1887–1948) and Margaret Mead (1901–1978) drew on their fieldwork in "primitive societies" to argue for the cultural relativity of gender norms.[30] By the 1950s, medical psychologist John Money (1921–2006) inferred from the clinical protocol of intersexual management a distinction of *gender* from biological *sex*. In 1955, Money used *gender role* to refer to "all those things that a person says or does to disclose himself or herself as having the status of boy or man, girl or woman," and *gender* to refer to "outlook, demeanor, and orientation."[31] But perhaps the most famous continuum example in modern sexology is none other than the seven-point homosexual-bisexual-heterosexual rating scale popularized by Alfred Kinsey (1894–1956) and his research team at Indiana University.[32]

The Benjamin scale emerged in the 1960s first and foremost as a culmination of these nineteenth- and twentieth-century developments in sexological continuum thinking. Not only did it account for the cross-dressing desire observed by Hirschfeld and other Victorian-era sexologists, it also incorporated both the sex object choice variable captured by the Kinsey scale and the more recent conception of gender role. Benjamin delineated transsexualism as a stand-alone diagnosis by adding the potential interest in surgery, hormonal medication, or psychotherapy to its underlying definition and his overall SOS taxonomy. At the same time, he understood transsexualism as a more extreme form of sex/gender disorientation than transvestism. According to Benjamin, "both can be considered symptoms or syndromes of the same underlying psychopathological condition, that of a sex or gender role disorientation and indecision. Transvestism is the minor though the more frequent, transsexualism the much more serious although rarer disorder."[33] He categorized transsexualism as Types IV to VI on the SOS continuum, while placing transvestism as Types I to III (adults with no cross-gender inclinations were given the rating of 0). The way that the continuum epistemology continued to inform midcentury sexological thinking is especially evident in the way Benjamin adhered to a relational link between transvestism and transsexualism. For Benjamin, "Cross-dressing exists (with few exceptions) in practically all transsexuals, while transsexual desires are not evident (although possibly latent) in most transvestites."[34] The language of exception and latency implies a nondefinitive difference between transsexualism and transvestism and draws attention to their mutual inclusivity.

In leaving room for overlaps and inclusion, Benjamin's tabulation of the SOS spectrum represented a moment of epistemic uncertainty. Sexological uncertainty, of course, predates the 1950s. From Benjamin's perspective, the coinage of "transsexualism" answered a long-standing plea made by patients who sought help from medicine to change their sex. Although Lili Elbe (1886–1931) is often credited as one of the first recipients of sex reassignment surgery (under Hirschfeld's supervision in Germany) in 1930, this kind of patient demand had existed prior to that.[35] Already in October 1920, for example, Hirschfeld received the following letter from K. S., a young man living in Frankfurt (figure 1.2):

Perhaps you remember my last letter of July 14, 1916, in which I spoke to you about my abdominal and sexual troubles, being more female than male. I was drafted and sent into the front lines in 1916, was operated on after a few weeks; the one diseased testicle, the cause of my illness, was not taken out at the time so that at present I have again the old pains. I have no idea of being a man, the female psyche is predominant in me, I feel more like a woman. . . . Would it be possible to remove the testicle and replace it by a female ovary? Perhaps in this way I could become a full fledged woman. . . . I am enclosing a small photo of myself dressed as a girl (nurse).[36]

The full extent of K. S.'s inquiry exceeded the framework of transvestism propounded by Hirschfeld. This scientific imprecision paved the way for Benjamin's later work on transsexualism, which was driven by patient

Fig. 1.2 K. S. in nurse's attire (1920).
Source: Courtesy of the Kinsey Institute Library and Special Collections.

request to alleviate gender discomfort. The gap of Hirschfeld's science eventually led to a new form of uncertainty surrounding Benjamin's distinction between transvestism and transsexualism. The continuum model of transgender expression bridges the two sexologists' oeuvre.

Based on his correspondence with transgender individuals, Benjamin embraced the idea that his sexology was both shaped by and shaping the experience and opinions of sexual minorities. One important voice that challenged, or was at least in dialogue with, Benjamin's research came from Louise Lawrence (1912–1976). A native of Northern California, Lawrence played an instrumental role in connecting the transgender community to sex researchers such as Kinsey and Benjamin.[37] Already in 1947, Kinsey's research team had interviewed nine male and two female transvestites.[38] By 1949, Kinsey was convinced by Lawrence that "no two [transvestites] are very much alike."[39] At this point Kinsey understood transvestism and homosexuality as two separate diagnoses: "it is only a small portion of such cases [transvestism] that are homosexual, and this is something that the psychiatrists have not begun to understand. I have seen them cause considerable confusion in a number of cases by encouraging a transvestite to become homosexual just because their theory demanded that transvestitism should be one of the products of homosexuality."[40] Despite this insistence, Kinsey considered transvestism, unlike homosexuality, a "relatively rare" phenomenon.[41]

Both Lawrence and Benjamin questioned Kinsey's minoritarian view of transgenderism. Lawrence advised Benjamin, "I am very sure that [transvestism] is much more common than most of us, even prominent doctors, are willing or able to admit."[42] Encouraged by Kinsey to collect more data on gender-variant individuals, Lawrence began to compile a list of transvestites from her personal network and hammered out a questionnaire. She observed, "Almost every day I run across something which leads me to believe more and more strongly that there are a great many more transvestites than most people are willing to admit."[43] Although Lawrence did not receive scientific or medical training, she was motivated by the promise of empirical science. And while she had neither Kinsey's caliber nor Benjamin's prestige in the medical community, Lawrence educated sex researchers by providing them important scientific data and bold interpretations on transgenderism.[44] Through close collaboration, Lawrence and Benjamin worked toward a new scientific understanding of cross-gender identification as more pervasive and universal than what had been previously assumed. Lawrence, in particular, sought to expand transvestism into a pluralist and diverse category.

Ultimately, Benjamin detected the conceptual imprecision of transvestism for grasping the most pressing concerns of his patients. Most of them did not find cross-dressing fulfilling and wanted instead to physically transform their sex. In May 1953, when discussing the case of Christine Jorgensen (1926–1989) with Kinsey, Benjamin proposed *transsexualism* as a new terminology:

> Transvestism does not adequately describe her case. It is only one of the symptoms of her condition. I think we might describe cases like hers as transsexualism. You have undoubtedly the histories of many, that is to say people who desperately want to belong to the opposite sex. They are probably all homosexual. A milder stage of the condition may be satisfied with one of the symptoms of transsexualism, that is to say with transvestism and they are frequently heterosexual (like Louise).[45]

Benjamin came to coin this neologism because he was increasingly convinced that what he encountered in the clinic differed from what Hirschfeld had called transvestism. For instance, in 1956, a young J. A. wrote to Benjamin from Fort Lauderdale:

> I'm 18 1/2 and I'm finally convinced that I'm a transsexual. Even my mother and my friends have finally come to that conclusion. For the last few months I've been searching for the right person to help me get the sex change operation. . . . About myself, I was [born] with the body of a boy, and the mind of a girl, there's nothing homosexual about me. I want the operation more than anything else in the world. . . . Please help me, I beg of you. . . . Once I get the operations I'll be the happiest person on this earth. . . . All I want to finally be is an ordinary housewife.[46]

For J. A., to be an ordinary housewife meant more than wearing women's clothes; it entailed the transformation of genital sex. Now finding transvestism an inadequate rubric, Benjamin developed the new vocabulary of transsexualism to address precisely the concerns raised by individuals like J. A. Between 1953 and 1966, Benjamin's taxonomy evolved from a TV-TS dichotomous model to an elaborate system accounting for different stages of intensity.[47] The SOS shades transgenderism in a variety of ways, establishing a multifarious spectrum between transvestism and transsexualism. In this way, the Benjamin scale was at once a response to scientific imprecision and a new measurement of infinite possibilities.

Throughout his career, Benjamin welcomed dissenting voices from sexual minorities. He practiced an ethics of transparency in advising his patients and listened to them carefully. In the 1950s and 1960s, Benjamin gave Jorgensen's story considerable weight for clarifying his notion of transsexualism.[48] But he also acknowledged that the Jorgensen story was unusual and represented only one end of the transgender spectrum. In 1953, Lawrence responded to Benjamin's interpretation of the Jorgensen case: "The fact that you say her urge goes much deeper than merely transvestism, that it is an 'obsessive urge to belong to the opposite sex,' I find very interesting but not surprising. I firmly believe that most transvestites have that same urge but in varying degrees and areas. Many of them want the role but not the sex. . . . I personally, have nothing against anyone wanting to belong to the opposite sex."[49] Similarly, female impersonator Edythe Ferguson, with whom Lawrence, Joan Thornton, and Virginia Prince (1912–2009) cofounded the magazine *Transvestia* in 1952, questioned the results of sex change operations. In a private letter, Ferguson called self-identified transsexuals really "a transvestic homosexual."[50] She viewed "surgical transmutation" as "always necessarily artificial and superficial." For Ferguson, "Absorption of a feminine entity by a genetic masculine . . . becomes possible and practical to a certain limited extent—with or without surgery—but never without cultivation, i.e., artistic training in femininity."[51] Such reactions from within the transgender community *resisted* Benjamin's nosology. The conceptual uncertainty in Benjamin's thinking on gender disorientation allowed for the input of sexual minority subjects, which in turn helped Benjamin to sharpen his taxonomic elaboration.[52] This might explain why Benjamin never jettisoned the category of transvestism altogether. Instead, he pitched it as a crucial anchor for constructing the full SOS horizon.

Some readers were so moved by Benjamin's work that they came up with their own way of helping other kindred spirits. For example, D. B., a female-to-male (FTM) employee at Merrill Lynch, met Benjamin in 1971, received the first stage of surgery at Stanford in May 1972, and announced three months later his intention to establish the D. Foundation while waiting for a penile construction operation. The Foundation aimed to educate the public about transsexuality and counsel other like-minded individuals. Confident in his capacity as a "counsellor," D. B. prided himself for being an insider. Unlike medical doctors, he was "a very experienced TS who could be a good *friend*."[53] Indeed, D. B. revealed that he had already handlifted many other transsexuals to date, referring many to Stanford for surgery in a timely manner. Though "deeply interested in the *whole spectrum* of Transsexuality," D. B. found that "all the different, complicated degrees now used to measure Transsexuality are not really necessary."[54] He proposed a simpler classification since "There are really only *three* kinds of Transsexuals, and those three categories are just as overlapping and interwoven as is just about everything else"—what he called "Low-Intensity Transsexual (LIT)," "Medium-Intensity Transsexual (MIT)," and "High-Intensity Transsexual (HIT)."[55] D. B. was adamant in endorsing the universalist interpretation of transgenderism: "We are comparable, as a group, only to a *complete cross-section of Society!*"[56] D. B. humorously remarked, "Some Queens are more beautiful than the average natural-born woman, and may still no more want surgery than Richard Nixon! Looks, having been married before, sexual preference, and what have you, have nothing to do whatsoever with the person's feelings regarding his gender."[57] In this way, D. B. forsook the complicated taxonomy of the Benjamin scale at the same time endorsing its underlying continuum epistemology.

Global Convergence

A product of intellectual culmination and synthesis, Benjamin's work on transsexualism occasioned an episode of *global convergence* in the history of sexual science. The history of sexology has typically been understood through the international networks surrounding key figures or institutional settings. Hirschfeld's Institute for Sexual Science in Berlin and the Kinsey Institute in Bloomington, Indiana, have thus far received the greatest measure of scholarly attention. This can be explained in part by the privileged focus on homosexuality in queer historiography and is substantiated by the numerous biographies of Hirschfeld and Kinsey available to date.[58] Over time, we do see a shift in the center of gravity in sexual scientific research from Western Europe to the United States as a result of World War II. This transatlantic shift was paralleled in other domains of science, such as biology, sociology, psychoanalysis, and physics.[59] Yet Benjamin's sexology, including his collaboration with sexual minorities like Lawrence, constitutes an important example that diversifies this narrative. One often-overlooked venue that took an unprecedented interest in gender variance in the midcentury is the

Bombay-based *International Journal of Sexology*. With A. P. Pillay (1889–1957) serving as its editor in chief, this publication made Western India a gateway to global networks of sexual science between 1947 and 1955.[60] Encouraged by Benjamin and Kinsey, Lawrence not only came to immerse herself in a network of at least 152 transvestites, but also contributed an article, "Transvestism: An Empirical Study," to Pillay's journal in 1951 (figure 1.3).[61] Cross-cultural data from Bali, Samoa, and American and Mexican indigenous communities led Lawrence to posit that "transvestism . . . is worldwide . . . and has existed in one form or another in every culture known to recorded history."[62] In fact, when Benjamin published his first official article on the topic of transsexualism two years later, titled "Transvestism and Transsexualism," it also appeared in the same journal.[63] Historicizing the context in which the SOS took shape thus reveals alternative routes of sex research, such as Benjamin's activities and the global circuit of transgender science shaped by them.

In the years leading up to the publication of *The Transsexual Phenomenon*, Benjamin became the key physician to which most male-to-females (MTF) and FTMs turned for help.[64] As historian Joanne Meyerowitz has argued, "into the 1960s, most roads led to Benjamin."[65] In 1968, one patient from Reading, Pennsylvania, approached Benjamin out of desperation, because his family physician and psychiatrist told him that "they have never heard of anything so absurd" as conversion operations.[66] Yet many readers identified with the conditions described in Benjamin's writings and began to appropriate his terminology. In 1970, Benjamin summarized his clinical work with internist Charles Ihlenfeld (b. 1937) in New York: "The diagnosis of transsexualism is most frequently made by the patient himself. Many have read *The Transsexual Phenomenon* . . . and have rated themselves according to the Sex Orientation Scale. . . . Most of our patients are Type 5 and 6, although frequently they may have appeared to be 3 or 4. All want and need endocrine treatment, and almost all, at least initially, desire conversion surgery both to alter the sex organs and to reverse the social gender."[67]

Even though Benjamin was based in New York and San Francisco, his work invited a global response. In the late 1960s and 1970s, readers from all over the world learned to situate themselves on the SOS continuum. After reading *The Transsexual Phenomenon*, R. B. from Santa Maria, Rio Grande do Sul, Brazil, informed Benjamin that "I would probably rate on your S.O.S. as Type II Transvestite." With "an understanding wife" who

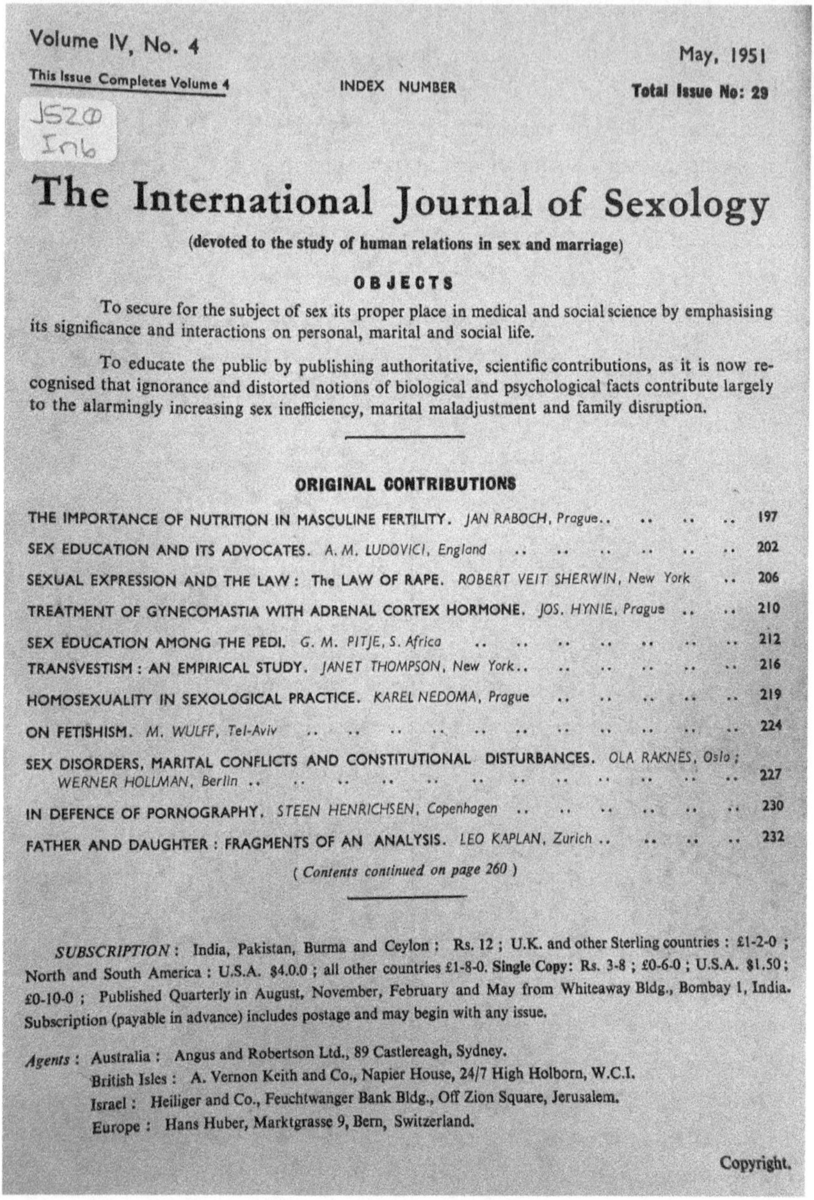

Volume IV, No. 4

May, 1951

This Issue Completes Volume 4

INDEX NUMBER

Total Issue No: 29

JS2⌀
Inb

The International Journal of Sexology

(devoted to the study of human relations in sex and marriage)

OBJECTS

To secure for the subject of sex its proper place in medical and social science by emphasising its significance and interactions on personal, marital and social life.

To educate the public by publishing authoritative, scientific contributions, as it is now recognised that ignorance and distorted notions of biological and psychological facts contribute largely to the alarmingly increasing sex inefficiency, marital maladjustment and family disruption.

ORIGINAL CONTRIBUTIONS

(Contents continued on page 260)

SUBSCRIPTION : India, Pakistan, Burma and Ceylon ; Rs. 12 ; U.K. and other Sterling countries : £1-2-0 ; North and South America : U.S.A. $4.0.0 ; all other countries £1-8-0. Single Copy: Rs. 3-8 ; £0-6-0 ; U.S.A. $1.50; £0-10-0 ; Published Quarterly in August, November, February and May from Whiteaway Bldg., Bombay 1, India. Subscription (payable in advance) includes postage and may begin with any issue.

Agents : Australia : Angus and Robertson Ltd., 89 Castlereagh, Sydney.
British Isles : A. Vernon Keith and Co., Napier House, 24/7 High Holborn, W.C.I.
Israel : Heiliger and Co., Feuchtwanger Bank Bldg., Off Zion Square, Jerusalem.
Europe : Hans Huber, Marktgrasse 9, Bern, Switzerland.

Fig. 1.3 The table of contents of the *International Journal of Sexology* issue in which Louise Lawrence's (Janet Thompson) "Transvestism" article appeared.
Source: *International Journal of Sexology* 4, no. 4 (1951).

"helps to ease the situation" at home, R. B. practiced transvestism quietly in Brazil.[68] In their correspondence, R. B. enclosed local news clippings, which he translated for Benjamin, about drag balls, the Carnival, sex reassignment, hormonal overdose, name change, and sex reregistration.[69] Benjamin introduced him to US-based magazines such as *Transvestia* and *Turnabout*.[70] In 1977, a correspondent from New Cumberland, Pennsylvania, who preferred to be addressed as "Minny" sought help from Benjamin after reading *The Transsexual Phenomenon*. Minny struggled for over five years in finding a sympathetic doctor who would take her concerns seriously. She had reached out to doctors at Stanford University, the University of Pennsylvania, Pennsylvania State University, and Johns Hopkins University, as well as clinics in Galveston, Memphis, and Cincinnati, to no avail. She explained to Benjamin that "From the S.O.S. Scale, I'd probably be between III and IV. . . . I would like Estrogen Therapy and the Conversion Operation." With a degree in chemistry and secondary education, Minny wanted to go on to live and work as a woman.[71] L. O., having identified herself as a "male transsexual" for over two decades, asked Benjamin to recommend a doctor in Canada from whom she might receive advice on hormones and surgery. In contrast to R. B. and Minny, L. O. considered her gender discomfort as the most severe form described by Benjamin: "I obtained your book, *The Transsexual Phenomenon*, from a Female (TS), and read it from cover to cover, and it confirmed me that I truly am No VI on the (SOS) Sex Orientation Scale."[72]

Benjamin also received letters from Asia. A reader in Hyderabad, West Pakistan, by the name of A. J. Q. wrote to Benjamin in the winter of 1969–1970: "After having read your book 'TS Phenomenon' I should frankly admit that it is the best book, I have read on the subject."[73] Taking up Benjamin's recommendation, A. J. Q. got in touch with the doctors at Johns Hopkins and ordered a copy of the book *Transsexualism and Sex Reassignment* by Richard Green (1836–2019) and John Money.[74] A. J. Q. wanted to know more. She asked specific questions about estrogen therapy, including whether it "helps in widening the pelvic bone and change of voice." She hoped Benjamin could put her "in contact with some wise patients, who have been successful in their life-long ambition of conversion and who may be willing to help me and give moral support, through correspondence."[75] A. J. Q. further requested "the addresses of doctors and hospitals who have been successful in this branch in the following countries: 1. Sweden, 2. Denmark, 3. Holland, 4. Japan, 5. Morocco

(Casablanca), 6. Italy, 7. Mexico, 8. U.S.A. (California & Hopkins)."[76] Their correspondence included "a photo—a life long ambition, which may some day turn into a reality" (figure 1.4).[77]

A. J. Q.'s inquiry about Japan is noteworthy given that Hyderabad is much closer to Japan than to the United States, where Benjamin was based. According to historian Mitsuhashi Junko, doctors at Tokyo's Nippon Medical University hospital performed Japan's first male-to-female sex change operation on cabaret singer Nagai Akiko (永井明子), the "Japanese Christine," in 1951.[78] (The first reported female-to-male case was that of the athletic star Tsutsumi Taeko.) Nagai's successful entertainment career inspired a generation of transgender individuals, also known as the "Blue Boys," to follow suit, but many did not choose to undergo full transformation.[79] Singer Carousel Maki, for example, received only castration in Japan but completed her transition in Morocco in 1973. Fear of being prosecuted for violating eugenic laws (which prohibited any sterilization surgery deemed unnecessary), Japanese doctors stopped performing such operations in 1965 (revived in 1998).[80] Therefore, regardless of Benjamin's awareness of the situation in Japan, by the time that A. J. Q.

Fig. 1.4 A. J. Q. from Hyderabad (1970).
Source: Courtesy of the Kinsey Institute Library and Special Collections.

reached out to him, Japan was no longer an international destination for genital surgery and would not be again for three decades.

In August 1972, another MTF, L. L. T., contacted Benjamin from Rizal, Philippines. L. L. T. implored, "I want to be myself . . . free of inhibitions, fears of unexplainable guilt feelings. I want to be a woman. Despite the cruel trick of anatomy, I still feel I was meant to be a woman."[81] In her letter to Benjamin, L. L. T. came right out and identified as a "true transsexual." "Though frightening," she continued, "I know that I am a type that most likely fits under Intensity VI" on the SOS scale.[82] This was corroborated by her psychiatrist, Dr. Gerardo Juan at the University of the Philippines, who told her that "I am truly sorry I cannot help you. You are decided and only a surgeon can help you."[83] By the time that Benjamin had heard from her, L. L. T. had seen at least a dozen doctors and psychologists. The Gender Identity Clinic at the Johns Hopkins Hospital filed her case under the name "Mrs. [L. L. T.]." By all counts, L. L. T. was determined to undergo genital conversion when she reached out to Benjamin and the Erickson Educational Foundation for financial assistance.[84] Like A. J. Q., L. L. T. enquired about the prospect of receiving the operation in Japan and sent Benjamin photos of herself in female attire (figure 1.5). These inquiries from Asia indicate that not only did Benjamin's writings have a non-Western impact, but readers residing in areas far removed from the United States took to the task of familiarizing themselves with and staying current on the literature on transsexuality. They cast a wide net in exploring surgical options near home and abroad.

The global response to Benjamin's work featured a prevailing interest in surgical intervention. In reaching out to Benjamin, F. C. from Farmingville, New York, insisted, "Please do not refer me to psychiatrists. I have spent much too much on them . . . they have failed."[85] Having "liv[ed] in the border of two worlds and suffering all time," F. L. from Stockholm wrote to Benjamin "to know all about operation."[86] D. H., an MTF from Frankfurt, took "an operation in consideration" and was ready to fly to the United States by the time he tried contacting Benjamin in summer 1974.[87] Many patients endorsed the transvestism-transsexualism continuum and explained that they started off identifying as a transvestite but were now ready to undergo surgery. In 1969, M. L. from Johannesburg disclosed, "I am a transvestite, a very unhappy and depressed one." M. L. entertained the idea of visiting the United States for a conversion operation but wanted to gather more information on this possibility before

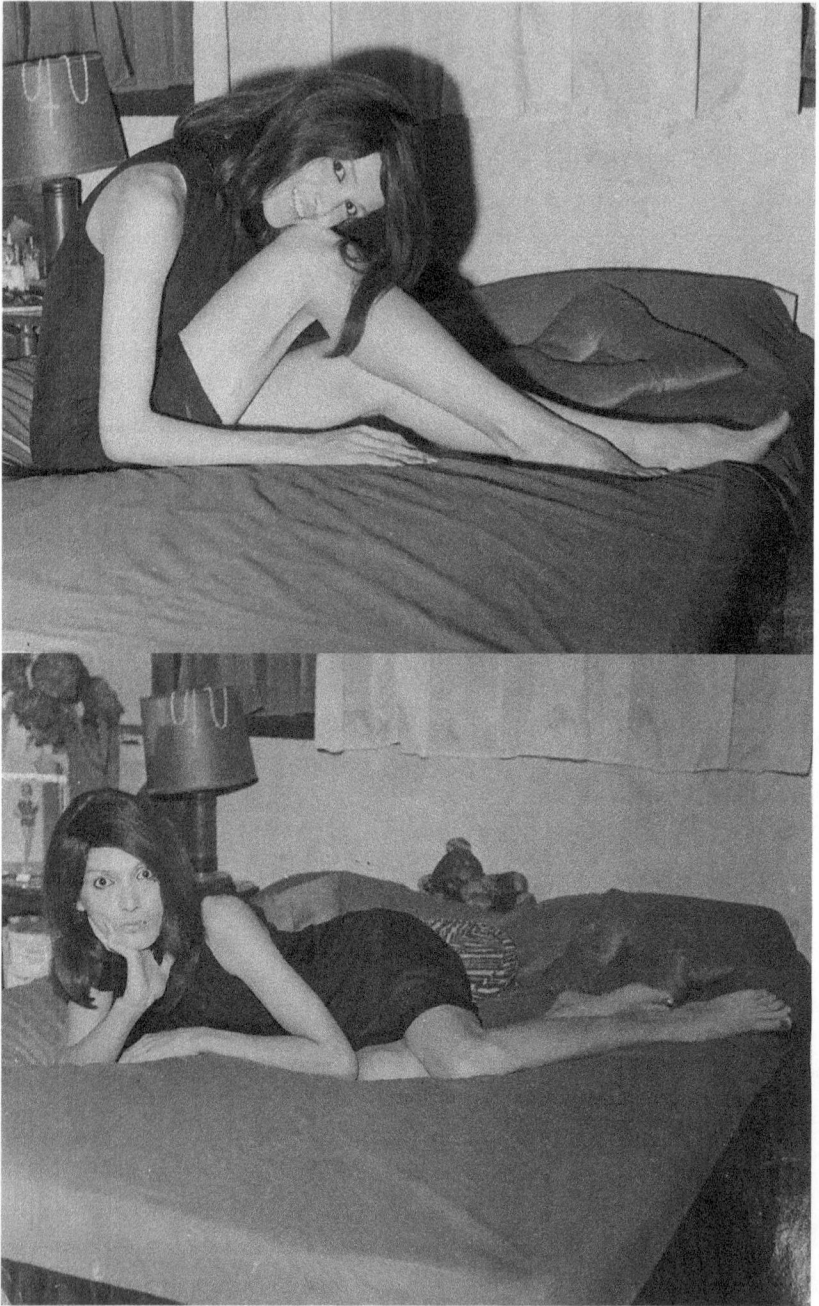

Fig. 1.5 L. L. T. from Rizal (1972).
Source: Courtesy of the Kinsey Institute Library and Special Collections.

taking action. As she explained in her letter, "You are my *very last* hope now Dr. Benjamin. If you can't help me, then my life is over. I have no intention of going on like this any longer."[88] In hoping to attain a more complete transformation, both R. B. (figure 1.6), an FTM from Switzerland, and N. B. (figure 1.7), an MTF from Germany, sent Benjamin photos of themselves dressed in the opposite gender.[89] In response to these desperate queries, Benjamin sometimes invited the correspondents, especially those already living in North America, to visit him for consultation.[90] More often, he provided as much information as possible over mail to help these patients and their physicians from afar.[91] He routinely acknowledged the limit of his assistance on account of being an endocrinologist rather than a surgeon.

Some correspondents made inquiries about two surgeons in particular: Georges Burou (1910–1987), who carried out the operation of Carousel Maki, in Casablanca and Jose Jesus Barbosa in Tijuana. In 1964, M. L. from St. Louis came across Benjamin's name in the magazine *Sexology* and decided to contact him about the surgeon who operated on the English model April Ashley (b. 1935). M. L.'s mother had allowed M. L. "to 'dress up' in some of her old clothes . . . when we were alone in our apartment" since the age of fourteen. When M. L.'s mother met Ashley in Europe, Burou's practice was brought to their attention, and M. L. began to envision devoting time to social work "such as being a Red Cross girl in a hospital" after undergoing surgery abroad.[92] Through Christine Jorgensen, H. L. in Jamaica reached out to Benjamin in 1965 "to know if it is possible to have sex-change operation in America." H. L. "was told there is a clinic in North Africa, where several Frenchmen had undergone [very successful] operations."[93] Benjamin confirmed the option of going to the French doctor in Casablanca for surgery. However, "you would have to . . . send a picture of yourself dressed as a woman before you can expect any appointment with him."[94] In a letter to a patient in Buenos Aires dated summer 1967, Benjamin identified two clinics in the United States (Johns Hopkins and Minnesota) and two abroad (Burou's in Morocco and Barbosa's in Mexico) where operation might be available with certain restrictions.[95] Benjamin became personally acquainted with Barbosa and continued to refer patients to his practice in Tijuana until at least 1969.[96]

In sum, the Benjamin scale is important to the global history of sexual science because it enables a new analytical perspective. This history has been narrated predominantly through the prisms of translation, circulation,

Fig. 1.6 R. B. (right) from Switzerland (1971).
Source: Courtesy of the Kinsey Institute Library and Special Collections.

Fig. 1.7 N. B. (right) from Germany (1974).
Source: Courtesy of the Kinsey Institute Library and Special Collections.

and exchange.[97] Certainly, all three lenses are important to my account of the Benjamin archive, but the example of the SOS also points to a somewhat different analytic: innovation.[98] Benjamin's development of the SOS went hand in hand with his effort to crystalize the diagnostic category of transsexualism. Not only did Benjamin's patients understand themselves by using the SOS classification, they also utilized its *full* spectrum to articulate their problems. That is, they navigated his sexological system for their own purposes, adapting it to their own needs. The continuum framework that underpinned the Benjamin scale made it possible for individuals with diverse cultural backgrounds and gender inclinations to associate themselves within the plurality of sexual knowledge. In other words, the scalar, rather than discrete, characteristics of Benjamin's transgender sexology easily lent itself to a global absorption of his ideas. Benjamin's work was in turn shaped by the global response it generated. Though Benjamin is often credited for popularizing the idea of transsexualism, his most original contribution perhaps lies in *the building of adjacent variations into a continuous epistemology of gender nonconformity*.[99] If we take the SOS as a new global technology of sexual selfhood—reciprocally produced by an international network of readers, patients, and correspondents—it is possible to reconceptualize the emergence of transsexuality in the mid-twentieth century as an intrinsically cross-regional and cross-temporal phenomenon, that is, the byproduct of a transtopian innovation.

Murderous Passion

Another thread of transtopian genealogy runs from an undercurrent in queer historiographical practice: the unstable consanguinity between cross-gender and homoerotic tendencies as the foci of historical analysis.[100] For instance, based on her global survey of the history of same-sex sexuality, historian Leila J. Rupp concludes that "sexual relations between two genitally alike (or originally alike) bodies are in many cases best defined as different-gender than same-sex relations."[101] Another incisive articulation of this insight can be found in Eve Kosofsky Sedgwick's *Epistemology of the Closet* (1990), which spotlights an "internal incoherence and mutual contradiction" in the binary definition of sexuality in the modern West.[102] Specifically, Sedgwick identifies "the contradiction between seeing same-sex object choice on the one hand as a matter of liminality or *transitivity* between genders, and seeing it on the other hand as reflecting an impulse of *separatism* . . . within each gender."[103] The framework of transtopia operates *at this very threshold* between gender transience and sameness, providing a structuralist impetus to defy transgender essentialism and congeal the tacit overlaps between queerness and transness.

Taking the contradiction between gender transitivity and gender separatism as an epistemologically productive cue, the second half of this chapter offers a "competitive comparison" of three temporally and geographically isolated episodes of a lesbian love murder story.[104] I focus on (1) the notorious trial of nineteen-year old Alice Mitchell, who took the life of seventeen-year old Freda Ward on February 23, 1892, in Memphis, Tennessee, the United States; (2) the lesser-known legal proceedings of twenty-two-year old Tao Sijin (陶思瑾), who killed twenty-year-old Liu Mengying (劉夢瑩) on February 11, 1932, in Hangzhou, Zhejiang, China; and (3) the well-documented prosecution of nineteen-year-old Mahin Padidarnazar, who murdered Zahra Amin on November 27, 1973, in Lahijan, Gilan, Iran.[105] My integrative reading of these incidents brackets homoeroticism as the *sole* analytical fulcrum, rather than jettisoning its pertinence altogether. Although the trials of Mitchell, Tao, and Mahin burst open public interest in female homosexuality in dispersed regions of the globe, the purported gender persona of the three protagonists diverged in significant ways. Public discourses uniformly depicted Mitchell and Mahin with a conspicuous masculine identity (gender transitivity); Tao, in contrast, was never understood by interested parties as anything other than normatively feminine (gender separatism).

Drawing on the strength of the tension between transitivity and separatism, I construe the cases of Mitchell, Tao, and Mahin as analogous in the sense of a *transtopian asymptote*. In mathematics, an asymptote describes a limiting behavior whereby a function, as expressed in a line or curve, approaches a given value but never reaches it. If we apply this concept to the comparability of Mitchell, Tao, and Mahin, it forges an unresolved limit at the nexus of gender/sexual subversion, so the transtopian nature of the cross-temporal analogy at once disrupts the epistemic priority of homoerotic over cross-gender subjectivity while nevertheless maintaining lesbianism as a meaningful ground of comparison. Alternatively put, the very undetermined status of the homosexual-transgender overtones ascribed to the three cases is precisely what a transtopian approach calls attention to, as opposed to something it seeks to overcome. Whereas the last section charts an international circuit of sexual knowledge emanating outward from a central focus on Benjamin's work, here I map three globally significant historical events—divided by time and place—onto one another in order to delineate a nodal core (the asymptotic value) by which they correlate but do not meet. Whether our view is centrifugally or centripetally oriented, the point, again, is to resist the temptation to identify who qualifies more or less as transgender (or lesbian) and, by extension, to conceive of transness as a social phenomenon with which different actors form contiguous orders of affinity.

Structurally, the three cases share certain similarities and differences. All three incidents were described as gruesome crimes of passion. Mitchell, Tao, and Mahin killed their lovers because they were too emotionally attached. The reckless murder may have arisen out of jealousy, possessiveness, selfishness, or other related inclinations, but the media brought all three "lesbian" relationships to public awareness in a swift and seemingly unambiguous fashion. The method of killing was also similar across the board. Mitchell slashed the throat of Ward with her father's razor; Tao disfigured at least sixteen places on Liu's body with knife wounds; and Mahin stabbed Zahra sixteen times with a switchblade knife that she was known for carrying around.[106] And all three couples entertained the idea of forming a lasting union in one way or another. Mitchell and Ward considered eloping; Tao and Liu swore to never enter a heterosexual marriage; and Mahin and Zahra "plotted running away together."[107] Of course, the historical circumstances were different: the Mitchell-Ward incident took place in the late-nineteenth-century American South, the Tao-Liu tragedy occurred in a Grand Canal–based city in interwar China, and the Mahin-Zahra affair happened in a small northern town of prerevolutionary Iran. Despite the contextual differences, my following analysis makes the strategic choice of averting chronological linearity in order to compress and translate the three episodes into a meaningful synthesis.

All three events drew a significant public following and turned the subsequent legal hearings into a dramatic spectacle. A newspaper story announced that the number of people, half of whom were women, who arrived in the Shelby County Criminal Court, in Tennessee, from February 23 to 25, 1892, was unprecedented in American history.[108] On April 1, 1932, the initially scheduled date for the first hearing of the Tao trial, an estimate of two thousand people, including female students, doctors, lawyers, professors, army recruits, reporters, and relatives and friends of Tao and Liu, flooded the Hangzhou district courtroom and broke the glass window of the front entrance. The judge had to delay the hearing due to the chaos.[109] The national dailies in Iran cultivated a nationwide obsession with the Mahin trial, which lasted a week, from July 18 to 25, 1974, in Rasht, the provincial capital of Gilan, and billed it as "one of the most clamorous trials of the year."[110]

The single most prominent feature shared by all three murder trials is the defendants' insanity plea. Their defense lawyers adopted this strategy to deflect the criminal responsibility of the accused by rerouting the juridical focus onto the plausibility of mental instability. In the case of Mahin, her lawyers downplayed the sexualized nature of her relationship with Zahra. Instead, they focused on her temporary insanity and turned the alleged mental disorder into the cause of her crime. According to her family lawyer, Ahmad Mu'tamidi, what Mahin suffered from was not sexual deviancy but a disorder of "double personality" (dau-shakhsiyati). Because Mu'tamidi's court statement integrated Mahin's gender transgression into an insanity defense, it is worth quoting at length:

Mahin was born in Lahijan and went to school at the age of six. . . . I spoke with her mother; she does not remember Mahin ever playing with dolls, she was never interested in girls' games. . . . From the fifth grade, that is, when her puberty was setting in and her personality was shaping, her temperament and her psyche suddenly changed such that she flunked the fifth grade. . . . She failed in high school as well. . . . Her father took her to Tehran, but there too she quarreled with teachers and students and they returned to Lahijan. . . . I checked with Dr. Ladan, Rasht's Legal Medical doctor. I asked him, considering Lahijan's climate, at what age girls begin to menstruate. He responded between eleven and twelve years of age. . . . But Mahin did not menstruate at ten, or fifteen, because her body's organism is not proper, she is ill. . . . She has an extra chromosome. She told me in jail that she had something like a one-day light menstruation but even that one day put her in an insane state of mind. . . . The day she committed injury with a knife, she was in the same abnormal state. . . . My client's character began to change radically; . . . at fourteen her situation ceased to be one of a woman; she began to wear male trousers and jacket, carry prayer beads and a knife, and imitate male gestures, wishing to become an army officer or a policeman on a motorcycle. Can she be considered a man then? No. . . . I say she has a masculine personality, a personality that has not been shaped properly. . . . I reject the charge of sexual deviancy and *homosexualité*. I say she has double personality. She has a personality deviancy not sexual deviancy.[111]

Mu'tamidi even produced a letter written by Mahin, dated April 15, 1973, seeking help from her brother to change sex: "Help me if you can, I cannot be a woman." Mu'tamidi used this letter as the basis for requesting a new medical and psychological examination of Mahin, which the court ultimately rejected. On her part, Mahin went along with her lawyers' strategy by describing herself as "ill and a nervous wreck."[112]

Outside the courtroom, reporters portrayed Mahin as a puzzling figure unhappy with her assigned gender at birth. The Iranian national daily that covered the case most extensively, *Ittila'at*, carried a front-page article on November 28, 1937, with the subheading, "The accused is known among her acquaintances and neighbors as '*jahil-i mahall*' [tough guy of the neighborhood]," and a fuller report on page 18 claiming that Mahin "always wears men's clothes."[113] As noted by historian Afsaneh Najmabadi, "This focus on her gender nonconformity continued to inform the presentation of Mahin by the press all the way to its end."[114] The mainstream newspapers

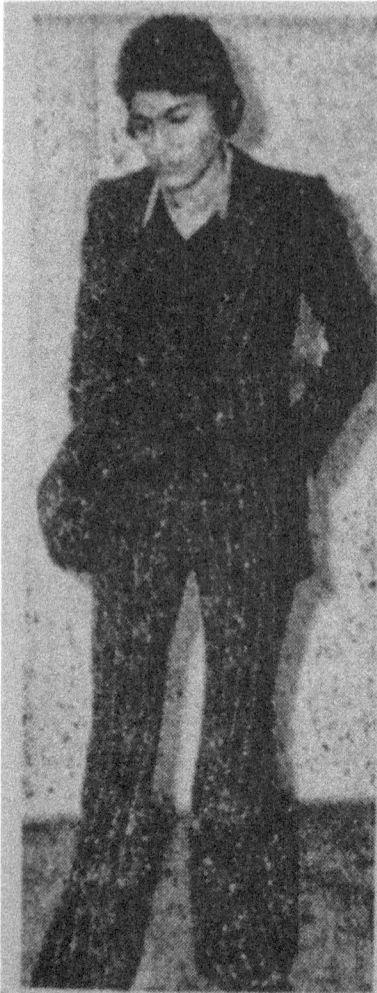

زهرا امین دختر جوانی که به
ضرب چاقوی دختر دیگری بقتل رسید

اشتباه نکنید صاحب این عکس که
کت وشلوار مردانه تن کرده پسر
نیست او خدیجهخانم بدبدارنظرمعروف
به مهین است که متهم به قتل زهرا
امین میباشد

Fig. 1.8 Mahin Padidarnazar (left) and
Zahra Amin (right).
Source: *Ittila'at*, November 29, 1973.

printed photographs of Mahin both before and during trial. Before trial,
Ittila'at contrasted the more masculine Mahin wearing a suit with the more
feminine Zahra (figure 1.8). During trial, the same daily featured a photograph of Mahin to reveal her "transformation" while in prison over the
previous months: "Mahin Padidarnazar . . . exhibits masculine behavior,

wears masculine clothes, and has a masculine hairstyle. This is one of her last photographs, which she has changed in this way while in prison, giving herself eyeglasses, mustache, and a beard" (figure 1.9).[115] When pressed by Pari Sekandari, the journalist who followed the Mahin-Zahra case most exhaustively, Mahin explained that "I have always considered myself psychologically a boy" even though "I swear that I am a girl." Mahin also admitted that she had desired to be surgically transformed into a boy "many times" and embraced the label of "same-sex playing."[116]

Mahin's family and friends provided further insight into her unconventional gender persona. When approached by Sekandari to comment on the case, Mahin's mother replied: "Of course my daughter was a very violent and bad girl. Actually we did not dare to call her 'girl.' If we did, she would become angry and curse us. She hated that she was a girl. She wished she could become a man. But Zahra was not innocent either. She used to come and visit my daughter all the time."[117] In this way, Mahin's mother hinted at something innate about Mahin's unusual gender orientation, rooted in her upbringing, and confirmed that her affection for Zahra was reciprocated. The plot thickened when Mahin's high school friends weighed in. In particular, their remarks suggested a circle of female same-sex friendships formed around Mahin. She stood as the central masculine figure in this circle, surrounded by admirers and potential lovers.[118] Yet no one surpassed Zahra in Mahin's mind. In her final defense in the courtroom, Mahin explained, "when I met Zari. I felt she was exactly what I had expected all these years. I attached myself strongly to Zari. My only companion and soulmate was Zari. . . . We sought solace in each other. She gave me hope in life."[119] Mahin concluded by reciting a poem she composed for Zahra, weeping uncontrollably before she could finish her defense. The trial ended on July 25, 1974, with Mahin receiving a life sentence.

Alice Mitchell's defense attorneys also pushed for an insanity plea. However, their position was somewhat atypical and differed from the one put forth by Mahin's legal team. Instead of pleading "not guilty" of murder by reason of insanity, Mitchell's attorneys presented a plea of "present insanity"—comparable to what is known as the plea of "incompetent to stand trial" today. As Judge DuBose explained for the jury in the Mitchell case, "The question is, whether the defendant has mental capacity sufficient to make a rational defense to the charge in the indictment."[120] Therefore, Mitchell appeared before the Criminal Court of Shelby County on July 18, 1892, to face a lunacy inquisition rather than a trial for

مهین بدردارنظر که بانهام هـل دوست و هـشاگردی سابق خود
مزهرا، در رست محاکمه مشود، رفتاری پـسرانه دارد و لباس پـسرانه
میـوند ومـوهایش ارایش پـسرانه مدهد .
این یکی از آخرین عکسهای مهین است که خود در زندان آن را به
این روز در آورده و برای خودش عـنک وریش و سبیل کشیده .

Fig. 1.9 Mahin displaying a masculine appearance.
Source: *Ittila'at*, July 21, 1974.

murder. Her family hired defense attorneys who consulted physicians and, by drawing on the latter's expertise, argued for committing her to the state lunatic asylum rather than putting her on trial for murder. In this way, the defense strategy protected the race- and class-based moral reputation of the Mitchell family, since it framed Mitchell as neither "bad" nor morally reprehensible but ill. The competing evidence offered by the prosecution attacked precisely Mitchell's respectability to hold her legally responsible for the murder. As historian Lisa Duggan has astutely observed, "Alice Mitchell's predicament required a 'responsible' woman's defense— one that would protect her family's reputation, while also containing any danger she might represent to the stability of the white home."[121]

Even though Mahin's lawyers and Mitchell's attorneys differed in their defense tactic, they shared a similar approach to demonstrating insanity based on evidence of gender transgression. In Mitchell's case, this evidentiary claim was built into the centerpiece of her defense—a "hypothetical case" constructed by her attorneys.[122] The hypothetical case synthesized the various aspects of Mitchell's life experience intended for presentation in court and translated them into a coherent narrative of illness akin to a "medical case" format. It was presented to expert witnesses, such as the physicians who offered diagnosis of the defendant based on its content. The opening of the hypothetical case, for example, suggested that Mitchell had inherited "mental alienation" from her mother's "puerperal insanity."[123] The testimony of all five physician experts confirmed this clinical portraiture and agreed on the etiology of her probably incurable insanity.[124] Both the prosecution and the defense could, in principle, deliver diverging hypothetical cases to the same experts for evaluation, but in Mitchell's case, only the defense generated a coherent narrative, which they circulated widely through the press. In this way, the hypothetical case at Mitchell's lunacy inquisition reached for three kinds of impact: medical, legal, and public. "The case's narrative," according to Duggan, "was therefore directed toward eliciting a diagnosis of medical pathology, meeting the legal standard for 'present insanity,' *and* persuading the jury and the public that, in commonsense terms, Alice Mitchell was crazy."[125]

The hypothetical case stressed Mitchell's deviation from gender norms. The two foremost clues came from Mitchell's long history of masculine temperament and Freda Ward's contrasting gender disposition (figures 1.10 and 1.11). The hypothetical case stated:

Fig. 1.10 Alice Mitchell.
Source: Outhistory.org.

ALICE MITCHELL.

Fig. 1.11 Freda Ward.
Source: Outhistory.org.

Miss Fred Ward in Life.

Alice was a nervous, excitable child, somewhat undersize. As she grew she did not manifest interest in those childish amusements and toys that girls are fond of. . . . She delighted in marbles and tops, in base ball and foot ball [*sic*], and was a member of the children's base ball nine. She spent much time with her brother Frank, who was next youngest, playing marbles and spinning tops. She preferred him and his sports to her sisters. He practiced with her at target shooting with a small rifle, to her great delight. She excelled this brother at tops, marbles and feats of activity. . . . She often rode [a horse] about the lot bareback, as a boy would. . . . To the family she seemed a regular tomboy. . . . She disliked sewing and needle work. Her mother could not get her to do such work. . . . She was wholly without that fondness for boys that girls usually manifest.[126]

When brought to the court, Mitchell's relatives, neighbors, and observers confirmed her boyish "peculiarities."[127] In contrast to Mitchell's preference for sports, games, and activities typically considered masculine, Ward was described in the hypothetical case as the couple's feminine half. Freda Ward was "girl-like," "tender and affectionate," and "took no pleasure in the boyish sports that Alice delighted in." Her "instincts and amusements were feminine." Mitchell and Ward "became lovers in the sense of that relationship between persons of different sexes."[128] In their love letters, Ward sometimes addressed Mitchell as "Alvin."[129] The defense juxtaposed Mitchell's masculinity against a soft and passive image of Ward, thereby conjuring a heteronormative script of mutual attraction.

The contrasting portraits of Mitchell and Ward served the defense's ultimate purpose: to explain, using the Victorian language of gender opposition, the two women's engagement as the conclusive proof of Mitchell's insanity. Shortly after the crime itself, the press issued an interview statement from Mitchell about her planned marriage with Ward.

> The day for our wedding was set, and then not all of the powers in the world could have separated us. It was our intention to leave here and go to St. Louis, and I would have been Freda's slave. I would have devoted my whole life to making her happy. . . . But when Freda returned my engagement ring it broke my heart. . . . Then, indeed, I resolved to kill Freda because I loved her so much that I wanted her to die loving me.[130]

The five medical experts who testified unanimously agreed that statements like these rendered Mitchell's intent to marry Ward as a "fixed delusion," an "insane idea," a "false judgement," or an "impossible idea."[131] Dr. John Hill Callendar, a Professor of Physiology and Psychology at the University of Nashville and Vanderbilt University, reprinted his assessment in the *Memphis Medical Monthly*:

> She seemed in her simplicity and weakness of mind to have no conception of the preposterous character of the marriage she looked for, and spoke in detail of the preparations as to man's apparel for the occasion, the procurement of a license for the ceremony, of the clipping of her hair after the fashion of men, the cultivation of a mustache, if Freda wanted her to wear one. The frankness and sincerity of her manner on this topic was evidence either of a gross delusion or the conception of a person imbecile.[132]

Mitchell's gender transgression thus lent weight to the insanity defense: the planned marriage was perceived as an indisputable sign of her lunacy. "Once Alice's lethal desperation led her to murder and put her on trial," explains Duggan, "the marriage proposal became evidence of insanity."[133] The court declared Mitchell insane on July 30, and she was committed to the Western State Insane Asylum at Bolivar, Tennessee, on August 1, 1892.

The Hangzhou Femme Fatale

The defense strategy in Tao Sijin's case was exceptional in that it struggled to frame a cogent narrative of insanity (figures 1.12 and 1.13). Like Mahin, Tao was never granted a psychiatric evaluation despite her lawyers' repeated emphases on its necessity.[134] Yet if Mu'tamidi proposed the specific diagnosis of "double personality" for Mahin's condition, Tao's attorneys, Li Baosen (李寶森) and Wang Shaogong (汪紹功), pushed for a more open-ended plea. When Tao appeared before the Hangzhou district court to face the murder trial on April 2, 1932, the defense counsel announced the "unusualness" of this case. Another key witness agreed that Tao showed symptoms of a neurotic disorder. The defense counsel immediately declared that Tao "suffered from neurasthenia" (神經衰弱病, *shenjing shuairuo bing*) and "psychological perversion" (變態心理, *biantai xinli*). They argued that a medical evaluation of Tao was necessary to determine her psychological fitness.[135] Later on, Li and Wang submitted a formal request "in the interest of juridical impartiality."[136] In this document and all subsequent arguments, the defense switched to a new diagnostic category called "the deterioration of the mental condition" (精神衰弱, *jingshen shuairuo*).[137] The allusion to neurasthenia's popular definition as the weakening of the nerves was unambiguous. Yet, in adopting the new language of *jingshen* (psyche), the defense argument moved away from a biological etiology rooted in the nervous system and toward a more psychologically grounded defense. As a highly educated young lady, Tao must have experienced a considerable level of trauma, which resulted in her delirious state of mind. Otherwise, the defense reasoning went, it would be difficult to explain the cause of such a tragedy.

The defense team compiled a list of factors that, when taken together, suggested the gravity of Tao's mental weakness: the intimate bond between Tao and Liu did not logically lead to a murderous act; the testimony of

Fig. 1.12 Tao Sijin.
Source: Current News Agency, *Tao Sijin yu Liu Mengying* [Tao Sijin and Liu Mengying] (陶思瑾與劉夢瑩) (Hangzhou: Shishi xinwenshe, 1932).

Fig. 1.13 Liu Mengying.
Source: Current News Agency, *Tao Sijin yu Liu Mengying* [Tao Sijin and Liu Mengying] (陶思瑾與劉夢瑩) (Hangzhou: Shishi xinwenshe, 1932).

another key witness explicitly pointed out Tao's mental debility;[138] and the accumulation of a series of events in the four years leading up to the murder undermined Tao's psychological well-being, such as the emotional residue from two prior suicidal attempts, the death of her brother, the death of Liu's father, the growing threats explicit in the letters from Liu, and even the physiological effects of the strongly scented fragrance and powder regularly used by Tao.[139] Li and Wang made a case for distinguishing what they called *jingshen shuairuo* from full-blown psychiatric disorders (精神病, *jingshen bing*), claiming that a person suffering from the former could easily slip into the latter under stressful circumstances. Legally speaking, whereas the severity of true psychiatric disorders would relieve the defendant's criminal responsibility by reason of insanity, *jingshen shuairuo* would still hold the accused accountable for the crime but with the possibility of receiving a lighter sentence. The rhetoric of Tao's insanity defense rested on the latter, that is, something akin to what is known as "moral insanity."[140] Citing Sigmund Freud and Josef Breuer, the defense team singled out Tao's homosexual relation (同性戀愛, *tongxing lian'ai*) with Liu as the major cause of psychological trauma and emotional battles that culminated in *jingshen shuairuo*.[141] It is important to note that throughout their argument, Li and Wang never specified the purpose of a potential medical evaluation: it was unclear whether its aim was to determine Tao's partial insanity when committing the crime (as in Mahin's case) or to confirm that she was mentally unfit to stand trial (as in Mitchell's case).

Tao's defense strategy also differed from the tactics used by Mahin's and Mitchell's lawyers in another subtle but notable respect. Whereas Mahin's and Mitchell's gender transgression underpinned their legal defense (presented as evidence for either the development of a personality disorder or the lunatic fantasy of a lesbian marriage), Tao's attorneys constructed a conventionally feminine image of Tao. In regard to the insanity plea, their description of Tao narrowed over time: they specifically homed in on matching Tao's symptoms to the typical clinical portrait of a female hysteric.[142] They referred to Tao's anxiety, insomnia, irritability, nervousness, psychological instability, traumatic emotions, and erratic behaviors, among other traits, to bolster her hyperfeminine impression.[143] The prosecution found this approach increasingly convincing and thus threatening, so they ultimately filed a motion to dismiss the request for psychiatric evaluation.[144] The prosecution explained the motion on three grounds: that Tao's mental capacity must have been stable enough to be admitted to a public fine arts institute in the first place, that her family members never cautioned against potential symptoms of hysteria when she lived by herself, and that the timing of Tao's insanity defense was too coincidental and it was only reasonable to suspect that the request came with the sole purpose of sentence reduction.[145] The Hangzhou district court did not grant a medical evaluation and sentenced Tao to life imprisonment.[146]

In their appeal to the Zhejiang provincial high court, Li and Wang challenged the severity of the original sentence by conforming Tao to normative gender stereotypes. This contrasted sharply with the widely circulated descriptions of Mahin and Mitchell in the press. Reports of Mahin's violent temper, including previous attempts to beat up her mother, and Mitchell's "man-like murder" served to reinforce the masculine signature of their lesbian desire that constituted a clue to their sadistic pathology.[147] On the contrary, Li and Wang insisted that the original penalty from the Hangzhou district court was too extreme because it was built on a misrepresentation of Tao's behavior as "ruthless" (殘忍, canren): "the criteria for defining a murderous act ruthless include the execution of cruel methods and merciless harm, such as gunning, burning, disembowelment, and continuous torture."[148] Yet Tao explained in court that she accidentally killed Liu because Liu approached her with a knife first, so the act was in many ways a self-defense. The defense rebutted the cutthroat depiction of Tao by characterizing her as a "naive," "frank," and "reasonable" girl.[149] Some experts attributed Tao's murderous act to her suffering from paranoia.[150] Others sympathized with the psychological duress that Tao had been under and pleaded for a lighter sentence.[151] The focus on her court appearance bolstered an image of uncontested femininity. When she appeared before the Zhejiang provincial high court on July 26, 1932, the press described her dress—from "a lavender long dress made of Indian silk with floral print" to her "beige stockings" and "yellow leather skimmers"—and her "lightly powdered face" in a "natural posture."[152] The Zhejiang provincial high court favored the prosecution and imposed a capital sentence, which was subsequently vacated by the Supreme Court in Beiping. The Supreme Court reinstated the penalty of life imprisonment handed down from the Hangzhou district court, but Tao was freed from prison, as part of a general amnesty, when the Japanese army occupied Hangzhou on December 24, 1937.[153]

To make a persuasive insanity plea, the defense in all three cases solicited expert commentary from medical professionals. Whether testifying in person or delivering written dispositions for court consideration, doctors dissected the gender and sexual symptoms of Mahin, Mitchell, and Tao through their life histories, diaries, poems, personal notes, and correspondences with the victims, many of which were subsequently published in the press.[154] In Mahin's case, psychologists, physicians, sociologists, and lawyers carried out extensive debates on female homosexuality and its relation to sex change outside the courtroom.[155] In their testimonies to support Mitchell's insanity, alienists and neurologists attributed her perversion to physical abnormalities, perhaps as a result of hermaphroditism or genital aberrations (e.g., enlarged clitoris).[156] Even though some doctors diagnosed Mitchell as suffering from an "emotional morbid impulse," none of those who testified questioned her insanity.[157] Similarly, Chinese medical experts attributed Tao's criminality and hysteric manifestations to physical causes, such as ovarian pathologies.[158] Pan Guangdan (潘光旦, 1899–1967), the sociologist who made eugenics (優生學, youshengxue) a household term in Republican China, anatomized Tao's case in a series of articles that advocated the expansion of forensic psychopathology and the mental hygiene movement.[159] Pan concluded that Tao was a "natural invert" and indeed mentally unstable in two essays, both of which were submitted to court by Tao's lawyers in support of her insanity plea.[160]

Perhaps most importantly, all three cases facilitated interconnections between local, national, and global networks of sexual knowledge. The deeply provincial nature of the Mahin-Zahra story made it a distinctively Iranian phenomenon. For readers in Iran, Mahin and Zahra were "'our lesbians,' not some Euro-American curiosity, not psycho-sexological cases analyzed in scientific textbooks or health pages of magazines, nor translations of 'foreign' science or 'alien' cultures."[161] The media portrayals of their passion, family history, gender traits, and eventual fate gave global concepts of sexual identity a native currency. Originating from Memphis, the Mitchell-Ward tragedy, too, exceeded the regional context despite its localization. Its escalated publicity cemented a transatlantic flow of Anglo-European sexual science. Not only did doctors in the United States draw on the writings of Krafft-Ebing and Ellis to make sense of Mitchell, her story subsequently made its way back into the European catalogue of sexological cases, including the 1906 edition of *Psychopathia Sexualis* and the 1915 edition of *Sexual Inversion*.[162]

Similarly, Chinese sexologists appropriated Western sexual science and psychoanalysis to diagnose Tao's mental health. Gu Yin (顧寅), a Suzhou-based physician well known for his expertise in sexual health, cited the theory of universal bisexuality and the latest endocrinological findings to explain Tao's condition as "a problem of glands and secretions."[163] In the 1920s, Gu had written about female masturbation, hysteria, psychoanalytic sublimation, sadism, masochism, fetishism, and neurasthenia in a series of articles published in *Life and Health*, a popular science journal founded by the Shanghai Life and Health Society in 1925.[164] In interpreting Tao's symptoms, Gu referenced Freud, Steinach, Hirschfeld, and Italian criminologist Cesare Lombroso (1835–1909), among many other foreign authorities, and argued that, during menstrual periods, women tended to be psychologically weak due to hormonal imbalance and thus particularly prone to acting out irrational, including criminal, behaviors.[165] By the time that Gu commented on Tao, the Mitchell-Ward case had already served as a template for European sexologists to explain female sexual inversion as, in Havelock Ellis's words, "a favorable soil for the seeds of passional crime, under those conditions of jealousy and allied emotions which must so often enter into the invert's life."[166] Gu mobilized this template to support his theory of how women who experienced "abnormal sexual excitation during menstrual periods, including homosexual arousal," were prone to "commit a murderous crime when rejected by her girlfriend."[167] Other observers broached the Tao-Liu romance as a prime example of the same-sex platonic love glorified by British sexologist Edward Carpenter.[168]

Across the board in the 1890s United States, 1930s China, and 1970s Iran, male sexologists focused on women's growing presence in the public sphere as a plausible clue to the emergence of "mannish" lesbians as new agents of social problem.[169] By making a scientific division between the normal and the pathological, they argued that these violent murders could be avoided even if they disagreed on the treatability of same-sex desire. Experts held parents and educators, in particular, responsible for preventing the intense same-sex friendships rampant in schools—itself becoming a global trend in the twentieth century—from turning into the morbid, pathological type of homosexuality that led to these cold-blooded crimes.[170] Yet, in retrospect, if lesbianism has served as a common ground for comparing the three murder stories in North America, East Asia, and the Middle East, that very possibility hinges on a divergence in the medico-legal characterizations of Mitchell's, Tao's, and Mahin's gender embodiment. The tension between homosexuality and gender variance had been contested but also intersected in the globally circulating sexological concept of inversion; that threshold also constitutes the unresolved limit that defines the transtopian asymptote of the Mitchell-Tao-Mahin analogy.

Trans in Relation

This chapter shifts the way we treat transgender as a category of historical analysis from a fixed set of meanings to a continuous structure, from an identitarian locus to a relational signifier within a connective system. Though a global history of transgenderism that accounts for all places and all times has yet to be written, the postidentitarian method advanced here takes a crucial step in thinking about the stakes and politics of such a project. Based in the

United States for most of his career, Benjamin created a conceptual instrument for capturing transgender variation that connected him to other minorities and experts around the world. Perhaps there were many others like Lawrence who organized informally and worked hard to change the minds of experts. It is probable that there were others who, without the ability to read English or access to Benjamin's work, inquired about changing their sex in different corners of the world. It is more than likely that the Benjamin archive represents only the tip of the iceberg. Nevertheless, the variety of experience present in the genealogy of the SOS complicates a monolithic understanding of to whom and where the "transsexual" label applies. The Mitchell, Tao, and Mahin cases, on the other hand, have been treated by historians as detached episodes of lesbian crime of passion, but comparing them in a commensurate frame brings to light the transgender, if not transtopian, traits of the queer protagonists in question. Given the existing theoretical tools, it would be difficult to locate the isolated experience of Tao squarely within transgender, rather than lesbian, historiography. Tao might not fit Halberstam's definition of "trans★" or Stryker's notion of "transgender," but an asymptotic genealogy of transtopia makes possible the imbrication of her story with the cross-cultural politics of transness.

By way of conclusion, I would like to put the Benjamin scale and the lesbian murders in dialogue with the history of "global Christine." This simultaneous occurrence in queer history refers to the refractions in Taiwan and Mexico of the saga of the American transsexual icon Christine Jorgensen. In 1950, Jorgensen traveled to Denmark to receive a series of sex reassignment surgeries. In December 1952, *New York Daily News* carried a front-page headline, "EX-GI Becomes Blonde Beauty: Operations Transform Bronx Youth," declaring her sex change to the world.[171] Jorgensen came back to New York in February 1953, surrendered to her fame, and embarked on a celebrity career. She glamorized sex reassignment and worked closely with Benjamin to turn "transsexuality" into a household term.[172] The presses in Taiwan and Mexico soon claimed that these countries, too, have their own Christine. Taiwanese newspapers broke the story of Xie Jianshun (b. 1918), the "Christine of Free China," in August 1953;[173] Mexico City dailies announced the sensational story of Marta Olmos (b. 1931), the Mexican Christine, in May 1954.[174] These reports announced that both Xie and Olmos, like Jorgensen, transformed into women through an array of medical interventions. Their stories drew media interest across the Pacific, appearing as far apart as in Singapore,

Hong Kong, Sydney, Melbourne, Maryborough, Torreón, and various cities in the United States (figure 1.14).[175]

Even though Jorgensen, Xie, and Olmos rose to stardom in the short span of a year and a half, their experience differed remarkably in terms of the narratives they generated about the "successful" outcome of sex reassignment. Sex change was a story of personal triumph for Jorgensen, but it translated into a remedy for treating the intersexuality of Xie, a Republican Chinese soldier who acquiesced to a total of nine surgeries with great reluctance. Olmos welcomed male-to-female genital reconstruction operations, which her medical team authorized and pitched as a solution to

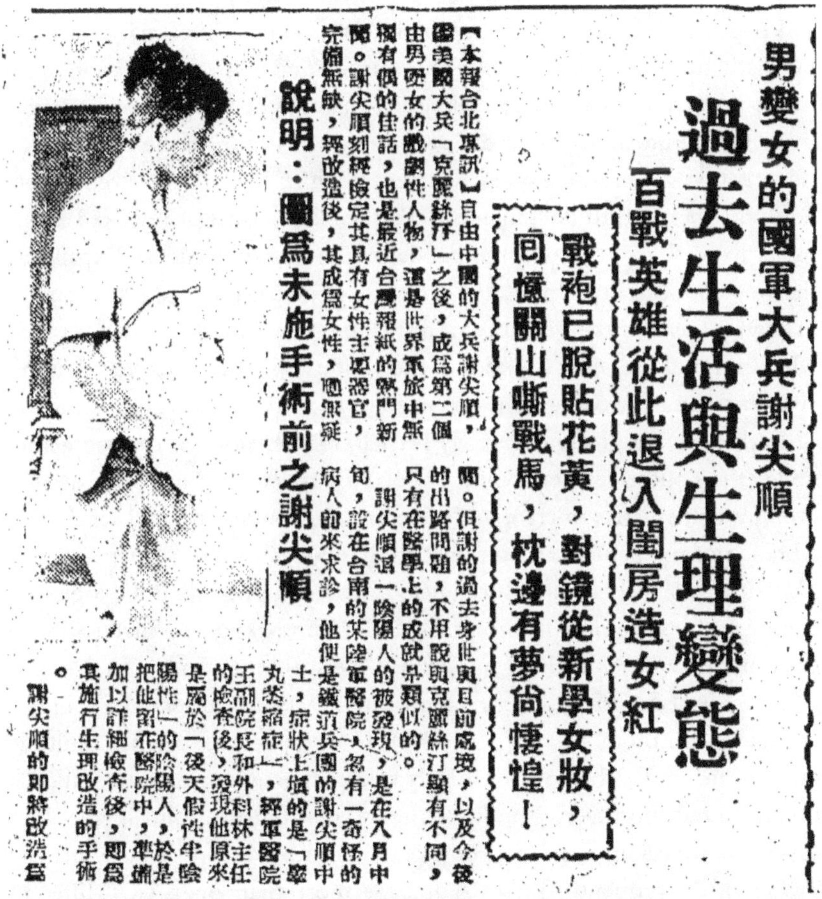

男變女的國軍大兵謝尖順

過去生活與生理變態

百戰英雄從此退入閨房造女紅

戰袍已脫貼花黃，對鏡從新學女妝，
回憶關山嘶戰馬，枕邊有夢尚悽惶！

【本報台北專訊】自由中國的大兵謝尖順，繼美國大兵「克麗絲汀」之後，成爲第二個由男變女的戲劇性人物，這是世界軍旅中無獨有偶的佳話，也是最近台灣報紙的熱門新聞。謝尖順刻經檢定其具有女性主要器官，完備無缺，經改造後，其成爲女性，毫無疑問。但謝的過去身世與目前處境，以及今後的出路問題，不用說與克麗絲汀頗有不同，只有在醫學上的成就是類似的。

謝尖順這一陰陽人的被發現，是在八月中旬，設在台南的某陸軍醫院，忽有一奇怪的病人前來求診，他便是鐵頭兵團的謝尖順中士，病狀上填的是「睪丸炎縮症」，經軍醫院王副院長和外科林主任的檢查後，發現他原來是屬於「後天假性半陰陽性」的陰陽人，於是把他留在醫院中，準備加以詳細檢查後，即爲其施行生理改造的手術。

謝尖順的即將改造爲

說明：圖爲未施手術前之謝尖順

Fig. 1.14 Report of Xie Jianshun in Hong Kong.
Source: *Kung Sheung Daily News*, September 2, 1953.

male homosexuality.[176] Media celebration bolstered a Cold War rhetoric of geopolitical sovereignty, often mediated by the rise of US global hegemony. Such mediation bespeaks the fluid configurations of national belonging (which region owned which version of transsexuality) as polities take form in relation to one another and cohere around certain imperial nuclei.[177] Throughout the 1950s, authoritarian regimes in both Taiwan and Mexico found a strong ally in the US government.[178] For our purposes, it is noteworthy that the coeval fashioning of the discrepant Christine narratives engendered a fluid spectrum of transgender meanings. Despite how the competing narratives all framed sex reassignment as the fulcrum of bodily experience, what the surgeries meant on personal and collective levels varied by region in significant ways.[179]

I began by stating that my approach to transtopian history is motivated by mathematical structuralism. The purpose of taking inspiration from math, however, is less about math itself than about yielding one possible mapping of historical structure. There are ways to connect the dots historically that do not presume queer coherence, which has characterized a more positivist approach to documenting transgender culture (as reflected in the intent to work from an overarching definition of trans/gender). Expanding the way connectivity typifies the concerns of global history, a structuralist mapping unearths the visibility of disjunctive resonances. To demonstrate what I mean, I will now summarize the various case studies explored in this chapter through two diagrams extracted from mathematical abstractions.

In the 1930s, a group of (mostly French) mathematicians came together under the collective pseudonym Nicolas Bourbaki.[180] Their goal was to ground mathematics in rigor and generality by moving toward set theory, a branch of mathematical logic that studies collections of objects ("sets"). Utilizing two of their models can help us come to grips with the logic and contours of transtopian historiography. The Bourbaki group invented such concepts as *surjection* and *injection*, which are still in use today, to describe mathematical functions, or a relationship between two sets (for simplicity, let us call them sets "A" and "B"). If an input in set A has multiple outputs in set B, the relationship between the sets cannot be called a function, but the reverse (multiple inputs to a single output) is fine. In a surjective function, every output ("value") in set B has *at least* one matching input ("argument") in set A (maybe more than one); two different arguments may potentially lead to the same value in surjection, and the key criterion here is that no "B" is left out. Conversely, in an injective function, *at most* one (including zero) input in set A can point to the same output in set B. Injection is also known as "one-to-one," so such functions cannot be many-to-one (which would be surjective) or one-to-many (not a function) between sets A and B. The way mathematicians conceptualize sets is comparable to the way scholars approach the collective units in which individual experience achieves meaning. Mathematical functions provide a heuristic analogy to understanding the broader patterns in which historical actors relate to the conceptual worlds they inhabit.

By keying the various examples from this chapter into a surjective and an injective function, the mathematical models shed figurative light on the epistemology of transgender continuum. The continuous paradigm under-lines the variability of transgender meanings across time and location even if certain practices (e.g., lesbian murder or sex change surgery) seem to share an identical set of historical import. The scientific assumption of universality in the Benjamin scale crucially blended sexological categories into a spectrum. The spectral perspective casts the origins of transgender embodiment in decisively malleable terms, always already trafficking in a transregional cir-cuit. Taking place across different time-place coordinates, the relationship of the three lesbian murder episodes to the gender transitive-separatist polarity can be interpreted in terms of a *surjective* function (figure 1.15).

In the Global Christine example, the surgical justification provided by medical experts conveys an *injective* relationship between the specific cases and the various sexological tools (figure 1.16). Whereas Benjamin considered Jorgenson an example of Type VI on his SOS, Olmos's doctors administered sex change as a cure for male homosexuality (Kinsey 6), and Xie's surgeons construed the operations as a treatment for neither gender discomfort nor homosexuality but intersexuality (neither SOS nor the Kinsey scale). Nota-bly, Benjamin did not consider the Kinsey scale sufficiently accurate to cap-ture Jorgenson's condition; Olmos's physicians did not approach her case on a par with the Benjamin spectrum; and Xie's doctors were more determined to demonstrate their surgical proficiency than concerned with either sexo-logical measurement. Even though this interpretation privileges the view of the doctors, and I am aware that the way we map these historical structures will change when accounting for other criteria (e.g., nonsexological ones), the examples of Jorgenson, Olmos, and Xie show that different formations of transness across time and location can be thought out as distinct *positions* in corresponding patterns. The math-inspired structures I depict here should not be viewed as prescriptive, definitive, or exclusive in shaping our historical

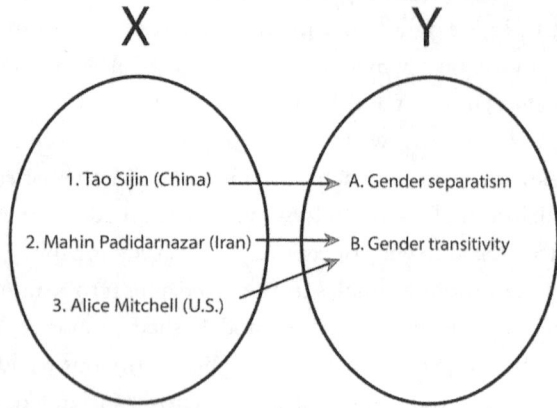

Fig. 1.15 Gender Expression as a Surjective Function of Lesbian Examples.
Source: Illustration by and copyright Howard Chiang.

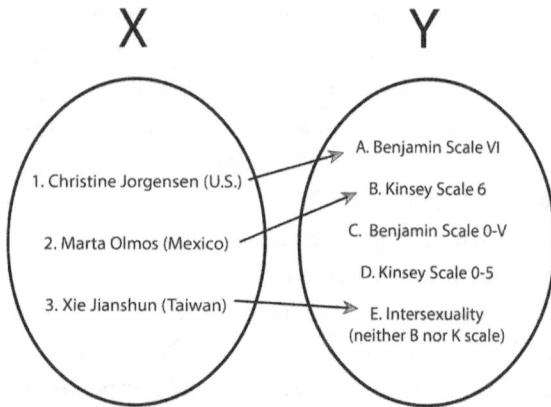

Fig. 1.16 Sexological Measurement as an Injective Function of Christine Examples.
Source: Illustration by and copyright Howard Chiang.

sensibility, but they disclose the utility of *relating* different actors and how they matter to continuum epistemologies.

My caveat all along is to deploy structuralist reasoning strategically. When brought together, the two transtopian genealogies suture a continuous axis on which transgender differences unfold. The significance of

Harry Benjamin's work and Christine Jorgensen's story does not lie in the exemplary version of transsexuality that they embody; rather, they catalyze historical change and differences by opening up a range of affinity with which gender agents come to embrace, contest, or remake. The importance of Mahin and Tao, or Olmos and Xie, can be attributed to not their nominal status as a non-Western variant of an original transgender prototype, but how they unsettle claims of transgender roots that are locked to a particular time, place, or set of social attributes. Taken together, Benjamin's sexual taxonomy, the lesbian crimes, and the postwar MTF celebrities represent dense points of signification that glide on a cross-cultural gradation of what "transgender" could mean historically. In part captured by the tools of surjective and injective abstraction, the two iterations of transtopia—innovation and asymptote—frustrate any definitive claim of transgender authenticity. It no longer makes sense to uphold a single figure, be it Jorgensen, Olmos, Mahin, or Tao, or any region for that matter, as the ultimate yardstick for measuring the historical production of transness. Their experiences are most meaningfully articulated in relation to one another and through the contestation of gender norms beyond a single location of time and space. Transtopia stipulates a nonhierarchal, commensurate range of embodied personhood on which transness *itself* transits as a polynodal construct without intrinsic coherence.

The experiences of Tao Sijin and Xie Jianshun suggest that transgender historiography as it is currently practiced can only be inadequate without accounting for the stabilizing *and* destabilizing effects of the non-West on the unity of transness. In explaining the broader significance of a global assemblage, this chapter has recounted two of its lateral genealogies to delineate the conceptual versatility of transtopia—proposed as a new way of interpreting the past. Instead of casting transness in terms of a relativist past, a transtopian approach departs from this familiar organization of world history and calls in its stead for the relational untangling of regional fabrics that interlace transness in the first place. At the same time that the stories of Tao and Xie begin to anchor a more interconnected web of transgender narration from the *Chinese* and *Sinophone* vicinities, a sophisticated execution of decolonial queer thinking needs to distinguish the heterogeneity of such spatial formations outside the West. The difference between these two geopolitical units—and why that difference is important—is where we turn next.

CHAPTER II

Stonewall Aside

Why Queer Theory Needs Sinophone Studies

I n June 1969, when police raided the Stonewall Inn, a gay bar in Man-
hattan, members of the LGBTQ community decided to fight back. In
the past, LGBTQ people typically retreated. But in this instance, they
came together, protested, and sustained a series of riots that lasted for five
days. Immediately, the Stonewall riots commended national and international
attention. Stonewall soon became a symbol of resistance to discrimination
that would inspire solidarity among gender and sexual minority groups
for decades. It catalyzed a transformation in the nature of gay activism, as
evident in the evolution from the conservative postwar homophile organizations to the militant Gay Liberation Front and Gay Activist Alliance.[1]
And it sparked the world's first gay pride marches in June 1970. Most historians consider the Stonewall rebellion as the founding moment of the
modern LGBTQ movement.[2] But what does it mean to reflect on this
historic turning point today, especially from a global viewpoint?

To think about the Stonewall uprising and its significance after half a
century raises a number of challenges. The most obvious, if not banal,
stems from an implied adherence to Western-centrism. Crudely put, rendering 1969 as a decisive rupture suggests that the West, whatever this
label holds, continues to serve as the entry point for thinking about an
"origin story" of queer history and sexual politics. Yet this critique immediately fractures upon a closer look at the diverse scholarship in LGBTQ
history.[3] Taking place in New York City, itself one of the most unusual

cities in the world, the Stonewall riots were a milestone, but not most representative of the concurrent queer happenings in North America and Europe outside Greenwich Village. An often-overlooked example is the Compton's Cafeteria Riot that occurred three years prior in San Francisco.[4] Though certain similarities across different social movements and activist moments can be deduced over time, and perhaps the incident of 1969 was more of a culminating episode than an origin story, Stonewall is historically significant because it was unusual *even within* the West.[5] The assumed coherence of Western-centrism needs to be debunked in order to appreciate the wider historical unevenness of the Stonewall legacy.

Yet a related challenge in reflecting on the Stonewall rebellion today precisely results from its presumed exemplarism. Scholars of Africa, Asia, Latin America, the Middle East, and other regions constantly confront intellectual problems intrinsic to a highly differentiated geopolitics, which can lead to two separate but interrelated interpretations of the division between these regions and the West.[6] First, with respect to LGBTQ activism, we might ask if its history in non-Western parts of the world merely represents a response to or reception of landmark achievements in the West. This would imply a *temporal lag*, which maps geographical difference onto an illusory race of cosmopolitan developmentalism.[7] Alternatively, scholars, especially in area studies, have sometimes valorized that very difference to argue for the exceptionalism of the non-West, so that LGBTQ experiences become not only a flattened supplement to a global logic but also the genuine example of cultural nativism or essentialized alterity.[8] Both understandings of the non-West as a promised marker of difference—demarcated from a coherent geopolitical center—reequivocate power so that the raison d'être of area studies derives from its very alienation by the supposed hegemon known as the West.

This chapter proceeds with bearing these challenges in mind. Though resolving them is beyond the scope here, I hope to use this occasion to reflect on the productive labor in reworking queer theory and history, especially in light of the kind of considerations enabled by treating Stonewall as a *lateral event*. This approach remembers the episode as just one of the many precedents in the global LGBTQ movement and restores its importance always in relative terms. In the last chapter, I introduced a theoretical framework to reconceptualize the malleability of transness from a cross-cultural historical viewpoint. The strategic structuralism of transtopia rethinks, rather than resists, the tensions and overlaps between queer expressions and transgender history—a strained coexistence that has ensued since the Stonewall uprising itself.[9] This chapter detaches our focal point on transgender articulations temporarily and, instead, draws on examples of same-sex intimacy to entertain the global legacy of Stonewall.[10] To explicate the theme of sovereign precarity in a region like Hong Kong, the principal aim here is to incorporate the analytical fulcrum of *geopolitics* into queer theoretical critique. Moving from epistemological history (last chapter) to disciplinary revamping (this chapter) "locates" this study in the geophysical nexus of the Sinophone Pacific.[11] As a scholar of Chinese and Sinophone cultures, I write from a viewpoint that neither glorifies the West nor nativizes the rest. In fact, the remainder of this chapter is less about Stonewall's political imprint than about the queering of China studies. Readers who long for an explication of Stonewall's impact on Chinese queer history might be disappointed. Others who wish to learn about the Chinese experience as an ethnic addendum to Stonewall historiography will equally find my deliberation unsatisfactory.

Or not. My working premise is to translate the scholarly possibilities exploded since the Stonewall aftermath into an opportunity for broadening the nature and future of queer analysis. As a historian, I consider critical theory not only a tool but very much a product of studying the past. Like many events aimed at challenging the status quo in human history, Stonewall continues to matter today because its relationship to us—in this chapter, I focus on intellectual and disciplinary concerns—promises the specter of unpredictability. Despite its canonical status, or precisely because of it, scholars have been prompted to identify other flashpoints or dictating variables of historical change.[12] The queerness of Stonewall therefore lies in its indeterminate prospect to initiate noncanonical modes of inquiry. As one scholar of South Asia has cautioned, if Stonewall has functioned "more as a site of historical metalepsis," it is no more than "an effect that was miscast as cause in global histories of sexuality."[13] Whereas the last chapter destabilized a fixed definition of trans/gender through the social grips of medical knowledge, this chapter seeks to diversify the meaning of queer/Stonewall resistance through the critical puncturing of Sinocentrism. With the recent rise of China, how do we study global queer experiences ethically and epistemologically?[14] If we approach China's ascendance itself as an unhinged experience in historical time, what can an antihegemonic investigation of queer China look like? How can queer theory be recalibrated and retooled accordingly? What if we put Stonewall *aside*, not behind, and start to worry less about "what's been central" and more about "what else"?[15]

Why Sinophone Studies?

One of the most notable developments in the last half-century concerns the geopolitical reorientation of China. The transformation of the PRC from spearheading the third world revolution under Mao to leading a neoliberal global economy in the twenty-first century demands a rethinking of the terms we use to interpret its recent history, culture, and global import.[16] In order to fully understand the relationship between the rise of global China and LGBTQ experience, I follow the work of scholars such as Shu-mei Shih, David Der-wei Wang, Jing Tsu, E. K. Tan, Alison Groppe, Brian Bernards, Lily Wong, and others to substitute what we have used to call the "Chinese diaspora" and "overseas Chinese" with the analytic concept of the "Sinophone."[17] In the landmark essay "The Concept of the Sinophone" (2011), Shih defines the field of Sinophone studies as "the study of Sinitic-language cultures on the margins of geopolitical nation-states and their hegemonic productions" and "locates its objects of attention at the conjuncture of China's internal colonialism and Sinophone communities everywhere immigrants from China have settled."[18] Sinophone communities and cultures bear a "precarious and problematic relationship" to China, similar to the relationships between the Anglophone world and England, the Francophone world and France, the Hispanophone world and Spain, the Lusophone world and Portugal, and so forth.[19]

Shih's conceptualization of the Sinophone, then, is a decisive riposte to the diaspora framework. To say that diaspora has an end date is to recognize that one cannot still be called diasporic after long periods of localization and heterogenization in regional communities.[20] This builds on the idea that what we mean by the word *Chinese* in Chinese literature, history, culture, politics, and so on tends to conflate nation, ethnicity, language, and culture in a chain of equivalence. The nested agenda is to move beyond national categories, and the Sinophone framework does so by turning our attention toward another unit of coherence around language and text, sound and script, and, as we will see later in the book, embodiment and mediality. Although Sinophone studies emerged from literary and cultural studies, historians now face a similar pressing task to redefine our discipline in light of China's rise as an economic superpower.[21] In what ways can scholars use the Sinophone as a heuristic lens to deconstruct how sexual normativity and contemporary PRC imperialism have been hegemonically produced through each other?[22] This chapter makes a preliminary inquiry into this question around lines of thought lost or overlooked during Stonewall's canonization. My thesis is that Sinophone studies ripened in this period as an unruly "queer" (酷兒, *ku'er*) progeny of Chinese studies.[23] The disruptive potential of Sinophone studies is adjacent to the effect of queer approaches on traditional gay and lesbian history and, by implication, Stonewall's capacity to unsettle historical understandings of political change.

But first, what are the contours of Sinophone history? In her definitive introduction to *Sinophone Studies: A Critical Reader* (2013), Shih identifies three main historical processes whereby Sinophone communities and cultures have come into being.[24] First, Shih builds on the insight of the field of New Qing history to draw attention to Qing *continental colonialism*.[25] This continent-oriented modality of colonialism exceeds our familiar notion of overseas expansion that characterizes much of modern European (and Japanese Pacific) empires.[26] The map of the PRC is inherited from the Qing, which doubled its size during the Qianlong reign (1735–1796) and brought Xinjiang, Mongolia, and Tibet into its territorial sovereignty.[27] Second, Shih draws on the Nationalist government's relocation to Taiwan to discuss *settler colonialism*.[28] The Nationalist Party's colonialism can be understood in terms of the way it reestablished itself as a hegemonic polity in Taiwan—instead of leaving the region—and continues to proclaim itself as the genuine "homeland" of Chinese culture.[29] Mirroring the single party-state on the mainland, the Nationalist regime's oppressive policies continued to shape the political atmosphere of the island well into the late 1980s. These policies have left a devastating legacy on the local Taiwanese and aboriginal populations.[30] Third, Shih points to *migration* as another key historical pillar of Sinophone communities and cultures. The examples of Southeast Asia and Asian America are telling in this regard. People conventionally viewed as "Chinese descents" in these regions are often trapped in the normative working of dual hegemonies. Because they are often sandwiched between assimilation/naturalization in the new country on the one hand and the presumed loyalty to the mother homeland on the other, a critical Sinophone perspective unravels that tension in order to give their voice a sorely needed platform.

Although Shih's coinage of the term *Sinophone* has consolidated into a coherent program at the intersection of post/colonial studies, ethnic studies, and area studies, it is worth noting that, before Sinophone studies, Sinologists had variously wrestled with the notion of *Chineseness* as both a cultural construct and a historical problem.[31] Scholars such as Wei-ming Tu attempted to decenter political China as a monolithic center by proposing what he called "cultural China."[32] Historian Gungwu Wang reconceptualized the focus of scholarly discussion on cultural China by crystallizing the very concept of Chineseness.[33] Starting in the mid-1990s, critics began to challenge the genealogy established by Tu and Wang, especially its embedded China-centrism and the presumed smooth continuum of cultural Chineseness spiraling outward from mainland China. Asian Americanist Ling-chi Wang refined the theoretical construct of Chineseness by identifying two, not one, geopolitical discursive hegemonies—the United States and China.[34] Cultural critic Ien Ang published a seminal essay called "Can One Say No to Chineseness?" (1998) to denaturalize a "surprising return to cultural essentialism—the ghost of the 'truly Chinese'" in much of the existing literature on the overseas Chinese.[35] Postcolonial theorist Rey Chow tackled Chineseness as less a cultural/historical category than a disciplinary problematic. By this, Chow called attention to the fact that with every major new theoretical trend, there can be a "Chinese" supplement, and this Chinese supplement amounts to nothing less or more than an ethnic supplement that promises a certain degree of non-Western recognition but at the same reghettoizes itself by way of ethnic, national labels.[36]

If we apply Chow's insight to queer studies, the task of bringing an area such as China to bear on critical gender/sexuality studies must avoid the foregone conclusion that only a China specialist can comment authoritatively on queer China and speak of Chinese queer theory.[37] On the contrary, a queer Sinophone intervention would activate a multidirectional critique that considers marginalization *itself* as a moving target of analysis. Such geopoliticization of queerness and Chineseness as mutually imbricated, in other words, counters the occlusion of the variant essentialisms—regional, cultural, gender, sexual, or otherwise—that work together to reauthorize disciplinary quandaries. In defense of queering area studies, feminist theorists Anjali Arondekar and Geeta Patel have relayed the "messy realignments" typically neglected by the segregation of area studies and queer studies into separate field formations.[38] Yet, as a prototype in the kind of area studies that flourished as an intelligence-gathering force for buttressing US power, the field of postwar China studies has never ceased to generate an "excess of power," whether the signifier *China* has taken on the form of a Cold War enemy, a third world leader, or a neoliberal alibi.[39] As scholar of colonial modernity Tani Barlow reminded us nearly three decades ago, "doubly displaced, colonialism nonetheless made Cold War area studies scholarship possible in the first place."[40]

The recent turn to Sinophone studies enables us to undo the erasure of colonialism in "China" studies. The delineation between the so-called Chinese canon and Sinophone cultures can be put into productive dialogue with queer theory to enrich ongoing critiques of queer displacement, mobility, and intersectionality.[41] The next two chapters will execute this agenda through the analytical praxis of body histories. This chapter pinpoints some programmatic rationales for unpacking the coproduction of heteronormativity and Sinocentrism. To quote anthropologist Martin Manalansan's remark on the twenty-fifth anniversary of the Stonewall riots, "the globalization of gay and lesbian oppression obfuscates hierarchical relations between metropolitan centers and sub-urban peripheries."[42] The queer Sinophone perspective I am advancing, twenty-five years after, further pluralizes our coordinates in understanding the way these hierarchies—of oppression, of cultural citizenship, of authenticity, and of globalization—have been transfigured laterally. This is especially urgent in an increasingly transnational and transcolonial world where the fetishization of a leftist counterhegemonic China is no more tenable than the nostalgic depiction of Stonewall as a crucible of queer liberation. For the remainder of this chapter, in order to flesh out this multifocal provocation, I outline seven reasons why queer theory needs Sinophone studies. Instead of casting the latter as a corrective to the shortcomings of the former, my more immediate goal is to underscore the kaleidoscopic range of illuminations made possible by their generative affinity.

Historicizing Translation

The first reason queer theory needs Sinophone studies is that it offers a rigorous context for historicizing the process of queer translation. A telling example is the history of how the Chinese term *tongzhi* (同志) has been used to translate the Western idea of "gay and lesbian." *Tongzhi* literally means "comrade" or "common will" in Chinese, and it typically referred to one's ordinary acquaintance in the high socialist period (1949–1976). Over time, however, the term has acquired a more specific, culturally subversive meaning: Chinese queer activists came to promote it as an umbrella category to designate individuals with nonnormative gender and erotic inclinations. Yet it is worth pointing out that the concept of *tongzhi* has historically been queered first and foremost in Sinophone locations; its queer appropriation and currency were *then* imported back into mainland China.[43] Hence Sinophone communities have served as the principal catalyst in mediating the "glocalization" of LGBTQ identities in East Asia.[44] In his groundbreaking study *Queer Comrades: Gay Identity and* Tongzhi *Activism in Postsocialist China* (2018), media scholar Hongwei Bao argues that "in contemporary China, the socialist 'comrade' and the postsocialist 'queer' are *mutually constitutive*. . . . That is to say, the socialist past laid the foundation and provided the inspiration for contemporary Chinese gay identity and queer politics, which are both produced by and pose resistance to the Chinese state, as well as to transnational capitalism."[45]

A Sinophone historicizing of *tongzhi*, on the other hand, harvests a more cautious approach to scrutinizing—even questioning—the historical nature of Bao's argument. Since what Bao proposes constitutes a genealogical claim about the epistemic traction of *tongzhi* as it transverses the socialist and postsocialist divide, it will be useful to recall the term's normative circulation in pre-1978 China.[46] Though making an intriguing claim, Bao does not actually seize evidence from the earlier period to arrive at his conclusion about the socialist precedent of the postsocialist queer. Based on the existing limited research on queer PRC history, it is not immediately obvious that *tongzhi* was used by sexual minorities in the Maoist era as either an linguistic marker of identification or an organizing principle for activism.[47] More often than not, people simply used *tongzhi* to describe each other's comradery, straight or unstraight. In fact, to be historically accurate, the queer notion of *tongzhi* as we understand it today is the product of a *cultural refraction* via such Sinophone communities as Hong Kong and Taiwan.[48]

Many critics have identified the popularization of the term in Sinophone queer cultural activism in the late 1980s and 1990s as a watershed turning point in the history of its lexical dissemination.[49] Most famously, playwright Edward Lam (Lam Yik-Wa 林奕華) used *tongzhi* to title the first Hong Kong Gay and Lesbian Film Festival in 1989. It is not going too far to argue that *tongzhi* could only be queered outside its heteronormalized circulation. It was precisely because *tongzhi* was not a fashionable concept in places like Hong Kong and Taiwan that its Sinophone deployment became a form of cultural subversion. *Tongzhi* would have never and indeed did not carry a queer-subversive content in Maoist China precisely due to the same reason—from the 1950s to the 1970s, it served to marginalize deviant sexual subjectivity in the mainland. The socialist conception of *tongzhi* may have stood for class, gender, and other forms of social egalitarianism, but it profoundly alienated sexual minorities (the Mao-era state discourse in fact condemned the very idea of bourgeois sexuality).[50] So historically speaking, a queer version of *tongzhi* has survived and circulated not in socialist China, but outside it. In the final chapter of this book, we will look into the conceptual transformation (in particular, transgendering) of *tongzhi* after the millennium. My point here is that the historical distinction between the PRC, on the one hand, and Sinophone communities such as Hong Kong and Taiwan, on the other, makes possible an understanding of queer/*tongzhi* China that is linguistically and historically sensitive.

Against Romanticizing China

The second reason queer theory needs Sinophone studies is that it allows us to study queer Asia in a transnational way that does not romanticize China and the non-West. This is a crucial response to another book that has garnered critical attention, *Queer Marxism in Two Chinas* (2015) by literary scholar Petrus Liu.[51] My remark in the previous section suggests that the conceptual stationing of *tongzhi* in such works has likely flattened the term's social connotation within Chinese history.[52] Here I wish to put forward another subtle query and ask if its idiosyncratic application in a work like Liu's may have also written off the leftist and radical politics of gay activism outside China, especially in areas where a strong heritage of anticapitalist queer critique exists.

Clearly, the socialist foundation of *tongzhi* in China presents a partially differentiated genealogy of queer activism in East Asia. That is, it pulls us out of an obsession with European Marxist traditions. One of Liu's main arguments is that "a unique local event has centrally shaped the development of Chinese queer [Marxist] thought: the 1949 division of China into the People's Republic of China (PRC) and the Republic of China on Taiwan (ROC)."[53] This version of queer Marxism, he tells us, "offers a nonliberal alternative to the Euro-American model of queer emancipation grounded in liberal values of privacy, tolerance, individual rights, and diversity."[54] The problem with Liu's assertion is that it blinds us from, rather than bringing us closer to, an understanding of the way global LGBTQ coalition politics has been made possible over time. Liu's version of *tongzhi* activism—deeply rooted in the views and activities of a highly niche, however radical, and self-referential circle in Taiwan—seems to repudiate the universal, not just liberal, importance of pluralist recognition and redistributive equality.[55]

A Sinophone vantage point recasts the queer rendition of *tongzhi* as a polyvalent synthesis of global leftist politics and identity politics—rather than something that is produced purely from within Chinese cultural contexts.[56] Historically, the homophile activism of the 1950s and the solidarity of gay and lesbian politics with the student, civil rights, antiwar, feminist, environmental, countercultural, and radical movements of the 1960s and 1970s provide concrete evidence for a leftist genealogy of gay activist history.[57] In academe, the scholarship of John D'Emilio, Lisa Duggan, Kevin Floyd, Diarmaid Kelliher, Peter Drucker, Emily Hobson, and many others has documented this history with nuance and complexity, and they are all bold proponents of Marxist critique.[58] The power differentials that bring queer resistance and the radical left together—or drive them apart—have always worked in uneven gradations unilaterally on a global scale.

What is decisively missing yet sorely needed is a Marxist analysis of Liu's queer Marxism, as well as an uncovering of the kind of China-centrism it conceals. An instance of Liu's romanticization of China can be seen in his definition of queer theory. By characterizing "queer theory as an incomplete project that is constantly transformed by China," Liu implies not only that the signifier "China" is doing the work of substituting for Marxist analysis, but also that China, or Marxism for that matter, is already a complete project or at least one that does not need to be transformed by queer theoretical critique.[59] *Pace* Liu, this chapter argues that what queer theory needs is not China but Sinophone studies.[60]

In this sense, the obsession with a "Chinese materialist queer theory that sets it apart from its Euro-American counterparts" not only begs the question of whose Chineseness is at stake, but also risks reifying the

East-West binary via what I have called "self- or re-Orientalization."[61] The title of Liu's book suggests that its focus is on both the PRC and the Republic of China (Taiwan), the homogenized "Two Chinas." However, Liu's study devotes only ten pages to the work of one PRC-based filmmaker, Cui Zi'en (崔子恩, b. 1958). Despite this skewed representation, Liu speaks of "Chinese" queer theory and Marxism throughout the book without making a distinction between the PRC and Sinophone Taiwan. In Liu's formulation, China is taken as given, self-consistent, internally productive of a bounded queer alternative to Euro-American queer articulations.[62] This unfortunate consequence shares a potential blind spot— and the word *potential* is crucial here—with cultural critic Kuan-Hsing Chen's injunction to use "Asia as method": namely, the essentialization of Asian nativism turns it into a privileged position for serious intellectual dialogue and thus completely isolates the work that scholars of Asia are doing from the heterogeneity of Western queer studies.[63] This is the very opposite of the disciplinary trap that Rey Chow has identified as ethnic supplementarity. Such marketing of China/Asia "meant that the philosophical and aesthetic investments in Chinese nativism and indigenism were set in motion at a steady pace of deterritorialization, in which the native or indigene, signifying the rooted, local knowledge that is associated with China and Chineseness, took on the exchange value of a marketable, because circulatable, transnational exhibit."[64] Therefore, how can we analyze queer Asia without romanticizing its past and upholding an "us-versus-them" mentality? Sinophone postcolonial perspectives, as I have been suggesting, provide a way out of that China-versus-the West binary deadlock. Queer theory needs Sinophone studies in this regard because it reminds us that the challenge to neoliberal capitalism in China is neither exceptional nor exemplary.

Global Indigeneity

The third reason queer theory needs Sinophone studies is that by focusing on *indigeneity* as a theoretical problem, it allows scholars to draw comparisons and connections across systems of oppression imposed on colonized people all over the world.[65] At this point it is imperative to think through the postcolonial purchase of Sinophone studies, especially in relation to the study of the contemporary PRC empire. Shu-mei Shih has recently suggested that "socialism in China could be seen as a postcolonial strategy against the imperial powers occupying parts of China in the first half of the twentieth century. If so, postsocialism of China then is post-postcolonial."[66] Building on this insight, we might ask, what is the value of labeling a phenomenon "post-postcolonial"? Do the two "posts" cancel each other out? Perhaps, in the more subtle way that Shih characterizes it, "postsocialism ought to be considered as a condition affecting the entire world."[67] A regrettable repercussion of the post–Cold War global reordering has been that some Chinese "New Left" intellectuals hasten to equate postsocialism with postcolonialism. Sinophone studies breaks from this conceptual ruse by challenging a monolithic postcolonial antipathy toward the West as depicted by predominantly Han Chinese intellectuals.

A queer Sinophone framework builds concerns of gender and sexual injustice into an analysis of how geopolitical others and ethnic minorities have been systematically marginalized by Han centrism. A promising recent development in queer theory synchronizes the power structures behind the definition of "indigeneity" with those that have come to shape the history of "queerness." Scholars working in the field of queer indigenous studies have delineated the history of epistemic violence and social oppression unduly experienced by North American Native queers.[68] Gender and sexual diversity among Native people has historically been interpreted by white colonists as signs of primitivity. This has bolstered the sedimentation over time of what anthropologist Scott Morgensen calls "settler sexuality": "a white national heteronormativity that regulates Indigenous sexuality and gender by supplanting them with sexual modernity of settler subjects."[69] The resistance to white homonationalist citizenship, we might add, is shared by not only oppressed Native subjects in the West but also LGBTQ minorities in other areas of the world.[70] Although media scholars such as Jia Tan have advocated for the "transversal queer alliance" between indigenous studies and area studies, their plea remains a minority.[71]

If the intersection of queerness with Han settler colonialism in Taiwan, the repression of ethnic minorities in the PRC, and the subjugation of migrant workers in Hong Kong, just to name a few, can be broached in conjunction with First Nation studies, queer theory can draw on Sinophone studies to enrich critical discussions of indigeneity (with its attendant critiques of progress, sovereignty, hierarchy, and so on) on a global and transcultural scale. These are questions that are of significance even for scholars who do not specialize in China. In fact, the three intersectional examples just mentioned have been studied in depth.[72] And in this way, perhaps the Stonewall revolution can be more appropriately "provincialized"—even criticized—for the way its alleged significance vindicates a template of settler homonationalism that is neither universal nor celebratory for "most of the world."[73] Conversely, we should also be asking why the category of indigeneity might stumble in certain places (e.g., does China have an indigenous population?), and how we can turn such a circumspection into a queer analytic of power differentiation within the family resemblance of nation-states (e.g., though home to a vibrant indigenous and LGBTQ rights movement, Taiwan has been without official nation-state status since 1971).[74] We will return to the queerness of Taiwan's global status in the next chapter. My point here is that by using Sinophone studies as an analytic lens, we can better diagnose how intersectional minority politics modulates into global (settler) colonial hierarchies, and vice versa, depending on the scale, angle, and parameters of our historical thinking.

Beyond Postsocialist China

Focusing our attention back on that geopolitical entity that we call "China," Sinophone studies acknowledges the historical tensions that have accumulated surrounding and outside it. In what ways can a queer analysis enhance this recognition, building on my earlier two points regarding the historicity of *tongzhi* and the pitfall of romanticizing China? To illustrate this, I propose to revisit one of the most celebrated films in which homosexual experience in the PRC is depicted, Stanley Kwan's *Lan Yu* (藍宇, 2001).[75] *Lan Yu* is easily mistaken for a mainland Chinese production, especially since it is adapted from the gay internet novel, *Beijing Story* (1998).[76] Yet precisely due to its vivid referencing of the Tiananmen Square incident, the significance of which I analyze in greater detail later, the author of *Beijing Story* could not find a publisher willing to publish the book in the PRC. Therefore, the author eventually published it online under the pseudonym "Beijing Tongzhi," which carries two further implications: (1) the availability of the novel in the virtual space of the World Wide Web invites a readership that is scattered throughout the globe (and thus not delimited by any national or geographical boundaries);[77] and (2) the queer meaning of *tongzhi* was already making its way back to mainland China by the late 1990s, giving further credence to my Sinophone refraction argument discussed earlier. In fact, critics have noted *Lan Yu*'s indebtedness to Taiwan, for the popularity of the film in Taiwan preceded that in China.[78]

Apart from being a gay film, *Lan Yu* is also instructive for our purpose given its plot enfoldment of the Tiananmen Square massacre, which took place two decades after Stonewall. As one of the most controversial topics in PRC history, the Tiananmen Square democracy movement spiraled from a rallying cry at the time known as the demand for a "fifth modernization."[79] This extraordinary populist insistence shares a civil discourse of political diversification that has fueled the growth of the gay and lesbian movement. Though fictional, *Lan Yu* provides a rare occasion to unpack the transformation of human rights rhetoric into multiple burdens in reform-era China.[80] My goal here is to zoom out from this queer text to elucidate the broader context of Sinophone historical and cultural analyses. Such a reading-effect will show that, and here is my fourth reason, queer theory needs Sinophone studies because it allows us to move beyond a "postsocialist" framework (a framework that, I would add, has long been an invention cherished by scholars based in the West but never been used systematically by commentators within the PRC).[81]

In an article that appeared as part of the 2010 special issue of *positions* on transnationalism and queer Chinese politics, Asian American specialist David Eng argues that what the film *Lan Yu* conveys is a "queer space of China." This is a space occupied by two contrasting figurations of political economy that have helped shape China's discrepant modernity—as best personified and embodied by the two protagonists: Handong (a successful businessman) and Lan Yu (a poor architecture student)—one capitalist, the other socialist.[82] The "postsocialist" plot unfolds as these two men fall in love after a one-night stand. Similar to this very first sexual transaction paid by Handong, their relationship revolves around, among other themes, money, consumerism, career, mobility, political turmoil, and familial responsibilities. However, if we reread the film through the Sinophone lens, the transnational logic of the film's biography, according to which its production, marketing, dissemination, and consumption have operated, raises poignant yet often overlooked questions. As Kwan explains in an interview from 2002, "For me, having been with my boyfriend for 11 years, there were a lot of things about the story I could relate to. In the end, I wanted to make the film because I was touched by the novel, but on some other level, I was probably using it as a lens to view my own relationship."[83] The queer space of China can been seen not as Eng does, but as a queer Sinophone space, one with both everyday quotidian effects (helping people like Kwan understand their relationships) as well as world-historical ones (about how to understand the politics of Hong Kong, Tiananmen, and Sinophone cultures at large).

In the process whereby *Lan Yu* becomes a "world picture," the immediate circulation of marginal desires is shot through public legitimation and international success in a Sinophone Hong Kong and Taiwan-based milieu of visuality, as opposed to an enclosed mainland China–based film industrial nexus.[84] In what ways has the global appreciation of mainland Chinese queer affect been cultivated through a "refracted" lens (through the liminality of Hong Kong)? According to Kwan's own reflection, the status of *Lan Yu* as an independent production licensed his team to do things that could not have been accomplished otherwise. The most telling example concerns whether the film could be set in Beijing, especially given the original story's eponymous reference of the city and, by extension, the Tiananmen Square protest:

> Even though I wanted to make the film, I had some reservations at first. I wasn't totally convinced it would be all right to shoot in Beijing, or that it'd be okay to shoot it as an independent production. When I made *Actress* and *Red Rose, White Rose* in Shanghai years before, I had to go through a lot of bureaucratic procedures, like script evaluation and so forth. So when I was told that I didn't need to do any of that [to make *Lan Yu*], I became immediately suspicious. Gradually, as evident during pre-production, I saw that it really was happening. Of course, the difference had a lot to do with the fact that this film was a Hong Kong–funded production and that this was an independent production. There wasn't any collaboration with any movie studios in mainland China. And I think for a Hong Kong production with a Hong Kong director, the worst that [the government] could do was to ban us from shooting in China. Once I set my mind to do the film and to use that production method, I couldn't worry about all the things that could possibly go wrong. Basically, if you're going to make that kind of movie and if you're going to use Beijing as the backdrop, you just have to know that certain difficulties will be impossible to avoid.[85]

The queerness and precarity of Hong Kong conditioned the making of *Lan Yu*. Therefore, the depiction of male homo-intimacy in the film registers an unruly tension of cultural and visual (dis)identification that transcends the ideological and even geopolitical contours of postsocialist China. The relationship between Handong and Lan Yu is as much a Sinophone construction as an abstract representation of the ongoing ideological struggle *within* the PRC's quest for a neoliberal order.

This strategy of mapping *Lan Yu* onto geopolitical concerns exemplifies the horizon of Sinophone cultural production, because its main historical pillars come from outside continental China proper. In other words, Kwan's production of *Lan Yu* is made possible by the convergence of the legacies of British postcolonialism, American neoimperialism, the Nationalist state's cosmopolitanism (including its film industry), and Hong Kong's cultural (which was, in turn, driven by economic) affiliations with other subregions of Cold War East Asia, such as Taiwan and Japan. As is well known, between the end of the Korean War in the mid-1950s and the reopening of the Chinese mainland in the late 1970s, Japan, Okinawa, South Korea, and Taiwan became US protectorates. "One of the lasting legacies of this period," quoting Kuan-Hsing Chen, "is the installation of the anticommunism-pro-Americanism structure in the capitalist zone of East Asia, whose overwhelming consequences are still with us today."[86] Inherent in the Sinophone concept lies a more calculated awareness of the role played by communist China in the way the Cold War structures the recent history of East Asia. Moving beyond a postsocialist framework this way, a queer Sinophone approach troubles the divide between the Cold War and after, tracing the historical agency of China in the Asia Pacific from the Korean War and the Third Indochina War to the ongoing South China Sea disputes as continuous and proactive, rather than passive, in nature.[87]

The year 1989 is a pivotal turning point for reflecting on the development of late-twentieth-century Chinese and Sinophone history.[88] The PRC government's military action to suppress the Tiananmen Square protests that year has been widely condemned by the international community.[89] Year after year, students in my Chinese history courses continue to be surprised by the scale of violence unleashed by the Chinese government, especially when juxtaposed against the degree of economic liberalization strong-armed by the same CCP leaders of the period. Taking place two years after the lifting of martial law in Taiwan, the incident has often been taken as a direct reflection of the sharp divergence in democratic characteristics of various Chinese-speaking communities (e.g., across the Taiwan strait). *Lan Yu* continues to be banned from public screening in the PRC, and we can reasonably assume that the reason for this censorship stems from its emplotment of the Tiananmen Square protest as much as its explicit portrayal of queer sexuality.

Handong's embrace of Lan Yu immediately after the Tiananmen Square incident, therefore, cannot simply be read as a syncretic moment when the seemingly diachronic socialist and postsocialist tendencies that constitute China's discrepant modernity intersect (figure 2.1). In terms of character development, it is a crucial turning point in the film where the couple explicitly accepts their desire and longing for each other. As Bao notes, prior to the mass protest, "Handong has refused to acknowledge his gay identity and recognize his feelings for Lan Yu as love. After the experience at Tiananmen, he finally comes to terms with his own sexuality."[90] The legibility of Tiananmen and queerness is thus mutually imbricated in denoting "knowing what not to know in contemporary China."[91] A similar embrace is repeated again midway through the film before Handong's arrest for business-related corruption. There, as before, it signals a new beginning. The reputable (if not *the* most famous and controversial) post-Tiananmen embrace in *Lan Yu* should be more adequately understood, then, as a subtle

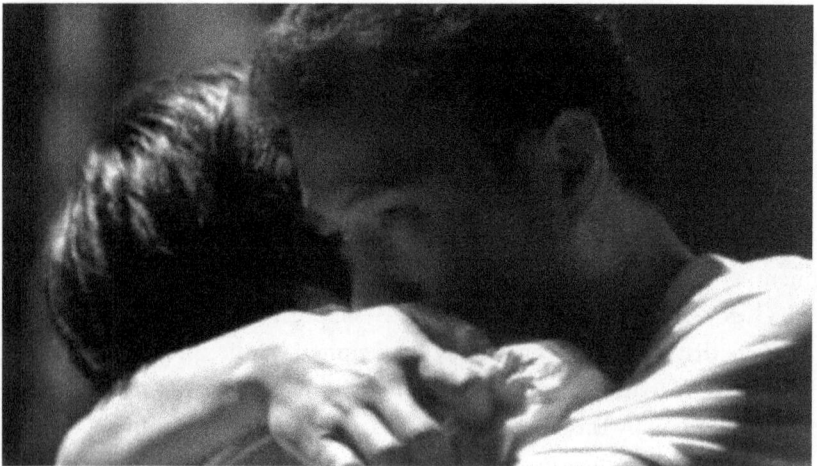

Fig. 2.1 Handong and Lan Yu's embrace after the Tiananmen Square incident.
Source: *Lan Yu* (2001), directed by Stanley Kwan, produced by Zhang Yongning.

yet contentious reflection (in part on behalf of the director) on the future anterior merging of the PRC and Sinophone communities. The scene is indicative of two overlapping historical forces: (1) the triangulation of geo-politics uniquely punctuated by the pulses and rhythms of queer intimacy and (2) the degree of difference between China and Sinitic-language cul-tures on its margins—between the PRC and the global sphere in which it is situated.

In the post-1987 (post–Martial Law) era, the Taiwanese social and cul-tural space soon became home to a vibrant group of queer authors, schol-ars, activists, and other public figures who passionately emulated North American gay and lesbian identity politics and queer theoretical dis-course.[92] Critics now tend to trace the roots of contemporary LGBTQ activism in mainland China to the rise of the *tongzhi* movement in Tai-wan and Hong Kong in the 1980s and 1990s.[93] Apart from social move-ment and academic theorization, gay men and lesbians in Taipei in par-ticular have constructed an urban geography of their own with unique subcultural fabrics. As Taiwan scholar Jens Damm has observed, "Taipei is the only city—probably not only in Taiwan but the whole of East Asia—where a huge open space, the Red House district, has been suc-cessfully developed into an area where gays and lesbians have openly cre-ated their own urban infrastructure, with bars, restaurants, shops and information exchange opportunities."[94] We will return to the issue of how Taipei came to host the first LGBT pride parade in the Sinophone world in 2003 in chapter 5. Hong Kong popular culture, too, especially in the cinematic realm, has developed a sophisticated arsenal of artistic creativity to capture, represent, and even transform the lives of the sexu-ally diverse, forging myriad variations of a sexual "undercurrent."[95] As cultural theorist Ackbar Abbas has remarked, "We get a better sense of Hong Kong through its new cinema (and architecture) than is currently available in any history book."[96] Lan Yu's death in the film, then, may suggest an implicit critique of PRC colonialism in Hong Kong, namely, the PRC should leave Hong Kong alone. But this is only one among the many possible readings from the Sinophone viewpoint, which can never be reduced to an anti-China critique.[97] Although the narrative currents of *Lan Yu* succumb to such an ostensible ending, the expressive yearning and desire for an alternative filmic departure precisely index the kind of *ambivalent* relationship between the PRC and Hong Kong that contin-ues to strike resonances across the Sinophone world. The queerness of

Sinophone relations descends from the poetics of this perennial ambivalence, uncertainty, and indeterminacy.

Minor-to-Minor Relations

Meant to fracture binary impasses, Sinophone interventions can destabilize the ontological position of the postmodern West as much as that of postsocialist China. My fifth reason for why queer theory needs Sinophone studies is that it provides a long overdue remedy to a lacuna in postcolonial studies: to push the field beyond an overwhelming preoccupation with "the West." Drawing on empirical examples mainly from the South Asian context, postcolonial scholars have problematized the West by either deconstructing it, deuniversalizing it, or provincializing it. These approaches can be found in such classics as Naoki Sakai's essay "Modernity and Its Critique: The Problem of Universalism and Particularism" (1988) and Dipesh Chakrabarty's "Provincializing Europe: Postcoloniality and the Critique of History" (1992).[98] At other times, critics have attempted to recuperate nativist examples from the histories of third world nations. Certain modern concepts often understood as imposed from the outside and sustained by the colonial system, they argue, were actually already internal to the indigenous civilization. The work of Ashis Nandy is exemplary in this regard.[99] But in all of these otherwise erudite discussions, the West has been analytically deployed as a universalized imaginary Other. That is, the West continues to function as "an opposing entity, a system of reference, an object from which to learn, a point of measurement, a goal to catch up with, an intimate enemy, and sometimes an alibi for serious discussion and action."[100]

In contrast, my earlier example of immersing *Lan Yu* in a web of Sinophone historical signification repositions our compass—and redraws our map—by spotlighting the non-West, Asia, and China more specifically. In *Asia as Method*, Kuan-Hsing Chen invites postcolonial scholars to "deimperialize" their own mode of investigation by moving beyond the fixation on "the West" as the sole historical-theoretical caliber of civilizational, national, imperial, colonial, and Cold War predicaments.[101] In his words,

In Asia, the deimperialization question cannot be limited to a reexamination of the impacts of Western imperialism invasion, Japanese colonial violence, and U.S. neoimperialist expansion, but must also include the oppressive practices of the Chinese empire. Since the status of China has shifted from an empire to a big country, how should China position itself now? In what new ways can it interact with neighboring countries? Questions like these can be productively answered only through deimperialized self-questioning, and that type of reflexive work has yet to be undertaken.[102]

Understanding *Lan Yu* in the language of queer Sinophone postcolonial theory takes a bold step in undertaking this type of reflexive work. It is an endeavor to refocus our attention from the "influence" of Western ideas (e.g., Western notions of homosexuality, the closet, and coming out) to the inter- and intra-Asian conditions of subject formation—from denaturalizing the West to provincializing China, Asia, and the rest.[103] By considering *Lan Yu* as a portrayal of Sinophone queerness rather than a monotonous representation of Chinese homosexuality, we are simultaneously repurposing the agenda and strengths of postcolonial studies. This expands the notion of *queer regionalism* that I have developed with queer theorist Alvin K. Wong, which "reckons with the vertical logics of Euro-American empire, but at the same time . . . signals greater attention to less orderly, bilateral, and horizontal intra-regional traffics of queerness across different countries and regions *in* Asia."[104]

The corollary argument I am making here is that a queer Sinophone synergism can serve as an interruptive worldview.[105] It not only breaks down the China-versus-the West binary, but also specifies the most powerful type, nature, and configuration of transnationalism, whose gravity must lie beyond the hegemonic constructions of the nation-state. A renewed understanding of how a certain *modularity* of transnationalism disturbs majoritarian forms of governance is especially meaningful as queer theory culls value from erased concerns or peripheral debates in critical area/regional studies.[106] According to Françoise Lionnet and Shumei Shih, the transnational "can be less scripted and more scattered" and "is not bound by the binary of the local and the global and can occur in national, local, or global spaces across different and multiple spatialities and temporalities."[107] If queer "China" and "Chineseness" indeed evolved in the course of the twentieth century from global sexual knowledge to neoliberal archetypes of biopolitics, what we witness over time has less to do with the "coming out" of sexual minorities per se (though this process certainly warrants historical and political recognition) than with the shift toward a *minor* transnational China (a less obvious sign of historical evolution).[108]

This notion of minor transnationalism focalizes the *rhizomic-horizontal* connectivity across postcolonial locations such as Taiwan, Hong Kong, Singapore, Malaysia, Indonesia, Philippines, Myanmar, and possibly even South Korea.[109] Cultural anthropologist Ting-Fai Yu, for instance, has examined the interarticulation of ethnic and sexual identities in the experience of queer Malaysian migrants in Taiwan and how this experience in turn shapes political activism back in Malaysia.[110] Regions that have not been colonized by foreign powers such as Thailand are equally germane.[111] The minor-to-minor relationality between any two or more of these regions guarantees a desubjugated historical spotlight that does not need to be routed through a center, be it China, Japan, Europe, or the United States. Rarely does queer studies in any of the earlier-mentioned *minor* places receive the measure of scholarly attention it deserves, unless it is pivoted against such *major* geopolitical rubrics as "East Asian studies," "Japanese colonial studies," or "Western imperialism." Bringing together minor area studies and queer theory in such a mutually syncopated fashion is "not about simplistic expansion into sites of alterity to reach a whole but a resistance to any form of totalizing knowledge."[112] The turn to minor transnationalism articulates the possibility of otherwise.

Queer Sonics

Sinophone studies is also useful for queer theory because it turns our analytic optic toward the queer potential of sound. One of the most powerful tools of queer Sinophone theory that has gone unnoticed, and herein lies my sixth reason, is the way it geopoliticizes the study of queer sonic cultures.[113] The *-phone* suffix in the Sinophone word indicates the speaking of a particular language, but it can also connote broader matters related to the register of sound. The queerness of sound is in some ways an old concern; the work done in the field of queer musicology comes to mind easily.[114] Nonetheless, this focus on sound stakes new opportunities for critical thinking in at least two ways: by expanding from a textual and visual theoretical abstraction occasioned by the "linguistic turn" of the 1980s and by integrating the auditory experience into the more recent "affective turn" in queer theory.[115] To hear queerness requires listening to the sur-prising ruptures of the norm, and these hearings elicit certain affective responses that could potentially transcend mechanisms of debilitation and social disparagement.[116] Sinophone studies, as a paradigm of historical and cultural critique, contextualizes these lines of inquiry on a concrete geo-political map. To illustrate what I mean, I would like to return to a crucial juncture in contemporary Chinese history—the handover of Hong Kong in 1997—from which to limn a minor transnational politics of sexuality through a Sinophone sonic lens.[117]

Specifically, I believe that a new queer reading of Wong Kar-wai's epic *Happy Together* (春光乍洩, 1997) is helpful to unmooring the geopolitics of Chineseness from historical queering, not the least because the film is a cultural commentary that is *produced during* as much as it is *about* the postcolonial transition.[118] For instance, the two protagonists' prehandover passports are shown in the film as belonging to the United Kingdom of Great Britain and Northern Ireland (figure 2.2). The weight of this colo-nial document thereby foreshadows the film's strong thematic allegory of borders and their crossings. In fact, as we will see, boundary transgression—sexual, sonic, geopolitical, or otherwise—in the film frequently operates in a South-to-South or minor-to-minor direction. More than two decades after its production, my following reading renders *Happy Together*

Fig. 2.2 Lai Yiu-fai's British passport.
Source: *Happy Together* (1997), directed by Wong Kar-wai, produced by Chan Ye-cheng.

as both a Sinophone cultural text about its time and a historical product of its time.

Critics have noted that Wong made two evasive, if not misleading, remarks at the time of the film's release. First, despite the film's overt portrayal of a strained relationship between two homosexual men, Wong insisted that *Happy Together* should not be read as a gay film: "In fact I don't like people to see this film as a gay film. It's more like a story about human relationships and somehow the two characters involved are both men."[119] Second, Wong intended to distance the film from Hong Kong's political crisis circa 1997. One reviewer goes so far as to claim that in the film "Argentina functions as a heterotopic metaphor for Hong Kong."[120] However, Wong subsequently conceded that his decision to film *Happy Together* as far away from Hong Kong as possible turned out to be an ironic failure. This self-defeating move cemented the topic of Hong Kong existentialism as one of the most enduring legacies in the film's critical reception. In his words, "One of the reasons I chose Argentina was that it is on the other side of the world, and I thought by going there, I would be able to stay away from 1997. But then, as you must understand, once you consciously try to stay away from something or to forget something, you will never succeed. That something is bound to be hanging in the air, haunting you."[121] By mapping the disappearance of colonial Hong Kong onto the potential public erasure of homosexuality after the PRC's takeover, *Happy Together* epitomizes the coimbrication of geopolitics and sexuality. This attests to film scholar Helen Leung's observation that "in the most innovative films of this period, the postcolonial predicament appears at most as an undercurrent, a not-quite-visible force that nonetheless animates what is amply visible on-screen."[122] Queer sex is often staged in Hong Kong cinema at the juncture of this collision between the visible and the invisible.

Existing readings of *Happy Together* tend to highlight the mainline story revolving around the two protagonists, Lai Yiu-fai and Ho Po-wing, two Hong Kong men who traveled to Argentina with the Iguazu Falls set as their final destination but were ultimately stranded in Buenos Aires when they ran out of money.[123] As literary scholar Carlos Rojas has shown, a central motif of the plot progression is proclaimed in the opening sequence of the film, when Ho says to Lai, "let's start over again."[124] This "seemingly simple and innocent plea . . . [for] *reiteration*," according to

Rey Chow, "makes sense only in the [logic of] supplementarity."[125] The perpetual desire to start over embodies the paradoxical nature of the relationship between Lai and Ho: the two men's yearning to start afresh, put the past behind, and transform their relationship into something more stable is constantly undercut by a recurring complication that drives that yearning in the first place. Throughout the story, Ho's persistent interest in anonymous sex clashes with Lai's strategic maneuvering to contain and domesticate their ostensible monogamy. Ultimately, it is when Lai begins to engage in anonymous sexual relations after Ho leaves him that Lai comes to acknowledge a version of Ho within himself. The recursive impetus to "start over" adumbrates their ultimate fate: Lai eventually returns to Hong Kong (via Taipei), leaving Ho behind to reenact the moments they shared in their old apartment in Buenos Aires. They never visited the Iguazu Falls together.

When I first watched *Happy Together* as a closeted high school student, my encounter was akin to what Shu-mei Shih later described as her experience in watching Ang Lee's *Crouching Tiger, Hidden Dragon* (臥虎藏龍, 2000): "The linguistic dissonance of the film registers the heterogeneity of Sinitic languages as well as their speakers living in different locales."[126] I say "akin" rather than "identical" because, unlike in *Crouching Tiger, Hidden Dragon*, the characters in *Happy Together* almost never converse in a seemingly unified yet heavily accented Mandarin, or *putonghua* (普通話). Instead, Lai and Ho speak Cantonese to each other (sometimes English to others), and when Lai engages in dialogues with his Taiwanese coworker at a Chinese restaurant, Chang, he speaks in Cantonese with Chang talking back in Mandarin. The film actually purports Lai's fluency in Mandarin (to be fair, Lai at times converses in mildly accented Mandarin) as well as Chang's ability to understand spoken Cantonese. Nevertheless, we might say that in this way *Happy Together* is an even more explicitly Sinophone film than *Crouching Tiger, Hidden Dragon*: "The Sinophone frustrates easy suturing, in this case, while foregrounding the value of difficulty, difference, and heterogeneity."[127] The cacophony along with the mutual readability of Sinitic language by Lai and Chang presumes a certain familiarity across the popular culture in Taiwan and Hong Kong that has existed since at least the 1950s.[128] Of course, lurking beneath the eclectic verbal bonding between the three male characters in *Happy Together* resides an ever-present threshold of homoerotic intimacy.

I dwell on the significance of the vocal and the sonic to illustrate the new possible angles of reading *Happy Together* based on a Sinophone analytic. To hark back to the minor transnational politics that I discussed earlier, a convincing queer reading of the film emerges from attending to the mutual refraction of *sound* and *minor relationality*. Whereas conventional analyses of the film have focused on the Lai-Ho homosexual relationship, I consider the Lai-Chang homosocial relationship (the film never disambiguates its erotic overtone) as what ultimately disrupts the queer futurity and utopian visions anticipated by the desire to "start over" between Lai and Ho.[129] To begin with, a queer reading is already hinted by my departure from the dominant focus on issues of queer sex, queer stardom, and queer reception centering on the Hong Kong actor Leslie Cheung (張國榮, 1956–2003), who played Ho.[130] The heterosexuality of both Tony Leung (梁朝偉, b. 1962), who played Lai, and Chang Cheng (張震, b. 1976), who played Chang, are well publicized. Thus the queerness of the Lai-Chang homoromance is accentuated by the actors' minor relationality to the characters in the film: two straight men playing queer and pseudoqueer roles respectively. What other kinds of queer irruptive reading can *Happy Together* yield from the minor vantage point of the Chang character?

In contrast to the vivid sex scenes in which Lai and Ho are portrayed, the film ultimately concludes with a sentimental portrayal of the Lai-Chang intimacy, with Lai stopping by Taipei and visiting the street stall run by Chang's family. Though Lai and Chang never had sex in the film, this critical sexual absence is perhaps what gives their affective tender ties and, in fact, the overall tenor of the film their queerest edge. The relationship between Lai and Chang is one that constantly subverts even as it contrasts with the major form of relationality that threads the plot development (Lai's gay partnership with Ho). The relevance of queer sound to the Lai-Chang minor relationality is especially evident by way of mutual refraction. Before Chang's departure for Ushuaia, he asks Lai to use his tape recorder to capture Lai's sadness (hinting at Chang's sensitivity to Lai's broken relationship with Ho), which he promises to take with him "to the end of the world" and leave it there (figure 2.3). Yet once he reaches Les Eclaireurs Lighthouse, Chang cannot hear anything on the recorder other than "some strange noise, like someone sobbing." Helen Leung has interpreted the inaudibility of Lai's

Fig. 2.3 Chang asks Lai to record Lai's sadness.
Source: Happy Together (1997), directed by Wong Kar-wai, produced by Chan Ye-cheng.

heartbreak as "the sound that we cannot quite hear" that "encapsulates everything that the film is about: loneliness, heartbreak, the futility of love, and the resilience of hope."[131]

I would go further and argue that the *trafficking* of this inaudible sound, which perversely irrupts the Sinitic dialects spoken throughout the film, is as important as its formal quality. The way that the queer Sinophone sound of Lai travels cannot be easily extricated from the minor relational nature of Lai's affect for Chang (and vice versa), a symbol of the minor transnationalism between Hong Kong and Taiwan. It is through Chang that Lai's queer voice arrives at the lighthouse at the end of the world. Moreover, this queer rerouting of non-Cantonese sound unveils the coexistence of multiple Hong Kongs, with Ho, now stranded in Buenos Aires without his prehandover passport (a reminder of the British colonial past), living by another form of queer silence in memory of what could have been—a perpetual "starting over." Though supposedly on his way back to Hong Kong, the final destination for Lai in the film turns out to be Taipei (a symbolic surrogate of homecoming).[132] But when he reaches the street stall run by Chang's family, Lai does not see Chang there. Instead, Lai sees a photo of Chang at the lighthouse and decides to take it with him, explaining that he does not know when he will see Chang again (figures 2.4 and 2.5). Reminiscent of the inaudible

Fig. 2.4 Lai sees a photograph of Chang at the lighthouse.
Source: *Happy Together* (1997), directed by Wong Kar-wai, produced by Chan Ye-cheng.

Fig. 2.5 A photograph of Chang at the lighthouse.
Source: *Happy Together* (1997), directed by Wong Kar-wai, produced by Chan Ye-cheng.

presence of Lai at the lighthouse scene, Chang claims his silent queer presence in the Taipei night market scene through Lai's Cantonese voiceover. The characters in *Happy Together* carry a certain "sonic" leverage with which to move across borders and through which it is possible to trace the transnational mobility of queer Sinophone subjects—in Argentina, Hong Kong, or Taiwan.

Saying No to Straight Sinology

Implicit in my analysis of *Lan Yu* and *Happy Together* lies my seventh reason for merging queer theory with Sinophone studies: to disrupt the spatial and temporal logics that have long defined the homophobic and transphobic contours of area studies, including China studies.[133] By provincializing China, the Sinophone framework enables us to see and think beyond the conventions of China studies. This radical mode of inquiry can be adapted to refuse an epistemological grid of heteronormativity. The rebuttal of *straight*-forwardness ensures the continual interrogation of a moving center from the margins of a margin.[134] In terms of the substantive objects of study, a growing number of Sinophone scholars have already ventured into multiple place-based analyses of literary and cinematic examples in a "transpacific" nexus, from Southeast Asia to Hong Kong, Taiwan to North America.[135] These localized examples in literature, film, and popular culture are rarely invoked in Chinese studies, Asian American studies, or other traditional (area studies) disciplines.[136] Sinophone studies, as "the 'study of China' that transcends China" (to borrow the phrase from Mizoguchi Yuzo), empowers those "queer" inquiries excluded from the time-honored Sinology that has formalized alongside the Cold War and its aftermath.[137]

In the spirit of marking out "a space in which unspoken stories and histories may be told,"[138] the queer Sinophone method raises a series of interrelated questions that continue to haunt a "China-centered perspective."[139] These are questions of cultural disparity as much as about geopolitical entanglement.[140] Is the kind of homosexual experience represented in *Lan Yu* and *Happy Together* "Chinese" or "Western" in nature? Homosexuality in whose sense of the term? Is it a foreign import, an expression (and thus internalization) of foreign imperialism, or a long-standing indigenous practice in a new light?[141] In what ways can we give serious attention and due consideration to the administrative reordering of Hong Kong in the late twentieth century? How do we make sense of the Special Administrative Region (SAR) as a newly invented political category? How about the impact of the Tiananmen Square protests on Sinophone communities? Is it possible to speak of an alternative Sinophone modernity that challenges the familiar socialist narrative of twentieth-century Chinese history?[142] Which China is alluded to by the various notions of

Chineseness depicted in the films? Is the handover of Hong Kong to the PRC another form of colonial (and imperial) domination? Or does it entail a different ordering of truth regimes and governing practices—what Foucault would call the microsites or "dense transfer point[s]" of power?[143] Evidently, the complexity of the history far exceeds the common terms we use to describe the historical characteristics of postcolonial Hong Kong (or Taiwan for that matter).[144] To conceive of the PRC in relation to Hong Kong circa 1997 as a regime from the outside or a colonial government only partially accounts for its proto-Chineseness or extra-Chineseness. Precisely due to the lack of a precedent and analogous situations, it is all the more difficult to historicize the social backdrop against which non-normative desires have been authenticated and circulated through overlapping grids of intelligibility and the "intimate frontiers" of empire.[145]

To Queer China Again

With the rise of China in the twenty-first century, it is all the more pressing to bring the scholarly practice of "queering" to bear on the study of "China." The world is occupied by 1.2 billion native speakers of the Sinitic-language family. That is more than three times the number of people for whom English is the mother tongue. Changing our purview from considering "China" as a national category to envisioning the "Sinophone" as a global concept reflects the fact that the area studies modus operandi of Sinology has long outlived its utility. The danger in criticizing "the West" from a seemingly harmless stance of nativist "China" can easily be neutralized by the self-fashioned postcolonial critic who works from a privileged position to marginalize ethnic, geopolitical, and gender/sexual others.[146] After all, there is no Stonewall in China, but that should not stop us from queering Chinese and Sinophone history. Similar to the way historians have recontextualized Stonewall time and again, queer Sinophone studies dispels the myth of a coherent *tongzhi* movement past and present. It is perhaps fitting, then, that even though I began with the injunction to treat Stonewall as a lateral event, this chapter concludes with the bid to put China aside or, alternatively put, to queer China again.

The rise of the PRC empire is perhaps one of the most underexplored topics in the critical humanities and social sciences today. Yet I write about this remiss at a moment when a significant number of historians continue to reference Stonewall as the inception of modern queer politics (think QHC19). My goal has been to consider both the Stonewall hegemony and contemporary Chinese imperialism as interconnected developments in world historiography—an instance of what Francophone writer Édouard Glissant has called the "poetics of relation."[147] The examples of the Tiananmen incident (1989) and the retrocession of Hong Kong (1997) highlight turning points other than 1969 in the globally intertwined history of dehumanization. In fact, if we bring this narrative to the present, Sinophone communities continue to occasion unforeseen possibilities for queer political action, such as the legalization of same-sex union in Taiwan and transgender marriage in Hong Kong.[148] Of course, there is no singular consensus on how the direction and contours of these new battles would impact the lives of LGBTQ people in the Asia Pacific.[149] But bringing to focus the geospatial complexities of the Sinitic language populations, at the very least, signals the death of two interconnected positivisms: a linear, evolutionary history of sexual liberation spawned from Stonewall and a neat compartmentalization of the non-West as a differential supplement. In this way queer theory needs Sinophone studies as a coproduced vector through which to double question its own essentialism, defined around any geocultural and temporal unit.

PART TWO

Uneven Paths

Three Methods

CHAPTER III

Titrating Transgender

Archiving Taiwan Through Renyao *History*

"H as the queer ever been human?"[1] Since queer theorists Dana Luciano and Mel Y. Chen posed this question in a special issue of *GLQ* (2015), the specter of humanity's limit has haunted queer studies unabatedly. In advancing the interest of those who have been unduly oppressed, the field has increasingly decried the privileging of human interest and subjectivity. Centering on the concept of *queer inhumanism*, this timely and provocative project draws attention to the often-ignored nonhuman realm.[2] This anti-anthropocentric turn augments an ongoing discussion on the role of affect, animal, object, environment, and other inanimate material agents in humanistic inquiries.[3] In their deliberation, Luciano and Chen confirm the enticing, productive, and contradictory effects of coupling—and rupturing—the terms *queer* and *human*: "*Yes*, because this sustained interrogation of the unjust dehumanization of queers insistently, if implicitly, posits the human as standard form, and also because many queer theorists have undeniably privileged the human body and human sexuality as the locus of their analysis. But *no* because queer theory has long been suspicious of the politics of rehabilitation and inclusion to which liberal-humanist values lead, and because 'full humanity' has never been the only horizon for queer becoming."[4] In short, it is high time to think about queerness not merely in relation to but also in terms of how it *continues to trouble* the uneven, recursive recognitions of being human—and becoming gendered.[5]

The absence of a sustained interest in the Asia Pacific marks a missed opportunity in this new exciting endeavor. After all, the boundaries between the human and the nonhuman, and between various gender types, have long preoccupied thinkers all over the world. This chapter refocuses the theorization of queer inhumanism through the lens of inter-Asian geopolitics, that is, the power dynamics behind the formation and differentiation of competing sovereignty regimes across Asia. By reconstructing the social life of renyao (人妖)—a Chinese category of transgenderism for which the best English translation is perhaps "human prodigy"—from Republican China to Nationalist Taiwan, it seeks to map the fluidity of transness (transtopian continuum) onto the volatility of Chineseness (Sinophone historicism). The terms under which this reciprocal interaction can be brought to light distinguish the central concern of the rest of this book. Because the nonoverlapping histories of renyao in mainland China and Taiwan constitute an important focus of this inquiry, I begin by drawing attention to the (in)significance of Taiwan in dominant Western academic thinking. This frame will lay the groundwork for my central argument that attending to this island's global alienation helps to illuminate renyao history and vice versa.

While the renyao figure has been understood to correlate with the motifs of gender dislocation, sex transformation, same-sex relations, the boundaries and meaning of humanism, and prostitution, this chapter historicizes the category apropos of a range of unexpected tropes, such as fraudulent behavior, intersexuality, incest, and ghosts. Before 1920, the Chinese discourse of renyao carried a definitional core of inhuman queerness, as the literal meaning of this compound term, "human (ren)-monster (yao)," already conveyed a threshold of dehumanization.[6] This spectral avatar accentuated—but also blurred—the boundaries of being human by underscoring what the category registers and fails to capture. More generally, renyao was frequently deployed to depict a troubling state of reproductive order, biological and social. In the 1920s and 1930s, the impact of Western medical science filtered the multiple meanings of renyao and uplifted the moral status of the category by associating it strictly with the more "humane" phenomenon of gender transgression.

After reclaiming renyao as an exemplary prototype of queer inhumanism, this chapter follows the history of renyao to Cold War Taiwan. Interweaving the public narratives of Zeng Qiuhuang (曾秋皇, b. 1909), arguably the most famous "human prodigy" in the 1950s, my investigation maps the region's marginality onto the peripheral potency of *renyao* embodiment. This archival destabilization interrupts the modalities of power that figure nonnormative genders and sexualities, however unsymmetrically and unevenly, into decolonial understandings of the past. Building on a thriving literature that interrogates the role of the archive in queer Asian history— from the heterogeneous constructions of a national queer archive in contemporary Korea to the precarious evidence of same-sex behavior in the legal archives of Qing China (1644–1912), and from the mundane impulse of recording perversity to the archival substantiation of possible queer afterlives in colonial India—this chapter uses the media sensationalism showered on gender plasticity to develop some tangible contours around the press sources as a corpus of evidentiary claims.[7] As a "Chinese" category, *renyao* has genealogical roots in mainland China, but its most pronounced and elaborate conceptual articulations in the mid-twentieth century transpired in Sinophone Taiwan.

A coupled rethinking of the conceptual parameters of archival utility and the normative cogency of human queerness reposes *archiving* itself as a problem of historical rumination and defetishizes the archive as an inevitably mediated corridor to the comprehensible past of queer lives and experiences. Taking cues from literary and historical deconstructions of colonial text and imagination, the challenge here is to unmoor the convention of archival rendering as an extractive enterprise of making access and enabling retrieval. In its stead, I argue for the palpability of absence assemblages through the retrospective traversing of the margins of postcolonial historicity *and* the gender and sexual peripheries of a postwar (imagined) national community.[8] Through these adjoining theoretical moves, this chapter posits a transtopian continuum that crosses the thresholds of the human/nonhuman divide. The evolution of this human/ nonhuman spectrum shadows the titration of the *renyao* category from continental China to Nationalist Taiwan. In the context of this chapter, titration refers to the proportional calibration of the way being cross-gendered and being human intersected, which grew into the overriding denotation of the *renyao* category by the 1950s.[9] In other words, *renyao* has historically operated as a signifier with the capacity to express the manifolds of corporeal arrangement, but its epistemic containment and gendered latitude condensed over time and space. This genealogical titration unearths the significance of Taiwan's global insignificance and accrues such displacement labor through the subversive and transversal effects of archiving transgender inhumanism as an allegorical archetype in queer Sinophone history.[10]

Chimera

Taiwan, the Republic of China, is a small island and has been without official nation-state status since 1971, the year in which Taiwan lost over to the PRC its membership in the United Nations. As such, scholarship on Taiwanese history and culture has been shaped by diverse political interests, a problem further amplified and complicated by the island's multiple colonial pasts as well as its highly contested relationship to a growing superpower. The field of Taiwanese studies, for instance, became institutionalized only in the twenty-first century, now bearing an uneasy tension with Sinology in Taiwanese academia. Native thinkers continue to debate the question of whether Taiwan can serve as an innovative site of theoretical knowledge production. Part of the contention concerns the specific *kinds* of political exploitation inflicted upon the region and its people historically. For example, northern Taiwan remained a small colony of the Spanish empire between 1626 and 1646, while southern Taiwan came under the colonial rule of the Dutch Republic from 1624 to 1662. Both of these regimes, and by extension their legacies in Taiwan, have been routinely excluded from mainstream discussions of (Western) modernity.[11] It is easy to consider inconsequential the interlacing of the Taiwanese experience with the saga of these early variants of European imperialism. Occupying a corner of the Chinese and Japanese empires subsequently, Taiwan's repressed sovereignty had further prevented itself from cultivating a distinctively robust epistemological tradition. Even with the burgeoning of critical theory among Taiwanese scholars in the late twentieth century, much of that vibrancy was facilitated by the global ascendance of US-based academic trends. Viewed from both without and within, Taiwan appears as an intellectual vacuum uncapable of generating its own theory that suited its own purpose.[12]

In light of these factors, Shu-mei Shih has noted the *illegibility* of Taiwan studies as an area of critical inquiry in the West:

Studying Taiwan is an *impossible* task. I say "impossible" because Taiwan is always already written out of mainstream Western discourse due to its *insignificance*. Taiwan, when any attention is given to it at all, is most often reduced to an object of empirical political analysis, and has been systematically dismissed as a worthwhile object of critical analysis in cultural and other humanistic studies with theoretical import. Taiwan is too small, too marginal, too ambiguous, and thus too insignificant. Taiwan does not enjoy the historical accident of having been colonised by a Western power in the nineteenth or twentieth century; instead it was colonised by other Asian powers: Japan (1895–1945) and the exiled Chinese Nationalist government (1945 to the late 1980s) respectively. If it had been colonised by Britain, Taiwan would have been able to share in the fashion of postcolonial theory. If it had been colonised by France, Taiwan would be part of Francophone studies. Colonisation by Japan and another ethnic Chinese regime effectively ghettoised Taiwan within the realm of "Asian studies," where it is further marginalised within so-called Sinology or Chinese Studies.[13]

Shih further points out that due to its connections to the American Right in the Cold War period, Taiwan has been strategically neglected by academics in North America. Studying Taiwan suggests that one is not sufficiently familiar with China and thus not worthy of being hired in the field of Chinese/East Asian studies. If only Taiwan had been a communist or socialist regime, then leftist scholars in the West could at least share some ideological sympathy with the region or hold it as a logical object of comparative analysis. The lingering effects of these prejudices—haunting scholarly interest in Taiwan's culture and history—motivated Shih to edit the special issue "Globalisation: Taiwan's (In)Significance" for the journal *Postcolonial Studies* in 2003.[14]

Although nearly two decades have passed since the publication of the special issue, the insignificance of Taiwan prevails in mainstream Western academic thought, and Taiwan's relevance remains hidden under the threatening shadow of China. To quote Gayatri Spivak from a different context, "the sophisticated vocabulary of much contemporary historiography *successfully* shields this cognitive *failure* and that this success-in-failure, this sanctioned ignorance, is inseparable from colonial domination."[15] A countermeasure to such "sanctioned ignorance" entails the careful placing of Taiwan on our educated radar. This should be executed not by reinforcing or elevating Taiwan-centrism but, on the contrary, by foregrounding Taiwan's abject status as situated at the intersections of various *margins*—geopolitical, sociocultural, and historiographical.[16] My recuperative stake thus joins the recent endeavors to investigate the mutual referentiality and disciplinary politics embedded in the relationship between China, Taiwan, and other Sinitic-language communities worldwide.[17] By looking from the outside in via competing angles of marginality, our grounding of Taiwan (more precisely, our appreciation of what it means to "be Taiwan") promises to denaturalize itself continuously.

Alighting on the immediate postwar years, *renyao*'s modernization gradually zooms in on a contextual frame in which the island earned for itself all the social and cultural weight of the postcolonial condition vis-à-vis the Japanese empire.[18] Meanwhile, this was the same volatile political moment when Taiwan underwent an increasingly violent acquisition by Chiang Kai-shek's US-backed Nationalist regime.[19] In the transitional period of the late 1940s, the Republic of China legal system gradually replaced Japanese laws on the island. Using press reports of *renyao* as the foci of analysis, my historicization supersedes existing readings that tend to emphasize the lifting of martial law in 1987 as the decisive turning point that enabled the flourishing of queer cultures and politics in late-capitalist Taiwan.[20] Considering the centrality of post–martial law political activism to dominant interpretations of Taiwan's sexual modernity, we can therefore locate accounts of gender transgression and sexual diversity in the "hypercolonial" 1950s as yet another one of the multiple peripheries from which the theoretical power of situating Taiwan in the present derives.[21]

Our undertaking here is to engage with the practice of *archiving* as a way of making visible the significance of Taiwan's historical ontology. This deepens recent ventures in literary and historical studies to enrich, problematize, or challenge the role of the archive in critical approaches to the past.[22] At the core of these debates sits a theoretical and empirical investment in questioning the existence of proof, the verifiability of evidence, and the pertinent styles of argumentation that unfurl from the mining of available sources. Despite the explosion of "archive fever" (to borrow Jacques Derrida's phrase), or precisely because of it, the archive has nonetheless "emerged as *the* register of epistemic arrangements, recording in its proliferating avatars the shifting tenor of debates around the production and ethics of knowledge."[23] Anjali Arondekar, in her erudite study of the relationship between sexuality and the colonial archive in India, urges us to acknowledge the simultaneous excess and limits of archival evidence as mutually co-constitutive, so that our reading practice produces subjects of futurity as it acknowledges the way it is circumscribed by the configuration of our source object.[24] According to anthropologist Ann Laura Stoler, (colonial) archives are "sites of the expectant and conjured—about dreams of comforting futures and forebodings of future failures."[25] Literary critic Lisa Lowe reformulates archival promise from "a source for knowledge retrieval" to "a site of knowledge production."[26] Yet if our approach to archival comprehension does not presume a complete, definitive, or successful disclosure of validity, then a queer *unknowing* of sorts proves to be conducive to a much richer set of possible answers, whatever our initial questions about the past may be.[27] In effect, it is at the moment when we surrender to a conviction about the ultimate truth measure of the archive—the moment that we privilege a propensity of satisfaction with what we have or have not uncovered—that our historicist sight becomes most shorted by a reductive complacency.[28] In what follows, I take up the kind of generative reading practices advanced by Arondekar, Stoler, Lowe, and others, but I also move in a slightly different direction with what I call archiving.

The move from probing the archive to the exercise of archiving bears conceptual symmetry to the divergence between executing the production of knowledge and knowing itself. Yet the politics of knowing, like the politics of archiving, routinely relies on the idioms of in/visibility when coupled with minoritized subject formations, such as in queer and postcolonial history, and thus upholds a triumphalist preference for the empirical record of "experience."[29] How does one study the relationship of queerness to the postcolonial archive, to quote Arondekar, "without fetishizing its historical formation, without relinquishing its epistemological possibilities, and without commodifying its political contexts?"[30] Part of the answer lies in the cross-examination of ostensibly freestanding analytical units. Despite the rise of transnational, interregional, and global history, many historians continue to situate the epistemological investment of their work comfortably within national confines. One of my main arguments is that by *archiving peripheral Taiwan*, we could register a more acute awareness of the mutating nature of our analytic categories, especially with respect to the ways in which their interdependent effects evolve over time. One such naturalized category that has been construed unproblematic time and again is the nation-state. In the case of Taiwan, this category raises immediate concern because for decades Taiwan has not (or never?) been fully considered as a true nation-state. The uncertainty of elision and abandonment, for instance, has led one author to identify Taiwan famously as an "orphan of Asia."[31] This liminality figures Taiwan as an emblematic queer state—defined as both a polity and a condition—in contemporary critical thought on the notions of region(alism), Asia, area, scale, and the globe.[32]

Other imbricated categories include historical gender and sexuality, especially since the 1950s has not been understood as a decade of visible gender and sexual variance in the dominant narratives of Chinese or Taiwanese history (or the history of the modern West for that matter).[33] As my archiving of Zeng Qiuhuang will demonstrate, the traditional "human-monster" expression, with its semantic governance of embodied historicity, indexes the *filtering* and *synthesis* of transgender meanings across time. Using titration as an analytic technique calibrates the specificity of *renyao* examples along the codependent axes of engendering and (de)humanization. By the 1950s, even the slippery category of the human fails to capture the range of nuances associated with human expression, the boundaries of humanhood, and the archival terms under which such epistemological configurations are collected and recalled. What the postwar discourse of *renyao* reveals and captures is the reciprocal chimera effect whereby the margins of sexuality and the periphery of "China" and "Chineseness" converge into the mimetic recalcitrant traces of the past: the prodigy of the human—*renyao*—configures the basis of archival imagination on which the prodigy of historical na(rra)tion—Taiwan—crystallizes with distinct tempos and visibility from the seemingly authentic repertoire of empirical retrieval, recovery, and access.

The act of archiving renders the task of the historian as much about producing the past as about engaging with it. In archival studies, there is a long-standing wisdom that separates the task of the archivist (overseeing the repository of information) from the work of the historian (accessing and producing knowledge about the past).[34] Labor historian Carolyn Steedman sums it up elegantly, "The Archive then is something that, through the cultural activity of History, can become Memory's potential space, one of the few realms of the modern imagination where hard-won and carefully constructed place can return to boundless, limitless space."[35] My following discussion brackets this distinction between the Archive and History by suggesting that *the act of history writing itself is a form of archiving*. In construing the historian as the archivist as such, or, more specifically, the production of the history of the human prodigy as an example of queer archiving, my purpose in reorienting the spaces of memory is threefold. First, I provide a comprehensive overview of the historiography of *renyao*. In doing so, I parse the various historical differentials available in an existing scholarly body of knowledge about the historicity of the concept. Canvassing the historiography of *renyao* thereby exemplifies the very practice of archiving—a mode of queering archival categories of legibility and knowledge. Second, I unpack the evolving lexicon of *renyao* in the Republican period in order to specify the sedimentary provisions of its later pronouncement outside mainland China. Finally, I offer a detailed analysis of the narratives about Zeng that loomed over the postwar Taiwanese press. This threefold agenda enunciates the excessive and limited "traces" of *renyao*, thereby destabilizing but also making apparent the mercurial vitality of this queer category.[36] The historian's desire for the past is thus routed not through attachments to a particular form of information but through a commitment to a strategy of knowledge production that accommodates, and even vindicates, stories of different shapes and memories.

Differentials

In engaging with an existing archive of knowledge, the act of archiving inevitably also transforms it, because it creates the possibility of unsettling the normativization of archival rubrics. In the historiography of gender and sexuality, the category of *renyao* has been scrutinized by scholars adopting various thematic, chronological, and methodological orientations. The major thematic components according to which *renyao* has been indexed in the existent literature include gender dislocation, sex transformation, same-sex relations, the boundaries and meaning of humanism, and prostitution. The chronological depth of this body of research spans from the Ming dynasty to the Cold War period, and the sources on which these studies draw include official records, anecdotal notations (筆記, *biji*), literary sources, medical treatises, mainstream journalism, and urban tabloid presses (小報, *xiaobao*).[37] Such a plethora of evidentiary trace reveals the impressive reach of the term *renyao* to different corners of Chinese cultural life for centuries. This section provides an exhaustive overview of the ways in which the concept of *renyao* has operated as a meaningful signifier in varying strands of critical inquiry. It aims to identify the multiple historical differentials of *renyao* and synthesize their anatomization by the most representative scholarship to date. In my later analysis of Zeng, the history of *renyao*, as a category of marginal subjectivities, will encompass all of these common denominators, but it will also subvert them on a novel basis in the context of mid-twentieth-century Taiwan.

One of the earliest lenses through which scholars have studied the history of *renyao* is gender dislocation. Literary scholar Judith Zeitlin in her seminal study of Pu Songling's *Strange Tales from a Chinese Studio* (聊齋誌異, *Liaozhai zhiyi*; written in the early Qing dynasty) proposes that the best translation of *renyao* is "human prodigy."[38] *Strange Tales* comprises nearly five hundred marvel stories (written in classical Chinese starting in the Tang dynasty), in which the boundaries between reality and the odd are blurred and a whole cast of ghosts, foxes, beasts, and spirits is introduced to contrast and thus call into question the status of the human, as exemplified by the more conventional characters of scholars, court officials, and husbands and wives. One of these stories is precisely titled "Renyao," in which a man disguised as the opposite gender to seduce a woman is ultimately castrated by her husband and becomes his concubine. As Zeitlin acknowledges, the most important message of this story concerns the way in which castration helps to reinstate a normative social order: "The important thing is not a search for truth and revelation but a search for rehabilitation and order."[39] Indeed, the removal of the protagonist's gender dislocation "can thus be seen as a perverse Confucian 'rectification of names,'" because "the prodigious has [now] been cut off from the human prodigy; what remains is merely the human being."[40] Castration therefore becomes "the means for [the protagonist's] reintegration into normal human society—as a concubine, he becomes a permanent member of the family and is even buried by the family tomb. The 'monster' is domesticated."[41]

In historicizing *renyao*, Zeitlin explains that the author Pu is drawing on an existing tradition of Chinese official thinking, which interprets social anomalies including gender transgression as a sign of moral disruption in the broader political cosmos:

The Chinese term *renyao* (human prodigy) originally denoted any human physical anomaly or freak. It was first employed in the philosophical writing of *Xunzi* (third c. B.C.), where it designated "human prodigies or portents" as implicitly opposed to "heavenly prodigies or portents" ([天妖] *tianyao*). Alongside this general meaning of human freak or monster, the term came to acquire an additional, more specialized usage: an impersonator of a member of the opposite sex. It was first used in this sense in the *History of the Southern Dynasties* ([南史] *Nan shi*) to criticize a lady named Lou Cheng who for years masqueraded as a man and held official post. The historians considered her an evil omen of a subsequent rebellion, for in their words, "you cannot have yin acting yang." Their interpretation follows the tradition of meticulously correlating irregularities in gender with specific political disasters.[42]

In this historiographical tradition, correlative epistemology—the linking of natural to social (dis)order on the basis of interrelated cosmological semblances—filters the concept of *renyao* through the differential of gender dislocation.

A second, related coordinate of *renyao* in historical hermeneutics is sex transformation. Historian Charlotte Furth's essay "Androgynous Males and Deficient Females: Biology and Gender Boundaries in Sixteenth- and Seventeenth-Century China" (1988) stands as the classic reference on this exegesis.[43] In mining through a series of male-to-female and female-to-male sex-reversal cases in the medical tracts, official notices, and informal writings of the Ming dynasty, Furth proposes that many of these should be more properly understood as examples of what modern Western biomedicine calls "hermaphroditism."[44] Furth also makes the interesting observation that starting in the second half of the Ming dynasty, female-to-male changes attracted a lesser degree of social hostility than transformations in the opposite direction: "Significantly, narratives of female-to-male changes were marked by a total suppression of the sexual in favour of the social. . . . The transition to male gender was presented as a psychologically unproblematic shift of role. Thus the discourse about transformations of sex subtly genderized the different protagonists' relationship to their bodily changes."[45] Building on this insight, Zeitlin suggests that stories of female-to-male transformations in the Ming-Qing period probably had a lesser impact on Pu's imagination.[46] Instead, both Furth and Zeitlin agree, the most obvious source for the "Renyao" story in *Strange Tales* was none other than the famous case of Sang Chong.[47] An orphan, Sang Chong of the Taiyuan prefecture in Shanxi was raised as a girl with bound feet during the Chenghua reign (1465–1488). Although Sang Chong stayed predominantly in women's quarters, his bodily biology was eventually discovered after a failed attempted rape by another man. According to Furth, "exposed, physically inspected and hauled before the magistrate's court, [Sang Chong] was pronounced a male 'monster' (*yao* [*r*]*en* [or prodigious human])—one who treacherously manipulated his genitals to appear female to the world, but male to the girls he lived to debauch."[48] In contrast to other accounts of the Sang Chong case that often ended with the public prosecution of the human prodigy, Pu's narration defies a strictly demonic view of this scandal saturated with sex, power, deceit, and violence.[49]

Adding to the historical residues of gender dislocation and sex transformation in the interpretation of *renyao* is the theme of same-sex relations. Building on the works of Zeitlin and Furth, historian Wenqing Kang extends the investigation of *renyao* into the Republican period. In *Obsession: Male Same-Sex Relations in China, 1900–1950* (2009), Kang argues that "in China during the first half of the twentieth century, men who were engaged in same-sex relations, especially those who were assumed to play the passive sexual role, and particularly male prostitutes, were sometimes called *renyao*."[50] Kang brings forward a number of examples in which male prostitutes and especially the *dan* actors (male actors playing female roles) of Peking opera were called *renyao* in the tabloid presses, as found in the Tianjin-based *Heavenly Wind* (天風報, *Tianfengbao*) and *Crystal* (晶報, *Jingbao*).[51] But he also notes that the category of *renyao* did not apply to men exclusively: "During the first half of the twentieth century, the prevalent understanding of *renyao* was one of men and women who appeared as the opposite gender, representing a potential threat to society and a bad omen for the country."[52] In many of the examples that Kang provides in his book, the label of *renyao* applied to both women and intersex individuals.[53] It is somewhat counterintuitive, then, for Kang to race to the following conclusion:

> On the one hand, *renyao*, men who had sex with other men, were considered to be male, and to the extent that they were considered male, they had transgressed existing sexual and gender norms. On the

other hand, because of their transgression, they were viewed as having lost their masculinity, and thus becoming women. This conceptual incoherence correlated with the internal contradiction between gender separatism and gender transitivity in the modern homo/heterosexual definition analyzed by [Eve Kosofsky] Sedgwick.[54]

Perhaps Kang has forced Sedgwick's gender separatism versus transitivity model onto Republican-era discourses of renyao too hastily by looking from the viewpoint of male homosexuality alone. In fact, one could argue that it is precisely due to the conceptual polyvalence of renyao that its historical purchase cannot be limited to an understanding rooted exclusively in men (or male same-sex relations). For instance, in the 1930s and 1940s, while the general move in the theatrical arts was to gender-straight acting (a trend that even Peking opera could not escape), the rise of all-women Yue troupes, especially in Shanghai, evolved in a decidedly opposite direction, making room for a variety of gender arrangements.[55] Homosexual relations or homoerotic sisterhood found a fleeting presence in Yue opera circles, and alternative gender subjecthood coexisted.[56] Furthermore, twentieth-century Chinese literature provides ample evidence for male elites' anxiety over lesbianism and gender inversion in women.[57] And as I will show later, anxious Republican-era commentators even went so far as to predict the extinction of masculine women once feminism has become an impasse. In other words, Sedgwick's gender separatism versus transitivity model applies as much to female same-sex intimacy and gender transgression as to an androcentric notion of renyao.[58] Still, to the extent that Kang's study sheds light on male social outcasts, at least in the cases of male prostitutes or the dan actors labeled renyao, male same-sex sexuality was foregrounded as a major conceptual coordinate in the popular understanding of this category in Republican-era tabloid sources.

Because renyao refers to a combination of opposing ideas concerning the natural (ren) and the supernatural worlds (yao), some scholars have probed its meaning within the broader horizon of humanness. In "Transgenderism as a Heuristic Device" (2012), for example, Alvin K. Wong demonstrates the fruitful endeavor of subjecting the signifier of renyao to cross-historical investigation.[59] To contest the modern transphobic usage of this compound word, Wong analyzes the ways in which the conceptual pillars of renyao transmutate across the literary and cultural texts of different periods: from Feng Menglong's Legend of the White Snake of the late

Ming to the short story "Renyao" written by May Fourth celebrity Yu Dafu (郁達夫, 1896–1945) in 1923, and from Hong Kong author Lilian Lee's (b. 1959) adaptation of the *Legend* in her novel *Green Snake* (1986) to the TV series adaptation *New Legend of Madame White Snake*, aired in Taiwan in 1992. In many ways, the direction of Wong's cross-historical study echoes the broader trajectory of the formation of Sinophone modernity: a centrifugal flow of Sinitic-language cultural forms and structural underpinnings from continental China to their peripheral localization.[60]

The most innovative part of Wong's analysis concerns his critical contextualization of Yu's "Renyao," a short story that had received limited scholarly attention. In situating Yu's story within a longer trajectory of Chinese transgender literary production surrounding the human-demon divide, Wong highlights the limits and boundaries of humanism as pivotal to debates raging within May Fourth literary circles. Unlike the themes of gender dislocation, sex transformation, and same-sex sexuality discussed earlier, Yu's rendition of the *renyao* figure squarely puts him alongside a cast of iconoclastic intellectuals, including Chen Duxiu (陳獨秀, 1879–1942), Lu Xun (魯迅, 1881–1936), Zhou Zuoren (周作人, 1885–1967), Hu Shi (胡適, 1891–1962), and Ba Jing (巴金, 1904–2005), among others, who vehemently questioned traditional (often dubbed Confucian) Chinese culture and pitched it as a ground of feudalism against which modernism, scientism, and the very optimism of human existence were juxtaposed.[61] As literary historian Ta-wei Chi has shown, both female impersonators and the Chinese past exemplify abjection in the novels of Ba Jin and others.[62] Rather than view *renyao* subjects as embodying a nonhuman condition of social pathology, Yu's "literary representation of the *renyao* figure work[s] against the assumption of nonhumanity by questioning what constitutes a human subject, narrated from the perspective of a young male who embraces feminine qualities."[63]

In the story, the male protagonist pursues transgender embodiment by making explicit the gender ambiguity of his own body and the bodies of other characters (including, most notably, an opera actress whom he stalked). The threshold of humanity, then, is made explicit with the continual deferral of a straightforward *gendered* reading of the characters, thereby always suspending and never resolving the tensions accumulated concerning the polarity of gender fictiveness and reality. By mapping the boundaries of human existence onto the metaphysical realms of gender expression, Yu's short story leaves behind another historical differential in the archiving of *renyao*: the meaning of being human. We will return to the legacy of May Fourth enlightenment and the way it generated a shift in the conceptualization of *renyao* in the 1920s and 1930s in the next section.

After Chiang Kai-shek's Nationalist regime retreated to Taiwan, where the Republic of China reclaimed its sovereignty, the group of social actors most frequently described by the mainstream press as *renyao* were male sex workers. In *Queer Politics and Sexual Modernity in Taiwan* (2011), cultural critic Hans Tao-Ming Huang explores the connections established by Taiwanese writers between the notion of *renyao* and male prostitution in the 1950s and 1960s.[64] Huang's work reveals that in the two decades following the Nationalist defeat in the civil war, the concept of *renyao* appeared in the Taiwanese press as a descriptor mainly of male sex workers, especially those based in the Wanhua district or the New Park in Taipei.[65] In this initial wave of press coverage, *renyao* was never interpreted in a psychologized language, such as the kind that framed the concept of sexuality (性心理, *xingxinli*) and that was advanced by the Chinese mental hygiene movement.[66] The psychologization of *renyao* was consolidated only in the 1970s, when mental health experts and journalists adopted "homosexuality" (同性戀, *tongxinglian*) as a discursive concept in Taiwan.[67] By the 1980s, the stigmatization of male same-sex relations took a decisive turn as AIDS became "homosexualized" in the mass media.[68] Throughout this period, the "glass clique" (玻璃圈, *boli quan*) label, an allegory of male prostitution, remained the reigning trope in the imagination of the queer community in Taipei. But when the *tongzhi* movement took off in the 1990s, homosexuality was finally dissociated from its conceptual attachment to prostitution.[69] Central to Huang's argument is the recuperation and celebration of Pai Hsien-yung's novel *Crystal Boys* (孽子, *Niezi*), published in 1983, by the *tongzhi* movement in the 1990s, by which point the broader context in which the novel was originally written no longer determined the contours of Taiwan's sexual mores.[70] From *renyao* to *tongzhi*, the role of prostitution in shaping the cultural perception of gender/sexual nonnormativity evolved from a centripetal to a centrifugal vector. This tentatively concludes our survey of the existing vectors of *renyao* knowability, the unity and discrepancy of which inevitably shape the ways we encounter the archival iterations of *renyao* in the record of Sinophone history.

(In)filtration

How did *renyao* become a bona fide transgender category that surrendered the nongender connotations of its literal inhumanism? Before we follow the fate of this category to postcolonial Taiwan, it is imperative to tackle this question and document the lexical evolution of *renyao* in the first half of the twentieth century. In the late Qing and early Republican periods, the concept of *renyao* enjoyed a wide currency in Chinese society. One of its most popular usages was in reference to biological deformity. Childbirth constituted a frequent site where many stories of such physical abnormality came to light. In 1909, for example, the Shanghai-based lithograph *Current Affairs* (時事報 圖畫新聞, *Shishibao tuhua xinwen*) published a report titled "Documenting *Renyao*" (figure 3.1).[71] Lithographs have long been considered by historians as a vivid source for interpreting the tangled social and cultural history of late Qing China.[72] Though most of them acquainted their readers with melodramatic stories, leaving a strong impression of sensationalism and shock, a careful reading suggests that these stories often embraced a consistent ambition of finding social order in chaos.[73] The *Current Affairs* lithograph on *renyao* can be viewed in this light.[74] A woman from Hukou County in Jiangxi delivered a boy with two heads. The baby's furry body had the shape of a dog, with one foot and three hooves. Constantly crying, the boy's twin red faces competed for breast milk from their mother. The woman's relatives considered this newborn a *yao* (monster), so they drowned the baby in a river. Significantly, this story of *renyao* contained no indication of gender dislocation or sexual transgression. The newborn acquired his prodigious status strictly through the animal-human hybridity of his body. His queerness, in other words, came not from hints of gender irregularity, but from the way that his two-headed configuration exceeded the ordinary parameters of human corporealism and, by implication, the acceptable boundaries of human subjectivity.

In the early twentieth century, the term *renyao* was frequently brought up in depictions of human-animal amalgam. In 1910, a *Yanbao Supplement* article used *renyao* to refer to the trespassing of, again, not gender but the human-animal boundary.[75] In Juzhou, an eight-year-old boy had gone missing for three years. For a long time, his family looked for him in vain. One day a trickster brought a midget with a dark body and a human face to the boy's home village. Among the curious many who gathered to

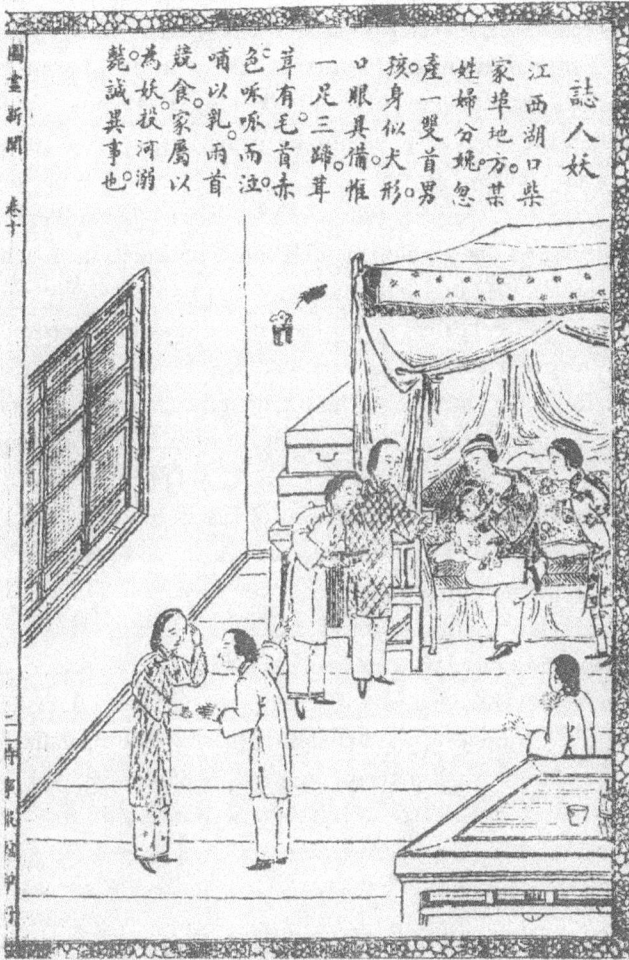

Fig. 3.1 "Documenting Renyao."
Source: Wushen Annual Pictorial (1909).

witness this odd creature, which the trickster named the "human-bear," stood the boy's older brother, who thought the midget looked familiar and called out the boy's name. The "human-bear" turned around and was thus discovered as the long missing child. After being interrogated by the provincial governor, the trickster revealed the process by which he turned the boy into a human monster. He scraped the skin off of a large dog, whom he killed, and wrapped the dog skin over the boy, whom he abducted, so that the boy's body would not grow in size. After punishing the trickster, the governor sent the boy home. However, upon meeting their returned son, the parents only found a highly incapable human. While the story aimed to caution people about an indecent mischief, it adopted the *renyao* label to highlight the inhumanism of the boy's "human-bear" spectacle. The label called into question not his gender presentation, but his astonishing and artificial appearance.[76]

Other accounts of *renyao* came under public scrutiny as a result of criminal prosecution. Indeed, since the sixteenth century, historical records of *renyao* have pinpointed the uncommon, bizarre, and peculiar behaviors as much as the gender and sexual subversion of the individual in question. Most of these misdemeanors fell outside the legally acceptable or legitimate realm of human conduct. As such, they were often charged with confusing the minds of people. In the case of Sang Chong studied by Zeitlin and Furth, for instance, the criminal was eventually executed alongside several named confederates.[77] The magistrate's pronouncement of Sang Chong as *yao*, therefore, was crucially linked to the illegality of his fraudulent acts. In the early nineteenth century, as Sinologist M. J. Meijer observes, "Travestites apparently were severely prosecuted, not so much because of homosexuality but because their activities were often narrowly related with sorcery and deceit."[78] This placement outside the normative social order made *renyao* a protoinhuman queer avant la lettre and presaged its unruly publicity in mid-twentieth-century Taiwan. Before modern science naturalized "sex" (性, *xing*) as the new interpretive discourse of the gendered body in the May Fourth era, criminal pursuits distinguished *renyao* as "problem bodies" that threatened public morale or the cultural imperative of verifiable identity.[79]

Two such cases of gender transgressive criminal behavior commended public attention in 1909 and 1910. In the first case, a thirty-one-year-old soldier by the name of Hsu was tried by the court of Yuanhe County in Suzhou (figure 3.2).[80] Because Hsu refused to cooperate, the county

Fig. 3.2 "Renyao."
Source: *Picture Daily* (1909).

magistrate Wu ordered a punishment of *chi* (笞) beating (beating with bamboo cane) on the buttocks. However, upon undressing Hsu's lower body, the court discovered her true (female) sex, and the magistrate reissued the punishment to a few hundred strokes of the (lighter) rattan cane. Hsu conceded that her husband had passed away many years earlier. Financial hardship led her to work as a soldier in Suzhou. Passing as a man, she subsequently abducted and sold a girl. Wu restrained Hsu in gyves before sentencing her to death by strangulation. Capital punishment might seem severe for transvestism, but in this case, Hsu's *renyao* status confounded gender deception with the abduction of a young girl. While Hsu's *renyao* embodiment may very well insinuate a breach of gender norms, this was largely overshadowed (and even absorbed) by the severity of her criminal offence—so severe that it earned her a death penalty, itself a statement about what her queer inhumanism deserved. It is worth noting that Hsu's interest in gender crossing did not form the decisive culprit of her public *renyao* recognition, a label reserved for marking her vulgar criminality.

The second case concerned a "handsome-looking" man named Huang from Fujian (figure 3.3).[81] Growing up, Huang felt increasingly uncomfortable with his physical appearance, so he decided to grow his hair, pierce his ears, and bind his feet. After a few months, he acquired a distinctively feminine look with long shiny black hair. Though eventually married to a woman, he still performed women's duties, including spinning and weaving. As time went on, no one noticed his true sex. But when the local magistrate Cao passed by his house one day, Cao misrecognized him as a prostitute showing a flamboyant and suggestive demeanor. After uncovering the truth, Cao punished Huang with three hundred strokes of the bamboo cane and the wearing of the cangue for public display at the Southern Gate. The severity of punishment did not reach the level of a death penalty, as in Hsu's fate discussed above, but it is unclear which law or statute Huang actually violated. In contrast to Hsu's case, Huang did not abduct anyone, nor was it obvious that Huang committed any criminal offense beyond passing as female. Therefore, the magistrate's decision to punish him isolated two particular aspects of this *renyao* story: Huang's cross-dressing *practice* and his *desire* to imitate the opposite gender. Here again, the human prodigy's criminality was imbricated with the danger of subterfuge and fraud unsanctioned in conventional legal terms.

Fig. 3.3 "Renyao."
Source: Shenzhou Pictorial (1910).

As China entered the May Fourth era, the literate public sought different ways to interpret *renyao* and reorganize it into a modern category. The cultural prestige of Western science penetrated different domains of Chinese intellectual life.[82] Modernizing elites heeded the potential power of science to explain the mysterious phenomenon of *renyao*. In 1913, Gu Mingsheng (顧鳴盛), a physician known for his syncretic approach to Chinese and Western medicine, published three cases of *renyao* in *Medicine World* (醫學世界, *Yiliao shijie*).[83] Building on the existing meaning of *renyao* to refer to natural malformations, the three examples Gu documented all came from the clinical site of newborn delivery. The first case involved an unmarried lady named Zhou in Shanyang County, Shangluo, Shaanxi. She was caught off-guard when her abdomen developed a large bulge that made weird noises. Her family suspected that it was an "unmentionable disease" (暗疾, *anji*), implying that she had contracted a venereal disease, but the growth was not cured after receiving medical treatment. One day, a small mass of flesh that was "neither human nor brute" (非人非畜, *feiren feichu*) carrying a large mouth-like opening that extended and contracted at will was dislodged from her body. After "giving birth" to this *renyao*, Zhou screamed before expiring with her body covered in blood. Discovered in the Dananmen area in Shanghai, the second case documented a woman named Zhu who gestated a fury creature that had "an upper body that looked like a gecko and a lower body that looked like a frog" (上體似壁虎 下替若田雞, *shangti si bihu xiati ruo tianji*). A third case involved a woman from Changzhou named Wu, who gave birth to a red-haired child that was "neither male nor female" (非男非女, *feinan feinü*) and made a creepy crying noise. Although himself a doctor and the article was published in a journal that promoted Western medicine, Gu concluded that "even if these cases piqued the interest of a modern biologist, there are still many obstacles to reaching a satisfactory and rational explanation of *renyao*."[84] Gu's report signaled the lingering definition of *renyao* as both the natural fusion of human and nonhuman forms and, to a lesser extent, the somatic indeterminacy of gender.

Starting in the 1920s, observers began to displace the nonhuman connotations of *renyao* and construe it as a specifically gender-ambiguous condition. This constitutes a midpoint threshold ("equivalence point") in the procedure of titrating transgender—whereby the patchy expression of transness and an assortment of corporealism in the historical semiotics of *renyao* are ascertained, calibrated, and distinguished—particularly through the interaction between old perceptions of gendered humanity and new ideas of modern science (figure 3.4). In order for *renyao* to assume an exclusively human signification, it had to shed its baggage of being perceived as a culturally backward sign. The biological concept of sex provided a key catalyst in its modernization. For example, a contributor to the Shanghai-based *Saturday*—a magazine that epitomized the evolving literary output of the so-called Mandarin Ducks and Butterflies

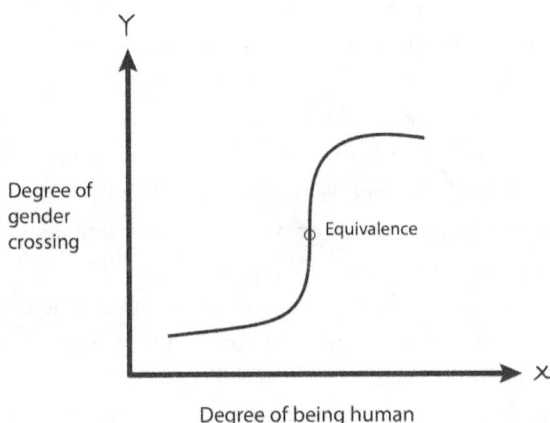

Fig. 3.4 Titration curve for historicizing *renyao*. Each example of *renyao* can be conceived as constituting a point on the curve. The part of the curve to the right of the equivalence point corresponds to the conventional understanding of *renyao* as a Chinese transgender category. When *renyao* is understood as a concept of human transgenderism, its history and cultural dissemination fall somewhere along the curve after the equivalence point. This chapter adds historical depth to the *renyao* category by bringing to light its queer inhuman connotations (with varying degrees of gender crossing). These historical examples are best placed somewhere on the curve prior to reaching the equivalence point. The y axis is typically considered a measurement of the degree of transness in dominant thinking in Western queer studies. The transtopian reframing of *renyao* broadens by supplementing an axial dimension to the meaning of transness: the extent of humanhood (the x axis). Although the curve is linear, it does not represent chronological movement. Time is neither an independent nor a dependent variable in this titration diagram. A temporally later example of *renyao* can fall somewhere on the curve before (to the left of) the equivalence point; a historically earlier example of *renyao* can be placed somewhere on the curve after (to the right of) the equivalence point.

Source: Illustration by and copyright Howard Chiang.

genre—identified *renyao* with the category of yin-yang person (陰陽人, *yinyang ren*).[85] The article documented a Shanghainese roughly at the age of thirty showing both male and female traits: the individual "acts and looks like a man but speaks with a feminine voice." Rumor had it that the individual typically switched sex in the middle of the month: s/he was usually *xiong* (雄, male) in the first half of the month and *ci* (雌, female) in the second. This pattern "repeated itself on a monthly basis" and, according to the article, confirmed that the case was "an example of yin-yang person."[86] Although the idea of a yin-yang person had long existed in traditional Chinese culture, it was now recast in the language of modern bioscience, specifically imbued with the categories of *ci* and *xiong*.[87]

As the social prestige of modern science reached a crescendo, Chinese sexologists reconceptualized the developmental basis of human intersexuality. In his widely read *ABC of Sexology*, sex educator Chai Fuyuan (柴福沅) defined "yin-yang persons" as "people with external male genitalia and internal female reproductive system or with external female genitalia and internal male reproductive system."[88] A keen reader who dug deeper into the medical literature would find similar descriptions that began to shift the definition of a yin-yang person away from reproductive capacity— an understanding rooted in classical Chinese medicine—and toward abnormal genital anatomy.[89] When natural scientist Liu Piji (劉丕基) carefully explained the difference between pseudo- and true hermaphroditism, he dismissed the validity of the traditional concept of *renyao*, which had circulated in Chinese discourses to describe a human diversity in ambiguous and, according to him, unscientific ways. In *Common Misinterpretations of Biology* (1928), Liu remarked that "our country has a long history of calling these individuals 'freaks' [怪胎, *guaitai*] or 'human prodigy.' Many of them are tortured to death, but even for the fortunate minority who survived, they have never been treated with moral decency."[90] Over time, urban writers increasingly drew on Western biomedical theories to bestow the category of *renyao* with a modern scientific meaning.

Whereas some commentators relied on the biological model of intersexuality to shed *renyao*'s traditional status, others took a more serious interest in the psychology of cross-gender inclination and sharpened an *exclusive* association of the *renyao* concept with the *desire* to cross-dress. In 1929, Zhou Shoujuan (周瘦鵑), the editor of the popular magazines *Saturday* and *Violet*, wrote an article that introduced a handful of famous male and female impersonators from nineteenth-century Europe, and in it he classified these individual under the sexological category of "sexual inversion" (顛倒性別, *diandao xingbie*) and called them "odd women and strange men."[91] In the same year, the *Literary Weekly* (文學週報, *Wenxue zhoubao*) featured a special issue denouncing female impersonation among Peking opera *dan* actors.[92] The twelve interlocutors targeted Mei Lanfang (梅蘭芳, 1894–1961) by calling him a "pervert" (變態人, *biantairen*) and a "*renyao*," describing him as "unnatural" and "aberrant," blaming his artistic performance for undermining China's image in the world, depicting his body as a "tool for the expression of sexual perversion," accusing him for spreading *meidu* (梅毒, "Mei poison" but also a homophone for syphilis), and organizing an "anti-Mei" social movement against him (倒梅運動, *daoMei yundong*) (figure 3.5).[93] *New Life Weekly* (新生活週刊, *Xinshenghuo zhoukan*) published a commentary in 1935 in which the writer recalled seeing a young man who dressed up like a girl on the street, labeled him a *renyao*, and blamed his cross-dressing motive on the negative repercussions of thriving cosmopolitanism, consumerism, and capitalism.[94]

How about women who passed as men? Under the influence of Western sexology, many Chinese cultural elites explained the growing visibility of mannish women as an outcome of women's greater access to the public, education, and political spheres. They associated women's desire to appear as socially male with the nascent feminist movement and argued, ironically, that once the feminist cause was achieved, cross-dressing among women would likely disappear altogether. According to one newspaper article, the phenomenon of "neither male nor female" and "the presence of *renyao*" were to be expected "before women have obtained equal rights as men."[95] A *Gossip Weekly* (人言週刊, *Renyan zhoukan*) essay from 1935 asserted that since "women have come to occupy a significant role in society" and "women's occupation has greatly expanded," the raison d'être of such phenomenon as "male cross-dressing among women" would "most definitely cease to exist in the future."[96]

In the interwar period, the most authoritative account of gender variance came from the work of the German-Jewish sexologist Magnus Hirschfeld, who visited China in 1931.[97] As we saw in chapter 1, Hirschfeld coined the concept of transvestism in his monumental work *Transvestites: The Erotic Drive to Cross Dress* (1910), to posit a spectrum of individuals who cross-dressed or had cross-gender identification.[98] Although Hirschfeld considered transvestism a "harmless inclination," when Chinese writers translated this term and introduced it to the Chinese public, it led to two

Fig. 3.5 Mei Lanfang on stage poses with water sleeves (undated by Vandamm Studios).
Source: Courtesy of Museum of Preperformance and Design, Performance Arts Library.

contradicting but related outcomes: at the same time that it acquired a stig-
matized meaning, the term was often invoked as an expression of modern
science—a symbol of enlightenment—to offset the derogatory connotations of *renyao*.[99] For example, in 1934, *Huanian Weekly* (華年週刊, *Huanian
zhoukan*) included an article titled "Renyao?" to make a case against that
very label.[100] The writer told a story about a forty-year-old male bookstore

manager named Fu in Neijiang, Sichuan. After studying in Japan, Fu came back to China to teach and eventually became the president of a middle school. Throughout this time, Fu appeared erudite and behaved with good manners, but he suddenly confronted a new irresistible obsession with dressing up as a woman. He enjoyed powdering his face, whether at home or in public. His inclination and conduct, the writer explained, earned him the *renyao* label.

In narrating the story of Fu, the *Huanian Weekly* article sought to dispel popular understandings of cross-gender identification that lacked a scientific basis. The writer insisted that "it simply isn't true that Fu emits goblin *qi* [妖氣, *yaoqi*]," but the problem with the *renyao* descriptor was that "people in Neijiang are fussing over something that they encounter only on occasion." Western sexology, the writer noted, provided useful knowledge to alleviate such backward mischaracterizations of a rare phenomenon:

Actually, Fu's inclination is a type of sexual perversion [性心理變態, *xingxinli biantai*]. Although it is uncommon, we easily come across one or two such cases if we pay enough attention. This form of sexual perversion has different names, but the most widely used version is "transvestism" [異性喬裝, *yixing qiaozhuang*]. The person who coined this term is none other than the German sexologist Magnus Hirschfeld who toured China two years ago. He published a book devoted to this topic more than two decades ago.

Like any other type of sexual perversion, "transvestism" is the result of both congenital and acquired factors. It will be difficult to ask those who are afflicted by this condition to suppress their cross-gender urges, just like how difficult it is to force people who are not afflicted by this condition to cross-dress. When we encounter transvestites—male or female—we must express some measure of sympathy. Even if we cannot offer any assistance, we should at the very least avoid condemnation by assigning them such derogatory labels as "renyao."[101]

By recasting the meaning of *renyao* through the scientific idioms of sexology, the writer further lamented the absence of empirical research into the psychology of *dan* actors in the past. This left open the question of whether their motivation to impersonate stemmed from strictly fulfilling a career ambition or satisfying a perverse form of personal pleasure.[102]

These various commentaries show that in condensing *renyao* into an anthropocentric rubric of gender transgression, the influx of Western sexology deracinated the other side of the term's lexical life: its less-than-human connotation especially discernible prior to the early Republican period. Rooted in May Fourth debates over gender and humanism, the nascent homology between a scientific revamping of *renyao* and Hirschfeld's transgender research instantiated an overhaul in the Chinese epistemological structure. By the late 1940s, mass media regularly used *renyao* to describe individuals with an outwardly opposite social gender, including Shen Junru (沈俊如) and Ju Guangzao (鞠光藻) in Shanghai and Wu Bangzhi (吳邦治) in Beijing, and reported on their involvement in various high-profile social incidents.[103] Yet the police investigation and court records show that rarely were these individuals arrested for gender crossing per se (in part because Republican China did not codify a law targeting transgender practice).[104] This historical bifurcation cemented the fate of *renyao*: by assuming an absolute definition of gender transgression in the public sphere, the category had shed its long-standing embeddedness of animalistic, monstrous, and hybrid references and that which ruptured the very category and corporeal integrity of the "human" in the realm of official repository. The unruly historicity of *renyao* makes it a foremost concept of queer inhumanism largely overlooked in inquiries preoccupied with the West as the engine of historical change.

Irruptions

The history of *renyao* features a plurality of differentials—gender dislocation, sex transformation, same-sex relations, prostitution, and being human—and in this final section, I show their potency and incompleteness by focusing on a widely reported case of *renyao* in postwar Taiwan: Zeng Qiuhuang. To further exemplify the exercise of archiving that I have been proposing, I document the various stories about Zeng—with all their shifting and intertwined multiplicities—that appeared in major Taiwanese newspapers such as the *United Daily News* (聯合報, *Lianhebao*), *People's Voice Daily* (民聲日報, *Minsheng ribao*), *China Times* (中國時報, *Zhongguo shibao*), and *Evening Independent* (自立晚報, *Zili wanbao*) throughout the 1950s. The archiving of Zeng demonstrates that each new episode of press coverage renders the category of *renyao* subversive to its past to varying degrees and that such a contested interaction itself changed over time. By making explicit the excessive and limited traces of *renyao*, the floods of stories not only denaturalize the historicity of this very category but also bring into sharper focus its guarantee to robust productive futurity. A detailed reading of this underappreciated chapter in Taiwan's history vis-à-vis Zeng therefore represents a critical ambition not predetermined by a singular blueprint of information, but one that is deeply invested in a mode of knowledge production that enables stories of different patterns and memories to reconfigure one another in a mutually generative fashion. Archiving *renyao* in 1950s Taiwan unveils the region's significance by throwing both a seemingly peripheral location and a multitude of marginal experience into the spotlight of historical narration.

In the first wave of press reports in 1951, the public was captivated by Zeng's *renyao* status primarily due to the ease with which he switched between genders when committing criminal offenses.[105] Born in Taichung, Taiwan, Zeng was forty-two years old when his name first hit newspaper headlines. According to one report, he had been carrying out a series of crimes since autumn 1950. In mid-October, he defrauded Zhong Zengmi and Zhong Linbing of $160 in Xizhou township, Taichung; in February 1951, he swindled $120 from Xu Zhenlin in Yuanlin township of Zhanghua county; two months after, in April, he deceived Lu Chenyun multiple times, for which he took away $874 in total and, among other items, a skein of grey yarn, a pair of underwear, and a watch. All four victims subsequently reported to the Taichung District Court and filed charges against Zeng. After a series of judicial hearings, the judges found him guilty of committing multiple fraudulent offenses (詐欺之罪, *zhaqi zhizui*) and sentenced him to three and a half years of imprisonment plus two years of forced labor. Zeng resented the decision and appealed. On October 18, the Taiwan High Court ruled in Zeng's favor and struck down the initial sentence. Instead, Zeng would spend one year in prison after which he would then serve an additional two years of forced labor administered by the Department of Labor.[106]

The national fascination with Zeng was driven by the rapid dissemination of his androgynous image in the media. For the appeal, he was transferred to the north on September 22, 1951, so the case could be heard by the Taiwan High Court in Taipei. On the following day, *United Daily News* announced "the arrival of *renyao* in Taipei" and offered a thorough description of Zeng's unusual appearance:

Zeng Qiuhuang wore a pair of white trousers. His hair was long. He looked like a man but not an authentic man; he looked like a woman but not a real woman [似男非男 似女非女, *sinan feinan sinü feinü*]. Zeng Qiuhuang had been married to a woman and had kids, but then [he] subsequently remarried to two husbands and committed fraudulent offenses in these marriages, for which [he] has been the subject of at least two legal charges.[107]

On the day before his case was heard before the Taiwan High Court, journalists described the crimes he committed as "obscene" and "fraudulent" in nature.[108] They also discussed the puzzlement in which Zeng put the police officers in Taipei: "When Zeng Qiuhuang was assigned to a holding cell in Taipei, the police guard did not know whether to assign him to a cell with male or female inmates, due to his legendary status as being a neither-man-nor-woman [不男不女, *bunan bunü*]."[109] *Evening Independent* seized this opportunity to dramatize the sexual ambiguity of Zeng's body, explaining that the term *renyao* did not mean "three-headed chimera with six arms" but referred instead to an individual with "an artificial and affected manner" (忸怩作態, *niuni zuotai*).[110]

After the Taiwan High Court delivered its verdict, newspapers reported that Zeng was extremely pleased with the success of his appeal. However, even here, the reports were often cloaked in a language that further staged Zeng as an object of spectacle based on his transgression of gender roles.[111] For example, one writer claimed that the most surprising aspect of Zeng's trials was not the series of crimes for which he was found guilty. Rather, "the most surprising part is that he was married to a woman with five children, and he still cross-dressed as a woman in order to commit swindling, for which he cohabitated with men and sold his body for sex."[112] Hinting at the jointure of prostitution and *renyao* embodiment, the writer underscored Zeng's cross-gender appearance: "although Zeng Qiuhuang dresses like a man, his voice and the way he walks [cause him to] bear [a] strikingly feminine composition. Upon discovering the success of his appeal, Zeng covered his smile with a handkerchief" (figure 3.6).[113]

From the beginning, part of the widespread interest in Zeng had to do with the analogy between his gender "deception" and his financial "fraud": his crimes (behavior) literalized his ontology or at least his way of being in the world.[114] In this initial wave of journalistic sensation, the

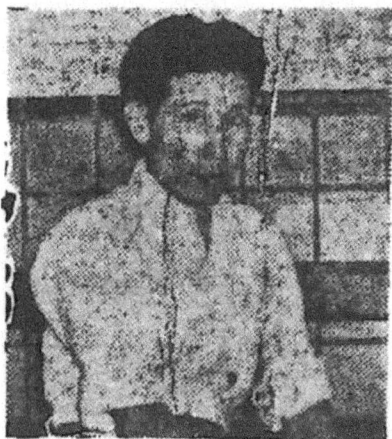

Fig. 3.6 Photograph of Zeng Qiuhuang printed in an article about the success of his appeal.
Source: United Daily News, October 23, 1951.

皇 秋 曾 妖 人

public awareness of Zeng's gender dislocation, sex transformation, homosexuality, nonhumanness, and tacit prostitution all came together to administer the intelligibility of his *renyao* designation. Zeng was a human prodigy because he appeared as someone who crossed genders, changed sex, engaged in romantic relationships with members of the same sex, committed crimes, used his malleable sexual appearance for illicit monetary gains, and, by implication, fell outside the legal parameters of being human. From the outset, the story of Zeng demonstrates that each of the differentials of *renyao* is both sufficient and limited in governing the category's coherence in the context of postcolonial Taiwan.

Soon after Zeng completed his labor service, he was arrested again. This time, however, the arrest resulted from stealing a chicken rather than committing fraudulent offenses. News broke in December 1954, exactly two years after he was released from prison. Upon visiting a lady named Miss Su in Yuanlin township of Zhanghua county, Zeng came across a chicken in the front yard of Su's residence. Since he did not see anyone in sight, the idea of stealing the chicken sprang to mind, and he quickly grabbed the chicken and tried to run away. Alarmed by the noises from the scene, Su rushed to her front yard to see what was going on. She witnessed Zeng's stealing, intervened successfully, and charged Zeng with larceny. The Taichung District Court found Zeng guilty and issued a nine-month prison sentence plus one year of forced labor. Zeng appealed again, and the Taiwan High Court removed the forced labor requirement. Zeng still had to serve the nine-month sentence, which the High Court ruled to be final and unappealable.[115]

Similar to what happened three years prior, the media gripped the public by spotlighting Zeng's unusual gender persona and sexual ambiguity. This second round of media coverage publicized aspects of Zeng's personal information previously unknown to the public. Living at No. 93 on Yongjing Street in Zhanghua county, Zeng's real name was Zeng Xiuqin (曾秀琴), reported to be forty-four years of age. About a decade ago, he dressed in female attire on a daily basis, and he had been married to a man named Su Tianci for seven years. According to the reporter, they were eventually separated "due to [his] neither-man-nor-woman status." After the divorce, he became more "masculine inclined" (男性傾向較濃, *nanxing qingxiang jiaonong*) and "started to wear men's clothes." By taking over the identification card of his deceased brother, he became Zeng Qiuhuang and married a woman. However, he ran into similar problems in the bedroom, so he got married to another man. This time, unlike in his first marriage, his fraudulent status was discovered, and after the court found him guilty of such charges, he went to prison for committing those offenses. When he was released in December 1952, Zeng decided to pursue a career in theater, so he joined the Zhanghua Theater Troupe (彰化藝華劇團, *Zhanghua yihua jutuan*). He was frequently assigned to play the role of *qingyi* (青衣), the virtuous lady, which was fitting for Zeng because, according to the reporter, "even though he had transitioned into a man, he still carried himself with effeminate manners [娘兒態, *niang'ertai*]." Zeng later left the troupe to attend to his mother, who was ill, and due to the resulting financial hardship, he stole Su's chicken and was imprisoned for it. As before, the question of to which gendered cell he most appropriately belonged came up again. According to Zeng's recollection, "when he was held in an all-male prison, his cellmate would always touch his face and make sexual advances." As a result, the guard was forced to put him in a single-bed cell by himself.[116]

By 1954, the idea of human sex change had circulated widely in Taiwan due to the nationwide publicity poured on the male-to-female transsexual Xie Jianshun. As we saw in chapter 1, Xie was frequently dubbed "the Chinese Christine," a Sinophone offshoot of the American ex-GI transsexual celebrity Christine Jorgensen.[117] Dazzled by the two glamorous

Christines, Zeng stated for the first time his determination to undergo sex reassignment. According to one reporter, "after serving his nine-month sentence, Zeng intends to opt for a surgery that could turn him into an authentic, healthy woman. Since he does not have the cash to cover the related medical expenses, he welcomes a proposal from any hospital that is willing to use him as an experimental subject for this kind of operation."[118] A *United Daily News* article documented the reason Zeng provided for preferring to assume the opposite gender: "When he took on the role of a wife previously, even though he could not satisfy his husband [sexually], he could always get on with an easy life. However, his subsequent decision to convert back into a 'man' led him to a destitute and troubled life."[119] Zeng made it known that he graduated from an all-girls junior high and had been previously employed as a nurse. Pledging a natural feminine predisposition, Zeng in his bodily constitution "shows a greater degree of femaleness." Zeng "always squats to pee" and claimed to experience "menstruation in seasonal cycles." Nevertheless, because his identification card classified him as male, the court still referred to Zeng as a man in finalizing their decision.[120]

In this second wave of press coverage, sex transformation became the leading conceptual quotient in the depiction of Zeng's *renyao* status. In the historiography of *renyao*, the category is often associated with individuals who switched their sex, especially in the late imperial period. However, what distinguished the context of post–World War II Taiwan was the emergence of *bianxingren* (變性人, transsexual) as an available identity category, whose popularity was conditioned by the publicized stories of Xie, the Chinese Christine. Even though Zeng's homoerotic relation with other prison inmates, positioning of himself outside the legal norms of human order, and ability to cross the borders of gender with ease were all made readily apparent, the theme of sex change—more precisely, his desire for a sex-reassignment surgery—became an unprecedented force in shaping the public understanding of his *renyao* embodiment.[121] This example demonstrates once again that the excess and inadequacy of the various differentials of *renyao* are never fixed but reconfigure themselves according to the contingencies of a given historical context. A few months after Zeng expressed interest in medical sex change, *People's Voice Daily* reported on the surgical transformation of a "true intersexual" (真性的陰陽人, *zhenxing de yiyangren*) in Tianzhong Township of Changhua County, echoing the famous story of Xie.[122]

Thinking about *renyao*, a recurrent concept, alongside *bianxingren*, a newly crystalized identity marker, reveals their interreferentiality in terms of a transtopian connection. Both categories, when treated in isolation, took form in seemingly separate Sinophone contexts. In our analysis so far, each term denotes a different configuration of transness. But both categories soon acquired new kinds of meaning and assumed particular urgency. Considering the transsexual more trans than the human prodigy flattens their historical resonance and cripples our queer sensibility. As Zeng's declaration makes clear, the two configurations of transness were reciprocally articulated and understood by actors in relation to one another on a historical continuum. The sex change differential of *renyao* becomes diversified—and made more poignant—when viewed through this model of a transtopian spectrum.

Despite the overwhelming emphasis that the media placed on Zeng's criminal behavior, the cause of his evolution into a distinct object of social ostracism clearly stemmed from his gender/sexual transgression. This was made nowhere more evident than during the third stream of Zeng's media exposure. In November 1955, Zeng was identified as a member of a team of bicycle thieves.[123] In an article titled "Suspect Zeng Qiuhuang Has Both Sexes: Being Both Male and Female and Married to Either Sex," he was described as "wearing female attire at the time of arrest" but later switched to "a complete male outfit by wearing a white shirt, a pair of blue pants, and a pair of white sneakers. His breasts are not very well developed, and his hairstyle seems neither masculine nor feminine [*feinan feinü*]. He speaks in a bashful manner [扭扭捏捏, *niuniu nienie*] with extremely feminine facial expressions."[124] At one o'clock AM on September 24, 1956, Zeng was brought to the police station again. The newspaper reporting on the incident called him a cross-dressing "yin-yang freak" (陰陽怪人, *yinyang guairen*) and documented his gendered androgyny with engrossing details: "His hair was permed like a lady; he wore a green silk dress, a laced undershirt, and a breast-holding bra; his face was powdered; he penciled his eyebrows, wore lipstick, and was in a pair of high-heel sandals; he wore a woman's dress, revealing a rough skin tone; he spoke like a woman, smiled, and coquetted frequently, but his voice sounded rather masculine." As before, the police found it difficult to assign him to a unisex cell, so they ended up, once again, putting him in a room by himself. However, the paper trail did not stop there. The news article went on to sketch a brief biography of Zeng. Most notably, the article highlighted his hidden intersexuality, which was revealed to the police and the public for the first time. Zeng was born with both male and female genitalia, but because his "female attributes predominated," his parents raised him as a girl. He even married a man. His intersexuality was not the only new factual information uncovered in his recent interaction with the police and journalists; concerning the rumor that he subsequently remarried a woman, Zeng clarified that "she was my sister-in-law!"[125] The specter of incest and its unusualness further intensified the perversity of his public image.

Interestingly, unlike what happened in 1951 and 1954, Zeng was furious about the arrest this time. The *United Daily News* reported:

> [Zeng] grumbles that he did not commit any crime, so on what basis could the police officer arrest him and keep him in custody? Even the act of putting on an unconventional attire resulting from some kind of psychological abnormality does not constitute a sufficient basis for being restrained in handcuffs overnight. Zeng points out that one of the police officers even attacked him with the handcuffs, resulting in two bruises on his head. He expresses grave intention to file charges against the police officer who attacked him.[126]

In contrast to previous instances in which he was arrested for the actual violation of law, Zeng's latest statement suggests that this arrest was caused by his well-known gender subversion and, relatedly, the prevailing biases that stereotyped his prodigious fame. The reporter ended the article with a brief summary of this incident. On the evening of September 23, while Zeng was visiting a friend in Taichung, he was stopped by a male acquaintance whom he knew from prison. Although he could not recall the name of the individual, who sexually courted but was rejected by him, the individual decided to file a "false accusation" (誣告, *wugao*) of fraudulent offense against Zeng.[127] After administering a gynecological exam mandated by the court on September 25, Dr. Hong confirmed that Zeng was 100 percent male.[128] Giving credence to Dr. Hong's finding, Zeng's father dismissed Zeng's self-proclaimed condition as either an intersexed or a half-woman.[129] On the following day, *People's Voice Daily* reported that Zeng's supposed "girlfriend" turned out to be a male guard of a holding cell.[130] Both of these revelations further obscured but also magnified Zeng's gender ambiguity.

In this third wave of press coverage, gender dislocation replaced sex transformation as the defining frame of Zeng's *renyao* status. Significantly, this was the only time that Zeng's exposure in the media did not result from committing an actual offense or crossing the legal boundaries of human order. Rather, this series of interrogations on Zeng's gender and sexual transgression emerged from a "false accusation" charged by someone who pursued (but was also turned down by) Zeng for sexual favors. Therefore, same-sex relations and the legal parameters of humanism remained as latent coefficients in the determination of Zeng's *renyao* public persona. The instability of Zeng's gender presentation, however, was the most immediate reason that captured the media spotlight, which further contributed to his unfortunate mistreatment by the police and harassment by others.

The final surge of publicity peaked in the summer of 1957, when Zeng was arrested again, but this time journalists focused on Zeng's attempt to disguise himself as a ghost rather than as the opposite sex (figure 3.7). At two in the morning on August 5, seventy-one-year-old Wang Chendui (王陳對), a resident in the Huatan township of Zhanghua county, was robbed of $114 after a strange event. She passed out from a concussion. It was not until the afternoon of that same day that she reported the incident to the police, after a community security guard found her in front of her house.[131] According to Wang, she was asleep before the incident occurred. In the middle of the night, a weird noise from outside of her house woke her up. She described the sound as unusually scary, making the hair stood up on the back of her neck. Wang got out of bed, approached the front of her house, and yelled: "I have lived my life for seventy-one years, and I am definitely not afraid of ghosts. If you are a human who is trying to put on a supernatural show, please leave immediately. However, if you are a real ghost, please stop making that noise; the Ghost Festival [中元節, *Zhongyuanjie*] is around the corner, and I will make you some offerings."[132] As soon as she finished the sentence, her head was hit by a stick, and the pouring of cold water followed. The $114 that she had with her was taken away. When she reported the incident to the police, she explained that the voice of the ghost thief sounded husky and "neither masculine nor feminine." Since her house had no electric lights, all of this took place in the dark. She was unable to take a good look at the thief. One reporter

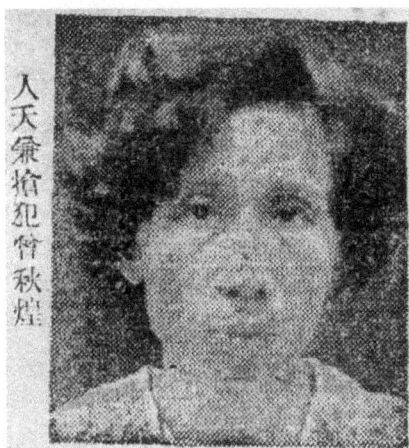

Fig. 3.7 Photograph of Zeng Qiuhuang printed in an article about his transformation from "prodigy" to "ghost." *Source: People's Voice Daily*, August 7, 1957.

surmised that Zeng deceived Wang by pretending to be a ghost because his "female impersonation" was "no longer convincing." Zeng therefore transformed himself "from a prodigy into a ghost" (由妖變鬼, *youyao biangui*), but "as soon as he went back to committing crimes again, he got arrested."[133] On August 26, the prosecutor considered Zeng to have violated the relevant article in the Republic of China Criminal Code concerning robbery offenses (掠奪罪, *luiduozui*). He recommended that the judges intensify the severity of punishment by one-half of what Zeng deserved.[134] The court eventually reached a verdict, finding Zeng guilty of committing robbery, and sentenced him to prison for three years and nine months.[135]

Not surprisingly, the press sought to valorize Zeng's *renyao* status, emphasizing again the difficulty of putting him in a cell that would be most appropriate for his gender. According to one article, "Given that this is the fourth time Zeng has been detained, the staff in the district prosecutor's office and the detention office in Taichung are anxious and baffled every time they see his face."[136] Previously, the jail guards had left Zeng in a separate cell by himself. However, this practice of single-celling apparently still caused them trouble:

When this *renyao* is assigned to a prison cell with other male inmates, he would self-identify as a woman in front of these *tongzhi*, leading to the offense of public indecency [傷風敗俗, *shangfeng baisu*]; when he is put in a cell with other women inmates, he would similarly make a move on them as well. . . . However, putting him in a single cell by himself is also not a solution. The reason is that the detention office is responsible for the health of the individuals in the remand, so the jailed individuals are not allowed to be kept in the cell for twenty-four consecutive hours in any given day. It is a mandatory requirement that single-cell inmates are released from their holding for exercise for at least one hour per day. It is during these brief periods of recess that the *renyao* starts to play mind games. He would babble excessively and incoherently like a mad person, attracting the attention of all the other inmates and causing disorder. This actually brings the guards further trouble.[137]

In this final episode of media exposure, Zeng's *renyao* embodiment becomes elusive with respect to the category's splitting differentials. As before, the themes of gender dislocation, sex transformation, same-sex relations, and the legal borders of human behavior lurked as a subtext in the popular imagination of Zeng's prodigious nonhumanity. However, what sets this episode apart from previous ones is his explicit attempt to disguise himself as a ghost, to supervene the possible present, thereby opening for the historical figuration of *renyao* a corridor to the supernatural world. By crossing the boundaries of humanhood, Zeng has essentially left a trace of himself as a queer ghost in the archiving of *renyao*. Over time, Zeng's fate came to be imbricated with Taiwan's twilight status in the world. As an orphan of the Cold War, Taiwan's diplomatic presence has forever haunted the (super)naturalization of other geopolitical giants.

Isomerism

This chapter began with the illegibility of Taiwan studies, and it concludes with the instability of *renyao* as a category of historical analysis, linking these two disparate modes of historiography through the processes of archiving. As the continuation of Zeng's media presence throughout the decade makes clear, he was arguably *the* most widely reported *renyao* in the 1950s Sinophone world.[138] In spite of his considerable celebrity, the discursive usage of the term *renyao* ultimately escapes a permanent epistemic closure from the world of the natural. To capture the transformation of this archival nature, we have established a scholarly canvas on which Taiwan's peripheral historical setting uncoils from the vexed adherence of the variegated and intersecting coordinates of marginal subjectivity. The multiple differentials examined in this chapter embody long-standing lexical histories from the Ming-Qing period, if not earlier, even as the epistemic congruity of *renyao* itself verges on becoming more hyperbolic over time.

As a "Chinese" category, *renyao* has genealogical roots in mainland China, but its most intricate elaborations in the mid-twentieth century came to light in Taiwan. Again, the point here is not to measure the earlier *renyao* examples against later ones, or other non-*renyao* queer subjects for that matter, with a preconceived ensemble of transgender criteria. The affinity between *renyao* and transgender is precisely what is at stake and needs to be thought through cautiously. By situating the cases discussed in this chapter on a continuum of transtopian commensurability, my goal has been to reveal how this spectrum evolved through time with respect to the moving baseline of gendered in/humanity. The overlapping structures of queerness and transness saturated the uneven manifestations of *renyao* from the late Qing to the Cold War periods. The method of *titrating transgender* enables us to map a specific genealogy of human transgression while accounting for the changing geopolitical nature of Chineseness. Interpreting the archival articulation of *renyao* in 1950s Taiwan as a mere extension of "Chinese history" misses the geopolitical wrestling that renders its conceptual purchase possible in the first place. In contemporary parlance, *renyao* incites an injurious locutionary effect. However, as this chapter has shown, this rhetorical perniciousness can be viewed as an outcome of the historical layering of an isomeric queerness approximating Taiwan's stature out of sync with the rectitude of such major imperial powers as China, Japan, and the United States.[139]

Like Taiwan, *renyao* has been left out of mainstream historical comprehension. Similar to *renyao*, Taiwan has been objectified as an aporia in a series of signification imposed by nationalism, colonialism, and cosmopolitanism.[140] The minor historicity of *renyao* as a metaphoric projection of Taiwan's global marginality emerges out of relational histories, relational at least in part because of the volatile competition and interdependence between the peripheral ontologies of the Republic of China and continental China after 1949.[141] This minor historicity percolates from the crossing of thresholds—a grand titration—that sutures the social epistemology of *renyao*, a recalibration of its transgender inhumanism in the Chinese and Sinophone cultural imaginations. Herein lies the palpability of absence assemblages where the inhuman and the postcolonial overhang. Herein also lies the very queerness of archiving a prodigy of historical narration, and nation, through the prodigy of the human: archival remnants promise futurity as they preemptively reserve the impossible determination of the historical desire for archiving and its absent presence.

CHAPTER IV

Inscribing Transgender

Intercorporeal Governance and the Logic of Sinophone Supplementarity

This study has alerted to the ways in which Sinophone studies exceeds a mimetic displacement of Chinese studies. The former presents a long overdue corrective to the disciplinary limitations of the latter, and in this sense, their sequence can be conceived in terms of a series of palimpsestic inscriptions. As a new paradigm that topples existing ethical presumptions, Sinophone critique calls for a rethinking of what the word *Chinese* encompasses and signifies, which often goes unquestioned in Sinological, transnational, and diaspora studies.[1] With an analytical calculus that is at once global and local in focus, it propagates a systematic intervention that takes China seriously as a growing global superpower. The Sinophone concept is germane to transgender studies in part because, as we saw earlier, the Chinese-speaking community encountered their first transsexual and postcolonial *renyao* in the specific context of 1950s Taiwan. This chapter widens the purview of Sinophone transtopia by examining the ways in which the Chinese castrated body has served as a nucleus for the co-contestations of gender idiosyncrasy and hegemonic Chineseness in transpacific circulations.

The theorization of the Sinophone analytic has attracted various criticisms to date, but here I would like to highlight two variants in particular: its tendency to reify language-centrism at the exclusion of thinking in terms of embodiment or styles and its limited attention to mediation or mediality.[2] In order to wrestle with these purported laxities, this chapter introduces the body as an interpretive vector in Sinophone studies and explores its currencies to traffic and mobilize the signifier *China* across time and space—that is, from the past to the present and between Asia and the West. My purpose here is to expose the relational fulcrum of the body in mediating the work of history in contemporary visual culture. In positing a continuum of corporeal signification from which transgender history can be inferred, I will show that embodiment offers a productive site of possibility for inscribing and translating meanings of gender across different medial expressions, artistic styles, and language-based cultures. Though scholars such as Jing Tsu have enriched the scope of Sinophone studies by advancing what she calls "linguistic governance," which interrogates the way different linguistic and translational capacities compete in material and political terms, the field remains relatively divorced from critical studies of medicine.[3] Probing into the broader ramifications of medical forms pluralizes the way Sinophone studies transgresses boundaries of culture via the mediality of material and bodily negotiation.

By casting corporeality as a tangible conduit of trans/gender epistemology, this chapter bridges the study of global Sinophone cultures, the history of the body, and the field of medical humanities. It assembles and analyzes a unique database—ranging from Tsui Hark's martial arts films to David Cronenberg's *M. Butterfly* (1993)—that features the theme of castration. Strictly speaking, *M. Butterfly* is an Anglophone rather than a Sinophone production, but a renewed focus on corporeal signs and iterability suggests the feasibility of otherwise. In bringing the film under the ambit of Sinophone investigation, my hope is to transfer the flexibility of cultural critique—with Chineseness serving as the linchpin of systematic scrutiny—onto a spectrum of transgender understandings parsed from the somatic order of the real. The unveiling of the diffused representations of castration supplies a methodical ground for comparing a body of works that tend to be considered separately. Such "entangled" comparison expands Sinophone studies in distinctively new directions.[4] Rather than an insistence on the struggle over language, sound, and script as chief concerns, I coin the concept of *intercorporeal governance* to refer to an alternative apparatus in which the grounds of tactical convergence and contestation assume urgency across scales of bodily signification. Governance, in this sense, is neither predetermined nor overdetermined by a top-down, state-centered authorization of historical production. Intercorporeal governance facilitates the relational modalities of power and recognition whereby it becomes possible to differentiate the body's sense of affinity or defiance to Chinese culture, place-based identity, and, above all, the contingent norms of personhood.[5] As we will see, when the malleability of the body and the mercurial nature of subjectivity activate hefty social troubling—such as the deconstruction of gender fixity—the basis of cultural governance transfigures from purely linguistic systems of negotiation into a postidentitarian circuitry of embodied histories.

In Sinophone cinema, martial arts prowess often denotes a crucial marker of the resulting embodiment of castration, a specific typological technique employed to distinguish the gender liminality of eunuchs. Because the immense physical power associated with eunuchs in these films exceeds the actual physical strength of eunuchs in China's past, this exceptional capture of castrated corporealism reveals a highly original expression in queer Sinophone production, contrasting contemporary *peripheral* adaptations against historical *mainland* Chinese culture.[6] On the other hand, whereas critics have tended to analyze *M. Butterfly* from the viewpoints of Asian American identity politics and, by extension, of anti-Orientalism, I resituate the film in a global Sinophone framework by arguing that despite its popular reception, one of its most often overlooked objects of critique is actually China. If *M. Butterfly* is contextualized in the global politics of the 1960s, China emerges as the Lacanian phallus embodied by the supposed Oriental "Butterfly"—as a phantom of the colonial project whose detachment from the French white man signifies its own demise.[7]

A medium- and corporeal-based reading of these otherwise unrelated films loosens representational claims about China from earnest ties to Sinitic languages, scripts, or texts; makes room for multi- and extralinguistic comparisons across shifting parameters of translation; and strategically aligns Chinese culture with the focal point of transnational Sinophone critique. A transtopian Sinophone reading forgoes the need to qualify individual bodies with degrees of transgender genuineness or Chinese persuasion; instead, it places a structural emphasis on the way different bodily configurations interrelate through the antihegemonic work of cross-historical mediation. The politics of Chineseness and the politics of transness reciprocally anchor a queer way of bringing history to life by visual means. Whereas the last chapter reorients the historical threshold of transgenderism by mapping it onto the human/nonhuman continuum, this chapter bursts open the material body as a spectrum of inscriptive possibilities from which the geopolitics of transgender history mutates, coalesces, and dissipates across regional and temporal divisions.

Monstrous Transmogrification

In *After Eunuchs* (2018), I traced a history of sex change from the demise of eunuchism in the late Qing to the emergence of transsexuality in Cold War Taiwan.[8] This narrative rests on the extinction of Chinese eunuchs in the last century. Indeed, the historical demise of eunuchism in the early twentieth century marked a transitional phase, when the castrated male body, women's bound feet, and the leper's crippled body all came to be disparaged as out of sync with the Chinese body politic at large.[9] The transcultural traffic of these corporeal "types" culminated from a longer historical process whereby the Chinese empire and body came to be associated with a distinctively pathological identity, as reflected in the stamping of the Qing regime as "the Sick Man of Asia" in nineteenth-century discourses.[10] The last Chinese eunuch, Sun Yaoting (孫耀庭, b. 1902), died in 1996, and his biography—translated into English in 2008—has made possible the global circulation of stories about the eunuchs of the last Chinese dynasty.[11] Despite the physical death of Qing eunuchs, castrated figures continue to fascinate popular cultural producers and consumers, and contemporary Sinophone cinema presents many examples of their cultural imagery, especially in *wuxia* films. Focusing on some of the best-known Sinophone films featuring castrated protagonists, my analysis utilizes transgender theories of embodiment to probe the representations and historicity of castration. By pinning extraordinary martial arts strength as a staple feature of castrated subjects, filmic production enables a queer articulation of eunuchism in the Sinophone peripheries even as the practice of castration itself has long disappeared from the center of Han Chinese history and culture.

In order to analyze the various bodily and subjective transformations in Sinophone films, I borrow the concept of *transmogrification* from queer theorist Nikki Sullivan.[12] Assigning the term a new theoretical edge, Sullivan challenges the exceptionality of any given type of body modification and, by extension, the moralistic tendency to dichotomize forms of embodiment by which oppositions are set up between, for instance, transsexualism and transgenderism, cosmetic surgery and "nonmainstream" body modification, conforming and subversive corporeal changes, or "bad" and "good" practices.[13] In considering all forms of body modification as distinct manifestations of "transmogrification," which she defines as "a process of (un)becoming strange and/or grotesque, of (un)becoming other," Sullivan acknowledges "important similarities, overlaps, resonances, and intersections between a range of modified bodies."[14] The trope of transmogrification helps to shed light on the connections across a range of corporeal transformations in Sinophone films. The cultural labor performed by castration can thus be saturated in a network of conjunctions with other examples of embodied and experiential change. Immersing castration in a web of bodily arrangements this way extends the nonhierarchal spectrum of embodied positionality that conditions and is pledged by the semiotics of transtopia.

Some of the earliest examples of castrated transmogrification can be found in films such as Jacob Cheung's *Lai Shi, China's Last Eunuch* (中國的最後一個太監, 1987), Chen Kaige's *Farewell My Concubine* (霸王別姬, 1993), and Ching Siu-tung and Tsui Hark's *Swordsman 2* (東方不敗, 1992).[15] First screened in Taiwan in 1987 and Hong Kong in 1988, *Lai Shi* is the first film that Cheung directed and thus cemented his successful transition from a film producer and screenwriter to a director. It also raised the profile of many of its cast, including the Hong Kong actor who played the leading role, Max Mo (莫少聰, b. 1960), whose performance scored the Best Actor nominations in the Eighth Annual Hong Kong Film Award and the Twenty-Fourth Annual Golden Horse Award. These recognitions completely transformed Mo's subsequent career in the Sinophone cinematic world. Adapted from Sun Yaoting's biography, *Lai Shi* tells a story of the last eunuch accepted into the Qing palace, Liu Laixi (劉來喜). Groomed by the aging loyal eunuch Ting, Laixi embarks on a mission to restore the last Qing emperor Pu Yi to the imperial throne. Conveying a humanistic message, the film refers to the last cohort of eunuchs dismissed by the Qing court as "victims of a grand transitional period" (大時代變遷的犧牲品, *dashidai bianqian de xishengpin*).[16]

The film drives home its historical eloquence through a Sinophone transposition of late Qing castration narratives, which retells Sun Yaoting's journey to becoming a eunuch through the story of Laixi's body transformation. Both born and raised in Jinghai District, Tianjin, Sun Yaoting and his fictionalized character, Laixi, aspire to become eunuchs from witnessing the successful career of late Qing eunuch Zhang Lande (張蘭德, 1876–1957) upon his return to Jinghai. The similarity in their castration experience is most telling. First, both Sun and Laixi are castrated by their fathers at home.[17] As I have argued elsewhere, this reveals one of the most significant parallels between footbinding and castration in Chinese history: the cultural survival of both practices entailed a homosocial environment in the occasion and demonstration of their corporeality.[18] Footbinding was a custom conducted by women and on women; castration was a practice performed by men and on men (in addition to fathers, some sources indicate that there was a group of "professional knifers" in China—again, all men— who carried out the castration operations on boys and young adults).[19] Moreover, both Sun Yaoting's and Laixi's childhood castration experiences confirm aspects of the procedure that was openly described by foreign observers in the late nineteenth century.[20] Sun's personal testimony and Laixi's filmic representation corroborate the necessity of placing a rod inside the main orifice after the operation to secure successful urination once the wound is healed.[21] In the film, Laixi's mother inserts a quill into his castrated site to prevent future urinary problems (figure 4.1). These life narratives, then, give rise to a subtle recognition of marginalized agency: the bodily involvement of eunuchs governs our understanding of the details of what it took to become and live as a Chinese eunuch, historically and historiographically—that is, both in historical real time and as vanguards of their own body history.

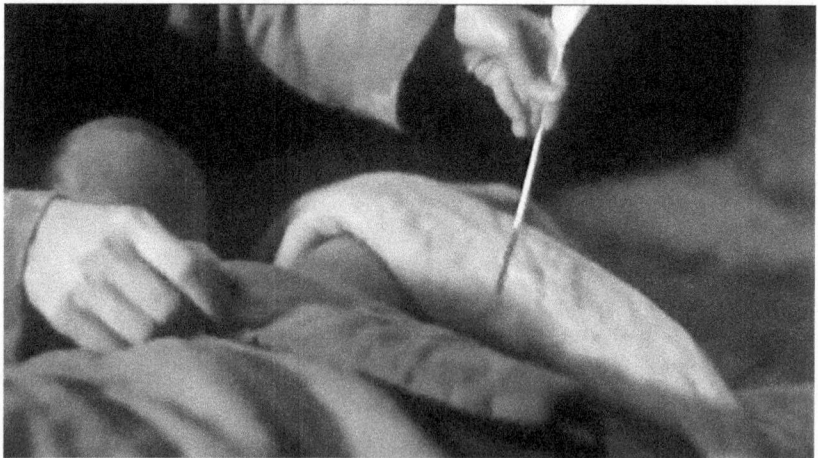

Fig. 4.1 Liu Laixi's mother removes a goose quill from his body to allow him to urinate. *Source*: *Lai Shi, China's Last Eunuch* (1987), directed by Jacob Cheung, produced by Sammo Hung.

Even as Laixi represents the Sinophone recapitulation of Sun, the film distinguishes Laixi's castration experience by connecting it to another kind of transmogrification notably absent in Sun's life story: female impersonation. Instead of reporting to the Qing palace directly, Laixi ends up working in a troupe in Beijing, apprenticing under a master to become a successful Peking opera *dan* actor. Historically speaking, due to the nature of their occupation, both opera actors and eunuchs were prohibited from advancing a career through the civil service examination system. The fusing of both historical subject positions in Laixi's character thus constitutes a parabolic commentary on their shared social status. Meanwhile, as discussed in the last chapter with respect to the evolving meaning of *renyao*, the practice of female impersonation among *dan* actors became a highly contested topic in the Republican era. Expressing a nationalist sentiment, Chinese modernizing elites who condemned the existence of *dan* actors castigated not only their cross-dressing behavior, but also their association with the vogue of male same-sex prostitution.[22] Both elements, as it turns out, play a central role in Laixi's transformation into a successful *dan* actor. Not only is he capable of giving an erudite performance of one of Mei Lanfang's masterpieces, *The Drunken Concubine* (貴妃醉酒, *Guifei zuijiu*), his feminine beauty mesmerizes Marshall Lei, who eventually invites him to a personal date and courts him aggressively (figure 4.2).[23] By portraying

Fig. 4.2 Liu Laixi gracefully performs *The Drunken Concubine*.
Source: *Lai Shi, China's Last Eunuch* (1987), directed by Jacob Cheung, produced by Sammo Hung.

the life of China's alleged last eunuch through the lens of the homoerotic journey of a *dan* actor, *Lai Shi* allegorizes China's cultural backwardness and "lack" in the overlapping destiny of a castrated subject living through the promise and pitfall of a nascent national modernity.

No other film has brought the topic of cross-dressing among *dan* actors to a more heated controversy in and out of China than *Farewell My Concubine*. In her essay "Trans on Screen" (2012), Helen Leung offers a refreshing reading of the character of Cheng Dieyi (程蝶衣) in the film precisely through the prism of transmogrification.[24] Although *Farewell My Concubine*, like *Lai Shi*, does not belong to the *wuxia* genre per se and has raised all sorts of problems for critics who try to identify a contemporary gay subjectivity in Dieyi's character, it merits some discussion in light of its unique deployments of gender (un)becoming.[25] Leung follows Sullivan's ethical imperative to bracket concerns about the "positive" versus "negative" representational effects of Dieyi's gender and sexual semiotics. Instead, Leung considers Peking opera training itself as a historically specific mode of transmogrification: "a life-long physical training that molds plaint bodies into stylized theatrical role-types."[26] In Dieyi's physical transformation from an untrained boy to a perfect *dan* actor, his extra finger is chopped off by his mother so that he can be accepted into and trained properly in the troupe; he endures recurrent merciless beating for the perfection of theatrical form and movement; and his body *transgenders* with the successful enunciation of the line "I am by nature born a girl" after repeated mistakes and corporal punishments (figure 4.3). Dieyi essentially exemplifies, quoting Susan Stryker's terminology, a "monstrous" trans subject, "not in the conventional identity sense but more provocatively in the sense that he assembles gender and constitutes his self within the contingent structure of power that produces him."[27] Not surprisingly, the film's closure seals the fate of such a doomed subject with the onstage realization of Dieyi's suicide—a fate mimicked in real life by the queer Sinophone icon who starred as the adult Dieyi, Leslie Cheung.[28]

Whereas Dieyi's transformation into a feminine subject unfolds in a series of corporeal changes that do not involve physical castration, the most direct example of male-to-female transmogrification can be found in the Dongfang Bubai (東方不敗) character in *Swordsman 2*. The arch villain in the film, Dongfang Bubai, castrates himself to practice a lethal form of martial art (documented in *The Precious Sunflower Scripture* [葵花寶典, *Kuihua baodian*]) that elevates his status to the top of the common martial

Fig. 4.3 Cheng Dieyi enunciates the line "I am by nature born a girl" after repeated mistakes and corporal punishments.
Source: *Farewell My Concubine* (1993), directed by Chen Kaige, produced by Hsu Feng.

world (江湖, *jianghu*). This accomplishment earns him the assignation of "the undefeated in the east," the literal meaning of his name and an unambiguous allusion to Mao Zedong's pompous appetite for power at the time when the original novel was written. According to Shu-mei Shih's reading, this loose filmic adaptation of Jin Yong's novel *The Smiling, Proud Wanderer* (笑傲江湖, *Xiao ao jianghu*), published in 1967, articulates a form of political satire that at once was conditioned by a localized diasporic subjectivity (both Tsui Hark and Jin Yong emigrated to Hong Kong where they launched successful careers) and parodied Hong Kong's social unrest under the impending pressure of the Chinese and British sovereignty contest.[29] Helen Leung has argued that the casting of Brigitte Lin (林青霞, b. 1954), an actress famous for her immense beauty, exemplifies a genuine attempt to enable certain aspects of transsexual subjectivity to emerge on the screen.[30] Above all, the telling differences between the novel (written in the Maoist era) and its cinematic rendering (produced in the context of increasing queer visibility in Hong Kong) complicate other homonormative critiques of the film.[31] Whereas Dongfang Bubai dies within a chapter in the four-volume novel, she becomes the most prominent character in the movie, usurping even the limelight of the male protagonist, Linghu Chong (令狐冲).[32] With its plot revolving around Dongfang Bubai's transmogrification, *Swordsman 2* also departs from the original novel by orchestrating an erotically charged relationship between Dongfang Bubai and Linghu Chong.

The casting of Brigitte Lin is significant in this regard, because it allows Dongfang Bubai to reemerge on screen as a beautiful *woman*, no longer a half-castrated man (figure 4.4).[33] The two protagonists first meet in a scene next to a lake where Dongfang Bubai rehearses the martial art scheme detailed in *The Precious Sunflower Scripture*, which she tries to keep in her possession by engraving the scripture on the inner layer of her garment. Initially hoping to battle as he approaches the person practicing this lethal

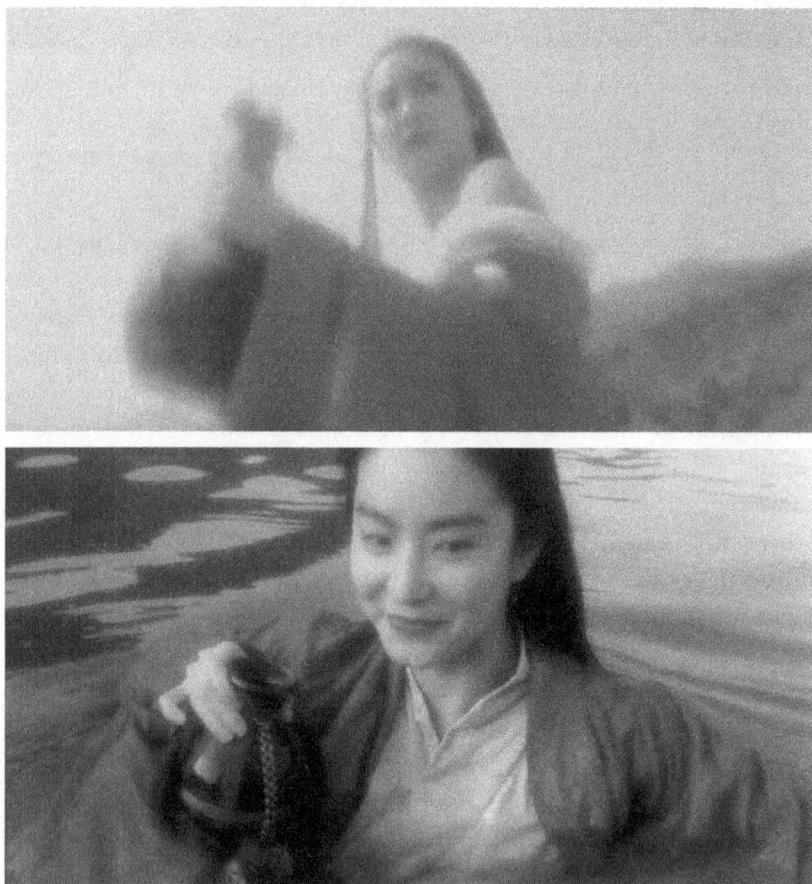

Fig. 4.4 Dongfang Bubai's first encounter with Linghu Chong, already appearing as a beautiful woman rather than a half-castrated man.
Source: *Swordsman 2* (1992), directed by Ching Siu-tung, produced by Tsui Hark.

form of martial art, Linghu Chong immediately retracts his sword and falls into the lake when he sees Dongfang Bubai's face, implying, quite notably, that he *already* (mis)recognizes Dongfang Bubai as female rather than half-male (and that he does not consider it possible for such a deadly force to have emanated from an attractive woman). After Dongfang Bubai joins Linghu Chong in the lake and exchanges her wine (a significant gesture of homosocial bonding), Linghu Chong shows irresistible adoration for her. Yet when he introduces himself and asks for her name by addressing her as a *guniang* (lady, 姑娘), Dongfang Bubai frowns and immerses herself fully in the lake in order to communicate to Linghu Chong through water—a technique that even Linghu Chong is incapable of performing—in her gender-neutral voice. Dongfang Bubai's realization that Linghu Chong already perceives her as a woman is of considerable consequence. To sustain this transsexual (mis)recognition, she maintains a hypersexual feminine visual imagery by concealing her auditory gender through a queer corpo-real enmeshment with the lake.

In a later reading, Leung draws attention to the negative connotations of Dongfang Bubai's transformation. According to Leung's reassessment, Dongfang Bubai's transsexuality "is explicitly figured in the film as evidence of the character's ruthless ambition, destructive power, and monstrosity. By intimately linking Dongfang Bubai's will to dominate the world with the transformation of her body from male to female, the film has displaced anxiety about totalitarian rule onto the sex-changed body, which it portrays to be both dangerously seductive and violently destructive."[34] For our purposes, it is worth noting that this displacement works only because Dongfang Bubai has been assigned a set of martial art skills unrivaled by others. Her self-inflicted sex change (as well as her calculated hiding of it from Linghu Chong), then, replicates not only the castration experience of Chinese eunuchs, but also their infamous image of being politically threatening agents. This embodiment of malicious insubordination—i.e., acquiring power through the elimination of the male sexual organ—enables castrated subjects to exhibit extraordinary skills superior to other gender-"normal" characters in the film, but, at the same time, demonizes their social role and significance. In this regard, eunuchs and castrated figures in Sinophone cinema represent, again, dehumanized subjects of what Stryker calls "transgender rage."[35]

In the postmillennial era, two films have appropriated and reinvented this image of eunuchs as at once powerful and demonic: Tsui Hark's

Flying Swords of Dragon Gate (龍門飛甲, 2011) and Su Chao-Bin and John Woo's *Reign of Assassins* (劍雨, 2010).[36] Set in the Ming dynasty—more precisely during the reign of Emperor Chenghua (成化, 1464–1487)—*Flying Swords* is in fact a sequel to the *New Dragon Gate Inn* (新龍門客棧, 1992).[37] By harking back to the historical context of the Ming dynasty, the film unambiguously renders the manipulative power of Ming eunuchs as a familiar cultural resource for demarcating the gender alterity of eunuchs in the film. As is well known, Emperor Chenghua (1447–1487) established the secret service Western Depot (西廠, *Xi Chang*) in 1477 under the directorship of the ruthless eunuch Wang Zhi (汪直), who, according to historian Henry Tsai, "practiced the worst aspects of terror during his tenure."[38] It is reasonable to assume, then, that Yu Huatian (雨化田), the most powerful eunuch character presiding over the Western Depot in *Flying Swords*, is a fictional representation of Wang. In the film, Yu attains his position and political power primarily through collaborating with the favorite imperial concubine of Chenghua, Consort Wan (萬貴妃, 1428–1487), for whom Wang also worked as a personal servant. Echoing the reputation of Wang's ruthless orchestration, the Western Depot under Yu's leadership offends many influential ministers, especially those working for the Eastern Depot (figure 4.5). To borrow from Tsai's depiction of Wang, "officials and ordinary were so frightened by [Yu's] entourage that everyone hid as soon as they heard the depot agents coming to their

Fig. 4.5 Presiding over the Western Depot, the powerful eunuch Yu Huatian visits the Eastern Depot and ridicules its staff as "moronic."
Source: *Flying Swords of Dragon Gate* (2011), directed and produced by Tsui Hark.

vicinity."[39] In fact, the storyline of *Flying Swords* mirrors the evolving circumstances of the Western Depot and its leaders—their eventual annihilation.

However, there are two notable differences between Yu in fictive construction and Wang in real life: Yu's romantic affair with Consort Wan and his martial art prowess. Although scholars have debated the nature and extent of Wang's collaboration with Consort Wan in their intrusion in Ming state affairs, the film takes Consort Wan's relationship with Yu to a new level by charging it with a heavy dose of eroticism (figure 4.6). And even though there is evidence to suggest that Wang loved martial arts and military science as a child, the physical power of Yu surpasses any truthful measure of imagination that can be applied to our understanding of Wang's military skill in terms of both degree and quality.[40] In short, by being Wang Zhi's Sinophone reincarnation, Yu Huatian exhibits "transsexual monstrosity" in ways similar to Dongfang Bubai. In spite of their invincible martial art strength, these characters take on the archenemy role in Sinophone films. Braided in the structural correlations of the body in both biopolitical and geopolitical terms, the transnational traffic of queer Sinophone production precipitates from the *peripheral* adaptation of historical *mainland* Chinese culture—a chronological leap in the appropriation of an antieunuchism that first emerged in the late Qing but continues to dwell and define the global engendering of Chinese historical fascination.

Fig. 4.6 Yu Huatian summoned by and flirting with Consort Wan.
Source: Flying Swords of Dragon Gate (2011), directed and produced by Tsui Hark.

Spontaneous Regeneration

Also set in the Ming dynasty, *Reign of Assassins* tells the story of an assassin gang, called the Dark Stone, whose goal is to collect all the mummified remains of an Indian Buddhist monk, Bodhi. Legend has it that Bodhi's remains, when unified, carry a kind of mystical power that allows the possessor to practice an insurmountable form of martial arts and thereby dominate the world. The Dark Stone gang's leader, Cao Feng (曹峰), is an accomplished martial artist and the master of the gang's top assassin, Drizzle. In a mission, Drizzle collects half of Bodhi's remains from Prime Minister Zhang and kills his family. However, Zhang's son, Zhang Renfong, gets away, while Drizzle, enlightened by a monk, decides to leave the Dark Stone for good and buries Bodhi's remains in a temple. Hoping to cut off from her old way of life, Drizzle turns to a famous surgeon, who changes her appearance. With a new identity, Drizzle eventually marries a man, who turns out to be Zhang Renfong himself, now also carrying a new look and new name after a changeover by the same surgeon that operated on Drizzle. Meanwhile, the leader of the Dark Stone, Cao, recruits and trains a new female assassin, Turquoise, a merciless girl who murdered her fiancé and in-laws on her wedding night. The bulk of the plot uncoils as the Dark Stone gang pursues a rigorous search for Drizzle and the missing half of Bodhi's remains.

In one of the most climatic and shocking moments in the film, Cao Feng is revealed as a eunuch who has served the imperial palace for over five decades but remains at the lowest rank of the nine-grade system of public servants (figure 4.7). His intention in tracking down and unifying the two halves of Bodhi's mummified remains is to stimulate the regrowth of his phallic organ by way of acquiring the mystical power promised by Bodhi's cadaver—in short, to reinstate his biological manhood through a miraculous spontaneous regeneration. This endeavor picks up a long-standing motif that has been circulating in China since at least the Han dynasty (206 BC–220 AD) according to which eunuchs regain their potency especially in times of political disorder and imperial weakness.[41] But Cao's hidden secret is only the tip of the iceberg. The story of *Reign of Assassins* unfolds with all of its major protagonists carrying *dual identities*. The film opens with Drizzle attempting to kill Zhang Renfang, but the two enemies go on to become husband and wife with new names and novel

Fig. 4.7 Cao Feng discovered by Zhang Renfong as a palace eunuch.
Source: *Reign of Assassins* (2010), directed by Su Chao-Bin and John Woo, produced by John Woo.

appearances not long after their respective plastic surgeries. Turquoise changes from an average girl into a powerful assassin after being recruited into the Dark Stone and, trained under Cao, becomes Drizzle's bona fide replacement on the team (though she never attains quite the same measure of military might). Throughout the film, Cao embodies two opposing social statuses, standing at both the top of the Dark Stone gang and the bottom of the Chinese imperial court.

The various transmutations of identity and the historical and cultural weight they carry in *Reign of Assassins* revolve around—and therefore must be decoded through the lens of—material corporeal change. The trope of transmogrification helps to recognize and theorize the connections across a range of embodied transformations in the film on a continuum, suggesting that Cao's castrated (un)becoming cannot be isolated as the apogee of its narrative development. Ideologically, this approach would merely reproduce the phallogocentric rationale behind the Dark Stone's mission. Rather, given the relatively minimal representations of Cao's castration throughout the film, a queer reading practice, drawing on the concept of transmogrification, steeps the signification of biological emasculation in a dense web of embodied (un)becoming and experiential refiguring. Unlike the evidentiary practice valorized by Chinese philologists, who "assumed that their only entrance to the realm of corporeality *in the past* was by way of written texts," the visual rendering of bodily changes in the film seams any rupture in the material presence of their historical "truth" and its embellishment in claims to a distanced past.[42]

In *Reign of Assassins*, the very notion of transmogrification demarcates the boundaries between dead and vital bodies. Whereas every living character participates in processes of transmogrification, the most prominent dead body in the film—Bodhi's mummified remains—operates along a radically different axis of ontological ubiquity. Namely, Bodhi's dead body presents itself as a token of exchange, legislating and circulating within a moral economy of the common martial world to which the Dark Stone gang belongs.[43] The belief that the unification of Bodhi's remains promises an invincible form of martial arts makes it the cardinal asset sought after by the most powerful fighters. The fact that the Dark Stone gang has been able to secure both parts of the remains, though the second half is hidden by Drizzle after she forsakes the team, implies that its leader, Cao Feng, is probably the strongest figure within the broader community of those martial artists who are interested in the acquisition of Bodhi's cadaver. Simply put, whoever puts his or her hand on Bodhi's dead body is honored with the recognition of being the most vicious martial artist in existence. This moral economy of the common martial world determines the fate of Bodhi's dead body—how and where it travels—as well as what it signifies with respect to the living persons who possess it. It is noteworthy that Bodhi's remains do not undergo a process of transmogrification. They simply go through processes of becoming and unbecoming in relation to the vital bodies that acquire or surrender them, and their social capital assumes value within a moral economy that dignifies superior martial art skills and justifies its varying proximity to different martial artists. This moral economy of life and death in *wuxia tianxia* (天下, all under heaven) predicates a queer form of regionalism in representing and recuperating the dynastic Chinese imperium. China, home to *wuxia tianxia*, is culturally fictionalized as a regionalized possibility of queerness that assumes its shape within the apparatus of Sinophone production and through the martial art prowess of the eunuch Cao, testifying to the embodiment of geopolitical marginality in the hallmark of his exclusive gender disparity.

In contrast to dead bodies, living bodies in the film always express themselves via transmogrification. It is interesting to note that if the diverse range of body modification practice studied by contemporary queer theorists overwhelmingly involves some kind of medical intervention (as is the case with sex transformation and various major and minor types of cosmetic surgery), the different examples of transmogrification represented in the film are almost always closely connected to medical practice as well.[44] Both Drizzle and Zhang, for example, seek a form of medical procedure in ancient China known as the "art of disguise" (*yirongshu*, 易容術), which radically transforms a person's physical (usually facial) appearance and considerably resembles modern plastic surgery. Through this invasive type of body modification, Drizzle and Zhang acquire not only new appearances, but also distinctively new identities. Drizzle's replacement in the Dark Stone, Turquoise, experiences a slightly different kind of embodied transformation: a merciless girl groomed into a fearless female assassin (and, as we will see, even a hypersexualized object of desire). Interestingly, the Dark Stone recruits Turquoise by feeding her a pill known as *guixidan* (歸西丹), which suppresses all the metabolic processes of a living body and thereby makes it appear dead for a fixed period of time. After the local magistrate disposes her body, Cao collects her after the effects of *guixidan* dissipates and says to her, "since I am the person who has given you a new life, you must do what I say from now on." From that point on, Turquoise becomes Drizzle's replacement—the only female assassin within the core group of the Dark Stone.

And Cao himself self-imposes transmogrification by lowering his voice every time he appears in front of the gang, mutating from a feminine-sounding, low-ranking eunuch to the most powerful martial artist taking charge of the Dark Stone. In fact, throughout the first half of the film, Cao, who is not yet known to be a eunuch, always appears on screen with a veil covering his face. With such visual and audial alterations, Cao's masculine identity goes unchallenged until his castrated body is discovered by Turquoise. If the "art of disguise" relocates Drizzle and Zhang from within to outside the moral economy of the common martial world, Cao's hunt for Bodhi's remains allows him to capitalize the measures of justice and respectability underlying the very same moral economy. We can even add here that the terminal goal of Cao is to undo his constant self-imposed transmogrification through an ultimate, once-and-for-all metamorphosis—to terminate the recursive role-switching between a eunuch and the Dark Stone leader by reversing his castration permanently. Similar to the way the Sinophone interrupts the desire for originality, interpreting Cao as a transtopian subject reveals the f(r)iction of transgender as a singular form of bodily change destined to "arrive" somewhere on a continuum of self-narrative.

If transmogrification distinguishes the vital from the dead, gender constitutes the preeminent variable forging the "intercorporeality" between bodies of life.[45] In the film, women's bodies serve the function of reaffirming the gender and sexual identities of men. Echoing Eve Kosofsky Sedgwick's identification of a male homosocial continuum triangulated through relations with women in English literature, the position of Drizzle, later replaced by Turquoise, in the Dark Stone mediates the very foundations of Cao's gender and sexual identity.[46] In the scene where Cao confronts the long-missing Drizzle, whose new residence has been tracked down by the gang, Cao takes a close look at her newlywed husband (Zhang), lying in bed after being drugged by Drizzle. Without a word, Cao uses his fingers to brush his own mustache, which, in a later scene, is shown to have been artificially affixed rather than naturally grown (figure 4.8). In confronting Drizzle's new lover, Cao seems to be fully aware of the reason for which Drizzle had left him years ago. Cao's self-referential comparison of biological masculinity, as expressed through his differentiation between Zhang's real and his own fake facial hair, suggests a hidden sentimental attraction that he had had for Drizzle when she was still a member of the Dark Stone. But did Drizzle leave the gang for a new life, or did she leave Cao for this new man? Or had Drizzle always known about Cao's castrated body, as implied in her repeated questioning about the reason for veiling his face?

As the only woman in the core group of the gang, Turquoise, now replacing Drizzle, magnifies her role as the sex object navigating the

Fig. 4.8 Cao Feng attaches a fake mustache to his face immediately before Turquoise enters the room.
Source: Reign of Assassins (2010), directed by Su Chao-Bin and John Woo, produced by John Woo.

boundaries of male masculine identity. In a series of scenes that depict Turquoise as the object of desire, she undresses herself and uses her naked body to show her affection for Cao *and* to seduce Zhang. Her affection for Cao reciprocally confirms Cao's earlier feelings toward Drizzle, which led to his immediate search for a bona fide substitute; her attempt to seduce Zhang, on the other hand, implies a self-reflective comparison of physical attraction with Drizzle, thereby consolidating the place of her character in the film whose import always lingers under the shadow of Drizzle. Even though there is an obvious gap in martial art skills between Drizzle and herself, these scenes suggest that Turquoise represents a hypersexualized object to a much greater extent than Drizzle did. The intercorporeality that develops and is shaped by the tensions between Cao's castrated body, Turquoise's trafficking body, and Drizzle's surgically altered body climaxes in Turquoise's second erotic confrontation with Cao. Although this scene of mutual affection is initiated by Cao, it leads to increasing aggressiveness on the part of Turquoise, who eventually corners Cao and discovers his phallic "lack."

Again, it is no coincidence that Ming China serves as the contextual referent, notorious for being one of the key historical epochs during which eunuchs wielded an unprecedented, enormous measure of political power.[47] When mapped onto Cao's martial arts invincibility, this form of political threat to the Chinese world order establishes precisely the historical backdrop against which the nationalist condemning rhetoric of eunuchs began to accumulate in the late nineteenth and early twentieth centuries.[48] The vilification of Cao in *Reign of Assassins*, therefore, resonates with the culmination of an antieunuch sentiment emerging from the waning decades of the Qing imperium. Like Dongfang Bubai in *Swordsman 2* and Yu Huatian in *Flying Swords*, Cao Feng exhibits a form of "transsexual monstrosity," underpinned by martial art prowess that surpasses all other gender-normative characters, at the same time being portrayed as the most malicious fighter in the film. Like Cheng Dieyi in *Farewell My Concubine*, Cao Feng's death issues a vigorous reminder of the kind of fate that eunuchs earned, or deserved, in the despotic past: to physically disappear from the world while posing an abiding phantasmic presence in the contemporary cultural register.

Reading these films as Sinophone rather than plainly Chinese brings into sharper focus the historically embedded and politically contested nature between the Sinophone world and China, mirroring (but not identical to) the fraught and troubled relation between the Anglophone world and England, the Francophone world and France, or the Hispanophone world and Spain. Cultural production firmly routed through and rooted in Sinophone arbitrations offers an opportunity to queer other regional scales and categories that have tended to be taken either for granted or as homogenous simply by virtue of its geographical location outside the West, such as "China."[49] In this light, it is not only feasible to speak of China as an empire, which reiterates the dynamism of this geobody's political past, it is also possible to exceed the framework of colonial modernity, which scholars have so frequently employed to deconstruct the transnational and semicolonial historicity of the very same geographical sphere.[50] The cross-temporal referentiality—a queer intercorporeal politics, if you will—between the demise of eunuchism around the turn of the twentieth century and the denigration of castrated bodies in present-day Sinophone cinema therefore unmasks the tactics of convergence and contestation between bodies of "Chineseness." If the Western gaze led the antieunuch discourse in the nineteenth century, the repetition of this focus through an act of reinscription in Sinophone cinemas grants castration "a stock symbolic meaning," whereby a timeless and placeless notion of both Chineseness and transness must be replaced with a historically and geographically sedimented gradation of bodily knowledge.[51]

The appropriation of late imperial Chinese eunuchism in contemporary Sinophone films draws attention to the ways in which Chineseness can be queered and mobilized in a heterogeneous fashion, both intraregionally within Asia and exterior to the West. Above all, this cultural reworking of corporeal signification bears witness to the ways in which "China," itself an evolving geobody, mutates as both a political signifier and a regional imaginary across time and space. Although there have been different attempts to deconstruct the conceptualizations of Asia as a region in various historical communities since the late nineteenth century, these otherwise innovative efforts often lack sustained treatments of queer topics, examples, or perspectives.[52] Rather than construing China as a queer region, this chapter has aimed to bring the spectrum of transgender corporeal (re)making to bear on the historicity of Asian regionalization. The project of queer(ing) regionalism opens up an analytical horizon that underscores the way queerness and queer bodies oftentimes index history as a source of cultural yearning, desire, and legibility.[53] In particular, through the cross-temporal resonances of eunuch corporeality, "Asia" and "region" gain an epistemic foothold by way of appropriating subversive symbols of the Chinese imperial past.[54] The way that dynastic China is enlivened by the Sinophone incarnations of eunuchism puts into motion a transgendering of Chinese history that, at the same time, defies the universalism of Western trans knowledge and iteration.[55]

The Butterfly Effect

Following my overture to think critically about queer regionalism and bodily scales of power, but also to inquire into how Chineseness can be *transgendered* across time and space, I would like to focus our attention back on the Western perception of China and Chineseness.[56] David Henry Hwang's *M. Butterfly* (1989) and its cinematic adaptation, directed by David Cronenberg (1993), have attracted considerable scholarly attention, but no critic has approached them from a decisively transfeminist perspective.[57] That is hardly to suggest, of course, that the transgender elements of the story—notably the gender transformations of the two protagonists, Song Liling and René Gallimard—have escaped existing readings of *M. Butterfly.* Nonetheless, most serious commentaries on the play or the film tend to center on the primacy of a *mimetic displacement* between gender, on the one hand, and other indexes of social identity, on the other. Thus, anthropologist Dorinne Kondo's deconstruction of the mutual assembly of racial and gender stereotypes and queer theorists David Eng's and Eng-Beng Lim's extension of such a method by way of incorporating sexuality often look *through* rather than *at* transgenderism as the epistemological tenor of political change.[58] Marjorie Garber's otherwise compelling reading highlights this potential pitfall most explicitly, claiming that transvestism operates in the story as symptomatic of what she calls a "category crisis"—since it is "once again, something to be looked *through* on the way to a story about men or women, Asian or European."[59]

The kind of transfeminist, antiphallocentric inquiry I propose here far exceeds a mere polemic about the cultural anxiety of cross-dressing. In extending other scholars' critique of the essentialist and overlapping constructions of gender, racial, and sexual identities, I argue that the category of transgenderism itself reorients the political agenda of feminism beyond a sheer intersection of gender with other grids of identitarian sedimentation. The globalization of feminist politics upends a quintessential root of cultural (dis)identification that has heretofore garnered insufficient attention in the case of *M. Butterfly*: the governing hegemony of nationalist fantasy.[60] By incorporating *M. Butterfly* into the remit of Sinophone investigation, my following analysis asks questions that are meant to acquire valence across different medial contexts. How does class revolution matter to *M. Butterfly*? Is the story a critique of Orientalism or the East, or more specifically, of American society, French politics, or China? Building on our excursion into queer inhumanism/monstrosity, we might also add: Is the butterfly a metaphor for displacing the boundaries of being human and, ultimately, embodiment itself?[61] In other words, can we consider the Butterfly—the metaphor as the real—leading a life of her own whose morphology persistently unsettles the gender of its corporal host? Our reading of Sinophone films so far enables further probing. In what ways can we map the cultural politics of life onto the geopolitics of history? How can we meaningfully approach the shifting grounds of imperial hegemony through the lens of gender and (trans)national entanglements? By making transfeminism the basis of a multidirectional critique, my goal is not to offer an inclusive, singular response to these questions.[62] Rather, I aim to probe a set of Sinophone modulations around the category of transgenderism to re-present the political ambition of *M. Butterfly* in a robust transcultural frame. These modulations develop a critique of the symbolic phallus in its imbrication with the cultural aegis of China's geopolitical rise.

A lasting legacy of *M. Butterfly* stems from its staging of a psychoanalytic catharsis culminating in the climax of its finale. The logic of this cathartic surprise could not have worked without a long-standing motif lurking in the popular imagination about cross-cultural romance, especially one between a Western man and an Asian woman.[63] In fact, the title of *M. Butterfly* proclaims itself unambiguously as a descendent of Puccini's infamous opera, *Madama Butterfly* (1904), one of the few well-known Italian operas that casted an (Orientalist) eye on Asia.[64] As the love story between Gallimard, a French accountant working in China, and Song, a Chinese opera singer, accrues its momentum, the audience is suddenly shocked by a dual gender inversion: not only does Song turn out to be a male spy working for the Chinese Communist Party, but after finding out—and resisting—Song's actual identity, Gallimard decides to transform himself into the Oriental butterfly that he has always fantasized.[65] This reciprocal inversion calls into question the very realness of their mutual attraction. Instead of the Asian heroine committing a suicide, a familiar ending in such tragedies as *Madama Butterfly*, the white male protagonist succumbs to his own death, an ironic sign of liberation.[66] The cathartic twist is only a shock insofar as it redirects dominant assumptions about cross-cultural sexual fantasy and the reciprocal intersections of gender and race in contemporary Western society.

Rather than seeking to uncover a "repressed truth" (the real penis, the real White or Asian subject, the real homosexual, the real lover, and so forth) behind this double gender reversal, it is perhaps more promising to view the gender transformations themselves as occupying some metaphysical primacy.[67] By this, I mean to consider gender as constitutive of the core parameters of being human and, accordingly, the transgender metamorphosis of the two protagonists as representing a more foundational political outlook on human life. This echoes Stryker's suggestion that the analytic power of transgenderism "promises to offer important new insights into such fundamental questions as how bodies mean or what constitutes human personhood."[68] Focusing transfeminism back on to the question of gender, phenomenologist Gayle Salamon has relatedly argued that "the transgendered subject is the constitutive outside of binary gender."[69] To bring in the relevance of class conflict, for example, or the cognate question of humanism into our reading, we must tackle the historical background of the 1960s, the communist fervor that fueled Maoist inclinations in Paris in particular, as the larger context for rethinking the transcultural nuance of *M. Butterfly*.[70]

It is useful to bear in mind that while the play *M. Butterfly* quickly built up its fame in New York City between March 20, 1988, and January 27, 1990 (and eventually around the world), a similar Broadway musical adaptation of Puccini's opera was premiered in London in September 1989: Claude-Michel Schönberg and Alain Boublil's *Miss Saigon*.[71] Evidently, there is a stark contrast in the geographical settings between the original opera, on the one hand, and the subsequent dramatic and musical adaptations, on the other. Whereas *Madama Butterfly* tells the story of an American naval officer and a Japanese well-to-do lady, in both *M. Butterfly* and *Miss Saigon*, the settings are relocated to a communist country: China and Vietnam, respectively. Moreover, the lead female character in *M. Butterfly* turns out to be a transvestite secret agent, whereas Miss Saigon earns her glamorous title only at the place where she works as a prostitute. There is one more subtle difference in the *M. Butterfly* variant: the Western man no longer comes from America, but France, which rekindles the social aura and political ambiance of the story through the May 1968 movement. In a different way, *Miss Saigon* also expands on the theme of communism in Cold War Asia by staging the Vietnam War and the Fall of Saigon as its historical context. If *M. Butterfly* presents a genuine critique of *Madama Butterfly*, one of its chief mechanisms concerns the narrative suturing of class struggle as the nodal point of a world revolutionary politics.

The centrality of global economic systems to the plot (un)layering of *M. Butterfly* embeds a different, perhaps more universal, sediment of social strife: the question of being human itself. As Kristin Ross, Richard Wolin, and other historians have convincingly demonstrated, French interest in Maoism reached a peak in the May 1968 movement, after which it evolved into a new vision of social democracy, grounded in a language of "human rights," for which French citizens have always prided themselves since its invention in the age of Enlightenment.[72] High-profile public intellectuals such as Jean-Paul Sartre, Michel Foucault, and Julia Kristeva weighed in, and their brief political allegiance with Maoism in the late 1960s was quite pivotal for their subsequent intellectual reorientation (e.g., resulting in, most notably, Foucault's conceptualization of biopolitics).[73] The French discourse of human rights as an axiom of human life, connected as it was to a communist rhetoric and more specifically to an ideological Sinophilia at the time, casts light on the mirroring of gender and cross-national mimicries between Song and Gallimard. This demands a rethinking of their transgender subjectivity on its own terms not as conditional of appending other social objectives, but as expressive of a broader historical struggle over the meaning and legitimacy of human organization.

The global politics of the 1960s, then, provides a key ingredient to our contextualization of the Song-Gallimard love story. This is a time in China when both Peking Opera and European operas are considered "bourgeois" and relics of the past. In 1968, at the peak of the Great Proletarian Cultural Revolution, Song is sent to a labor camp for "reeducation." While the camp's loudspeaker is gradually replaced by the familiar music of *Madama Butterfly*, the scene of Song in the camp fades and the camera shifts to Paris 1968, where Gallimard is watching a performance of the opera in tears. Afterward, Gallimard reminisces about China in a bar, and the man sitting next to him looks out of the window and complains that Paris is looking more like the revolutionary East, with young students rioting in the streets and rehearsing Maoist slogans: "Talk about China!

I'll bet that if you go out that door, you'll think you're back in Beijing!" As the work of Wolin and others has shown, this initial upsurge of mass student interest in Maoism emerged from French students' decisive *lack* of concrete engagement with Chinese culture. "Cultural Revolutionary China," to quote Wolin's assessment, "became a projection screen, a Rorschach test, for their innermost radical political hopes and fantasies."[74] The meaning of "cultural revolution" in Paris changed over time as the educated class became disillusioned with Maoism, but here it unveils a dirty secret of the Butterfly fantasy. As Rey Chow puts it,

> Is "revolution" itself, the film seems to say, not simply another type of "fantasy stereotype"—the fantasy stereotype that exploits in the name of the collective, the people? If we mobilize, as we must, criticism against Western "orientalist" and "imperialist" fantasies about the East, then should the cruelties committed by way of this other fantasy stereotype not also be under attack? The pro-Chinese Communist fervor in France of the 1960s—is it an awakening from western imperialism and orientalism, or is it not simply the other side of that dream called Butterfly, which fetishizes the East this time not in the form of an erotic object but in the form of a political object, not in the form of the beautiful "oriental woman" but in the form of the virile oriental man, the Great Helmsman, Mao Zedong?[75]

Perhaps the dream of the Western masculine subject has never been of possessing a submissive butterfly, but of desiring a revolutionary prototype (from the Middle Kingdom) with the vision and power to overthrow the conditional present and inculcate a utopian future.

This connection between Paris and Beijing, therefore, suggests that the gender crossings of Song and Gallimard constitute a deeper simulacrum of cross-national politicization. This conflation, convergence, and confluence between gender transgression and interregional mimesis is driven home most forcefully by the most famous and yet controversial scene in *M. Butterfly*. This is the concluding scene in which Gallimard decides to transform himself from a white, middle-class, and supposedly heterosexual man into an Oriental butterfly (he announces, "My name is René Gallimard, also known as Madame Butterfly"). After putting on a wig, applying thick layers of lipstick and facial powder, and wearing a kimono, Gallimard commits suicide by cutting his throat with a piece of mirror

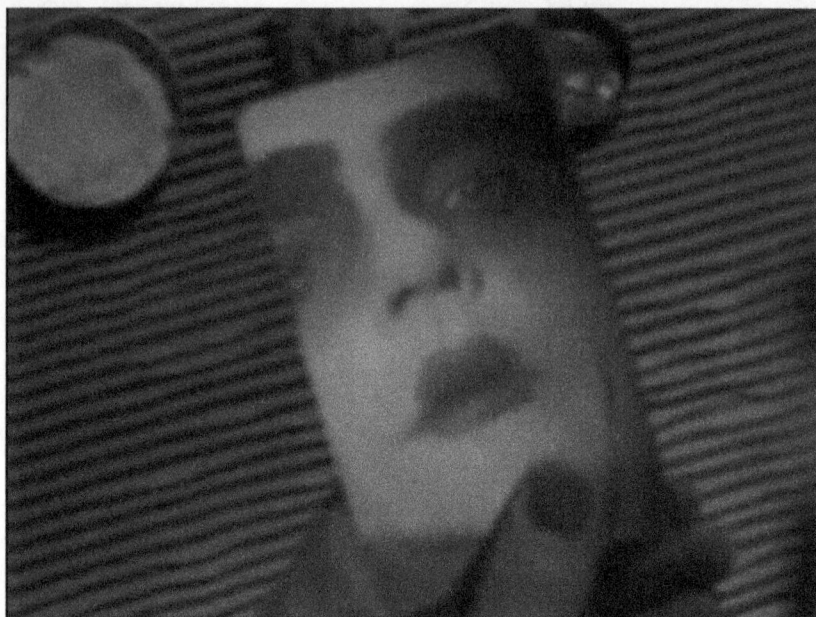

Fig. 4.9 After transforming himself into Madame Butterfly, René Gallimard looks into the mirror with which he eventually takes his life.
Source: *M. Butterfly* (1993), directed by David Cronenberg, produced by Gabriella Martinelli.

(figure 4.9). While critics have approached Gallimard's fate differently, I consider his suicidal transgenderism to symbolize an abrupt about-face of the processual manifestations of castration. Throughout the bulk of the story, Song is depicted as the "castrated" (wo)man, but *M. Butterfly* actually concludes with Gallimard castrating himself. However, what Gallimard castrates is not his sex, race, or gender. These readings would lure themselves into the myth of a "repressed truth," because they merely reify the normativity of the real penis, the real Whiteness (or Asianness), and the real androcentric manhood. Rather, borrowing from Chow's description of Gallimard's final gesture as exemplifying the visible painting of fantasy, I consider what he castrates in the very act of slashing his throat to be *the projection of political and erotic fantasy.*[76] The cut signals the white man's death, but it also represents an act of removing the symbolic phallus—the quintessential ground of white masculine identity.

If *M. Butterfly* is historicized vis-à-vis the global politics of the 1960s, China emerges as the Lacanian phallus embodied by the supposed Oriental butterfly—an ontological symbol that signifies its detachment from the French white man (the real Oriental woman, however ironically) the moment such relinquishment defines his death.[77] China, it seems, carries the seat of hypervirile masculinity, having long been considered the historical origins of all things "under heaven" (*tianxia*) through and beyond the Maoist period.[78] Indeed, the film ends with the "butterfly" (Song) flying back to China. With that, France is left in a vacuum—a dispossession—of Maoist passion, and we are left not with the Western misperception of the East, but with the decolonizing traces of communist China itself.

As I have been suggesting, Gallimard's transmogrification is a form of castration, compounding ethics and aesthetics, but it is not simply a sexual, racial, or gender castration on the level of bodily erasure. Instead, his self-slashing castrates the promise of projecting a political and sexual fantasy. This is mirrored in Song's double inversion (from a man into a woman and back into a man). Again, at the end of the film the butterfly flies back to China. But Song is no longer Gallimard's butterfly by this point in the story; rather, Song's very presence implies the symbolic status of China as the phallus that has been cut off from the white man's identity constitution. In other words, this ending makes a powerful statement about China itself: that Gallimard's death also resembles the death of China's own projection of political fantasy. Much like the way that scholars have understood empires to contain the origins of their own decline, Song's homecoming to China echoes the demise of Maoism in Paris in the late 1960s: a political formation that sets into motion its own undoing from the very beginning. The colonial phallus, after all, retracts back to its homeland under a different guise and relinquishes its project(ion) of political desire.

Whereas most critics have construed Hwang's play as an effort to challenge Orientalism from the viewpoint of disenfranchised minorities, my rendering of Song's and Gallimard's gender transitions as a political end per se, rather than a means through which to look, makes possible understanding *M. Butterfly* as a critique of global "China" as much as it is one of late capitalist America. The different crossovers featured in the film oftentimes subvert wider national and geopolitical trappings at the same time that they trouble gender. Gallimard's transformation into a Japanese butterfly makes the Orient more opaque than a simple citationality of the aesthetics of Chinese operatic arts; Song's conversion into a powerful communist spy highlights the trope of class struggle (as political struggle) absent in Puccini's opera from which the power of his romance narrative with Gallimard originally derived; and Hwang's rerouting of the racial and gender oppression of Asian Americans through a historical context rooted in both a European genealogy of human rights and a revolutionary modularity of Sinocentrism undermines any subsidiary articulation of nationalism for anchoring a story about, above all, transgenderism itself. Heretofore, this study has refrained from defining transtopia nominally as either a utopia or a dystopia of trans existence, but cross-gender practices in *M. Butterfly* embody precisely the possibility of these ideological fissures and fusions.

Supplemental Fabulations

Rey Chow defines "entanglements" as "the linkages and enmeshments that keep things apart; the voidings and uncoverings that hold things together."[79] This chapter has unearthed the fate of transmogrified subjects as the common ground around which the entangled meanings of castration cohere in Sinophone cultures across the Pacific. By incorporating *M. Butterfly* into a critique of global China, and with a focus on the role of the body as a medial fulcrum of historical affinity, my goal has been to supersede the lingo-centric and translational limitations of Sinophone theory. The representations of castration in Sinophone *wuxia* films are often deliberated through the embodied experience of martial art prowess, a cinematic technique that foregrounds the gender liminality of eunuchs. At the same time, this unorthodox personification functions as an expedient ground for the social denigration of castrated subjects—taken as symptomatic of their incredible "transsexual monstrosity." The Sinophone filmic articulation of castration thus emanates from a contemporary adaptation in the cultural periphery of an earlier antieunuch sentiment that epitomized the heart of fin-de-siècle revolutionary Chinese consciousness. On the other hand, castration in *M. Butterfly* is most vividly depicted in Gallimard's transmogrification from a French white male accountant into an Oriental Butterfly. Yet his transformation climaxes as the enactment of his suicidal outro, representing the eradication of the possibility of projecting a political and sexual ambition, a resisting denunciation of Maoist colonial fantasy. The kaleidoscopic operations of "castration" converge in its fatal excess—death as the common destiny of feminine subjects, whether it is Cheng Dieyi or René Gallimard—across different medial contexts within and beyond the cultural signifier "China."

It goes without saying that not all cinematic representations of eunuchs come in the fixed persona of a fierce, diabolical martial artist. The portrayal of the alleged last Chinese eunuch in *Lai Shi* makes this readily evident. One could go so far as to argue that the death of Laixi's mentor, Eunuch Ting, resembles a determined critique of his inadequate combatant strength: again, an insinuation of China's "lack" and the weakness of the late Qing body politic. Even the *wuxia* films surveyed almost always feature a spectrum of diverse martial art skills. The plot of *Flying Swords*, for instance, unfolds with the Western Depot's second-in-command, Ma Jinniang, playing an indispensable role but commanding a different kind of militant power than Yu Huatian. A similar dynamic is apparent in the Cao Feng/Drizzle pair in the *Reign of Assassins* or the Dongfang Bubai/Ren Woxing duo in *Swordsman 2*. Even though, as archvillains, Dongfang Bubai, Yu Huatian, and Cao Feng are all crowned as the head of *jianghu* in their respective ways, their claims to such representational propriety rely on the presence of other characters— transmogrified or not—who assert highly differentiated acumens in their dexterity to fight.

In contrast and response to the portrayal of nefarious castrated fighters in Sinophone films, the more recent delineation of "super eunuchs" in films produced in the PRC goes so far as to exceed a referential frame solidified through martial art strength alone. The super eunuch unequivocally lacks martial art training, but he is blessed with the marvelous superpower of turning any object into anything he desires, vital or inanimate. The polarizing depictions of the "good" super eunuch, Da Bao (大寶), and the "evil" Ming eunuch, Cao Huachun (曹化淳), in Jiao Yang's *Super Eunuch* (超能太監, 2016) is telling in this regard (figure 4.10).[80] The powerful Cao is a fictive representation of the infamous Ming eunuch with an identical name, echoing, again, the ways in which Yu Huatian embodies Wang Zhi in the *Flying Swords*. Despite his power and strength, Cao is killed by Lao Wang, the person who castrated Da Bao, but Da Bao ends up killing Lao Wang with his spectacular superhuman power. This new cinematic technique that uses extraordinary techno-scientific superpower—rather than martial arts prowess—to demarcate the newly improved "super" mainland eunuch from the old, militarily potent

土豆 茄子 辣椒
potato, eggplant and chilipermanently.

Fig. 4.10 In the final battle scene where Da Bao (right) attempts to turn Cao Huachun (left) into a potato, an eggplant, and a chili with his superpower.
Source: *Super Eunuch* (2016), directed by Stephen Jiao Yang.

Sinophone eunuch brings us full circle to the relationship between Chinese history and contemporary Sinophone culture.

By putting the spotlight on matters of mediality and corporeality in this chapter, I have tried to complicate the ways in which *China* signifies both the lure of implicit resistance and the object of symbolic seduction. With that in mind, I want to conclude by recasting the relationship between Chinese history and global Sinophone cultures in the Derridean framework of supplementarity.[81] In Jacques Derrida's well-cited (but often misunderstood) logic of *le supplément*, the representation or the imitation troubles the binary logic of the real and the nonreal, carrying the elusive, threatening potential to operate as and even exceed the very presence of what it claims to supplement. A supplement, on the one hand, confirms the completeness of an originary presence, but, on the other, reveals the lack or deficiency of a presence that calls for supplementation in the first place. For Derrida, these seemingly contradictory significations of the supplement must in fact be understood as operatively intertwined: that which is being supplemented is also a supplement to begin with. "The concept of origin or nature," Derrida writes in *Of Grammatology*, "is nothing but the myth of addition, of supplementarity annulled by being purely additive. It is the myth of the effacement of the trace, that is to say of an originary differance that is neither absence nor presence, neither negative nor positive."[82]

The Sinophone bartering of an elusive "Chinese" origin, in this sense, incites the affective politics of fear and desire: "A terrifying menace, the supplement is also the first and most secure protection; against that very menace."[83] By "procuring an absent presence through its image" and "the proxy [*procuration*] of the sign," the logic of Sinophone supplementarity is therefore always "a necessarily indefinite process . . . sign of a sign," permitting itself as the authentic deception of an imitated origin.[84] According to Barbara Johnson, this is how the logic of supplementarity works, where A is the supplement and B is the thing supplemented:

A is added to B.
A substitutes for B.
A is a superfluous addition to B.
A makes up for the absence of B.
A usurps the place of B.
A makes up for B's deficiency.
A corrupts the purity of B.
A is necessary to that B can be restored.
A is an accident alienating B from itself.
A is that without which B would be lost.
A is that through which B is lost.
A is a danger to B.
A is a remedy to B.
A's fallacious charm seduces one away from B.
A can never satisfy the desire for B.
A protects against direct encounter with B.[85]

With an eye on the global trafficking of the castrated body as both a moving historical referent and a medium of transgender inscription, it is now possible to substitute "Sinophone culture" for "A" and "Chinese history" for "B" in these statements. This substitution makes it possible to confront a series of interrelationships between A and B. So: Sinophone culture is that without which Chinese history would be lost; Sinophone culture is that through which Chinese history is lost; Sinophone culture is a danger to Chinese history; Sinophone culture is a remedy to Chinese history; Sinophone culture's fallacious charm seduces one away from Chinese history; Sinophone culture can never satisfy the desire for Chinese history (recall that the Butterfly itself is insufficient, but one has to become the Butterfly to satisfy the desire for the Orient); Sinophone culture protects against direct encounter with Chinese history; and so forth. We have already seen how Sinophone films feature a remarkably creative expression by portraying castration as a form of transmogrification and exceptional martial art vigor as its outcome. The demonization of gender liminality through the physical power of eunuchs therefore marks Sinophone *différance*. Drawing on the resource of imperial Chinese history, this folding of difference and deferral of meaning works as a supplement to the tradition of anticastration nationalism, a rhetoric that first arose out of the late Qing period and decisively turned China "inside-out" in the aftermath of the Opium Wars and the Taiping Rebellion.[86]

The more recent projection of "super eunuchs" in PRC-produced films suggests that China bears an uneasy but imperative relation to the Sinophone world. An implicit recognition of loss through incorporation figures centrally in any relational modality that conditions the charge of imperial agitation—an urgent comparative point of departure that exposes the chain of supplementarity between Sinophone, Anglophone, and Francophone cultural deconstructions.[87] In the context of the *Super Eunuchs* duology, its incorporation of Sinophone eunuchism (embodied by the character Cao Huachun) helps to remedy the fear of the loss of the Chinese empire in two ways: first, by juxtaposing a new, scientifically marvelous ("super") eunuch against an old but physically powerful eunuch and, second, by defining the super eunuch as a fully supplemented eunuch that absorbs but also supersedes Sinophone figuration. The second strategy is most striking in the sequel, *Super Eunuch 2: Golden Right Hand* (超能太監 2: 黃金右手, 2016), which revamps the controversial protagonist Wei Xiaobao from Wong Jing's *Royal Tramp* (鹿鼎記, 1992).[88] As is well known, *Royal Tramp* itself is a loose adaptation of Jin Yong's last and longest novel, *The Dear and the Cauldron* (1969).[89] Through this double refraction, then, the new Wei Xiaobao in *Super Eunuch 2* kills the antagonist Oboi (a prominent Manchu military commander and courtier) with a deadly form of qigong known as the "golden right hand," which supplements and is supplemented by the "bone-dissolving soft palm" (化骨綿掌, *huagu mianzhang*) technique, which he had learned from Eunuch Hai. This is a distinctively *tertiary* circulation of Sinophone articulation because the "bone-dissolving soft palm" technique is practiced by the empress dowager in Jin Yong's original novel (primary circulation), but it becomes the secret weapon of Eunuch Hai in *Royal Tramp* (secondary circulation) and eventually *Super Eunuch 2* (tertiary circulation).[90] Epitomizing the fantasy of conquest, the body of the super eunuch thus tells a recursive morality tale about the nightmare of diffusing Chinese history through the amending and amelioration of Sinophone culture.

Similarly, when contextualized in the global politics of the 1960s, the renowned cross-cultural romance in M. Butterfly entails the functioning of "China" as an indispensable supplement in global Sinophone imaginations. From the Maoist inclinations of Parisian students and intellectuals to the critique of Western Orientalism and imperialism underlying the transgender attainment of Song and Gallimard, M. Butterfly refuses to settle on a frame of transference rooted in a single nation, given region, or fixed place. It is a story about the politically layered supplementary logic at once between legendary Maoism and radical France, third-world sexuality and first-world racism, Cold War communism and the capitalist spirit, and, as I have been suggesting, Chinese history and transpacific Sinophone culture. The elusory yearnings of Western—and Chinese—domination end up being overdetermined by their own erotic allegories, which amount to a prevailing critique of why and how trans/gender itself matters. The transfeminist Butterfly evades mortal flesh by camouflaging the body of a communist spy and transposing and inscribing its immortal eminence onto the fantasy prison of a dreamful accountant.

Whereas this chapter began by looking at the global perception of China's lack, it now concludes by thinking through the Sinophone trafficking of China's presence. The Sinophone is thus an imitation or representation that prevents one from recalling the absence of the real. Frequently denied the foil of the native claim, the Sinophone must confront its own presence in the chain of supplementarity and recognize that it, too, "is a substitute for an anterior presence, an indication of a void that precedes and thus necessitates [its] own presence."[91] Because the Sinophone renders certain queer forms possible and ontologically viable in ways that "China" cannot (e.g., the beautiful Dongfang Bubai or the French Butterfly), Sinophone cultures—as supplemental virtue and events—adduce how the historical premise and promise of transgender inscriptions can be.

CHAPTER V

Creolizing Transgender

Citizenship Contest in the New Millennium

S o far I have outlined two procedures through which the category of transgender acquires mobility and currency in Sinophone historical contexts. The variation of transness across time and place, such as from late-imperial and Republican-era China to post–World War II Taiwan, Hong Kong, and Asian America, attests to the urgency of redefining the foundation of our geopolitical reasoning. The method of titrating transgender (chapter 3) charts the evolving historicity of *renyao* in relation to the precarious hold of Chineseness and the hauntological threshold of inhumanism.[1] Sinophone contextualization unwinds the layering of trans/ gendered meanings on how the human prodigy came to hasten Taiwan's liminal sovereignty. The method of inscribing transgender (chapter 4) reorients such contextualization beyond purely linguistic circuits and into nexuses of intercorporeal governance. Sinophone embodiment traffics the mutual constructions of queerness and "Chinese" affinity with gradations of historical durability. A cornerstone of this work has been the reminder that the identitarian impetus of political fracturing since the 1970s is no longer efficacious in the current st/age of global cross-referencing.[2] This hardly invalidates the ongoing multitude of assertions of transgender identification; it simply acknowledges the structural demand, means, and shape of antitransphobic struggle.[3] The programmatic contours of Sinophone transtopia reorganize the spatial and conceptual grid of LGBTQ history.

Now we arrive at what is perhaps the ultimate utility of historicizing LGBTQ experience from the corner of the world that I call the Sinophone Pacific: to account for how inequitable notions of citizenship have come to be contested cross-culturally. In a thread of critical inquiry that deliberates the so-called antisocial thesis, US-based queer theorists have debated the relationship of queer subject positions to civic responsibility, socialization, and meaningful and livable life.[4] The most radical critique of normalized sociality can be found in Lee Edelman's *No Future* (2004), in which Edelman construes the reproductive investment in the figure of the child as the antonym of queer livelihood.[5] On the other end of the spectrum sits scholars such as José Muñoz, who in *Cruising Utopia* (2009) contends that queers have sustained futurity through alternative temporal arrangements with the past—a utopian stance of "not yet here."[6] Other theorists have contributed to this debate from different angles, such as Tim Dean and David Halperin on sexual risk, Elizabeth Freeman on temporality, Jack Halberstam on archive, and Sara Ahmed, Lauren Berlant, and Michael Snediker on affect.[7] The overriding concern of this antisocial turn tackles—and questions—the centrality of progression, trajectory, and certainty to a relational framing of queerness. This becomes most saliently articulated in the controversy surrounding same-sex marriage *within* the LGBTQ movement: Is the battle for marriage equality a complicit nod to the procreative logic of the heterosexist state or a radical step that diverts its unfolding?[8] Since same-sex union is not legally sanctioned in most of the world, it is long overdue to reconsider the ramification of this question from an intercultural perspective.

Given that notions of citizenship cannot be neatly segregated from normative claims of culture, be it on a national, hemispheric, or transregional scale, it is somewhat surprising that the antisocial thesis debate in queer theory has not engaged with the literature on creolization. Most commonly evoked in the Atlantic context, creolization refers to the development of new cultural subjectivities as a result of European, African, and Indigenous American mixtures in the "New World" colonies.[9] Henceforth, creole subjects imply an uneven social affinity to both non- (or pre)creolized political communities and the dispersed specter of empire. These two components of creolized subjectivity raise important questions about queer citizenship unanswered by a debate routinely routed through the optic of marriage (or other similar state-sanctioned practices) in Euro-America. Our consideration of transgender Sinophone politics thus mirrors the uneven affinity between creole production and the hegemonic origins of power—be it China or the West. By using *creolize* as a transitive verb, I emphasize the way actors actively take materials from existing systems of sociality, reshape them, and incorporate them into something new.[10] In the context of this chapter, it underscores the syncretism of transness that eschews a stable division between indigeneity and exogeneity in its cultural-political formation. Antisocial or not, creole/queer subjects make new life.

Creole cultures have been studied with respect to a wide spectrum of social domains, including religion, language, food, and the arts, but the most sophisticated expositions tend to limit themselves to the black Atlantic and, to a lesser extent, Indian Ocean histories. Geographically, this chapter joins the work of scholars such as Celina Hung, E. K. Tan, and Brian Bernards to expand the postcolonial study of creolization into the Pacific fold.[11] The Chinese Mestizos in Spanish Manila, the Peranakans in the port cities of Dutch Java, and the Baba Chinese in the British Straits Settlements of Singapore, Malacca, and Penang (including the Nyonyas), among other ethnic-social groups, exemplify the broader process of creolizing the Sinophone Pacific: the culture-remaking of Sinitic-language communities as they migrated from Southern China to the "South Seas," or the *Nanyang* (南洋).[12]

Theoretically, creolization serves as a useful analogy for interrogating sexual sociality, because it resembles a queering of cultural authenticity without losing sight of the colonial legacy, or what Stuart Hall calls the "unfinished relation to history."[13] Despite the warning of Michel-Rolph Trouillot, Stephan Palmie, and other anthropologists against overstretching its applicability, the concept of creolization is invoked here not merely to capture empirical reality, but also to parse out the experiential folding of subalternity.[14] Akin to the reactionary stance coagulated in the socially embedded hierarchy of the plantation systems, queer resistance "striv[es] to express something it is forbidden to refer to and find[] risky retorts to this organic censorship over time."[15] Like creole languages, the subversive script of queer politics "renew(s) itself every instance on the basis of a series of forgetting. Forgetting, that is, integration, of what it starts from."[16] The process of creolization generates lasting consequences—invented and reinvented ongoingly—oftentimes entwined into place-based articulations, unlike the more transient nature and celebratory optimism of cultural hybridity.[17] And in this sense, it is perhaps equally useful to conceptualize creolization in terms of a continuum akin to transtopia.[18]

Wedding this theoretical borrowing to the antisocial debate, this chapter delineates a third method of historical analysis that I call *creolizing transgender*, which registers the political currency of the category of transgender through the way it grounds regionally based claims of LGBTQ citizenship. The decolonizing overtone of creolization underlines the cultural sedimentation and fluid amalgamation of transness. Whereas other critics have focused on the postcolonial creolization of language-based cultures, this chapter builds on my effort in this book to affix transness to the nodal density of change. What if gender intentionality, rather than linguistic or cultural expression per se, defines creole constituency *itself*? Shifting the ontological focus from bodily inscription to citizenship contest, this chapter depicts Sinophone queer activism as conditional of transgender creolization in contemporary Taiwan and Hong Kong. By focusing on the contested notions of queer sociality, normative or otherwise, we can approach transgender as neither a globally coherent concept, a wholly nativist construct, nor an epistemic product overdetermined by Western homogenization.

In particular, I analyze two examples in which the concept of transgender has been creolized to unsettle the universal forces of gender-normative coercion. First, the turn of the twenty-first century witnessed a retooling of the Chinese notion of *tongzhi*: it was substantially reworked to adapt to local transgender rights activism and, by extension, to appropriate and resignify the work of queering in contemporary East Asia. Observers often date the first queer invocation of *tongzhi* to 1989, when the theater director Edward Lam used the term to name the first lesbian and gay film festival in Hong Kong.[19] But the presumed all-embracing queerness of *tongzhi* since that designation warrants further scrutiny. By probing into the term's circulation in the events that led to the first gay pride in Taiwan in 2003, I will show that the political mobilization of *tongzhi* was overwhelmingly driven by lesbian and gay interest before 2000. The immediate postmillennial era saw the radical transformation of *tongzhi* into an umbrella category that absorbed the epistemic fluidity of *ku'er* (酷兒, queer). The key stimulant to this transformation is the increasing visibility and promotion of transgender rights, which facilitated the gradual symmetry between *tongzhi* and *LGBT* in twenty-first century Taiwan. In this way, the creolization of the Western notion of transgender has aligned its political urgency with the Sinophone expansion of *tongzhi*.

Next, I turn to the battle for marriage equality to examine the capacious and interconnected symptoms of transphobia and homophobia in Sinophone societies. Numerous studies of queer kinship have critiqued the neoliberal agenda of the mainstream gay and lesbian movement.[20] By incorporating state instrumentalization into the remit of transtopian analysis, I make a case for bringing such critiques to bear on the struggle for transgender rights. Centering on the *W v Registrar of Marriages* court case in 2013 in Hong Kong, the second half of the chapter highlights the epistemic rigidity and dogmatism nested in the judgment and, from there, the geopolitical precarity qua postcolonial locality of the Hong Kong legal system. In this example, the creolization of transgender has inadvertently deepened a heterosexist and gender normative state apparatus. A sustained attention to how transphobia and homophobia reinforce each other speaks to the asymptotic nature of a transtopian threshold, an idea I first introduced in the comparative analysis of historical lesbianism in chapter 1. Whereas the redeployment of *tongzhi* in Taiwan reflects the radicalizing effect of the category of transgender, the *W* court history throws light on the conservative concealment of heteronormativity by the state mobilization of the very same category. Taken together, this chapter seeks to map these two asymmetrical ends of a political continuum that disrupts the coercive power of gender/sexual norms in the postcolonial Sinophone Pacific.

Working with the social, cultural, and legal articulations of citizenship, I pivot creolization as a structuralist fulcrum that relinquishes the need for a decisive definition of being trans.[21] Instead, by looking at the context-specific production of transness, the analytic of creolization unearths the diversified nuance of how "transgender" coevolves over time and place. As such, the method of creolizing transgender builds on the craft of historicism.[22] Without historicizing the divergence in the cultural ecology and political dynamics in which transgender activism operated across Taiwan and Hong Kong, it would be difficult to grasp how queer actors position their nonnormative attributes along the axis of social belonging.[23] Although it is not my intention here to resolve the antisocial thesis debate, treating transgender creolization as a coeval historical process, I propose, sheds light on the ethical purchase of viewing transness as a saturated structure rather than a minoritarian identity. The two examples examined in this chapter syncopate a modular understanding of LGBTQ citizenship that crisscrosses regional and global scales.[24] Queers in postmillennial

Taiwan and Hong Kong have laid *regional* claims to citizenship vis-à-vis the slippery sovereignty of these Sinophone locations, meanwhile resting such claims on the projected allegiance to a *global* LGBTQ community.[25] Homonationalism sees its limit; transtopia "cruises," in the Muñozian sense, the subtle but subversive minor-to-minor poetics of relation.

Queering *Tongzhi*: A Sinophone Reconfiguration

A consideration of how *tongzhi* has been queered over time needs to exceed a political agenda calibrated according to lesbian and gay interest alone, or "homonormativity" for short.[26] To accomplish that goal requires us to turn to twenty-first-century Taiwan, where the Chinese concept of *tongzhi* has been substantially reworked in response to local transgender rights activism, and to resignify the work of queering in the Asia Pacific.[27] Whereas the lifting of Martial Law in 1987 is often heralded as a watershed turning point that enabled the blossoming of queer cultural politics in Taiwan, as we saw in chapter 3, the region's queer history goes much further back in time.[28] This genealogical extension complicates a singular fixation on the liberal tendencies of the 1990s.[29] But what happened to this genealogy in the post-1990s era? In mapping the way that the discourse of *tongzhi* came to assume the epistemic fluidity of *ku'er*, as opposed to rendering this process as inevitable (which would mean a teleological development), I argue that any historical understanding of *tongzhi* is incomplete without accounting for the increasing visibility and promotion of transgender rights. Sinophone queering did not stop in the 1980s and 1990s (as especially evident in Hong Kong cinema or Taiwanese literature); the Western category of transgender has been creolized by Sinophone activists to redefine and retool the political expediency of *tongzhi* in the new millennium.

My following discussion centers on two landmark developments that catalyzed this radical transformation of *tongzhi*. The first is the unprecedented collaboration between feminists and gay and lesbian activists in the legislation of the Gender Equity Education Act (性別平等教育法, *Xingbie pingdeng jiaoyufa*) in 2004. This partnership overturned the narrow preoccupation with women's rights in the feminist movement and with the politics of sexuality in the gay and lesbian movement.[30] The second crucial development can be seen in the role of the government and the

Tongzhi Hotline Association (同志諮詢熱線協會, *Tongzhi zixun rexian xie-hui*) in organizing the Taipei LGBT Civil Rights Movement Festival, the precursor to the first official Taiwanese LGBT pride (itself the first of its kind in the global Sinophone community, held in 2003). Through these two examples, I unpack how the growing political traction of the concept of transgender contributed to the reconfiguration of the *tongzhi* movement and, conversely, how *tongzhi* politics has elevated a platform for transgender expressions. The unruly history and circulation of *tongzhi*—from "comrades" in socialist China to "gay and lesbian" in postcolonial Hong Kong to "queer" in late capitalist Taiwan—inflect the perverse articulations of Chineseness across communities marked by different motors of civic activism.[31]

From Sex Equality to Gender Equity

The first and foremost milestone toward the queering of *tongzhi* in Taiwan is the legislation of the Gender Equity Education Act of 2004, which consolidated a broad-based public awareness of gender fluidity. The Act was initially called the "Equality of the Two Sexes Education Act" (兩性平等教育法, *Liangxing pingdeng jiaoyufa*). Formalized in 2002, the decision to rename the Act played a determinant role in raising public awareness of gender nonconformity and attenuating the rigid perception of a masculine-feminine dichotomy. "The renaming process had significant meaning," observes feminist scholar Yang Chia-Ling, "since it extended the binary understanding of gender to a post-structural one."[32] The eventual legislation of the Act in 2004 anchored the social conceptualization of a gender spectrum not delimited by two immutable paragons. As we will see, the subsequent integration of the "T" into the redefinition of *tongzhi* relied on this very foundation to comprehend gender expression beyond binary fixity. But first, let us turn to the tragic event that called attention to the significance of gender variance and animated the momentum to rebrand the Act: the high-profile Yeh Yung-chih (葉永鋕, 1985–2000) incident.

The story began on April 20, 2000, at the Gaoshu Junior High School in Pingtung County of Southern Taiwan. Five minutes before a class session ended on that day, ninth grader Yeh raised his hand to seek permission to use the bathroom (figure 5.1). With the teacher's permission, Yeh left the classroom. Instead of returning to class afterward, however, Yeh

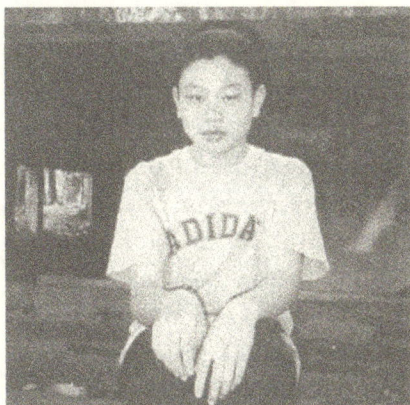

Fig. 5.1 Yeh Yung-chih (1985–2000). *Source*: Courtesy of Taiwan Gender Equity Education Association.

was found lying in a pool of blood in the bathroom. His classmates found him trembling in pain with signs of a head injury. The school immediately sent him to the emergency room in a nearby hospital. But the medical team was unable to save him. He passed away on the next morning. On the day of the incident, the school cleansed the bathroom swiftly and thoroughly without filing a police report. Subsequently, Yeh's family requested the Pingtung District Prosecutors' Office to carry out a forensic determination of the cause of his death.[33]

In June, the Ministry of Education's Committee for the Equality of the Two Sexes Education (the committee changed its name to the Committee for Gender Equity Education after the passing of the Act in 2004) convened an emergency subcommittee to investigate this case. The subcommittee was chaired by Chi Hui-Jung (紀惠容), CEO of the Garden of Hope Foundation (an NGO aimed to protect women's rights, with a focus on intervening in cases of sexual assault and domestic violence, disseminating knowledge about birth control, and offering assistance to single parents), and comprised Wang Lih-rong (王儷容), a Professor of Social Work at the National Taiwan University (NTU); Bih Herng-Dar (畢恆達), an NTU Professor of Building and Planning known for his expertise in the spatial analysis of gender; and Su Chien-ling (蘇芊玲), a prominent feminist activist-scholar based at Ming Chuan University and founder of the first Sinophone feminist bookstore—Fembooks (女書店, *Nüshudian*)—in Taipei. They began the investigation at Gaoshu Junior High later that month, looking into the procedures by which the school handled the case, the gender friendliness of the campus environment, and any prior record of campus violence. Completed toward the end of July, their report highlighted a correlation between the Yeh case and the existing structural tolerance of gender discrimination and related incidents of violence on campus. Based on the investigation, the subcommittee included a series of policy proposals in their final report.[34]

During the formation of the subcommittee, the Pingtung district attorney charged the following three administrators of Gaoshu Junior High with professional negligence: the principal, the director of general affairs, and the section chief of purchase and maintenance. Between June 2000 and September 2006, this case was heard at the Pingtung District Court, the Taiwan High Court Kaohsiung Branch Court, and the Supreme Court, which sent it back to the High Court. It was then appealed to the Supreme Court but was returned to the High Court Kaohsiung Branch Court again. For nearly six years, the three administrators of Gaoshu Junior High were found innocent as the various judges insisted on holding no one responsible for Yeh's death. This changed in September 2006, when the Kaohsiung Branch High Court reversed its earlier decision. This time the High Court made a nonappealable ruling, convicting the principal, the director of general affairs, and the purchase and maintenance section chief of negligent homicide (業務過失致死罪, yewu guoshi zhisizui). The court sentenced them to five, four, and three months of imprisonment, respectively. This final judgment concluded the judicial proceedings of the Yeh case.[35]

Attracting wide-scale media attention, the Yeh story adumbrated the enrichment of gender understandings that were to shape Taiwanese public policies in the years to come (figure 5.2). One of the most significant consequences of the incident was the revamping of the "Equality of the Two Sexes Education Act" in 2002. During their investigation of the Gaoshu Junior High, the emergency subcommittee learned that Yeh had been a persistent victim of campus-wide ostracism, profiling, and bullying due to his "feminine temperament" (女性特質, nüxing tezhi). People at the school knew that Yeh enjoyed cooking, doing housework, and singing and that he behaved in an outwardly girly manner (figure 5.3). For that, he was constantly harassed by his classmates, such as by being forced to drop his pants to reveal his genitals.[36] Many students made fun of him; sometimes they would go further and play mischievous pranks that targeted his gender nonconformity. That was the main culprit behind his habit of using the restroom immediately before class sessions ended. Chen Hwei-Syin (陳惠馨), a Professor of Law at the National Chengchi University, reflected

Fig. 5.2 The Yeh Yung-chih Incident Fifth Anniversary Press Conference, Kaohsiung, Taiwan (December 17, 2005).
Source: Courtesy of Taiwan Gender Equity Education Association.

Fig. 5.3 Yeh Yung-chih (1985–2000).
Source: Courtesy of Taiwan Gender
Equity Education Association.

on her experience in chairing the Gender Equity Education Act Proposal
Research Project (2000–2004):

> Yeh's death pushed us to recognize the necessity of respecting stu-
> dents with diverse gender orientations in educational settings and
> the utmost importance of securing a safe learning environment. As
> such, we proposed renaming the "Equality of the Two Sexes Education

Act" proposal to the "Gender Equity Education Act" proposal. . . . Through the eventual passing of the Act, we hoped that schools would start paying attention to the plight of gender minorities so that fatal tragedies, such as what happened to Yeh, could be avoided in the future.[37]

The seminal impact of the Yeh incident reflected the changing nature of feminist and *tongzhi* activism. When the Ministry of Education formed the Committee for the Equality of the Two Sexes Education in 1997, members of the Committee conceded that its purpose might not be sustainable after the decline in social interest/pressure or the reorganization of the Committee. To redress this potential recession, they appointed a subcommittee to draft a proposal for a bill that would reflect the work done by the Committee. This led to the establishment of the Equality of the Two Sexes Education Act Proposal Research Project, headed by Chen Hwei-Syin. By the time that Chen's group began to hammer out the details of the proposal, however, the feminist movement had educated the Taiwanese public about women's rights and a more egalitarian view of the relationship between men and women in society for over a decade.[38] Meanwhile, the *tongzhi* movement that blossomed in the 1990s had distinguished eroticism as a separate sphere of public representation and political intervention.[39] Though developed in parallel, the two social movements broadened the vocabulary of sex (as in 兩性, *liangxing*) and sexuality (as in 性傾向, *xingqinxiang*) simultaneously.

Therefore, when news of the Yeh story broke in 2000, it did not single-handedly create a sophisticated lexicon of gender, a nodal concept that had intersected with the language of "two sexes" in feminist contention and "sexual desire" in *tongzhi* discourse since the 1980s (if not earlier). But the story did serve as an important catalyst to shake up people's awareness of gender expression beyond binary essentialism. As Su Chien-ling, who served on both the emergency subcommittee for the investigation of the Gaoshu Junior High and the Equality of the Two Sexes Education Act Proposal Research Project, later recalled:

The Yeh incident opened a door for Taiwanese people, especially those concerned with gender education, by bringing to sharper focus the importance of gender temperament. Indeed, campus bullying targets not only men, women, or people with different sexual orientation, but also those whose gender traits are different [不同性別特質, *butong xingbie tezhi*]. . . . Although it is not entirely accurate to say that people began to acknowledge the insufficiency of a binary gender system only due to the Yeh incident, it was a pivotal driving force . . . behind our decision to amend the name of our proposal to Gender Equity Education Act.[40]

The decision to rename the Act captured the way that both feminists and gay and lesbian activists came to realize the limiting capacity of their independent political battles. In the early 2000s, feminist and sexual minority rights activists began to work together to elevate a public consciousness of gender fluidity. This overturned at once the long-standing focus on women's rights within the feminist movement and the exclusive preoccupation with sexual politics in the gay and lesbian movement. The incorporation of gender diversity conditioned a reframing of the meaning of *tongzhi* activism in the context of millennial Taiwan.[41]

From Inclusion to Redistribution

Although public discourses rarely associated Yeh with the label of transgender, his tragedy instigated a systemic reconsideration of gender as a nonbinary, multifaceted attribute. A small cohort of queer theorists in the 1990s tried to open up a space on Taiwan's social margins for the articulation of antinormative genders and sexualities.[42] But that had yet to generate a nationwide interest. The postmillennial trend in the social mainstream following the Yeh incident served as the backdrop for the gender/sexual minority subculture to undergo a significant epistemic shift: the incorporation of the "T" (alongside the "B") into a renewed definition of *tongzhi*. This discursive reconceptualization was most explicitly crystalized in 2003, when the first LGBTQ pride took place in Taipei.[43] If one were to account for the roots of this social change, it is evident that the second catalyst transforming *tongzhi* into a more inclusive umbrella category was the precursor to the first official Taiwanese pride: the Taipei LGBT Civil Rights Movement Festival (台北同玩節, *Taibei tongwanjie*), launched in 2000.[44]

The Taipei LGBT Civil Rights Movement Festival materialized during an era of great political upheaval.[45] The year 2000 marked the triumph of the Democratic Progressive Party (DPP) in winning the presidential election, thereby ending more than five decades of Kuomintang (KMT, Nationalist Party) hegemony on the island. Concurrent with the flowering of human rights organizations, the feminist movement, and *tongzhi* politics, the DPP matured during the post–Martial Law period.[46] Yet one cannot overlook the fact that the feasibility of the Festival was itself rooted in a decade-long struggle of lesbian and gay activism. One of the most famous episodes of this struggle occurred in 1995, when the Taipei city mayor, Chen Shui-Bian (later the elected president from 2000 to 2008), decided to subject the New Park to urban replanning.[47] Lesbian and gay groups immediately responded by forging a "Tongzhi Spatial Action Front" (同志空間行動陣線, *Tongzhi kongjian xingdong zhenxian*), a social protest that lasted from December 1995 to June 1996.[48] The Front challenged the city government's attempt to efface the historic and symbolic importance of the New Park as a long-standing center of *tongzhi* activities and socialization. The Front coordinated a series of demonstrations and cultural events, rendering the New Park as both a rallying cry and an urgent site for *tongzhi* memorialization. Even though the government ultimately redesignated the park as the 228 Peace Memorial Park in 1998, the Front delivered an unambiguous message in regards to grounding a new form of cultural citizenship in queer sexual desire.[49]

Between 1996 and 2000, the *tongzhi* movement in Taiwan grew at an unprecedented rate and with extraordinary momentum. The first Buddhist *tongzhi* organization, Buddhist Youth Abode (童梵精舍, *Tongfan jingshe*), was established by Wu Chen-feng (吳辰風) toward the end of 1996.[50] Wu likely drew inspiration from the Tong-Kwang Light House Presbyterian Church, which was founded in May 1996.[51] The Tongzhi Citizen Action Front (同志公民行動陣線, *Tongzhi gongmin xingdong zhenxian*), or the "Second Front," was founded in December 1996 as the reincarnation of the earlier Spatial Action Front.[52] The police raid of a house party on Changde Street in Taipei in July 1997, also known as the Changde Street incident, prompted the Tongzhi Citizen Action Front to form an emergency working group.[53] The working group organized a series of initiatives to document the unjust treatment of the gay men arrested by the police, forming a resistance force that questioned the legitimacy of such discriminatory practices in social governance.[54] This in turn set the stage for the formation of the first *tongzhi* consultation group, the Tongzhi Assistance Association (同志助人者協會, *Tongzhi zhurenzhe xiehui*), in

November 1997.[55] Founded in 1998, the group Queer'n Class later changed its name to Gender/Sexuality Rights Association Taiwan for official registration in May 1999.[56] In 2004, the G/STRAT won the Felipa de Souza Award conferred by the International Gay and Lesbian Human Rights Commission (now OutRight Action International).

It is also to this period that some scholars have dated the origin of the transgender movement in Taiwan, with activist-scholar Josephine Ho (何 春蕤, b. 1951) acting as the key advocate spearheading the movement. The cornerstone publication that gave it its initial thrust was her essay "Call Me 'Transgender': Transgender Subjectivity and Gender/Sexual Liberation Movement" (1998), which appeared in the leftist publication *Pots Weekly*.[57] According to Ho, "drag queens, drag kings, effeminate men, tom boys, t-po lesbians, transsexuals, intersexuals, transvestites, third sex hostesses, and other emerging gender variant types" constituted the range of minority subjects previously overlooked by both the feminist movement and the *tongzhi* movement.[58] However, it is important to note that, in the context of the 1990s, neither this initial agitation nor the existing third sex "hostess" culture and drag shows in Taiwan typified the grassroots character of Western transgender activism.[59] Many male drag performers at the time justified their onstage cross-dressing by *distancing* themselves from the people they called the "perverted" transsexuals.[60] It is also noteworthy that Ho singled out the mainstream feminist and *tongzhi* movements together, especially their "simple view on gender subjectivity," as the obstacle that her newly envisioned transgender movement sought to overcome.[61] The implication here is that a trans-oriented agenda had been excluded from the political tenor of *tongzhi* activism.[62] By the time that various lesbian and gay groups came together to cofound the landmark Tongzhi Hotline Association, which became the first *tongzhi* corporation officially registered with the Ministry of the Interior (MOI) in June 2000, there existed a growing alertness to the scattered subgroups that had been marginally positioned in relation to the mainstream gay and lesbian movement.[63]

As the first large-scale event hosted by the Tongzhi Hotline Association, the Taipei LGBT Civil Rights Movement Festival, in essence, queered *tongzhi* by bringing the fluid definition of gender into the wider context of political activism. Whereas the name of the inaugural 2000 Festival adopted the English translation, "Lesbian and Gay Civil Rights Movement," in the short span of three years, the Festival rebilled its mission to serve the "Taiwan LGBT Community."[64] In 2003, the Festival operated as the programmer of Taiwan's first pride parade. Two of the foremost organizers of the Festival, the Taipei government (which budgeted one million New Taiwan Dollars for the inaugural Festival) and the Tongzhi Hotline Association, collaborated in the publication of a signature pamphlet for the Festival called *A Handbook on Tongzhi* (認識同志手冊, *Renshi tongzhi shouce*). A new edition of the *Handbook* was updated every year, but all carried the consistent aim to educate the general public in order to demystify the LGBTQ community. Published annually, the *Handbook* typically contained a glossary of terms associated with LGBTQ subculture, brief essays and commentaries on politics and current events, biographical and autobiographical stories, and lists of bookstores and other LGBTQ-friendly venues (figure 5.4). A few examples from the 2003 edition of the *Handbook* will reveal the conceptual evolution of *tongzhi*, which both reflected and contributed to the growing visibility of the transgender community in Taiwan.

A candid indication of the new direction taken by the Festival in 2003 came from the pride organizers themselves. The mayor of Taipei city, Ma Ying-jeou (later the elected president from 2008 to 2016), wrote a preface for the *Handbook*. In his prefatory remark, he lamented learning about the tragic fate of Yeh Yung-chih, as well as that of fictional characters in films such as *Boys Don't Cry*. He claimed that he had heart-achingly come to a realization: "the victims of many tragic incidents involving human rights violation or safety impeachment are homosexuals, bisexuals, transgender individuals, and men whom society considers 'effeminate' and women

▲請問你／妳能分辨他／她的性別嗎？或者說性別是什麼？真的「有那麼嚴重嗎？」

Fig. 5.4 An illustration from *A Handbook on Tongzhi* (2003, p. 55) with the accompanying text: "Can you distinguish his/her gender? Or what is gender? Is it 'that serious'?" *Source*: Courtesy of Tongzhi Hotline Association.

'masculine.'"[65] Citing Pai Hsien-yung's *Crystal Boys*, which was set in Taipei (and, more symbolically, the New Park), Ma expressed optimism toward the prospect for the nation's capital to become a more inclusive place with a human face (人情味, *renqingwei*). The expansion of the *Handbook* to include discussions of bisexuality and transsexuality, he hoped, would cultivate greater respect for those people whom "society currently does not understand . . . and yet [upon whom it] inflicts harm."[66]

The educational intent of the pamphlet was similarly acknowledged by the editorial team. As one of the main editors, Lai Yu-lin (賴鈺麟), noted, in the previous Festival, "very few people would question" the taken-for-granted "equation of *tongzhi* with homosexuality." But in 2003, the *Handbook* distinguished itself from earlier editions by "adding 'bisexuality' and 'transgenderism' to the editorial team's rethinking of what *tongzhi* refers to."[67] According to Lai, the pamphlet from 2003 may have failed to spell out a crystal clear definition of *tongzhi*; the point, nonetheless, was to "stimulate questioning, thinking, and reflection on the controversial nature of sexual orientation [*xingqingxiang*] and gender traits [性別特質, *xingbie tezhi*]."[68] This refusal to stabilize a coherent definition of *tongzhi*, alongside the insistence on its critical potential to challenge given assumptions (including ones that continued to haunt the lesbian and gay movement), represents a queering of *tongzhi* that resulted from a resolute interest in transgender experience and alternative sexual configurations.

Another way to consider the relationship between terms such as *bisexuality* and *transgenderism* to the newly minted agenda of the Festival is through redistributive politics. Similar to Ma and Lai, Xiaocao (小草), another contributing editor to the 2003 *Handbook*, observed that the time was ripe to amend the meaning of *tongzhi* after a decade of lesbian and gay activism. Yet for Xiaocao, this renewed effort cannot be reduced to mere categorical expansion. "To be more precise, [this year's *Handbook*] tries hard to make room in the category of *tongzhi*, a concept long occupied by 'homosexuality,' for subjects typically marginalized or minoritized within the gender/sexual sphere."[69] The insertion of bisexuality and transgender into the new parameters of *tongzhi*, therefore, reclaimed the space traditionally taken up by homosexual subjects and redistributed it to previously disenfranchised groups. It at once foregrounded a "novel attitude of inclusion" and averted an "older, regressive road of exclusion."[70]

In line with this approach to forging new forms of solidarity, the glossary of the 2003 *Handbook* introduced a novel subsection on *kuaxingbie*

(跨性別, transgender), defined as a phenomenon "that challenges mainstream social suppositions about the correlation between gender expression and biological sex" and that characterizes a group of minority subjects "already included in the LGBT [*tongzhi*] movement in most countries elsewhere."[71] This category included individuals who self-identify as transsexuals, transvestites, FTMs, MTFs, and intersexed.[72] The glossary also featured new terms such as *zhitongzhi* (直同志), which literally means "straight comrade." The editors defined *zhitongzhi* as the merging of "straight" or "heterosexuality" with *tongzhi* to designate those nonqueer allies who "understand *tongzhi*, are friendly to *tongzhi*, and subvert hegemonic gender constructs."[73] The expansion of the glossary to include *kuaxingbie* and *zhitongzhi* undermines the predominance of the textual space traditionally reigned over by terms related to homosexual subcultural practice and identification.

The most indicative evidence of the way that the Yeh incident transformed the *tongzhi* movement can be found in the 2004 edition of the *Handbook*, which was published a month before the second LGBT annual pride took place in November that year. As Ma Ying-jeou noted, this edition elaborated on the topic of *tongzhi* human rights in a manner much more explicit than before.[74] Following the mayor's preface, Su Chien-ling introduced the 2004 handbook by commenting directly on the significance of the Gender Equity Education Act, which passed the Executive Yuan meeting on March 31 and was formally implemented nationwide in June (figure 5.5). As the Act entered the stage of legislation, the Tongzhi Hotline Association joined forces with the feminist organization Awakening Foundation to form the NGO League of Promoting Gender Equity Education Act.[75] Su reflected on a decade of labor dedicated to the advancement of women's rights, stressing the importance of the linguistic shift from "two sexes" (*liangxing*) to "gender" (性別, *xingbie*) in this activist history.[76] Her involvement in the Yeh incident convinced her that the country's judiciary branch had been transformed as a result. She used her ordinary experience in the classroom to generalize about larger patterns of social change, whereby Taiwan's society, legal system, and young people came to pay increasing attention to the needs and rights of gender and sexual-variant subjects.[77] Therefore, as the first LGBTQ prides in the Sinophone world unfolded in Taipei, an enlarged, inclusive, and redistributed notion of queerness had begun to formalize within the *tongzhi* movement that stood by, rather than excluded, transgender interest. This owed

Fig. 5.5 The Passing of the Gender Equity Education Act at Executive Yuan (March 31, 2004).
Source: Courtesy of Taiwan Gender Equity Education Association.

in large part to the ratification of the Gender Equity Education Act following the Yeh tragedy. Interpreting this history through the framework of transtopia allows us to acknowledge the importance of the Yeh incident to the *tongzhi* movement without assuming a prototransgender identity in Yeh.

Lopsided Equality: The Polite Residuals of Heteronormativity

After looking at the radical edge of the "T" that transformed the nature of *tongzhi* politics in postmillennial Taiwan, we now turn to contemporary Hong Kong to track a much more curtailed social pattern in the pursuit of transgender rights. To analyze the political currency of transness in postcolonial Hong Kong, I will perform a close reading of the landmark court case *W v. Registrar of Marriages* (2013).[78] The protagonist Ms. W, a Hong Kong resident, entered the world as a boy, but was subsequently diagnosed with gender identity disorder. She started receiving medical treatments in 2005 and underwent sex reassignment surgery in 2008. As a result of her gender transitioning, the government issued her a new identity card and a new passport reflecting her sex now as female. In 2008, she hired a lawyer to approach the Registrar of Marriages to inquire about her right to marry in her acquired gender rather than biological sex at birth. The Registrar denied W the right to marry her male partner on the ground that same-sex marriage was not (and is still not) recognized in Hong Kong. For the purposes of marriage at the time, the legal attribution of gender for transsexuals was still determined by the biological sex indicated on the birth certificate regardless of the new identity card or passport.[79]

Believing that the Registrar's refusal had violated her constitutional right to marry as well as her right to privacy, W brought the case to court for judicial review. However, both the Court of First Instance and the Court of Appeal upheld the Registrar's decision in 2010 and 2011, respectively.[80] This ruling attracted a significant measure of scholarly discussion critiquing the judgment from various perspectives in its immediate aftermath.[81] Moreover, it did not stop W from pushing the envelope further. She subsequently appealed her case to the Court of Final Appeal and, on May 13, 2013, in a four to one decision, the Court of Final Appeal overturned the Registrar's decision and held that W could marry her boyfriend (figure 5.6).[82] This has been widely perceived as a landmark judgment that grants transgender people in Hong Kong the right to marry in their identified gender rather than their biological sex at birth.[83]

Although there is much to be commended about the *W v Registrar of Marriages* ruling, I would like to open up discussions about what it forecloses, especially in light of how its narrative of success strikingly rests on a presumed *irrelevance* of gay and lesbian political ambition. Queering *W* in such a way subverts the pervasive usage of "transgender," to borrow Susan Stryker's astute insight, "as the site in which to contain all gender trouble, thereby helping secure both homosexuality and heterosexuality as stable categories of personhood."[84] In fact, it is not difficult to discern that the question of same-sex marriage was implicated in this judicial consideration from the start. The Registrar initially denied W the right to marry her male partner because same-sex marriage has not been legally sanctioned in Hong Kong; the Court of Final Appeal overturned that decision on the basis that the relationship between W and her spouse represents a strictly heterosexual union, disavowing—if not

Fig. 5.6 Michael Vidler, lawyer for W, speaks to the press outside the Court of Final Appeal in Hong Kong (May 13, 2013).
Source: Copyright Philippe Lopez/AFP/Getty Images.

evading altogether—any ancillary space for destabilizing the coproduction of gender and sexual subject positions.

The issue of same-sex marriage has drawn a divisive line within the LGBTQ community, and this is far from the place to claim a resolution to that debate.[85] Nonetheless, to assess the ramifications of *W,* I believe there is much to be gained from turning that debate on its head: if gay marriage has been critiqued vociferously on the ground of its exclusionary blind spots that further marginalize underprivileged social groups and bolster the heteronormative power of the state, can the legitimation of nonheterosexual partnership be similarly conceived as a vital oversight in the intelligibility of transgender marriage? If existing discussions of queer antisociality tend to presume a universal congruity, such metaphysical presumption is unwarranted when one considers the uneven progress of the marriage equality movement worldwide, as exemplified by the double-edged consequences of *W v Registrar of Marriages.* W's court battles bring to sharp focus the *differential* creolization of transness and, by extension, the discrepant unfolding of queer citizenship contest in postmillennial Hong Kong and Taiwan. Inasmuch as the *W* case brings transgender politics to the fore, same-sex couples, to borrow Muñoz's words, "are not the sovereign princes of futurity."[86] The juxtaposition between Hong Kong and Taiwan, especially in terms of the asymptotic tension between queerness and transness, illumines queer antisociality and its ethical obligation in the intercultural specificity of the Sinophone Pacific.

Building on a growing body of literature that brings the issue of queer kinship to the heart of discussions about global configurations of power, I propose an alternative reading of *W* that foregrounds the geopolitical positioning of Hong Kong.[87] This reading underscores the danger of eclipsing the reciprocal masking of homophobia and transphobia when the state's interest in setting them apart as mutually distinct political agendas rearticulates itself in powerful ways behind definitive court decisions.[88] I will first shed light on Hong Kong's geopolitical salience by exploring the international jurisprudence history within which the *W* judgment is nested. In many ways, my comparative perspective simply adds further weight to legal scholar Marco Wan's claim that "giving transsexuals the right to marry in Hong Kong at the present time represents a logical development in [the history of marriage]."[89] My analysis also extends cultural critic John Erni's insight that in ruling the position of the Registrar of Marriages unconstitutional, the Court of Final Appeal "has sent a strong message of anti-discrimination to society."[90]

Yet I also go beyond these observations by suggesting that neither England nor Europe alone deserves a taken-for-granted place in the process of historical referentiality. Our interrogation must take into account the increasingly charged relationship between the Hong Kong Special Administrative Region (HKSAR) and the PRC, one that is frequently neglected in Anglocentric critical legal analyses.[91] Accordingly, I will elaborate on the mutual imbrication of juridical conservatism and gender/sexual geopolitics through a critical reappraisal of the *W* judgment. In the legal deliberation of *W*, the liberal framing of transgender marriage rights engenders what I call the *polite residuals of heteronormativity*, which figures the advancement of queer interest by concealing certain implicit forms of gender and sexual oppression within a broader outlook of political progressiveness.[92] I use the keyword *residual* to signal the postcolonial contingency of such regions as Hong Kong, alerting to the way traces from past colonial regimes "reside in" contemporary Sinophone communities and cultures. This form of "residing in" is always already conditioned by the postcolonial present. As we will see in the case of *W*, Hong Kong's precarity is characterized by its struggle with the growing global hegemony of the PRC state, at the same time proceeding through the reification of difference and protection by its Basic Law system. The polite residuals of heteronormativity capture a twofold process: the lingering presence of discrimination hidden in ostensibly respectful emancipatory discourses and the articulation of sexual minority rights through the remains and grip of European jurisprudence logic.

The Weight of a Fairer Past

The majority opinion in favor of W's appeal, delivered by Chief Justice Geoffrey Ma and Permanent Judge Robert Ribeiro, raises a long-standing subject of contention in the history of marriage rights: the separation of procreation from the legal definition of marriage. Specifically, a leading assumption of Hong Kong Basic Law that the judges wished to overturn was the idea that procreation is a necessary condition for defining "a man and a woman" and, therefore, the legitimation of marriage. Similar to most judicial rulings, the W case had a long history of related court battles from which to infer, albeit mainly outside Hong Kong, in order to arrive at a compelling conclusion about the nature of the relationship between sex and marriage deemed most appropriate for contemporary Hong Kong society. The issue of whether marriage ought to be legally inclusive of procreation, however, was from the outset conflated with a narrow understanding of sexual intercourse. One could reasonably claim that the right of transsexuals to marry in their acquired gender became a possible question only after gender reassignment was made available.[93] Indeed, both Justices Ma and Ribeiro made this poignant observation in their deliberation.[94] Nonetheless, the first time that a European court faced the challenge of resolving this issue goes back to 1969 in the case of *Corbett v Corbett (Otherwise Ashley)*. Since this case served as the starting point for the unfolding of the W judgment, our historical contextualization begins there.

Heard in late 1969 with a decision delivered in February 1970, *Corbett* was a divorce case in which the plaintiff, Arthur Corbett, a British aristocrat, petitioned to nullify his marriage to the transsexual model April Ashley. Corbett sought to dissolve his marriage based on two grounds: first, at the time of their marriage ceremony in 1963 Ashley was still a person of the male sex (whereas the legal definition of marriage involved the union of a man and a woman); and second, the marriage was never consummated due to Ashley's incapacity or her intentional refusal to consummate the marriage. Though Ashley brought a petition under the Matrimonial Causes Act of 1965 for maintenance, the court ultimately ruled in favor of Corbett. The judge who presided this case, Justice Roger Ormrod, explained that since it was impossible to change a person's biological sex, and yet marriage was by definition a union between a man and a woman, their marriage was void ab initio. His decision rested on a biologistic understanding of sex in relation to marriage:

> sex is clearly an essential determinant of the relationship called marriage, because it is and always has been recognised as the union of man and woman. It is the institution on which the family is built, and in which the capacity for natural heterosexual intercourse is an essential element . . .
>
> Having regard to the essentially heterosexual character of the relationship which is called marriage, the criteria must, in my judgment, be biological, for even the most extreme degree of transsexualism in a male or the most severe hormonal imbalance which can exist in a person with male chromosomes, male gonads and male genitalia cannot reproduce a person who is naturally capable of performing the essential role of a woman in marriage. In other words, the law should adopt, in the first place, the first three of the doctors' criteria, [i.e.,] the chromosomal, gonadal and genital tests, and, if all three are congruent, determine the sex for the purpose of marriage accordingly, and ignore any operative intervention. . . . My conclusion, therefore, is that the respondent is not a woman for the purposes of marriage but is a biological male and has been so since birth. It follows that the so-called marriage of 10th September 1963 is void.[95]

In defining procreative intercourse as the "essential" constituent of marriage at common law, Justice Ormrod laid down four foundational criteria for determining the legal sex of transsexuals: chromosomal factors, gonadal factors, genital factors (including internal sex organs), and psychological factors to which transsexualism was understood to belong. This definition was endorsed as the "present state of English law regarding the sex of transsexual people" until as late as 2003 in *Bellinger v Bellinger*, and it was overturned only with the introduction of the Gender Recognition Act 2004—to which we will return.[96]

In drawing on the *Corbett* case, Justices Ma and Ribeiro distinguished two components in the legal definition of sex central to Justice Ormrod's decision: consummation and the four psychobiological factors. However, they were quick to reject nonconsummation as a reasonable ground for voiding a marriage:

> We will content ourselves with saying that we are not convinced that the existence of non-consummation as a ground for voidability has any necessary connection with procreation as an essential purpose of marriage. The test for consummation has traditionally been regarded as full coital penetration but without any requirement of emission, far less of conception. Moreover, there is in any event authority to support the view that consummation can be achieved where the woman has had a surgically constructed vagina, suggesting that there is no legal impediment to consummating a marriage with a post-operative transsexual woman who is able to engage in sexual intercourse. We are therefore not persuaded that the existence or otherwise of non-consummation as a ground for avoiding a marriage is of any present relevance.[97]

In other words, the focus of their attention immediately shifted to the question of who qualified as a "man" or a "woman" for the purposes of marriage irrespective of consummation. In the case of W, the more relevant question became: Could a postoperative male-to-female (MTF) transsexual person be treated as a "woman" for those purposes?

In establishing their decision, Justices Ma and Ribeiro acknowledged three considerable challenges to the United Kingdom's adherence to the *Corbett* approach in the twelve years between 1986 and 1998. In 1986, the European Court of Human Rights (ECHR) interpreted the right of transsexuals to marry in the case of *Rees v UK* in a way similar to *Corbett*.[98] Mark Rees was a postoperative transsexual man who had been refused the alteration of his birth certificate so as to reflect his posttransition sex. The ECHR ruled against Rees on the ground that it did not consider his marriage right infringed: "In the Court's opinion, the right to marry guaranteed by Article 12 (art. 12) refers to the traditional marriage between persons of opposite biological sex. This appears also from the wording of the Article which makes it clear that Article 12 is mainly concerned to protect marriage as the basis of the family."[99] The fifteen judges presiding the *Rees v UK* case held *unanimously* that there was no violation of Article 12 of the Convention for the Protection of Human Rights and Fundamental Freedoms (hereafter "the Convention"). Four years later, the ECHR considered a similar case, *Cossey v UK*, but this time involving a postoperative transsexual woman, Miss Cossey, who had been engaged to two men sequentially by the time of her application. In viewing the issues confronting her case as akin to those arising in the *Rees* case, the ECHR again held (by fourteen votes to four) that there was no violation of Article 12.[100]

The question of whether a transsexual's right to marry is violated under Article 12 resurfaced again in 1998, when the European Commission of Human Rights referred two complaints to the ECHR, together constituting the case of *Sheffield and Horsham v UK*. MTF Kristina Sheffield and Rachel Horsham objected to the nullity of their potential marriage with a male partner under English Law since a male-to-female transsexual was still considered a man for legal purposes (and since same-sex marriage was not yet recognized). In holding (by eighteen votes to two) again that there was no violation of Article 12, the Court recalled that

> in its Cossey judgement it found that the attachment to the traditional concept of marriage which underpins Article 12 of the Convention provides sufficient reason for the continued adoption by the respondent State of biological criteria for determining a person's sex for the purposes of marriage, this being a matter encompassed within the power of the Contracting States to regulate by national law the exercise of the right to marry.[101]

Again, by "the traditional concept of marriage," the ECHR was referring to the original formulation of legal sexual criteria first articulated in *Corbett*. In the twelve years from *Rees* to *Sheffield and Horsham*, the ECHR maintained that the biological characteristics of sex fixed at the time of birth provided the sufficient measures for determining an individual's right to marry. Yet "in each of those cases," Justices Ma and Ribeiro observed, "the Court noted that questions regarding the rights of transsexual persons arose in an area of legal, social and scientific change, acknowledging the need to keep the position under review."[102]

The opportunity for a watershed turning point came in 2002, when the ECHR sat as a Grand Chamber in the landmark judgment of *Goodwin v UK*. The postoperative MTF Christine Goodwin claimed a violation of Articles 8, 12, 13, and 14 of the Convention and applied (under Article 41) for just satisfaction. Overturning the decisions in *Rees, Cossey,* and *Sheffield and Horsham,* the ECHR decided on this occasion that, despite the absence of a common European approach to the legal resolution of the practical problems faced by transsexuals, the time had come to take on board "the clear and uncontested evidence of a continuing international trend in favour not only of increased social acceptance of transsexuals but of legal recognition of the new sexual identity of post-operative transsexuals."[103] As such,

> The Court is not persuaded that at the date of this case it can still be assumed that these terms must refer to a determination of gender by purely biological criteria (as held by Ormrod J. in the case of *Corbett v. Corbett,* paragraph 21 above). There have been major social changes in the institution of marriage since the adoption of the Convention as well as dramatic changes brought about by developments in medicine and science in the field of transsexuality. The Court has found above, under Article 8 of the Convention, that a test of congruent biological factors can no longer be decisive in denying legal recognition to the change of gender of a post-operative transsexual. There are other important factors—the acceptance of the condition of gender identity disorder by the medical professions and health authorities within Contracting States, the provision of treatment including surgery to assimilate the individual as closely as possible to the gender in which they perceive that they properly belong and the assumption by the transsexual of the social role of the assigned gender.[104]

By the same measure, the ECHR held that the right to found a family was not a necessary condition of the right to marry, and it also no longer considered the chromosomal element or a congruent test of biological factors decisive in denying the legal recognition to the gender change of a post-operative transsexual. Incorporating these revolutionary amendments, the judges now assessed Goodwin's right to marry in the following light: "The applicant in this case lives as a woman, is in a relationship with a man and would only wish to marry a man. She has no possibility of doing so. In the Court's view, she may therefore claim that the very essence of her right to marry has been infringed."[105] For the first time in the history of transsexual rights, the ECHR held unanimously that transgender people's right to marry has been infringed upon under Article 12 of the Convention.

By referencing three decades of European jurisprudence history from *Corbett* to *Goodwin* to explain how they arrived at their position, Justices Ma and Ribeiro highlighted the flexibility of British law, mediated by the ECHR decisions, especially as it adapted to the evolving international social environment. According to their judgment, Hong Kong must be placed squarely within this context of historical legal transformation: "the Basic Law [of Hong Kong] . . . are living instruments intended to meet changing needs and circumstances. . . . When the position in Hong Kong in 2013 is examined, it is in our view clear that there have been significant changes which call into question the concept of marriage adopted as a premise by Ormrod J and also the criteria which he deduced therefrom."[106] In order to drive home their conclusion that procreation was no longer an essential criterion for the legal legitimation of marriage, Justices Ma and Ribeiro pointed to the changing social conditions in Hong Kong, with an emphasis on its increasing openness and cultural diversity.

> In present-day multi-cultural Hong Kong where people profess many different religious faiths or none at all and where the social conditions described by Thorpe LJ by and large prevail, *procreation is no longer (if it ever was) regarded as essential to marriage*. There is certainly no justification for regarding the ability to engage in procreative sexual intercourse as a sine qua non of marriage and thus as the premise for deducing purely biological criteria for ascertaining a person's sex for marriage purposes.[107]

Their strategic decision to echo the ECHR's approach in *Goodwin* underscores an important feature that sets HKSAR apart from the rest of the PRC, the evolving Portuguese civil law system in Macau notwithstanding: namely, the region's unique legal system resulting from its former British colonial status. In contrast to mainland China's civil law system, Hong Kong continues to follow the English Common Law tradition established under British rule.[108] By transposing the flexibility of British law onto Hong Kong Basic Law, Justices Ma and Ribeiro executed a set of juridical practices that extended the lingering shadow of the British imperial reach, rendering "Europe" as a goal to catch up with for a region situated precisely at the interstitial space between China and the West.[109]

The irony here is that the mainland Chinese government had already granted a marriage license to Zhang Lin, an MTF from Chengdu, Sichuan, in 2004.[110] Legal scholar Guo Xiaofei has recently highlighted the British colonial legacy in Hong Kong as a reason for the sharp contrast between the disquieting jurisprudence transformations occasioned by *W* and the relatively "silent and subtle" legalization of marriage rights for gender-reassigned individuals in the present-day PRC.[111] Therefore, it is interesting to note that the nonpermanent judge Kemal Bockhary, concurring with the majority's decision in *W,* was the only member of the court to point out the fact of Hong Kong's lagging behind in the area of transsexual marriage rights: "This country China, of which Hong Kong is a part, will be fully within the international trend to which Lord Nicholls referred if we in Hong Kong uphold the right of a post-operative transsexual to marry in the reassigned capacity. I say that because such a right is recognized in the Mainland."[112] Yet whether the alibi for taking the transformation of the legal system in Hong Kong seriously is Europe or China, the message remains clear: the extraordinary geopolitical position of Hong Kong makes a seemingly straightforward issue of human rights (i.e., the right to marry) fundamentally difficult to grasp without assigning global giants such as China or Britain an epistemologically and ontologically privileged position.

The Veil of Queer Interpellations

Although the ruling of *W* allows ample room for inferring radical implications about the separation of procreation from the legal definition of marriage, the court decision ultimately reauthorizes certain heteronormative assumptions about gender and sexuality. Despite its queer potential and legalization of transsexual marriage rights, the outcome of *W* engenders what I call the polite residuals of heteronormativity for three reasons. First, the decision rested on the ideological perpetuation, rather than troubling, of the heterosexual-homosexual binary that has endemically fractured our epistemological organization of sexuality, rendering marriage as an entirely straight institution.[113] From the outset, Justices Ma and

Ribeiro foreclosed the potential of using this case to transform the institution of marriage and its meaning through the possible prism of homo-intimacy: "We should make it clear that nothing in this judgment is intended to address the question of same sex marriage."[114] Even from W's perspective, "it is not part of the appellant's case that same sex marriage should be permitted. The contention advanced is that she is for legal purposes a woman and entitled to marry a person of the opposite sex."[115] Although the debate on gay marriage is far from settled in the LGBT community, both at the grass-roots level and within scholarly discourses, what remains unchallenged in the successful appeal of W is the strict definition of marriage as a union between a man and a woman. Though the legal criteria for who qualifies as a man or a woman may have undergone a drastic transformation (and this should certainly be lauded in its own right), the broader heterosexist framework of marriage has not. The predicament of cross-sex desires continues to be *naturalized* through these judicial conversations about transgender rights.[116]

Second, by reinforcing a heterosexist institutionalization of marriage, the W case elides the radical queer potential of the notion of *trans* itself.[117] In striving to convince the judges that the category of woman includes postoperative MTF transsexuals, the arguments put forth by W and her legal representatives essentially absorb the immensely disruptive power of "trans" into an epistemic fixity and boundedness of gender. Perhaps this is the flip side of the same coin with respect to my last critique, in which a consideration of *sexuality* (gay, straight, and so on) in the legal reconceptualization of marriage sheds light on where transsexual rights may have fallen short in obscuring the possible horizons of queerness. Here, the turning of our analytic lens to *gender* addresses the problem of homonormativity in the strategic queering of marriage, but it fails to adjure what such queering can do to expose the pluralistic and inclusive spectrum of gender expressions.[118] As trans theorists Susan Stryker, Paisley Currah, and Lisa Jean Moore have argued, a compelling purchase of "trans" resists "seeing genders as classes or categories that by definition contain only one kind of thing" and instead "understand[s] genders as potentially porous and permeable spatial territories (arguable numbering more than two), each capable of supporting rich and rapidly proliferating ecologies of embodied difference."[119] Through its contrived intervention in the regulatory governmentality of Hong Kong Basic Law, the W case ultimately fails to bring the fluid ecologies of gender embodiment to bear on the juridical lexicon of marriage rights beyond redressing the question of who qualifies as a man or a woman. In fact, its success precisely reconsolidates this question in the subsequent jurisprudence importance of the case.

A potential counterpoint to my argument may be identified in the judges' decision to endorse the United Kingdom's Gender Recognition Act of 2004 (GRA). The Act "does not lay down a bright line test for when a transsexual person does or does not qualify for recognition in his or her acquired gender. Instead, the Act sets up a panel with legal and medical members which hears applications for gender recognition and requires the panel to grant a gender recognition certificate."[120] In other words, rather than drawing an arbitrary line at some point in transitioning (usually in the sex reassignment process) to serve as a universal litmus test for the judicial recognition of gender change, this approach determines legal gender status on a case-by-case basis via an expert panel without imposing an undesirable coercive effect on persons who may not wish to undergo surgery.[121] In transferring this method of "sex determination" from Britain to Hong Kong, the majority of *W* judges have certainly allowed for more flexibility in the proper recognition of wide-ranging transgender expressions not preemptively axed by the fulcrum of sex change operations or by the biological determinism of *Corbett.*

However, two problems arising from this approach form the basis of my third critique of the *W* judgment. The first problem with this approach is that it reauthorizes the same legal and medical regimes that have sub-jected transgender individuals to oppressive scrutiny in the first place.[122] Calling the state determination to establish a trans person's gender status a process of "getting sex right," constitutional law expert David Cruz has argued that this

> "getting sex right" approach fails to appreciate how legal sex is a normative, regulatory tool, not a natural fact. "Getting sex right" risks unaccountable legal decision-making and transfers of power to an alternative regime, that of medicine, that may seem more conge-nial than the legal arena at the current moment, but which is not guaranteed to promote the liberty and equality of transgender, or indeed any, persons.[123]

Instead of supporting the equal existence of gender diverseness without the systematic intrusion of the state, the GRA approach reaffirms the importance for pertinent legal, medical, and scientific experts to ensure "getting sex right" and prioritizes the power of these authorities over the voice of gender-variant people in legal sex determination, if legal sex determination is even a desirable and necessary precondition.

Second, the appropriation of the GRA method undermines the subversive geopolitical potential of Hong Kong as a region situated at the intersections of British postcolonialism and the PRC's growing global dominance. If Hong Kong has indeed become increasingly incorporated into the geocultural Sinosphere (and has increasingly been steered away from the Anglosphere), and if the mainland Chinese state has already legalized trans people's right to marry in their identified gender, why is it still necessary to codify a legislative intervention in the form of a gender recognition panel for future considerations of transgender legal claims? Again, from the perspective of cultural critique, it is not going too far to suggest that such a strategic resolution to recentering the GRA approach in future judicial conversations about transgender rights merely reinforces the West as a normative frame of intelligibility in a region commonly deemed to be a territorial propriety of China. In some ways, the ensuing articulation of proximate British legal practices in a Chinese-speaking region resuscitates the static binary of China-versus-the West and, by extension, obscures an immensely powerful realization of Hong Kong's queer regionalism.[124] It significantly diminishes the profound potential of flexible gender expression—and recognition—for accounting for queer selves in the name of sensible law. In the way it fought for the state recognition of transsexuality, *W v Registrar of Marriages* instrumentalized a limiting legal *and* geopolitical apparatus that resists the more open-ended, flexible, and egalitarian definition of transness central to the conceptual foundation of transtopia. To paraphrase Shu-mei Shih, when transtopian expressions become complicit with heteronormativity, they lose their articulatory function as the pivot of resistance and transformative identities.[125]

Ironically, despite its troublesome agenda, the dissenting opinion of Justice Chan illustrates a potentially *queerer* intervention in comparison to the majority judgment. (However, as I shall also point out, his heterosexist and transphobic motives preclude the realization of such queer potential.) First, this can be inferred from Justice Chan's invention of a new category called "transsexual marriage" in his opening declaration: "I am not persuaded that there is justification for extending the meaning of 'marriage' in art 37 of the Basic Law to include a transsexual marriage."[126] This statement implies that the traditional institution of marriage excludes the type of union that Justice Chan calls "transsexual marriage" and that the prospect of including the latter would merely be an extension of the former, reflecting their presumed mutual exclusivity. Yet what exactly does "transsexual marriage" refer to, and what work is it actually doing for judicial reasoning?

In fact, Justice Chan's remark leaves room for two diverging interpretations, and a queerness of some sorts can be inferred from such interpretive instability. On the one hand, his comment is an utterly transphobic statement in its failure to respect why the legal and medical acceptance of transsexuality is important. By confining transsexuals to a legal position relative to the institution of marriage as that distinct from gender-normative men and women, it dismisses the legal acknowledgement of full gender transitioning as a serious advancement in the interest of trans people. On the other hand, this depiction of transgender exceptionalism accentuates the liminal autonomy of the trans category itself, rather than the normative operation of gender binaries. In this sense, "trans" acts as a mediating conceptual anchor that exceeds those hegemonic definitions of gender that have traditionally consolidated the cultural traction of heterosexual marriage. The conceptual ambiguity in the idea of transsexual marriage, if mobilized strategically so as to destabilize the coherence and expose the artifice of gender, provides a potentially radical space for broadening and transforming the very meaning of marriage itself. Unfortunately, this was the opposite of what Justice Chan sought to accomplish with his newly invented label. By transsexual marriage, he merely referred to those unions involving gender non-conforming individuals whose interest does not deserve state sanctioning.

In addition to inventing the category of transsexual marriage, Justice Chan bases his dissenting judgment on the queer geopolitical relationality of Hong Kong, a way to unravel the politicity of Hong Kong overshadowed in the majority reasoning. Specifically, he distinguishes Hong Kong from other major nation-states that have advanced the legal interest of transsexuals to marry in their acquired gender. This formulation construes HKSAR as a minor region—minor in the Deleuzian sense. In their decisive characterization of minor literature, Deleuze and Guattari argue that "a minor literature doesn't come from a minor language; it is rather that which a minority constructs within a major language."[127] Similarly, the minor regionalism of Hong Kong is not derived from a minor statist polity per se; it is rather that which a minority constructs within and between major statist polities such as the British empire and the PRC. Hong Kong society, incidentally, continues to be geographically situated in *marginal relations* to the cultural spheres of such major languages as English or Mandarin Chinese.

The queer peripheral realism of Hong Kong is most powerfully articulated in Justice Chan's explanation for why he refuses to follow the logic of international human rights rulings.[128] All other members of the judgment team agreed with W's legal representative that an increasing trend of tolerance in international jurisprudence has been evident of late: Australia, New Zealand, Singapore, Canada, parts of the United States, and, above all, the United Kingdom in the aftermath of *Goodwin*. Justice Chan responded by dismissing these discerning references: "With respect, I would approach these authorities and legislative changes with caution since the social conditions in different countries are obviously not the same."[129] On the question of applying the principles behind these changes from abroad to Hong Kong, he continued:

> While the situations overseas are clearly relevant and must be taken into account in the interpretation of art 37, one must bear in mind that the culture and social conditions in each place are not the same. For the purpose of the interpretation and application of the Basic Law, I think the principal consideration must be the circumstances in Hong Kong, just as the ECHR was more concerned with the situations among its member states.
>
> In my view, the present position in Hong Kong is quite different from that in Europe and the UK when *Goodwin* was decided. While there was evidence of the changing attitudes in both Europe and the UK, I do not think there is sufficient evidence to show that the circumstances in Hong Kong are such as to justify the Court giving an interpretation to art 37 to include transsexual men and women for the purpose of marriage. As pointed out earlier, there is no evidence showing that for the purpose of marriage, the ordinary meanings of man and woman in Hong Kong have changed to accommodate a transsexual man and woman. More importantly, there is no evidence that the social attitudes in Hong Kong towards the traditional concept of marriage and the marriage institution have fundamentally

altered. Nor is there evidence on the degree of social acceptance of transsexualism.[130]

Whereas the other judges stressed the need for Hong Kong to be made legislatively similar to overseas nation-states, Justice Chan precisely used Hong Kong's difference to back transphobic assumptions about the virtue of holding on to enduring vestiges of social discrimination. Similar to what the category of transsexual marriage could have done for the subversion of gender norms, the queer/minor regionalism of Hong Kong could have been productively mobilized to contest the critical operation of the West—or China for that matter—as a source of imperial citationality.[131] But instead, Justice Chan's delineation turned this recognition into a mere arbiter of difference for displacing the privileged status of global superpowers as a pedagogical model. The vision of Hong Kong nativism expressed in his judgment ends up reinforcing the widespread disapproval of transsexuality in Hong Kong society.

Comparative Creolization

China's image in mainstream Western discourses often withstands an oxymoronic depiction: as a growing yet threatening international superpower on the one hand, and as the antithesis of human rights on the other.[132] The burden of this entrenched binarism has been felt most intimately by disenfranchised groups, including lesbians, gay men, bisexuals, trans-identified individuals, and queers, especially those living in geographies sandwiched between China and the West. Critics frequently bring up Taiwan as a reference point for making lateral comparisons with Hong Kong, especially in light of their shared resistance to Beijing political hegemony.[133] Both regions embody what Gayatri Spivak calls "the postcoloniality in the space of difference, *in decolonized terrain.*"[134] Yet if this postcoloniality conventionally refers to the legacy of Japanese colonialism or British imperialism, it is high time to introduce the PRC into our conceptual resystematization. Using Taiwan as a case study, literary scholar Petrus Liu has argued against the popular perception of Taiwan as epitomizing a more progressive sexual politics than mainland China.[135] Although Liu is correct to note that the movement behind the legalization of same-sex marriage in Taiwan "reveals the complexity of the discourse of queer human rights when it is compounded with the 'China question,'" his work fails to intervene at the conjuncture where transgender and gay rights intersect so as to overcome a homonormative framing of queerness.[136]

By situating the Sinophone creolization of transgender in a comparative framework, this chapter has focalized queer citizenship contest to overcome a flattened assertion about the Taiwan-China comparison. It is important to consider the postmillennial queering of *tongzhi* as a Sinophone—not just Chinese or Taiwanese—reconfiguration for at least two reasons. First, the eventual connectivity between Western *transgender* and Taiwanese *tongzhi* depended on a locally urgent, widely publicized episode: the Yeh Yung-chih incident. This syncretism must be understood as a form of creolization because the way that transgender activism gained a foothold in Taiwan was at once a postidentitarian phenomenon (e.g., Yeh never identified as transgender) and born out of historical contingency (e.g., the unforeseen convergence of the feminist and *tongzhi* movements in the early 2000s). The political landscape of post-KMT hegemony Taiwan witnessed the radicalizing potential of transgender activism to overturn the status quo; in this sense, the path toward a greater advocacy of gender nonconformity was *not* merely circumscribed by the opposing tensions between the cultural particularism of Taiwanese nativism and the universal imperialism of "Western" transgenderism. That is, with the Yeh incident serving as a catalyst, the legislative decision to move away from "sex equality" and endorse "gender equity" did not amount to a simple critique of the imposition of Western transgender identities. On the contrary, the Act and its renaming are best understood as developing alongside and contributing to a blossoming worldwide awareness to legitimate, protect, and sanction the nonpredetermined and the diversification of gender formations.[137] It is perhaps more accurate to conceive of the legislation as a broader step toward the protection of transtopian, rather than purely transgender, rights.

Second, the creolization of transgender in Taiwan has been further made possible by a Sinophone definition of *ku'er* that from the start disavowed any strict loyalty to Western conceptions of queer.[138] This established the basis for the Sinophone revamping of *tongzhi* to formalize the epistemic overlap between transness and queerness in extra-Chinese, nonsocialist settings in the twenty-first century. On the one hand, the trajectory from the Yeh incident to the Gender Equity Education Act and the first Sinophone LGBT pride puts Taiwan ahead of many countries in the area of gender and sexual rights activism. The global significance has been evinced by the fact that Taiwan became the twenty-ninth state in the world, and the first in Asia, to legalize same-sex marriage in May 2019. On the other hand, the conceptual expansion of *tongzhi* came to denote the most radical meaning of queerness both through the incorporation of the "T" (and "B") and by contrasting itself against the heteronormative circulation of "comrade" in socialist China. The enduring plurality of Sinophone queering makes it unambiguous *why* and *how* the Taiwanese subversion of *tongzhi* constitutes a multidirectional form of resistance.

One final example will suffice to bring home the comparative creolization of transgender politics. In the midst of W's victory, the union between two self-identified genderqueers, Wu Yi-ting (吳伊婷) and Wu Zhi-yi (吳芷儀), generated a media storm in Taiwan. Their case provides a useful window into understanding the state response to the *mutual constructions of gender and sexuality* as codified through the legislation of marriage in Sinophone communities.[139] Both born male, Wu and Wu successfully applied for a marriage license in 2012 after one of them, Yi-ting, received MTF reassignment. The operation ensured that their union was heterosexual by definition in congruence with their opposite legal gender status. However, later when Zhi-yi also underwent full gender transition, they received a letter from the MOI requesting them to de-register their marriage. Facing immense pressure from experts and activists, the MOI decided in August 2013 to allow Yi-ting and Zhi-yi to retain their marriage certificate. The MOI justified the legality of their marriage by defining it as a union between a man and a woman *at the time of registration*. In the same year, Yi-ting officially founded the Intersex, Transgender and Transsexual People Care Association (ITTPCA).[140] The ITTPCA has campaigned vociferously for the removal of a surgical requirement in the change of legal gender status. On this subject, the association clashed head on with the long-standing TG Butterfly Garden (TG 蝶園, *Dieyuan*), founded by Josephine Ho in 2000.[141]

The Wu-Wu case also prepared the historical context for a watershed event taking place two months later in October 2013, when the Marriage Equality Bill (婚姻平權草案, *hunyin pingquan cao'an*) gained sufficient support and signatures and was successfully delivered to the Legislative Yuan of the Republic of China for consideration. Many have lauded this landmark petition delivery for making possible the eventual legalization of gay marriage in Taiwan.[142] Evidently, the issue of transgender marriage rights and that of same-sex marriage rights have been intertwined in state logic from the start. This entanglement led the MOI, for instance, to try to retrieve the certification of the Wu-Wu union in order to preserve a heterosexualized coherence of the marriage institution in Taiwan. Above all, what this example reveals is a broader transnational context in which Sinophone communities such as Hong Kong and Taiwan articulate a vision of sexual politics that is grounded in both a demand of pluralist recognition and a shared legal "difference/distance" from mainland China. In effect, the geopolitics of sexuality in the Sinophone world complicates the superpower vs. antihuman rights polarizing image of "Chinese" culture within prevailing Western discourses.[143]

The *W v Registrar of Marriages* case represents another iteration where the adhesion of such projected dualism collapses. The court decision of 2013, heralded as an important milestone in LGBT rights, highlights the ways in which queer agendas and the unique political position of Hong Kong are articulated in and through each other. By borrowing European jurisprudence history as a pretext, the legal reasoning behind the *W* judgment provincializes China from the strategic geopolitical standpoint of Hong Kong.[144] Since the mainland government had already granted transsexuals the right to marry in their posttransition gender nearly a decade prior, such a legible right seems to have come rather late and far behind in Hong Kong even as the *W* ruling maintains European legal frameworks as useful models to emulate. However, it is worth pointing out that there are perilous side effects to the approach adopted by the PRC government, as outlined in the document "Sex Change Operation Technical Management Standard" (变性手术技术管理规范, *bianxing shoushu jishu guanli guifan*).[145] For example, Chinese citizens who wish to undergo gender-affirming surgery are required to procure the full support, approval, and signatures of their parents. This requirement of parental consent violates the international standard of self-determination as the guiding factor of policy making.[146] Moreover, even though an individual can change a gender marker on identification documents (the earliest one can undergo surgery is at the age of twenty), this cannot be applied retroactively to such crucial records as an education diploma.[147]

Returning to *W*, precisely due to the postcolonial historicity of Hong Kong (interceded between the waning British empire and the expanding

PRC hegemony), the judges' recommendation to endorse the GRA approach in future legal attributions of gender identity aims to keep separate the issue of transgender marriage rights from that of same-sex marriage rights, which is still nonexistent in the PRC (and Asia more broadly). The *W* judgment brings into effect what I have called a transtopian asymptote—deepening an unresolved limit where gender and sexual transgressions approach each other but do not meet—and makes it a risky target for Hong Kong's antidiscriminatory political culture. Whereas the creolization of transgender in Taiwan underwent a politics of redistribution to achieve the integration of "T" into *tongzhi* emancipation, the creolization of transgender in Hong Kong leveraged a particular affirmative legal stance at the expense of further distancing the "T" from the rest of queer citizenship.

This book has aimed to surpass a fixation on standardizing narratives of transitioning or transness. In light of the way trans thematization has revamped queer theory in the last two decades, it is all the more urgent to consider "transgender" as a discursively embedded category that indexes interposing forms of oppression, be they subjective, geopolitical, or otherwise. As this chapter has shown, a neat conceptual separation of gender from sexuality not only is impractical, but easily reproduces the biopolitical apparatus of the heteronormative state that deliberately distinguishes transgender from gay and lesbian political aspirations.[148] This further exacerbates the subtle but far-reaching ways in which homophobia and transphobia conceal—and congeal—each other, as well as the fragility of certain geopolitical bodies lingering as derivatives or afterthoughts under the threatening shadow of contending global superpowers. If queer studies has evolved from an explicit antihomophobic inquiry into a concomitant antitransphobic critique, one can no longer ignore the "politics of the governed . . . in most of the world."[149] Minor transnational regions such as Taiwan and Hong Kong can operate as ontological sites for voicing diverging legal opinions about privacy interest and social membership, all the while providing a powerful ground on which unpredictable forms of queer citizenry, antisocial or not, acquire valence throughout the Sinophone world.[150] Echoing the recalcitrant effects of creolization, transtopia's refusal to authenticate a singular template of queerness secures the state of gender as being akin to a more equitable, and habitable, global ecosystem.

Conclusion

An Antidote Approach

This book has developed a new paradigm for doing transgender history in which geopolitics assumes central importance. Transtopia can be conceived as an antidote approach. Socially, it counters transphobia in all of its varieties; pragmatically, transtopia licenses a solution to many of the ongoing problems besieging the field of transgender studies. These problems have led some critics to claim that "trans studies is over." This statement appeared in a dialogue on "After Trans Studies" between two gender critics, Andrea Long Chu and Emmett Harsin Drager, in 2019. Pronouncing the death of trans studies, Chu explains, "Thus far, trans studies has largely failed to establish a robust, compelling set of theories, methods, and concepts that would distinguish itself from gender studies or queer studies."[1] In response, Drager endorses some of the spirit: "Trans studies is not over, but it does need to learn to stand on its own, not as an addendum or a hyphen or an asterisk to something else."[2] Both interlocutors call attention to a "narrative problem" that trans studies has inherited from queer studies.[3] On the one hand, they argue that trans theory has failed to materialize fully, because trans studies lacks a core theoretical-methodological canon that separates its goal from the tenor of gender and queer analysis. On the other hand, in labeling trans scholarship as "junk DNA," they are "politically optimistic" about the attachment scholars maintain to trans studies.[4] That is, such attachment, if independently and successfully erected, carries the potential of breathing life into the dead.

This book presents transtopia as a vibrant theoretical vocabulary with which transgender studies can readily distinguish itself. The concept designates both a mode of being in the world (ontology) and a way of reorienting the existing structures of knowledge (epistemology). By setting transgender as its specific object of analysis, transtopian studies surpasses an analytical fulcrum that continues to circle back to the question of binary gender expressions, even if only to undermine it. Switching from gender to transgender continuum as its cardinal principle, transtopia renders transness as something that bears a universal affinity to all of us. As such, it is high time to denaturalize the transgender–cisgender divide. I consider this an especially urgent move, because the sequential effect embedded in this very binary structure conceals more than what it reveals. Etymologically, "cisgender" is a neologism developed *after* "transgender" has acquired widespread currency, but the incitement of "cisgender" captures a hegemonic structure that *precedes* the circulation of "transgender." This disclosure of the norm-as-novelty inflicts epistemic harm by occluding transphobia in the legibility—and thus normativity—of a preexisting form of oppression disguised as a new lexical negation. Throughout human history, conventions and scripts of gender shift across time and space. One's cisgenderness may very well turn into transgenderness in a different historical or cultural context. Similarly, most of us inhabit gender embodiment that at one point or another cuts across the dichotomy of cis- and trans-gender. So upholding the notion of cisgenderism as a given state of being undermines the principle of inclusion, diversity, and difference. Transtopia imagines a universe in which transgender is not the exception but the norm by which all embodied subjects can be calibrated and understood.

By replacing the cisgender-transgender binary with a definition of transtopia as the antidote to transphobia, this book maintains the difference between transness and queerness as a generative ground for contesting the status quo. Transphobia, like homophobia, has critically shaped the historical and structural development of human culture. In the last century, the borders of gender and sexual injustice have intersected with the vicissitudes of *renyao*, castrated subjects, and those outlaws whose lives pushed the boundaries of medicine, law, culture, and social acceptance. Updating Eve Kosofky Sedgwick's thesis, then, virtually any aspect of human culture must be not merely incomplete, but damaged in its central substance to the degree that it does not incorporate a conjunctural analysis of transphobia and homophobia.[5]

This is precisely what the antidote approach of transtopia remedies. One the one hand, many of the protagonists whose stories are told in the preceding chapters have for a long time been viewed by critics as "gay" or "lesbian" subjects par excellence: Alice Mitchell, Mahin Madidarnazar, Tao Sijin, Zeng Qiuhuang, Chen Dieyi, and René Gallimard, to name just a few. This book recasts their experience in a new transgender light, thereby drawing attention to the conceptual slipperiness between queer and trans. On the other hand, stories such as that of Yeh Yung-chih and W caution against an impervious distinction between queer and trans interest in the quest for social citizenry. The absolute distillation of gender from sexuality easily reinstates the heteronormative and gender-coercive apparatus of the biopolitical state.[6] What these two motifs share is the way transtopia transforms the productive tensions between queerness and transness into a style of conceptual precision. Chu and Drager are correct in noting the similarity in the analytical work performed by the categories of "queer" and "trans." This study has attempted to dissolve this alleged crisis of equivalence by mobilizing the two terms' resonances and contradictions in order to restore both into a shared basis of political and theoretical action. As a counterpart to queering, transtopian thinking destabilizes the coherence of *both* gay/lesbian and transgender subjectivities.

To render transgender incoherent does not mean incapacitating the task of writing transgender history. Quite the contrary. Transtopia responds to the growing need—indeed, a long-standing calling—for a different type of history. "Global queering" has alerted us to the peril of subsuming the diversity of gender and sexual expressions under the cohesion of modern Western categories.[7] Settler colonial studies has similarly challenged the integrity of these categories from the viewpoint of the oppressed *within* the West.[8] Transtopia charts a terrain not as an alternative to but as an entrée into a commensurate dialogue with transgender taxonomic practice. This book shows that there is not one stable point of origin in trans history; transness has always (already) been produced from multiple geographical and temporal sites. Any inquiry into the history of transgender experience in a single region needs to account for the coeval development of transness elsewhere. Chapter 1 made this point unambiguously in regard to the historical import of sex change surgery: Jorgensen's global narrative was shaped by as much as it impacted the experience of Nagai in Japan, Xie in Taiwan, and Olmos in Mexico. By conceptualizing transgender expressions and politics on the basis of a continuum model, transtopia makes for a more potent coalitional solidarity. This sits in stark contrast to a discrete minoritarian or essentialist model, which immensely restricts the terms and scope of recognition. By placing the diverse cast of queer subjects in this book on a spectrum, a transtopian hermeneutics refuses to single out any one of their experiences as the privileged ground on which claims of social, civic, and political justice should be laid.

As a postidentitarian approach to historical inquiry, transtopia brings to the fore the ethical predicaments of academic knowledge production. One of my chief concerns has been to refute a static conception of spatial difference and, in so doing, to address the limits of certain ongoing debates in transnational sexuality studies, particularly the debate between proponents of the "Global Gays" and opponents of the "Gay International."[9] Navigating the ethical dilemma of such a debate requires that we bear in mind two variables at once: (1) *the limits of nativism*, by which I mean the assumed guarantee of "native informants" as subjects providing material that is never falsifiable or data elevated to a status that allegedly trumps any external bias; and (2) *the agency of mobile subjects*, which comprise individuals who have the capacity to claim mobility or have access to the way knowledge circulates, traffics, and connects across rigidly policed geographical borders.[10] With these two variables in sight, a postidentitarian approach also brings to life a post–area studies mode of critical intervention (that is, post–American studies, post–Asian studies, and so on). As we saw in chapter 2, it is not only possible but imperative to *treat routes as roots*, to deconstruct both "China" and "the West" simultaneously as the sole alibi for serious discussion, the only perpetrator of cultural imperialism, or the mere object of praise or blame.[11] Even though subjects whose interest the Gay International claims to protect may be vulnerable to the effects of Western cultural imperialism, it is not viable—and, indeed, I would argue, *un*ethical—when such an argument expands into a claim about an a priori lack of queer historical depth in any region, Western or not.[12] The Sinophone Pacific provides an acutely charged political and cultural climate for the recalibration of this debate, with transness serving as a key frame of reference. To trouble transgender is to also dismantle the geographical fetishism that has come to characterize transnational queer studies and academic research at large.

Even though the focus on gender variability might seem narrow, this study has sought to enrich a broader set of conversations in the theory of history.[13] As a new historiographical intervention, transtopia represents a standpoint epistemology: it debunks cisgenderism, relates transness to queerness, and posits a nonhierarchical paradigm of embodied personhood. Yet for this paradigm to work in historical analysis, transtopia also denotes a set of distinct practices. The second part of this book, in particular, brought these practices into action: the approaches of titrating, inscribing, and creolizing the category of transgender. Chapter 3 showed how the queer concept of *renyao* came to acquire a modernized intelligibility of transness, titrated from its earlier dehumanized historicity, as it moved across temporal and geopolitical borders—from late imperial China to postcolonial Taiwan. Chapter 4 traced the specter of gender liminality in the inscriptive visualization of castrated bodies, a transcultural signifier reincarnated from dynastic China and transposed onto the screen of Sinophone cinema. Chapter 5 tracked the creolization of transgender as a basis of political movement whose traction and purchase bifurcated across the Taiwan-Hong Kong activist world.

The indeterminacy of transness—the mainstay of this book—is continually motivated by the question of what counts as human or inhuman, the interreferentiality between Chinese corporeality and Sinophone embodiment, and the contest over sovereignty and social citizenry. Through these motors of debate and change, the young field of trans history provides imaginative tools to enhance the devices we use to construct persuasive accounts of the past, that is, the rhetoric of history. The methods of titration, inscription, and creolization allow us to deconstruct the doctrines of linearity, essentialism, and uniformity—elements so familiar to a mode of emplotment in which human, not just queer, history is reduced time and again to a story of progression, liberation, and even redemption. The threshold of recognition and the politics of visibility must never be treated as stable or unchanging over time, for they mutually syncopate as a variable of context. Always more than an act of recuperation, history creates the unforeseen opportunities in which the meaning of the past becomes legible, authorized, and enlivened.

Abbreviations

EFC	Edythe Ferguson Collection, KI
HBC	Harry Benjamin Collection, KI
HN	*Huanian* 華年 [Chinese maturity]
IJS	*International Journal of Sexology*
KI	The Kinsey Institute for Research in Sex, Gender, and Reproduction, Indiana University, Bloomington
LHB	*Lianhebao* 聯合報 [United daily news]
LLC	Louise Lawrence Collection, KI
MHC	Magnus Hirschfeld Collection, KI
MSRB	*Minsheng ribao* 民聲日報 [People's voice daily]
SMA	Shanghai Municipal Archive
SMYJK	*Shengming yu jiankang* 生命與健康 [Life and health]
TSYLM	Current News Agency 時事新聞社. 1932. *Tao Sijin yu Liu Mengying* 陶思瑾與劉夢瑩 [Tao Sijin and Liu Mengying]. Hangzhou: Shishi xinwenshe.
VPC	Virginia Prince Collection, Oviatt Library, California State University at Northridge
WXZB	*Wenxue zhoubao* 文學週報 [Literary weekly]
XSH	*Xin Shanghai* 新上海 [New Shanghai]
YMS	Chien-ling Su 蘇芊玲 and Jau-jiun Hsiao 蕭紹君, eds. 2006. *Yongbao meigui shaonian* 擁抱玫瑰少年 [Embrace the rose lad]. Taipei: Fembooks.
ZGSB	*Zhongguo shibao* 中國時報 [China times]
ZJWX	*Zhuanji wenxue* 傳記文學 [Biography literature]
ZLWB	*Zili wanbao* 自立晚報 [Evening independent]

Notes

Introduction

1. "QHC19" is the official acronym for the Queer History Conference, the first conference that the Committee on Lesbian, Gay, Bisexual, and Transgender (LGBT) History organized in the forty years of its existence. An official affiliate of the American Historical Association, the Committee was founded in 1979 to promote the historical study of homosexuality. It subsequently changed its name in 2009 to reflect the inclusion of bisexual and transgender history. On the basis of its nomenclature alone, the Committee welcomes the study of queer history in any region and time period. For a formal report on QHC19, see Julio Capó and Emily K. Hobson, "Co-Chairs' Column," *Committee on Lesbian, Gay, Bisexual, and Transgender History Newsletter* 33, no. 2 (2019): 1–4.

2. The Committee on LGBT History's goal to be inclusive of all regional and temporal focus was in some ways reflected in the QHC19 program. As is often the case with fields animated by minority politics in the United States (a parallel example is race and ethnic studies), however, the constituency of the Committee—and the presentations at QHC19—have largely focused their scholarly energy on the Euro-American experience. As a member of the conference program committee and the society's governing board, I organized and chaired the only panel on queer Asian history—out of a total of forty-one formal sessions. On the history of ethnic studies, see, for example, Rudolfo Acuna, *Occupied America*, 3rd ed. (New York: Harper and Row, 1988); Glenn Omatsu, ed., "Salute to the 60s and 70s: Legacy of the San Francisco State Strike," special issue, *Amerasia Journal* 15, no. 1 (1989): i–352; Darlene Clark Hine, "The Black Studies Movement: Afrocentric-Traditionalist-Feminist Paradigms for the Next Stage," *Black Scholar* 22 (Summer 1992): 11–18; and Evelyn Hu-DeHart, "The History, Development, and Future of Ethnic Studies," *Phi Delta Kappan* 75, no. 1 (1993): 50–54. Although scholars of East Asia have

begun to treat race and racism as the foci of historical analysis, this has yet to develop into a coherent and systematic program. See, for example, Frank Dikötter, *The Discourse of Race in Modern China* (Stanford: Stanford University Press, 1992); Frank Dikötter, ed., *The Construction of Racial Identities in China and Japan* (Honolulu: University of Hawaii Press, 1998); Rotem Kowner and Walter Demel, eds., *Race and Racism in Modern East Asia: Western and Eastern Constructions* (Leiden: Brill, 2012); and Rotem Kowner and Walter Demel, eds., *Race and Racism in Modern East Asia: Interactions, Nationalism, Gender and Lineage* (Leiden: Brill, 2015).

3. On September 4, 2019, the Hong Kong Special Administrative Region chief executive Carrie Lam announced that she would formally withdraw the bill in October and introduce additional measures to calm the situation. On October 23, the secretary for security, John Lee, officially withdrew the bill. The protests came to be overshadowed by the global response to the coronavirus (COVID-19) outbreak in early 2020.

4. Roda Mushkat, *One Country, Two International Legal Personalities: The Case of Hong Kong* (Hong Kong: Hong Kong University Press, 1997); Yash P. Ghai, *Hong Kong's New Constitutional Order: The Resumption of Chinese Sovereignty and the Basic Law* (Hong Kong: Hong Kong University Press, 1999). On the historical roots of the democracy movement in Hong Kong, see also the essays in Ming K. Chan, ed., *The Challenge of Hong Kong's Reintegration with China* (Hong Kong: Hong Kong University Press, 1997).

5. Susan Stryker, "Stonewall in the Middle: Reperiodizing Queer History" (keynote presented at the 2019 Queer History Conference, San Francisco, California, June 17, 2019).

6. E. P. Thompson, *The Making of the English Working Class* (London: Victor Gollancz, 1963). This comment implies a shift in perspective from critiquing capitalism and material deprivation to focusing on moral and social desolation. On the history of this latter intellectual trend, see Tim Rogan, *The Moral Economists: R. H. Tawney, Karl Polanyi, E. P. Thompson, and the Critique of Capitalism* (Princeton: Princeton University Press, 2017).

7. Amnesty International, "Verified: Hong Kong Police Violence Against Peaceful Protestors," www.amnesty.org/en/latest/news/2019/06/hong-kong-police-violence -verified/.

8. I borrow the notion of planetarity from Gayatri Spivak. See Gayatri Spivak, *Death of a Discipline* (New York: Columbia University Press, 2003). This stands in juxtaposition against the use of the "planet" as a catachresis for establishing the rightful premise of collective responsibility.

9. Howard Chiang, "Gay Marriage in Taiwan and the Struggle for Recognition," *Current History: A Journal of Contemporary World Affairs* 118 (September 2019): 241–243.

10. Heather Love, *Feeling Backward: Loss and the Politics of Queer History* (Cambridge, MA: Harvard University Press, 2007). On the queer politics of shame, see David Halperin and Valerie Traub, eds., *Gay Shame* (Chicago: University of Chicago Press, 2009).

11. The idea of the contact zone comes from Mary Louise Pratt, "Arts of the Contact Zone," *Profession* (1991): 33–40. On the interconnected cultural history of Asia and Asian America, see, for example, David Palumbo-Liu, *Asian/American: Historical Crossings of a Racial Frontier* (Stanford: Stanford University Press, 1999); Jodi Kim, *Ends of Empire: Asian American Critique and Cold War Compositions* (Minneapolis: University of Minnesota Press, 2010); Matthew D. Rothwell, *Transpacific Revolutions: The Chinese Revolution in Latin*

America (London: Routledge, 2012); Chih-ming Wang, *Transpacific Articulations: Student Migration and the Remaking of Asian America* (Honolulu: University of Hawaii Press, 2013); Janet Alison Hoskins and Viet Thanh Nguyen, eds., *Transpacific Studies: Framing an Emerging Field* (Honolulu: University of Hawaii Press, 2014); Richard Jean So, *Transpacific Community: America, China, and the Rise and Fall of a Cultural Network* (New York: Columbia University Press, 2016); Yasuko Takezawa and Gary Y. Okihiro, eds., *Trans-Pacific Japanese American Studies* (Honolulu: University of Hawaii Press, 2016); Lisa Yoneyama, *Cold War Ruins: Transpacific Critiques of American Justice and Japanese War Crimes* (Durham: Duke University Press, 2016); Simeon Man, *Soldiering Through Empire: Race and the Making of the Decolonizing Pacific* (Berkeley: University of California Press, 2018); and Lily Wong, *Transpacific Attachments: Sex Work, Media Networks, and Affective Histories of Chineseness* (New York: Columbia University Press, 2018).

12. Aihwa Ong, *Flexible Citizenship: The Cultural Logics of Transnationality* (Durham: Duke University Press, 1999); Johannes Fabian, *Time and the Other: How Anthropology Makes Its Objects* (New York: Columbia University Press, 1983).

13. Howard Chiang and Ari Larissa Heinrich, eds., *Queer Sinophone Cultures* (London: Routledge, 2013); and Howard Chiang and Alvin K. Wong, eds., *Keywords in Queer Sinophone Studies* (London: Routledge, 2020).

14. For a remarkable ethnography that disrupts the disconnection between LGBTQ politics and dominant civil political discourses through a queering of the Umbrella movement in Hong Kong, see Lucetta Y. L. Kam, "Return, Come Out: Queer Lives in Postcolonial Hong Kong," in *Hong Kong Culture and Society in the New Millennium*, ed. Yiu-Wai Chu (Singapore: Springer, 2017), 165–178.

15. On the insignificance of Hong Kong, see Rey Chow, "Between Colonizers: Hong Kong's Postcolonial Self-Writing in the 1990s," *Diaspora* 2, no. 2 (1992): 151–170, especially on p. 152. On the insignificance of Taiwan, see Shu-mei Shih, "Globalisation and the (In)Significance of Taiwan," *Postcolonial Studies* 6, no. 2 (2003): 143–153.

16. For historical scholarship on queer Asia, see, for example, Bret Hinsch, *Passions of the Cut Sleeve: The Male Homosexual Tradition in China* (Berkeley: University of California Press, 1990); Peter A. Jackson, *Dear Uncle Go: Male Homosexuality in Thailand* (Bangkok: Bua Luang, 1995); Gary Leupp, *Male Colors: The Construction of Homosexuality in Tokugawa Japan* (Berkeley: University of California Press, 1997); Jennifer Robertson, *Takarazuku: Sexual Politics and Popular Culture in Modern Japan* (Berkeley: University of California Press, 1998); Gregory M. Pflugfelder, *Cartographies of Desire: Male-Male Sexuality in Japanese Discourse* (Berkeley: University of California Press, 1999); Matthew Sommer, *Sex, Law, and Society in Late Imperial China* (Stanford: Stanford University Press, 2002); Tze-Lan D. Sang, *The Emerging Lesbian: Female Same-Sex Desire in Modern China* (Chicago: University of Chicago Press, 2003); Tom Boellstorff, *The Gay Archipelago: Sexuality and Nation in Indonesia* (Princeton: Princeton University Press, 2005); Mark McLelland, *Queer Japan from the Pacific War to the Internet Age* (Lanham, MD: Rowman and Littlefield 2005); James Riechert, *In the Company of Men: Representations of Male-Male Sexuality in Meiji Literature* (Stanford: Stanford University Press, 2006); Anjali Arondekar, *For the Record: On Sexuality and the Colonial Archive in India* (Durham: Duke University Press, 2009); Wenqing Kang, *Obsession: Male Same-Sex Relations in China, 1900–1950* (Hong Kong: Hong Kong

University Press, 2009); Michael G. Peletz, *Gender Pluralism: Southeast Asia Since Early Modern Times* (London: Routledge, 2009); Jonathan D. Mackintosh, *Homosexuality and Manliness in Postwar Japan* (London: Routledge, 2010); Fran Martin, *Backward Glances: Contemporary Chinese Cultures and the Female Homoerotic Imaginary* (Durham: Duke University Press, 2010); Hans Tao-Ming Huang, *Queer Politics and Sexual Modernity in Taiwan* (Hong Kong: Hong Kong University Press, 2011); Giovanni Vitiello, *The Libertine's Friend: Homosexuality and Masculinity in Late Imperial China* (Chicago: University of Chicago Press, 2011); Howard Chiang, ed., *Transgender China* (New York: Palgrave Macmillan, 2012); J. Keith Vincent, *Two-Timing Modernity: Homosocial Narrative in Modern Japanese Fiction* (Cambridge, MA: Harvard University Press, 2012); Cuncun Wu, *Homoerotic Sensibilities in Late Imperial China* (London: Routledge, 2012); Howard Chiang, *After Eunuchs: Science, Medicine, and the Transformation of Sex in Modern China* (New York: Columbia University Press, 2018); Jessica Hinchy, *Governing Gender and Sexuality in Colonial India: The Hijra, c. 1850–1900* (Cambridge: Cambridge University Press, 2019); and Todd A. Henry, ed., *Queer Korea* (Durham: Duke University Press, 2020). As a tip of the iceberg, this list excludes many important works in queer Asian studies, such as scholarship rooted in anthropological methods.

17. In a broad sense, transtopia binds the *temporal* designation of change in the *trans-* prefix to the *spatial* projection of difference implicated in the *-topia* suffix. Conceptualizing transtopia as an alternative "place" frozen in or across time does not account for its entire theoretical force; transtopia must also be thought of as an alternative "chronotype" that transcends specific geographic units.

18. Dung Kai-cheung, *Atlas: The Archaeology of an Imagined City*, trans. Dung Kai-cheung, Anders Hansson, and Bonnie S. McDougall (New York: Columbia University Press, 2012), 33.

19. On the history of utopia and dystopia, see, for example, Michael D. Gordin, Helen Tilley, and Gyan Prakash, eds., *Utopia/Dystopia: Conditions of Historical Possibility* (Princeton: Princeton University Press, 2010). On heterotopia, see Michel Foucault, "Of Other Places," in *Heterotopia and the City: Public Space in a Postcivil Society*, ed. Michiel Dehaene and Lieven De Cauter (London: Routledge, 2008), 13–30.

20. Eve Kosofsky Sedgwick, *Epistemology of the Closet* (Berkeley: University of California Press, 1990), 1.

21. On the practice of critical history, see Ethan Kleinberg, Joan Wallach Scott, and Gary Wilder, "Theses on Theory and History" (May 2018), http://theoryrevolt.com/#history.

22. This resounds anthropologist Michael Peletz's utilization of transgenderism as an analytical category in his textured study of Southeast Asia: "transgendered persons provide a powerful lens through which to view pluralism, partly because for this region and period the vicissitudes of transgenderism index processes that have occurred across a number of culturally and analytically interlocked domains. These processes include: the increased formalization and segregation of gender roles; the distancing of women from loci of power and prestige; the narrowed range of legitimacy concerning things intimate, erotic and sexual; and the construction of pluralistic gender sensibilities as a whole, which, in recent times (since the 1980s), has gone hand in hand with a proliferation of diversity and the emergence of new loci of legitimacy." Peletz, *Gender Pluralism*, 5.

23. While some critics might find the divergence from queer studies to be a positive move-ment in trans studies, I will argue throughout this book that the coupling of *queer*, either as an adjective or as a verb, and *trans* ensures a productive way to deconstruct the mutual imbrication of gender and sexuality.

24. Sedgwick, *Epistemology of the Closet*, 22.

25. David Valentine, *Imagine Transgender: An Ethnography of a Category* (Durham: Duke University Press, 2007). For Susan Stryker's response with reference to Chinese transgender stud-ies, see Susan Stryker, "De/Colonizing Transgender Studies of China," in Chiang, *Trans-gender China*, 287–292. My formulation of transtopia takes up Aren Aizura's injunction to "oppose trans epochalism" by "look[ing] for the ways that somatechnic embodiment takes place in the past and in non-modern spaces without posing them as the backward past pre-ceding the postmodern, technologized Global North." Aren Z. Aizura, *Mobile Subjects: Transnational Imaginaries of Gender Reassignment* (Durham: Duke University Press, 2018), 56.

26. See, for example, Clare Sears, *Arresting Dress: Cross-Dressing, Law, and Fascination in Nineteenth-Century San Francisco* (Durham: Duke University Press, 2015); Emily Skidmore, *True Sex: The Lives of Trans Men at the Turn of the Twentieth Century* (New York: New York University Press, 2017); C. Riley Snorton, *Black on Both Sides: A Racial History of Trans Identity* (Minneapolis: University of Minnesota Press, 2017); and Jen Manion, *Female Hus-bands: A Trans History* (Cambridge: Cambridge University Press, 2020).

27. Rey Chow, "Introduction: On Chineseness as a Theoretical Problem," *boundary 2* 25, no. 3 (1998): 1–24, on 4–5.

28. This is a paraphrase of Shu-mei Shih's critique of Chineseness. See Shu-mei Shih, *Visu-ality and Identity: Sinophone Articulations Across the Pacific* (Berkeley: University of Cali-fornia Press, 2007), 26–27.

29. M. W. Bychowski, Howard Chiang, Jack Halberstam, Jacob Lau, Kathleen P. Long, Mar-cia Ochoa, and C. Riley Snorton, "Trans*historicities," *TSQ: Transgender Studies Quar-terly* 5, no. 4 (2018): 658–685, on 660.

30. The scholarship on these non-Western concepts of gender diversity is too vast to be cited adequately here. For representative studies, see, for example, Walter L. Williams, *The Spirit and the Flesh: Sexual Diversity in American Indian Culture* (Boston: Beacon, 1986); Will Roscoe, *The Zuni Man-Woman* (Albuquerque: University of New Mexico Press, 1991); Sue-Ellen Jacobs, Wesley Thomas, and Sabine Lang, *Two Spirit People: Native American Gender Identity, Sexuality, and Spirituality* (Urbana: University of Illinois Press, 1997); Peter A. Jackson, "Gay Adaptation, Tom-Dee Resistance, and Kathoey Indifference: Thai-land's Gender/Sex Minorities and the Episodic Allure of Queer English," in *Speaking in Queer Tongues: Globalization and Gay Language*, ed. William L. Leap and Tom Boellstorff (Urbana: University of Illinois Press, 2004), 202–230; Boellstorff, *The Gay Archipelago*; Gayatri Reddy, *With Respect to Sex: Negotiating Hijra Identity in South India* (Chicago: University of Chicago Press, 2005); Peletz, *Gender Pluralism*; Dredge Kang, "*Kathoey* 'In Trend': Emergent Genderscapes, National Anxieties, and the Re-Signification of Male-Bodied Effeminacy in Thailand," *Asian Studies Review* 36, no. 4 (2012): 475–494; and Alfredo Mirandé, *Behind the Mask: Gender Hybridity in a Zapotec Community* (Tuc-son: University of Arizona Press, 2017). The history of *renyao* is examined in greater depth in chapter 3 of this book.

31. Corporate institutions such as the Human Rights Campaign who sponsor rights-based legislation reform—based on discrete, insular minority status with immutable traits—are some of the most discernible agents that promote the identitarian definitions of transgender.

32. For a set of critical essays on the postidentitarian approach to Chinese transgender studies, see Chiang, *Transgender China*.

33. James L. Hevia, *Cherishing Men from Afar: Qing Guest Ritual and the Macartney Embassy of 1793* (Durham: Duke University Press, 1995), 248.

34. The subversive capability of transtopia resembles other accounts of minoritization articulated through the object instead of the subject of critique (e.g., race or the body). See, for example, Kandice Chuh, *Imagine Otherwise: On Asian Americanist Critique* (Durham: Duke University Press, 2003); Gayle Salamon, *Assuming a Body: Transgender and Rhetorics of Materiality* (New York: Columbia University Press, 2010).

35. On the genealogy of "transversality" in the Atlantic world, see Snorton, *Black on Both Sides*, 9–10. Snorton's book makes a case for the transversality of blackness and transness in the US context. This book extends this conversation into the Pacific fold, using Chineseness as a leading nodal point for deconstructing queer race, language, and nation-ness.

36. Hevia, *Cherishing Men from Afar*, 248.

37. See, for example, Michael Warner, *The Trouble with Normal: Sex, Politics, and the Ethics of Queer Life* (New York: Free Press, 1999); Lisa Duggan, *The Twilight of Equality?: Neoliberalism, Cultural Politics, and the Attack on Democracy* (Boston: Beacon, 2003); and Ryan Conrad, ed., *Against Equality: Queer Revolution, Not Mere Inclusion* (Oakland: AK Press, 2014).

38. Jasbir Puar, *Terrorist Assemblages: Homonationalism in Queer Times* (Durham: Duke University Press, 2007).

39. By *pinkwashing*, I adopt the definition of "a form of discourse, frequently political, in which a government or activist highlights the progressive nature of a country, political party, or organization in order to distract people from, or conceal, other ways in which said country, political party, or organization behaves in an oppressive and/or nonprogressive manner toward other peoples or groups." Jedidiah Anderson, "Pinkwashing," in *Global Encyclopedia of Lesbian, Gay, Bisexual, Transgender, and Queer (LGBTQ) History*, ed. Howard Chiang (Farmington Hills, MI: Charles Scribner's Sons, 2019), 1244–1248, on 1244. For the application of these concepts to various Asian societies, see Jun Zubillaga-Pow, "The Negative Dialectics of Homonationalism, or Singapore English Newspapers and Queer World-Making," in *Queer Singapore: Illiberal Citizenship and Mediated Cultures*, ed. Audrey Yue and Jun Zubillaga-Pow (Hong Kong: Hong Kong University Press, 2012), 149–159; Petrus Liu, *Queer Marxism in Two Chinas* (Durham: Duke University Press, 2015); John Whittier Treat, "The Rise and Fall of Homonationalism in Singapore," *positions: asia critique* 23, no. 2 (2015): 349–365; Michelle M. Lazar, "Homonationalist Discourse as a Politics of Pragmatic Resistance in Singapore's Pink Dot Movement: Towards a Southern Praxis," *Journal of Sociolinguistics* 21, no. 3 (2017): 420–441; Oishik Sircar and Dipika Jain, eds., *New Intimacies, Old Desire: Caw, Culture and Queer Politics in Neoliberal Times* (New Delhi: Zubaan, 2017); Alvin K. Wong, "Queering the Quality of Desire: Perverse Use-Value in Transnational Chinese Cultures," *Culture, Theory and Critique* 58, no. 2 (2017): 209–225; Hongwei Bao, *Queer Comrades: Gay Identity and Tongzhi Activism in Postsocialist*

China (Copenhagen: Nordic Institute of Asian Studies Press, 2018); and Travis S. K. Kong, "Transnational Queer Sociological Analysis of Sexual Identity and Civic-Political Activism in Hong Kong, Taiwan, and Mainland China," *British Journal of Sociology* 70, no. 5 (2019): 1904–1925, on 1914–1915.

40. As cultural anthropologist Chris Tan has remarked, interpreting an event such as Pink Dot in Singapore through the lens of homonationalism "ignores non-capitalist economic practices that co-exist with neoliberal relationship of profit and debt." Chris K. K. Tan, "A 'Great Affective Divide': How Gay Singaporeans Overcome Their Double Burden," *Anthropological Forum: A Journal of Social Anthropology and Comparative Sociology* 26, no. 1 (2016): 17–36, on 29. For a similar critique in the Israel-Palestine context, see Jason Ritchie, "Pinkwashing, Homonationalism, and Israel-Palestine: The Conceits of Queer Theory and the Politics of the Ordinary," *Antipode: A Radical Journal of Geography* 47, no. 3 (2015): 616–634. For critiques of this concept in the Indian context, see Stephen Legg and Srila Roy, "Neoliberalism, Postcolonialism and Hetero-Sovereignties: Emergent Sexual Formations in Contemporary India," *Interventions: International Journal of Postcolonial Studies* 15, no. 4 (2013): 461–473; and Svati P. Shah, "Queering Critiques of Neoliberalism in India: Urbanism and Inequality in the Era of Transnational 'LGBTQ' Rights," *Antipode* 47, no. 3 (2015): 635–651. For Puar's view on the transnational adaptability of the concept, see Jasbir Puar, "Rethinking Homonationalism," *International Journal of Middle Eastern Studies* 45 (2013): 336–339.

41. Susan Stryker, "Transgender History, Homonormativity, and Disciplinarity," *Radical History Review*, no. 100 (2008): 145–157.

42. Margot Canaday, "Thinking Sex in the Transnational Turn: An Introduction," *American Historical Review* 114, no. 5 (2009): 1250–1257. Notable exceptions include Ong, *Flexible Citizenship*; and Françoise Lionnet and Shu-mei Shih, eds., *Minor Transnationalism* (Durham: Duke University Press, 2005).

43. See, for example, Liu, *Queer Marxism in Two Chinas*.

44. The refusal to neatly segregate transness from queerness echoes Valerie Traub's defense of opaqueness in the practice of queer historicism. See Valerie Traub, *Thinking Sex with the Early Moderns* (Philadelphia: University of Pennsylvania Press, 2015).

45. Shih, *Visuality and Identity*, 4.

46. The concept of *différance* was coined by Jacques Derrida. See Derrida, *Writing and Difference*, trans. A. Bass (London: Routledge, 1978), 75.

47. Although the "Sinophone Pacific" encompasses a wide geographical reach, this book mainly focuses on queer and trans examples in Taiwan, Hong Kong, and Asian America due to the limitation of my expertise. Much more work needs to be done to explore other sites across the Pacific, including, most notably, Southeast Asia. As Shih notes, "the purpose of Sinophone studies is not to construct yet another universal category such as the Chinese diaspora and 'Cultural China' with obligatory relationship to China, but rather to examine how the relationship becomes more and more various and problematic and how it becomes but one of the many relationships that define the Sinophone in the multiangulated and multiaxiological contexts of the local, the global, the national, the transnational, and, above all, the place of settlement and everyday practice." Shih, *Visuality and Identity*, 31.

48. Shu-mei Shih, "On the Conjunctive Method," in Chiang and Heinrich, *Queer Sinophone Cultures*, 223–225.

49. Roger Smith, *Being Human: Historical Knowledge and the Creation of Human Nature* (New York: Columbia University Press, 2007); Howard Chiang, ed., *The Making of the Human Sciences in China: Historical and Conceptual Foundations* (Leiden: Brill, 2019).

50. Shih, *Visuality and Identity*; Jing Tsu, *Sound and Script in Chinese Diaspora* (Cambridge, MA: Harvard University Press, 2010); Jing Tsu and David Der-wei Wang, eds., *Global Chinese Literature: Critical Essays* (Leiden: Brill, 2010); Shu-mei Shih, Chien-hsin Tsai, and Brian Bernards, eds., *Sinophone Studies: A Critical Reader* (New York: Columbia University Press, 2013).

51. A noncontinuum model of transgender expression oftentimes imposes a hierarchy of transness. In fact, it would validate a hierarchy of discrete trans categories. Since the larger trans community has become ever more politicized and divisive, both within and outside academia, my hope is that transtopia can serve as another method of building alliance and solidarity that overcomes those divisions. On the recuperative politics of feminist history, see, for example, Joan W. Scott, *Gender and the Politics of History* (New York: Columbia University Press, 1988); Tani Barlow, *The Question of Women in Chinese Feminism* (Durham: Duke University Press, 2004); and Claire Goldberg Moses, " 'What's in a Name?': On Writing the History of Feminism," *Feminist Studies* 38, no. 3 (2012): 757–779.

52. Hayden V. White, *Metahistory: The Historical Imagination in Nineteenth-Century Europe* (Baltimore: Johns Hopkins University Press, 1973); Hayden V. White, "The Value of Narrativity in the Representation of Reality," *Critical Inquiry* 7, no. 1 (1980): 5–27.

53. On the use of footnotes and citations in the historical profession, see J. H. Hexter, "The Rhetoric of History," *History and Theory* 6, no. 1 (1967): 3–13.

54. Hexter, 11.

55. The classic study that interrogates the notion of linear history from the viewpoint of modern China is Prasenjit Duara, *Rescuing History from the Nation: Questioning Narratives of Modern China* (Chicago: University of Chicago Press, 1995).

56. On the master metaphor of inscription, see Andrea Bachner, *The Mark of Theory: Inscriptive Figures, Poststructuralist Prehistories* (New York: Fordham University Press, 2017).

57. On the Sinophone democracy movements, see Ian Rowen, "Inside Taiwan's Sunflower Movement: Twenty-Four Days in a Student-Occupied Parliament, and the Future of the Region," *Journal of Asian Studies* 74, no. 1 (2015): 5–21; Richard C. Bush, *Hong Kong in the Shadow of China: Living with the Leviathan* (Washington, DC: Brookings Institution Press, 2016); Tsung-gan Kong, *Umbrella: A Political Tale from Hong Kong* (Harrisburg, PA: PEMA Press, 2017); Francis L. F. Lee and Joseph M. Chan, eds., *Media and Protest Logic in the Digital Era: The Umbrella Movement in Hong Kong* (Oxford: Oxford University Press, 2018); and Ming-sho Ho, *Challenging Beijing's Mandate of Heaven: Taiwan's Sunflower Movement and Hong Kong's Umbrella Movement* (Philadelphia: Temple University Press, 2019). For an erudite study of student activism in the May Fourth era, see Fabio Lanza, *Behind the Gate: Inventing Students in Beijing* (New York: Columbia University Press, 2010).

58. Prasenjit Duara, "The Regime of Authenticity: Timelessness, Gender, and National History in Modern China," *History and Theory* 37, no. 3 (1998): 287–308.

59. Karen Barad, *Meeting the Universe Halfway: Quantum Physics and the Entanglement of Matter and Meaning* (Durham: Duke University Press, 2007); Nicole Shukin, *Animal Capital: Rendering Life in Biopolitical Time* (Minneapolis: University of Minnesota Press, 2009); Lydia H. Liu, *The Freudian Robot: Digital Media and the Future of Unconscious* (Chicago: University of Chicago Press, 2011); and Ari Larissa Heinrich, *Chinese Surplus: Biopolitical Aesthetics and the Medically Commodified Body* (Durham: Duke University Press, 2018). One scientist whose work on epistemology and structuralist philosophy has been largely overlooked is eminent developmental psychologist Jean Piaget, who compared Foucault's notion of episteme to Thomas Kuhn's idea of paradigm. See Jean Piaget, *Structuralism* (New York: Harper and Row, 1970). On paradigm, see Thomas Kuhn, *The Structure of Scientific Revolutions* (Chicago: University of Chicago Press, 1962). On episteme, see Michel Foucault, *The Order of Things: An Archaeology of the Human Sciences* (New York: Vintage, 1973).

60. STEM is a term/acronym used to group together the disciplines in science, technology, engineering, and mathematics.

61. Hayden V. White, "The Burden of History," *History and Theory* 5, no. 2 (1966): 111–134. On the "two cultures," see C. P. Snow, *The Two Cultures* (1959; Cambridge: University of Cambridge Press, 2001).

62. White, "The Burden of History," 124 (emphasis in original).

63. Jacques Rancière, *The Names of History: On the Poetics of Knowledge*, trans. Hassan Melehy (Minneapolis: University of Minnesota Press, 1994).

64. On gender performativity, see Judith Butler, *Gender Trouble: Feminism and the Subversion of Identity* (New York: Routledge, 1990).

65. Michel Foucault, "Critical Theory/Intellectual History," in *Critique and Power: Recasting the Foucault/Habermas Debate*, ed. Michael Kelly (Cambridge, MA: MIT Press, 1994), 109–137, on 124. See also Frederic Jameson, *The Prison-House of Language: A Critical Account of Structuralism and Russian Formalism* (Princeton: Princeton University Press, 1972), 101–216; Paul Allen Miller, "The Classical Roots of Poststructuralism: Lacan, Derrida, and Foucault," *International Journal of the Classical Tradition* 5, no. 2 (1998): 204–225; Paul Harrison, "Poststructuralist Theories," in *Approaches to Human Geography*, ed. Stuart Aitken and Gill Valentine (London: Sage, 2006), 122–135; and Paul Allen Miller, *Postmodern Spiritual Practices: The Construction of the Subject and the Reception of Plato in Lacan, Derrida, and Foucault* (Columbus: Ohio State University Press, 2007).

1. Transstopia

1. David Valentine, *Imagining Transgender: An Ethnography of a Category* (Durham: Duke University Press, 2007).

2. For an early attempt to historicize gender variance through the Western framework of transgender, see Leslie Feinberg, *Transgender Warriors: Making History from Joan of Arc to Dennis Rodman* (Boston: Beacon, 1996). For a sexological approach, see Vern L. Bullough and Bonnie Bullough, *Cross Dressing, Sex, and Gender* (Philadelphia: University of Pennsylvania Press, 1993).

3. Genny Beemyn, "A Presence in the Past: A Transgender Historiography," *Journal of Women's History* 25, no. 4 (2013): 113–121; Susan Stryker and Aren Aizura, "Introduction: Transgender Studies 2.0," in *Transgender Studies Reader 2*, ed. Susan Stryker and Aren Aizura (New York: Routledge, 2013), 1–12; and Leah DeVun and Zeb Tortorici, "Trans, Time, and History," *TSQ: Transgender Studies Quarterly* 5, no. 4 (2018): 518–539.

4. On the impact of mathematical structuralism on the social sciences, see Amir D. Aczel, *The Artist and the Mathematician: The Story of Nicolas Bourbaki, the Genius Mathematician Who Never Existed* (New York: Thunder's Mouth, 2006).

5. On this point, I am especially inspired by Laura Doan, *Disturbing Practices: History, Sexuality, and Women's Experience of Modern War* (Chicago: University of Chicago Press, 2013).

6. My notion of strategic structuralism echoes Gayatri Spivak's proposal of "a strategic use of positivist essentialism in a scrupulously visible political interest." See Gayatri Chakravorty Spivak, "Subaltern Studies: Deconstructing Historiography," in *Selected Subaltern Studies*, ed. Ranajit Guha and Gayatri Chakravorty Spivak (New York: Oxford University Press, 1988), 3–32, on 13. Note Spivak has subsequently disavowed the concept altogether. See Gayatri Chakravorty Spivak, *Other Asias* (Malden, MA: Blackwell, 2008), 260. Like Spivak, I am unwilling to return to positivist essentialism, strategic or not.

7. Jack Halberstam, *Trans*: A Quick and Quirky Account of Gender Variability* (Oakland: University of California Press, 2018), 4.

8. Susan Stryker, *Transgender History* (Berkeley: Seal, 2008), 1.

9. Halberstam, *Trans**, 131.

10. Clare Sears, *Arresting Dress: Cross-Dressing, Law, and Fascination in Nineteenth-Century San Francisco* (Durham: Duke University Press, 2015), 9. For a different iteration of "transing" in historical analysis, see Afsaneh Najmabadi, "Transing and Transpassing Across Sex-Gender Walls in Iran," *WSQ: Women's Studies Quarterly* 36, nos. 3–4 (2008): 23–42.

11. Adrienne Rich, "Compulsory Heterosexuality and Lesbian Existence," *Signs: Journal of Women and Culture in Society* 5, no. 4 (1980): 631–660.

12. C. L. Cole and Shannon L. C. Cate, "Compulsory Gender and Transgender Existence: Adrienne Rich's Queer Possibility," *WSQ: Women's Studies Quarterly* 36, nos. 3–4 (2008): 279–287, on 282 (emphasis added).

13. See, for example, Unni Wikan, "Man Becomes Woman: Transsexualism in Oman as a Key to Gender Roles," *Man* 12 (1977): 304–319; Gilbert Herdt, ed., *Third Sex, Third Gender: Beyond Sexual Dimorphism in Culture and History* (New York: Zone, 1993); Will Roscoe, *Changing Ones: Third and Fourth Genders in Native North America* (New York: St. Martin's, 1998); Rosalind C. Morris, "Three Sexes and Four Sexualities: Redressing the Discourses on Gender and Sexuality in Contemporary Thailand," *positions: east asia cultures critique* 2, no. 1 (1994): 15–43; Stephen O. Murray and Will Roscoe, *Islamic Homosexualities: Culture, History, and Literature* (New York: New York University Press, 1997); and Walter Penrose, "Hidden in History: Female Homoeroticism and Women of a 'Third Nature' in the South Asian Past," *Journal of the History of Sexuality* 10, no. 1 (2001): 3–39. For a critique of such an approach in the historiography of gender and sexuality outside the modern West, see Afsaneh Najmabadi, "Mapping Transformations of Sex, Gender, and Sexuality in Modern Iran," *Social Analysis* 49, no. 2 (2005): 54–77; Afsaneh Najmabadi, *Women with Mustaches and Men Without Beards: Gender and Sexual Anxieties of Iranian*

Modernity (Berkeley: University of California Press, 2005); and Afsaneh Najmabadi, "Beyond the Americas: Are Gender and Sexuality Useful Categories of Analysis?," *Journal of Women's History* 18, no. 1 (2006): 11–21.

14. For a sophisticated analysis of the "border wars" in female masculinities between FTMs and lesbian butches, see Judith Halberstam, "Transgender Butch: Butch/FTM Border Wars and the Masculine Continuum," *GLQ: A Journal of Lesbian and Gay Studies* 4, no. 2 (1998): 287–310; and J. Halberstam, "Global Female Masculinities," *Sexualities* 15, nos. 3–4 (2012): 336–354. Similar to Halberstam's refusal "to invest in the notion of some fundamental antagonism between lesbian and FTM subjectivities" ("Transgender Butch," 293), my goal here is to seize the fluidity of the transgender continuum to share political affinity with non-Butch lesbians and non-FTM men as well. The asymptotic approach described in this chapter takes seriously Halberstam's injunction that "studies of transsexuality and of lesbianism must attempt to account for historical moments when the difference between gender deviance and sexual deviance is hard to discern" ("Transgender Butch," 303). In this sense, I prefer a more "slippery and porous" understanding of the border wars over "some notion of territories to be defended" ("Transgender Butch," 304). On the tenuous connection between historical lesbianism and female masculinities, see Judith Halberstam, *Female Masculinity* (Durham: Duke University Press, 1998); Jay Prosser, "'Some Primitive Thing Conceived in a Turbulent Age of Transition': The Transsexual Emerging from *The Well*," in *Palatable Poison: Critical Perspectives on* The Well of Loneliness, ed. Laura Doan and Jay Prosser (New York: Columbia University Press, 2001), 129–144; and Laura Doan, *Fashioning Sapphism: The Origins of a Modern English Lesbian Culture* (New York: Columbia University Press, 2001).

15. One familiar point of convergence from which most histories of female masculinity descend is Radclyffe Hall's novel *Well of Loneliness* (1928), with a particular focus on its protagonist Stephen Gordon. In addition to the work of Halberstam, Prosser, and Doan cited earlier, see, among others, Esther Newton, "The Mythic Mannish Lesbian: Radclyffe Hall and the New Woman," *Signs: Journal of Women in Culture and Society* 9, no. 4 (1984): 557–575.

16. Aczel, *The Artist and the Mathematician.*

17. Georges Canguilhem, *The Normal and the Pathological*, trans. Carolyn R. Fawcett and Robert S. Cohen (New York: Zone, 1991); Michel Foucault, *The Order of Things: An Archaeology of the Human Sciences* (New York: Vintage, 1973); and Michel Foucault, *The History of Sexuality*, vol. 1, *An Introduction*, trans. Robert Hurley (New York: Vintage, 1990); Ian Hacking, *The Social Construction of What?* (Cambridge, MA: Harvard University Press, 1999); Ian Hacking, *Historical Ontology* (Cambridge, MA: Harvard University Press, 2002).

18. I thank Susan Stryker for inspiring me to come to this theoretical summation. On assemblage (note that the original word in French is *agencement*), see Gilles Deleuze and Félix Guattari, *A Thousand Plateaus: Capitalism and Schizophrenia*, trans. Brian Massumi (Minneapolis: University of Minnesota Press, 1987).

19. For a study of how Rich grapples with the tensions between the particular and the universal from the 1980s onward, especially with respect to her increasing engagement in Jewish heritage and identity, see Hannah Edber, "'This Poem Which Is Not Your

Language': Jewishness, Translation, and the Historical Philosophy of Adrienne Rich, 1968–1991" (MA thesis, University of California, Santa Cruz, 2017).

20. Joanne Meyerowitz, *How Sex Changed: A History of Transsexuality in the United States* (Cambridge, MA: Harvard University Press, 2002), 6.

21. Harry Benjamin, *The Transsexual Phenomenon* (New York: Julian, 1966).

22. Alfred C. Kinsey, Wardell B. Pomeroy, and Clyde E. Martin, *Sexual Behavior in the Human Male* (Philadelphia: W. B. Saunders, 1948). Benjamin mapped the Kinsey scale onto Types I–VI of his SOS classification. It is crucial to note that even as he mapped the Kinsey scale onto his SOS taxonomy, Benjamin made it clear that transsexualism and homosexuality should not be confounded: "Is the 'new woman' still a homosexual man? 'Yes,' if pedantry and technicalities prevail. 'No' if reason and common sense are applied and if the respective patient is treated as an individual and not as a rubber stamp." In other words, Benjamin called into question the equating of Kinsey type 6 with SOS type VI. Benjamin, *The Transsexual Phenomenon*, 27. On the Kinsey scale, see, among others, Simon LeVay, *Queer Science: The Use and Abuse of Research Into Homosexuality* (Cambridge, MA: MIT Press, 1996), 47–50; Stephanie H. Kenen, "Who Counts When You're Counting Homosexuals? Hormones and Homosexuality in Mid-Twentieth-Century America," in *Science and Homosexualities*, ed. Vernon A. Rosario (London: Routledge, 1997), 197–218, on 208–209; and Jennifer Terry, *An American Obsession: Science, Medicine, and Homosexuality in Modern Society* (Chicago: University of Chicago Press, 1999), 299–302.

23. Benjamin, *The Transsexual Phenomenon*, 11.

24. Richard von Krafft-Ebing, *Psychopathia Sexualis with Special Reference to Contrary Sexual Instinct: A Medico-Legal Study*, trans. Charles Gilbert Chaddock (Philadelphia: F. A. Davis, 1894), 216; Havelock Ellis, *Studies in the Psychology of Sex*, vol. 7, *Eonism and Other Supplementary Studies* (Philadelphia: F. A. Davis, 1928). Ellis initially proposed the term *sexoaesthetic inversion* to address the affective and emotional sphere of inversion not captured by Hirschfeld's "transvestism." See Havelock Ellis, "Sexo-Aesthetic Inversion," *Alienist and Neurologist* 34, no. 2 (1913): 249–279, on 273. For important discussions of the role of autobiographical accounts in these sexological treatises, see Ivan Crozier, "Havelock Ellis, Eonism and the Patient's Discourse; Or, Writing a Book About Sex," *History of Psychiatry* 11 (2000): 125–154; Harry Oosterhuis, *Stepchildren of Nature: Krafft-Ebing, Psychiatry, and the Making of Sexual Identity* (Chicago: University of Chicago Press, 2000); and Katie Sutton, "Sexological Cases and the Prehistory of Transgender Identity Politics in Interwar Germany," in *Case Studies and the Dissemination of Knowledge*, ed. Joy Damousi, Birgit Lang, and Katie Sutton (London: Routledge, 2015), 85–103.

25. Magnus Hirschfeld, *Transvestites: The Erotic Drive to Cross Dress*, trans. Michael A. Lombardi-Nash (Buffalo, NY: Prometheus, 1991), 219. On the evolution of Hirschfeld's scientific views, see Elena Mancini, *Magnus Hirschfeld and the Quest for Sexual Freedom: A History of the First International Sexual Freedom Movement* (New York: Palgrave Macmillan, 2010), 31–86.

26. George Henry, *Sex Variants: A Study in Homosexual Patterns*, 2 vols. (New York: Paul B. Hoeber, the Medical Book Department of Harper and Brothers, 1941). For sophisticated accounts of the Committee for the Study of Sex Variants led by Henry, see Terry, *An American Obsession*, 178–267; and Henry L. Minton, *Departing from Deviance: A History of*

Homosexual Rights and Emancipatory Science in America (Chicago: University of Chicago Press, 2002).

27. Ernst Laqueur, Elisabeth Dingemanse, P. C. Hart, and S. E. de Jongh, "Female Sex Hormone in Urine of Men," *Klinische Wochenschrift* 6 (1927): 1859; Bernhard Zondek, "Mass Excretion of Oestrogenic Hormone in the Urine of the Stallion," *Nature* 133 (1934): 209–210. For compelling analyses of the history of sex endocrinology, see Nelly Oudshoorn, *Beyond the Natural Body: An Archaeology of Sex Hormones* (London: Routledge, 1994); Adele E. Clarke, *Disciplining Reproduction: Modernity, American Life Sciences, and the Problems of Sex* (Berkeley: University of California Press, 1998); and Chandak Sengoopta, *The Most Secret Quintessence of Life: Sex, Glands, and Hormones, 1850–1950* (Chicago: University of Chicago Press, 2006). On the "Latin circuit" of sex endocrinology, see Chiara Beccalossi, "Italian Sexology, Nicola Pende's Biotypology and Hormone Treatments in the 1920s," *Histoire, médecine et santé* 12 (2017): 73–97; Chiara Beccalossi, "Latin Eugenics and Sexual Knowledge in Italy, Spain, and Argentina: International Networks Across the Atlantic," in *A Global History of Sexual Science, 1880–1960*, ed. Veronika Fuechtner, Douglas E. Haynes, and Ryan M. Jones (Oakland: University of California Press, 2018), 205–329; and Kurt MacMillan, "'Forms So Attenuated That They Merge Into Normality Itself': Alexander Lipschütz, Gregorio Marañón, and Theories of Intersexuality in Chile, Circa 1930," in *A Global History of Sexual Science, 1880–1960*, ed. Veronika Fuechtner, Douglas E. Haynes, and Ryan M. Jones (Oakland: University of California Press, 2018), 330–352.

28. For accounts of the theory of bisexuality in psychoanalytic discourse, see Meyerowitz, *How Sex Changed*, 23–27; Chandak Sengoopta, *Otto Weininger: Sex, Science, and Self in Imperial Vienna* (Chicago: University of Chicago Press, 2000); and Sandor Rado's review of the literature and critique of the concept in "A Critical Examination of the Concept of Bisexuality," *Psychosomatic Medicine* 2, no. 4 (1940): 459–467.

29. Lewis M. Terman and Catharine Cox Miles, *Sex and Personality: Studies in Masculinity and Femininity* (New York: McGraw-Hill, 1936).

30. Ruth Benedict, *Patterns of Culture* (1934; Boston: Houghton Mifflin, 1959); Margaret Mead, *Sex and Temperament in Three Primitive Societies* (New York: Morrow, 1935). For an interpretation of the two books as a dialogue, see Lois W. Banner, "Mannish Women, Passive Men, and Constitutional Types: Margaret Mead's *Sex and Temperament in Three Primitive Societies* as a Response to Ruth Benedict's *Patterns of Culture*," *Signs: Journal of Women in Culture and Society* 28, no. 3 (2003): 833–858.

31. John Money, "Hermaphroditism, Gender, and Precocity in Hyperadrenocorticism," *Bulletin of the Johns Hopkins Hospital* 96 (1955): 253–264, on 254, 258. On the relationship of Money's clinical formulation to the history of the feminist movement and feminist scholarship, see Joanne Meyerowitz, "A History of 'Gender,'" *American Historical Review* 113, no. 5 (2008): 1346–1356, especially on 1353–1356.

32. Kinsey, Pomeroy, and Martin, *Sexual Behavior in the Human Male*; Alfred C. Kinsey, Wardell B. Pomeroy, Clyde E. Martin, and Paul H. Gebhard, *Sexual Behavior in the Human Female* (Philadelphia: W. B. Saunders, 1953).

33. Benjamin, *The Transsexual Phenomenon*, 17.

34. Benjamin, 17.

35. Niels Hoyer, ed., *Man Into Woman: An Authentic Record of a Change of Sex* (New York: E. P. Dutton, 1933). On Hirschfeld's involvement in the Elbe case, see Meyerowitz, *How Sex Changed*, 20–21.

36. K. S. to Magnus Hirschfeld, October 5, 1920, Hirschfeld Scrapbook, p. 72, MHC. To protect the privacy of the individuals who wrote to sexologists, I anonymize all archival correspondences except for those penned by people whose identity is already publicly known.

37. Louise Lawrence acted as an intermediary between the Mattachine Society, one of the earliest homophile organizations in the United States, and these sex researchers. See Louise Lawrence to Alfred C. Kinsey, April 16, 1955, folder 1, box 1, Series IB, LLC. On the history of the Mattachine Society, see John D'Emilio, *Sexual Politics, Sexual Communities: The Making of a Homosexual Minority in the United States, 1940–1970* (Chicago: University of Chicago Press, 1983); and Martin Meeker, *Contacts Desired: Gay and Lesbian Communications and Community, 1940s–1970s* (Chicago: University of Chicago Press, 2005). Louise Lawrence also worked closely with Karl Bowman, the president of the American Psychiatric Association from 1944 to 1946.

38. Joanne Meyerowitz, "Sex Research at the Borders of Gender: Transvestites, Transsexuals, and Alfred C. Kinsey," *Bulletin of the History of Medicine* 75 (2001): 72–90, on 75.

39. Kinsey to Lawrence, October 10, 1949, folder 1, box 1, Series IB, LLC.

40. Kinsey to Lawrence, October 10, 1949, folder 1, box 1, Series IB, LLC.

41. Lawrence to Harry Benjamin, c. December 1949, folder 2, box 1, Series IB, LLC.

42. Lawrence to Benjamin, c. December 1949, folder 2, box 1, Series IB, LLC.

43. Lawrence to Benjamin, May 8, 1950, folder 2, box 1, Series IB, LLC.

44. Joanne Meyerowitz, "Louise Lawrence," in *Encyclopedia of Lesbian, Gay, Bisexual, and Transgender History in America*, ed. Marc Stein (New York: Charles Scribner's Sons, 2004), 151–152.

45. Benjamin to Kinsey, May 19, 1953, Kinsey Era Correspondence, KI.

46. J. A. to Benjamin, January 18, 1956, J. A. folder, box 3, Series IIC, HBC.

47. For an overview of how Benjamin's taxonomy evolved over time, compare Harry Benjamin, "Transvestism and Transsexualism," *IJS* 7, no. 1 (1953): 12–14; Harry Benjamin, "Transsexualism and Transvestism as Psycho-Somatic and Somato-Psychic Syndromes," *American Journal of Psychotherapy* 8, no. 2 (1954): 219–230; Harry Benjamin, "Nature and Management of Transsexualism: With a Report on Thirty-One Operated Cases," *Western Journal of Surgery, Obstetrics and Gynecology* 72 (1964): 105–111; Harry Benjamin, "Transvestism and Transsexualism in the Male and Female," *Journal of Sex Research* 3, no. 2 (1967): 107–127; and Harry Benjamin, "Should Surgery Be Performed on Transsexuals," *American Journal of Psychotherapy* 25, no. 1 (1971): 74–82.

48. See, for example, Benjamin, "Transvestism and Transsexualism," 12.

49. Lawrence to Benjamin, April 24, 1953, folder 2, box 1, Series IB, LLC.

50. Edythe Ferguson (Edward G. Bourke) to D. E. A., September 29, 1954, EFC.

51. Edythe Ferguson, "Transvestic Outlines," unpublished manuscript (1951–55), p. 7, EFC.

52. Benjamin, *The Transsexual Phenomenon*, 24.

53. D. D. B. to Benjamin, August 18, 1972, D. D. B. folder, box 3, Series IIC, HBC (emphasis in original).

54. D. D. B. to Benjamin, August 18, 1972, D. D. B. folder, box 3, Series IIC, HBC (emphasis added).

55. D. D. B. to Benjamin, August 18, 1972, D. D. B. folder, box 3, Series IIC, HBC (emphasis in original).

56. D. D. B. to Benjamin, August 18, 1972, D. D. B. folder, box 3, Series IIC, HBC (emphasis in original).

57. D. D. B. to Benjamin, August 18, 1972, D. D. B. folder, box 3, Series IIC, HBC.

58. For biographies of Kinsey, see Cornelia Christenson, *Kinsey: A Biography* (Bloomington: Indiana University Press, 1971); Wardell Pomeroy, *Dr. Kinsey and the Institute for Sex Research* (New York: Harper and Row, 1972); James H. Jones, *Alfred C. Kinsey: A Public/ Private Life* (New York: Norton, 1997); Jonathan Gathorne-Hardy, *Sex the Measure of All Things: A Life of Alfred C. Kinsey* (London: Chatto and Windus, 1998); Peter Hagarty, *Gentlemen's Disagreement: Alfred Kinsey, Lewis Terman, and the Sexual Politics of Smart Men* (Chicago: University of Chicago Press, 2013); and Donna J. Drucker, *The Classification of Sex: Alfred Kinsey and the Organization of Knowledge* (Pittsburgh: University of Pittsburgh Press, 2014). For biographies of Hirschfeld, see James D. Steakley, *The Homosexual Emancipation Movement in Germany* (New York: Arno, 1975); Charlotte Wolff, *Magnus Hirschfeld: A Portrait of a Pioneer in Sexology* (London: Quartet, 1986); Mancini, *Magnus Hirschfeld and the Quest for Sexual Freedom*; Ralf Dose, *Magnus Hirschfeld: The Origins of the Gay Liberation Movement* (New York: Monthly Review Press, 2014); and Heike Bauer, *The Hirschfeld Archives: Violence, Death, and Modern Queer Culture* (Philadelphia: Temple University Press, 2017).

59. The literature on émigré scientists is too vast to be cited adequately here. See, for example, Pnina G. Abir-Am, "From Multidisciplinary Collaboration to Transnational Objectivity: International Space as Constitutive of Molecular Biology, 1930–1970," in *Denationalizing Science: The Contexts of International Scientific Practice*, ed. E. Crawford, T. Shinn, and S. Sorlin (Dordrecht: Kluwer Academic, 1993), 153–186; Mitchell G. Ash, and Alfons Söllner, eds., *Forced Migration and Scientific Change: German-Speaking Scientists and Scholars After 1933* (Cambridge: Cambridge University Press, 1996); and John Forrester, *Thinking in Cases* (Cambridge: Polity, 2017).

60. Sanjam Ahluwalia, " 'Tyranny of Orgasm': Global Convergence of Sexuality from Bombay, 1930s–1950s," in *A Global History of Sexual Science, 1880–1960*, ed. Veronika Fuechtner, Douglas E. Haynes, and Ryan M. Jones (Oakland: University of California Press, 2018), 353–373.

61. Lawrence published this article under the pseudonym Janet Thompson: Janet Thompson (Louise Lawrence), "Transvestism: An Empirical Study," *IJS* 4, no. 4 (1951): 216–219. On the number of transvestites Lawrence came to know, see Meyerowitz, "Louise Lawrence," 152.

62. Lawrence, "Transvestism," 217.

63. Benjamin, "Transvestism and Transsexualism."

64. The Harry Benjamin Collection at the Kinsey Institute contains a voluminous collection of patient correspondence. From the 1950s on, many adopted Benjamin's terminology from *The Transsexual Phenomenon* in writing to Benjamin.

65. Meyerowitz, *How Sex Changed*, 133.

66. L. L. to Benjamin, March 25, 1968, L. L. folder, box 6, Series IIC, HBC.

67. Harry Benjamin and Charles L. Ihlenfeld, "The Nature and Treatment of Transsexual-ism," *Medical Opinion and Review* 6, no. 11 (1970): 24–35, on 26. Benjamin and Ihlenfeld also mention their use of the SOS scale in their clinical practice in "Transsexualism," *American Journal of Nursing* 73, no. 3 (1973): 457–461.

68. R. B. to Benjamin, April 10, 1967, R. B. folder, box 3, Series IIC, HBC.

69. R. B. to Benjamin, May 14, 1967, R. B. folder, box 3, Series IIC, HBC; R. B. to Ben-jamin, June 9, 1967, R. B. folder, box 3, Series IIC, HBC; R. B. to Benjamin, July 17, 1967, R. B. folder, box 3, Series IIC, HBC; and R. B. to Benjamin, November 11, 1967, R. B. folder, box 3, Series IIC, HBC.

70. Benjamin to R. B., April 25, 1967, R. B. folder, box 3, Series IIC, HBC.

71. J. B. I. to Benjamin, September 4, 1977, J. I. folder, box 5, Series IIC, HBC.

72. L. O. to Benjamin, December 5, 1967, L. O. folder, box 6, Series IIC, HBC.

73. A. J. Q. to Benjamin, January 23, 1970, folder 27, box 25, HBC.

74. Benjamin to A. J. Q., December 28, 1969, folder 27, box 25, HBC.

75. A. J. Q. to Benjamin, January 23, 1970, folder 27, box 25, HBC.

76. A. J. Q. to Benjamin, December 15, 1969, folder 27, box 25, HBC.

77. A. J. Q. to Benjamin, January 23, 1970, folder 27, box 25, HBC.

78. Mitsuhashi Junko 三橋順子, "'Sei tenkan' no shakaishi (1): Nihon ni okeru 'sei tenkan' gainen no keisei to sono jittai, 1950−60 nendai o chūshin ni" '性転換'の社会史 (1)—日本における'性転換'概念の形成とその実態、1950−60年代を中心に [A social history of "sex change" (1): The emergence and reality of the "sex change concept" in Japan, 1950–1960], in *Sengo Nihon josō dōseiai kenkyū* 戦後日本女装・同性愛研究 [Research in postwar Japa-nese transvestism and homosexuality], ed. 矢島正見 Yajima Masami (Tokyo: Chuo Uni-versity Press, 2006), 397–435, on 405.

79. Mark McLelland, *Queer Japan from the Pacific War to the Internet Age* (Lanham, MD: Row-man and Littlefield, 2005), 113.

80. McLelland, 116.

81. L. L. T. to Benjamin, August 25, 1972, L. L. T. folder, box 8, Series IIC, HBC.

82. L. L. T. to Benjamin, August 25, 1972, L. L. T. folder, box 8, Series IIC, HBC.

83. L. L. T. to Benjamin, August 25, 1972, L. L. T. folder, box 8, Series IIC, HBC.

84. On the Erickson Educational Foundation, see Aaron Devor and Nicholas Matte, "Build-ing a Better World for Transpeople: Reed Erickson and the Erickson Educational Foun-dation," *International Journal of Transgenderism* 10, no. 1 (2007): 47–68.

85. F. C. to Benjamin, March 9, 1970, F. C. folder, box 3, Series IIC, HBC. See also W. M. to Benjamin, November 26, 1969, W. M. folder, box 6, Series IIC, HBC.

86. F. L. to Benjamin, April 1, 1967, F. L. folder, box 6, Series IIC, HBC.

87. D. H. to Benjamin, August 4, 1974, D. H. folder, box 5, Series IIC, HBC.

88. M. L. to Benjamin, undated (likely late 1969), M. L. folder, box 6, Series IIC, HBC.

89. R. B. to Benjamin, January 23, 1971, R. B. folder, box 3, Series IIC, HBC; N. B. to Benjamin, December 3, 1974, N. B. folder, box 3, Series IIC, HBC.

90. Benjamin to F. C., April 19, 1970, F. C. folder, box 3, Series IIC, HBC.

91. Benjamin to F. L., April 17, 1967, F. L. folder, box 6, Series IIC, HBC; Benjamin to M. L., January 17, 1969, M. L. Folder, box 6, Series IIC, HBC; Benjamin to R. B., February 3,

1971, R. B. folder, box 3, Series IIC, HBC; Benjamin to N. B., December 27, 1974, N. B. folder, box 3, Series IIC, HBC.

92. M. L. to Benjamin, August 26, 1964, M. L. folder, box 6, Series IIC, HBC.

93. H. L. to Benjamin, June 1, 1965, H. L. folder, box 5, Series IIC, HBC.

94. Benjamin to H. L., June 8, 1965, H. L. folder, box 5, Series IIC, HBC.

95. Benjamin to H. A., June 23, 1967, H. A. folder, box 3, Series IIC, HBC.

96. Benjamin to Jose Jesus Barbosa, March 22, 1969, Jose Jesus Barbosa folder, box 3, Series IIC, HBC.

97. See the essays in Heike Bauer, ed., *Sexology and Translation: Cultural and Scientific Encounters Across the Modern World* (Philadelphia: Temple University Press, 2015); and Veronika Fuechtner, Douglas E. Haynes, and Ryan M. Jones, eds., *A Global History of Sexual Science, 1880–1960* (Oakland: University of California Press, 2018). For a critique of the popular dissemination model, see Laura Doan, "Troubling Popularisation: On the Gendered Circuits of a 'Scientific' Knowledge of Sex," *Gender and History* 31, no. 2 (2019): 1–15.

98. On the historiography of scientific innovation, including critiques of the framework, see, for example, David Edgerton, "From Innovation to Use: Ten Eclectic Theses on the Historiography of Technology," *History and Technology* 16, no. 2 (1999): 111–136; Francesca Bray, "Towards a Critical History of Non-Western Technology," in *China and Historical Capitalism: Genealogies of Sinological Knowledge*, ed. Timothy Brook and Gregory Blu (Cambridge: Cambridge University Press, 2002), 158–209; Sean Hsiang-lin Lei, *Neither Donkey nor Horse: Medicine in the Struggle Over China's Modernity* (Chicago: University of Chicago Press, 2014), 141–166; Dagmar Schäfer and Marcu Popplow, "Technology and Innovation Within Expanding Webs of Exchange," in *The Cambridge World History*, vol. 5, *Expanding Webs of Exchange and Conflict, 500 CE—1500 CE*, ed. Benjamin Z. Kedar (Cambridge: Cambridge University Press, 2015), 309–338; and Benoît Godin, *Models of Innovation: The History of an Idea* (Cambridge, MA: MIT Press, 2017).

99. One could argue that Hirschfeld made a similar case in his formulation of "sexual intermediaries," but Benjamin's "transsexualism" distinguished itself by adding the desire for bodily change as a central domain of gender nonconformity. With respect to the cross-cultural transmission of medical knowledge, Benjamin's name was widely known to psychiatrists and surgeons in the Sinophone world, especially since his name was attached to the Harry Benjamin International Gender Dysphoria Association (now the World Professional Association for Transgender Health) and its product, the Standards of Care for the Health of Transsexual, Transgender, and Gender Nonconforming People (formerly known as the Harry Benjamin Standards of Care). Starting in the 1980s, when Taiwanese psychiatrists such as Jung-Kwang Wen (文榮光) began to treat transsexual patients on a more systematic basis, they tried to come up with their own standards of care that followed the Benjamin protocol but would be more suited for Taiwan. Personal interview with Jung-Kwang Wen on March 20, 2008. On Wen's involvement in Taiwan's transsexual history, see Hsu Su-Ting 徐淑婷, "Bianxingyuzheng huanzhe bianxing shoushu hou de shenxin shehui shiying" 變性慾症患者變性手術後的身心社會適應 [The physical, psychological and social adaptation among transsexuals after sex reassignment surgery: A study of six cases] (MA thesis, Kaohsiung Medical University, 1998).

100. For a historical elucidation of this nexus in the contemporary Iranian context, see Afsaneh Najmabadi, *Professing Selves: Transsexuality and Same-Sex Desire in Contemporary Iran* (Durham: Duke University Press, 2014).

101. Leila J. Rupp, "Toward a Global History of Same-Sex Sexuality," *Journal of the History of Sexuality* 10, no. 2 (2001): 287–302, on 293.

102. Eve Kosofsky Sedgwick, *Epistemology of the Closet* (Berkeley: University of California Press, 1990), 1.

103. Sedgwick, 1–2 (emphasis added).

104. Brad Epps, "Comparison, Competition, and Cross-Dressing: Cross-Cultural Analysis in a Contested World," in *Islamicate Sexualities: Translations Across Temporal Geographies of Desire*, ed. Kathryn Babayan and Afsaneh Najmabadi (Cambridge, MA: Harvard University Press, 2008), 114–160. On the signification of the figure of the murderer in Western history, see Lisa Downing, *The Subject of Murderer: Gender, Exceptionality, and the Modern Killer* (Chicago: University of Chicago Press, 2013).

105. On the Mitchell-Ward case, see Lisa J. Lindquist, "The Images of Alice: Gender, Deviancy, and a Love Murder in Memphis," *Journal of the History of Sexuality* 6, no. 1 (1995): 30–61; and Lisa Duggan, *Sapphic Slashers: Sex, Violence, and American Modernity* (Durham: Duke University Press, 2001). On the Tao-Liu case, see Peter J. Carroll, "'A Problem of Glands and Secretions': Female Criminality, Murder, and Sexuality in Republican China," in *Sexuality in China: Histories of Power and Pleasure*, ed. Howard Chiang (Seattle: University of Washington Press, 2018), 99–124. On the Mahin-Zara case, see Najmabadi, *Professing Selves*, 75–119. The following analysis synthesizes my own primary research and a comparative distillation of these secondary sources.

106. Duggan, *Sapphic Slashers*, 10; *TSYLM*, 65; Najmabadi, *Professing Selves*, 109.

107. Duggan, *Sapphic Slashers*, 48; *TSYLM*, 12; Najmabadi, *Professing Selves*, 98. On the history of the "marriage resistance" movement and a sisterhood of sworn spinsters in late Qing Canton, see Andrea Sankar, "Sisters and Broters, Lovers and Enemies: Marriage Resistance in Southern Kwangtung," *Journal of Homosexuality* 11 (1986): 69–82; Janice E. Stockard, *Daughters of the Canton Delta: Marriage Patterns and Economic Strategies in South China, 1860–1930* (Stanford: Stanford University Press, 1989).

108. Duggan, *Sapphic Slashers*, 69.

109. *TSYLM*, 87.

110. Najmabadi, *Professing Selves*, 107.

111. Najmabadi, 111.

112. Najmabadi, 112.

113. Najmabadi, 78.

114. Najmabadi, 78.

115. Najmabadi, 108.

116. Najmabadi, 114.

117. Najmabadi, 88.

118. Najmabadi, 97.

119. Najmabadi, 113.

120. Duggan, *Sapphic Slashers*, 90.

121. Duggan, 91.

122. For the full text of the hypothetical case, see F. L. Sim, "Alice Mitchell Adjudged Insane," *Memphis Medical Monthly* 12, no. 8 (August 1892): 377–428, on 377–390.

123. Sim, 379.

124. Duggan, *Sapphic Slashers*, 99.

125. Duggan, 92 (emphasis in original).

126. Sim, "Alice Mitchell Adjudged Insane," 379.

127. Duggan, *Sapphic Slashers*, 95.

128. Sim, "Alice Mitchell Adjudged Insane," 380.

129. Sim, 382.

130. Duggan, *Sapphic Slashers*, 48.

131. Duggan, 101.

132. Sim, "Alice Mitchell Adjudged Insane," 409.

133. Duggan, *Sapphic Slashers*, 118.

134. As historian Emily Baum has shown, since its erection in 1908, the Beijing Municipal Asylum increasingly functioned as a physical place to detain the criminally insane—to provide a middle ground "between outright punishment and absolute freedom." Emily Baum, *The Invention of Madness: State, Society, and the Insane in Modern China* (Chicago: University of Chicago Press, 2018), 61. In 1932, the judges presiding over Tao's trial concluded that there was no equipped professional to perform the psychiatric evaluation requested by the defense attorneys. But this merely exemplified a long-standing pattern in the Chinese judicial system. Baum documents one case in as early as 1916 in which the court could not reach a conclusion concerning the sanity of the convicted and the appropriate measures (including whom to turn to) for determining it. See Baum, *The Invention of Madness*, 60. These legal uncertainties were further complicated by the ambiguous wording of the Republican penal code of 1912, according to which "deviant acts committed by the insane should 'not be considered a crime' but that the lunatic should nevertheless be 'incarcerated and penalized' according to the facts of the case." The penal code failed to specify *where* the legally culpable would be incarcerated and *how* he or she would be penalized. Cited in Baum, *The Invention of Madness*, 58. The first national penal code enacted on September 1, 1928, maintained this ambiguous language. According to section 4, article 31, "Those who have lost their minds should not be [legally] punished," but should still be "incarcerated and penalized in according with the details of the crime." This is Baum's translation: see *The Invention of Madness*, 116. It was only when the Nationalist government revised the penal code in 1935, three years after the Tao hearings, that the ambiguity found a clearer resolution. According to Article 87 of the revised code, "Those who have lost their minds should not be punished, but should be sent to an appropriate facility and placed under guardianship." This revision, according to Baum, "purposely relieved the mentally ill of both legal responsibility *and* moral culpability. For the first time since the waning years of the Qing dynasty, the Chinese government had excised the stipulation that mentally ill people be disciplined for their wrongdoings." Moreover, this was the first that the Nationalist government specified "an appropriate facility" where the mentally unsound would be placed under guardianship, as opposed to being locked in a prison or confined in the home. Baum, *The Invention of Madness*, 132 (emphasis in original). For the original text, see "Xin Zhonghua minguo

xingfa" 新中華民國刑法 [New penal code for the Republic of China], *Zhonghua minguo xingfa xinjiu quanwen duizhao biao* 中華民國刑法新舊全文對照表 [Comparison chart of the old and new Republican penal codes] (Beiping: n.p., 1935).

135. *TSYLM*, 91.

136. *TSYLM*, 92.

137. *TSYLM*, 92.

138. *TSYLM*, 93.

139. *TSYLM*, 94.

140. *TSYLM*, 93.

141. *TSYLM*, 94.

142. *TSYLM*, 120. On the association of hysteria with the feminine gender, see Carroll Smith-Rosenberg, "The Hysterical Woman: Sex Roles and Role Conflict in Nineteenth Century America," *Social Research* 39, no. 4 (1972): 652–678; Barbara Ehrenreich and Deirdre English, *Complaints and Disorders: The Sexual Politics of Sickness* (New York: Feminist Press, 1973); Graham Barker-Benefield, *The Horrors of the Half-Known Life: Male Attitudes Toward Woman and Sexuality in Nineteenth Century America* (New York: Harper and Row, 1976); Barbara Ehrenreich and Deirdre English, *For Her Own Good: 150 Years of the Experts' Advice to Women* (New York: Doubleday, 1978); Elaine Showalter, *The Female Malady: Women, Madness, and English Culture, 1830–1980* (New York: Pantheon, 1985); Ornella Moscucci, *The Science of Woman: Gynaecology and Gender in England, 1800–1929* (Cambridge: Cambridge University Press, 1990); Laura Briggs, "The Race of Hysteria: 'Overcivilization' and the 'Savage' Woman in Late Nineteenth-Century Obstetrics and Gynecology," *American Quarterly* 52, no. 2 (2000): 246–273; and Andrew Scull, *Hysteria: The Biography* (Oxford: Oxford University Press, 2009).

143. *TSYLM*, 122–123. On the eclectic symptomatology and highly porous, constantly evolving diagnostic criteria of hysteria in late Victorian–era medicine, see Mark S. Micale, "On the 'Disappearance' of Hysteria: A Study in the Clinical Deconstruction of a Diagnosis," *Isis* 84, no. 3 (1993): 496–529.

144. *TSYLM*, 126–129.

145. *TSYLM*, 128.

146. *TSYLM*, 139.

147. Najmabadi, *Professing Selves*, 89; Lindquist, "The Images of Alice," 43.

148. *TSYLM*, 187.

149. *TSYLM*, 175.

150. Pan Guangdan 潘光旦, "TaoLiu dusha'an de xinli beijin" 陶劉妒殺案的心裡背景 [The psychological background of the Tao-Liu jealousy murder case], *HN* 1, no. 1 (1932): 4–5.

151. Shen Xiaoxiang 沈孝祥, "Tongxing cansha'an Tao Sijin chusixing tantao" 同性慘殺案陶思瑾處死刑探討 [Discussing the death penalty of Tao Sijin in a homosexual murder case], *Shiyejie zhuankan* 實業界專刊 [Industry column] 3 (1932): 17–19.

152. *TSYLM*, 207.

153. Carroll, "'A Problem of Glands and Secretions,'" 120.

154. Najmabadi, *Professing Selves*, 91–94, 97; Duggan, *Sapphic Slashers*, 213–231; *TSYLM*, 16–18, 25–29, 57–59, 75, 129–132.

155. Najmabadi, *Professing Selves*, 100–107.

156. Duggan, *Sapphic Slashers*, 106.

157. Duggan, 104.

158. Gu Yin 顧寅, "Cong TaoLiu dusha shuodao nüzi tongxing'ai he nüxing fanzui yu xingjineng (zhong)" 從陶劉妒殺說到女子同性愛和女性犯罪與性機能 (中) [Speaking of women's criminality and sexual function from the perspective of the Tao Liu jealousy murder (middle)], *Doubao* 斗報 2, no. 10 (1932): 5–7; Gu Yin, "Cong TaoLiu dusha shuodao nüzi tongxing'ai he nüxing fanzui yu xingjineng (xia)" 從陶劉妒殺說到女子同性愛和女性犯罪與性機能 (下) [Speaking of women's criminality and sexual function from the perspective of the Tao Liu jealousy murder (final)], *Doubao* 斗報 2, no. 11 (1932): 3–5; and "Yuejing yu chunü mo: Tao Sijin shengli shang yanjiu" 月經與處女膜：陶思瑾生理上研究 [Menstruation and the hymen: on Tao Sijin's physiology], *Shibao* 時報 [Eastern times], June 9, 1932.

159. Pan, "TaoLiu dusha'an de xinli beijing"; Pan Guangdan, "TaoLiu dusha'an de shehui zeren" 陶劉妒殺案的社會責任 [The social responsibility of the Tao-Liu jealousy murder case], *HN* 1, no. 2 (1932): 25–26; Pan Guangdan, "Zaiti TaoLiu dusha'an" 再提陶劉妒殺案 [Revisiting the Tao-Liu jealousy murder case], *HN* 1, no. 5 (1932): 82–83; Pan Guangdan, "Wudu you'ou de tongxing jiansha'an" 無獨有偶的同性姦殺案 [Not a singular case of homosexual love murder], *HN* 1, no. 11 (1932): 205; Pan Guangdan, "Zailun TaoLiu an de diaocha buzu" 再論陶劉案的調查不足 [Revisiting the insufficient investigation into the Tao-Liu case], *HN* 1, no. 26 (1932): 504–505. On the mental hygiene movement in Republican China, see Geoffrey Blowers and Shelley Wang, "Gone with the *West Wind*: The Emergence and Disappearance of Psychotherapeutic Culture in China (1936–1968)," in *Psychiatry and Chinese History*, ed. Howard Chiang (London: Pickering and Chatto, 2014), 143–160; Wen-Ji Wang, "*West Wind Monthly* and the Popular Mental Hygiene Discourse in Republican China," *Taiwanese Journal for Studies of Science, Technology and Medicine* 13 (2011): 15–88; Emily Baum, "Healthy Minds, Compliant Citizens: The Politics of 'Mental Hygiene' in Republican China, 1938–1937," *Twentieth-Century China* 42, no. 3 (2017): 215–233; Baum, *The Invention of Madness*, 137–158; Jinping Ma, "Remoulding the Chinese Mind: Mental Hygiene Promotion in Republican Shanghai" (PhD diss., University of Warwick, 2019); and Wen-Ji Wang and Hsuan-Ying Huang, "Mental Health," in *The Making of the Human Sciences in China: Historical and Conceptual Foundations*, ed. Howard Chiang (Leiden: Brill, 2019), 460–488.

160. Pan, "TaoLiu dusha'an de shehui zeren," 26; Pan, "Zaiti TaoLiu dusha'an," 83.

161. Najmabadi, *Professing Selves*, 118.

162. Duggan, *Sapphic Slashers*, 25–26, 163, 174.

163. Gu, "Cong TaoLiu dusha shuodao nüzi tongxing'ai he nüxing fanzui yu xingjineng (zhong)."

164. See, for example, Gu Yin, "Xingyu zhi shenghua" 性慾之昇華 [The sublimation of libido], *SMYJK*, no. 38 (1926): 89–92; Gu Yin, "Nüzi de shouyin" 女子的手淫 [Female masturbation], *SMYJK*, no. 42 (1926): 136–138; Gu Yin, "Luozhe biantai xingyu de shehui canju" 絡著變態性慾的社會慘劇 [Social tragedy emanating from perverse sexuality], *SMYJK* 3 (1929): 3, 6–7.

165. Gu, "Cong TaoLiu dusha shuodao nüzi tongxing'ai he nüxing fanzui yu xingjineng (xia)."

166. Duggan, *Sapphic Slashers*, 174.

167. Gu, "Cong TaoLiu dusha shuodao nüzi tongxing'ai he nüxing fanzui yu xingjineng (xia)," 4.

168. Zhi Shui 止水, "Guanyu Tao Sijin Liu Mengying de guangan" 關於陶思瑾劉夢瑩的觀感 [A perspective on Tao Sijin and Liu Mengying], *Doubao* 斗報 2, no. 8 (1932): 7–10. For Carpenter's original views, see Edward Carpenter, *The Intermediate Sex: A Study of Some Transitional Types of Men and Women* (London: Allen and Unwin, 1908). For a Chinese translation of the second chapter on "The Intermediate Sex," see Zheng Sheng 正聲, trans., "Zhongxinglun" 中性論 [The intermediate sex], *Funü zazhi* 婦女雜誌 [Ladies journal] 6, no. 8 (1920): 1–14. For a Chinese translation of the third chapter on "The Homogenic Attachment," see Qiu Yuan 秋原 (possibly Hu Qiuyuan, 胡秋原), trans., "Tongxinglian'ai lun" 同性戀愛論 [On same-sex romantic love], *Xin nüxing* 新女性 [New woman] 4, no. 4 (1929): 513–534; and 4, no. 5 (1929): 605–628.

169. Lillian Faderman and Ann Williams, "Radclyffe Hall and the Lesbian Image," *Conditions* 1, no. 1 (1977): 31–41; Blanche Wiesen Cook, "'Women Alone Stir My Imagination': Lesbianism and the Cultural Tradition," *Signs: Journal of Women in Culture and Society* 4, no. 4 (1979): 718–739; Lillian Faderman, *Surpassing the Love of Men: Romantic Friendship and Love Between Women from the Renaissance to the Present* (New York: William Morrow, 1981), 322–323; Newton, "The Mythic Mannish Lesbian"; and Carroll Smith-Rosenberg, *Disorderly Conduct: Visions of Gender in Victorian America* (New York: Knopf, 1985), 245–296.

170. Najmabadi, *Professing Selves*, 75, 87, 100; Duggan, *Sapphic Slashers*, 178; Tze-lan Sang, *The Emerging Lesbian: Female Same-Sex Desire in Modern China* (Chicago: University of Chicago Press, 2003), 99–126; Gregory M. Pflugfelder, "'S' Is for Sister: Schoolgirl Intimacy and 'Same-Sex Love' in Early Twentieth-Century Japan," in *Gendering Modern Japanese History*, ed. Barbara Molony and Kathleen Uno (Cambridge, MA: Harvard University Asia Center, 2005), 133–190; Fran Martin, *Backward Glances: Contemporary Chinese Cultures and the Female Homoerotic Imaginary* (Durham: Duke University Press, 2010), 29–48; Carroll, "'A Problem of Glands and Secretions'"; and Howard Chiang, *After Eunuchs: Science, Medicine, and the Transformation of Sex in Modern China* (New York: Columbia University Press, 2018), 125–177.

171. "Ex-GI Becomes Blond Beauty," *New York Daily News*, December 1, 1952.

172. Meyerowitz, *How Sex Changed*.

173. Chiang, *After Eunuchs*, 237–281.

174. Ryan M. Jones, "Mexican Sexology and Male Homosexuality: Genealogies and Global Contexts, 1860–1957," in *A Global History of Sexual Science, 1880–1960*, ed. Veronika Fuechtner, Douglas E. Haynes, and Ryan M. Jones (Oakland: University of California Press, 2018), 232–257.

175. For early reports of Xie in Hong Kong, Singapore, and Torreón, see "Guojun shibing Xie Jianshun shoushuhou bian nüren" 國軍士兵謝尖順施手術後變女人 [After operation, the KMT solider Xie Jianshun became a woman], *Kung Sheung Daily News*, August 22, 1953; "Nan biannü de guojun dabing Xie Jianshun guoqu de shenghuo yu shengli biantai" 男變女的國軍大兵謝尖順過去的生活與生理變態 [The life history and physical pathology of the Male-to-Female KMT Soldier Xie Jianshun], *Kung Sheung Daily News*, September 2, 1953; "Dabing bianxing qiankun yiding Xie Jianshun jingshi nü'er shen" 大兵變性乾坤已定謝尖

順竟是女兒身 [The situation of the transsexual soldier is now clear, Xie Jianshun has a female body], *Wah Kiu Yat Po*, September 15, 1955; "Soldier May Become Woman," *Singapore Free Press Straits*, August 22, 1953; and "Soldado Chino Convertido en Mujer," *El Siglo de Torreón*, August 22, 1953. I thank Ryan Jones for bringing the Torreón coverage to my attention. For reports of Olmos in the United States and Australia, see "Before and After Sex Change," folder 24, box 1, series I, VPC; and relevant discussions in Emily Skidmore, "Constructing the 'Good Transsexual': Christine Jorgensen, Whiteness, and Heteronormativity in the Mid-Twentieth Century Press," *Feminist Studies* 37, no. 2 (2011): 270–300; Ryan M. Jones, " 'Now I Have Found Myself, and I Am Happy:' Marta Olmos, Debates on Sex-Reassignment, and Mexico on a Global Stage, 1952–1957," *Journal of Latin American Studies* (under review).

176. As Ryan Jones has shown, even though Olmos's doctors saw the surgeries as a cure for homosexuality, Marta's story is more complex and deserves a more rigorous analysis in its own right. In a similar spirit, the formulation of transtopia envisions an analytical platform that gives the transness of historical subjects such as Marta its due attention. For a more detailed analysis of Marta's case, see Jones, " 'Now I Have Found Myself, and I Am Happy.' "

177. Prasenjit Duara, *Rescuing History from the Nation: Questioning Narratives of Modern China* (Chicago: University of Chicago Press, 1995).

178. See, for example, Peter H. Smith, "Mexico Since 1946: Dynamics of an Authoritarian Regime," in *Mexico Since Independence*, ed. Leslie Bethell (New York: Cambridge University Press, 1991), 321–396; Richard C. Bush, *At Cross Purposes: U.S.-Taiwan Relations Since 1942* (Armonk, NY: M. E. Sharpe, 2004); Joseph Contreras, *In the Shadow of the Giant: The Americanization of Modern Mexico* (New Brunswick, NJ: Rutgers University Press, 2009); and Robert F. Alegre, *Railroad Radicals in Cold War Mexico: Gender, Class, and Memory* (Lincoln: University of Nebraska Press, 2013).

179. On the deconstruction of stabilized narratives of the transgender body, see, among others, Gayle Salamon, *Assuming a Body: Transgender and Rhetorics of Materiality* (New York: Columbia University Press, 2010); Carlos Rojas, "Writing the Body," in *Transgender China*, ed. Howard Chiang (New York: Palgrave Macmillan, 2012), 199–223.

180. Maurice Mashaal, *Bourbaki: A Secret Society of Mathematicians*, trans. Anna Pierrehumbert (Providence, RI: American Mathematical Society, 2006).

2. Stonewall Aside

1. The Gay Liberation Front and the Gay Activist Alliance were both founded in 1969. On the homophile movement, see John D'Emilio, *Sexual Politics, Sexual Communities: The Making of a Homosexual Minority in the United States, 1940–1970* (Chicago: University of Chicago Press, 1983); Martin Meeker, *Contacts Desired: Gay and Lesbian Communications and Community, 1940s–1970s* (Chicago: University of Chicago Press, 2006); Marcia M. Gallo, *Different Daughters: A History of the Daughters of Bilitis and the Rise of the Lesbian Rights Movement* (Emeryville, CA: Seal, 2007); David S. Churchill, "Transnationalism and Homophile Political Culture in the Postwar Decades," *GLQ: A Journal of Lesbian*

and Gay Studies 15, no. 1 (2008): 31–66; Leila J. Rupp, "The Persistence of Transnational Organizing: The Case of the Homophile Movement," *American Historical Review* 116, no. 4 (2011): 1014–1039; Craig M. Loftin, *Masked Voices: Gay Men and Lesbians in Cold War America* (Albany: State University of New York Press, 2012); and Victor M. Macias-González, "The Transnational Homophile Movement and the Development of Domesticity in Mexico City's Homosexual Community," *Gender and History* 26, no. 3 (2014): 519–554.

2. The definitive study of the Stonewall riots is Martin Duberman, *Stonewall* (New York: Dutton, 1993). See also David Carter, *Stonewall: The Riots That Sparked the Gay Revolution* (New York: St. Martin's, 2004); and Marc Stein, *The Stonewall Riots: A Documentary History* (New York: New York University Press, 2019).

3. The historiography of LGBTQ history is too extensive to be cited adequately here. For recent overviews of US queer history, within which the Stonewall rebellion is typically situated, see Michael Bronski, *A Queer History of the United States* (Boston: Beacon, 2011); Vicki L. Eaklor, *Queer America: A People's GLBT History of the United States* (New York: New Press, 2011); Marc Stein, *Rethinking the Gay and Lesbian Movement* (London: Routledge, 2012); Lilian Faderman, *The Gay Revolution: The Story of the Struggle* (New York: Simon and Schuster, 2016); and the essays in Don Romesburg, ed., *The Routledge History of Queer America* (London: Routledge, 2018). For a global overview, see Martin Duberman, Martha Vicinus, and George Chauncey, eds., *Hidden from History: Reclaiming the Gay and Lesbian Past* (New York: New American Library, 1989); and Howard Chiang, ed., *Global Encyclopedia of Lesbian, Gay, Bisexual, Transgender, and Queer (LGBTQ) History* (Farmington Hills, MI: Scribner's, 2019).

4. Susan Stryker, *Transgender History*, 2nd ed. (New York: Seal, 2017). Stryker has used the Compton's Riot to develop a larger critique of disciplinary "homonormativity" in LGBTQ history. See Susan Stryker, "Transgender History, Homonormativity, and Disciplinarity," *Radical History Review*, no. 100 (2008): 145–157.

5. An obvious way to think about the unusualness of Stonewall is by decentering queer urbanity. See, for example, John Howard, *Men Like That: A Southern Queer History* (Chicago: University of Chicago Press, 1999); Judith Halberstam, *In a Queer Time and Place: Transgender Bodies, Subcultural Lives* (New York: New York University Press, 2005); Colin R. Johnson, *Just Queer Folks: Gender and Sexuality in Rural America* (Philadelphia: Temple University Press, 2013); and Mary L. Gray, Colin R. Johnson, and Brian J. Gilley, eds., *Queering the Countryside: New Frontiers in Rural Queer Studies* (New York: New York University Press, 2016). Some historians have assigned the transnational homophile movement of the 1950s a middle position between the interwar World League for Sexual Reform and the gay and lesbian movement in the 1970s. See Rupp, "The Persistence of Transnational Organizing."

6. For a critique of the desire for the incommensurability of the "Rest," see Anjali Arondekar, "Geopolitics Alert!," *GLQ: A Journal of Lesbian and Gay Studies* 10, no. 2 (2004): 236–240; Anjali Arondekar, "Thinking Sex with Geopolitics," *WSQ: Women's Studies Quarterly* 44, nos. 3–4 (2016): 332–335.

7. The scholar with whom the "global queering" hypothesis is typically associated is Dennis Altman. See Dennis Altman, *Global Sex* (Chicago: University of Chicago Press, 2001).

See also Neil Miller, *Out in the World: Gay and Lesbian Life from Buenos Aires to Bangkok* (London: Penguin, 1992); Ken Plummer, "Speaking Its Name: Inventing a Gay and Lesbian Studies," in *Modern Homosexualities: Fragments of Lesbian and Gay Experience*, ed. Ken Plummer (London: Routledge, 1992), 3–28; Peter Drucker, " 'In the Tropics There Is No Sin': Sexuality and Gay-Lesbian Movements in the Third World," *New Left Review* 218 (1996): 75–101; Peter Jackson, "An Explosion of Thai Identities: Global Queering and Reimagining Queer Theory," *Culture, Health, and Sexuality* 2 (2000): 405–424. Jackson has recently nuanced this thesis by drawing on the history of capitalism in Asia: see Peter Jackson, "Capitalism and Global Queering: National Markets, Parallels Among Sexual Cultures, and Multiple Queer Modernities," *GLQ: A Journal of Lesbian and Gay Studies* 15, no. 3 (2009): 357–395.

8. A critique of the West from the viewpoint of cultural nativism and essentialized alterity is best captured in Joseph Massad, *Desiring Arabs* (Chicago: University of Chicago Press, 2007).

9. Susan Stryker, "Transgender Studies: Queer Theory's Evil Twin," *GLQ: A Journal of Lesbian and Gay Studies* 10, no. 2 (2004): 212–215; David Valentine, *Imagining Transgender: An Ethnography of a Category* (Durham: Duke University Press, 2007).

10. My decision to focus on homoerotic examples in this chapter is intentional to the effect of making an independent case for bringing Sinophone studies into the ambit of queer theory.

11. On epistemological history and its corollary, historical epistemology, see, for example, Arnold I. Davidson, *The Emergence of Sexuality: Historical Epistemology and the Formation of Concepts* (Cambridge, MA: Harvard University Press, 2001); Ian Hacking, *Scientific Reason* (Taipei: National Taiwan University Press, 2009); Howard Chiang, ed., *Historical Epistemology and the Making of Modern Chinese Medicine* (Manchester: Manchester University Press, 2015).

12. One important "precursor" to the formalization of modern homosexual identities and subcultures can be found in the molly houses of early modern England. See Randolph Trumbach, "The Birth of the Queen: Sodomy and the Emergence of Gender Equality in Modern Culture, 1660–1750," in *Hidden from History: Reclaiming the Gay and Lesbian Past*, ed. Martin Duberman, Martha Vicinus, and George Chauncey (New York: New American Library, 1989), 129–140. Another important episode in the global history of sexual reform can be identified with the international network surrounding the activities of Jewish sexologist Magnus Hirschfeld. For Hirschfeld's global impact, see the essays in Veronika Fuechtner, Douglas E. Haynes, and Ryan M. Jones, eds., *A Global History of Sexual Science, 1880–1960* (Oakland: University of California Press, 2018).

13. Anjali Arondekar, "The Sex of History, or Object/Matters," *History Workshop Journal*, no. 89 (2020): 207–213, on 207.

14. Although various scholars have made a convincing case for preferring a "transnational" over a "global" framework in order to overcome the Western-centrism of LGBTQ studies, I strategically invoke "global" in this essay for two reasons. First, theories of transnationalism have tended to provide a limited historical understanding of global and interregional processes (e.g., colonialism). Second, in the spirit of this essay, the term *global* indicates a polycentric worldview so that whatever hegemonic implications it

carries with respect to Western cultural imperialism, the imposition of other imperialistic visions, including China-centrism, must be introduced as a coeval variable in our understanding of the global. My interest in the global underpinnings of LGBTQ history thus follows Arjun Appadurai's observation that "Globalization is . . . [an] uneven and even *localizing* process. Globalization does not necessarily or even frequently imply homogenization or Americanization." Arjun Appadurai, *Modernity at Large: Cultural Dimensions of Globalization* (Minneapolis: University of Minnesota Press, 1996), 17 (emphasis in original). See also Fran Martin, Peter Jackson, Mark McLelland, and Audrey Yue, eds., *AsiaPacifiQueer: Rethinking Genders and Sexualities* (Urbana: University of Illinois Press, 2008). On transnational approaches to sexuality, see Elizabeth A. Povinelli and George Chauncey, "Thinking Sexuality Transnationally: An Introduction," *GLQ: A Journal of Lesbian and Gay Studies* 5, no. 4 (1999): 439–450; Inderpal Grewal and Caren Kaplan, "Global Identities: Theorizing Transnational Studies of Sexuality," *GLQ: A Journal of Lesbian and Gay Studies* 7, no. 4 (2001): 663–679; and Margot Canaday, "Thinking Sex in the Transnational Turn: An Introduction," *American Historical Review* 114, no. 5 (2009): 1250–1257.

15. This notion of putting Stonewall aside draws inspiration from the following collection of essays: Jason Potts and Daniel Stout, eds., *Theory Aside* (Durham: Duke University Press, 2014).

16. For an authoritative exploration of China's transformation in this period, see Maurice Meisner, *Mao's China and After: A History of the People's Republic*, 3rd ed. (New York: Free Press, 1999). On the history of global Maoism, see Alexander C. Cook, ed., *Mao's Little Red Book: A Global History* (Cambridge: Cambridge University Press, 2014); and Julia Lovell, *Maoism: A Global History* (London: Bodley Head, 2019). On China's transformation after Mao, see, for example, David M. Lampton, *Following the Leader: Ruling China, from Deng Xiaoping to Xi Jinping* (Berkeley: University of California Press, 2014).

17. Shu-mei Shih, "Global Literature and the Technologies of Recognition," *PMLA* 119, no. 1 (2004): 16–30; Shu-mei Shih, *Visuality and Identity: Sinophone Articulations Across the Pacific* (Berkeley: University of California Press, 2007); Jing Tsu and David Der-wei Wang, eds., *Global Chinese Literature: Critical Essays* (Leiden: Brill, 2010); Jing Tsu, *Sound and Script in Chinese Diaspora* (Cambridge, MA: Harvard University Press, 2010); Shu-mei Shih, Chien-hsin Tsai, and Brian Bernards, eds., *Sinophone Studies: A Critical Reader* (New York: Columbia University Press, 2013); E. K. Tan, *Rethinking Chineseness: Translational Sinophone Identities in the Nanyang Literary World* (Amherst, NY: Cambria, 2013); Alison M. Groppe, *Sinophone Malaysian Literature: Not Made in China* (Amherst, NY: Cambria, 2013); Brian Bernards, *Writing the South Seas: Imagining the Nanyang in Chinese and Southeast Asian Postcolonial Literature* (Seattle: University of Washington Press, 2015); and Lily Wong, *Transpacific Attachments: Sex Work, Media Networks, and Affective Histories of Chineseness* (New York: Columbia University Press, 2018). For authoritative discussions of Sinophone studies in Chinese, see David Der-wei Wang 王德威, Chia-cian Ko 高嘉謙, and Kam Loon Woo 胡金倫, eds., *Huayifeng: Huayuyuxi wenxue duben* 華夷風: 華語語系文學讀本 [Sinophone/Xenophone: Contemporary Sinophone literature reader] (Taipei: Linking, 2016); Shu-mei Shih 史書美, *Fanlisan: Huayuyuxi yanjiulun* 反離散: 華語語系研究論 [Against diaspora: Discourses on Sinophone studies] (Taipei: Linking,

2017); and Yu-lin Lee 李育霖, ed., *Huayuyuxi shijiang* 華語語系十講 [Ten lectures on Sino-phone studies] (Taipei: Linking, 2020).

18. Shu-mei Shih, "The Concept of the Sinophone," *PMLA* 126, no. 3 (2011): 709–718, on 710. In Shih's original formulation, the Sinophone world is defined as "a network of places of cultural production outside of China and on the margins of China and Chine-seness, where a historical process of heterogenizing and localizing of continental Chi-nese culture has been taking place for several centuries." Shih, *Visuality and Identity*, 4.

19. Shih, *Visuality and Identity*, 30.

20. Shu-mei Shih, "Against Diaspora: The Sinophone as Places of Cultural Production," in *Global Chinese Literature: Critical Essays*, ed. Jing Tsu and Davd Der-wei Wang (Leiden: Brill, 2010), 29–48.

21. For an insightful consideration of China's capital investment in Africa, see Ching Kwan Lee, *The Specter of Global China: Politics, Labor, and Foreign Investment in Africa* (Chicago: University of Chicago Press, 2017). I introduce the heuristic value of the Sinophone for historians in another essay: Howard Chiang, "Sinophone Modernity: History, Culture, Geopolitics," in *Composing Modernist Connections in China and Europe*, ed. Chunjie Zhang (London: Routledge, 2019), 142–167.

22. This chapter aims to extend the theoretical and empirical horizons explored in Howard Chiang and Ari Larissa Heinrich, eds., *Queer Sinophone Cultures* (New York: Routledge, 2013); and Howard Chiang and Alvin K. Wong, eds., *Keywords in Queer Sinophone Studies* (London: Routledge, 2020). See also Fran Martin, "Transnational Queer Sinophone Cul-tures," in *Routledge Handbook of Sexuality Studies in East Asia*, ed. Mark McLelland and Vera Mackie (London: Routledge, 2014), 35–48; and Zoran Lee Pecic, *New Queer Sinophone Cinema: Local Histories, Transnational Connections* (New York: Palgrave Macmillan, 2016).

23. The word choice here is intentional: "queer" is translated into Chinese by Taiwanese writers in the 1990s as 酷兒 (*ku'er*), which literally means a "cool child."

24. Shu-mei Shih, "Introduction: What Is Sinophone Studies?," in *Sinophone Studies: A Crit-ical Reader*, ed. Shu-mei Shih, Chien-hsin Tsai, and Brian Bernards (New York: Colum-bia University Press, 2013), 1–16.

25. An important essay that marked a decisive turn toward New Qing history is Evelyn Rawski, "Reenvisioning the Qing: The Significance of the Qing Period in Chinese His-tory," *Journal of Asian Studies* 55, no. 4 (1996): 829–850.

26. For a revisionist study that places oceanic interest at the center of Qing history, see Ron-ald Po, *The Blue Frontier: Maritime Vision and Power in the Qing Empire* (Cambridge: Cambridge University Press, 2018).

27. Peter C. Perdue, *China Marches West: The Qing Conquest of Central Eurasia* (Cambridge, MA: Belknap Press of Harvard University Press, 2005).

28. On settler colonialism, see Lorenzo Veracini, *Settler Colonialism: A Theoretical Overview* (New York: Palgrave Macmillan, 2010); Edward Cavanagh and Lorenzo Veracini, eds., *The Routledge Handbook of the History of Settler Colonialism* (London: Routledge, 2017); Penelope Edmonds and Amanda Nettelbeck, eds., *Intimacies of Violence in the Settler Colony: Economies of Dispossession Around the Pacific Rim* (New York: Palgrave Macmillan, 2018); and Yu-ting Huang and Rebecca Weaver-Hightower, eds., *Archiving Settler Colonialism: Culture, Space and Race* (London: Routledge, 2019).

29. Steven Phillips, *Between Assimilation and Independence: The Taiwanese Encounter Nationalist China, 1945–1950* (Stanford: Stanford University Press, 2003); Melissa J. Brown, *Is Taiwan Chinese?: The Impact of Culture, Power, and Migration on Changing Identities* (Berkeley: University of California Press, 2004); and Dominic Meng-Hsuan Yang, *The Great Exodus from China: Trauma, Memory, and Identity in Modern Taiwan* (Cambridge: Cambridge University Press, 2020).

30. On the intersections of Taiwanese identity and bioscientific research, see Jennifer Liu, "Making Taiwanese (Stem Cells): Identity, Genetics, and Purity," in *Asian Biotech: Ethics and Communities of Fate*, ed. Aihwa Ong and Nancy Chen (Durham: Duke University Press, 2010), 239–262; Mark Munsterhjelm, *Living Dead in the Pacific: Contested Sovereignty and Racism in Genetic Research on Taiwanese Aborigines* (Vancouver: University of British Columbia Press, 2014); and Jennifer Liu, "Postcolonial Biotech: Taiwanese Conundrums and Subimperial Desires," *East Asian Science, Technology and Society* 11, no. 4 (2017): 563–588.

31. In addition to the review below, see also Aihwa Ong, *Flexible Citizenship: The Cultural Logics of Transnationality* (Durham: Duke University Press, 1999); Philip A. Kuhn, *Chinese Among Others: Emigration in Modern Times* (Lanham, MD: Rowman and Littlefield, 2008); Shelly Chan, *Diaspora's Homeland: Modern China in the Age of Global Migration* (Durham: Duke University Press, 2018).

32. Wei-ming Tu, "Cultural China: The Periphery as Center," *Daedalus* 120, no. 2 (1991): 1–32.

33. Gungwu Wang, "Chineseness: The Dilemmas of Place and Practice," in *Cosmopolitan Capitalists: Hong Kong and the Chinese Diaspora*, ed. Gary G. Hamilton (Seattle: University of Washington Press, 1999), 118–134. See also Gungwu Wang, *The Chinese Overseas: From Earthbound China to the Quest for Autonomy* (Cambridge, MA: Harvard University Press, 2000). On Wang's scholarly contribution, see Jianli Huang, "Conceptualizing Chinese Migration and Chinese Overseas: The Contribution of Wang Gungwu," *Journal of Chinese Overseas* 6, no. 1 (2010): 1–21.

34. Ling-chi Wang, "The Structure of Dual Domination: Toward a Paradigm for the Study of the Chinese Diaspora in the United States," *Amerasia Journal* 21, no. 1 (1995): 149–169.

35. Ien Ang, "Can One Say No to Chineseness?," *boundary 2* 25, no. 3 (1998): 223–242.

36. Rey Chow, "Introduction: On Chineseness as a Theoretical Problem," *boundary 2* 25, no. 3 (1998): 1–24.

37. When queer theorists such as Eve Sedgwick readily acknowledged the limit of their focus on the "Euro-American male" experience in the early 1990s, they had already anticipated the diversification of queer critical praxis across uneven global spaces. The queer/Sinophone intersection advanced in this book is best situated within an ongoing project of letting queer experience speak across its differentially situated contexts, whereupon one can build a field of inquiry welcome to "the widest possible range of other and even contradictory availabilities." Eve Kosofsky Sedgwick, *The Epistemology of the Closet* (Berkeley: University of California Press, 1990), 14. I thank Mark McConaghy for drawing my attention to this point.

38. Anjali Arondekar and Geeta Patel, "Area Impossible: Notes Toward an Introduction," *GLQ: A Journal of Lesbian and Gay Studies* 22, no. 2 (2016): 151–171, on 154.

39. Robert B. Hall, *Area Studies: With Special Reference to Their Implications for Research in the Social Sciences* (New York: Social Science Research Council, 1947), 82.

40. Tani E. Barlow, "~~Colonialism~~'s Career in Postwar China Studies," *positions: east asia cultures critique* 1, no. 1 (1993): 224–267, on 225.

41. Cindy Patton and Benigno Sánchez-Eppler, eds., *Queer Diasporas* (Durham: Duke University Press, 2000); Arnaldo Cruz-Malavé and Martin F. Manalansan, eds., *Queer Globalizations: Citizenship and the Afterlife of Colonialism* (New York: New York University Press, 2002); Martin F. Manalansan, *Global Divas: Filipino Gay Men in Diaspora* (Durham: Duke University Press, 2003); William L. Leap and Tom Boellstorff, eds., *Speaking in Queer Tongues: Globalization and Gay Language* (Urbana: University of Illinois Press, 2004); Gayatri Gopinath, *Impossible Desires: Queer Diasporas and South Asian Public Cultures* (Durham: Duke University Press, 2005); Eithne Luibhéid and Lionel Cantú Jr., eds., *Queer Migrations: Sexuality, U.S. Citizenship, and Border Crossing* (Minneapolis: University of Minnesota Press, 2005); Tom Boellstorff, *A Coincidence of Desires: Anthropology, Queer Studies, Indonesia* (Durham: Duke University Press, 2007); Lawrence La Fountain-Stokes, *Queer Ricans: Cultures and Sexualities in the Diaspora* (Minneapolis: University of Minnesota Press, 2009); David L. Eng, *The Feeling of Kinship: Queer Liberalism and the Racialization of Intimacy* (Durham: Duke University Press, 2010); Nadia Ellis, *Territories of the Soul: Queered Belonging in the Black Diaspora* (Durham: Duke University Press, 2015); Jarrod Hayes, *Queer Roots for the Diaspora: Ghosts in the Family Tree* (Ann Arbor: University of Michigan Press, 2016); Gayatri Gopinath, *Unruly Visions: The Aesthetic Practices of Queer Diaspora* (Durham: Duke University Press, 2018); and Eithne Luibhéid and Karma R. Chávez, eds., *Queer and Trans Migration: Dynamics of Illegalization, Detention, and Deportation* (Urbana: University of Illinois Press, 2020).

42. Marin F. Manalansan, "In the Shadows of Stonewall: Examining Gay Transnational Politics and the Diasporic Dilemma," *GLQ: A Journal of Lesbian and Gay Studies* 2, no. 4 (1995): 425–438, on 426.

43. Martin, "Transnational Queer Sinophone Cultures," 43. On the meaning, history, and politics of the term *tongzhi*, see Wah-shan Chou, *Tongzhi: Politics of Same-Sex Eroticism in Chinese Societies* (New York: Haworth, 2000); and Ta-wei Chi, *Tongzhi wenxueshi: Taiwan de faming* 同志文學史：台灣的發明 [A queer invention in Taiwan: A history of tongzhi literature] (Taipei: Linking, 2017), 379–392. A parallel example of lexical circulation is the Chinese vernacular translation of "lesbian" into *lala*: see Loretta Wing Wah Ho, *Gay and Lesbian Subculture in Urban China* (London: Routledge, 2010); Lucetta Kam, *Shanghai Lalas: Female Tongzhi Communities and Politics in Urban China* (Hong Kong: Hong Kong University Press, 2012); and Elisabeth L. Engebretsen, *Queer Women in Urban China: An Ethnography* (London: Routledge, 2014). On *tongzhi* digital activism in contemporary China, see Elisabeth L. Engebretsen, William F. Schroeder, and Hongwei Bao, eds., *Queer/Tongzhi China: New Perspectives on Research, Activism and Media Cultures* (Copenhagen: Nordic Institute of Asian Studies Press, 2015); Hongwei Bao, *Queer China: Lesbian and Gay Literature and Visual Culture Under Postsocialism* (London: Routledge, 2020).

44. Victor Roudometof, *Glocalization: A Critical Introduction* (London: Routledge, 2016).

45. Hongwei Bao, *Queer Comrades: Gay Identity and Tongzhi Activism in Postsocialist China* (Copenhagen: Nordic Institute of Asian Studies Press, 2018), 5.

46. I highlight the year 1978 due to the historic significance of the Third Plenum of the Eleventh Party Congress held in December 1978, to which scholars tend to attribute the consolidation of Deng Xiaoping's power in the CCP and the launching of his "reform and opening" program. Other possible dates to demarcate the Maoist/post-Mao eras include 1976 (the year Mao died) and 1980 (the trial of the Gang of Four).

47. Wenqing Kang, "The Decriminalization and Pathologization of Homosexuality in China," in *China in and Beyond the Headlines*, ed. Timothy B. Weston and Lionel M. Jensen (Lanham, MD: Rowman and Littlefield, 2012), 231–248; Qingfei Zhang, "Representation of Homoeroticism by the *People's Daily* Since 1949," *Sexuality and Culture* 18, no. 4 (2014): 1010–1024; Yixiong Huang, "Media Representation of *Tongxinglian* in China: A Case Study of the *People's Daily*," *Journal of Homosexuality* 65, no. 3 (2018): 338–360; Wenqing Kang, "Male Same-Sex Relations in Socialist China," *PRC History Review* 3, no. 1 (2018): 20–22; Shana Ye, "A Reparative Return to 'Queer Socialism': Male Same-Sex Desire in the Cultural Revolution," in *Sexuality in China: Histories of Power and Pleasure*, ed. Howard Chiang (Seattle: University of Washington Press, 2018), 142–162; and Wenqing Kang, "Queer Life, Communities, and Activism in Contemporary China," *Cross-Currents: East Asian History and Culture Review* 31 (2019): 226–230.

48. On queer politics and culture in late twentieth-century Hong Kong, see Helen Hok-Sze Leung, *Undercurrents: Queer Culture and Postcolonial Hong Kong* (Vancouver: University of British Columbia Press, 2008); Travis S. K. Kong, *Chinese Male Homosexualities: Memba, Tongzhi, and Golden Boy* (London: Routledge, 2011); and Denise Tse-Shang Tang, *Conditional Spaces: Hong Kong Lesbian Desires and Everyday Life* (Hong Kong: Hong Kong University Press, 2011). On queer Taiwan, see Antonia Chao, "Global Metaphors and Local Strategies in the Construction of Taiwan's Lesbian Identities," *Culture, Health, and Sexuality* 2 (2000): 377–390; Antonia Chao, "Drink, Stories, Penis, and Breasts: Lesbian Tomboys in Taiwan from the 1960s to the 1990s," *Journal of Homosexuality* 40 (2001): 185–209; Fran Martin, *Situating Sexualities: Queer Representation in Taiwanese Fiction, Film, and Public Culture* (Hong Kong: Hong Kong University Press, 2003); Tze-lan D. Sang, *The Emerging Lesbian: Female Same-Sex Desire in Modern China* (Chicago: University of Chicago Press, 2003); Hans Tao-Ming Huang, *Queer Politics and Sexual Modernity in Taiwan* (Hong Kong: Hong Kong University Press, 2011); Liang-ya Liou, "Taiwan's Postcolonial and Queer Discourses in the 1990s," in *Comparatizing Taiwan*, ed. Shu-mei Shih and Ping-hui Liao (London: Routledge, 2015), 259–277; Howard Chiang and Yin Wang, eds., *Perverse Taiwan* (London: Routledge, 2016); Po-Han Lee, "Queer Activism in Taiwan: An Emergent Rainbow Coalition from the Assemblage Perspective," *Sociological Review* 65, no. 4 (2017): 682–698; and Amy Brainer, *Queer Kinship and Family Change in Taiwan* (New Brunswick, NJ: Rutgers University Press, 2019).

49. See, for example, Song Hwee Lim, "How to Be Queer in Taiwan: Translation, Appropriation, and the Construction of a Queer Identity in Taiwan," in *AsiaPacifiQueer: Rethinking Genders and Sexualities*, ed. Fran Martin, Peter Jackson, Mark McLelland, and Audrey Yue (Urbana: University of Illinois, 2004), 235–250; Song Hwee Lim, "Queer Theory Goes to Taiwan," in *The Ashgate Research Companion to Queer Theory*, ed. Noreen Giffney and Michael O'Rourke (Aldershot, UK: Ashgate, 2009), 257–275; Audrey Yue, "Queer Asian Cinema and Media Studies: From Hybridity to Critical

Regionality," *Cinema Journal* 53, no. 2 (2014): 145–151; Travis S. K. Kong, Sky H. L. Lau, and Amory H. W. Hui, "*Tongzhi*," in *Global Encyclopedia of Lesbian, Gay, Bisexual, Transgender, and Queer (LGBTQ) History*, ed. Howard Chiang (Farmington Hills, MI: Charles Scribner's Sons, 2019), 1603–1609.

50. Scholars have begun to revise the repressive hypothesis for studying heterosexual intimacy in the Maoist period. See, for example, Harriet Evans, *Women and Sexuality in China: Dominant Discourses of Female Sexuality and Gender Since 1949* (Cambridge: Polity, 1997); Wendy Larson, "Never This Wild: Sexing the Cultural Revolution," *Modern China* 25, no. 4 (1999): 423–450; Emily Honig, "Socialist Sex: The Cultural Revolution Revisited," *Modern China* 29, no. 2 (2003): 143–175; Yunxiang Yan, *Private Life Under Socialism: Love, Intimacy, and Family Change in a Chinese Village, 1949–1999* (Stanford: Stanford University Press, 2003); Everett Yuehong Zhang, "Rethinking Sexual Repression in Maoist China: Ideology, Structure, and the Ownership of the Body," *Body and Society* 11, no. 3 (2005): 1–25; and Everett Yuehong Zhang, *The Impotence Epidemic: Men's Medicine and Sexual Desire in Contemporary China* (Durham: Duke University Press, 2015).

51. Petrus Liu, *Queer Marxism in Two Chinas* (Durham: Duke University Press, 2015).

52. See, for example, Liu, 41–45. In chapter 5, I will call attention to the ways in which the absence of a critical attention to trans politics undermines the queerness of *tongzhi*.

53. Liu, *Queer Marxism in Two Chinas*, 4.

54. Liu, 7.

55. See, for example, Iris Marion Young, *Justice and the Politics of Difference* (Princeton: Princeton University Press, 1990); Nancy Fraser, *Justice Interruptus: Critical Reflections on the "Postsocialist" Condition* (London: Routledge, 1997).

56. Alvin K. Wong, "Queer Sinophone Studies as Anti-Capitalist Critique: Mapping Queer Kinship in the Works of Chen Ran and Wong Bik-wan," in *Queer Sinophone Cultures*, ed. Howard Chiang and Ari Larissa Heinrich (London: Routledge, 2013), 109–129; Howard Chiang and Alvin K. Wong, "Queering the Transnational Turn: Regionalism and Queer Asias," *Gender, Place and Culture: A Journal of Feminist Geography* 23, no. 11 (2016): 1643–1656; Howard Chiang and Alvin K. Wong, "Asia Is Burning: Queer Asia as Critique," *Culture, Theory and Critique* 58, no. 2 (2017): 121–126; and Alvin K. Wong, "Queering the Quality of Desire: Perverse Use-Values in Transnational Chinese Cultures," *Culture, Theory and Critique* 58, no. 2 (2017): 209–225.

57. See, for example, Jonathan Ned Katz, *Gay American History: Lesbians and Gay Men in the U.S.A.* (New York: Crowell, 1976); D'Emilio, *Sexual Politics, Sexual Communities*; Lillian Faderman, *Odd Girls and Twilight Lovers: A History of Lesbian Life in Twentieth-Century America* (New York: Columbia University Press, 1991); John Loughery, *The Other Side of Silence: Men's Lives and Gay Identities: A Twentieth-Century History* (New York: Henry Holt, 1998); Marc Stein, *City of Sisterly and Brotherly Loves: Lesbian and Gay Philadelphia, 1945–1972* (Chicago: University of Chicago Press, 2000); Justin David Suran, "Coming Out Against the War: Antimilitarism and the Politicization of Homosexuality in the Era of Vietnam," *American Quarterly* 53, no. 3 (2001): 452–488; Nan Alamilla Boyd, *Wide Open Town: A History of Queer San Francisco to 1965* (Berkeley: University of California Press, 2003); Meeker, *Gay and Lesbian Communications and Community*; and Loftin, *Masked Voices*.

58. John D'Emilio, "Capitalism and Gai Identity," in *Powers of Desire: The Politics of Sexuality*, ed. Ann Snitow, Christine Stansell, and Sharon Thompson (New York: Monthly Review Press, 1983), 100–113; Lisa Duggan, *The Twilight of Equality?: Neoliberalism, Cultural Politics, and the Attack on Democracy* (Boston: Beacon, 2003); Kevin Floyd, *The Reification of Desire: Toward a Queer Marxism* (Minneapolis: University of Minnesota Press, 2009); Diarmaid Kelliher, "Solidarity and Sexuality: Lesbians and Gays Support the Miners 1984–5," *History Workshop Journal* 77 (2014): 240–262; Peter Drucker, *Warped: Gay Normality and Queer Anti-Capitalism* (Leiden: Brill, 2015); Emily K. Hobson, *Lavender and Red: Liberalism and Solidarity in the Gay and Lesbian Left* (Oakland: University of California Press, 2016). See also the essay, Aaron Lecklider, "Coming to Terms: Homosexuality and the Left in American Culture," *GLQ: A Journal of Lesbian and Gay Studies* 18, no. 1 (2012): 179–195, and the works reviewed in it.

59. Liu, *Queer Marxism in Two Chinas*, 21.

60. For an early statement of Liu's view, see Petrus Liu, "Why Does Queer Theory Need China?," *positions: east asia cultures critique* 18, no. 2 (2010): 291–320.

61. Liu, *Queer Marxism in Two Chinas*, 6. On self- or re-Orientalization, see Howard Chiang, "Epistemic Modernity and the Emergence of Homosexuality in China," *Gender and History* 22, no. 3 (2010): 629–657, on 634; Howard Chiang, "(De)Provincializing China: Queer Historicism and Sinophone Postcolonial Critique," in *Queer Sinophone Cultures*, ed. Howard Chiang and Ari Larissa Heinrich (London: Routledge, 2013), 19–51, on 32. On the way this concept applies to the "Asian values" discourse, see Michael G. Peletz, *Gender Pluralism: Southeast Asia Since Early Modern Times* (London: Routledge, 2009), 201–203.

62. A Sinophone epistemology would never take "China" or "Chinese" as a complete project in and of itself, always insisting on and pointing out its internal slippages. Whether "China" or "Chinese" signifies a series of languages, a cultural heritage, a nation-state, or an ethnocultural formation, such phenomena are always in the process of dynamic formation and reformation, restaging, and reframing, negotiated on the myriad grounds of differential localities. I thank Mark McConaghy for enlightening me on this point.

63. Kuan-Hsing Chen, *Asia as Method: Toward Deimperialization* (Durham: Duke University Press, 2010). See also Kuan-Hsing Chen and Chua Beng Huat, "Introduction: The *Inter-Asia Cultural Studies: Movements* Project," in *The Inter-Asia Cultural Studies Reader*, ed. Kuan-Hsing Chen and Chua Beng Huat (London: Routledge, 2007), 1–5.

64. Rey Chow, *Entanglements, or Transmedial Thinking About Capture* (Durham: Duke University Press, 2012), 171.

65. This insight builds on the expanding literature on comparative imperial studies. See, for example, Ann Laura Stoler, ed., *Haunted by Empire: Geographies of Intimacy in North American History* (Durham: Duke University Press, 2006); Ann Laura Stoler, Carole McGranahan, and Peter C. Perdue, eds., *Imperial Formations* (Santa Fe, NM: School for Advanced Research Press, 2007); Jane Burbank and Frederick Cooper, *Empires in World History: Power and the Politics of Difference* (Princeton: Princeton University Press, 2010); and Lisa Lowe, *The Intimacies of Four Continents* (Durham: Duke University Press, 2015).

66. Shu-mei Shih, "Is the *Post-* in Postsocialism the *Post-* in Posthumanism?," *Social Text*, no. 110 (2012): 27–50, on 29.

67. Shih, 28. See also Jason McGrath, *Postsocialist Modernity: Chinese Cinema, Literature, and Criticism in the Market Age* (Stanford: Stanford University Press, 2008), 14–15.

68. Qwo-Li Driskill, Chris Finley, Brian Joseph Gilley, and Scott Lauria Morgensen, eds., *Queer Indigenous Studies: Critical Interventions in Theory, Politics, and Literature* (Tucson: University of Arizona Press, 2011); Scott Lauria Morgensen, *Spaces Between Us: Queer Settler Colonialism and Indigenous Decolonization* (Minneapolis: University of Minnesota Press, 2011); Qwo-Li Driskill, *Asegi Stories: Cherokee Queer and Two-Spirit Memory* (Tucson: University of Arizona Press, 2016); and Joanne Barker, ed., *Critically Sovereign: Indigenous Gender, Sexuality, and Feminist Studies* (Durham: Duke University Press, 2017).

69. Scott Lauria Morgensen, "Settler Homonationalism: Theorizing Settler Colonialism within Queer Modernities," *GLQ: A Journal of Lesbian and Gay Studies* 16, nos. 1–2 (2010): 105–131, on 106.

70. On homonatioanlism, see Jasbir Puar, *Terrorist Assemblages: Homonationalism in Queer Times* (Durham: Duke University Press, 2007).

71. Jia Tan, "Beijing Meets Hawai'i: Reflections on *Ku'er*, Indigeneity, and Queer Theory," *GLQ: A Journal of Lesbian and Gay Studies* 23, no. 1 (2017): 137–150.

72. Wen-Ling Lin, "Buluo 'jiemei' zuo xingbie: Jiaozhi zai xieqin, yinqin, diyuan yu shengchan laodong zhijian" 部落「姊妹」做性別：交織在血親、姻親、地緣與生產勞動之間 ["Sisters" making gender: Between everyday work and social relations], *Taiwan: A Radical Quarterly in Social Studies* 86 (2012): 51–98; Francisca Yuenki Lai, "Migrant and Lesbian Activism in Hong Kong: A Critical Review of Grassroots Politics," *Asian Anthropology* 17, no. 2 (2018): 135–150; Francisca Yuenki Lai, "Sexuality at Imagined Home: Same-Sex Desire Among Indonesian Migrant Domestic Workers in Hong Kong," *Sexualities* 21, nos. 5–6 (2018): 899–913; Séagh Kehoe and Chelsea E. Hall, "Tibet," in *Global Encyclopedia of Lesbian, Gay, Bisexual, Transgender, and Queer (LGBTQ) History*, ed. Howard Chiang (Farmington Hills, MI: Charles Scribner's Sons, 2019), 1597–1601; and Kyle Shernuk, "A Queerness of Relation: The Plight of the 'Ethnic Minority' in Chan Koon-Chung's *Bare Life*," in *Keywords in Queer Sinophone Studies*, ed. Howard Chiang and Alvin K. Wong (London: Routledge, 2020), 80–102.

73. Dipesh Chakrabarty, *Provincializing Europe: Postcolonial Thought and Historical Thought* (Princeton: Princeton University Press, 2000); Partha Chatterjee, *The Politics of the Governed: Reflections on Popular Politics in Most of the World* (New York: Columbia University Press, 2004).

74. On the notion of family resemblance, see Ludwig Wittgenstein, *Philosophical Investigations* (Oxford: Blackwell, 1997).

75. *Lan Yu*, directed by Stanley Kwan (2001; Hong Kong: Universe, 2002), DVD. In this sense, I follow historian Paul Pickowicz's lead to use cinematic examples to reflect on the viability of postsocialism as an analytical framework, a historical condition, and a cultural phenomenon. See Paul G. Pickowicz, "Huang Jianxin and the Notion of Post-socialism," in *New Chinese Cinemas: Forms, Identities, Politics*, ed. Nick Browne, Paul G. Pickowicz, Vivian Sobchack, and Esther Yau (Cambridge: Cambridge University Press, 1994), 57–87.

76. For an English translation of this novel, see Bei Tong, *Beijing Comrades*, trans. Scott E. Myers (New York: Feminist Press, 2016).

77. Based on my anecdotal conversations with Hongwei Bao and anthropologist Hoching Jiang, both *Lan Yu* and *Beijing Story* have served as an important focus of discussion and queer bonding *across* the PRC and global Sinophone communities. This possibility of crossing and, for the lack of a better way to characterize it, globalization disrupts any attempt to return a debate on the parameters of Sinophone studies to ground zero centering on inclusionary/exclusionary criteria. On Internet literature and control in the PRC, see Michel Hockx, *Internet Literature in China* (New York: Columbia University Press, 2015).

78. *Lan Yu*'s first major recognition came with Stanley Kwan receiving the Best Director award and Liu Ye, who played Lan Yu, receiving the Best Lead Actor award from the 38th Taipei Golden Horse Film Festival in 2001. The film scored the highest number of awards (four) and nominations (ten) at the Golden Horse that year. After being acclaimed by the Gold Horse, *Lan Yu* then attracted extensive coverage in the Taiwanese media, which gave rise to the film's popularity first in Sinophone Taiwan and then elsewhere.

79. Jingsheng Wei, "The Fifth Modernization: Democracy (December 1978)," in *The Courage to Stand Alone: Letters from Prison and Other Writings* (New York: Viking, 1997), 201–212.

80. On social organization in authoritarian China, see Timothy Hildebrandt, *Social Organizations and the Authoritarian State in China* (Cambridge: Cambridge University Press, 2013).

81. See, for example, Arif Dirlik, "Postsocialism? Reflections on 'Socialism with Chinese Characteristics,'" *Bulletin of Concerned Asian Scholars* 21, no. 1 (1989): 33–44; Pickowicz, "Huang Jianxin"; Sheldon H. Lu, *Chinese Modernity and Global Biopolitics: Studies in Literature and Visual Culture* (Honolulu: University of Hawai'i Press, 2007), 204–210; and Lisa Rofel, *Desiring China: Experiments in Neoliberalism, Sexuality, and Public Culture* (Durham: Duke University Press, 2007). This is not to suggest that the framework of "postsocialist China" leaves no room for meaningful explorations in the areas of gender and sexuality. Scholars such as Shana Ye have usefully probed its production under the pressures of disciplinary norms and transpacific political economic formations. See Shana Ye, "The Love That Does Not Speak Its Name: Affect and Transnational Production of 'Queer China'" (PhD diss., University of Minnesota, 2017). Cf. Bao, *Queer China*. For an argument that reform-era China represents not an abandonment of socialism but its complex transformation, see Lin Chun, *The Transformation of Chinese Socialism* (Durham: Duke University Press, 2006).

82. David L. Eng, "The Queer Space of China: Expressive Desire in Stanley Kwan's *Lan Yu*," *positions: east asia cultures critique* 18, no. 2 (Fall 2010): 459–487.

83. Fiona Ng, "Interview: Love in the Time of Tiananmen," *IndieWire*, www.indiewire.com /2002/07/interview-love-in-the-time-of-tiananmen-stanley-kwans-lan-yu-80279/. For a reflection on the intertwined nature of Kwan's personal history and filmmaking career, see Song Hwee Lim, *Celluloid Comrades: Representations of Male Homosexuality in Contemporary Chinese Cinemas* (Honolulu: University of Hawai'i Press, 2006), 153–179.

84. I borrow the notion of a "world picture," with an intentional pun on the word *picture*, from Martin Heidegger, *The Question Concerning Technology, and Other Essays*, trans William Lovitt (New York: Harper and Row, 1977).

85. Ng, "Interview: Love in the Time of Tiananmen."

86. Chen, *Asia as Method*, 7.

87. Jian Chen, *Mao's China and the Cold War* (Chapel Hill: University of North Carolina Press, 2001).

88. Wang Hui, "The Year 1989 and the Historical Roots of Neoliberalism in China," in *The End of Revolution: China and the Limits of Modernity* (London: Verso, 2009), 19–66.

89. On the history of the Tiananmen Square protests, see Timothy Brook, *Quelling the People: The Military Suppression of the Beijing Democracy Movement* (New York: Oxford University Press, 1992); Dingxin Zhao, *The Power of Tiananmen: State-Society Relations and the 1989 Beijing Student Movement* (Chicago: University of Chicago Press, 2001); and Louisa Lim, *The People's Republic of Amnesia: Tiananmen Revisited* (New York: Oxford University Press, 2015).

90. Bao, *Queer China*, 72.

91. Margaret Hillenbrand, *Negative Exposures: Knowing What Not to Know in Contemporary China* (Durham: Duke University Press, 2020).

92. See, for example, Martin, *Situating Sexualities*; Li-fen Chen, "Queering Taiwan: In Search of Nationalism's Other," *Modern China* 37, no. 4 (2011): 384–412; Chiang and Wang, *Perverse Taiwan*; Lee, "Queer Activism in Taiwan." For an historical overview of the discourses and cultures of same-sex desire in Taiwan in the two decades preceding the lifting of the martial law, see Jens Damm, "Same-Sex Desire and Society in Taiwan, 1970–1987," *China Quarterly* 181 (2005): 67–81.

93. Jens Damm, "The Impact of the Taiwanese LGBTQ Movement in Mainland China with a Specific Focus on the Case of the 'Chinese Lala Alliance' and 'Marriage Equality in Chinese Societies,'" in *Connecting Taiwan: Participation—Integration—Impacts*, ed. Carsten Storm (London: Routledge, 2018), 146–166.

94. Jens Damm, "Discrimination and Backlash Against Homosexual Groups," in *Politics of Difference in Taiwan*, ed. Tak-Wing Ngo and Hong-zen Wang (London: Routledge, 2011), 152–80, on 172.

95. Leung, *Undercurrents*.

96. Ackbar Abbas, *Hong Kong: Culture and the Politics of Disappearance* (Minneapolis: University of Minnesota Press, 1997), 27.

97. Shih, *Fanlisan*, 225.

98. Naoki Sakai, "Modernity and Its Critique: The Problem of Universalism and Particularism," *South Atlantic Quarterly* 87, no. 3 (1988): 475–504; Dipesh Chakrabarty, "Provincializing Europe: Postcoloniality and the Critique of History," *Cultural Studies* 6, no. 3 (1992): 337–357.

99. Ashis Nandy, *The Intimate Enemy: Loss and Recovery of Self Under Colonialism* (New York: Oxford University Press, 1984).

100. Chen, *Asia as Method*, 216.

101. Chen, 211–55.

102. Chen, 197.

103. On the sexological discourse of homosexuality in Republican China, see Sang, *The Emerging Lesbian*, 99–126; Wenqing Kang, *Obsession Male Same-Sex Relations in China, 1900–1950* (Hong Kong: Hong Kong University Press, 2009), 41–59; Fran Martin, *Backward Glances: Contemporary Chinese Culture and the Female Homoerotic Imaginary* (Durham:

Duke University Press, 2010), 29–48; and Howard Chiang, *After Eunuchs: Science, Medicine, and the Transformation of Sex in Modern China* (New York: Columbia University Press, 2018), 125–177.

104. Chiang and Wong, "Queering the Transnational Turn," 1645 (emphasis added).

105. I borrow the idea of Sinophone interruptions from Shu-mei Shih, "Theory, Asia and the Sinophone," *Postcolonial Studies* 13, no. 4 (2010): 465–484.

106. Arondekar and Peetal, "Area Impossible"; Chiang and Wong, "Queering the Transnational Turn"; Chiang and Wong, "Asia Is Burning." On modularity, see also Partha Chatterjee, *The Nation and Its Fragments: Colonial and Postcolonial Histories* (Princeton: Princeton University Press, 1993), 3–13.

107. Françoise Lionnet and Shu-mei Shih, "Introduction: Thinking Through the Minor, Transnationally," in *Minor Transnationalism*, ed. Françoise Lionnet and Shu-mei Shih (Durham: Duke University Press, 2005), 1–23, on 5, 6.

108. Chiang, *After Eunuchs*. See also Alvin K. Wong, "Queer Vernacularism: Minor Transnationalism Across Hong Kong and Singapore," *Cultural Dynamics* 32, nos. 1–2 (2020): 49–67.

109. On queer Taiwan, see, for example, Martin, *Situating Sexualities*; Huang, *Queer Politics and Sexual Modernity in Taiwan*; Liu, *Queer Marxism in Two Chinas*; and Chiang and Wang, *Perverse Taiwan*. On queer Hong Kong, see, for example, Leung, *Undercurrents*; Yau Ching, ed., *As Normal as Possible: Negotiating Sexuality and Gender in Mainland China and Hong Kong* (Hong Kong: Hong Kong University Press, 2010); Kong, *Chinese Male Homosexualities*; and Tang, *Conditional Spaces*. On queer Singapore, see, for example, Audrey Yue and Jun Zubillaga-Pow, eds., *Queer Singapore: Illiberal Citizenship and Mediated Cultures* (Hong Kong: Hong Kong University Press, 2012); Lynette J. Chua, *Mobilizing Gay Singapore: Rights and Resistance in an Authoritarian State* (Philadelphia: Temple University Press, 2014); Shawna Tang, *Postcolonial Lesbian Identities in Singapore* (London: Routledge, 2018); and Natalie Oswin, *Global City Futures: Desire and Development in Singapore* (Athens: University of Georgia Press, 2019). On queer Malaysia, see, for example, Michael G. Peletz, *Gender Pluralism: Southeast Asia Since Early Modern Times* (London: Routledge, 2009); Joseph N. Goh, *Living Out Sexuality and Faith: Body Admissions of Malaysian Gay and Bisexual Men* (London: Routledge, 2018); Shanah Shah, *The Making of a Gay Muslim: Religion, Sexuality and Identity in Malaysia and Britain* (New York: Palgrave Macmillan, 2018); and Joseph N. Goh, *Becoming a Malaysian Trans Man: Gender, Society, Body and Faith* (Singapore: Palgrave Macmillan, 2020). On queer Indonesia, see, for example, Tom Boellstorff, *The Gay Archipelago: Sexuality and Nation in Indonesia* (Princeton: Princeton University Press, 2005); Tom Boellstorff, *A Coincidence of Desires: Anthropology, Queer Studies, Indonesia* (Durham: Duke University Press, 2007); Evelyn Blackwood, *Falling Into the Lesbi World: Desire and Difference in Indonesia* (Honolulu: University of Hawai‘i Press, 2010); and Sharyn Graham Davies, *Gender Diversity in Indonesia: Sexuality, Islam and Queer Selves* (London: Routledge, 2010). On queer Philippines, see, for example, J. Neil Garcia, *Philippine Gay Culture: Binabae to Bakla, Silahis to MSM* (Quezon City: University of Philippine Press, 1996); Mark Johnson, *Beauty and Power: Transgendering and Cultural Transformation in the Philippines* (Oxford: Berg, 1997); Bobby Benedicto, *Under Bright Lights: Gay Manila and the Global Scene* (Minneapolis:

University of Minnesota Press, 2014); and Victor Román Mendoza, *Metroimperial Intimacies: Fantasy, Racial-Sexual Governance, and the Philippines in U.S. Imperialism, 1899– 1913* (Durham: Duke University Press, 2015). On queer Myanmar, see Lynette J. Chua, *The Politics of Love in Myanmar: LGBT Mobilization and Human Rights as a Way of Life* (Stanford: Stanford University Press, 2018). On queer Korea, see Todd A. Henry, ed., *Queer Korea* (Durham: Duke University Press, 2020).

110. Ting-Fai Yu, "Queer Migration Across the Sinophone World: Queer Chinese Malaysian Students' Educational Mobility to Taiwan," *Journal of Ethnic and Migration Studies*, www.tandfonline.com/doi/full/10.1080/1369183X.2020.1750946.

111. On queer Thailand, see, for example, Peter A. Jackson, *Male Homosexuality in Thailand* (New York: Global Academic, 1989); Megan Sinnott, *Toms and Dees: Transgender Identity and Female Same-Sex Relationships in Thailand* (Honolulu: University of Hawaiʻi Press, 2004); LeeRay M. Costa and Andrew Matzner, *Male Bodies, Women's Souls: Personal Narratives of Thailand's Transgender Youth* (New York: Haworth, 2007); and Peter A. Jackson, ed., *Queer Bangkok: 21st Century Markets, Media, and Rights* (Hong Kong: Hong Kong University Press, 2011). For an erudite study of colonial modernity in Thai gender and sexual history, see Tamara Loos, *Subject Siam: Family, Law, and Colonial Modernity in Thailand* (Ithaca, NY: Cornell University Press, 2006). On the issue of colonialism in the formation of Thai nationalism, see Thongchai Winichakul, *Siam Mapped: A History of the Geo-Body of a Nation* (Honolulu: University of Hawaiʻi Press, 1994).

112. Arondekar and Peetal, "Area Impossible," 155.

113. On sound studies, see Michael Bull and Les Back, eds., *The Auditory Culture Reader* (Oxford: Berg, 2003); Jonathan Sterne, ed., *The Sound Studies Reader* (London: Routledge, 2012); and David Novak and Matt Sakakeeny, eds., *Keywords in Sound* (Durham: Duke University Press, 2015). While sound studies represents an emerging field, a sustained scholarly attention to its intersection with queer theory has yet to formalize. For some preliminary investigations, see Drew Daniel, "Queer Sound," *WIRE*, no. 333 (2011): 42–46; and Sarah E. Truman and David Ben Shannon, "Queer Sonic Cultures: An Affective Walking-Composing Project," *Capacious: Journal for Emerging Affective Inquiry* 1, no. 3 (2018): 58–77.

114. See, for example, Wayne Koestenbaum, *The Queen's Throat: Opera, Homosexuality, and the Mystery of Desire* (New York: Poseidon, 1993); Sophie Fuller and Lloyd Whitesell, eds., *Queer Episodes in Music and Modern Identity* (Urbana: University of Illinois Press, 2002); Nadine Hubbs, *The Queer Composition of America's Sound: Gay Modernists, American Music, and National Identity* (Berkeley: University of California Press, 2004); Philip Brett, Elizabeth Wood, and Gary C. Thomas, eds., *Queering the Pitch: The New Gay and Lesbian Musicology*, 2nd ed. (London: Routledge, 2006); Judith Peraino, *Listening to the Sirens: Musical Technologies of Queer Identity from Homer to Hedwig* (Berkeley: University of California Press, 2006); Sheila Whiteley, ed., *Queering the Popular Pitch* (London: Routledge, 2006); Rachel Lewis, "What's Queer About Musicology Now?," *Women and Music: A Journal of Gender and Culture* 13 (2009): 43–53; Nadine Hubbs, *Rednecks, Queers, and Country Music* (Berkeley: University of California Press, 2014); and L. H. Stallings, *Funk the Erotic: Transaesthetics and Black Sexual Cultures* (Urbana: University of Illinois Press, 2015).

115. On the linguistic turn of the 1980s, see the essays in Victoria E. Bonnell and Lynn Hunt, eds., *Beyond the Cultural Turn: New Directions in the Study of Society and Culture* (Berkeley: University of California Press, 1999). On the affective turn in queer theory, see, for example, Eve Kosofsky Sedgwick, *Touching Feeling: Affect, Pedagogy, Performativity* (Durham: Duke University Press, 2003); Sarah Ahmed, *The Cultural Politics of Emotions* (Edinburgh: Edinburgh University Press, 2004); Heather Love, *Feeling Backward: Loss and the Politics of Queer History* (Cambridge, MA: Harvard University Press, 2007); and the essays in David M. Halperin and Valerie Traub, eds., *Gay Shame* (Chicago: University of Chicago Press, 2009).

116. Brian Massumi, *Politics of Affect* (Cambridge: Polity, 2015); Jasbir Puar, *The Right to Maim: Debility, Capacity, Disability* (Durham: Duke University Press, 2017).

117. My approach builds on and synthesizes the recent analyses of Audrey Yue and Helen Leung, who have considered Wong's oeuvre from a Sinophone and a queer angle, respectively. See Audrey Yue, "The Sinophone Cinema of Wong Kar-wai," in *A Companion to Wong Kar-wai*, ed. Martha P. Nochimson (Malden, MA: Wiley-Blackwell, 2016), 232–249; Helen Hok-Sze Leung, "New Queer Angles on Wong Kar-wai," in *A Companion to Wong Kar-wai*, ed. Martha P. Nochimson (Malden, MA: Wiley-Blackwell, 2016), 250–271.

118. *Happy Together*, directed by Wong Kar-wai (Hong Kong: Jet Tone, 1997).

119. Quoted in Marc Siegel, "The Intimate Spaces of Wong Kar-wai," in *At Full Speed: Hong Kong Cinema in a Borderless World*, ed. Esther C. M. Yau (Minneapolis: University of Minnesota Press, 2001), 277–294, on 279.

120. Chris Berry, "Happy Alone?," *Journal of Homosexuality* 39, nos. 3–4 (2000): 187–200, on 193.

121. Jimmy Ngai, "A Dialogue with Wong Kar-wai: Cutting Between Time and Two Cities," in *Wong Kar-wai*, ed. Jean-Marc Lalanne, David Martinez, Ackbar Abbas, and Jimmy Ngai (Paris: Dis Voir, 1997), 83–117, on 112.

122. Helen Leung, "Queerscapes in Contemporary Hong Kong Cinema," *positions: east asia cultures critique* 9, no. 2 (2001): 423–447, on 424.

123. See, for example, Rey Chow, "Nostalgia of the New Wave: Structure in Wong Kar-wai's *Happy Together*," *Camera Obscura* 14, no. 3 (1999): 30–49; Berry, "Happy Alone?"; Leung, "Queerscapes in Contemporary Hong Kong Cinema"; Siegel, "The Intimate Spaces of Wong Kar-wai;" Lim, *Celluloid Comrades*, 99–125; David L. Eng, *The Feeling of Kinship: Queer Liberalism and the Racialization of Intimacy* (Durham: Duke University Press, 2010); 58–92; Carlos Rojas, "Queer Utopias in Wong Kar-wai's *Happy Together*," in *A Companion to Wong Kar-wai*, ed. Martha P. Nochimson (Malden, MA: Wiley-Blackwell, 2016), 508–521; and Alvin K. Wong, "Postcoloniality Beyond China-Centrism: Queer Sinophone Transnationalism in Hong Kong Cinema," in *Keywords in Queer Sinophone Studies*, ed. Howard Chiang and Alvin K. Wong (London: Routledge, 2020), 62–79.

124. Rojas, "Queer Utopias in Wong Kar-wai's *Happy Together*."

125. Chow, "Nostalgia of the New Wave," 34 (emphasis in original).

126. Shih, *Visuality and Identity*, 4.

127. Shih, 5.

128. I thank Alvin K. Wong for pointing this out to me.

129. Rojas, "Queer Utopias in Wong Kar-wai's *Happy Together*."

130. On the queer stardom of Leslie Cheung, see Helen Hok-Sze Leung, *Undercurrents*, 85–105.

131. Leung, "New Queer Angles on Wong Kar-wai," 269.

132. For insightful analyses of queer kinship and homecoming in the Sinophone contexts, see E. K. Tan, "A Queer Journey Home in *Solos*: Rethinking Kinship in Sinophone Singapore," in *Queer Sinophone Cultures*, ed. Howard Chiang and Ari Larissa Heinrich (London: Routledge, 2013), 130–146; and Alvin K. Wong, "Queer Sinophone Studies as Anti-Capitalist Critique: Mapping Queer Kinship in the Work of Chen Ran and Wong Bik-wan," *Queer Sinophone Cultures*, ed. Howard Chiang and Ari Larissa Heinrich (London: Routledge, 2013), 109–129.

133. Although my discussion primarily focuses on China studies, it is equally imperative to point out the way that the Sinophone framework troubles the methods of American studies. Notably, scholars continue to neglect the experience of LGBTQ subjects in Asian American history. Some promising discussions can be found in Eric C. Wat, *The Making of a Gay Asian Community: An Oral History of Pre-AIDS Los Angeles* (Lanham, MD: Rowman and Littlefield, 2002); Peter Boag, *Same-Sex Affairs: Constructing and Controlling Homosexuality in the Pacific Northwest* (Berkeley: University of California Press, 2003); Nayan Shah, "Between 'Oriental Depravity' and 'Natural Degenerates': Spatial Borderlands and the Making of Ordinary Americans," *American Quarterly* 57, no. 3 (2005): 703–725; Judy Tze-Chun Wu, *Doctor Mom Chung of the Fair-Haired Bastards: The Life of a Wartime Celebrity* (Berkeley: University of California Press, 2005); and Amy Sueyoshi, *Queer Compulsions: Race, Nation, and Sexuality in the Affairs of Yone Noguchi* (Honolulu: University of Hawai'i Press, 2012). Sinophone studies provides a useful barometer to (1) study the queer experience of non-English speakers in North America, (2) queer the "homosocial normativity" of Chinese bachelor societies, especially its overlap with other forms of marginalization (linguistic, racial, cultural, economic, legal, and so on), (3) question the resistance of Asian American scholars to take gender and sexual oppression seriously, and (4) challenge their insistence on certain Asian values (e.g., Confucianism) as explanatory vectors for cultural conservativism or denial within Asian American communities. On the "homosocial normativity" of Chinese bachelor societies, see Madeline Y. Hsu, "Unwrapping Orientalist Constraints: Restoring Homosocial Normativity to Chinese American History," *Amerasia Journal* 29, no. 2 (2003): 230–253. On the latter two problems, see Amy Sueyoshi, "Queer Asian American Historiography," in *The Oxford Handbook of Asian American History* (New York: Oxford University Press, 2016), 267–278. See also David L. Eng, *Racial Castration: Managing Masculinity in Asian America* (Durham: Duke University Press, 2001); and Cynthia Wu, *Sticky Rice: A Politics of Intraracial Desire* (Philadelphia: Temple University Press, 2018).

134. Shih, "Theory, Asia and the Sinophone."

135. See, for example, Shih, *Visuality and Identity*; Tsu, *Sound and Script*; Tsu and Wang, *Global Chinese Literature*; Shih, Tsai, and Bernards, *Sinophone Studies*; Tan, *Rethinking Chineseness*; Groppe, *Sinophone Malaysian Literature*; Chiang and Heinrich, *Queer Sinophone Cultures*; Audrey Yue and Olivia Khoo, eds., *Sinophone Cinemas* (New York: Palgrave Macmillan, 2014); Bernards, *Writing the South Seas*; Christopher Lupke, *The Sinophone Cinema*

of Hou Hsiao-hsien: Culture, Style, Voice, and Motion (Amherst, NY: Cambria, 2016); Chia-rong Wu, *Supernatural Sinophone Taiwan and Beyond* (Amehrst, NY: Cambria, 2016); Wong, *Transpacific Attachments*; and Wai-Siam Hee, *Remapping the Sinophone: The Cultural Production of Chinese-Language Cinema in Singapore and Malaya Before and During the Cold War* (Hong Kong: Hong Kong University Press, 2019).

136. On the limitations of "diaspora" for the study of Chinese cinemas, see Shu-mei Shih, "Forward: The Sinophone as History and the Sinophone as Theory," *Journal of Chinese Cinemas* 6, no. 1 (2012): 5–7; Audrey Yue and Olivia Khoo, "From Diasporic Cinemas to Sinophone Cinemas: An Introduction," *Journal of Chinese Cinemas* 6, no. 1 (2012): 9–13.

137. Mizoguchi Yuzo, *Ribenren shiyezhong de zhongguoxue* 日本人視野中的中國學 [China as method], trans. Li Suping 李甦平, Gong Ying 龔穎, and Xu Tao 徐滔 (Beijing: Chinese People's University Press, 1996 [1989]), 93. Of course, the discipline of Sinology has a history that goes back to the pre–Cold War period, but my concern here focuses on its transformation in an era when the area studies paradigm came to dominate.

138. Chen, *Asia as Method*, 120.

139. For a historiographical rendition of the "China-centered perspective," see Paul A. Cohen, *Discovering History in China: American Historical Writing on the Recent Chinese Past*, new ed. (1984; New York: Columbia University Press, 2010).

140. Chow, *Entanglements*.

141. On the history of male same-sex relations in China, see Bret Hinsch, *Passions of the Cut Sleeve: The Male Homosexual Tradition in China* (Berkeley: University of California Press, 1990); Cuncun Wu, *Homoerotic Sensibilities in Late Imperial China* (New York: Routledge, 2004); Kang, *Obsession*; and Giovanni Vitiello, *The Libertine's Friend: Homosexuality and Masculinity in Late Imperial China* (Chicago: University of Chicago Press, 2011).

142. See my discussion in *After Eunuchs* and "Sinophone Modernity."

143. Michel Foucault, *The History of Sexuality*, vol. 1, *An Introduction*, trans. Robert Hurley (New York: Vintage, 1990), 103.

144. For a promising approach, see Yiu-Wai Chu, *Lost in Transition: Hong Kong Culture in the Age of China* (Albany: State University of New York Press, 2013).

145. On "grids of intelligibility," see Hubert L. Dreyfus and Paul Rabinow, *Michel Foucault: Beyond Structuralism and Hermeneutics* (Chicago: University of Chicago Press, 1982), 120–121. On "intimate frontiers," see Albert L. Hurtado, *Intimate Frontiers: Sex, Gender, and Culture in Old California* (Albuquerque: University of New Mexico Press, 1999).

146. Kwame Anthony Appiah, "Is the Post- in Postmodernism the Post- in Postcolonial?," *Critical Inquiry* 17, no. 2 (1991): 336–357.

147. Édouard Glissant, *Poetics of Relation*, trans. Betsy Wing (Ann Arbor: University of Michigan Press, 1997).

148. On gay marriage activism in Taiwan, see Hoching Jiang, "Marriage, Same-Sex, in Taiwan," in *Global Encyclopedia of Lesbian, Gay, Bisexual, Transgender, and Queer (LGBTQ) History*, ed. Howard Chiang (Farmington Hills, MI: Charles Scribner's Sons, 2019), 1004–1008; Howard Chiang, "Gay Marriage in Taiwan and the Struggle for Recognition," *Current History: A Journal of Contemporary World Affairs* 118 (2019): 241–243; and Po-Han Lee, "First in Asia, Now What? Taiwan and Marriage Quasi-Equality," *Kyoto Journal* 96 (2019): 36–39. On the *W v. Registrar of Marriages* (2013) landmark court case granting

transgendered persons the right to marry in Hong Kong, see John Nguyet Erni, "Disrupting the Colonial Transgender/Law Nexus: Reading the Case of W in Hong Kong," *Cultural Studies—Critical Methodologies* 16, no. 4 (2016): 351–360. See also chapter 5 of this book.

149. See, for example, Joseph M. K. Cho and Lucetta Y. L. Kam, "Same-Sex Marriage in China, Hong Kong and Taiwan: Ideologies, Spaces and Developments," in *Contemporary Issues in International Political Economy*, ed. Fu-Lai Tony Yu and Diana S. Kwan (Singapore: Palgrave Macmillan, 2019), 289–306; Denise Tse-Shang Tang, Diana Khor, and Yi-Chien Chen, "Legal Recognition of Same-Sex Partnerships: A Comparative Study of Hong Kong, Taiwan, and Japan," *Sociological Review* 68, no. 1 (2020): 192–208.

3. Titrating Transgender

1. Dana Luciano and Mel Y. Chen, "Has the Queer Ever Been Human?," *GLQ: A Journal of Lesbian and Gay Studies* 21, nos. 2–3 (2015): 183–207.

2. The genealogy of this mode of thinking dates further back in time. See, for example, Noreen Giffney and Myra J. Hird, eds., *Queering the Non/Human* (Burlington, VT: Ashgate, 2008); Mel Y. Chen, *Animacies: Biopolitics, Racial Mattering, and Queer Affect* (Durham: Duke University Press, 2012); Mel Y. Chen and Dana Luciana, eds., "Queer Inhumanism," special issue, *GLQ: A Journal of Lesbian and Gay Studies* 21, nos. 2–3 (2015): 183–458; and Eva Hayward and Jami Weinstein, eds., "Tranimalities," special issue, *TSQ: Transgender Studies Quarterly* 2, no. 2 (2015): 184–363.

3. See, for example, Sara Ahmed, *Queer Phenomenology: Orientations, Objects, Others* (Durham: Duke University Press, 2006); Bruno Latour, *Reassembling the Social: An Introduction to Actor-Network-Theory* (Oxford: Oxford University Press, 2007); Jasbir Puar, *Terrorist Assemblages: Homonationalism in Queer Times* (Durham: Duke University Press, 2007); Patricia Ticento Clough, ed., *The Affective Turn: Theorizing the Social* (Durham: Duke University Press, 2007); Diana Coole and Samantha Frost, eds., *New Materialisms: Ontology, Agency, and Politics* (Durham: Duke University Press, 2010); Catriona Mortimer-Sandilands and Bruce Erickson, eds., *Queer Ecologies: Sex, Nature, Politics, Desire* (Bloomington: Indiana University Press, 2010); Robert Azzarello, *Queer Environmentality: Ecology, Evolution, and Sexuality in American Literature* (Burlington, VT: Ashgate, 2012); Jeffrey J. Cohen, "Queering the Inorganic," in *Queer Futures: Reconsidering Ethics, Activism, and the Political*, ed. Elahe Haschemi Yekani, Eveline Killian, and Beatrice Michaels (Surrey, UK: Ashgate, 2013), 149–165; Nicole Seymour, *Strange Natures: Futurity, Empathy, and the Queer Ecological Imagination* (Urbana: University of Illinois Press, 2013); Scott Herring, *The Hoarders: Material Deviance in American Culture* (Minneapolis: University of Minnesota Press, 2014); Donna J. Haraway, *Staying with the Trouble: Making Kin in the Chthulucene* (Durham: Duke University Press, 2016); Elizabeth A. Povinelli, *Geontologies: A Requiem to Late Liberalism* (Durham: Duke University Press, 2016); Jasbir Puar, *The Right to Maim: Debility, Capacity, Disability* (Durham: Duke University Press, 2017); and Lily Wong, *Transpacific Attachments: Sex Work, Media Networks, and Affective Histories of Chineseness* (New York: Columbia University Press, 2018). On the

way magic and magical thinking were incorporated into sexual science in the nineteenth century, see Benjamin Kahan, *The Book of Minor Perverts: Sexology, Etiology, and the Emergence of Sexuality* (Chicago: University of Chicago Press, 2019), 66–84.

4. Luciano and Chen, "Has the Queer Ever Been Human," 188.

5. As Eve Kosofsky Sedgwick has pointed out, "The word 'queer' itself means across—it comes from the Indo-European root-*twerkw*, which also yields the German *quer* (transverse), Latin *torquere* (to twist), English *athwart*." Eve Kosofsky Sedgwick, *Tendencies* (Durham: Duke University Press, 1993), xii. For an illuminating account of the politics of recognition, see Pheng Cheah, "The Biopolitics of Recognition: Making Female Subjects of Globalization," *boundary 2* 40, no. 2 (2013): 81–112.

6. In U.S. history, the expression of "man-monster" was used to describe the black crossdresser Mary Jones (Peter Sewally), who was tried for grand larceny in New York City in June 1836. However, unlike the long history of *renyao* in Chinese and Sinophone cultures told in this chapter, this singular incidence neither generated nor sustained a recursive/common usage of "man-monster" as a trans descriptor in the Anglophone world. The story of Jones is detailed in Timothy J. Gilfoyle, *City of Eros: New York City, Prostitution, and the Commercialization of Sex, 1790–1920* (New York: Norton, 1992), 136–137; Jonathan Ned Katz, *Love Stories: Sex Between Men Before Homosexuality* (Chicago: University of Chicago Press, 2001), 81–84; Tavia Nyong'o, *The Amalgamation Waltz: Race, Performance, and the Ruses of Memory* (Minneapolis: University of Minnesota Press, 2009), 96–102; and C. Riley Snorton, *Black on Both Sides: A Racial History of Trans Identity* (Minneapolis: University of Minnesota Press, 2017), 59–66.

7. Todd Henry, "A Documentary Impulse: The Historical Imagination of Queer Films in Contemporary South Korea" (paper presented at the annual meeting of the Association for Asian Studies, San Diego, California, March 21–23, 2013); Matthew H. Sommer, "Confusion in the Archive: Qing Dynasty Sodomy Cases from the Ba County Court" (paper presented at the Queer Asia as Historical Critique conference, University of Warwick, May 25, 2013); Anjali Arondekar, "In the Absence of Reliable Ghosts: Sexuality, Historiography, South Asia," *differences* 25, no. 3 (2014): 98–122; and Jessica Hinchy, "The Eunuch Archive: Colonial Records of Non-Normative Gender and Sexuality in India," *Culture, Theory, and Critique* 58, no. 2 (2017): 127–146.

8. See, for example, Nancy Rose Hunt, *A Colonial Lexicon: Of Birth Ritual, Medicalization, and Mobility in Colonial Congo* (Durham: Duke University Press, 1999); Nancy Rose Hunt, *A Nervous State: Violence, Remedies, and Reveries in Colonial Congo* (Durham: Duke University Press, 2016); and Ann Laura Stoler, *Duress: Imperial Durabilities in Our Times* (Durham: Duke University Press, 2016). On the imagined accumulations of national communities, see Benedict Anderson, *Imagined Communities: Reflections on the Origins and Spread of Nationalism* (New York: Verso, 1983).

9. My borrowing of *titration* from the language of chemistry both resonates with and differs from Joseph Needham's notion of "grand titration" in his study of the history of Western and Chinese science. The similarity resides in our ambition to execute a more robust cross-cultural approach to historical inquiry. Like science, queer inhumanism deserves a critical lens that is grounded beyond a Western-centric source base. However, Needham and I differ in the way we borrow the scientific metaphor of titration.

For Needham, his goal was to titrate Chinese against European traditions of scientific practice in order to discern who deserves credit for the discovery or invention of scientific ideas. In contrast, my "chemical reaction" in this chapter is conducted less between Western and Chinese/Sinophone examples of embodiment than between the various ideas and tropes of corporeal experience to ascertain with precision the way they ascribe transness to the *renyao* category across temporal and geographical scales. The queer potency of *renyao* is partly "dissolved" by and through its various iterations in history. On Needham's initial usage, see Joseph Needham, *The Grand Titration: Science and Society in East and West* (London: Allen and Unwin, 1969).

10. For a general critique of humanism, see, for example, Iain Chambers, *Culture After Humanism: History, Culture, Subjectivity* (London: Routledge, 2001); and Pheng Cheah, *Inhuman Conditions: On Cosmopolitanism and Human Rights* (Cambridge, MA: Harvard University Press, 2006). By bringing the transgender inhumanism of *renyao* into a global conversation about Taiwan, I aim to extend Cheah's thinking on inhumanism into the postcolonial cosmopolitanism of Sinophone production. See Pheng Cheah, *What Is a World?: On Postcolonial Literature as World Literature* (Durham: Duke University Press, 2016).

11. Walter D. Mignolo, *The Darker Side of the Renaissance: Literacy, Territoriality, and Colonization* (Ann Arbor: University of Michigan Press, 1995); Walter D. Mignolo, *The Darker Side of Western Modernity: Global Futures, Decolonial Options* (Durham: Duke University Press, 2011).

12. For a compelling rebuttal of this view, see the essays collected in Shu-mei Shih 史書美, Chia-Ling Mei 梅家玲, Chaoyang Liao 廖朝陽, and Dung-Sheng Chen 陳東升, eds., *Zhishi Taiwan: Taiwan lilun de kenengxing* 知識臺灣: 臺灣理論的可能性 [Knowledge Taiwan: The possibility of Taiwanese theory] (Taipei: Rye Field, 2016).

13. Shu-mei Shih, "Globalisation and the (In)Significance of Taiwan," *Postcolonial Studies* 6 (2003): 143–153, on 144.

14. Shu-mei Shih, ed., "Globalisation: Taiwan's (In)Significance," special issue, *Postcolonial Studies* 6, no. 2 (2003): 143–249.

15. Gayatri Chakravorty Spivak, "Subaltern Studies: Deconstructing Historiography," in *Selected Subaltern Studies*, ed. Ranajit Guha and Gayatri Chakravorty Spivak (New York: Oxford University Press, 1988), 3–32, on 6 (emphasis in original).

16. Two important role models for my thinking on the historiographical significance of Taiwan are Kuan-Hsing Chen, *Asia as Method: Toward Deimperialization* (Durham: Duke University Press, 2010); and Xiaojue Wang, *Modernity with a Cold War Face: Reimagining the Nation in Chinese Literature Across the 1949 Divide* (Cambridge, MA: Harvard University Press, 2013). See also the essays in Shu-mei Shih and Ping-hui Liao, eds., *Comparatizing Taiwan* (London: Routledge, 2015).

17. David Der-Wei Wang and Shu-mei Shih, "'Huayu yuxi yu Taiwan' zhuti luntan" 「華語語系與台灣」主題論壇 [Forum on Sinophone.Taiwan], *Zhongguo xiandai wenxue* 中國現代文學 [Modern Chinese literature], no. 32 (2017): 75–94. See also other essays in Yu-lin Lee and Howard Chiang, eds., "Taiwan yu huayu yuxi yanjiu" 台灣與華語語系研究 [Taiwan and Sinophone Studies], special issue, *Zhongguo xiandai wenxue*, no. 32 (2017): 1–94.

18. Ping-hui Liao and David Der-wei Wang, eds., *Taiwan Under Colonial Rule: History, Culture, Memory* (New York: Columbia University Press, 2006).

19. See, for example, Steven E. Phillips, *Between Assimilation and Independence: The Taiwanese Encounter Nationalist China, 1945–1950* (Stanford: Stanford University Press, 2003).

20. On the emergence of queer cultures in post–martial law Taiwan, see Fran Martin, *Situating Sexualities: Queer Representation in Taiwanese Fiction, Film, and Public Culture* (Hong Kong: Hong Kong University Press, 2003); and Jens Damm, "Discrimination and Backlash Against Homosexual Groups," in *Politics of Difference in Taiwan*, ed. Tak-Wing Ngo and Hong-zen Wang (London: Routledge, 2011), 152–180. For a succinct analysis of the discourse of same-sex desire in Taiwan in the two decades preceding the lifting of martial law, see Jens Damm, "Same-Sex Desire and Society in Taiwan, 1970–1987," *China Quarterly* 181 (2005): 67–81. For a remarkable study of postmillennial queer Taiwan, see Amy Brainer, *Queer Kinship and Family Change in Taiwan* (New Brunswick, NJ: Rutgers University Press, 2019).

21. I borrow the term *hypercolony* from Ruth Rogaski's study of health and hygiene in Tianjin history. See Ruth Rogaski, *Hygienic Modernity: Meanings of Health and Disease in Treaty-Port China* (Berkeley: University of California Press, 2004), 11. On sexual modernity in Taiwan, see Martin, *Situating Sexualities*; and Hans Tao-Ming Huang, *Queer Politics and Sexual Modernity in Taiwan* (Hong Kong: Hong Kong University Press, 2011); and Howard Chiang and Yin Wang, eds., *Perverse Taiwan* (London: Routledge, 2016).

22. See, for example, Jacques Derrida, *Archive Fever: A Freudian Impression*, trans. Eric Prenowitz (Chicago: University of Chicago Press, 1995); Carolyn Steedman, *Dust* (Manchester: Manchester University Press, 2001); Antoinette Burton, *Dwelling in the Archive: Women Writing House, Home, and History in Late Colonial India* (New York: Oxford University Press, 2003); Ann Cvetkovich, *An Archive of Feelings: Trauma, Sexuality, and Lesbian Public Culture* (Durham: Duke University Press, 2003); Antoinette Burton, ed., *Archive Stories: Facts, Fictions, and the Writing of History* (Durham: Duke University Press, 2005); Charles Merewhether, *The Archive* (Cambridge: MIT Press, 2006); Anjali Arondekar, *For the Record: On Sexuality and the Colonial Archive in India* (Durham: Duke University Press, 2009); Ann Laura Stoler, *Along the Archival Grain: Epistemic Anxieties and Colonial Common Sense* (Princeton: Princeton University Press, 2009); Kathryn Burns, *Into the Archive: Writing and Power in Colonial Peru* (Durham: Duke University Press, 2010); and Zeb Tortorici, *Sins Against Nature: Sex and Archives in Colonial New Spain* (Durham: Duke University Press, 2018).

23. Derrida, *Archive Fever*; Arondekar, *For the Record*, 2.

24. Arondekar, *For the Record*.

25. Stoler, *Along the Archival Grain*, 1.

26. Lisa Lowe, "The Intimacies of Four Continents," in *Haunted by Empire: Geographies of Intimacy in North American History*, ed. Ann Laura Stoler (Durham: Duke University Press, 2006), 191–212, on 203. See also Ann Laura Stoler, "Colonial Archives and the Arts of Governance," *Archival Science* 2 (2002): 87–109, on 90. Working on the transatlantic slave trade, historian Stephanie Smallwood understands "the archive itself as embodying part of the process of colonial violence." See Stephanie E. Smallwood, "The Politics of the Archive and History's Accountability to the Enslaved," *History of the Present* 6, no. 2 (2016): 117–132, on 124.

27. My notion of queer unknowing draws on recent scholarly approaches to queering failure and problematizing success. See, e.g., Heather Love, *Feeling Backward: Loss and the*

Politics of History (Cambridge, MA: Harvard University Press, 2007); Lauren Berlant, *Cruel Optimism* (Durham: Duke University Press, 2011); Judith Halberstam, *The Queer Art of Failure* (Durham: Duke University Press, 2011); and Lauren Berlant and Lee Edelman, *Sex, or the Unbearable* (Durham: Duke University Press, 2013).

28. For a compelling defense of historicism as a queer scholarly intervention, see David Halperin, *How to Do the History of Homosexuality* (Chicago: University of Chicago Press, 2002). See also Valerie Traub, *Thinking Sex with the Early Moderns* (Philadelphia: University of Pennsylvania Press, 2015).

29. Joan W. Scott, "The Evidence of Experience," *Critical Inquiry* 17, no. 4 (1991): 773–797. For an interrogation of this problem in queer history, see Lisa Duggan, "The Discipline Problem: Queer Theory Meets Lesbian and Gay History," *GLQ: Journal of Lesbian and Gay Studies* 2, no. 3 (1995): 179–191.

30. Arondekar, *For the Record*, 2.

31. Zhouliu Wu, *Orphan of Asia*, trans. Ioannis Mentzas (New York: Columbia University Press, 2006). For insightful analyses of this novel, see Yu-lin Lee, *Writing Taiwan: A Study of Taiwan's Nativist Literature* (Saarbrücken, Germany: VDM, 2008); Chien-heng Wu, " 'Tiger's Leap Into the Past': Comparative Temporality and the Politics of Redemption in The Orphan of Asia," in *Comparatizing Taiwan*, ed. Shu-mei Shih and Ping-hui Liao (London: Routledge, 2015), 33–58; and Chien-hsin Tsai, *A Passage to China: Literature, Loyalism, and Colonial Taiwan* (Cambridge, MA: Harvard University Asia Center, 2017), 251–280. There are undoubtedly other "orphans" in the Asia Pacific, including but not limited to East Timor and Okinawa, whose historical queerness deserves sustained analysis in its own right. On the distinctiveness of Okinawa, see Wendy Matsumura, *The Limits of Okinawa: Japanese Capitalism, Living Labor, and Theorizations of Community* (Durham: Duke University Press, 2015).

32. Antonia Chao, "The Logic of Power in Imagining the Nation-State: Diaspora, Public Sphere, and Modernity in Fifties Taiwan," *Taiwan: A Radical Quarterly in Social Studies* 35 (1999): 37–83; Howard Chiang and Yin Wang, "Perverse Taiwan," in *Perverse Taiwan*, ed. Howard Chiang and Yin Wang (London: Routledge, 2016), 1–17. On the theorization of the state in a time of globalization, see Judith Butler and Gayatri Chakravorty Spivak, *Who Sings the Nation-State?: Language, Politics, Belonging* (Oxford: Seagull, 2007).

33. For revisionist accounts of gender and sexuality in the 1950s in the United States and Europe, see the essays in Joanne Meyerowitz, ed., *Not June Cleaver: Women and Gender in Postwar America, 1945–1960* (Philadelphia: Temple University Press, 1994); and Heike Bauer and Matt Cook, eds., *Queer 1950s: Rethinking Sexuality in the Postwar Years* (New York: Palgrave Macmillan, 2012). The revisionist scholarship on Maoist China is more limited, see, for example, Harriet Evans, *Women and Sexuality in China: Dominant Discourses of Female Sexuality and Gender Since 1949* (Cambridge: Polity, 1997); Everett Zhang, "Rethinking Sexual Repression in Maoist China: Ideology, Structure, and the Ownership of the Body," *Body and Society* 11, no. 3 (2005): 1–25; and Wenqing Kang, "The Decriminalizaiton and Depathologization of Homosexuality in China," in *China in and Beyond the Headlines*, ed. Timothy B. Weston and Lionel M. Jensen (Lanham, MD: Rowman and Littlefield, 2012), 231–248.

34. There is a growing number of researchers actively working against this dichotomy. See, for example, Francis X. Blouin and William G. Rosenberg, *Processing the Past: Contesting Authorities in History and the Archives* (Oxford: Oxford University Press, 2011).

35. Carolyn Steedman, "The Space of Memory: In an Archive," *History of the Human Sciences* 11 (1998): 65–83, on 78.

36. On trace, see Jacques Derrida, *Of Grammatology*, trans. Gayatri Chakravorty Spivak (Baltimore: Johns Hopkins University Press, 1976); Jacques Derrida, *Writing and Difference*, trans. Alan Bass (London: Routledge, 1978).

37. On the nature of tabloid newspapers as a historical source, see Li Nan 李楠, *WanQing Minguo shiqi Shanghai xiaobao* 晚清民國時期上海小報 [Shanghai tabloid newspapers during the late Qing and Republican period] (Beijing: Renmin wenxue chubanshe, 2006).

38. Judith Zeitlin, *Historian of the Strange: Pu Songling and the Chinese Classical Tale* (Stanford: Stanford University Press, 1993), 98.

39. Zeitlin, 102.

40. Zeitlin, 102.

41. Zeitlin, 103.

42. Zeitlin, 104.

43. Charlotte Furth, "Androgynous Males and Deficient Females: Biology and Gender Boundaries in Sixteenth- and Seventeenth-Century China," *Late Imperial China* 9 (1988): 1–31.

44. Furth, 19.

45. Furth, 18.

46. Zeitlin, *Historian of the Strange*, 107.

47. Furth, "Androgynous Males and Deficient Females," 22–24; Zeitlin, *Historian of the Strange*, 109–116.

48. Furth, "Androgynous Males and Deficient Females," 22.

49. Furth, 22; Zeitlin, *Historian of the Strange*, 114.

50. Wenqing Kang, *Obsession: Male Same-Sex Relations in China, 1900–1950* (Hong Kong: Hong Kong University Press, 2009), 33.

51. Kang, 36–38. Interestingly, the labeling of Mei as a *renyao* reappeared in the context of Cold War Taiwan. See "Suzu wenhua yishutuanti fangwen youhaoguojia" 速組文化藝術團體 訪問友好國家 [Formation of Culture and Arts Group for Visiting Friendly Countries], *LHB*, May 27, 1956. In Taiwan during the Japanese colonial period, the Chinese section of such newspapers as *Taiwan Nichinichi Shinpō* 臺灣日日新報 [Taiwan daily news] carried sporadic stories of *renyao*. See Chen Pei-jean, "Xiandai 'xing' yu diguo 'ai': Taihan zhimin shiqi tongxingai zaixian" 現代「性」與帝國「愛」: 台韓殖民時期同性愛再現 [Colonial modernity and the empire of love: The representation of same-sex love in colonial Taiwan and Korea], *Taiwan wenxue xuebao* 台灣文學學報 23 (2013): 101–136, on 116.

52. Kang, *Obsession*, 34.

53. Kang, 35–36.

54. Kang, 38. On Sedgwick's original formulation, see Eve Kosofsky Sedgwick, *Epistemology of the Closet* (Berkeley: University of California Press, 1990), 1–65.

55. Jin Jiang, *Women Playing Men: Yue Opera and Social Change in Twentieth-Century Shanghai* (Seattle: University of Washington Press, 2009), 51–59.

56. Jiang, 205–208.

57. Tze-lan D. Sang, *The Emerging Lesbian: Female Same-Sex Desire in Modern China* (Chicago: University of Chicago Press, 2003).

58. See chapter 1 of this book.

59. Alvin K. Wong, "Transgenderism as a Heuristic Device: On the Cross-Historical and Transnational Adaptations of the *Legend of the White Snake*," in *Transgender China*, ed. Howard Chiang (New York: Palgrave Macmillan, 2012), 127–158.

60. On the formation of queer Sinophone modernity, see Howard Chiang, "(De)Provincializing China: Queer Historicism and Sinophone Postcolonial Critique," in *Queer Sinophone Cultures*, ed. Howard Chiang and Ari Larissa Heinrich (London: Routledge, 2013), 19–51; Howard Chiang, "Sinophone Modernity: History, Culture, Geopolitics," in *Composing Modernist Connections in China and Europe*, ed. Chunjie Zhang (London: Routledge, 2019), 142–167.

61. For a more in-depth discussion of the polarizing debates on literary humanism in the New Culture period, see Lydia H. Liu, *Translingual Practice: Literature, National Culture, and Translated Modernity—China, 1900–1937* (Stanford: Stanford University Press, 1995), 239–258. On related accounts of humanism and monstrosity in Chinese literary modernity, see Shu-mei Shih, *The Lure of the Modern: Writing Modernism in Semicolonial China, 1917–1937* (Berkeley: University of California Press, 2001); and David Der-wei Wang, *The Monster That Is History: History, Violence, and Fictional Writing in Twentieth-Century China* (Berkeley: University of California Press, 2004). On scientism as a dominant intellectual trend in early-twentieth-century China, see D. W. Y. Kwok, *Scientism in Chinese Thought: 1900–1950* (New Haven: Yale University Press, 1965); Charlotte Furth, *Ting Wen-chiang: Science and China's New Culture* (Cambridge, MA: Harvard University Press, 1970); and Hui Wang, "Scientific Worldview, Culture Debates, and the Reclassification of Knowledge in Twentieth-Century China," *boundary 2* 35 (2008): 125–155. For a more recent collection of essays that move beyond the simplistic paradigm of scientism in modern China, see Jing Tsu and Benjamin A. Elman, eds., *Science and Technology in Modern China, 1880s–1940s* (Leiden: Brill, 2014). On the limitation of this paradigm, see also Howard Chiang, *After Eunuchs: Science, Medicine, and the Transformation of Sex in Modern China* (New York: Columbia University Press, 2018), 70–124.

62. Ta-wei Chi, "Performers of the Paternal Past: History, Female Impersonators, and Twentieth-Century Chinese Fiction," *positions: east asia cultures critique* 15, no. 3 (2007): 580–608.

63. Wong, "Transgenderism as a Heuristic Device," 137.

64. Huang, *Queer Politics and Sexual Modernity in Taiwan*, 53–81. Although Huang discusses the media blitz on Zeng briefly (pp. 54–55), this chapter offers a more contextualized reading of the Zeng trials, including the details of not only the initial press coverage but also the subsequent stories about him, which introduced him to the Taiwanese public. See also Antonia Chao, "Fengnan shuonü, fengnü shuonan—renyao zhapianshi" 逢男說女，逢女說男-人妖詐騙史 [A history of renyao fraud], *Zili zaobao* (自立早報), October 22, 1997.

65. Huang, *Queer Politics and Sexual Modernity in Taiwan*, 55–59.

66. Huang, 57. The Chinese mental hygiene movement was founded at the National Central University in Nanjing in 1936 and rerooted in Taiwan in the 1950s. On the history of the movement in Republican China and postwar Taiwan, see Geoffrey Blowers and Shelley Wang, "Gone with the *West Wind*: The Emergence and Disappearance of Psychotherapeutic Culture in China (1936–1968)," in *Psychiatry and Chinese History*, ed. Howard Chiang (London: Pickering and Chatto, 2014), 143–160; Huang, *Queer Politics and Sexual Modernity in Taiwan*, 31–52; Wen-Ji Wang, "*West Wind Monthly* and the Popular Mental Hygiene Discourse in Republican China," *Taiwanese Journal for Studies of Science, Technology and Medicine* 13 (2011): 15–88; Emily Baum, "Healthy Minds, Compliant Citizens: The Politics of 'Mental Hygiene' in Republican China, 1938–1937," *Twentieth-Century China* 42, no. 3 (2017): 215–233; and Emily Baum, *The Invention of Madness: State, Society, and the Insane in Modern China* (Chicago: University of Chicago Press, 2018), 137–158.

67. Huang, *Queer Politics and Sexual Modernity in Taiwan*, 59–66. On "cut-sleeve *pi*" as a descriptor of male homoromance in premodern China, see Bret Hinsch, *Passions of the Cut Sleeve: The Male Homosexual Tradition in China* (Berkeley: University of California Press, 1990). On the discursive deployment of *tongxinglian* in Republican China, see Howard Chiang, "Epistemic Modernity and the Emergence of Homosexuality in China," *Gender and History* 22, no. 3 (2010): 629–657.

68. Huang, *Queer Politics and Sexual Modernity in Taiwan*, 73–81.

69. Huang, 66–73. On the queering of *tongzhi* in postsocialist China, see Hongwei Bao, "Queer Comrades: Transnational Popular Culture, Queer Sociality, and Socialist Legacy," *English Language Notes* 49 (2011): 131–137; Hongwei Bao, *Queer Comrades: Gay Identity and Queer Activism in Postsocialist China* (Copenhagen: Nordic Institute of Asian Studies Press, 2018); Hongwei Bao, *Queer China: Lesbian and Gay Literature and Visual Culture Under Postsocialism* (London: Routledge, 2020). On the politics of the term, see also Wah-shan Chou, *Tongzhi: Politics of Same-Sex Eroticism in Chinese Societies* (New York: Haworth, 2000). See also my discussion of this term in chapters 2 and 5 of this book.

70. Huang, *Queer Politics and Sexual Modernity in Taiwan*, 113–142. See also Jonathan Te-hsuan Yeh 葉德宣, "Yinhun busan de jiating zhuyi chimei: due quanyi *Niezi* zhuwen de lunshu fenxi" 陰魂不散的家庭主義魑魅: 對詮釋《孽子》諸文的論述分析 [The haunting spectre of familialism: A discursive analysis of interpretations of *Niezi*], *Chung-Wai Literary Monthly* 中外文學 24, no. 7 (1995): 66–88; Jonathan Te-hsuan Yeh, "Liangzhong luying/yin de fangfa: *Yongyuan de yinxueyan* he *Niezi*" 兩種露營/淫的方法: 永遠的《尹雪豔》和《孽子》 [Go camping: Gender crossing in *Yongyuan de yinxuanya* and *Niezi*], *Chung-Wai Literary Monthly* 中外文學 26, no. 12 (1998): 67–89; Jonathan Te-hsuan Yeh, "Cong jiating shouxun dao jingju wenxun: *Niezi* zhong fuxi guo/jia de shenti guixun dijing" 從家庭授勳到警局問訊:《孽子》中父系國／家的身體規訓地景 [From Familial decoration to police interrogation: Bodily discipline by the patrilineal nation/family in *Crystal Boys*], *Chung-Wai Literary Monthly* 中外文學 30, no. 2 (2001): 124–154; Ta-wei Chi 紀大偉, *Tongzhi wenxue shi: Taiwan de faming* 同志文學史: 台灣的發明 [A queer invention in Taiwan: A history of tongzhi literature] (Taipei: Linking, 2017), 275–339. For contrasting perspectives, see Hsiu-ping Tseng 曾秀萍, *Guchen, Niezi, Taibeiren: Bai Xianyong tongzhi xiaoshuolun* 孤臣・孽子・台北人: 白先勇同志小說論 [Alienated courtiers, impious sons, and Taipei ren: Essays on Pai Hsien-yung's tongzhi fictions] (Taipei: Elite, 2003). Whereas

most of these discussions center on gay male literature, for a discussion of contemporary Taiwanese lesbian literature, see Pei-ling Lin 林佩苓, *Yiwei yu zhongxin yu bianchui zhijian: Taiwan dangdai jingying nütongzhi xiaoshuo yanjiu* 依違於中心與邊陲之間: 臺灣當代菁英女同志小說研究 [Between center and periphery: Research on contemporary Taiwanese elite lesbian fictions] (Taipei: Showwe, 2015).

71. "Zhi renyao" 誌人妖 [Documenting renyao], *Shishi baoguan wushen quannian huabao* 時事報館戊申全年畫報 [Current affairs annual pictorial] 30 (1909): *juan* 10.

72. See Don J. Cohn, *Vignettes from the Chinese: Lithographs from Shanghai in the Late Nineteenth Century* (Hong Kong: Chinese University of Hong Kong Press, 1987); Wang Erhmin 王爾敏, "Zhongguo jindai zhishi pujihua chuanbo zhi tushuo xingshi—Dianshizhai huabaoli" 中國近代知識普及化傳播之圖說形式——點石齋畫報例 [The illustrated form of news for the diffusion of the modern world knowledge in nineteenth-century China: The Tien-Shih-Chai pictorial newspaper, 1884–1900], *Bulletin of the Institute of Modern History Academia Sinica* 19 (1990): 135–172; Wu Youru 吳有如 et al., ed., *Qingmuo fushihui: Dianshizhai huabao jingxuanji* 清末浮世繪: 《點石齋畫報》精選集 [Late Qing lithographs: Best collections of *Dianshizhai huabao*] (Taipei: Yuanliu, 2008). On the impact of the early periodical press on Chinese politics, including gender politics, see Joan Judge, *Print and Politics: "Shibao" and the Culture of Reform in Late Qing China* (Stanford: Stanford University Press, 1996); Barbara Mittler, *A Newspaper for China?: Power, Identity, and Change in Shanghai's News Media, 1872–1912* (Cambridge, MA: Harvard East Asia Monographs, 2004); Christopher Reed, *Gutenberg in Shanghai: Chinese Print Capitalism, 1876–1937* (Vancouver: University of British Columbia Press, 2004); and Joan Judge, *Republican Lens: Gender, Visuality, and Experience in the Early Chinese Periodical Press* (Berkeley: University of California Press, 2015).

73. Li Peifen 李佩芬, "*Dianshizhai huabao* zhong de zhixuguan (1884–1898)" 《點石齋畫報》中的秩序觀 [1884–1898] [The perspectives on order in *Dianshizhai huabao*] (MA thesis, National Taiwan Normal University, 2008).

74. On *Current Affairs*, see Chen Pingyuan 陳平原, *Tuxiang Wan Qing: Dianshizhai huabao zhiwai* 圖像晚清: 《點石齋畫報》之外 [Picturing the Late Qing: Outside the world of *Dianshizhai huabao*] (Shanghai: Dongfang, 2014), 130–150.

75. "Renyao tan" 人妖談 [Discussions on renyao], *Yanbao fuzhang* 燕報附張 [Yanbao supplement], no. 16 (January 21, 1910).

76. For another story of a human-animal *renyao*, see "Renyao helai" 人妖何來 [Where does renyao come from], *Yanbao fuzhang* (January 10, 1910).

77. Furth, "Androgynous Males and Deficient Females," 22.

78. M. J. Meijer, "Homosexual Offences in Ch'Ing Law," *T'oung Pao* 71, no. 1 (1985): 109–133, on 115.

79. On the modern scientific construction of "sex" in China, see Chiang, *After Eunuchs*. I borrow the notion of "problem bodies" from Clare Sears, *Arresting Dress: Cross-Dressing, Law, and Fascination in Nineteenth-Century San Francisco* (Durham: Duke University Press, 2015), 10–12.

80. "Renyao" 人妖 [Human prodigy], *Tuhua ribao* 圖畫日報 [Pictorial daily], no. 166 (1909): 12.

81. "Renyao" 人妖 [Human prodigy], *Shenzhou huabao* 神州畫報 [Shenzhou pictorials] (1910).

82. See, for example, Benjamin Elman, *A Cultural History of Modern Science in China* (Cambridge, MA: Harvard University Press, 2006); Sean Hsiang-lin Lei, *Neither Donkey nor Horse: Medicine in the Struggle Over China's Modernity* (Chicago: University of Chicago Press, 2014); and the essays in Tsu and Elman, *Science and Technology in Modern China.*

83. Gu Mingsheng 顧鳴盛, "Renyao" 人妖 [Human prodigy], *Yixue shijie* 醫學世界 [Medicine world] 22 (1913): 4–5. On the syncretism of Chinese and Western medicine, see Bridie Andrews, *The Making of Modern Chinese Medicine, 1850–1960* (Vancouver: University of British Columbia Press, 2014); and Lin, *Neither Donkey nor Horse.*

84. Gu, "Renyao," 5.

85. Tuisi Zhaizhu 退思齋主, "Renyao" 人妖 [Human prodigy], *Libailiu* 禮拜六 [Saturday], no. 191 (1922): 23–24. On the role of this genre in Shanghai's literary production, see Zhu Rutong 朱汝瞳, *Zhongguo xiandai wenxue liupai mantan* 中國現代文學流派漫談 [Modern Chinese literary schools] (Taipei: Showwe, 2010), 18; Bin Li, "The School of Mandarin Duck and Butterfly's Creative Push on Early Chinese Publishing Industry," *Asian Social Science* 8, no. 12 (2012): 164–170. The classic study of this genre is Perry Link, *Mandarin Ducks and Butterflies: Popular Fiction in Early Twentieth Century Chinese Cities* (Berkeley: University of California Press, 1981).

86. Tuisi Zhaizhu, "Renyao," 24.

87. On the scientific constructions of *ci* and *xiong*, see Howard Chiang, "The Conceptual Contours of Sex in the Chinese Life Sciences: Zhu Xi (1899–1962), Hermaphroditism, and the Biological Discourse of *Ci* and *Xiong*, 1920–1950," *East Asian Science, Technology and Society: An International Journal* 2, no. 3 (2008): 401–430; Chiang, *After Eunuchs*, 70–124. For the history of sexual science, see also Frank Dikötter, *Sex, Culture and Modernity in China: Medical Science and the Construction of Sexual Identities in the Early Republican Period* (Hong Kong: Hong Kong University Press, 1995).

88. Chai Fuyuan 柴福沅, *Xingxue ABC* 性學 ABC [ABC of sexology] (1928; Shanghai: Shijie shuju, 1932), 116.

89. See, for example, Ding Fubao 丁福保, "Ban yinyang yili" 半陰陽一例 [A case of half yinyang], *The Shin Yih Yaw* 新醫藥 [New medicine] 4, no. 9 (September 1936): 973–977.

90. Liu Piji 劉丕基, *Renjian wujie de shengwu* 人間誤解的生物 [Common misinterpretations of biology] (1928; Shanghai: Commercial Press, 1935), 82.

91. Zhou Shoujuan 周瘦鵑, "Diandao xingbie zhi guainü qinan" 顛倒性別之怪女奇男 [Odd women and strange men of sexual inversion], *Ziluolan* 紫羅蘭 [Violet] 4, no. 5 (1929): 1–6. On this magazine, see Pan Shaw-yu 潘少瑜, "Shishang wuzui: *Ziluolan* banyuekan de luoji meixue, zhengzhi yishi yu wenhua xiangxiang" 時尚無罪：《紫羅蘭》半月刊的邏輯美學、政治意識與文化想像 [Fashion is no crime: The aesthetics of editorship, political awareness and cultural imaginary of the semimonthly *Ziluolan*], *Chung Cheng Chinese Studies* 中正漢學研究, no. 22 (2013): 271–302.

92. Special issue on Mei Lanfang, *WXZB* 8, no. 353 (1929): 62–90. On the cross-dressing practice of *dan* actors, see Min Tian, "Male Dan: The Paradox of Sex, Acting, and Perception of Female Impersonation in Traditional Chinese Theatre," *Asia Theatre Journal* 17, no. 1 (2000): 78–97; Siu Leung Li, *Cross-Dressing in Chinese Opera* (Hong Kong: Hong Kong University Press, 2003); Joshua Goldstein, *Drama Kings: Players and Publics in the Re-Creation of Peking Opera* (Berkeley: University of California Press, 2007); and

Wenqing Kang, *Obsession: Male Same-Sex Relations in China, 1900–1950* (Hong Kong: Hong Kong University Press, 2009), 115–144.

93. Xi Yuan 西源, "Dadao danjiao de daibiaoren Mei Lanfang" 打倒旦角的代表人梅蘭芳 [Defeating Mei Lanfang, the representative dan], *WXZB* 8, no. 353 (1929): 62–65, on 64; Ying Yi 影憶, "Fanchang shehui de chanwu" 反常社會的產物 [An abnormal product of society], *WXZB* 8, no. 353 (1929): 66–72, on 71; Qi Fan 豈凡, "Mei Lanfang yangming haiwai zhiyi kaocha" 梅蘭芳揚名海外之一考察 [An investigation into Mei Lanfang's reputation abroad], *WXZB* 8, no. 353 (1929): 72–76; Pu Shui 蒲水, "Jiujiu guoji shangde mingyu ba" 救救國際上的名譽吧 [Save the international reputation], *WXZB* 8, no. 353 (1929): 77–78; Yu Ke 雨殼, "Nanban nüzhuang de Mei Lanfang" 男扮女裝的梅蘭芳 [Female impersonating Mei Lanfang], *WXZB* 8, no. 353 (1929): 82–84, on 83; Dao Mei 倒霉, "Gongju" 工具 [Tool], *WXZB* 8, no. 353 (1929): 84; Jue Gen 掘根, "Dao Mei yundong zhi xianjue wenti" 倒梅運動之先決問題 [The primary challenges of the anti-Mei movement], *WXZB* 8, no. 353 (1929): 84–85.

94. "Aimei" 愛美 [Beauty], *Xinshenghuo zhoukan* 新生活週刊 [New life weekly] 1, nos. 72–73 (1935): 18.

95. "Shishi xianping: renyao" 時事閒評：人妖 [Current affairs: renyao], *Xinshijie xiaoshuo shebao* 新世界小說社報 [New world fiction house magazine], no. 7 (1906): 1.

96. Qi Fan 豈凡, "Nübiannan yu nübannan" 女變男與女扮男 [Woman becoming man and woman dressing up as man], *Renyan zhoukan* 人言週刊 [Gossip weekly] 2, no. 9 (1935): 171.

97. Magnus Hirschfeld, *Men and Women: The World Journey of a Sexologist*, trans. O. P. Green (New York: G. P. Putnam's Sons, 1935), 65.

98. Magnus Hirschfeld, *Transvestites: The Erotic Drive to Cross Dress*, trans. Michael A. Lombardi-Nash (1910; Buffalo, NY: Prometheus, 1991).

99. Hirschfeld, *Transvestites*, 256.

100. "Renyao" 人妖 [Human prodigy], *HN* 3, no. 4 (1934): 62–63.

101. "Renyao," *HN* 3, no. 4 (1934): 62.

102. "Renyao," *HN* 3, no. 4 (1934): 63.

103. See, for example, Xi Liu 細柳, "Xiandai renyao Shen Junru: Shanghai zhongshengxiang" 現代人妖沈俊如：上海眾生相 [Modern human prodigy Shen Junru: Public appearance in Shanghai], *Yisiqi huabao* 一四七畫報 [One four seven pictorial] 12 (1947): 4–5; "Renyao 'Shen Wuye' beibu!: Yilishabo gongyu puohuo mimi yinku" 人妖「沈五爺」被捕！：依利莎伯公寓破獲秘密淫窟 [Human prodigy Shen Wuye arrested!: Elizabeth Apartment discovered to hide a lust cave], *XSH* no. 67, May 2, 1947; "'Renyao' beibu zhi qianyin houguo" 「人妖」被捕之前因後果 [The reasons and consequences of the arrest of "renyao"], *XSH*, no. 83 (September 11, 1947); "Qishi niannian you jinnia renyao duo: Nanban nüzhuang guairenyao" 奇事年年有 今年人妖多：男扮女裝怪人妖 [Strange things happen annually, numerous human prodigies witnessed this year: Male cross-dressing weird human prodigy], *Zhongwai Chunqiu* 中外春秋 [Sino-Foreign annals], no. 51 (September 17, 1947).

104. The nonimplementation of *renyao* as a legal language in the prosecution of these individuals does not mean their gender-transgressive conduct received no policing or legal scrutiny whatsoever. There were other ways for the police to arrest trans subjects or for

a prosecutor to file charges against them, such as by way of referencing criminal codes on fraud and swindling or subjecting them to trials of civil law (e.g., marriage disputes). For the police and court records of the Shen Junru case, see SMA Q131-5-6190, Q185-2-23279, and Q188-2-2920. For the records of the Ju Guangzao case, see SMA Q185-2-21657, Q185-2-25565, Q185-3-17428, and Q188-2-5018. In these folios comprising more than fourteen hundred pages of archival documents concerning the Shen and Ju cases, only *once* did I come across the mentioning of *renyao* in passing: the category made a brief appearance in SMA Q185-2-21657 as a borrowing of Ju's popular depiction in the news media.

105. While noting the intrinsic limitations, I use the masculine pronoun to refer to Zeng for two reasons. First, this usage conforms to the convention adopted in most historical records on Zeng. Second, Zeng at one point declared interest in a sex change surgery to transition into a woman. It is unclear, however, if Zeng followed through with this intent, but the implication is that Zeng's biological and social sex was still perceived by himself and others as predominantly male. Nonetheless, I acknowledge the problems with using the masculine pronoun exclusively in analyzing Zeng's experience, especially since Zeng's desire for transitioning suggests a deep-seated identification with the opposite gender. See, for example, "Renyao fuchuxian: Zhuangnan ban nüzhuang" 人妖復出現 壯男扮女裝 [Human prodigy reappears: A strong man dressed as a woman], *MSRB*, July 20, 1957. Moreover, some newspaper accounts of Zeng that appeared later in the decade suggested the possibility that Zeng was an intersexed person. The earliest report of the Zeng case might be "Renyao Zeng Qiuhuang" 人妖曾秋煌 [Human prodigy Zeng Qiuhuang], *MSRB*, May 26, 1951. In this account, Zeng was described as having both yin and yang bodily features. The piece was subtitled as "With a Wife and a Son, Zeng Enjoys the Company of Men."

106. "Renyao zhaqi'an zuofupan Zeng Qiuhuang gaichuxing yinian" 人妖詐欺案昨覆判 曾秋煌改處刑一年 [The Case of human prodigy reheard yesterday: Zeng Qiuhuang resentenced to one year], *LHB*, October 23, 1951.

107. "Renyao jiedi Taibei: Gaoyuan zuowenxun" 人妖解抵台北 高院昨間訊 [The Human prodigy arrived in Taipei and was interrogated by the High Court yesterday], *LHB*, September 23, 1951.

108. "Renyao Zeng Qiuhuang wushi Zeng Chaodong mingri fenbie shousheng" 「人妖」曾秋皇 「舞師」曾朝東 明日分別受審 [The "human prodigy" Zeng Qiuhuang and the "dance teacher" Zeng Chaodong to be investigated individually tomorrow], *LHB*, October 17, 1951.

109. "Renyao Zeng Qiuhuang nanweile kanshou" 人妖曾秋皇 難為了看守 [The human prodigy Zeng Qiuhuang gave the guard a hard time], *LHB*, October 18, 1951.

110. "Renyao Zeng Qiuhuang an gaoyuan shengxun zhongjie" 人妖曾秋煌案 高院審訊終結 [The investigation of the case of the human prodigy Zeng Qiuhuang by the High Court concluded], *ZLWB*, October 18, 1951.

111. "Renyaoan fusheng xuanpan" 人妖案複審宣判 [The appeal of the human prodigy case was ruled], *ZLWB*, October 22, 1951.

112. "Renyao zhaqi'an zuofupan Zeng Qiuhuang gaichuxing yinian."

113. "Renyao zhaqi'an zuofupan Zeng Qiuhuang gaichuxing yinian."

114. I thank Benjamin Kahan for drawing my attention to this point.

115. "Aile zhongnian bunan bunü hunpei liangdu yifuyiqi" 哀樂中年不男不女 婚配兩度亦夫亦妻 [The mid-aged intersex married twice to a husband and a wife, respectively], *LHB*, December 24, 1954.

116. "Aile zhongnian bunan bunü hunpei liangdu yifuyiqi."

117. For more details on Xie, see Chiang, *After Eunuchs*, 236–286. On Christine Jorgensen, see David Harley Serlin, "Christine Jorgensen and the Cold War Closet," *Radical History Review* 62 (1995): 137–165; Joanne Meyerowitz, *How Sex Changed: A History of Transsexuality in the United States* (Cambridge, MA: Harvard University Press, 2002); Susan Stryker, *Transgender History* (Berkeley: Seal, 2008); and Emily Skidmore, "Constructing the 'Good Transsexual': Christine Jorgensen, Whiteness, and Heteronormativity in the Mid-Twentieth-Century Press," *Feminist Studies* 37 (2011): 270–300.

118. "Aile zhongnian bunan bunü hunpei liangdu yifuyiqi."

119. "Aile zhongnian bunan bunü hunpei liangdu yifuyiqi."

120. "Aile zhongnian bunan bunü hunpei liangdu yifuyiqi."

121. On the role of sex-reassignment surgery in shaping the concept of gender in the United States, see Bernice Hausman, *Changing Sex: Transsexualism, Technology, and the Idea of Gender* (Durham: Duke University Press, 1995).

122. "Tianzhongzhen faxian zhenxing yinyangren" 田中鎮發現 真性陰陽人 [Tianzhong Township discovers a true hermaphrodite], *MSRB*, April 16, 1955.

123. "Yiyiwang dajin quanan jiangyisong fayuan" 已一網打盡 全案將移送法院 [Completely under control: The entire case is now being delivered to the court for investigation], *ZGSB*, November 14, 1955.

124. "Congfan Zeng Qiuhuang jianliangxing yinanyinü ququjiaren" 從犯曾秋皇 兼兩性 亦男亦女娶妻嫁人 [Suspect Zeng Qiuhuang has both sexes: Being both male and female and married to either sex], *ZGSB*, November 14, 1955.

125. "Qiankun hunyuan yiti cixiong jingneng liangquan" 乾坤混元一體 雌雄竟能兩全 [Male and female hybridized into one: Maleness and femaleness can functionally coexist], *LHB*, September 25, 1956.

126. "Qiankun hunyuan yiti cixiong jingneng liangquan."

127. "Taizhongshi renyao chuxian: Xunluojing mangqing ruju" 台中市人妖出現 巡邏警忙請入局 [Human prodigy appears in Taizhong City again: Police took him to the station], *MSRB*, September 25, 1956; "Zeng Qiuhuang yijie Yuanlin" 曾秋皇 移解員林 [Zeng Qiuhuang released in Yuanlin], *LHB*, September 26, 1956.

128. "Renyao jieshou tijian: Chunyang haobu shenyin" 人妖接受體檢 純陽毫不滲陰 [Human prodigy found completely male after medical exam], *MSRB*, September 26, 1956.

129. "Renyao yiyu Yunlin: Laofu mata buxiao" 人妖移玉雲林 老父罵他不孝 [Human prodigy relocated to Yunlin: Father calls him unfilial], *MSRB*, September 27, 1956.

130. "Renyao nüyou quishi nanren" 人妖女友 卻是男人 [Human prodigy's girlfriend is a man], *MSRB*, September 26, 1956.

131. "Yinyang guaiqi renyao zhuangshen banggui xingqiang" 陰陽怪氣人妖 裝神扮鬼行搶 [Enigmatic human prodigy assumes supernatural status for robbery], *MSRB*, August 7, 1957.

132. "Laoyu yugui jingcha qinyao" 老嫗遇鬼 警察擒妖 [Old woman ran into a ghost: The cops caught the prodigy], *LHB*, August 7, 1957.

133. "Laoyu yugui jingcha qinyao."

134. "Renyao Zeng Qiuhuang beitiqi gongsu" 人妖曾秋煌 被提起公訴 [Charges filed against the human prodigy Zeng Qiuhuang], *LHB*, August 26, 1957; "Renyao Zeng Qiuhuang beitiqi gongsu" 人妖曾秋煌 被提起公訴 [Charges filed against the human prodigy Zeng Qiuhuang], *MSRB*, August 26, 1957.

135. "Renyao zuoerduo tiechuang suiyue chang" 人妖作惡多 鐵窗歲月長 [Human prodigy receives a long sentence for wrongdoing], *MSRB*, September 1, 1957; "Yinyangren Zeng Qiuhuang chuxing sannian jiuyue" 陰陽人曾秋煌 處刑三年九月 [The yin-yang person Zeng Qiuhuang received a three-year-and-nine-month sentence], *ZGSB*, September 14, 1957.

136. "Zhuoyao rongyi jingyaonan Zeng Qiuhuang nanyu anpai" 捉妖容易禁妖難 曾秋煌難於安排 [The prodigy is easy to catch but hard to keep: The difficulty of allocating Zeng Qiuhuang], *LHB*, August 8, 1957.

137. "Zhuoyao rongyi jingyaonan."

138. Searching for "renyao" in the database of *People's Daily* (the official newspaper of the Central Committee of the Chinese Communist Party), trans scholar Qing Fei Zhang finds no occurrence of this keyword in the newspaper in the Maoist era (1949–1976). According to Zhang, the first time that *renyao* appeared in *People's Daily* was in an article dated October 8, 1982. Titled "A Glance at Social Problems in Taiwan," the article used the transgender performance of Taiwanese *renyao* artists as the basis for criticizing Taiwan for importing a "foreign and base" culture. See Qing Fei Zhang, "Transgender Representation by the People's Daily Since 1949," *Sexuality and Culture: An Interdisciplinary Quarterly* 18, no. 1 (2014): 180–195, on 188.

139. On the intercultural citationality of *renyao* between Taiwan and other Asian countries such as Singapore, Thailand, and Japan since the 1970s, see Chen Wei-Jhen 陳薇真, *Taiwan kuaxingbie qianshi: Yiliao, fengsu yu yaji zaofeng* 台灣跨性別前史：醫療、風俗誌與亞際遭逢 [Pretransgender history in Taiwan: Medical treatment, hostess clubs and inter-Asia encounters] (New Taipei City: Transgender Punk Activist Publishing, 2016), 175–227. Similar to the cultural transformation of the word *queer*, *yao* has been reclaimed by gender-variant individuals as a subversive concept. On the discourse of *yao* among sex workers in the contemporary PRC, see Dennis Lin 林純德, "'Yao' xinggongzuozhe yanjiu: Shijiao yu fangfa" 「妖」性工作者研究：視角與方法 [Research on "yao" sex workers: Perspectives and methods] (paper presented at the 8th Theory and Practice of the Sociology of Sex Graduate Workshop, Harbin, People's Republic of China, June 28 to July 5, 2017). On the Hong Kong sex worker Kiki, who uses *yao* to queer transgenderism, see Yiu Fai Chow, "*Yao*, More or Less Human," *TSQ: Transgender Studies Quarterly* 5, no. 3 (2018): 464–472.

140. I borrow this insight from Spivak's discussion of the postcolonial differentiation of gender in Gayatri Chakravorty Spivak, "Woman in Difference: Mahashweta Devi's 'Douloti the Bountiful,'" *Cultural Critique* 14 (1989–1990): 105–128. On Taiwan's cosmopolitanism, see Shu-mei Shih, *Visuality and Identity: Sinophone Articulations Across the Pacific* (Berkeley: University of California Press, 2007), 165–182.

141. My notion of minor historicity is adapted from the idea of "minor literature" developed by Gilles Deleuze and Félix Guattari. See Gilles Deleuze and Félix Guattari, *Kafka: Toward a Minor Literature*, trans. Dana Polan (Minneapolis: University of Minnesota Press, 1986).

4. Inscribing Transgender

1. In addition to the works cited in previous chapters, see also Andrea Bachner, *Beyond Sinology: Chinese Writing and the Scripts of Culture* (New York: Columbia University Press, 2014); Sheng-mei Ma, *Sinophone-Anglophone Cultural Duet* (New York: Palgrave Macmillan, 2017); and Hsiao-yen Peng and Ella Raidel, eds., *The Politics of Memory in Sinophone Cinemas and Image Culture: Altering Archives* (London: Routledge, 2018).

2. On this point, I have learned enormously from extended conversations with Andrea Bachner and Yu-lin Lee.

3. Jing Tsu, *Sound and Script in the Chinese Diaspora* (Cambridge, MA: Harvard University Press, 2010).

4. Rey Chow, *Entanglements, or Transmedial Thinking About Capture* (Durham: Duke University Press, 2012).

5. On the concept of intercorporeality, see Gail Weiss, *Body Images: Embodiment as Intercorporeality* (London: Routledge, 1998).

6. On queer Sinophone production, see Howard Chiang, "(De)Provincializing China: Queer Historicism and Sinophone Postcolonial Critique," in *Queer Sinophone Cultures*, ed. Howard Chiang and Ari Heinrich (London: Routledge, 2013), 19–51; and Howard Chiang and Alvin K. Wong, "Queer Sinophone Studies: Interdisciplinary Synergies," in *Keywords in Queer Sinophone Studies*, ed. Howard Chiang and Alvin K. Wong (London: Routledge, 2020), 1–15.

7. On the convergence of anti-Chinese politics and cross-dressing discourses in the turn-of-the-twentieth-century United States, see Clare Sears, *Cross-Dressing, Law, and Fascination in Nineteenth-Century San Francisco* (Durham: Duke University Press, 2015), 121–138.

8. Howard Chiang, *After Eunuchs: Science, Medicine, and the Transformations of Sex in Modern China* (New York: Columbia University Press, 2018).

9. Dorothy Ko, *Cinderella's Sisters: A Revisionist History of Footbinding* (Berkeley: University of California Press, 2005); Angela Ki Che Leung, *Leprosy in China: A History* (New York: Columbia University Press, 2009); and Howard Chiang, "How China Became a 'Castrated Civilization' and Eunuchs a 'Third Sex,'" in *Transgender China*, ed. Howard Chiang (New York: Palgrave Macmillan, 2012), 23–66.

10. Ari Larissa Heinrich, *The Afterlife of Images: Translating the Pathological Body Between China and the West* (Durham: Duke University Press, 2008); Yang Ruisong 楊瑞松, *Bingfu, huanghuo yu shuishi: "Xifang" shiye de zhongguo xingxiang yu jindai Zhongguo guozu lunshu xiangxiang* 病夫, 黃禍與睡獅: 「西方」視野的中國形象與近代中國國族論述想像 [Sick man, yellow peril, and sleeping lion: The images of China from the Western perspectives and the discourses and imagination of Chinese national identity] (Taipei: Chengchi

University Press, 2010); and Carlos Rojas, *Homesickness: Culture, Contagion, and National Reform in Modern China* (Cambridge, MA: Harvard University Press, 2015). On the transcultural traffic of the sleeping lion image, see also Ari Larissa Heinrich, *Chinese Surplus: Biopolitical Aesthetics and the Medically Commodified Body* (Durham: Duke University Press, 2018), 25–48.

11. Yinghua Jia, *The Last Eunuch of China: The Life of Sun Yaoting*, trans. Sun Haichen (Beijing: China Intercontinental, 2008). For the original Chinese edition, see Jia Yinghua 賈英華, *Modai taijian miwen: Sun Yaoting zhuan* 末代太監秘聞: 孫耀庭傳 [The secret life of the last eunuch: A biography of Sun Yaoting] (Beijing: Zhishi chubanshe, 1993).

12. Nikki Sullivan, "Transmogrification: (Un)becoming Other(s)," in *The Transgender Studies Reader*, ed. Susan Stryker and Stephen Whittle (London: Routledge, 2006), 553–563.

13. On the queer appropriation of transgenderism at the expense of excluding transsexualism, see Jay Prosser, *Second Skins: The Body Narratives of Transsexuality* (New York: Columbia University Press, 1998), 21–60. Cf. Judith Butler, *Bodies That Matter: On the Discursive Limits of "Sex"* (London: Routledge, 1993).

14. Sullivan, "Transmogrification," 561.

15. *Lai Shi, China's Last Eunuch* 中國的最後一個太監, dir. Chi Leung Jacob Cheung (Hong Kong: Golden Harvest, 1987); *Swordsman 2* 東方不敗, dir. Ching Siu-tung (Hong Kong: Mei Ah, 1992); *Farewell My Concubine* 霸王別姬, dir. Chen Kaige (Hong Kong: Tomson, 1993).

16. On Pu Yi's dismissal of eunuchs in the 1920s, see *After Eunuchs*, 63–66.

17. On Sun, see Sun Yaoting 孫耀庭, "Wozai mingguo zuo taijian" 我在民國作太監 [Being a eunuch in the Republican period], *ZJWX* 57, no. 2 (1990): 113–133; Sun Yaoting, "Wozai mingguo zuo taijian" 我在民國作太監 [Being a eunuch in the Republican period], *ZJWX* 57, no. 3 (1990): 115–134; Yang Zhengguang 楊爭光, *Zhongguo zuihou yige taijian* 中國最後一個太監 [The last eunuch in China] (Beijing: Qunzhong chubanshe, 1991); Jia, *Modai taijian miwen*; Ling Haicheng 凌海成, *Zhongguo zuihou yige taijian* 中國最後一個太監 [The last eunuch in China] (Hong Kong: Heping tushu, 2003), 17–21.

18. Chiang, "How China Became a 'Castrated Civilization' and Eunuchs a 'Third Sex,'" 50.

19. See Jennifer W. Jay, "Another Side of Chinese Eunuch History: Castration, Adoption, Marriage, and Burial," *Canadian Journal of History* 28, no. 3 (1993): 459–478; Jennifer W. Jay, "Castration and Medical Images of Eunuchs in Traditional China," in *Current Perspectives in the History of Science in East Asia*, ed. Yun-sik Kim and Francesca Bray (Seoul: Seoul National University Press, 1999), 385–394; and Melissa Dale, "Understanding Emasculation: Western Medical Perspectives on Chinese Eunuchs," *Social History of Medicine* 23, no. 1 (2010): 38–55. On the identity of eunuchs as "masculine" relatives in kinship organization, see Gilbert Chan, "Castration and Connection: Kinship Organization Among Ming Eunuchs," *Journal of Ming Studies* 74 (2016): 27–47. For a revisionist study of Qing eunuchs, see Norman A. Kutcher, *Eunuch and Emperor in the Great Age of Qing Rule* (Oakland: University of California Press, 2018). For a more critical perspective, see Chiang, "How China Became a 'Castrated Civilization.'"

20. See, for example, Georges Morache, *Pékin et ses habitants: Étude d'hygiene* (Paris: J.-B. Baillière, 1869), 133–135; G. Carter Stent, "Chinese Eunuchs," *Journal of the North China*

Branch of the Royal Asiatic Society 11 (1877): 143–184; and Jean-Jacques Matignon, "Les eunuques du Palais Impérial à Pékin," Bulletins de la Société d'anthropologie de Paris 7, no. 4 (1896): 325–336.

21. Sun, "Wozai mingguo zuo taijian," ZJWX 57, no. 2 (1990): 124–125; a more dramatized account of Sun's castration can be found in Jia, Modai taijian miwen, 24–26.
22. Min Tian, "Male Dan: The Paradox of Sex, Acting, and Perception of Female Impersonation in Traditional Chinese Theatre," Asia Theatre Journal 17, no. 1 (2000): 78–97; Siu Leung Li, Cross-Dressing in Chinese Opera (Hong Kong: Hong Kong University Press, 2003); Joshua Goldstein, Drama Kings: Players and Publics in the Re-Creation of Peking Opera (Berkeley: University of California Press, 2007); Wenqing Kang, Obsession: Male Same-Sex Relations in China, 1900–1950 (Hong Kong: Hong Kong University Press, 2009), 115–144; Howard Chiang, "Epistemic Modernity and the Emergence of Homosexuality in China," Gender and History 22, no. 3 (2010): 629–657; and David E. Mungello, Western Queers in China: Flight to the Land of Oz (Lanham, MD: Rowman and Littlefield, 2012), 25–40.
23. On Mei, see, for example, Joshua Goldstein, "Mei Lanfang and the Nationalization of Peking Opera, 1912–1930," positions: east asia cultures critique 7, no. 2 (1999): 377–420; John Zou, "Cross-Dressed Nation: Mei Lanfang and the Clothing of Modern Chinese Men," in Embodied Modernities: Corporeality, Representation, and Chinese Cultures, ed. Fran Martin and Ari Larissa Heinrich (Honolulu: University of Hawai'i Press, 2006), 79–97; and Min Tian, Mei Lanfang and the Twentieth-Century International Stage: Chinese Theatre Placed and Displaced (New York: Palgrave Macmillan, 2012).
24. Helen Hok-Sze Leung, "Trans on Screen," in Transgender China, ed. Howard Chiang (New York: Palgrave Macmillan, 2012), 183–198.
25. See Leung's insightful analysis of this problem in her book Farewell My Concubine: A Queer Film Classic (Vancouver: Arsenal Pulp Press, 2010). See also Chris Berry, "Farewell My Concubine: At What Price Success?" Cinemaya 20 (1993): 20–22; Shu Kei, "Farewell to My Concubine: A Letter to Chen Kaige," Cinemaya 20 (1993): 18–20; Max Tessier, "Farewell to My Concubine: Art Over Politics," Cinemaya 20 (1993): 16–18; E. Ann Kaplan, "Reading Formations and Chen Kaige's Farewell My Concubine," in Transnational Chinese Cinemas: Identity, Nationhood, Gender, ed. Sheldon Hsiao-peng Lu (Honolulu: University of Hawai'i Press, 1997), 265–275; Wendy Larson, "The Concubine and the Figure of History: Chen Kaige's Farewell My Concubine," in Transnational Chinese Cinemas: Identity, Nationhood, Gender, ed. Sheldon Hsiao-peng Lu (Honolulu: University of Hawai'i Press, 1997), 331–346; Teri Silvo, "Chinese Opera, Global Cinema, and the Ontology of the Person: Chen Kaige's Farewell My Concubine," in Between Opera and Cinema, ed. Jeongwon Joe and Rose Theresa (New York: Routledge, 2002), 177–197; Song Hwee Lim, Celluloid Comrades: Representations of Male Homosexuality in Contemporary Chinese Cinemas (Honolulu: University of Hawai'i Press, 2006), 69–98; and Jen-Hao Hsu, "Queering Chineseness: The Queer Sphere of Feelings in Farewell My Concubine and Green Snake," Asian Studies Review 36 (2012): 1–17.
26. Leung, "Trans on Screen," 194.
27. Leung, 196–197; Susan Stryker, "My Words to Victor Frankenstein Above the Village of Chamounix: Performing Transgender Rage," GLQ: A Journal of Lesbian and Gay Studies 1, no. 3 (1994): 237–254.

28. For an illuminating account of Cheung's queer iconicity, see Helen Hok-Sze Leung, *Undercurrents: Queer Culture and Postcolonial Hong Kong* (Vancouver: University of British Columbia Press, 2008), 85–105. Cheung also played the gay character Ho Po-wing in Wong Kar-wai's *Happy Together* (1997), which was discussed in chapter 2 of this book.

29. Jin Yong 金庸, *Xiao Ao Jiang Hu* 笑傲江湖 [The smiling, proud wanderers], 4 vols. (Hong Kong: Minghe She, 1980); Shu-mei Shih, *Fanlisan: Huayuyuxi yanjiulun* 反離散: 華語語系研究論 [Against diaspora: Discourses on Sinophone studies] (Taipei: Linking, 2017), 139–160.

30. Leung, *Undercurrents*, 71–77.

31. For homonormative critiques of the film, see Wah-Shan Chou 周華山, *Tongzhilun* 同志論 [On tongzhi] (Hong Kong: Xianggang Tongzhi Yanjiushe, 1995), 300; Ching Yau 游靜, *Lingqi luzao* 另起爐灶 [Starting another stove] (Hong Kong: Youth Literary Bookstore, 1996), 165.

32. I switch my usage of gender pronoun in referring to Dongfang Bubai here to reflect both my argument about her sex change and the gendered nature of the reciprocal erotic attraction between Ling Huchong and her in the film.

33. Leung, *Undercurrents*, 73. Given the accentuation of Dongfang Bubai's feminine beauty in the film, I retain the feminine pronoun when referring to the Dongfang Bubai character in my subsequent analysis.

34. Leung, "Trans on Screen," 188.

35. Stryker, "My Words to Victor Frankenstein."

36. *Reign of Assassins* 劍雨, dir. Su Chao-pin and John Woo (Hong Kong: Media Asia and Beijing: Beijing Galloping Horse Group, 2010); *Flying Swords of Dragon Gate* 龍門飛甲, dir. Tsui Hark (Hong Kong: Distribution Workshop, 2011).

37. *New Dragon Gate Inn* 新龍門客棧, dir. Raymond Lee (Hong Kong: Golden Harvest, 1992).

38. Henry Shi-shan Tsai, *The Eunuchs in the Ming Dynasty* (Albany: State University of New York Press, 1996), 115.

39. Tsai, 115.

40. Tsai, 116.

41. Keith McMahon, "The Pornographic Doctrine of a Loyalist Ming Novel: Social Decline and Sexual Disorder in *Preposterous Words* (Guwangyan)," in *Sexuality in China: Histories of Power and Pleasure*, ed. Howard Chiang (Seattle: University of Washington Press, 2018), 50–75, on 64.

42. This quotation is taken from Dorothy Ko's examination of the footbinding origin discourses penned by Chinese philologists from the twelfth century onward. Ko, *Cinderella's Sisters*, 112.

43. On the original formulation of "moral economy" in the context of British working-class social history, see Edward P. Thompson, "The Moral Economy of the English Crowd in the Eighteenth Century," *Past and Present*, no. 50 (1971): 76–136.

44. See, e.g., Nikki Sullivan and Samantha Murray, eds., *Somatechnics: Queering the Technologisation of Bodies* (Farham, Surrey, UK: Ashgate, 2009).

45. Weiss, *Body Images*.

46. Eve Kosofsky Sedgwick, *Between Men: English Literature and Male Homosocial Desire* (New York: Columbia University Press, 1985).

47. Tsai, *The Eunuchs in the Ming Dynasty*.

48. Chiang, "How China Became a 'Castrated Civilization.'"

49. Shih, "The Concept of the Sinophone," *PMLA* 126, no. 3 (2011): 709–718.

50. The term *geobody* is first proposed by Thongchai Winichakul in *Siam Mapped: A History of the Geo-Body of a Nation* (Honolulu: University of Hawai'i Press, 1994). On the historical relationship between China's geobody and the human body as viewed through the lenses of war and military activities, see Jinlin Hwang 黃金麟, *Lishi, shenti, guojia: Jindai zhongguo de shenti xingcheng, 1895–1937* 歷史、身體、國家：近代中國的身體形成，1895–1937 [History, the body, the nation: The formation of the body of modern China, 1895–1937] (Taipei: Linking, 2001); Jinlin Hwang, *Zhanzhen, shenti, xiandaixing: Xiandai Taiwan de junshi zhili yu shenti, 1895–2005* 戰爭、身體、現代性：近代台灣的軍事治理與身體，1895–2005 [War, the body, and modernity: Military governmentality and the body in modern Taiwan, 1895–2005] (Taipei: Linking, 2009). On the framework of colonial modernity, see the essays in Tani E. Barlow, ed., *Formations of Colonial Modernity in East Asia* (Durham: Duke University Press, 1997). On the bypassing of the colonial modernity paradigm in the study of queer Sinophone cultures, see Chiang, "(De)Provincializing China."

51. Shu-mei Shih, *Visuality and Identity: Sinophone Articulations Across the Pacific* (Berkeley: University of California Press, 2007), 84.

52. See, for example, Rebecca Karl, "Creating Asia: China in the World at the Beginning of the Twentieth Century," *American Historical Review* 103, no. 4 (1998): 1096–1118; Prasenjit Duara, "Asia Redux: Conceptualizing a Region for Our Times," *Journal of Asian Studies* 69, no. 4 (2010): 963–983; Hui Wang, "The Idea of Asia and Its Ambiguities," *Journal of Asian Studies* 69, no. 4 (2010): 985–989.

53. Howard Chiang and Alvin K. Wong, "Queering the Transnational Turn: Regionalism and Queer Asias," *Gender, Place and Culture: A Journal of Feminist Geography* 23, no. 1 (2016): 1643–1656.

54. Howard Chiang and Alvin K. Wong, "Asia Is Burning: Queer Asia as Critique," *Culture, Theory and Critique* 58, no. 2 (2017): 121–126.

55. Susan Stryker, "De/Colonizing Transgender Studies of China," in *Transgender China*, ed. Howard Chiang (New York: Palgrave Macmillan, 2012), 287–292.

56. For a rigorous historical contextualization of the modern Western perceptions of China, see Yang, *Bingfu, huanghuo yu shuishi*.

57. David Henry Hwang, *M. Butterfly* (New York: Plume, 1989); *M. Butterfly*, dir. David Cronenberg (Burbank, CA: Warner, 1993).

58. Dorine Kondo, "*M. Butterfly*: Orientalism, Gender, and a Critique of Essentialist Identity," *Cultural Critique* 16 (1990): 5–29; David Eng, "In the Shadows of a Diva: Committing Homosexuality in David Henry Hwang's *M. Butterfly*," *Amerasia Journal* 20, no. 1 (1994): 93–116; David Eng, *Racial Castration: Managing Masculinity in Asian America* (Durham: Duke University Press, 2001), 137–166; Eng-Beng Lim, *Brown Boys and Rice Queens: Spellbinding Performance in the Asias* (New York: New York University Press, 2014), 138–143.

59. Marjorie Garber, *Vested Interests: Cross-Dressing and Cultural Anxiety* (London: Routledge, 1992), 17.

60. On minority subjects' negotiation with mainstream culture, see José Esteban Muñoz, *Disidentifications: Queers of Color and the Performance of Politics* (Minneapolis: University of Minnesota Press, 1999).

61. On the history of being human, see Roger Smith, *Being Human: Historical Knowledge and the Creation of Human Nature* (New York: Columbia University Press, 2007). On the scientific constructions of being human in late imperial and modern China, see Howard Chiang, ed., *The Making of the Human Sciences in China: Historical and Conceptual Foundations* (Leiden: Brill, 2019).

62. Anne Enke, ed., *Transfeminist Perspectives: In and Beyond Transgender and Gender Studies* (Philadelphia: Temple University Press, 2012); Susan Stryker and Talia M. Bettcher, eds., "Trans/Feminisms," special issue, *TSQ: Transgender Studies Quarterly* 3, nos. 1–2 (2016): 1–329.

63. Teresa de Lauretis, "Popular Culture, Public and Private Fantasies: Femininity and Fetishism in David Cronenberg's *M. Butterfly*," *Signs: Journal of Women in Culture and Society* 24, no. 2 (1999): 303–334.

64. Nicolas Tarling, *Orientalism and the Operatic World* (Lanham, MD: Rowman and Littlefield, 2015). To be historically accurate, John Luther Long's short story "Madame Butterfly" was published in 1898 and dramatized in 1900 by David Belasco, which Puccini saw and which inspired his opera. Long's story is indebted to Pierr Loti's *Madame Chrysanthème* (published in 1887) as well. Either Long or Loti is the more appropriate site of origin for *M. Butterfly*. See Jan van Rij, *Madame Butterfly: Japaonisme, Puccini, and the Search for the Real Cho-Cho-San* (Berkeley, CA: Stone Bridge, 2001); Jonathan Wisenthal, Sherrill Grace, Melinda Boyd, Brian McIlroy, and Vera Micznik, eds., *A Vision of the Orient: Texts, Intertexts, and Context of Madame Butterfly* (Toronto: University of Toronto Press, 2006).

65. Hwang's play is based on an actual court case involving Shi Pei Pu and Bernard Boursicot. See Joyce Wadler, "The True Story of M. Butterfly: The Spy Who Fell in Love with a Shadow," *New York Times*, August 15, 1993.

66. Catharine Clément, *Opera, or the Undoing of Women*, trans. Betsy Wing (Minneapolis: University of Minnesota Press, 1988), 43–47.

67. Rey Chow, "The Dream of a Butterfly," in *Human, All Too Human*, ed. Diana Fuss (London: Routledge, 1996), 61–92, on 70.

68. Susan Stryker, "The Transgender Issue: An Introduction," *GLQ: A Journal of Lesbian and Gay Studies* 4, no. 2 (1998): 145–158, on 155.

69. Gayle Salamon, "Transfeminism and the Future of Gender," in *Women's Studies on the Edge*, ed. Joan Wallach Scott (Durham: Duke University Press, 2008), 115–136, on 118.

70. Julian Bourg, "The Red Guards of Paris: French Student Maoism of the 1960s," *History of European Ideas* 31, no. 4 (2004): 472–490.

71. Edward Behr and Mark Steyn, *The Story of Miss Saigon* (New York: Arcade, 1991).

72. Kristin Ross, *May '68 and Its Afterlives* (Chicago: University of Chicago Press, 2002); Richard Wolin, *The Wind from the East: French Intellectuals, the Cultural Revolution, and the Legacy of the 1960s* (Princeton: Princeton University Press, 2010); Camille Robcis, "'China in Our Heads': Althusser, Maoism, and Structuralism," *Social Text* 30, no. 1 (2012): 51–69.

73. See, for example, Julia Kristeva, *About Chinese Women* (London: Boyars, 1977); Wolin, *The Wind from the East*, 179–232 and 288–349. See also the essays in François Lionnet and Shu-mei Shih, eds., *The Creolization of Theory* (Durham: Duke University Press, 2011).

74. Wolin, *The Wind from the East*, 3.

75. Chow, "The Dream of a Butterfly," 79–80.

76. Chow, 84–85. Here, Chow is drawing on Lacan: see Jacques Lacan, *The Four Fundamental Concepts of Psycho-Analysis*, ed. Jacques-Alain Millers and trans. Alan Sheridan (New York: Norton, 1981), 91–104.

77. Although de Lauretis calls attention to Song's yearning in intriguing ways, her reading tends to take for granted the homosexual nature of Song's desire and inadvertently risks ontologizing the myth of a "repressed truth" about the normativity of the real penis—Song's penis. Regardless of their physical makeup, the butterfly fantasy can easily operate in a reciprocal fashion between Song and Gallimard, making a primordial presupposition of homosexuality always volatile. De Lauretis, "Popular Culture, Public and Private Fantasies," 330.

78. See, for example, Rey Chow, *Writing Diaspora: Tactics of Intervention in Contemporary Cultural Studies* (Bloomington: Indiana University Press, 1993); Jian Chen, *Mao's China and the Cold War* (Chapel Hill: University of North Carolina Press, 2001); Susan D. Blum and Lionel M. Jensen, eds., *China Off Center: Mapping the Margins of the Middle Kingdom* (Honolulu: University of Hawai'i Press, 2002); and Sherman Cochran and Paul G. Pickowicz, eds., *China on the Margins* (Honolulu: University of Hawai'i Press, 2010). On the problem of "global hypermasculinity" in contemporary East Asia in relation to the West, see Lily H. M. Ling, "Sex Machine: Global Hypermasculinity and the Image of Asian Woman in Modernity," *positions: east asia cultures critique* 7, no. 2 (1999): 277–306. For a fuller development of this thesis, see Lily Ling, *Postcolonial International Relations: Conquest and Desire Between Asia and the West* (New York: Palgrave Macmillan, 2002). For a groundbreaking collection of essays on East Asian masculinity, see Xiaodong Lin, Chris Haywood, and Martin Mac an Ghaill, eds., *East Asian Men: Masculinity, Sexuality, and Desire* (New York: Palgrave Macmillan, 2017). Cf. Kam Louie and Morris Low, eds., *Asian Masculinities: The Meaning and Practice of Manhood in China and Japan* (London: Routledge, 2003); Kam Louie, *Chinese Masculinities in a Globalizing World* (London: Routledge, 2015); and Kam Louie, ed., *Changing Chinese Masculinities: From Imperial Pillars of State to Global Real Men* (Hong Kong: Hong Kong University Press, 2016).

79. Chow, *Entanglements*, 12.

80. *Super Eunuch* 超能太監, dir. Jiao Yang (Beijing: Seven Entertainment, Huayi Brothers, and Beijing Skylimit and Culture Media, 2016).

81. My proposition therefore adds a new perspective on the relationship between Chinese culture and the Sinophone world that has been articulated variously in Shih, *Visuality and Identity*; Tsu, *Sound and Script in the Chinese Diaspora*; Jing Tsu and David Der-wei Wang, "Introduction: Global Chinese Literature," in *Global Chinese Literature: Critical Essays*, ed. Jing Tsu and David Der-wei Wang (Leiden: Brill, 2010), 1–14; and David Der-wei Wang, " 'Gen' de zhengzhi, 'shi' de shixue: Huayu lunshu yu Zhongguo wenxue"「根」的政治,「勢」的詩學:華語論述與中國文學 [The politics of "root," the poetics of

"propensity": Sinophone discourse and Chinese literature], *Zhongguo xiandai wenxue* 中國現代文學 [Modern Chinese literature] 24 (2013): 1–18.

82. Jacques Derrida, *Of Grammatology*, trans. Gayatri Chakravorty Spivak (Baltimore: John Hopkins University Press, 1976), 181.

83. Derrida, 168. The best study of Sinophone culture through the lens of affective politics to date is Lily Wong, *Transpacific Attachments: Sex Work, Media Networks, and Affective Histories of Chineseness* (New York: Columbia University Press, 2018).

84. Derrida, *Of Grammatology*, 168, 306.

85. Barbara Johnson, "Writing," in *Critical Terms for Literary Study*, ed. Frank Lentricchia and Thomas McLaughlin (Chicago: University of Chicago Press, 1990), 39–49, on 45.

86. Meng Yue, *Shanghai and the Edges of Empire* (Minneapolis: University of Minnesota Press, 2006). For example, late Qing Western missionary narratives of the "natural" body worked to *expose* men's castrated body and women's bound feet precisely to counter their cultural endurance, which worked in a logic of *concealment*. See Ko, *Cinderella's Sisters*; Chiang, "How China Became a 'Castrated Civilization.'"

87. See, for example, Nancy Rose Hunt, *A Colonial Lexicon: Of Birth Ritual, Medicalization, and Mobility in the Congo* (Durham: Duke University Press, 1999); Johannes Fabian, *Out of Our Minds: Reason and Madness in the Exploration of Central Africa* (Berkeley: University of California Press, 2000); Ann Laura Stoler, *Carnal Knowledge and Imperial Power: Race and the Intimate in Colonial Rule* (Berkeley: University of California Press, 2002); and Andrea Smith, *Conquest: Sexual Violence and American Indian Genocide* (Durham: Duke University Press, 2015).

88. *Royal Tramp* 鹿鼎記, dir. Jing Wong (Hong Kong: Golden Harvest, 1992); *Super Eunuch 2: Golden Right Hand* 超能太監 2: 黃金右手, dir. Jiao Yang (Beijing: Seven Entertainment, Huayi Brothers, and Beijing Skylimit and Culture Media, 2016).

89. Jin Yong 金庸, *Lu Ding Ji* 鹿鼎記 [The dear and the cauldron], 5 vols. (Hong Kong: Minghe She, 1981).

90. For a theoretical exposition of articulation as a discursive social practice, see Ernesto Laclau and Chantel Mouffe, *Hegemony and Socialist Strategy: Towards a Radical Democratic Politics* (London: Verso, 1985), 105–114.

91. Anjali Arondekar, *For the Record: On Sexuality and the Colonial Archive in India* (Durham: Duke University Press, 2009), 124.

5. Creolizing Transgender

1. On hauntology, see Jacques Derrida, *Spectres of Marx: The State of Debt, the Work of Mourning, and the New International*, trans. Peggy Kamuf (London: Routledge, 1994).

2. Daniel T. Rodgers, *Age of Fracture* (Cambridge, MA: Belknap Press, 2011).

3. On the plurality of stories about transgender lives, see, for example, Jay Prosser, *Second Skins* (New York: Columbia University Press, 1998); Genny Beemyn and Susan Rankin, *The Lives of Transgender People* (New York: Columbia University Press, 2011); and Laura Erickson-Schroth, ed., *Trans Bodies, Trans Selves* (New York: Oxford University Press, 2014). For a phenomenological account of corporeal narrativity, see Gayle Salamon,

Assuming a Body: Transgender and the Rhetorics of Materiality (New York: Columbia University Press, 2010).

4. Robert L. Caserio, "The Antisocial Thesis in Queer Theory," *PMLA* 121, no. 3 (2006): 819–821; Lee Edelman, "Antagonism, Negativity, and the Subject of Queer Theory," *PMLA* 121, no. 3 (2006): 821–823; Judith Halberstam, "The Politics of Negativity in Recent Queer Theory," *PMLA* 121, no. 3 (2006): 823–825; Jóse Esteban Muñoz, "Thinking Beyond Antirelationality and Antiutopianism in Queer Critique," *PMLA* 121, no. 3 (2006): 825–826; and Tim Dean, "The Antisocial Homosexual," *PMLA* 121, no. 3 (2006): 826–828. The antisocial thesis is first definitively formulated in Leo Bersani, *Homos* (Cambridge, MA: Harvard University Press, 1996). See also Judith Halberstam, "The Anti-Social Turn in Queer Studies," *Graduate Journal of Social Science* 5, no. 2 (2008): 140–156.

5. Lee Edelman, *No Future: Queer Theory and the Death Drive* (Durham: Duke University Press, 2004).

6. Jóse Esteban Muñoz, *Cruising Utopia: The Then and There of Queer Futurity* (New York: New York University Press, 2009). See also Jill Dolan, *Utopia in Performance: Finding Hope at the Theatre* (Ann Arbor: University of Michigan Press, 2005).

7. Tim Dean, *Unlimited Intimacy: Reflections on the Subculture of Barebacking* (Chicago: University of Chicago Press, 2009); David Halperin, *What Do Gay Men Want?: An Essay on Sex, Risk, and Subjectivity* (Ann Arbor: University of Michigan Press, 2007); Elizabeth Freeman, *Time Binds: Queer Temporalities, Queer Histories* (Durham: Duke University Press, 2010); Judith Halberstam, *In a Queer Time and Place: Transgender Bodies, Subcultural Lives* (New York: New York University Press, 2005); Judith Halberstam, *The Queer Art of Failure* (Durham: Duke University Press, 2011); Sara Ahmed, *The Cultural Politics of Emotions* (New York: Routledge, 2004); Sara Ahmed, *The Promise of Happiness* (Durham: Duke University Press, 2010); Lauren Berlant, *Cruel Optimism* (Durham: Duke University Press, 2011); and Michael D. Snediker, *Queer Optimism: Lyric Personhood and Other Felicitous Persuasions* (Minneapolis: University of Minnesota Press, 2009). The "temporal" turn in queer theory is also threaded by, for example, Carolyn Dinshaw, *Getting Medieval: Sexualities and Communities, Pre- and Postmodern* (Durham: Duke University Press, 1999); and Carla Freccero, *Queer/Early/Modern* (Durham: Duke University Press, 2006). This is sutured to the "affective" turn: see Ann Cvetkovich, *An Archive of Feelings: Trauma, Sexuality, and Lesbian Public Cultures* (Durham: Duke University Press, 2003); Clare Hemmings, "Invoking Affect: Cultural Theory and the Ontological Turn," *Cultural Studies* 19, no. 5 (2005): 546–567; Heather Love, *Feeling Backward: Loss and the Politics of Queer History* (Cambridge, MA: Harvard University Press, 2007); and Linda Åhäll, "Affect as Methodology: Feminism and the Politics of Emotion," *International Political Sociology* 12, no. 1 (2018): 36–52.

8. For a historical perspective on gay marriage in the U.S. context, see George Chauncey, *Why Marriage: The History Shaping Today's Debate Over Gay Equality* (New York: Basic, 2004).

9. The literature on creolization is too extensive to be cited adequately here. For informative overviews, see, for example, Robin Cohen, "Creolization and Cultural Globalizations: The Soft Sounds of Fugitive Power," *Globalizations* 4, no. 3 (2007): 369–384; Charles Stewart, ed., *Creolization: History, Ethnography, Theory* (Walnut Creek, CA: Left Coast, 2007);

Jacqueline Knörr, "Contemporary Creoleness; or, The World in Pidginization?," *Current Anthropology* 51, no. 6 (2010): 731–759; and Richard Price, "The Concept of Creolization," in *The Cambridge World History of Slavery*, vol. 3, *AD 1420–AD 1804*, ed. David Eltis and Stanley L. Engerman (Cambridge: Cambridge University Press, 2011), 513–537.

10. I thank John Smolenski for drawing my attention to this point.

11. Tzu-hui Celina Hung, " 'There Are No Chinamen in Singapore': Creolization and Self-Fashioning of the Straits Chinese in the Colonial Contact Zone," *Journal of Chinese Overseas* 5, no. 2 (2009): 257–290; Tzu-hui Celina Hung, "Hunxie(yu)hua mailuo Zhong de huayuyuxi yanjiu" 混血(語)化脈絡中的華語語系研究 [Sinophone studies through the lens of creolization], *Sun Yat-sen Journal of Humanities* 35 (2013): 47–67; E. K. Tan, *Rethinking Chineseness: Translational Sinophone Identities in the Nanyang Literary World* (Amherst, NY: Cambria, 2013); Brian Bernards, *Writing the South Seas: Imagining the Nanyang in Chinese and Southeast Asian Postcolonial Literature* (Seattle: University of Washington Press, 2015); and Brian Bernards, "Reanimating Creolization Through Pop Culture: Yasmin Ahmad's Inter-Asian Audio-Visual Integration," *Asian Cinema* 28, no. 1 (2017): 55–71.

12. On the history of the *Nanyang*, see, for example, Michael R. Godley, *The Mandarin-Capitalists from Nan-Yang: Overseas Chinese Enterprise in the Modernization of China, 1893–1911* (Cambridge: Cambridge University Press, 1981); Ching-hwang Yen, *A Social History of the Chinese in Singapore and Malaya, 1800–1911* (Singapore: Oxford University Press, 1986); Gungwu Wang, *China and the Chinese Overseas* (Singapore: Times Academic Press, 1991); Anthony Reid and Kristine Alilunas Rodgers, eds., *Sojourners and Settlers: Histories of Southeast Asia and the Chinese* (Honolulu: University of Hawai'i Press, 1996); G. William Skinner, "Creolized Chinese Societies in Southeast Asia," in *Sojourners and Settlers: Histories of Southeast Asia and the Chinese*, ed. Anthony Reid and Kristine Alilunas Rodgers (Sydney: Allen and Unwin, 1996), 51–93; Adam McKeown, "Conceptualizing Chinese Diasporas, 1842 to 1949," *Journal of Asian Studies* 58, no. 2 (1999): 306–331; Gungwu Wang, *The Chinese Overseas: From Earthbound China to the Quest for Autonomy* (Cambridge, MA: Harvard University Press, 2000); Philip A. Kuhn, *Chinese Among Others: Emigration in Modern Times* (Lanham, MD: Rowman and Littlefield, 2008); Deborah L. Madsen and Andrea Riemenschnitter, eds., *Diasporic Histories: Cultural Archives of Chinese Transnationalism* (Hong Kong: Hong Kong University Press, 2009); Adam McKeown, "Chinese Emigration in Global Context, 1850–1940," *Journal of Global History* 5, no. 1 (2010): 95–124; Shelly Chan, *Diaspora's Homeland: Modern China in the Age of Globalization* (Durham: Duke University Press, 2018); and Kwa Chong Guan and Kua Bak Lim, eds., *A General History of the Chinese in Singapore* (Singapore: World Scientific, 2019).

13. Stuart Hall, "Créolité and the Process of Creolization," in *The Creolization Reader: Studies in Mixed Identities and Cultures*, ed. Robin Cohen and Paola Taninato (London: Routledge, 2010), 26–38, on 29. This statement brings theories of creolization into dialogue with the anthropological discussion of "other" times. See Johannes Fabian, *Time and the Other: How Anthropology Makes Its Objects* (New York: Columbia University Press, 1983). On the historiography of the colonial legacy, see Martin J. Wiener, "The Idea of 'Colonial Legacy' and the Historiography of Empire," *Journal of the Historical Society* 13, no. 1 (2013): 1–32.

14. My usage of creolization takes cues from the epistemological model that "indexes flexibility" as developed by Franćois Lionnet and Shu-mei Shih in *The Creolization of Theory* (Durham: Duke University Press, 2011), 2. This descends from the Francophone usage in the Caribbean. See Édouard Glissant, *Poetics of Relation*, trans. Betsy Wing (Ann Arbor: University of Michigan Press, 1997). Richard Price distinguishes the Anglophone usage of *creolization* by anthropologists and historians from the Francophone concept of *créolisation* as championed by Glissant. See Richard Price, "*Créolisation*, Creolization, and *Créolité*," *Small Axe* 21, no. 1 (2017): 211–219. On the caution against facile appropriations of the concept, see, for example, Michel-Rolph Trouillot, "Culture on the Edges: Caribbean Creolization in Historical Context," in *From the Margins: Historical Anthropology and Its Futures*, ed. Brian Ketih Axel (Durham: Duke University Press, 2002), 189–210; and Stephen Palmie, "Creolization and Its Discontents," *Annual Review of Anthropology* 35 (2006): 433–456.

15. Glissant, *Poetics of Relation*, 68–69.

16. Glissant, 69.

17. On postcolonial hybridity, see Homi K. Bhabha, *The Location of Culture* (London: Routledge, 1994). For critiques of its celebratory tone, see, for instance, Ella Shohat, "Notes on the 'Post-Colonial,'" *Social Text*, nos. 31–32 (1992): 99–113; Aijaz Ahmad, "The Politics of Literary Postcoloniality," *Race and Class* 36, no. 3 (1995): 1–20; and Jacqueline Lo, "Beyond Happy Hybridity: Performing Asian Australian Identities," in *Alter/Asians: Asian-Australian Identities in Art, Media and Popular Culture*, ed. Ien Ang, Sharon Chalmers, Lisa Law, and Mandy Thomas (Sydney: Pluto, 2000), 152–168. For a defense of hybridity, see Ien Ang, "Together-in-Difference: Beyond Diaspora, Into Hybridity," *Asian Studies Review* 27, no. 2 (2003): 141–154.

18. Derek Bickerton, "The Nature of a Creole Continuum," *Language* 49, no. 3 (1973): 640–669.

19. For the best treatment of the history of *tongzhi* to date, see Ta-wei Chi, *Tongzhi wenxueshi: Taiwan de faming* 同志文學史：台灣的發明 [A queer invention in Taiwan: A history of tongzhi literature] (Taipei: Linking, 2017), 376–392. See also Wah-shan Chou, *Tongzhi: Politics of Same-Sex Eroticism in Chinese Societies* (New York: Haworth, 2000).

20. See, for example, Michael Warner, *The Trouble with Normal: Sex, Politics, and the Ethics of Queer Life* (New York: Free Press, 1999); Judith Butler, "Is Kinship Always Already Heterosexual?," *differences: A Journal of Feminist Cultural Studies* 13, no. 1 (2002): 14–44; Lisa Duggan, *The Twilight of Equality?: Neoliberalism, Cultural Politics, and the Attack on Democracy* (Boston: Beacon, 2003); Jack Halberstam, *Gaga Feminism: Sex, Gender, and the End of Normal* (Boston: Beacon, 2012), 95–129; and Peter Drucker, *Warped: Gay Normality and Queer Anti-Capitalism* (Leiden: Brill, 2015).

21. The classic formulation of social citizenship is Thomas Humphrey Marshall, "Citizenship and Social Class," in *The Citizenship Debates: A Reader*, ed. Gershon Shafir (Minneapolis: University of Minnesota Press, 1998), 93–112. An amended view from the feminist angle can be found in Iris Marion Young, "Polity and Group Difference: A Critique of the Ideal of Universal Citizenship," *Ethics* 99, no. 2 (1989): 250–274. For legal approaches in the tradition of American gender history, see, for example, Linda K. Kerber, "The Meanings of Citizenship," *Journal of American History* 84, no. 3 (1997): 833–854; Nancy F. Cott, "Marriage and Women's Citizenship in the United States, 1830–1934,"

American Historical Review 103, no. 54 (1998): 1440–1474; Linda K. Kerber, *No Constitutional Right to Be Ladies: Women and the Obligations of Citizenship* (New York: Hill and Wang, 1998); Nancy F. Cott, *Public Vows: A History of Marriage and the Nation* (Cambridge, MA: Harvard University Press, 2000); and Margot Canaday, *The Straight State: Sexuality and Citizenship in Twentieth-Century America* (Princeton: Princeton University Press, 2009). On cultural citizenship, see, for example, Aihwa Ong, "Cultural Citizenship as Subject-Making," *Current Anthropology* 37, no. 5 (1996): 737–762; Aihwa Ong, *Flexible Citizenship: The Cultural Logic of Transnationality* (Durham: Duke University Press, 1999); Leti Volpp, "The Culture of Citizenship," *Theoretical Inquiries in Law* 8, no. 2 (2007): 571–602; and Jean Beaman, "Citizenship as Cultural: Towards a Theory of Cultural Citizenship," *Sociology Compass* 10 (2016): 849–857. For the study of cultural citizenship in queer Asian contexts, see Peter Jackson, "Capitalism and Global Queering: National Markets, Parallels Among Sexual Cultures, and Multiple Queer Modernities," *GLQ: A Journal of Lesbian and Gay Studies* 15, no. 3 (2009): 357–395; Peter Jackson, *Queer Bangkok: Twenty-First Century Markets, Media, and Rights* (Hong Kong: Hong Kong University Press, 2011); Travis Kong, *Chinese Male Homosexualities: Memba, Tongzhi, and Golden Boy* (London: Routledge, 2011); and Audrey Yue and Jun Zubillaga-Pow, *Queer Singapore: Illiberal Citizenship and Mediated Cultures* (Hong Kong: Hong Kong University Press, 2012).

22. The celebrity literature on queer historicism includes David Halperin, *One Hundred Years of Homosexuality, and Other Essays on Greek Love* (London: Routledge, 1990); Joan W. Scott, "The Evidence of Experience," *Critical Inquiry* 17, no. 4 (1991): 773–797; Lisa Duggan, "The Discipline Problem: Queer Theory Meets Lesbian and Gay History," *GLQ: A Journal of Lesbian and Gay Studies* 2 (1995): 179–191; Arnold I. Davidson, *The Emergence of Sexuality: Historical Epistemology and the Formation of Concepts* (Cambridge, MA: Harvard University Press, 2001); David Halperin, *How to Do the History of Homosexuality* (Chicago: University of Chicago Press, 2002); and Valerie Traub, *Thinking Sex with the Early Moderns* (Philadelphia: University of Pennsylvania, 2015). See also Susan McCabe, "To Be and to Have: The Rise of Queer Historicism," *GLQ: A Journal of Lesbian and Gay Studies* 11, no. 1 (2005): 119–134.

23. One of the foremost transformations in the cultural ecology and political dynamics of post-2000 Taiwan and Hong Kong is the growing strength of right-wing and conservative religious groups. This anti-LGBTQ social trend is beyond the scope of this chapter, but important discussions of this topic can be found in Josephine Ho, "Is Global Governance Bad for East Asian Queers?," *GLQ: A Journal of Lesbian and Gay Studies* 14, no. 4 (2008): 457–479; Ying-Chao Kao, "Organizing Transnational Moral Conservatism: How U.S. Christian and Taiwanese 'Pro-Family' Movements Converge, Diverge, and Collide" (PhD diss., Rutgers University, 2018); and Joseph M. K. Cho 曹文傑, Lucetta Y. L. Kam 金曄路, and Francisca Y. K. Lai 賴婉琪, "Qianxi nianhou de Xianggang tongzhi yundong tuxiang: Lianjie, chongtu, han xianzhi" 千禧年後的香港同志運動圖像: 連結、衝突和限制 [The depiction of the tongzhi movement in postmillennial Hong Kong: Links, conflicts, and limitations], in *Sheyun niandai: Xianggang kangzheng zhengzhi de guiji* 社運年代：香港抗爭政治的軌跡 [The era of social movement: The paths of

political resistance in Hong Kong], ed. Zheng Wei 鄭煒 and Yuan Weixi 袁瑋熙 (Hong Kong: Chinese University Press, 2018), 115–140.

24. On queer citizenship, see, for example, Duggan, *The Twilight of Equality*; Paisley Currah, Richard M. Juang, and Shannon Price Minter, eds., *Transgender Rights* (Minneapolis: University of Minnesota Press, 2006); Canaday, *The Straight State*; Julie A. Greenberg, *Intersexuality and the Law: Why Sex Matters* (New York: New York University Press, 2012); Jami K. Taylor and Donald P. Haider-Markel, *Transgender Rights and Politics: Groups, Issue Framing, and Policy Adoption* (Ann Arbor: University of Michigan Press, 2014); and Francesca Stella, Yvette Taylor, Tracey Reynolds, and Antoine Rogers, eds., *Sexuality, Citizenship and Belonging: Trans-National and Intersectional Perspectives* (London: Routledge, 2016). Queer theorists have termed the reciprocal production of neoliberal nationalism and queer identities "homonationalism." The original formulation can be found in Jasbir Puar, *Terrorist Assemblages: Homonatioanlism in Queer Times* (Durham: Duke University Press, 2007). The most vibrant region in Asia to which this concept has been applied is Singapore. See Yue and Zubillaga-Pow, *Queer Singapore*; Robert Phillips, "'And I Am Also Gay': Illiberal Pragmatics, Neoliberal Homonormativity and LGBT Activism in Singapore," *Anthropologica* 56, no. 1 (2014): 45–51; John Whittier Treat, "The Rise and Fall of Homonationalism in Singapore," *positions: asia critique* 23, no. 2 (2015): 349–365; and Michelle M. Lazar, "Homonationalist Discourse as a Politics of Pragmatic Resistance in Singapore's Pink Dot Movement: Towards a Southern Praxis," *Journal of Sociolinguistic* 21, no. 3 (2017): 420–442.

25. Although scholars such as Lisa Rofel, Loretta Ho, and Hongwei Bao have examined a similar "transcultural" space in which gayness and national belonging are interarticulated in postsocialist China, the contest of queer citizenship examined in this chapter exceeds a purely "Chinese" framework. I argue that the kind of citizenship status that queers attempt to claim in Taiwan and Hong Kong should not be viewed, at least in the historical period under consideration, as identical to the articulations of queer citizenship in mainland China. See Lisa Rofel, *Desiring China: Experiments in Neoliberalism, Sexuality, and Public Culture* (Durham: Duke University Press, 2007); Loretta Wing Wah Ho, *Gay and Lesbian Subculture in Urban China* (London: Routledge, 2010); and Hongwei Bao, *Queer Comrades: Gay Identity and Tongzhi Activism in Postsocialist China* (Copenhagen: Nordic Institute of Asian Studies, 2018).

26. Susan Stryker, "Transgender History, Homonormativity, and Disciplinarity," *Radical History Review*, no. 100 (2008): 145–157.

27. For an insightful ethnography of queer and transgender kinship in postmillennial Taiwan, see Amy Brainer, *Queer Kinship and Family Change in Taiwan* (New Brunswick, NJ: Rutgers University Press, 2019).

28. See also Ta-wei Chi, "Plural Not Singular: Homosexuality in Taiwanese Literature of the 1960s," in *Perverse Taiwan*, ed. Howard Chiang and Yin Wang (London: Routledge, 2016), 44–63.

29. Jen-Peng Liu and Naifei Ding, "Reticent Poetics, Queer Politics," *Inter-Asia Cultural Studies* 6 (2005): 30–55; Ho, "Is Global Governance Bad for East Asian Queers?;" Josephine Ho, "Queer Existence Under Global Governance: A Taiwan Exemplar," *positions:*

east asia cultures critique 18 (2010): 537–554; Hans Tao-Ming Huang, *Queer Politics and Sexual Modernity in Taiwan* (Hong Kong: Hong Kong University Press, 2011); and Petrus Liu, *Queer Marxism in Two Chinas* (Durham: Duke University Press, 2015).

30. On the divergence in the political strategies of the mainstream feminist and *tongzhi* movements in 1990s Taiwan, see Huang, *Queer Politics and Sexual Modernity in Taiwan*, 113–200.

31. Chou, *Tongzhi*; Bao, *Queer Comrades*; Howard Chiang and Yin Wang, eds., *Perverse Taiwan* (London: Routledge, 2016).

32. Chia-Ling Yang, "Challenges to LGBTI Inclusive Education and Queer Activism in Taiwan," in *Queer Social Movements and Outreach Work in Schools: A Global Perspective*, ed. Dennis A. Francis, Jón Ingvar Kjaran, and Jukka Lehtonen (Cham: Palgrave Macmillan, 2020), 52–92, on 67. I thank Adam Dedman for bringing this article to my attention.

33. Herng-Dar Bih 畢恆達, "Ye·Yong-Zhi buwang" 夜·永誌不忘 [Night·memorializing Yung-chih], in *YMS*, 28–36.

34. Hwei-Syin Chen 陳惠馨, "Renzhen duidai xingbie pingdeng jiaoyufa: Xingbie pingdeng jiaoyufa zhi lifa yu zhanwang" 認真對待性別平等教育法: 性別平等教育法之立法與展望 [Treating the Gender Equity Education Act seriously: The legislation and prospect of the Gender Equity Education Act], *Guojia zhengce jikan* 國家政策季刊 [National policy quarterly] 4, no. 1 (2005): 21–32, on 23–24.

35. You-mei Lai 賴友梅, "Ye Yong-Zhi dashiji" 葉永誌案大事紀 [Chronicle of events in the Yeh Yung-chih case], in *YMS*, 37–43.

36. Bih, "Ye·Yongzhi buwang," 32.

37. Hwei-Syin Chen 陳惠馨, "Xingbie pingdeng jiaoyu fa: Taiwan xingbie jiaoyu zhi jiwang yu kailai" 性別平等教育法: 台灣性別教育之繼往與開來 [Gender Equity Education Act: The Past and future of gender education in Taiwan], *Xingbie pingdeng jiaoyu jikan* 性別平等教育季刊 [Gender equity education quarterly], no. 30 (2005): 115–129, on 127.

38. The most representative voice of radical feminism in this period is Josephine Ho 何春蕤, *Haoshuang nüren: Nüxing zhuyi yu xing jiefang* 豪爽女人: 女性主義與性解放 [The gallant woman: Feminism and sex emancipation] (Taipei: Crown, 1994). See the historicization of late-twentieth-century Taiwanese feminism in Miao-hung Lee 李妙虹, "Zhanhou Taiwan funü de shehui diwei (1970–2000)" 戰後臺灣婦女的社會地位 (1970–2000) [Women's status in postwar Taiwanese society] (MA thesis, National Chung Hsing University, 2003); Daiwie Fu 傅大為, *Yaxiya de xinshenti: Xingbie, yiliao yu jindai Taiwan* 亞細亞的新身體: 性別、醫療與近代台灣 [Assembling the new body: Gender/sexuality, medicine, and Taiwan] (Taipei: Socio, 2005), 283–313; Fang-Mei Lin, "Women's Organizations and the Changing State/Society Relationship: Resistance, Co-Optation by the State, or Partnership?," *Taiwan in Comparative Perspective* 2 (2008): 47–64; Huang, *Queer Politics and Sexual Modernity in Taiwan*, 134–139; Liu, *Queer Marxism in Two Chinas*, 58–72.

39. Chou, *Tongzhi*; Jens Damm, "Discrimination and Backlash Against Homosexual Groups," in *Politics of Difference in Taiwan*, ed. Tak-Wing Ngo and Hong-zen Wang (London: Routledge, 2011), 152–180; Fran Martin, *Situating Sexualities: Queer Representation in Taiwanese Fiction, Film and Public Culture* (Hong Kong: Hong Kong University Press, 2003); Tze-lan Sang, *The Emerging Lesbian: Female Same-Sex Desire in Modern China* (Chicago: University of Chicago Press, 2003), 225–274; Hans Tao-Ming Huang, "From Glass Clique to *Tongzhi* Nation: *Crystal Boys*, Identity Formation, and the Politics of

Sexual Shame," *positions: east asia cultures critique* 18, no. 2 (2010): 373–398; Fran Martin, *Backward Glances: Contemporary Chinese Cultures and the Female Homoerotic Imaginary* (Durham: Duke University Press, 2010), 118–146; and Chi, *Tongzhi wenxueshi*, 341–408.

40. Yun-Xiu Lee 李昀修, "Chongdu xingping jiaoyu fa: Yu Su Chien-ling laoshi de fangtan" 重讀性平教育法: 與蘇芊玲老師的訪談 [Rereading the Gender Equity Education Act: An interview of Professor Chien-ling Su], *Renben jiaoyu zhaji* 人本教育札記 [Humanities Education Foundation magazine], June 1, 2017, http://hefmag.dudaone.com/my-post41. On the history of the Act, especially in relation to the tongzhi movement in Taiwan, see Yang, "Challenges to LGBTI Inclusive Education."

41. In addition to serving as a social lubrication between the feminist movement and the lesbian and gay movement, the Yeh incident also cemented the formal inauguration of "men's studies" in Taiwan. The establishment of "men's studies" as a separate field of scholarly inquiry further pushed the feminist agenda beyond an overwhelming preoccupation with women's issues to consider gender as a useful category of analysis across different "bodily manifestations." See, for example, the essays in "Nanxing yanjiu" 男性研究 [Men's studies], special issue, *Liangxing pingdeng jiaoyu jikan* 兩性平等教育季刊 [Equality of two sexes education quarterly], no. 12 (2000): 1–142.

42. See, for example, Ta-wei Chi 紀大偉, "Ku'er lun: Sikao dangdai Taiwan ku'er yu ku'er wensue" 酷兒論: 思考當代台灣酷兒與酷兒文學 [On *ku'er*: Thoughts on *ku'er* and *ku'er* literature in contemporary Taiwan], in *Ku'er kuanghuan jie* 酷兒狂歡節 [Queer Carnival], ed. Ta-wei Chi (Taipei: Meta Media, 1997), 9–28; Josephine Ho, ed., *Ku'er: Lilun yu zhengzhi* 酷兒: 理論與政治 [Queer politics and queer theory], special issue, *Working Papers in Gender/Sexuality Studies*, nos. 3–4 (Jungli, Taiwan: National Central University Center for the Study of Sexualities, 1998), 47–87.

43. Liao Shuhui 廖淑惠, "Xiayuechu tongzhi dayouxin" 下月初 同志大遊行 [Tongzhi pride parade early next month], *LHB*, October 18, 2003; Liao Shuhui 廖淑惠, "Taibei Tongwanjie tongzhi mingtian caijie" 台北同玩節 同志明天彩街 [Taipei LGBT Civil Rights Movement Festival tomorrow on the streets], *LHB*, October 31, 2003; Chen Yingzi 陳英姿, "Tongzhi youxing lizheng jiehun lingyangquan" 同志遊行 力爭結婚、領養權 [Tongzhi pride parade fighting for marriage and adoption rights], *LHB*, November 2, 2003.

44. Jian Zhujun 簡竹君, "Tongzhi fei tongzhi dajia yiqilai" 同志非同志 大家一起來 [Tongzhi or not everyone comes along], *LHB*, August 26, 2000; Qin Fuzhen 秦富珍, "Tongwanjie 9 yue 2 ri dengchang" 同玩節 9月2日登場 [Taipei LGBT Civil Rights Movement Festival starts on September 2], *LHB*, August 28, 2000; Zhang Renhao 張仁豪, "Renshi tongxinglian Taibei Tongwanjie zhoumuo dengchang" 認識同性戀 台北同玩節周末登場 [Getting to know homosexuality Taipei LGBT Civil Rights Movement Festival begins this weekend], *LHB*, September 2, 2000; Zhang Renhao 張仁豪, "Tongxinglian jianian huahui biekai shengmian" 同性戀嘉年華會 別開生面 [Homosexual carnival breathes new life], *LHB*, September 3, 2000. For the coverage of this landmark event in tongzhi publications, see, for example, Yuxuan Aiji 魚玄阿璣 et al., "Taibei Tongwanjie zhuanti" 台北同玩節專題 [Feature articles on the Taipei lesbian and gay festival], *Nü pengyou* 女朋友 [Girlfriend], no. 33 (2000): 6–23.

45. Liang Yufang 梁玉芳, "Zongtong jiejian tongzhi gongzuozhe" 總統接見同志工作者 [President meets tongzhi worker], *LHB*, September 5, 2000.

46. Tak-Wing Ngo and Hong-zen Wang, eds., *Politics of Difference in Taiwan* (London: Routledge, 2011); Dafydd Fell, *Government and Politics in Taiwan*, 2nd ed. (London: Routledge, 2018); and Yun Fan, *Social Movements in Taiwan's Democratic Transition* (London: Routledge, 2018).

47. Yang Jinyan 楊金嚴, "Taibei gongyuan gengming jiangli liangkuai beiwen" 台北公園更名 將立兩塊碑文 [Taipei Park renamed with two epitaphs], *LHB*, March 16, 1995.

48. Shen Changlu 沈長祿, "Tongxinglian tuanti panhuo zunzhong" 同性戀團體 盼獲尊重 [Homosexual groups seeking respect], *LHB*, February 8, 1996.

49. Xie Peijuan 謝佩娟, "Taibei Xingongyuan tongzhi yundong: Qingyu zhuti de shehui shijian" 台北新公園同志運動：情慾主體的社會實踐 [Gay movement in Taipei New Park: The social practices of sexual subjectivity] (MA thesis, National Taiwan University, 1999); Wang Zhihong 王志弘, "Taibei Xingongyuan de qingyu dilixue: Kongjian zaixian yu nan tongxinglian rentong" 台北新公園的情慾地理學：空間在線與男同性戀認同 [Erotic geographies of Taipei New Park: Spatial representations of gay identity], *Taiwan: A Radical Quarterly in Social Sciences* 22 (1996): 195–218.

50. Liang Yufang 梁玉芳, "Tongxinglian fojiaotu zucheng Tongfan jingshe" 同性戀佛教徒組成童梵精舍 [Homosexual Buddhist groups form Tongfan jingshe], *LHB*, April 6, 1997; Yang Huinan 楊惠南, "Tongxin fanxing: Dangdai Taiwan fojiao tongzhi pingquan yundong" 童心梵行：當代台灣佛教同志平權運動 [Childish heart, brahma behaviour: Contemporary Taiwanese Buddhist gay and lesbian equality movement]," *Dangdai* 當代 [Contemporary] 173 (2002): 30–51; Su Lin 蘇林, "Yang Huinan *Ai yu xinyang* guanhuai fojiao tongzhi tuanti" 楊惠南《愛與信仰》 關懷佛教同志團體 [Yang Huinan's *Love and Belief* attends to Buddhist gay and lesbian groups], *LHB*, January 30, 2005.

51. Yang, "Tongxin fanxing."

52. Shao Bingru 邵冰如, "Taiwan caihongguo yaoban menggongyuan" 台灣彩虹國 要辦夢公園 [Taiwan's rainbow nation organizes dream park], *LHB*, June 19, 1997; Liang Yufang 梁玉芳, "Jiaoshi 'tong' meng yaodui xuesheng jihui jiaoyu" 教師「同」盟 要對學生機會教育 [Teachers alliance offers students a strategic education], *LHB*, June 30, 1997; Liang Yufang 梁玉芳, "Qingzhu tongxinglian yue Taiwan tongzhi jianianhua" 慶祝同性戀月 台灣同志嘉年華 [Celebrating the homosexual month at the Taiwan gay and lesbian carnival], *LHB*, June 30, 1997.

53. Liang Yufang 梁玉芳, "Tongzhen kangyi jingfang lanyong gongquanli chengli 'zhuan'an xiaozu'" 同陣抗議警方濫用公權力 成立「專案小組」 [Tongzhi Front protests the abuse of power by police by forming a "special committee"], *LHB*, August 10, 1997; Lü Lingling 呂玲玲, "Huanwo renquan tongzhi fanpu" 還我人權 同志反撲 [Give me back human rights homosexuals react], *LHB*, August 19, 1997.

54. Shao Bingru 邵冰如, "Tongzhi jinye jiti sanbu" 同志今夜 集體散步 [Gay and lesbians take it to the streets together this evening], *LHB*, August 9, 1997; Liang Yufang 梁玉芳, "Tongzhi kongjian zhongneng bubei darao" 同志空間 終能不被打擾 [Homosexual space will not be disturbed], *LHB*, December 15, 2001.

55. Liang Yufang 梁玉芳, "Tongzhi zixun rexian meizhou santian" 同志諮詢熱線 每周三天 [Tongzhi consultation hotline open three days a week], *LHB*, November 23, 1998.

56. For a partial overview of the Gender/Sexuality Rights Association Taiwan, see Liu, *Queer Marxism in Two Chinas*, 72–76.

57. Josephine Ho 何春蕤, "Jiaowo 'kuaxingren': kuaxingbie zhuti yu xingbie jiefang yun-dong" 叫我「跨性人」——跨性別主體與性別解放運動 [Call me "transgender": Transgender subjectivity and gender/sexual liberation movement], *Po zhoubao 破週報* [Pots weekly], March 17, 1998. References to Ho's effort can be found in Sang, *The Emerging Lesbian*, 260–261; Chen Wei-Jhen 陳薇真, *Taiwan kuaxingbie qianshi: Yiliao, fengsu yu yaji zaofeng* 台灣跨性別前史：醫療、風俗誌與亞際遭逢 [Pretransgender history in Taiwan: Medical treatment, hostess clubs and inter-Asia encounters] (New Taipei City: Transgender Punk Activist Publishing, 2016), 90.

58. Ho, "Jiaowo 'kuaxingren.'"

59. On the history of the third sex hostess culture, see Chen, *Taiwan kuaxingbie qianshi*, 89–174. On the cross-dressing performances, see Ivy I-Chu Chang 張靄珠, "Xingbie fan-chuan, yizhi kongjian, yu houzhimin bianzhuang huanghou de wenhua xianji" 性別反串、異質空間、與後殖民變裝皇后的文化溿忌 [Cross-dressing, heterotopia, and the cultural ambivalence of postcolonial drag], *Chung Wai Literary Monthly* 29, no. 7 (2000): 139–157; Chao-Jung Wu, "Performing Transgender Desire: Male Cross-Dressing Shows in Taiwan," in *Transgender China*, ed. Howard Chiang (New York: Palgrave Macmillan, 2012), 225–262; and Chao-Jung Wu, "Performing Hybridity: The Music and Visual Politics of Male Cross-Dressing Performance in Taiwan," in *Perverse Taiwan*, ed. Howard Chiang and Yin Wang (London: Routledge, 2016), 131–160.

60. See Hsiao-hung Chang 張小虹, *Qingyu weiwu lun* 情慾微物論 [On the microphysics of sexuality] (Taipei: Datian, 1998), 123–124.

61. Ho, "Jiaowo 'kuaxingren.'"

62. My periodization of how transgender rights came to be incorporated into *tongzhi* citizenship thus sides with literary scholar Wei-cheng Chu's critique. See Wei-cheng Chu 朱偉誠, "Kuaxingbie yundong de Taiwan sisuo" 跨性別運動的台灣思索 [Reflections on the transgender movement in Taiwan], *Chengpin haodu 誠品好讀*, no. 5 (2000): 8–10. Josephine Ho continued to promote transgender studies into the twenty-first century. See Josephine Ho, ed., *Kuaxingbie 跨性別* [Transgender] (Chungli, Taiwan: Center for the Study of Sexualities, National Central University, 2003); and Fran Martin and Josephine Ho, eds., "Trans/Asia, Trans/Gender," special issue, *Inter-Asia Cultural Studies* 7, no. 2 (2006): 185–318.

63. Liang Yufang 梁玉芳, "QuanTai shouge hefa tongzhi tuanti xiayue chengli" 全台首個合法同志團體 下月成立 [The first legal gay and lesbian group in Taiwan to be established next month], *LHB*, May 28, 2000.

64. Wei-Jhen Chen 陳薇真, "'Tongzhi baokuo LGBT': Taiwan tongzhi zhishiyu 2000–2005 nian de yuyishi yu dangqian" 「同志包括 LGBT」：台灣同志知識域 2000–2005 年的語意史與當前 ["Tongzhi includes LGBT": The linguistic history of Taiwanese tongzhi knowledge field from 2000 to 2005 and the present] (paper presented at the Cultural Studies Association, Taiwan, January 4–5, 2014). I thank Wei-Jhen for sharing with me a draft of her conference paper.

65. Taiwan Tongzhi Hotline Association, *Renshi tongzhi shouce* 認識同志手冊 [A handbook on tongzhi] (Taipei: Taipei City Government Department of Civil Affairs, 2003), 3.

66. Taiwan Tongzhi Hotline Association, 3.

67. Taiwan Tongzhi Hotline Association, 6.

68. Taiwan Tongzhi Hotline Association, 6.

69. Taiwan Tongzhi Hotline Association, 7.

70. Taiwan Tongzhi Hotline Association, 7.

71. Taiwan Tongzhi Hotline Association, 10.

72. Taiwan Tongzhi Hotline Association, 10.

73. Taiwan Tongzhi Hotline Association, 9.

74. Taiwan Tongzhi Hotline Association, *Renshi tongzhi shouce* 認識同志手冊 [A handbook on tongzhi] (Taipei: Taipei City Government Department of Civil Affairs, 2004), 1.

75. In the mid-1990s, a heated debate within Awakening Foundation called attention to its compulsory heterosexuality and homophobia. This led to the falling out of several pro-lesbian feminists, including Wang Ping 王蘋 and Ni Jiazhen 倪家珍. Therefore, the new collaboration between the Tongzhi Hotline Association and Awakening Foundation in 2004 can be viewed as a new phase in both the feminist and the tongzhi movements in Taiwan. See Wang Ping, Ni Jiazhen, et al., "Xingbie zhengzhi yu tongzhi yundong" 性別政治與同志運動 [Gender politics and lesbian/gay movement], in *Huaren tongzhi xin duben* 華人同志新讀本 [A new reader on Chinese *tongzhi*], ed. Lu Jianxiong 盧劍雄 (Hong Kong: Huasheng shudian, 1999), 87–90. For the politics of lesbianism in Taiwanese feminist activism in the 1990s, see Sang, *The Emerging Lesbian*, 235–246.

76. Taiwan Tongzhi Hotline Association, *Renshi tongzhi shouce* (2004), 2.

77. Taiwan Tongzhi Hotline Association, 3.

78. *W v Registrar of Marriages* [2013] HKCFA 39.

79. For an overview of the case, see John Nguyet Erni, "*W v. Registrar of Marriages* (2013)," in *Global Encyclopedia of Lesbian, Gay, Bisexual, Transgender, and Queer (LGBTQ) History*, ed. Howard Chiang (Farmington Hills, MI: Charles Scribner's Sons, 2019), 1713–1717.

80. *W v Registrar of Marriages* [2010] 6 HKC 359; *W v Registrar of Marriages* [2012] 1 HKC 88.

81. Karen L. M. Yee, "*W v Registrar of Marriages*: From Transsexual Marriage to Same-Sex Marriage?," *Hong Kong Law Journal* 40, no. 3 (2010): 549–562; Cora Chan, "Deference and the Separation of Powers: An Assessment of the Court's Constitutional and Institutional Competence," *Hong Kong Law Journal* 41, no. 1 (2011): 7–25; Christopher Hutton, "Objectification and Transgender Jurisprudence: The Dictionary as Quasi-Statute," *Hong Kong Law Journal* 41, no. 1 (2011): 27–47; Pujai Kapai, "A Principled Approach Towards Judicial Review: Lessons from *W v Registrar of Marriages*," *Hong Kong Law Journal* 41, no. 1 (2011): 49–74; Holning Lau and Derek Loh, "Misapplication of ECHR Jurisprudence in *W v Registrar of Marriages*," *Hong Kong Law Journal* 41, no. 1 (2011): 75–87; Athena Liu, "Exacerbating *Corbett*: *W v Registrar of Marriages*," *Hong Kong Law Journal* 41, no. 3 (2011): 759–783; Kelley Loper, "*W v Registrar of Marriages* and the Right to Equality in Hong Kong," *Hong Kong Law Journal* 41, no. 1 (2011): 88–107; Jens M. Scherpe, "Changing One's Legal Gender in Europe—the 'W' Case in Comparative Perspective," *Hong Kong Law Journal* 41, no. 1 (2011): 109–123; Marco Wan, "Doing Things with the Past: A Critique of the Use of History by Hong Kong's Court of First Instance in *W v Registrar of Marriages*," *Hong Kong Law Journal* 41, no. 1 (2011): 125–138; Marco Wan, "What's So Unusual About W?," *Hong Kong Law Journal* 41, no. 1 (2011): 5–6; Sam Winter, "Transgender Science: How Might It Shape the Way We Think About Transgender Rights?," *Hong Kong Law Journal* 41, no. 1 (2011): 139–153; Athena Liu, "Understanding *Goodwin*: *W v Registrar of Marriages*,"

Hong Kong Law Journal 42, no. 2 (2012): 403–430; and Carole J. Petersen, "Sexual Orientation and Gender Identity in Hong Kong: A Case for the Strategic Use of Human Rights Treaties at the International Reporting Process," *Asian-Pacific Law and Policy Journal* 14, no. 2 (2012): 28–83.

82. As Joseph Cho and Lucetta Kam have noted, a wide disparity exists between the Court of Appeal and the Court of Final Appeal in Hong Kong in matters concerning the legal recognition of queer gender and sexual expressions. Joseph M. K. Cho and Lucetta Y. L. Kam, "Same-Sex Marriage in China, Hong Kong and Taiwan: Ideologies, Spaces and Developments," in *Contemporary Issues in International Political Economy*, ed. Fu-Lai Tony Yu and Diana S. Kwan (Singapore: Palgrave Macmillan, 2019), 289–306, on 302.

83. For a discussion of how W's case played a pivotal role in giving strength and momentum to the nascent transgender movement in Hong Kong, see Pui Kei Eleanor Cheung, "Transgenders in Hong Kong: From Shame to Pride," in *Transgender China*, ed. Howard Chiang (New York: Palgrave Macmillan, 2012), 263–284. Outside the courtroom for W, trans solidarity has existed in Hong Kong since the beginning of the twenty-first century, despite some internal fractures within the transgender community. A case in point is the formation of the Hong Kong Transgender Equality and Acceptance Movement (TEAM). See, for example, Robyn Emerton, "Finding a Voice, Fighting for Rights: The Emergence of the Transgender Movement in Hong Kong," *Inter-Asia Cultural Studies* 7, no. 2 (2006): 243–269.

84. Susan Stryker, "Transgender Studies: Queer Theory's Evil Twin," *GLQ: A Journal of Lesbian and Gay Studies* 10, no. 2 (2004): 212–215, on 214.

85. Morris. B. Kaplan, "Intimacy and Equality: The Question of Lesbian and Gay Marriage," *Philosophical Forum* 25, no. 4 (1994): 333–360; Lisa Bower, "Queer Problems/Straight Solutions: The Limits of a Politics of 'Official Recognition,'" in *Playing with Fire: Queer Politics, Queer Theories*, ed. Shane Phelan (London: Routledge, 1997), 267–291; Warner, *The Trouble with Normal*; Butler, "Is Kinship Always Already Heterosexual?"; and Duggan, *The Twilight of Equality*.

86. Muñoz, *Cruising Utopia*, 95.

87. Elizabeth Freeman, "Queer Belongings: Kinship Theory and Queer Theory," in *A Companion to Lesbian, Gay, Bisexual, Transgender, and Queer Studies*, ed. George E. Haggerty and Molly McGarry (Oxford: Blackwell, 2007), 295–314; David L. Eng, *The Feeling of Kinship: Queer Liberalism and the Racialization of Intimacy* (Durham: Duke University Press, 2010); Meg Wesling, "Neocolonialism, Queer Kinship, and Diaspora: Contesting the Romance of the Family in Shani Mootoo's *Cereus Blooms at Night* and Edwidge Danticat's *Breath, Eyes, Memory*," *Textual Practice* 25, no. 4 (2011): 649–670; Lucetta Y. L. Kam, *Shanghai Lalas: Female Tongzhi Communities and Politics in Urban China* (Hong Kong: Hong Kong University Press, 2012); E. K. Tan, "A Queer Journey Home in *Solos*: Rethinking Kinship in Sinophone Singapore," in *Queer Sinophone Cultures*, ed. Howard Chiang and Ari Larissa Heinrich (London: Routledge, 2013), 130–146; Alvin K. Wong, "Queer Sinophone Studies as Anti-Capitalist Critique: Mapping Queer Kinship in the Work of Chen Ran and Wong Bik-wan," in *Queer Sinophone Cultures*, ed. Howard Chiang and Ari Larissa Heinrich (London: Routledge, 2013), 109–129; and Elisabeth L. Engebretsen, *Queer Women in Urban China: An Ethnography* (London: Routledge, 2014).

88. For an analysis of how wider transphobic social structures disenfranchise transgender persons through multiple forms of "imprisonment," including gender and sexual essentialism, see John Nguyet Erni, "Legitimating Transphobia: The Legal Disavowal of Transgender Rights in Prison," *Cultural Studies* 27, no. 1 (2013): 136–159.

89. Wan, "Doing Things with the Past," 126.

90. John Nguyet Erni, "Marriage Rights for Transgender People in Hong Kong: Reading the W Case," in *Wives, Husbands, and Lovers: Marriage and Sexuality in Hong Kong, Taiwan, and Urban China*, ed. Deborah S. Davis and Sara L. Friedman (Stanford: Stanford University Press, 2014), 189–216, on 210. In this essay, Erni makes a slightly more positive assessment of the court case than I do: "That a post-operative transsexual woman has not only not deviated from 'womanhood' as a necessary category in marriage but has also *transformed* its meaning from the inside out. Aside from the legal recognition of her female identity as bestowed by the state (for example, issuance of a new identity card, legal acceptance of her using a public toilet for women), Miss W is a woman *in otherness*. Her lived gender asserts her womanhood as a *new sign* fit for marriage" (209–210, emphasis in original).

91. For an excellent treatment of this intricate relation through the lens of queer cultural production in postcolonial Hong Kong, see Helen Hok-Sze Leung, *Undercurrents: Queer Culture and Postcolonial Hong Kong* (Vancouver: University of British Columbia Press, 2008). As cultural studies scholars such as Leung have already begun to give this realm of theoretical critique its due, this chapter supplements their effort by utilizing legal history and case studies to explore the overlapping social ramifications of queer activism and trans recognition, especially in transnational Sinophone contexts. For an overview of the transgender movement in Hong Kong, see Cheung, "Transgenders in Hong Kong"; Emerton, "Finding a Voice, Fighting for Rights." See also Howard Chiang, "Transgender in China," in *Handbook on the Family and Marriage in China*, ed. Xiaowei Zang and Lucy Xia Zhao (Cheltenham, UK: Edward Elgar, 2017), 392–408.

92. I borrow the descriptor "polite" from Takashi Fujitani's comparative work on the "polite racism" of the Japanese and Americans in the context of the Asia-Pacific War. See Takashi Fujitani, *Race for Empire: Koreans as Japanese and Japanese as Americans During World War II* (Berkeley: University of California Press, 2011). By describing the kind of residual heteronormativity examined in this chapter as "polite," I do not mean to deny the existence of more vulgar, blatant, and atrocious forms of transphobia in Hong Kong society.

93. On the medical history of transsexuality, see Bernice Hausman, *Changing Sex: Transsexualism, Technology, and the Idea of Gender* (Durham: Duke University Press, 1995); Joanne Meyerowitz, *How Sex Changed: A History of Transsexuality in the United States* (Cambridge, MA: Harvard University Press, 2002); Afsaneh Najmabadi, *Professing Selves: Transsexuality and Same-Sex Desire in Contemporary Iran* (Durham: Duke University Press, 2013); and Howard Chiang, *After Eunuchs: Science, Medicine, and the Transformation of Sex in Modern China* (New York: Columbia University Press, 2018).

94. *W v Registrar of Marriages* [2013] HKCFA 39: § 26.

95. *Corbett v Corbett (Otherwise Ashley)* [1971] P83.

96. *Bellinger v Bellinger* [2003] 2 AC 467: § 11.

97. *W v Registrar of Marriages* [2013] HKCFA 39: § 55.

98. For an analysis of the European Court of Human Rights' jurisprudence in respect of sexual orientation, see Paul Johnson, *Homosexuality and the European Court of Human Rights* (London: Routledge, 2012).

99. *Rees v UK* (1986) 9 EHRR 56: § 49.

100. *Cossey v UK* (1990) 13 EHRR 622.

101. *Sheffield and Horsham v UK* (1998) 27 EHRR 163: § 67.

102. *W v Registrar of Marriages* [2013] HKCFA 39: § 75.

103. *Goodwin v UK* (2002) 35 EHRR 18: § 85.

104. *Goodwin v UK* (2002) 35 EHRR 18: § 100.

105. *Goodwin v UK* (2002) 35 EHRR 18: § 101.

106. *W v Registrar of Marriages* [2013] HKCFA 39: § 84.

107. *W v Registrar of Marriages* [2013] HKCFA 39: § 89, emphasis added.

108. Carole Petersen has observed that due to its "lack of democracy," Hong Kong in the colonial period lagged behind England with respect to promoting human rights through legal reform. See Petersen, "Sexual Orientation and Gender Identity in Hong Kong," 32.

109. Dipesh Chakrabarty, *Provincializing Europe: Postcolonial Thought and Historical Difference* (Princeton: Princeton University Press, 2000); Kuan-hsing Chen, *Asia as Method: Toward Deimperialization* (Durham: Duke University Press, 2010).

110. Hao Qian 郝倩, "Zhongguo shoulie bianxingren hunyin de ganga" (中國首例變性人婚姻的尷尬) [The awkwardness of the first case of transsexual marriage in China], *Xiandai kuaibao*, March 16, 2004, http://big5.huaxia.com/xw/shgj/00186663.html.

111. Xiaofei Guo 郭曉飛, "Wusheng wuxi de bianqian: Zhongguofa shiyiexia de bianxingren hunyinquan" 無聲無息的變遷：中國法視野下的變性人婚姻權 [A silent and subtle transformation: Transsexual marriage rights in China] (paper presented at the "Twenty Years of Gender/Sexualities" conference [organized by the Centre for the Study of Sexualities at National Central University], Taipei, Taiwan, May 16, 2015).

112. *W v Registrar of Marriages* [2013] HKCFA 39: § 203.

113. Eve Kosofsky Sedgwick, *Epistemology of the Closet* (Berkeley: University of California Press, 1990); Butler, "Is Kinship Always Already Heterosexual?"

114. *W v Registrar of Marriages* [2013] HKCFA 39: § 2.

115. *W v Registrar of Marriages* [2013] HKCFA 39: § 2.

116. Terry S. Kogan, "Transsexuals, Intersexuals, and Same-Sex Marriage," *Brigham Young University Journal of Public Law* 18, no. 2 (2003): 371–418.

117. For a historical overview of the tensions between gender pluralism and the umbrella coherence of the transgender rights movement in the United States, see Paisley Currah, "Gender Pluralisms Under the Transgender Umbrella," in *Transgender Rights*, ed. Paisley Currah, Richard M. Juang, and Shannon Price Minter (Minneapolis: University of Minnesota Press, 2006), 3–31.

118. Although the concept of homonormativity has been used by queer theorists such as Lisa Duggan and Jasbir Puar to refer to the imitative constructs of heterosexual norms within mainstream neoliberal gay and lesbian politics, my usage in this context—as throughout most of the book—sides with Susan Stryker, who adopts the term to describe the normative imposition of a gay and lesbian agenda over the concerns of transgender people

on the margins of sexual politics and history. See Duggan, *The Twilight of Equality*; Puar, *Terrorist Assemblages*; and Stryker, "Transgender History, Homonormativity, and Disciplinarity."

119. Susan Stryker, Paisley Currah, and Lisa Jean Moore, "Introduction: Trans-, Trans, or Transgender?," *WSQ: Women's Studies Quarterly* 36, nos. 3–4 (2008): 11–22, on 12.

120. *W v Registrar of Marriages* [2013] HKCFA 39: § 139.

121. *W v Registrar of Marriages* [2013] HKCFA 39: § 136.

122. Judith Butler, "Undiagnosing Gender," in *Transgender Rights*, ed. Paisley Currah, Richard M. Juang, and Shannon Price Minter (Minneapolis: University of Minnesota Press, 2006), 274–298.

123. David B. Cruz, "Getting Sex 'Right': Heteronormativity and Biologism in Trans and Intersex Marriage Litigation and Scholarship," *Duke Journal of Gender Law and Policy* 18 (2010): 203–222, on 203.

124. Howard Chiang and Alvin K. Wong, "Queering the Transnational Turn: Regionalism and Queer Asias," *Gender, Place and Culture: A Journal of Feminist Geography* 23, no. 11 (2016): 1643–1656.

125. Shu-mei Shih, *Visuality and Identity: Sinophone Articulations Across the Pacific* (Berkeley: University of California Press, 2007), 192.

126. *W v Registrar of Marriages* [2013] HKCFA 39: § 152.

127. Gilles Deleuze and Félix Guattari, *Kafka: Toward a Minor Literature*, trans. Dana Polan (Minneapolis: University of Minnesota Press, 1986), 16.

128. On the use of peripheral realism in literary aesthetics, see Jed Esty and Colleen Lye, "Peripheral Realisms Now," *Modern Language Quarterly* 73, no. 3 (2012): 269–288.

129. *W v Registrar of Marriages* [2013] HKCFA 39: § 171.

130. *W v Registrar of Marriages* [2013] HKCFA 39: § 187–188.

131. Chiang and Wong, "Queering the Transnational Turn."

132. David L. Eng, Teemu Ruskola, and Shuang Shen, "Introduction: China and the Human," *Social Text* 29, no. 4 (2011): 1–27.

133. See the productive endeavor of "comparatizing" Taiwan in Shu-mei Shih and Ping-hui Liao, eds., *Comparatizing Taiwan* (London: Routledge, 2015). Another important Sinophone site that is often referenced for comparative purposes is Singapore, which falls beyond the scope of the present study. See, for example, Audrey Yue and Helen Hok-Sze Leung, "Notes Towards the Queer Asian City: Singapore and Hong Kong," *Urban Studies* 54, no. 3 (2017): 747–764. On the transgender history of Singapore, the center of sex-reassignment surgeries in the Sinophone world in the 1970s, see Audrey Yue, "Trans-Singapore: Some Notes Toward Queer Asia as Method," *Inter-Asia Cultural Studies* 18, no. 1 (2017): 10–24.

134. Gayatri Chakravorty Spivak, "Woman in Difference: Mahashweta Devi's 'Douloti the Bountiful,'" *Cultural Critique*, no. 14 (1989–1990): 105–128, on 105 (emphasis original).

135. Liu, *Queer Marxism in Two Chinas*, 138–169.

136. Petrus Liu, "Queer Human Rights in and Against China: Marxism and the Figuration of the Human," *Social Text* 30, no. 1 (2012): 71–89, on 81. In *Queer Marxism in Two Chinas*, Liu summons the empty ghosts of "People living with AIDS, transgendered individuals, non-monogamous gay people, drag queens, transsexuals, drug-users,

prostitutes, and their clients" to recalibrate his definition of queer human (163). However, the book lacks sustained attention to transgender subjectivity and routinely prioritizes gay and lesbian positionality in its treatment of Chinese queerness. The book also fails to envision a program of sexual emancipation that addresses social inequalities in countries with socialist governments, including China. This implies a highly selective deployment of what Liu calls queer Marxism.

137. In this sense, the connectivity between Western *transgender* and Taiwanese *tongzhi* differs from the kind of queer hybridity as theorized by Fran Martin and others, because cultural hybrids, if not read as an aversion to colonial authority, could easily be understood as the very symptoms of colonization. See Martin, *Situating Sexualities*, 36. As Ella Shohat has noted, "A celebration of syncretism and hybridity per se, if not articulated in conjunction with questions of hegemony and neo-colonial power relations, runs the risk of appearing to sanctify the fait accompli of colonial violence." See Shohat, "Notes on the 'Post-Colonial,'" 109. The framework of creolization gives foremost weight to the cross-fertilization between different cultures as they interact. According to Robin Cohen, "When creolization occurs, participants select particular elements from incoming or inherited cultures, endow these with meanings different from those they possessed in the original cultures and then creatively merge these to create new varieties that supersede the prior forms." See Cohen, "Creolization and Cultural Globalization," 369. On the similarities and differences between creolization and hybridity, see also Charles Stewart, "Creolization, Hybridity, Syncretism, Mixture," *Portuguese Studies* 27, no. 1 (2011): 48–55.

138. For an incisive critique of the desire to align Taiwanese *ku'er* with Western "queer," see Chi, *Tongzhi wenxueshi*, 393. As Chi points out, one of the unruliest—and thus queerest—consequences in "translingual practice" is precisely to not glorify an "original" standard, which would otherwise imply the always-inferior status of the "copy." On translingual practice, see Lydia H. Liu, *Translingual Practice: Literature, National Culture, and Translated Modernity—China, 1900–1937* (Stanford: Stanford University Press, 1995). See also Ta-wei Chi, "Ku'er" 酷兒 [Queer], in *Taiwan lilun guanjianci* 台灣理論關鍵詞 [Keywords of Taiwan theory], ed. Shu-mei Shih, Chia-ling Mei, Dung-sheng Chen, and Chaoyang Liao (Taipei: Linking, 2019), 325–334.

139. Yi Chien Chen, "Asian Queering: Narratives, Lives, and Law: Legal Queeries Refabrication in Taiwan" (paper presented at the Inter-Asia Cultural Studies Conference, Singapore, July 3–5, 2013); Sara L. Friedman, "Stranger Anxiety: Failed Legal Equivalences and the Challenges of Intimate Recognition in Taiwan," *Public Culture* 29 (2017): 433–455.

140. The Intersex, Transgender and Transsexual People Care Association is the brainchild of Beyond Gender Alliance (性別不明行動聯盟, *xingbie buming xingdong lianmeng*), originally founded in 2009.

141. According to one of the current leaders of TG Butterfly Garden, Gao Xukuan 高旭寬, the very existence of a gender category on identification cards is a regulatory regime—an institutionalized weapon—wielded by the state. Therefore, Gao considered the fight for getting rid of the surgical requirement shortsighted. See Xu Xiangyun 徐湘芸, Wang Ruoying 王若穎, and Luo Wenyu 羅文妤, "Kuabuguo de 'lan': Xing/bie shehui zhong

yincang de kuaxingbie zhe" 跨不過的「欄」——性／別社會中隱藏的跨性別者 [The border that cannot be crossed: The hidden transgender individuals in sexed/gendered society], *Zhengda daxue bao* 政大大學報 [NCCU news], no. 1681 (June 21, 2018), https://unews.nccu.edu.tw/unews/跨不過的「欄」-性%EF%BC%8F別社會中隱藏的跨性別者/. For a middle-ground position, see Wei-Jhen Chen 陳薇真, "Haizai shenqing luowu de 'mian shoushu huanzheng'?: 'Wu tiaojian huanzheng' caishi renquan chaoliu!" 還在申請落伍的「免手術換證」？「無條件換證」才是人權潮流！ [Still applying for the nonsurgical requirement to change sex? Nonconditional requirement to change sex is the human rights trend], *Feng chuanmei* 風傳媒 [The storm media], April 17, 2016, www.storm.mg/lifestyle/103826?srcid=73746f726d2e6d675f62363535626533653365538306537663961_1562603620. For a history of Josephine Ho's involvement with the TG Butterfly Garden, see her autobiographical reflection: Josephine Ho, "Wode kuaxingbie jiachushi: Jianlun Taiwan TG Dieyuan" 我的跨性別接觸史：兼論台灣 TG 蝶園 [My engagement with transgender history: A corollary discussion of Taiwan's TG butterfly garden] (paper presented at the "Northeast *Yao* Lecture: Trans/Gender History and the Present" [東北妖講座：跨／性別越界的歷史與現在], Taipei, Taiwan, November 11, 2017). According to Ho, the TG Butterfly Garden entered an incubation phase in 2017.

142. Critics have pointed out the insufficiency of the Marriage Equality Bill. If the legal definition of kinship limits its expansion to same-sex monogamous unions, it falls short of achieving the range of civic rights that the remainder of the Diversified Family Formation Petition (多元成家立法草案, *duoyuan chengjia lifa cao'an*) sets out to legislate. The other two parts of the Diversified Family Formation Petition include (1) Civil Partnership System Bill (伴侶制度草案, *banlü zhidu cao'an*), which seeks to legalize civil unions (not marriage) between two adults (akin to the French civil solidarity pact, or *pacte civil de solidarité*, but with an expanded set of rights such as adoption rights), and (2) Multiple-Person Family System Bill (家屬制度草案, *jiashu zhidu cao'an*), which seeks to broaden the legal definition of kinship beyond the institutionalization of blood ties and marriage. For a remarkable study of structuralist familialism in contemporary French law and policy debates, see Camille Robcis, *The Law of Kinship: Anthropology, Psychoanalysis, and the Family in France* (Ithaca: Cornell University Press, 2013).

143. Howard Chiang and Ari Larissa Heinrich, eds., *Queer Sinophone Cultures* (London: Routledge, 2013); Howard Chiang and Alvin K. Wong, eds., *Keywords in Queer Sinophone Studies* (London: Routledge, 2020).

144. Howard Chiang, "(De)Provincializing China: Queer Historicism and Sinophone Postcolonial Critique," in *Queer Sinophone Cultures*, ed. Howard Chiang and Ari Larissa Heinrich (London: Routledge, 2013), 19–51.

145. This document was first published in 2002 by the General Office of the Ministry of Health (卫生部办公厅, *weishengbu bangongting*) and was updated in 2008.

146. Ausma Bernotaite, Lukas Berredo, and H.c Zhuo, "Chinese Trans Advocates Organizing Nationally: A Conference Report," *TSQ: Transgender Studies Quarterly* 5, no. 3 (2018): 473–486, on 479.

147. Bernotaite, Berredo, and Zhuo, 480.

148. Some of the most productive dialogues on this point have taken place in the field of Middle Eastern history: see, for example, Afsaneh Najmabadi, *Women with Mustaches and Men*

Without Beards: Gender and Sexual Anxieties of Iranian Modernity (Berkeley: University of California Press, 2005); Afsaneh Najmabadi, "Beyond the Americas: Are Gender and Sexuality Useful Categories of Historical Analysis?," *Journal of Women's History* 18, no. 1 (2006): 11–21; and the essays in Kathryn Babayan and Afsaneh Najmabadi, eds., *Islamicate Sexualities: Translation across Temporal Geographies of Desire* (Cambridge, MA: Harvard University Press, 2008).

149. Partha Chatterjee, *The Politics of the Governed: Reflection on Popular Politics in Most of the World* (New York: Columbia University Press, 2004). Drawing on his experience in working with civil society groups in 1990s Taiwan, Kuan-Hsing Chen has engaged with Chatterjee's concept of "political society" in the East Asian context. Chen's project treats Asia not as an object of analysis but as a means of transforming knowledge production. See Chen, *Asia as Method*, 224–245.

150. On minor transnationalism, see Françoise Lionnet and Shu-mei Shih, eds., *Minor Transnationalism* (Durham: Duke University Press, 2005).

Conclusion

1. Andrea Long Chu and Emmett Harsin Drager, "After Trans Studies," *TSQ: Transgender Studies Quarterly* 6, no. 1 (2019): 103–116, on 103.

2. Chu and Drager, 104.

3. Chu and Drager, 105.

4. Chu and Drager, 103, 106.

5. Eve Kosofsky Sedgwick, *Epistemology of the Closet* (Berkeley: University of California Press, 1990), 1.

6. Afsaneh Najmabadi, "Are Gender and Sexuality Useful Categories of Historical Analysis?," *Journal of Women's History* 18, no. 1 (2006): 11–21.

7. For an early synthesis of this idea, see Dennis Altman, *Global Sex* (Chicago: University of Chicago Press, 2001). For a revised perspective that accounts for market economies, see Peter Jackson, "Capitalism and Global Queering: National Markets, Parallelism Among Sexual Cultures, and Multiple Queer Modernities," *GLQ: A Journal of Lesbian and Gay Studies* 15, no. 3 (2009): 357–395.

8. See, for example, Qwo-Li Driskill, Chris Finley, Brian Joseph Gilley, and Scott Lauria Morgensen, eds., *Queer Indigenous Studies: Critical Interventions in Theory, Politics, and Literature* (Tucson: University of Arizona Press, 2011); Scott Lauria Morgensen, *Spaces Between Us: Queer Settler Colonialism and Indigenous Decolonization* (Minneapolis: University of Minnesota Press, 2011); Qwo-Li Driskill, *Asegi Stories: Cherokee Queer and Two-Spirit Memory* (Tucson: University of Arizona Press, 2016); and Joanne Barker, ed., *Critically Sovereign: Indigenous Gender, Sexuality, and Feminist Studies* (Durham: Duke University Press, 2017).

9. The idea of "Global Gays" is proposed by Dennis Altman and the "Gay International" by Joseph Massad. See Dennis Altman, "Global Gaze/Global Gays," *GLQ: A Journal of Lesbian and Gay Studies* 3, no. 4 (1997): 417–436; Joseph Massad, "Re-Orienting Desire: The Gay International and the Arab World," *Public Culture* 14, no. 2 (2002): 361–385.

10. I borrow the phrase "mobile subjects" from Aren Z. Aizura, *Mobile Subjects: Transnational Imaginaries of Gender Reassignment* (Durham: Duke University Press, 2018).

11. On "routes as roots," see Shu-mei Shih, *Visuality and Identity: Sinophone Articulations Across the Pacific* (Berkeley: University of California Press, 2007), 190.

12. As feminist scholar Sahar Amer has argued in an incisive review, "Based on *Desiring Arabs*, there are no gays in the Arab world prior to Western imperialism; there is no romantic love between members of the same-sex either, only same-sex desire (consummation)." Sahar Amer, "Joseph Massad and the Alleged Violence of Human Rights," *GLQ: A Journal of Lesbian and Gay Studies* 16, no. 4 (2010): 649–653, on 652.

13. On the theorization of history from the perspective of the history of sexuality, see, for example, Laura Doan, *Disturbing Practices: History, Sexuality, and Women's Experience of Modern War* (Chicago: University of Chicago Press, 2013); Susan S. Lanser, *The Sexuality of History: Modernity and the Sapphic, 1565–1830* (Chicago: University of Chicago Press, 2014); and Valerie Traub, *Thinking Sex with the Early Moderns* (Philadelphia: University of Pennsylvania Press, 2015).

Bibliography

Abbas, Ackbar. *Hong Kong: Culture and the Politics of Disappearance*. Minneapolis: University of Minnesota Press, 1997.

Abir-Am, Pnina G. "From Multidisciplinary Collaboration to Transnational Objectivity: International Space as Constitutive of Molecular Biology, 1930–1970." In *Denationalizing Science: The Contexts of International Scientific Practice*, edited by E. Crawford, T. Shinn, and S. Sorlin, 153–186. Dordrecht: Kluwer Academic, 1993.

Acuna, Rudolfo. *Occupied America*, 3rd ed. New York: Harper and Row, 1988.

Aczel, Amir D. *The Artist and the Mathematician: The Story of Nicolas Bourbaki, the Genius Mathematician Who Never Existed*. New York: Thunder's Mouth Press, 2006.

Ähäll, Linda. "Affect as Methodology: Feminism and the Politics of Emotion." *International Political Sociology* 12, no. 1 (2018): 36–52.

Ahluwalia, Sanjam. "'Tyranny of Orgasm': Global Convergence of Sexuality from Bombay, 1930s–1950s." In *A Global History of Sexual Science, 1880–1960*, edited by Veronika Fuechtner, Douglas E. Haynes, and Ryan M. Jones, 353–373. Oakland: University of California Press, 2018.

Ahmad, Aijaz. "The Politics of Literary Postcoloniality." *Race and Class* 36, no. 3 (1995): 1–20.

Ahmed, Sarah. *The Cultural Politics of Emotions*. Edinburgh: Edinburgh University Press, 2004.

——. *The Promise of Happiness*. Durham: Duke University Press, 2010.

——. *Queer Phenomenology: Orientations, Objects, Others*. Durham: Duke University Press, 2006.

"Aile zhongnian bunan bunü hunpei liangdu yifuyiqi" 哀樂中年不男不女 婚配兩度亦夫亦妻 [The mid-aged intersex married twice to a husband and a wife, respectively]. *LHB*, December 24, 1954.

"Aimei" 愛美 [Beauty]. *Xinshenghuo zhoukan* 新生活週刊 [New life weekly] 1, nos. 72–73 (1935): 18.

Aizura, Aren Z. *Mobile Subjects: Transnational Imaginaries of Gender Reassignment*. Durham: Duke University Press, 2018.

Alegre, Robert F. *Railroad Radicals in Cold War Mexico: Gender, Class, and Memory*. Lincoln: University of Nebraska Press, 2013.

Altman, Dennis. "Global Gaze/Global Gays." *GLQ: A Journal of Lesbian and Gay Studies* 3, no. 4 (1997): 417–436.

——. *Global Sex*. Chicago: University of Chicago Press, 2001.

Amer, Sahar. "Joseph Massad and the Alleged Violence of Human Rights." *GLQ: A Journal of Lesbian and Gay Studies* 16, no. 4 (2010): 649–653.

Amnesty International. "Verified: Hong Kong Police Violence Against Peaceful Protestors." www.amnesty.org/en/latest/news/2019/06/hong-kong-police-violence-verified/.

Anderson, Benedict. *Imagined Communities: Reflections on the Origins and Spread of Nationalism*. New York: Verso, 1983.

Anderson, Jedidiah. "Pinkwashing." In *Global Encyclopedia of Lesbian, Gay, Bisexual, Transgender, and Queer (LGBTQ) History*, edited by Howard Chiang, 1244–1248. Farmington Hills, MI: Charles Scribner's Sons, 2019.

Andrews, Bridie. *The Making of Modern Chinese Medicine, 1850–1960*. Vancouver: University of British Columbia Press, 2014.

Ang, Ien. "Can One Say No to Chineseness?" *boundary 2* 25, no. 3 (1998): 223–242.

——. "Together-in-Difference: Beyond Diaspora, Into Hybridity." *Asian Studies Review* 27, no. 2 (2003): 141–154.

Appadurai, Arjun. *Modernity at Large: Cultural Dimensions of Globalization*. Minneapolis: University of Minnesota Press, 1996.

Appiah, Kwame Anthony. "Is the Post- in Postmodernism the Post- in Postcolonial?" *Critical Inquiry* 17, no. 2 (1991): 336–357.

Arondekar, Anjali. *For the Record: On Sexuality and the Colonial Archive in India*. Durham: Duke University Press, 2009.

——. "Geopolitics Alert!" *GLQ: A Journal of Lesbian and Gay Studies* 10, no. 2 (2004): 236–240.

——. "In the Absence of Reliable Ghosts: Sexuality, Historiography, South Asia." *differences* 25, no. 3 (2014): 98–122.

——. "The Sex of History, or Object/Matters." *History Workshop Journal*, no. 89 (2020): 207–213.

——. "Thinking Sex with Geopolitics." *WSQ: Women's Studies Quarterly* 44, nos. 3–4 (2016): 332–335.

Arondekar, Anjali, and Geeta Patel. "Area Impossible: Notes Toward an Introduction." *GLQ: A Journal of Lesbian and Gay Studies* 22, no. 2 (2016): 151–171.

Ash, Mitchell G., and Alfons Söllner, eds. *Forced Migration and Scientific Change: German-Speaking Scientists and Scholars After 1933*. Cambridge: Cambridge University Press, 1996.

Azzarello, Robert. *Queer Environmentality: Ecology, Evolution, and Sexuality in American Literature*. Burlington, VT: Ashgate, 2012.

Babayan, Kathryn, and Afsaneh Najmabadi, eds. *Islamicate Sexualities: Translation Across Temporal Geographies of Desire*. Cambridge, MA: Harvard University Press, 2008.

Bachner, Andrea. *Beyond Sinology: Chinese Writing and the Scripts of Culture.* New York: Columbia University Press, 2014.

——. *The Mark of Theory: Inscriptive Figures, Poststructuralist Prehistories.* New York: Fordham University Press, 2017.

Banner, Lois W. "Mannish Women, Passive Men, and Constitutional Types: Margaret Mead's *Sex and Temperament in Three Primitive Societies* as a Response to Ruth Benedict's *Patterns of Culture.*" *Signs: Journal of Women in Culture and Society* 28, no. 3 (2003): 833–858.

Bao, Hongwei. *Queer China: Lesbian and Gay Literature and Visual Culture Under Postsocialism.* London: Routledge, 2020.

——. *Queer Comrades: Gay Identity and* Tongzhi *Activism in Postsocialist China.* Copenhagen: Nordic Institute of Asian Studies Press, 2018.

——. "Queer Comrades: Transnational Popular Culture, Queer Sociality, and Socialist Legacy." *English Language Notes* 49 (2011): 131–137.

Barad, Karen. *Meeting the Universe Halfway: Quantum Physics and the Entanglement of Matter and Meaning.* Durham: Duke University Press, 2007.

Barker, Joanne, ed. *Critically Sovereign: Indigenous Gender, Sexuality, and Feminist Studies.* Durham: Duke University Press, 2017.

Barker-Benefield, Graham. *The Horrors of the Half-Known Life: Male Attitudes Toward Woman and Sexuality in Nineteenth Century America.* New York: Harper and Row, 1976.

Barlow, Tani E. "Colonialism's Career in Postwar China Studies." *positions: east asia cultures critique* 1, no. 1 (1993): 224–267.

——, ed. *Formations of Colonial Modernity in East Asia.* Durham: Duke University Press, 1997.

——. *The Question of Women in Chinese Feminism.* Durham: Duke University Press, 2004.

Bauer, Heike, ed. *The Hirschfeld Archives: Violence, Death, and Modern Queer Culture.* Philadelphia: Temple University Press, 2017.

——, ed. *Sexology and Translation: Cultural and Scientific Encounters Across the Modern World.* Philadelphia: Temple University Press, 2015.

Bauer, Heike, and Matt Cook, eds. *Queer 1950s: Rethinking Sexuality in the Postwar Years.* New York: Palgrave Macmillan, 2012.

Baum, Emily. "Healthy Minds, Compliant Citizens: The Politics of 'Mental Hygiene' in Republican China, 1938–1937." *Twentieth-Century China* 42, no. 3 (2017): 215–233.

——. *The Invention of Madness: State, Society, and the Insane in Modern China.* Chicago: University of Chicago Press, 2018.

Beaman, Jean. "Citizenship as Cultural: Towards a Theory of Cultural Citizenship." *Sociology Compass* 10 (2016): 849–857.

Beccalossi, Chiara. "Italian Sexology, Nicola Pende's Biotypology and Hormone Treatments in the 1920s." *Histoire, médecine et santé* 12 (2017): 73–97.

——. "Latin Eugenics and Sexual Knowledge in Italy, Spain, and Argentina: International Networks Across the Atlantic." In *A Global History of Sexual Science, 1880–1960,* edited by Veronika Fuechtner, Douglas E. Haynes, and Ryan M. Jones, 205–329. Oakland: University of California Press, 2018.

Beemyn, Genny. "A Presence in the Past: A Transgender Historiography." *Journal of Women's History* 25, no. 4 (2013): 113–121.

Beemyn, Genny, and Susan Rankin. *The Lives of Transgender People*. New York: Columbia University Press, 2011.

Behr, Edward, and Mark Steyn. *The Story of Miss Saigon*. New York: Arcade, 1991.

Bei Tong. *Beijing Comrades*. Translated by Scott E. Myers. New York: Feminist Press, 2016.

Bellinger v Bellinger [2003] 2 AC 467.

Benedict, Ruth. *Patterns of Culture*. 1934; Boston: Houghton Mifflin, 1959.

Benedicto, Bobby. *Under Bright Lights: Gay Manila and the Global Scene*. Minneapolis: University of Minnesota Press, 2014.

Benjamin, Harry. "Nature and Management of Transsexualism: With a Report on Thirty-One Operated Cases." *Western Journal of Surgery, Obstetrics and Gynecology* 72 (1964): 105–111.

——. "Should Surgery Be Performed on Transsexuals." *American Journal of Psychotherapy* 25, no. 1 (1971): 74–82.

——. "Transsexualism and Transvestism as Psycho-Somatic and Somato-Psychic Syndromes." *American Journal of Psychotherapy* 8, no. 2 (1954): 219–230.

——. *The Transsexual Phenomenon*. New York: Julian, 1966.

——. "Transvestism and Transsexualism." *IJS* 7, no. 1 (1953): 12–14.

——. "Transvestism and Transsexualism in the Male and Female." *Journal of Sex Research* 3, no. 2 (1967): 107–127.

Benjamin, Harry, and Charles L. Ihlenfeld. "The Nature and Treatment of Transsexualism." *Medical Opinion and Review* 6, no. 11 (1970): 24–35.

——. "Transsexualism." *American Journal of Nursing* 73, no. 3 (1973): 457–461.

Berlant, Lauren. *Cruel Optimism*. Durham: Duke University Press, 2011.

Berlant, Laren, and Lee Edelman. *Sex, or the Unbearable*. Durham: Duke University Press, 2013.

Bernards, Brian. "Reanimating Creolization Through Pop Culture: Yasmin Ahmad's Inter-Asian Audio-Visual Integration." *Asian Cinema* 28, no. 1 (2017): 55–71.

——. *Writing the South Seas: Imagining the Nanyang in Chinese and Southeast Asian Postcolonial Literature*. Seattle: University of Washington Press, 2015.

Bernotaite, Ausma, Lukas Berredo, and H.c Zhuo. "Chinese Trans Advocates Organizing Nationally: A Conference Report." *TSQ: Transgender Studies Quarterly* 5, no. 3 (2018): 473–486.

Berry, Chris. "Farewell My Concubine: At What Price Success?" *Cinemaya* 20 (1993): 20–22.

——. "Happy Alone?" *Journal of Homosexuality* 39, nos. 3–4 (2000): 187–200.

Bersani, Leo. *Homos*. Cambridge, MA: Harvard University Press, 1996.

Bhabha, Homi K. *The Location of Culture*. London: Routledge, 1994.

Bickerton, Derek. "The Nature of a Creole Continuum." *Language* 49, no. 3 (1973): 640–669.

Bih, Herng-Dar 畢恆達. "Ye·Yong-Zhi buwang" 夜·永誌不忘 [Night·memorializing Yungchih]. In *YMS*, 28–36.

Blackwood, Evelyn. *Falling Into the Lesbi World: Desire and Difference in Indonesia*. Honolulu: University of Hawai'i Press, 2010.

Blouin, Francis X., and William G. Rosenberg. *Processing the Past: Contesting Authorities in History and the Archives*. Oxford: Oxford University Press, 2011.

Blowers, Geoffrey, and Shelley Wang. "Gone with the *West Wind*: The Emergence and Disappearance of Psychotherapeutic Culture in China (1936–1968)." In *Psychiatry and Chinese History*, edited by Howard Chiang, 143–160. London: Pickering and Chatto, 2014.

Blum, Susan D., and Lionel M. Jensen, eds. *China Off Center: Mapping the Margins of the Middle Kingdom.* Honolulu: University of Hawai'i Press, 2002.

Boag, Peter. *Same-Sex Affairs: Constructing and Controlling Homosexuality in the Pacific Northwest.* Berkeley: University of California Press, 2003.

Boellstorff, Tom. *A Coincidence of Desires: Anthropology, Queer Studies, Indonesia.* Durham: Duke University Press, 2007.

———. *The Gay Archipelago: Sexuality and Nation in Indonesia.* Princeton: Princeton University Press, 2005.

Bonnell, Victoria E., and Lynn Hunt, eds. *Beyond the Cultural Turn: New Directions in the Study of Society and Culture.* Berkeley: University of California Press, 1999.

Bourg, Julian. "The Red Guards of Paris: French Student Maoism of the 1960s." *History of European Ideas* 31, no. 4 (2004): 472–490.

Bower, Lisa. "Queer Problems/Straight Solutions: The Limits of a Politics of 'Official Recognition.'" In *Playing with Fire: Queer Politics, Queer Theories,* edited by Shane Phelan, 267–291. London: Routledge, 1997.

Boyd, Nan Alamilla. *Wide Open Town: A History of Queer San Francisco to 1965.* Berkeley: University of California Press, 2003.

Brainer, Amy. *Queer Kinship and Family Change in Taiwan.* New Brunswick, NJ: Rutgers University Press, 2019.

Bray, Francesca. "Towards a Critical History of Non-Western Technology." In *China and Historical Capitalism: Genealogies of Sinological Knowledge,* edited by Timothy Brook and Gregory Blu, 158–209. Cambridge: Cambridge University Press, 2002.

Brett, Philip, Elizabeth Wood, and Gary C. Thomas, eds. *Queering the Pitch: The New Gay and Lesbian Musicology.* 2nd ed. London: Routledge, 2006.

Briggs, Laura. "The Race of Hysteria: 'Overcivilization' and the 'Savage' Woman in Late Nineteenth-Century Obstetrics and Gynecology." *American Quarterly* 52, no. 2 (2000): 246–273.

Bronski, Michael. *A Queer History of the United States.* Boston: Beacon, 2011.

Brook, Timothy. *Quelling the People: The Military Suppression of the Beijing Democracy Movement.* New York: Oxford University Press, 1992.

Brown, Melissa J. *Is Taiwan Chinese? The Impact of Culture, Power, and Migration on Changing Identities.* Berkeley: University of California Press, 2004.

Bull, Michael, and Les Back, eds. *The Auditory Culture Reader.* Oxford: Berg, 2003.

Bullough, Vern L., and Bonnie Bullough. *Cross Dressing, Sex, and Gender.* Philadelphia: University of Pennsylvania Press, 1993.

Burbank, Jane, and Frederick Cooper. *Empires in World History: Power and the Politics of Difference.* Princeton: Princeton University Press, 2010.

Burns, Kathryn. *Into the Archive: Writing and Power in Colonial Peru.* Durham: Duke University Press, 2010.

Burton, Antoinette, ed. *Archive Stories: Facts, Fictions, and the Writing of History.* Durham: Duke University Press, 2005.

———. *Dwelling in the Archive: Women Writing House, Home, and History in Late Colonial India.* New York: Oxford University Press, 2003.

Bush, Richard C. *At Cross Purposes: U.S.-Taiwan Relations Since 1942.* Armonk, NY: M. E. Sharpe, 2004.

——. *Hong Kong in the Shadow of China: Living with the Leviathan.* Washington, DC: Brookings Institution Press, 2016.

Butler, Judith. *Bodies That Matter: On the Discursive Limits of "Sex."* London: Routledge, 1993.

——. *Gender Trouble: Feminism and the Subversion of Identity.* London: Routledge, 1990.

——. "Is Kinship Always Already Heterosexual?" *differences: A Journal of Feminist Cultural Studies* 13, no. 1 (2002): 14–44.

——. "Undiagnosing Gender." In *Transgender Rights,* edited by Paisley Currah, Richard M. Juang, and Shannon Price Minter, 274–298. Minneapolis: University of Minnesota Press, 2006.

Butler, Judith, and Gayatri Chakravorty Spivak. *Who Sings the Nation-State? Language, Politics, Belonging.* Oxford: Seagull, 2007.

Bychowski, M. W., Howard Chiang, Jack Halberstam, Jacob Lau, Kathleen P. Long, Marcia Ochoa, and C. Riley Snorton. "Trans★historicities." *TSQ: Transgender Studies Quarterly* 5, no. 4 (2018): 658–685.

Canaday, Margot. *The Straight State: Sexuality and Citizenship in Twentieth-Century America.* Princeton: Princeton University Press, 2009.

——. "Thinking Sex in the Transnational Turn: An Introduction." *American Historical Review* 114, no. 5 (2009): 1250–1257.

Canguilhem, Georges. *The Normal and the Pathological.* Translated by Carolyn R. Fawcett and Robert S. Cohen. New York: Zone, 1991.

Capó, Julio, and Emily K. Hobson. "Co-Chairs' Column." *Committee on Lesbian, Gay, Bisexual, and Transgender History Newsletter* 33, no. 2 (2019): 1–4.

Carpenter, Edward. *The Intermediate Sex: A Study of Some Transitional Types of Men and Women.* London: Allen and Unwin, 1908.

Carroll, Peter J. "'A Problem of Glands and Secretions': Female Criminality, Murder, and Sexuality in Republican China." In *Sexuality in China: Histories of Power and Pleasure,* edited by Howard Chiang, 99–124. Seattle: University of Washington Press, 2018.

Carter, David. *Stonewall: The Riots That Sparked the Gay Revolution.* New York: St. Martin's, 2004.

Caserio, Robert L. "The Antisocial Thesis in Queer Theory." *PMLA* 121, no. 3 (2006): 819–821.

Cavanagh, Edward, and Lorenzo Veracini, eds. *The Routledge Handbook of the History of Settler Colonialism.* London: Routledge, 2017.

Chai Fuyuan 柴福沅. *Xingxue ABC* 性學 ABC [ABC of sexology]. Shanghai: Shijie shuju, 1932 (1928).

Chakrabarty, Dipesh. "Provincializing Europe: Postcoloniality and the Critique of History." *Cultural Studies* 6, no. 3 (1992): 337–357.

——. *Provincializing Europe: Postcolonial Thought and Historical Thought.* Princeton: Princeton University Press, 2000.

Chambers, Iain. *Culture After Humanism: History, Culture, Subjectivity.* London: Routledge, 2001.

Chan, Cora. "Deference and the Separation of Powers: An Assessment of the Court's Constitutional and Institutional Competence." *Hong Kong Law Journal* 41, no. 1 (2011): 7–25.

Chan, Gilbert. "Castration and Connection: Kinship Organization Among Ming Eunuchs." *Journal of Ming Studies*, no. 74 (2016): 27–47.

Chan, Ming K., ed. *The Challenge of Hong Kong's Reintegration with China*. Hong Kong: Hong Kong University Press, 1997.

Chan, Shelly. *Diaspora's Homeland: Modern China in the Age of Global Migration*. Durham: Duke University Press, 2018.

Chang, Hsiao-hung 張小虹. *Qingyu weiwu lun* 情慾微物論 [On the microphysics of sexuality]. Taipei: Datian, 1998.

Chang, Ivy I-Chu 張靄珠. "Xingbie fanchuan, yizhi kongjian, yu houzhimin bianzhuang huanghou de wenhua xianji" 性別反串、異質空間、與後殖民變裝皇后的文化羨忌 [Cross-dressing, heterotopia, and the cultural ambivalence of postcolonial drag]. *Chung Wai Literary Monthly* 29, no. 7 (2000): 139–157.

Chao, Antonia. "Drink, Stories, Penis, and Breasts: Lesbian Tomboys in Taiwan from the 1960s to the 1990s." *Journal of Homosexuality* 40 (2001): 185–209.

——. "Fengnan shuonü, fengnü shuonan—renyao zhapianshi" 逢男說女，逢女說男-人妖詐騙史 [A history of renyao fraud]. *Zili zaobao* 自立早報, October 22, 1997.

——. "Global Metaphors and Local Strategies in the Construction of Taiwan's Lesbian Identities." *Culture, Health, and Sexuality* 2 (2000): 377–390.

——. "The Logic of Power in Imagining the Nation-State: Diaspora, Public Sphere, and Modernity in Fifties Taiwan." *Taiwan: A Radical Quarterly in Social Studies* 35 (1999): 37–83.

Chatterjee, Partha. *The Nation and Its Fragments: Colonial and Postcolonial Histories*. Princeton: Princeton University Press, 1993.

——. *The Politics of the Governed: Reflections on Popular Politics in Most of the World*. New York: Columbia University Press, 2004.

Chauncey, George. *Why Marriage: The History Shaping Today's Debate Over Gay Equality*. New York: Basic, 2004.

Cheah, Pheng. "The Biopolitics of Recognition: Making Female Subjects of Globalization." *boundary 2* 40, no. 2 (2013): 81–112.

——. *Inhuman Conditions: On Cosmopolitanism and Human Rights*. Cambridge, MA: Harvard University Press, 2006.

——. *What Is a World? On Postcolonial Literature as World Literature*. Durham: Duke University Press, 2016.

Chen, Hwei-Syin 陳惠馨. "Renzhen duidai xingbie pingdeng jiaoyufa: Xingbie pingdeng jiaoyufa zhi lifa yu zhanwang" 認真對待性別平等教育法: 性別平等教育法之立法與展望 [Treating the Gender Equity Education Act seriously: The legislation and prospect of the Gender Equity Education Act]. *Guojia zhengce jikan* 國家政策季刊 [National policy quarterly] 4, no. 1 (2005): 21–32.

——. "Xingbie pingdeng jiaoyu fa: Taiwan xingbie jiaoyu zhi jiwang yu kailai" 性別平等教育法: 台灣性別教育之繼往與開來 [Gender Equity Education Act: The Past and future of gender education in Taiwan]. *Xingbie pingdeng jiaoyu jikan* 性別平等教育季刊 [Gender equity education quarterly], no. 30 (2005): 115–129.

Chen, Jian. *Mao's China and the Cold War*. Chapel Hill: University of North Carolina Press, 2001.

Chen Kaige, dir. *Farewell My Concubine* 霸王別姬. Hong Kong: Tomson, 1993.

Chen, Kuan-Hsing. *Asia as Method: Toward Deimperialization*. Durham: Duke University Press, 2010.

Chen, Kuan-Hsing, and Chua Beng Huat. "Introduction: The *Inter-Asia Cultural Studies: Movements* Project." In *The Inter-Asia Cultural Studies Reader*, edited by Kuan-Hsing Chen and Chua Beng Huat, 1–5. London: Routledge, 2007.

Chen, Li-fen. "Queering Taiwan: In Search of Nationalism's Other." *Modern China* 37, no. 4 (2011): 384–412.

Chen, Mel Y. *Animacies: Biopolitics, Racial Mattering, and Queer Affect*. Durham: Duke University Press, 2012.

Chen, Mel Y., and Dana Luciana, eds. "Queer Inhumanism," *GLQ: A Journal of Lesbian and Gay Studies* 21, nos. 2–3 (2015): 183–458.

Chen, Pei-jean. "Xiandai 'xing' yu diguo 'ai': Taihan zhimin shiqi tongxingai zaixian" 現代「性」與帝國「愛」: 台韓殖民時期同性愛再現 [Colonial modernity and the empire of love: The representation of same-sex love in colonial Taiwan and Korea]. *Taiwan wenxue xuebao* 台灣文學學報 23 (2013): 101–136.

Chen Pingyuan 陳平原. *Tuxiang Wan Qing:* Dianshizhai huabao *zhiwai* 圖像晚清: 《點石齋畫報》之外 [Picturing the Late Qing: Outside the World of *Dianshizhai huabao*]. Shanghai: Dongfang, 2014.

Chen Wei-Jhen 陳薇真. "Haizai shenqing luowu de 'mian shoushu huanzheng?' 'Wu tiaojian huanzheng' caishi renquan chaoliu!" 還在申請落伍的「免手術換證」?「無條件換證」才是人權潮流! [Still applying for the non-surgical requirement to change sex? Nonconditional requirement to change sex is the human rights trend]. *Feng chuanmei* 風傳媒 [The storm media], April 17, 2016. www.storm.mg/lifestyle/103826?srcid=73746f726d2e6d675f62363 535626533656538306537663961_1562603620.

——. *Taiwan kuaxingbie qianshi: Yiliao, fengsu yu yaji zaofeng* 台灣跨性別前史: 醫療、風俗誌與亞際遭逢 [Pretransgender history in Taiwan: Medical treatment, hostess clubs and inter-Asia encounters]. New Taipei City: Transgender Punk Activist Publishing, 2016.

——. "'Tongzhi baokuo LGBT': Taiwan tongzhi zhishiyu 2000–2005 nian de yuyishi yu dangqian" 「同志包括 LGBT」: 台灣同志知識域 2000–2005 年的語意史與當前 ["Tongzhi includes LGBT": The linguistic history of Taiwanese tongzhi knowledge field from 2000 to 2005 and the present]. Paper presented at the Cultural Studies Association, Taiwan, January 4–5, 2014.

Chen, Yi Chien. "Asian Queering: Narratives, Lives, and Law: Legal Queeries Refabrication in Taiwan." Paper presented at the Inter-Asia Cultural Studies Conference, Singapore, July 3–5, 2013.

Chen Yingzi 陳英姿. "Tongzhi youxing lizheng jiehun lingyangquan" 同志遊行 力爭結婚、領養權 [Tongzhi pride parade fighting for marriage and adoption rights]. *LHB*, November 2, 2003.

Cheung, Chi Leung Jacob, dir. *Lai Shi, China's Last Eunuch* 中國的最後一個太監. Hong Kong: Golden Harvest, 1987.

Cheung, Pui Kei Eleanor. "Transgenders in Hong Kong: From Shame to Pride." In *Transgender China*, edited by Howard Chiang, 263–284. New York: Palgrave Macmillan, 2012.

Chi, Ta-wei 紀大偉. "Ku'er" 酷兒 [Queer]. In *Taiwan lilun guanjianci* 台灣理論關鍵詞 [Keywords of Taiwan theory], edited by Shu-mei Shih, Chia-ling Mei, Dung-sheng Chen, and Chaoyang Liao, 325–334. Taipei: Linking, 2019.

——. "Ku'er lun: Sikao dangdai Taiwan ku'er yu ku'er wensue" 酷兒論: 思考當代台灣酷兒與酷兒文學 [On *ku'er*: Thoughts on *ku'er* and *ku'er* literature in contemporary Taiwan]. In *Ku'er kuanghuan jie* 酷兒狂歡節 [Queer Carnival], edited by Ta-wei Chi, 9–28. Taipei: Meta Media, 1997.

——. "Performers of the Paternal Past: History, Female Impersonators, and Twentieth-Century Chinese Fiction." *positions: east asia cultures critique* 15, no. 3 (2007): 580–608.

——. "Plural Not Singular: Homosexuality in Taiwanese Literature of the 1960s." In *Perverse Taiwan*, edited by Howard Chiang and Yin Wang, 44–63. London: Routledge, 2016.

——. *Tongzhi wenxueshi: Taiwan de faming* 同志文學史：台灣的發明 [A queer invention in Taiwan: A history of tongzhi literature]. Taipei: Linking, 2017.

Chiang, Howard. *After Eunuchs: Science, Medicine, and the Transformation of Sex in Modern China*. New York: Columbia University Press, 2018.

——. "The Conceptual Contours of Sex in the Chinese Life Sciences: Zhu Xi (1899–1962), Hermaphroditism, and the Biological Discourse of *Ci* and *Xiong*, 1920–1950." *East Asian Science, Technology and Society: An International Journal* 2, no. 3 (2008): 401–430.

——. "(De)Provincializing China: Queer Historicism and Sinophone Postcolonial Critique." In *Queer Sinophone Cultures*, edited by Howard Chiang and Ari Larissa Heinrich, 19–51. London: Routledge, 2013.

——. "Epistemic Modernity and the Emergence of Homosexuality in China." *Gender and History* 22, no. 3 (2010): 629–657.

——. "Gay Marriage in Taiwan and the Struggle for Recognition." *Current History: A Journal of Contemporary World Affairs* 118 (September 2019): 241–243.

——, ed. *Global Encyclopedia of Lesbian, Gay, Bisexual, Transgender, and Queer (LGBTQ) History*. Farmington Hills, MI: Charles Scribner's Sons, 2019.

——, ed. *Historical Epistemology and the Making of Modern Chinese Medicine*. Manchester: Manchester University Press, 2015.

——. "How China Became a 'Castrated Civilization' and Eunuchs a 'Third Sex.'" In *Transgender China*, edited by Howard Chiang, 23–66. New York: Palgrave Macmillan, 2012.

——, ed. *The Making of the Human Sciences in China: Historical and Conceptual Foundations*. Leiden: Brill, 2019.

——. "Sinophone Modernity: History, Culture, Geopolitics." In *Composing Modernist Connections in China and Europe*, edited by Chunjie Zhang, 142–167. London: Routledge, 2019.

——, ed. *Transgender China*. New York: Palgrave Macmillan, 2012.

——. "Transgender in China." In *Handbook on the Family and Marriage in China*, edited by Xiaowei Zang and Lucy Xia Zhao, 392–408. Cheltenham, UK: Edward Elgar, 2017.

Chiang, Howard, and Ari Larissa Heinrich, eds. *Queer Sinophone Cultures*. London: Routledge, 2013.

Chiang, Howard, and Yin Wang. "Perverse Taiwan." In *Perverse Taiwan*, edited by Howard Chiang and Yin Wang, 1–17. London: Routledge, 2016.

——, eds. *Perverse Taiwan*. London: Routledge, 2016.

Chiang, Howard, and Alvin K. Wong. "Asia Is Burning: Queer Asia as Critique." *Culture, Theory and Critique* 58, no. 2 (2017): 121–126.

——, eds. *Keywords in Queer Sinophone Studies*. London: Routledge, 2020.

———. "Queering the Transnational Turn: Regionalism and Queer Asias." *Gender, Place and Culture: A Journal of Feminist Geography* 23, no. 11 (2016): 1643–1656.

———. "Queer Sinophone Studies: Interdisciplinary Synergies." In *Keywords in Queer Sinophone Studies*, edited by Howard Chiang and Alvin K. Wong, 1–15. London: Routledge, 2020.

Ching Siu-tung, dir. *Swordsman 2* 東方不敗. Hong Kong: Mei Ah, 1992.

Cho, Joseph M. K., and Lucetta Y. L. Kam. "Same-Sex Marriage in China, Hong Kong and Taiwan: Ideologies, Spaces and Developments." In *Contemporary Issues in International Political Economy*, edited by Fu-Lai Tony Yu and Diana S. Kwan, 289–306. Singapore: Palgrave Macmillan, 2019.

Cho, Joseph M. K. 曹文傑, Lucetta Y. L. Kam 金曄路, and Francisca Y. K. Lai 賴婉琪. "Qianxi nianhou de Xianggang tongzhi yundong tuxiang: Lianjie, chongtu, han xianzhi" 千禧年後的香港同志運動圖像: 連結、衝突和限制 [The depiction of the tongzhi movement in post-millennial Hong Kong: Links, conflicts, and limitations]. In *Sheyun niandai: Xianggang kangzheng zhengzhi de guiji* 社運年代：香港抗爭政治的軌跡 [The era of social movement: The paths of political resistance in Hong Kong], edited by Zheng Wei 鄭煒 and Yuan Weixi 袁瑋熙, 115–140. Hong Kong: Chinese University Press, 2018.

Chou, Wah-shan 周華山. *Tongzhi: Politics of Same-Sex Eroticism in Chinese Societies*. New York: Haworth, 2000.

———. *Tongzhilun* 同志論 [On tongzhi]. Hong Kong: Xianggang Tongzhi Yanjiushe, 1995.

Chow, Rey. "Between Colonizers: Hong Kong's Postcolonial Self-Writing in the 1990s." *Diaspora* 2, no. 2 (1992): 151–170.

———. "The Dream of a Butterfly." In *Human, All Too Human*, edited by Diana Fuss, 61–92. London: Routledge, 1996.

———. *Entanglements, or Transmedial Thinking About Capture*. Durham: Duke University Press, 2012.

———. "Introduction: On Chineseness as a Theoretical Problem." *boundary 2* 25, no. 3 (1998): 1–24.

———. "Nostalgia of the New Wave: Structure in Wong Kar-wai's *Happy Together*." *Camera Obscura* 14, no. 3 (1999): 30–49.

———. *Writing Diaspora: Tactics of Intervention in Contemporary Cultural Studies*. Bloomington: Indiana University Press, 1993.

Chow, Yiu Fai. "*Yao*, More or Less Human." *TSQ: Transgender Studies Quarterly* 5, no. 3 (2018): 464–472.

Christenson, Cornelia. *Kinsey: A Biography*. Bloomington: Indiana University Press, 1971.

Chu, Andrea Long, and Emmett Harsin Drager. "After Trans Studies." *TSQ: Transgender Studies Quarterly* 6, no. 1 (2019): 103–116.

Chu, Wei-cheng 朱偉誠. "Kuaxingbie yundong de Taiwan sisuo" 跨性別運動的台灣思索 [Reflections on the transgender movement in Taiwan]. *Chengpin haodu* 誠品好讀, no. 5 (2000): 8–10.

Chu, Yiu-Wai. *Lost in Transition: Hong Kong Culture in the Age of China*. Albany: State University of New York Press, 2013.

Chua, Lynette J. *Mobilizing Gay Singapore: Rights and Resistance in an Authoritarian State*. Philadelphia: Temple University Press, 2014.

——. *The Politics of Love in Myanmar: LGBT Mobilization and Human Rights as a Way of Life.* Stanford: Stanford University Press, 2018.

Chuh, Kandice. *Imagine Otherwise: On Asian Americanist Critique.* Durham: Duke University Press, 2003.

Churchill, David S. "Transnationalism and Homophile Political Culture in the Postwar Decades." *GLQ: A Journal of Lesbian and Gay Studies* 15, no. 1 (2008): 31–66.

Clarke, Adele E. *Disciplining Reproduction: Modernity, American Life Sciences, and the Problems of Sex.* Berkeley: University of California Press, 1998.

Clément, Catharine. *Opera, or the Undoing of Women.* Translated by Betsy Wing. Minneapolis: University of Minnesota Press, 1988.

Clough, Patricia Ticento ed. *The Affective Turn: Theorizing the Social.* Durham: Duke University Press, 2007.

Cochran, Sherman, and Paul G. Pickowicz, eds. *China On the Margins.* Honolulu: University of Hawai'i Press, 2010.

Cohen, Jeffrey J. "Queering the Inorganic." In *Queer Futures: Reconsidering Ethics, Activism, and the Political,* edited by Elahe Haschemi Yekani, Eveline Killian, and Beatrice Michaels, 149–165. Surrey, UK: Ashgate, 2013.

Cohen, Paul A. *Discovering History in China: American Historical Writing on the Recent Chinese Past.* New ed. 1984; New York: Columbia University Press, 2010.

Cohen, Robin. "Creolization and Cultural Globalizations: The Soft Sounds of Fugitive Power." *Globalizations* 4, no. 3 (2007): 369–384.

Cohn, Don J. *Vignettes from the Chinese: Lithographs from Shanghai in the Late Nineteenth Century.* Hong Kong: Chinese University of Hong Kong Press, 1987.

Cole, C. L., and Shannon L. C. Cate. "Compulsory Gender and Transgender Existence: Adrienne Rich's Queer Possibility." *WSQ: Women's Studies Quarterly* 36, nos. 3–4 (2008): 279–287.

"Congfan Zeng Qiuhuang jianliangxing yinanyinü quqijiaren" 從犯曾秋皇 兼兩性 亦男亦女娶妻嫁人 [Suspect Zeng Qiuhuang has both sexes: Being both male and female and married to either sex]. *ZGSB,* November 14, 1955.

Conrad, Ryan, ed. *Against Equality: Queer Revolution, Not Mere Inclusion.* Oakland: AK Press, 2014.

Contreras, Joseph. *In the Shadow of the Giant: The Americanization of Modern Mexico.* New Brunswick, NJ: Rutgers University Press, 2009.

Cook, Alexander C., ed. *Mao's Little Red Book: A Global History.* Cambridge: Cambridge University Press, 2014.

Cook, Blanche Wiesen. " 'Women Alone Stir My Imagination': Lesbianism and the Cultural Tradition." *Signs: Journal of Women in Culture and Society* 4, no. 4 (1979): 718–739.

Coole, Diana, and Samantha Frost, eds. *New Materialisms: Ontology, Agency, and Politics.* Durham: Duke University Press, 2010.

Corbett v Corbett (Otherwise Ashley) [1971] P83.

Cossey v UK (1990) 13 EHRR 622.

Costa, LeeRay M., and Andrew Matzner. *Male Bodies, Women's Souls: Personal Narratives of Thailand's Transgender Youth.* New York: Haworth, 2007.

Cott, Nancy F. "Marriage and Women's Citizenship in the United States, 1830–1934." *American Historical Review* 103, no. 54 (1998): 1440–1474.

——. *Public Vows: A History of Marriage and the Nation.* Cambridge, MA: Harvard University Press, 2000.

Cronenberg, David. *M. Butterfly*, dir. Burbank, CA: Warner, 1993.

Crozier, Ivan. "Havelock Ellis, Eonism and the Patient's Discourse; Or, Writing a Book About Sex." *History of Psychiatry* 11 (2000): 125–154.

Cruz, David B. "Getting Sex 'Right': Heteronormativity and Biologism in Trans and Intersex Marriage Litigation and Scholarship." *Duke Journal of Gender Law and Policy* 18 (2010): 203–222.

Cruz-Malavé, Arnaldo, and Martin F. Manalansan, eds. *Queer Globalizations: Citizenship and the Afterlife of Colonialism.* New York: New York University Press, 2002.

Currah, Paisley. "Gender Pluralisms Under the Transgender Umbrella." In *Transgender Rights*, edited by Paisley Currah, Richard M. Juang, and Shannon Price Minter, 3–31. Minneapolis: University of Minnesota Press, 2006.

Currah, Paisley, Richard M. Juang, and Shannon Price Minter, eds. *Transgender Rights.* Minneapolis: University of Minnesota Press, 2006.

Cvetkovich, Ann. *An Archive of Feelings: Trauma, Sexuality, and Lesbian Public Culture.* Durham: Duke University Press, 2003.

"Dabing bianxing qiankun yiding Xie Jianshun jingshi nü'er shen" 大兵變性乾坤已定謝尖順竟是女兒身 [The situation of the transsexual soldier is now clear, Xie Jianshun has a female body]. *Wah Kiu Yat Po*, September 15, 1955.

Dale, Melissa. "Understanding Emasculation: Western Medical Perspectives on Chinese Eunuchs." *Social History of Medicine* 23, no. 1 (2010): 38–55.

Damm, Jens. "Discrimination and Backlash Against Homosexual Groups." In *Politics of Difference in Taiwan*, edited by Tak-Wing Ngo and Hong-zen Wang, 152–180. London: Routledge, 2011.

——. "The Impact of the Taiwanese LGBTQ Movement in Mainland China with a Specific Focus on the Case of the 'Chinese Lala Alliance' and 'Marriage Equality in Chinese Societies.'" In *Connecting Taiwan: Participation—Integration—Impacts*, edited by Carsten Storm, 146–166. London: Routledge, 2018.

——. "Same-Sex Desire and Society in Taiwan, 1970–1987." *China Quarterly* 181 (2005): 67–81.

Daniel, Drew. "Queer Sound." *WIRE*, no. 333 (2011): 42–46.

Dao Mei 倒霉. "Gongju" 工具 [Tool]. *WXZB* 8, no. 353 (1929): 84.

Davidson, Arnold I. *The Emergence of Sexuality: Historical Epistemology and the Formation of Concepts.* Cambridge, MA: Harvard University Press, 2001.

Davies, Sharyn Graham. *Gender Diversity in Indonesia: Sexuality, Islam and Queer Selves.* London: Routledge, 2010.

Dean, Tim. "The Antisocial Homosexual." *PMLA* 121, no. 3 (2006): 826–828.

——. *Unlimited Intimacy: Reflections on the Subculture of Barebacking.* Chicago: University of Chicago Press, 2009.

de Lauretis, Teresa. "Popular Culture, Public and Private Fantasies: Femininity and Fetishism in David Cronenberg's *M. Butterfly*." *Signs: Journal of Women in Culture and Society* 24, no. 2 (1999): 303–334.

Deleuze, Gilles, and Félix Guattari. *Kafka: Toward a Minor Literature.* Translated by Dana Polan. Minneapolis: University of Minnesota Press, 1986.

——. *A Thousand Plateaus: Capitalism and Schizophrenia.* Translated by Brian Massumi. Minneapolis: University of Minnesota Press, 1987.

D'Emilio, John. "Capitalism and Gai Identity." In *Powers of Desire: The Politics of Sexuality,* edited by Ann Snitow, Christine Stansell, and Sharon Thompson, 100–113. New York: Monthly Review Press, 1983.

——. *Sexual Politics, Sexual Communities: The Making of a Homosexual Minority in the United States, 1940–1970.* Chicago: University of Chicago Press, 1983.

Derrida, Jacques. *Archive Fever: A Freudian Impression.* Translated by Eric Prenowitz. Chicago: University of Chicago Press, 1995.

——. *Of Grammatology.* Translated by Gayatri Chakravorty Spivak. Baltimore: Johns Hopkins University Press, 1976.

——. *Spectres of Marx: The State of Debt, the Work of Mourning, and the New International.* Translated by Peggy Kamuf. London: Routledge, 1994.

——. *Writing and Difference.* Translated by A. Bass. London: Routledge, 1978.

Devor, Aaron, and Nicholas Matte. "Building a Better World for Transpeople: Reed Erickson and the Erickson Educational Foundation." *International Journal of Transgenderism* 10, no. 1 (2007): 47–68.

DeVun, Leah, and Zeb Tortorici. "Trans, Time, and History." *TSQ: Transgender Studies Quarterly* 5, no. 4 (2018): 518–539.

Dikötter, Frank, ed. *The Construction of Racial Identities in China and Japan.* Honolulu: University of Hawai'i Press, 1998.

——. *The Discourse of Race in Modern China.* Stanford: Stanford University Press, 1992.

——. *Sex, Culture and Modernity in China: Medical Science and the Construction of Sexual Identities in the Early Republican Period.* Hong Kong: Hong Kong University Press, 1995.

Ding Fubao 丁福保. "Ban yinyang yili" 半陰陽一例 [A case of half yin-yang]. *The Shin Yih Yaw* 新醫藥 [New medicine] 4, no. 9 (September 1936): 973–977.

Dinshaw, Carolyn. *Getting Medieval: Sexualities and Communities, Pre- and Postmodern.* Durham: Duke University Press, 1999.

Dirlik, Arif. "Postsocialism? Reflections on 'Socialism with Chinese Characteristics.'" *Bulletin of Concerned Asian Scholars* 21, no. 1 (1989): 33–44.

Doan, Laura. *Disturbing Practices: History, Sexuality, and Women's Experience of Modern War.* Chicago: University of Chicago Press, 2013.

——. *Fashioning Sapphism: The Origins of a Modern English Lesbian Culture.* New York: Columbia University Press, 2001.

——. "Troubling Popularisation: On the Gendered Circuits of a 'Scientific' Knowledge of Sex." *Gender and History* 31, no. 2 (2019): 1–15.

Dolan, Jill. *Utopia in Performance: Finding Hope at the Theatre.* Ann Arbor: University of Michigan Press, 2005.

Dose, Ralf. *Magnus Hirschfeld: The Origins of the Gay Liberation Movement.* New York: Monthly Review Press, 2014.

Downing, Lisa. *The Subject of Murderer: Gender, Exceptionality, and the Modern Killer.* Chicago: University of Chicago Press, 2013.

Dreyfus, Hubert L., and Paul Rabinow. *Michel Foucault: Beyond Structuralism and Hermeneutics*. Chicago: University of Chicago Press, 1982.

Driskill, Qwo-Li. *Asegi Stories: Cherokee Queer and Two-Spirit Memory*. Tucson: University of Arizona Press, 2016.

Driskill, Qwo-Li, Chris Finley, Brian Joseph Gilley, and Scott Lauria Morgensen, eds. *Queer Indigenous Studies: Critical Interventions in Theory, Politics, and Literature*. Tucson: University of Arizona Press, 2011.

Drucker, Donna J. *The Classification of Sex: Alfred Kinsey and the Organization of Knowledge*. Pittsburgh: University of Pittsburgh Press, 2014.

Drucker, Peter. "'In the Tropics There Is No Sin': Sexuality and Gay-Lesbian Movements in the Third World." *New Left Review* 218 (1996): 75–101.

——. *Warped: Gay Normality and Queer Anti-Capitalism*. Leiden: Brill, 2015.

Duara, Prasenjit. "Asia Redux: Conceptualizing a Region for Our Times." *Journal of Asian Studies* 69, no. 4 (2010): 963–983.

——. "The Regime of Authenticity: Timelessness, Gender, and National History in Modern China." *History and Theory* 37, no. 3 (1998): 287–308.

——. *Rescuing History from the Nation: Questioning Narratives of Modern China*. Chicago: University of Chicago Press, 1995.

Duberman, Martin. *Stonewall*. New York: Dutton, 1993.

Duberman, Martin, Martha Vicinus, and George Chauncey, eds. *Hidden from History: Reclaiming the Gay and Lesbian Past*. New York: New American Library, 1989.

Duggan, Lisa. "The Discipline Problem: Queer Theory Meets Lesbian and Gay History." *GLQ: Journal of Lesbian and Gay Studies* 2, no. 3 (1995): 179–191.

——. *Sapphic Slashers: Sex, Violence, and American Modernity*. Durham: Duke University Press, 2001.

——. *The Twilight of Equality?: Neoliberalism, Cultural Politics, and the Attack on Democracy*. Boston: Beacon, 2003.

Dung Kai-cheung. *Atlas: The Archaeology of an Imagined City*. Translated by Dung Kai-cheung, Anders Hansson, and Bonnie S. McDougall. New York: Columbia University Press, 2012.

Eaklor, Vicki L. *Queer America: A People's GLBT History of the United States*. New York: New Press, 2011.

Edber, Hannah. "'This Poem Which Is Not Your Language': Jewishness, Translation, and the Historical Philosophy of Adrienne Rich, 1968–1991." MA thesis, University of California, Santa Cruz, 2017.

Edelman, Lee. "Antagonism, Negativity, and the Subject of Queer Theory." *PMLA* 121, no. 3 (2006): 821–823.

——. *No Future: Queer Theory and the Death Drive*. Durham: Duke University Press, 2004.

Edgerton, David. "From Innovation to Use: Ten Eclectic Theses on the Historiography of Technology." *History and Technology* 16, no. 2 (1999): 111–136.

Edmonds, Penelope, and Amanda Nettelbeck, eds. *Intimacies of Violence in the Settler Colony: Economies of Dispossession Around the Pacific Rim*. New York: Palgrave Macmillan, 2018.

Ehrenreich, Barbara, and Deirdre English. *Complaints and Disorders: The Sexual Politics of Sickness*. New York: Feminist Press, 1973.

——. *For Her Own Good: 150 Years of the Experts' Advice to Women*. New York: Doubleday, 1978.

Ellis, Havelock. "Sexo-Aesthetic Inversion." *Alienist and Neurologist* 34, no. 2 (1913): 249–279.

———. *Studies in the Psychology of Sex.* Vol. 7, *Eonism and Other Supplementary Studies.* Philadelphia: F. A. Davis, 1928.

Ellis, Nadia. *Territories of the Soul: Queered Belonging in the Black Diaspora.* Durham: Duke University Press, 2015.

Elman, Benjamin. *A Cultural History of Modern Science in China.* Cambridge, MA: Harvard University Press, 2006.

Emerton, Robyn. "Finding a Voice, Fighting for Rights: The Emergence of the Transgender Movement in Hong Kong." *Inter-Asia Cultural Studies* 7, no. 2 (2006): 243–269.

Eng, David L. *The Feeling of Kinship: Queer Liberalism and the Racialization of Intimacy.* Durham: Duke University Press, 2010.

———. "In the Shadows of a Diva: Committing Homosexuality in David Henry Hwang's *M. Butterfly.*" *Amerasia Journal* 20, no. 1 (1994): 93–116.

———. "The Queer Space of China: Expressive Desire in Stanley Kwan's *Lan Yu.*" *positions: east asia cultures critique* 18, no. 2 (Fall 2010): 459–487.

———. *Racial Castration: Managing Masculinity in Asian America.* Durham: Duke University Press, 2001.

Eng, David L., Teemu Ruskola, and Shuang Shen. "Introduction: China and the Human." *Social Text* 29, no. 4 (2011): 1–27.

Engebretsen, Elisabeth L. *Queer Women in Urban China: An Ethnography.* London: Routledge, 2014.

Engebretsen, Elisabeth L., William F. Schroeder, and Hongwei Bao, eds. *Queer/Tongzhi China: New Perspectives on Research, Activism and Media Cultures.* Copenhagen: Nordic Institute of Asian Studies Press, 2015.

Enke, Anne, ed. *Transfeminist Perspectives: In and Beyond Transgender and Gender Studies.* Philadelphia: Temple University Press, 2012.

Epps, Brad. "Comparison, Competition, and Cross-Dressing: Cross-Cultural Analysis in a Contested World." In *Islamicate Sexualities: Translations Across Temporal Geographies of Desire,* edited by Kathryn Babayan and Afsaneh Najmabadi, 114–160. Cambridge, MA: Harvard University Press, 2008.

Erickson-Schroth, Laura ed. *Trans Bodies, Trans Selves.* New York: Oxford University Press, 2014.

Erni, John Nguyet. "Disrupting the Colonial Transgender/Law Nexus: Reading the Case of W in Hong Kong." *Cultural Studies—Critical Methodologies* 16, no. 4 (2016): 351–360.

———. "Legitimating Transphobia: The Legal Disavowal of Transgender Rights in Prison." *Cultural Studies* 27, no. 1 (2013): 136–159.

———. "Marriage Rights for Transgender People in Hong Kong: Reading the W Case." In *Wives, Husbands, and Lovers: Marriage and Sexuality in Hong Kong, Taiwan, and Urban China,* edited by Deborah S. Davis and Sara L. Friedman, 189–216. Stanford: Stanford University Press, 2014.

———. "*W v. Registrar of Marriages* (2013)." In *Global Encyclopedia of Lesbian, Gay, Bisexual, Transgender, and Queer (LGBTQ) History,* edited by Howard Chiang, 1713–1717. Farmington Hills, MI: Charles Scribner's Sons, 2019.

Esty, Jed, and Colleen Lye. "Peripheral Realisms Now." *Modern Language Quarterly* 73, no. 3 (2012): 269–288.

Evans, Harriet. *Women and Sexuality in China: Dominant Discourses of Female Sexuality and Gender Since 1949.* Cambridge: Polity, 1997.

"Ex-GI Becomes Blond Beauty." *New York Daily News,* December 1, 1952.

Fabian, Johannes. *Out of Our Minds: Reason and Madness in the Exploration of Central Africa.* Berkeley: University of California Press, 2000.

——. *Time and the Other: How Anthropology Makes Its Objects.* New York: Columbia University Press, 1983.

Faderman, Lillian. *The Gay Revolution: The Story of the Struggle.* New York: Simon and Schuster, 2016.

——. *Odd Girls and Twilight Lovers: A History of Lesbian Life in Twentieth-Century America.* New York: Columbia University Press, 1991.

——. *Surpassing the Love of Men: Romantic Friendship and Love Between Women from the Renaissance to the Present.* New York: William Morrow, 1981.

Faderman, Lillian, and Ann Williams. "Radclyffe Hall and the Lesbian Image." *Conditions* 1, no. 1 (1977): 31–41.

Fan, Yun. *Social Movements in Taiwan's Democratic Transition.* London: Routledge, 2018.

Feinberg, Leslie. *Transgender Warriors: Making History from Joan of Arc to Dennis Rodman.* Boston: Beacon, 1996.

Fell, Dafydd. *Government and Politics in Taiwan.* 2nd ed. London: Routledge, 2018.

Floyd, Kevin. *The Reification of Desire: Toward a Queer Marxism.* Minneapolis: University of Minnesota Press, 2009.

Forrester, John. *Thinking in Cases.* Cambridge: Polity, 2017.

Foucault, Michel. "Critical Theory/Intellectual History." In *Critique and Power: Recasting the Foucault/Habermas Debate,* edited by Michael Kelly, 109–137. Cambridge, MA: MIT Press, 1994.

——. *The History of Sexuality.* Vol. 1, *An Introduction.* Translated by Robert Hurley. New York: Vintage, 1990.

——. "Of Other Places." In *Heterotopia and the City: Public Space in a Postcivil Society,* edited by Michiel Dehaene and Lieven De Cauter, 13–30. London: Routledge, 2008.

——. *The Order of Things: An Archaeology of the Human Sciences.* New York: Vintage, 1973.

Fraser, Nancy. *Justice Interruptus: Critical Reflections on the "Postsocialist" Condition.* London: Routledge, 1997.

Freccero, Carla. *Queer/Early/Modern.* Durham: Duke University Press, 2006.

Freeman, Elizabeth. "Queer Belongings: Kinship Theory and Queer Theory." In *A Companion to Lesbian, Gay, Bisexual, Transgender, and Queer Studies,* edited by George E. Haggerty and Molly McGarry, 295–314. Oxford: Blackwell, 2007.

——. *Time Binds: Queer Temporalities, Queer Histories.* Durham: Duke University Press, 2010.

Friedman, Sara L. "Stranger Anxiety: Failed Legal Equivalences and the Challenges of Intimate Recognition in Taiwan." *Public Culture* 29 (2017): 433–455.

Fu, Daiwie 傅大為. *Yaxiya de xinshenti: Xingbie, yiliao yu jindai Taiwan* 亞細亞的新身體: 性別、醫療與近代台灣 [Assembling the new body: Gender/sexuality, medicine, and Taiwan]. Taipei: Socio, 2005.

Fuechtner, Veronika, Douglas E. Haynes, and Ryan M. Jones, eds. *A Global History of Sexual Science, 1880–1960.* Oakland: University of California Press, 2018.

Fujitani, Takashi. *Race for Empire: Koreans as Japanese and Japanese as Americans During World War II*. Berkeley: University of California Press, 2011.

Fuller, Sophie, and Lloyd Whitesell, eds. *Queer Episodes in Music and Modern Identity*. Urbana: University of Illinois Press, 2002.

Furth, Charlotte. "Androgynous Males and Deficient Females: Biology and Gender Boundaries in Sixteenth- and Seventeenth-Century China." *Late Imperial China* 9 (1988): 1–31.

——. *Ting Wen-chiang: Science and China's New Culture*. Cambridge, MA: Harvard University Press, 1970.

Gallo, Marcia M. *Different Daughters: A History of the Daughters of Bilitis and the Rise of the Lesbian Rights Movement*. Emeryville, CA: Seal, 2007.

Garber, Marjorie. *Vested Interests: Cross-Dressing and Cultural Anxiety*. London: Routledge, 1992.

Garcia, J. Neil. *Philippine Gay Culture: Binabae to Bakla, Silahis to MSM*. Quezon City: University of Philippine Press, 1996.

Gathorne-Hardy, Jonathan. *Sex the Measure of All Things: A Life of Alfred C. Kinsey*. London: Chatto and Windus, 1998.

Ghai, Yash P. *Hong Kong's New Constitutional Order: The Resumption of Chinese Sovereignty and the Basic Law*. Hong Kong: Hong Kong University Press, 1999.

Giffney, Noreen, and Myra J. Hird, eds. *Queering the Non/Human*. Burlington, VT: Ashgate, 2008.

Gilfoyle, Timothy J. *City of Eros: New York City, Prostitution, and the Commercialization of Sex, 1790–1920*. New York: Norton, 1992.

Glissant, Édouard. *Poetics of Relation*. Translated by Betsy Wing. Ann Arbor: University of Michigan Press, 1997.

Godin, Benoît. *Models of Innovation: The History of an Idea*. Cambridge, MA: MIT Press, 2017.

Godley, Michael R. *The Mandarin-Capitalists from Nan-Yang: Overseas Chinese Enterprise in the Modernization of China, 1893–1911*. Cambridge: Cambridge University Press, 1981.

Goh, Joseph N. *Becoming a Malaysian Trans Man: Gender, Society, Body and Faith*. Singapore: Palgrave Macmillan, 2020.

——. *Living Out Sexuality and Faith: Body Admissions of Malaysian Gay and Bisexual Men*. London: Routledge, 2018.

Goldstein, Joshua. *Drama Kings: Players and Publics in the Re-Creation of Peking Opera*. Berkeley: University of California Press, 2007.

——. "Mei Lanfang and the Nationalization of Peking Opera, 1912–1930." *positions: east asia cultures critique* 7, no. 2 (1999): 377–420.

Goodwin v UK (2002) 35 EHRR 18.

Gopinath, Gayatri. *Impossible Desires: Queer Diasporas and South Asian Public Cultures*. Durham: Duke University Press, 2005.

——. *Unruly Visions: The Aesthetic Practices of Queer Diaspora*. Durham: Duke University Press, 2018.

Gordin, Michael D., Helen Tilley, and Gyan Prakash, eds. *Utopia/Dystopia: Conditions of Historical Possibility*. Princeton: Princeton University Press, 2010.

Gray, Mary L., Colin R. Johnson, and Brian J. Gilley, eds. *Queering the Countryside: New Frontiers in Rural Queer Studies*. New York: New York University Press, 2016.

Greenberg, Julie A. *Intersexuality and the Law: Why Sex Matters*. New York: New York University Press, 2012.

Grewal, Inderpal, and Caren Kaplan. "Global Identities: Theorizing Transnational Studies of Sexuality." *GLQ: A Journal of Lesbian and Gay Studies* 7, no. 4 (2001): 663–679.

Groppe, Alison M. *Sinophone Malaysian Literature: Not Made in China*. Amherst, NY: Cambria, 2013.

Gu Mingsheng 顧鳴盛. "Renyao" 人妖 [Human prodigy]. *Yixue shijie* 醫學世界 [Medicine world] 22 (1913): 4–5.

Gu Yin 顧寅. "Cong TaoLiu dusha shuodao nüzi tongxing'ai he nüxing fanzui yu xingjineng (xia)" 從陶劉妒殺說到女子同性愛和女性犯罪與性機能 (下) [Speaking of women's criminality and sexual function from the perspective of the Tao Liu jealousy murder (final)]. *Doubao* 斗報 2, no. 11 (1932): 3–5.

——. "Cong TaoLiu dusha shuodao nüzi tongxing'ai he nüxing fanzui yu xingjineng (zhong)" 從陶劉妒殺說到女子同性愛和女性犯罪與性機能 (中) [Speaking of women's criminality and sexual function from the perspective of the Tao Liu jealousy murder (middle)]. *Doubao* 斗報 2, no. 10 (1932): 5–7.

——. "Luozhe biantai xingyu de shehui canju" 絡著變態性慾的社會慘劇 [Social tragedy emanating from perverse sexuality]. *SMYJK* 3 (1929): 3, 6–7.

——. "Nüzi de shouyin" 女子的手淫 [Female masturbation]. *SMYJK*, no. 42 (1926): 136–138.

——. "Xingyu zhi shenghua" 性慾之昇華 [The sublimation of libido]. *SMYJK*, no. 38 (1926): 89–92.

Guan, Kwa Chong, and Kua Bak Lim, eds. *A General History of the Chinese in Singapore*. Singapore: World Scientific, 2019.

Guo, Xiaofei 郭曉飛. "Wusheng wuxi de bianqian: Zhongguofa shiyiexia de bianxingren hunyinquan" 無聲無息的變遷：中國法視野下的變性人婚姻權 [A silent and subtle transformation: Transsexual marriage rights in China]. Paper presented at the Twenty Years of Gender/Sexualities conference (organized by the Centre for the Study of Sexualities at National Central University), Taipei, Taiwan, May 16, 2015.

"Guojun shibing Xie Jianshun shoushuhou bian nüren" 國軍士兵謝尖順施手術後變女人 [After operation, the KMT solider Xie Jianshun became a woman]. *Kung Sheung Daily News*, August 22, 1953.

Hacking, Ian. *Historical Ontology*. Cambridge, MA: Harvard University Press, 2002.

——. *Scientific Reason*. Taipei: National Taiwan University Press, 2009.

——. *The Social Construction of What?* Cambridge, MA: Harvard University Press, 1999.

Hagarty, Peter. *Gentlemen's Disagreement: Alfred Kinsey, Lewis Terman, and the Sexual Politics of Smart Men*. Chicago: University of Chicago Press, 2013.

Halberstam, J. "The Anti-Social Turn in Queer Studies." *Graduate Journal of Social Science* 5, no. 2 (2008): 140–156.

——. *Female Masculinity*. Durham: Duke University Press, 1998.

——. *Gaga Feminism: Sex, Gender, and the End of Normal*. Boston: Beacon, 2012.

——. "Global Female Masculinities." *Sexualities* 15, nos. 3–4 (2012): 336–354.

——. *In a Queer Time and Place: Transgender Bodies, Subcultural Lives*. New York: New York University Press, 2005.

———. "The Politics of Negativity in Recent Queer Theory." *PMLA* 121, no. 3 (2006): 823–825.

———. *The Queer Art of Failure*. Durham: Duke University Press, 2011.

———. *Trans*: A Quick and Quirky Account of Gender Variability*. Oakland: University of California Press, 2018.

———. "Transgender Butch: Butch/FTM Border Wars and the Masculine Continuum." *GLQ: A Journal of Lesbian and Gay Studies* 4, no. 2 (1998): 287–310.

Hall, Robert B. *Area Studies: With Special Reference to Their Implications for Research in the Social Sciences*. New York: Social Science Research Council, 1947.

Halperin, David. *How to Do the History of Homosexuality*. Chicago: University of Chicago Press, 2002.

———. *One Hundred Years of Homosexuality, and Other Essays on Greek Love*. London: Routledge, 1990.

———. *What Do Gay Men Want? An Essay on Sex, Risk, and Subjectivity*. Ann Arbor: University of Michigan Press, 2007.

Halperin, David, and Valerie Traub, eds. *Gay Shame*. Chicago: University of Chicago Press, 2009.

Hao, Qian 郝倩. "Zhongguo shoulie bianxingren hunyin de ganga" (中國首例變性人婚姻的尷尬) [The awkwardness of the first case of transsexual marriage in China]. *Xiandai kuaibao*, March 16, 2004. http://big5.huaxia.com/xw/shgj/00186663.html.

Haraway, Donna J. *Staying with the Trouble: Making Kin in the Chthulucene*. Durham: Duke University Press, 2016.

Harrison, Paul. "Poststructuralist Theories." In *Approaches to Human Geography*, edited by Stuart Aitken and Gill Valentine, 122–135. London: Sage, 2006.

Hausman, Bernice. *Changing Sex: Transsexualism, Technology, and the Idea of Gender*. Durham: Duke University Press, 1995.

Hayes, Jarrod. *Queer Roots for the Diaspora: Ghosts in the Family Tree*. Ann Arbor: University of Michigan Press, 2016.

Hayward, Eva, and Jami Weinstein, eds. "Tranimalities." *TSQ: Transgender Studies Quarterly* 2, no. 2 (2015): 184–363.

Hee, Wai-Siam. *Remapping the Sinophone: The Cultural Production of Chinese-Language Cinema in Singapore and Malaya Before and During the Cold War*. Hong Kong: Hong Kong University Press, 2019.

Heidegger, Martin. *The Question Concerning Technology, and Other Essays*. Translated by William Lovitt. New York: Harper and Row, 1977.

Heinrich, Ari Larissa. *The Afterlife of Images: Translating the Pathological Body Between China and the West*. Durham: Duke University Press, 2008.

———. *Chinese Surplus: Biopolitical Aesthetics and the Medically Commodified Body*. Durham: Duke University Press, 2018.

Hemmings, Clare. "Invoking Affect: Cultural Theory and the Ontological Turn." *Cultural Studies* 19, no. 5 (2005): 546–567.

Henry, George. *Sex Variants: A Study in Homosexual Patterns*. 2 vols. New York: Paul B. Hoeber, the Medical Book Department of Harper and Brothers, 1941.

Henry, Todd A. "A Documentary Impulse: The Historical Imagination of Queer Films in Contemporary South Korea." Paper presented at the annual meeting of the Association for Asian Studies, San Diego, California, March 21–23, 2013.

——, ed. *Queer Korea*. Durham: Duke University Press, 2020.

Herdt, Gilbert, ed. *Third Sex, Third Gender: Beyond Sexual Dimorphism in Culture and History*. New York: Zone, 1993.

Herring, Scott. *The Hoarders: Material Deviance in American Culture*. Minneapolis: University of Minnesota Press, 2014.

Hevia, James L. *Cherishing Men from Afar: Qing Guest Ritual and the Macartney Embassy of 1793*. Durham: Duke University Press, 1995.

Hexter, J. H. "The Rhetoric of History." *History and Theory* 6, no. 1 (1967): 3–13.

Hildebrandt, Timothy. *Social Organizations and the Authoritarian State in China*. Cambridge: Cambridge University Press, 2013.

Hillenbrand, Margaret. *Negative Exposures: Knowing What Not to Know in Contemporary China*. Durham: Duke University Press, 2020.

Hinchy, Jessica. "The Eunuch Archive: Colonial Records of Non-Normative Gender and Sexuality in India." *Culture, Theory and Critique* 58, no. 2 (2017): 127–146.

——. *Governing Gender and Sexuality in Colonial India: The* Hijra, *c. 1850–1900*. Cambridge: Cambridge University Press, 2019.

Hine, Darlene Clark. "The Black Studies Movement: Afrocentric-Traditionalist-Feminist Paradigms for the Next Stage." *Black Scholar* 22 (Summer 1992): 11–18.

Hinsch, Bert. *Passions of the Cut Sleeve: The Male Homosexual Tradition in China*. Berkeley: University of California Press, 1990.

Hirschfeld, Magnus. *Men and Women: The World Journey of a Sexologist*. Translated by O. P. Green. New York: G. P. Putnam's Sons, 1935.

——. *Transvestites: The Erotic Drive to Cross Dress*. Translated by Michael A. Lombardi-Nash. 1910; Buffalo, NY: Prometheus, 1991.

Ho, Josephine 何春蕤. *Haoshuang nüren: Nüxing zhuyi yu xing jiefang* 豪爽女人：女性主義與性解放 [The gallant woman: Feminism and sex emancipation]. Taipei: Crown, 1994.

——. "Is Global Governance Bad for East Asian Queers?" *GLQ: A Journal of Lesbian and Gay Studies* 14, no. 4 (2008): 457–479.

——. "Jiaowo 'kuaxingren': kuaxingbie zhuti yu xingbie jiefang yundong" 叫我「跨性人」——跨性別主體與性別解放運動 [Call me 'transgender': Transgender subjectivity and gender/sexual liberation movement]. *Po zhoubao* 破週報 [Pots weekly], March 17, 1998.

——, ed. *Kuaxingbie* 跨性別 [Transgender]. Chungli, Taiwan: Center for the Study of Sexualities, National Central University, 2003.

——, ed. *Ku'er: Lilun yu zhengzhi* 酷兒：理論與政治 [Queer politics and queer theory]. *Working Papers in Gender/Sexuality Studies* nos. 3–4. Jungli, Taiwan: National Central University Center for the Study of Sexualities, 1998.

——. "Queer Existence Under Global Governance: A Taiwan Exemplar." *positions: east asia cultures critique* 18 (2010): 537–554.

——. "Wode kuaxingbie jiachushi: Jianlun Taiwan TG Dieyuan" 我的跨性別接觸史：兼論台灣 TG 蝶園 [My engagement with transgender history: A corollary discussion of Taiwan's TG butterfly garden]. Paper presented at the "Northeast *Yao* Lecture: Trans/Gender History and the Present" (東北妖講座：跨／性別越界的歷史與現在), Taipei, Taiwan, November 11, 2017.

Ho, Loretta Wing Wah. *Gay and Lesbian Subculture in Urban China*. London: Routledge, 2010.

Ho, Ming-sho. *Challenging Beijing's Mandate of Heaven: Taiwan's Sunflower Movement and Hong Kong's Umbrella Movement*. Philadelphia: Temple University Press, 2019.

Hobson, Emily K. *Lavender and Red: Liberalism and Solidarity in the Gay and Lesbian Left*. Oakland: University of California Press, 2016.

Hockx, Michel. *Internet Literature in China*. New York: Columbia University Press, 2015.

Honig, Emily. "Socialist Sex: The Cultural Revolution Revisited." *Modern China* 29, no. 2 (2003): 143–175.

Hoskins, Janet Alison, and Viet Thanh Nguyen, eds. *Transpacific Studies: Framing an Emerging Field*. Honolulu: University of Hawai'i Press, 2014.

Howard, John. *Men Like That: A Southern Queer History*. Chicago: University of Chicago Press, 1999.

Hoyer, Niels, ed. *Man Into Woman: An Authentic Record of a Change of Sex*. New York: E. P. Dutton, 1933.

Hsu, Jen-Hao. "Queering Chineseness: The Queer Sphere of Feelings in *Farewell My Concubine* and *Green Snake*." *Asian Studies Review* 36 (2012): 1–17.

Hsu, Madeline Y. "Unwrapping Orientalist Constraints: Restoring Homosocial Normativity to Chinese American History." *Amerasia Journal* 29, no. 2 (2003): 230–253.

Hsu Su-Ting 徐淑婷. "Bianxingyuzheng huanzhe bianxing shoushu hou de shenxin shehui shiying" 變性慾症患者變性手術後的身心社會適應 [The physical, psychological and social adaptation among transsexuals after sex reassignment surgery: A study of six cases]. MA thesis, Kaohsiung Medical University, 1998.

Huang, Hans Tao-Ming. "From Glass Clique to *Tongzhi* Nation: *Crystal Boys*, Identity Formation, and the Politics of Sexual Shame." *positions: east asia cultures critique* 18, no. 2 (2010): 373–398.

——. *Queer Politics and Sexual Modernity in Taiwan*. Hong Kong: Hong Kong University Press, 2011.

Huang, Jianli. "Conceptualizing Chinese Migration and Chinese Overseas: The Contribution of Wang Gungwu." *Journal of Chinese Overseas* 6, no. 1 (2010): 1–21.

Huang, Yixiong. "Media Representation of *Tongxinglian* in China: A Case Study of the People's Daily." *Journal of Homosexuality* 65, no. 3 (2018): 338–360.

Huang, Yu-ting, and Rebecca Weaver-Hightower, eds. *Archiving Settler Colonialism: Culture, Space, and Race*. London: Routledge, 2019.

Hubbs, Nadine. *The Queer Composition of America's Sound: Gay Modernists, American Music, and National Identity*. Berkeley: University of California Press, 2004.

——. *Rednecks, Queers, and Country Music*. Berkeley: University of California Press, 2014.

Hu-DeHart, Evelyn. "The History, Development, and Future of Ethnic Studies." *Phi Delta Kappan* 75, no. 1 (1993): 50–54.

Hung, Tzu-hui Celina. "Hunxie(yu)hua mailuo Zhong de huayuyuxi yanjiu" 混血(語)化脈絡中的華語語系研究 [Sinophone studies through the lens of creolization]. *Sun Yat-sen Journal of Humanities* 35 (2013): 47–67.

——. "'There Are No Chinamen in Singapore': Creolization and Self-Fashioning of the Straits Chinese in the Colonial Contact Zone." *Journal of Chinese Overseas* 5, no. 2 (2009): 257–290.

Hunt, Nancy Rose. *A Colonial Lexicon: Of Birth Ritual, Medicalization, and Mobility in Colonial Congo.* Durham: Duke University Press, 1999.

———. *A Nervous State: Violence, Remedies, and Reveries in Colonial Congo.* Durham: Duke University Press, 2016.

Hurtado, Albert L. *Intimate Frontiers: Sex, Gender, and Culture in Old California.* Albuquerque: University of New Mexico Press, 1999.

Hutton, Christopher. "Objectification and Transgender Jurisprudence: The Dictionary as Quasi-Statute." *Hong Kong Law Journal* 41, no. 1 (2011): 27–47.

Hwang, David Henry. *M. Butterfly.* New York: Plume, 1989.

Hwang, Jinlin 黃金麟. *Lishi, shenti, guojia: Jindai zhongguo de shenti xingcheng, 1895–1937* 歷史、身體、國家：近代中國的身體形成，1895–1937 [History, the body, the nation: The formation of the body of modern China, 1895–1937]. Taipei: Linking, 2001.

———. *Zhanzhen, shenti, xiandaixing: Xiandai Taiwan de junshi zhili yu shenti, 1895–2005* 戰爭、身體、現代性：近代台灣的軍事治理與身體，1895–2005 [War, the body, and modernity: Military governmentality and the body in modern Taiwan, 1895–2005]. Taipei: Linking, 2009.

Jackson, Peter A. "Capitalism and Global Queering: National Markets, Parallels Among Sexual Cultures, and Multiple Queer Modernities." *GLQ: A Journal of Lesbian and Gay Studies* 15, no. 3 (2009): 357–395.

———. *Dear Uncle Go: Male Homosexuality in Thailand.* Bangkok: Bua Luang, 1995.

———. "An Explosion of Thai Identities: Global Queering and Reimagining Queer Theory." *Culture, Health, and Sexuality* 2 (2000): 405–424.

———. "Gay Adaptation, Tom-Dee Resistance, and Kathoey Indifference: Thailand's Gender/Sex Minorities and the Episodic Allure of Queer English." In *Speaking in Queer Tongues: Globalization and Gay Language,* edited by William L. Leap and Tom Boellstorff, 202–230. Urbana: University of Illinois Press, 2004.

———. *Male Homosexuality in Thailand.* New York: Global Academic, 1989.

———, ed. *Queer Bangkok: 21st Century Markets, Media, and Rights.* Hong Kong: Hong Kong University Press, 2011.

Jacobs, Sue-Ellen, Wesley Thomas, and Sabine Lang. *Two Spirit People: Native American Gender Identity, Sexuality, and Spirituality.* Urbana: University of Illinois Press, 1997.

Jameson, Frederic. *The Prison-House of Language: A Critical Account of Structuralism and Russian Formalism.* Princeton: Princeton University Press, 1972.

Jay, Jennifer W. "Another Side of Chinese Eunuch History: Castration, Adoption, Marriage, and Burial." *Canadian Journal of History* 28, no. 3 (1993): 459–478.

———. "Castration and Medical Images of Eunuchs in Traditional China." In *Current Perspectives in the History of Science in East Asia,* edited by Yun-sik Kim and Francesca Bray, 385–394. Seoul: Seoul National University Press, 1999.

Jia Yinghua 賈英華. *The Last Eunuch of China: The Life of Sun Yaoting.* Translated by Sun Haichen. Beijing: China Intercontinental, 2008.

———. *Modai taijian miwen: Sun Yaoting zhuan* 末代太監秘聞：孫耀庭傳 [The secret life of the last eunuch: A biography of Sun Yaoting]. Beijing: Zhishi chubanshe, 1993.

Jian Zhujun 簡竹君. "Tongzhi fei tongzhi dajia yiqilai" 同志非同志 大家一起來 [Tongzhi or not everyone comes along]. *LHB,* August 26, 2000.

Jiang, Hoching. "Marriage, Same-Sex, in Taiwan." In *Global Encyclopedia of Lesbian, Gay, Bisexual, Transgender, and Queer (LGBTQ) History*, edited by Howard Chiang, 1004–1008. Farmington Hills, MI: Charles Scribner's Sons, 2019.

Jiang, Jin. *Women Playing Men: Yue Opera and Social Change in Twentieth-Century Shanghai*. Seattle: University of Washington Press, 2009.

Jin Yong 金庸. *Lu Ding Ji* 鹿鼎記 [The dear and the cauldron]. 5 vols. Hong Kong: Minghe She, 1981.

——. *Xiao Ao Jiang Hu* 笑傲江湖 [The smiling, proud wanderers]. 4 vols. Hong Kong: Minghe She, 1980.

Johnson, Barbara. "Writing." In *Critical Terms for Literary Study*, edited by Frank Lentricchia and Thomas McLaughlin, 39–49. Chicago: University of Chicago Press, 1990.

Johnson, Colin R. *Just Queer Folks: Gender and Sexuality in Rural America*. Philadelphia: Temple University Press, 2013.

Johnson, Mark. *Beauty and Power: Transgendering and Cultural Transformation in the Philippines*. Oxford: Berg, 1997.

Johnson, Paul. *Homosexuality and the European Court of Human Rights*. London: Routledge, 2012.

Jones, James H. *Alfred C. Kinsey: A Public/Private Life*. New York: Norton, 1997.

Jones, Ryan M. "Mexican Sexology and Male Homosexuality: Genealogies and Global Contexts, 1860–1957." In *A Global History of Sexual Science, 1880–1960*, edited by Veronika Fuechtner, Douglas E. Haynes, and Ryan M. Jones, 232–257. Oakland: University of California Press, 2018.

——. "'Now I Have Found Myself, and I Am Happy': Marta Olmos, Debates on Sex-Reassignment, and Mexico on a Global Stage, 1952–1957." Forthcoming.

Judge, Joan. *Print and Politics: "Shibao" and the Culture of Reform in Late Qing China*. Stanford: Stanford University Press, 1996.

——. *Republican Lens: Gender, Visuality, and Experience in the Early Chinese Periodical Press*. Berkeley: University of California Press, 2015.

Jue Gen 掘根. "Dao Mei yundong zhi xianjue wenti" 倒梅運動之先決問題 [The primary challenges of the anti-Mei movement]. *WXZB* 8, no. 353 (1929): 84–85.

Kahan, Benjamin. *The Book of Minor Perverts: Sexology, Etiology, and the Emergence of Sexuality*. Chicago: University of Chicago Press, 2019.

Kam, Lucetta Y. L. "Return, Come Out: Queer Lives in Postcolonial Hong Kong." In *Hong Kong Culture and Society in the New Millennium*, edited by Yiu-Wai Chu, 165–178. Singapore: Springer, 2017.

——. *Shanghai Lalas: Female Tongzhi Communities and Politics in Urban China*. Hong Kong: Hong Kong University Press, 2012.

Kang, Dredge. "*Kathoey* 'In Trend': Emergent Genderscapes, National Anxieties, and the Re-Signification of Male-Bodied Effeminacy in Thailand." *Asian Studies Review* 36, no. 4 (2012): 475–494.

Kang, Wenqing. "The Decriminalization and Pathologization of Homosexuality in China." In *China in and Beyond the Headlines*, edited by Timothy B. Weston and Lionel M. Jensen, 231–248. Lanham, MD: Rowman and Littlefield, 2012.

——. "Male Same-Sex Relations in Socialist China." *PRC History Review* 3, no. 1 (2018): 20–22.

——. *Obsession: Male Same-Sex Relations in China, 1900–1950.* Hong Kong: Hong Kong University Press, 2009.

——. "Queer Life, Communities, and Activism in Contemporary China." *Cross-Currents: East Asian History and Culture Review* 31 (2019): 226–230.

Kao, Ying-Chao. "Organizing Transnational Moral Conservatism: How U.S. Christian and Taiwanese 'Pro-Family' Movements Converge, Diverge, and Collide." PhD diss., Rutgers University, 2018.

Kapai, Pujai. "A Principled Approach Towards Judicial Review: Lessons from *W v Registrar of Marriages.*" *Hong Kong Law Journal* 41, no. 1 (2011): 49–74.

Kaplan, E. Ann. "Reading Formations and Chen Kaige's *Farewell My Concubine.*" In *Transnational Chinese Cinemas: Identity, Nationhood, Gender*, edited by Sheldon Hsiao-peng Lu, 265–275. Honolulu: University of Hawai'i Press, 1997.

Kaplan, Morris. B. "Intimacy and Equality: The Question of Lesbian and Gay Marriage." *Philosophical Forum* 25, no. 4 (1994): 333–360.

Karl, Rebecca E. "Creating Asia: China in the World at the Beginning of the Twentieth Century." *American Historical Review* 103, no. 4 (1998): 1096–1118.

Katz, Jonathan Ned. *Gay American History: Lesbians and Gay Men in the U.S.A.* New York: Crowell, 1976.

——. *Love Stories: Sex Between Men Before Homosexuality.* Chicago: University of Chicago Press, 2001.

Kehoe, Séagh, and Chelsea E. Hall. "Tibet." In *Global Encyclopedia of Lesbian, Gay, Bisexual, Transgender, and Queer (LGBTQ) History*, edited by Howard Chiang, 1597–1601. Farmington Hills, MI: Charles Scribner's Sons, 2019.

Kelliher, Diarmaid. "Solidarity and Sexuality: Lesbians and Gays Support the Miners 1984–5." *History Workshop Journal*, no. 77 (2014): 240–262.

Kenen, Stephanie H. "Who Counts when You're Counting Homosexuals? Hormones and Homosexuality in Mid-Twentieth-Century America." In *Science and Homosexualities*, edited by Vernon A. Rosario, 197–218. London: Routledge, 1997.

Kerber, Linda K. "The Meanings of Citizenship." *Journal of American History* 84, no. 3 (1997): 833–854.

——. *No Constitutional Right to Be Ladies: Women and the Obligations of Citizenship.* New York: Hill and Wang, 1998.

Kim, Jodi. *Ends of Empire: Asian American Critique and Cold War Compositions.* Minneapolis: University of Minnesota Press, 2010.

Kinsey, Alfred C., Wardell B. Pomeroy, and Clyde E. Martin. *Sexual Behavior in the Human Male.* Philadelphia: W. B. Saunders, 1948.

Kinsey, Alfred C., Wardell B. Pomeroy, Clyde E. Martin, and Paul H. Gebhard. *Sexual Behavior in the Human Female.* Philadelphia: W. B. Saunders, 1953.

Kleinberg, Ethan, Joan Wallach Scott, and Gary Wilder. "Theses on Theory and History." http://theoryrevolt.com/#history.

Knörr, Jacqueline. "Contemporary Creoleness; or, The World in Pidginization?" *Current Anthropology* 51, no. 6 (2010): 731–759.

Ko, Dorothy. *Cinderella's Sisters: A Revisionist History of Footbinding.* Berkeley: University of California Press, 2005.

Koestenbaum, Wayne. *The Queen's Throat: Opera, Homosexuality, and the Mystery of Desire.* New York: Poseidon, 1993.

Kogan, Terry S. "Transsexuals, Intersexuals, and Same-Sex Marriage." *Brigham Young University Journal of Public Law* 18, no. 2 (2003): 371–418.

Kondo, Dorine. "*M. Butterfly*: Orientalism, Gender, and a Critique of Essentialist Identity." *Cultural Critique*, no. 16 (1990): 5–29.

Kong, Travis S. K. *Chinese Male Homosexualities: Memba, Tongzhi, and Golden Boy.* London: Routledge, 2011.

——. "Transnational Queer Sociological Analysis of Sexual Identity and Civic-Political Activism in Hong Kong, Taiwan, and Mainland China." *British Journal of Sociology* 70, no. 5 (2019): 1904–1925.

Kong, Travis S. K., Sky H. L. Lau, and Amory H. W. Hui. "*Tongzhi.*" In *Global Encyclopedia of Lesbian, Gay, Bisexual, Transgender, and Queer (LGBTQ) History*, edited by Howard Chiang, 1603–1609. Farmington Hills, MI: Charles Scribner's Sons, 2019.

Kong, Tsung-gan. *Umbrella: A Political Tale from Hong Kong.* Harrisburg, PA: PEMA, 2017.

Kowner, Rotem, and Walter Demel, eds. *Race and Racism in Modern East Asia: Interactions, Nationalism, Gender and Lineage.* Leiden: Brill, 2015.

——, eds. *Race and Racism in Modern East Asia: Western and Eastern Constructions.* Leiden: Brill, 2012.

Krafft-Ebing, Richard von. *Psychopathia Sexualis with Special Reference to Contrary Sexual Instinct: A Medico-Legal Study.* Translated by Charles Gilbert Chaddock. Philadelphia: F. A. Davis, 1894.

Kristeva, Julia. *About Chinese Women.* London: Boyars, 1977.

Kuhn, Philip A. *Chinese Among Others: Emigraiton in Modern Times.* Lanham, MD: Rowman and Littlefield, 2008.

Kuhn, Thomas. *The Structure of Scientific Revolutions.* Chicago: University of Chicago Press, 1962.

Kutcher, Norman A. *Eunuch and Emperor in the Great Age of Qing Rule.* Oakland: University of California Press, 2018.

Kwan, Stanley, dir. *Lan Yu.* 2001; Hong Kong: Universe, 2002. DVD.

Kwok, D. W. Y. *Scientism in Chinese Thought, 1900–1950.* New Haven: Yale University Press, 1965.

Lacan, Jacques. *The Four Fundamental Concepts of Psycho-Analysis.* Edited by Jacques-Alain Millers. Translated by Alan Sheridan. New York: Norton, 1981.

Laclau, Ernesto, and Chantel Mouffe. *Hegemony and Socialist Strategy: Towards a Radical Democratic Politics.* London: Verso, 1985.

La Fountain-Stokes, Lawrence. *Queer Ricans: Cultures and Sexualities in the Diaspora.* Minneapolis: University of Minnesota Press, 2009.

Lai, Francisca Yuenki. "Migrant and Lesbian Activism in Hong Kong: A Critical Review of Grassroots Politics." *Asian Anthropology* 17, no. 2 (2018): 135–150.

——. "Sexuality at Imagined Home: Same-Sex Desire Among Indonesian Migrant Domestic Workers in Hong Kong." *Sexualities* 21, nos. 5–6 (2018): 899–913.

Lai, You-mei 賴友梅. "Ye Yong-Zhi dashiji" 葉永鋕案大事紀 [Chronicle of events in the Yeh Yung-chih case]. In *YMS*, 37–43.

Lampton, David M. *Following the Leader: Ruling China, from Deng Xiaoping to Xi Jinping*. Berkeley: University of California Press, 2014.

Lanser, Susan S. *The Sexuality of History: Modernity and the Sapphic, 1565–1830*. Chicago: University of Chicago Press, 2014.

Lanza, Fabio. *Behind the Gate: Inventing Students in Beijing*. New York: Columbia University Press, 2010.

"Laoyu yugui jingcha qinyao" 老嫗遇鬼 警察擒妖 [Old woman ran into a ghost: The cops caught the prodigy]. *LHB*, August 7, 1957.

Laqueur, Ernst, Elisabeth Dingemanse, P. C. Hart, and S. E. de Jongh. "Female Sex Hormone in Urine of Men." *Klinische Wochenschrift* 6 (1927): 1859.

Larson, Wendy. "The Concubine and the Figure of History: Chen Kaige's *Farewell My Concubine*." In *Transnational Chinese Cinemas: Identity, Nationhood, Gender*, edited by Sheldon Hsiao-peng Lu, 331–346. Honolulu: University of Hawai'i Press, 1997.

——. "Never This Wild: Sexing the Cultural Revolution." *Modern China* 25, no. 4 (1999): 423–450.

Latour, Bruno. *Reassembling the Social: An Introduction to Actor-Network-Theory*. Oxford: Oxford University Press, 2007.

Lau, Holning, and Derek Loh. "Misapplication of ECHR Jurisprudence in *W v Registrar of Marriages*." *Hong Kong Law Journal* 41, no. 1 (2011): 75–87.

Lazar, Michelle M. "Homonationalist Discourse as a Politics of Pragmatic Resistance in Singapore's Pink Dot Movement: Towards a Southern Praxis." *Journal of Sociolinguistics* 21, no. 3 (2017): 420–441.

Leap, William L., and Tom Boellstorff, eds. *Speaking in Queer Tongues: Globalization and Gay Language*. Urbana: University of Illinois Press, 2004.

Lecklider, Aaron. "Coming to Terms: Homosexuality and the Left in American Culture." *GLQ: A Journal of Lesbian and Gay Studies* 18, no. 1 (2012): 179–195.

Lee, Ching Kwan. *The Specter of Global China: Politics, Labor, and Foreign Investment in Africa*. Chicago: University of Chicago Press, 2017.

Lee, Francis L. F., and Joseph M. Chan, eds. *Media and Protest Logic in the Digital Era: The Umbrella Movement in Hong Kong*. Oxford: Oxford University Press, 2018.

Lee, Miao-hung 李妙虹. "Zhanhou Taiwan funü de shehui diwei (1970–2000)" 戰後臺灣婦女的社會地位 (1970–2000) [Women's status in postwar Taiwanese society]. MA thesis, National Chung Hsing University, 2003.

Lee, Po-Han. "First in Asia, Now What? Taiwan and Marriage Quasi-Equality." *Kyoto Journal* 96 (2019): 36–39.

——. "Queer Activism in Taiwan: An Emergent Rainbow Coalition from the Assemblage Perspective." *Sociological Review* 65, no. 4 (2017): 682–698.

Lee, Raymond, dir. *New Dragon Gate Inn* 新龍門客棧. Hong Kong: Golden Harvest, 1992.

Lee, Yu-lin 李育霖, ed. *Huayuyuxi shijiang* 華語語系十講 [Ten lectures on Sinophone studies]. Taipei: Linking, 2020.

——. *Writing Taiwan: A Study of Taiwan's Nativist Literature*. Saarbrücken, Germany: VDM, 2008.

Lee, Yu-lin, and Howard Chiang, eds. "Taiwan yu huayu yuxi yanjiu" 台灣與華語語系研究 [Taiwan and Sinophone studies]. *Zhongguo xiandai wenxue*, no. 32 (2017): 1–94.

Lee, Yun-Xiu Lee. "Chongdu xingping jiaoyu fa: Yu Su Chien-ling laoshi de fangtan" 重讀性平教育法: 與蘇芊玲老師的訪談 [Rereading the Gender Equity Education Act: An interview of Professor Chien-ling Su]. *Renben jiaoyu zhaji* 人本教育札記 [Humanities Education Foundation magazine], June 1, 2017. http://hefmag.dudaone.com/my-post41.

Legg, Stephen, and Srila Roy. "Neoliberalism, Postcolonialism and Hetero-Sovereignties: Emergent Sexual Formations in Contemporary India." *Interventions: International Journal of Postcolonial Studies* 15, no. 4 (2013): 461–473.

Lei, Sean Hsiang-lin. *Neither Donkey nor Horse: Medicine in the Struggle Over China's Modernity*. Chicago: University of Chicago Press, 2014.

Leung, Angela Ki Che. *Leprosy in China: A History*. New York: Columbia University Press, 2009.

Leung, Helen Hok-Sze. *Farewell My Concubine: A Queer Film Classic*. Vancouver: Arsenal Pulp, 2010.

——. "New Queer Angles on Wong Kar-wai." In *A Companion to Wong Kar-wai*, edited by Martha P. Nochimson, 250–271. Malden, MA: Wiley-Blackwell, 2016.

——. "Queerscapes in Contemporary Hong Kong Cinema." *positions: east asia cultures critique* 9, no. 2 (2001): 423–447.

——. "Trans on Screen." In *Transgender China*, edited by Howard Chiang, 183–198. New York: Palgrave Macmillan, 2012.

——. *Undercurrents: Queer Culture and Postcolonial Hong Kong*. Vancouver: University of British Columbia Press, 2008.

Leupp, Gary. *Male Colors: The Construction of Homosexuality in Tokugawa Japan*. Berkeley: University of California Press, 1997.

LeVay, Simon. *Queer Science: The Use and Abuse of Research Into Homosexuality*. Cambridge, MA: MIT Press, 1996.

Lewis, Rachel. "What's Queer About Musicology Now?" *Women and Music: A Journal of Gender and Culture* 13 (2009): 43–53.

Li, Bin. "The School of Mandarin Duck and Butterfly's Creative Push on Early Chinese Publishing Industry." *Asian Social Science* 8, no. 12 (2012): 164–170.

Li Nan 李楠. *WanQing Minguo shiqi Shanghai xiaobao* 晚清明國時期上海小報 [Shanghai tabloid newspapers during the late Qing and Republican period]. Beijing: Renmin wenxue chubanshe, 2006.

Li Peifen 李佩芬. "*Dianshizhai huabao* zhong de zhixuguan (1884–1898)" 《點石齋畫報》中的秩序觀 (1884–1898) [The perspectives on order in *Dianshizhai huabao* (1884–1898)]. MA thesis, National Taiwan Normal University, 2008.

Li, Siu Leung. *Cross-Dressing in Chinese Opera*. Hong Kong: Hong Kong University Press, 2003.

Liang Yufang 梁玉芳. "Jiaoshi 'tong' meng yaodui xuesheng jihui jiaoyu" 教師「同」盟 要對學生機會教育 [Teachers alliance offers students a strategic education]. *LHB*, June 30, 1997.

——. "Qingzhu tongxinglian yue Taiwan tongzhi jianianhua" 慶祝同性戀月 台灣同志嘉年華 [Celebrating the homosexual month at the Taiwan gay and lesbian carnival]. *LHB*, June 30, 1997.

——. "QuanTai shouge hefa tongzhi tuanti xiayue chengli" 全台首個合法同志團體 下月成立 [The first legal gay and lesbian group in Taiwan to be established next month]. *LHB*, May 28, 2000.

——. "Tongxinglian fojiaotu zucheng Tongfan jingshe" 同性戀佛教徒 組成童梵精舍 [Homosexual Buddhist groups form Tongfan jingshe]. *LHB*, April 6, 1997.

——. "Tongzhen kangyi jingfang lanyong gongquanli chengli 'zhuan'an xiaozu'" 同陣抗議 警方濫用公權力 成立「專案小組」 [Tongzhi Front protests the abuse of power by police by forming a "special committee"]. *LHB*, August 10, 1997.

——. "Tongzhi kongjian zhongneng bubei darao" 同志空間 終能不被打擾 [Homosexual space will not be disturbed]. *LHB*, December 15, 2001.

——. "Tongzhi zixun rexian meizhou santian" 同志諮詢熱線 每周三天 [Tongzhi consultation hotline open three days a week]. *LHB*, November 23, 1998.

——. "Zongtong jiejian tongzhi gongzuozhe" 總統接見同志工作者 [President meets tongzhi worker]. *LHB*, September 5, 2000.

Liao, Ping-hui, and David Der-wei Wang, eds. *Taiwan Under Colonial Rule: History, Culture, Memory.* New York: Columbia University Press, 2006.

Liao Shuhui 廖淑惠. "Taibei Tongwanjie tongzhi mingtian caijie" 台北同玩節 同志明天彩街 [Taipei LGBT Civil Rights Movement Festival tomorrow on the streets]. *LHB*, October 31, 2003.

——. "Xiayuechu tongzhi dayouxin" 下月初 同志大遊行 [Tongzhi pride parade early next month]. *LHB*, October 18, 2003.

Lim, Eng-Beng. *Brown Boys and Rice Queens: Spellbinding Performance in the Asias.* New York: New York University Press, 2014.

Lim, Louisa. *The People's Republic of Amnesia: Tiananmen Revisited.* New York: Oxford University Press, 2015.

Lim, Song Hwee. *Celluloid Comrades: Representations of Male Homosexuality in Contemporary Chinese Cinemas.* Honolulu: University of Hawai'i Press, 2006.

——. "How to Be Queer in Taiwan: Translation, Appropriation, and the Construction of a Queer Identity in Taiwan." In *AsiaPacifiQueer: Rethinking Genders and Sexualities*, edited by Fran Martin, Peter Jackson, Mark McLelland, and Audrey Yue, 235–250. Urbana: University of Illinois Press, 2004.

——. "Queer Theory Goes to Taiwan." In *The Ashgate Research Companion to Queer Theory*, edited by Noreen Giffney and Michael O'Rourke, 257–275. Aldershot, UK: Ashgate, 2009.

Lin Chun. *The Transformation of Chinese Socialism.* Durham: Duke University Press, 2006.

Lin, Dennis 林純德. "'Yao' xinggongzuozhe yanjiu: Shijiao yu fangfa" 「妖」性工作者研究：視 角與方法 [Research on "yao" sex workers: Perspectives and methods]. Paper presented at the 8th Theory and Practice of the Sociology of Sex Graduate Workshop, Harbin, People's Republic of China, June 28 to July 5, 2017.

Lin, Fang-Mei. "Women's Organizations and the Changing State/Society Relationship: Resistance, Co-Optation by the State, or Partnership?" *Taiwan in Comparative Perspective* 2 (2008): 47–64.

Lin, Pei-ling 林佩苓. *Yiwei yu zhongxin yu bianchui zhijian: Taiwan dangdai jingying nütongzhi xiaoshuo yanjiu* 依違於中心與邊陲之間：臺灣當代菁英女同志小說研究 [Between center and periphery: Research on contemporary Taiwanese elite lesbian fictions]. Taipei: Showwe, 2015.

Lin, Wen-Ling. "Buluo 'jiemei' zuo xingbie: Jiaozhi zai xieqin, yinqin, diyuan yu shengchan laodong zhijian" 部落「姊妹」做性別：交織在血親、姻親、地緣與生產勞動之間 ["Sisters" making gender: Between everyday work and social relations]. *Taiwan: A Radical Quarterly in Social Studies* 86 (2012): 51–98.

Lin, Xiaodong, Chris Haywood, and Martin Mac an Ghaill, eds. *East Asian Men: Masculinity, Sexuality, and Desire*. New York: Palgrave Macmillan, 2017.

Lindquist, Lisa J. "The Images of Alice: Gender, Deviancy, and a Love Murder in Memphis." *Journal of the History of Sexuality* 6, no. 1 (1995): 30–61.

Ling Haicheng 凌海成. *Zhongguo zuihou yige taijian* 中國最後一個太監 [The last eunuch in China]. Hong Kong: Heping tushu, 2003.

Ling, Lily H. M. *Postcolonial International Relations: Conquest and Desire Between Asia and the West*. New York: Palgrave Macmillan, 2002.

——. "Sex Machine: Global Hypermasculinity and the Image of Asian Woman in Modernity." *positions: east asia cultures critique* 7, no. 2 (1999): 277–306.

Link, Perry. *Mandarin Ducks and Butterflies: Popular Fiction in Early Twentieth Century Chinese Cities*. Berkeley: University of California Press, 1981.

Lionnet, Françoise, and Shu-mei Shih, eds. *The Creolization of Theory*. Durham: Duke University Press, 2011.

——. "Introduction: Thinking Through the Minor, Transnationally." In *Minor Transnationalism*, edited by Françoise Lionnet and Shu-mei Shih, 1–23. Durham: Duke University Press, 2005.

——, eds. *Minor Transnationalism*. Durham: Duke University Press, 2005.

Liou, Liang-ya. "Taiwan's Postcolonial and Queer Discourses in the 1990s." In *Comparatizing Taiwan*, edited by Shu-mei Shih and Ping-hui Liao, 259–277. London: Routledge, 2015.

Liu, Athena. "Exacerbating *Corbett: W v Registrar of Marriages*." *Hong Kong Law Journal* 41, no. 3 (2011): 759–783.

——. "Understanding *Goodwin: W v Registrar of Marriages*." *Hong Kong Law Journal* 42, no. 2 (2012): 403–430.

Liu, Jennifer. "Making Taiwanese (Stem Cells): Identity, Genetics, and Purity." In *Asian Biotech: Ethics and Communities of Fate*, edited by Aihwa Ong and Nancy Chen, 239–262. Durham: Duke University Press, 2010.

——. "Postcolonial Biotech: Taiwanese Conundrums and Subimperial Desires." *East Asian Science, Technology and Society* 11, no. 4 (2017): 563–588.

Liu, Jen-Peng, and Naifei Ding. "Reticent Poetics, Queer Politics." *Inter-Asia Cultural Studies* 6 (2005): 30–55.

Liu, Lydia H. *The Freudian Robot: Digital Media and the Future of Unconscious*. Chicago: University of Chicago Press, 2011.

——. *Translingual Practice: Literature, National Culture, and Translated Modernity—China, 1900–1937*. Stanford: Stanford University Press, 1995.

Liu, Petrus. "Queer Human Rights in and Against China: Marxism and the Figuration of the Human." *Social Text* 30, no. 1 (2012): 71–89.

——. *Queer Marxism in Two Chinas*. Durham: Duke University Press, 2015.

——. "Why Does Queer Theory Need China?" *positions: east asia cultures critique* 18, no. 2 (2010): 291–320.

Liu Piji 劉丕基. *Renjian wujie de shengwu* 人間誤解的生物 [Common misinterpretations of biology]. 1928; Shanghai: Commercial, 1935.

Lo, Jacqueline. "Beyond Happy Hybridity: Performing Asian Australian Identities." In *Alter/ Asians: Asian-Australian Identities in Art, Media and Popular Culture*, edited by Ien Ang, Sharon Chalmers, Lisa Law, and Mandy Thomas, 152–168. Sydney: Pluto, 2000.

Loftin, Craig M. *Masked Voices: Gay Men and Lesbians in Cold War America*. Albany: State University of New York Press, 2012.

Loos, Tamara. *Subject Siam: Family, Law, and Colonial Modernity in Thailand*. Ithaca: Cornell University Press, 2006.

Loper, Kelley. "*W v Registrar of Marriages* and the Right to Equality in Hong Kong." *Hong Kong Law Journal* 41, no. 1 (2011): 88–107.

Loughery, John. *The Other Side of Silence: Men's Lives and Gay Identities: A Twentieth-Century History*. New York: Henry Holt, 1998.

Louie, Kam, ed. *Changing Chinese Masculinities: From Imperial Pillars of State to Global Real Men*. Hong Kong: Hong Kong University Press, 2016.

——. *Chinese Masculinities in a Globalizing World*. London: Routledge, 2015.

Louie, Kam, and Morris Low, eds. *Asian Masculinities: The Meaning and Practice of Manhood in China and Japan*. London: Routledge, 2003.

Love, Heather. *Feeling Backward: Loss and the Politics of Queer History*. Cambridge, MA: Harvard University Press, 2007.

Lovell, Julia. *Maoism: A Global History*. London: Bodley Head, 2019.

Lowe, Lisa. "The Intimacies of Four Continents." In *Haunted by Empire: Geographies of Intimacy in North American History*, edited by Ann Laura Stoler, 191–212. Durham: Duke University Press, 2006.

——. *The Intimacies of Four Continents*. Durham: Duke University Press, 2015.

Lü Lingling 呂玲玲. "Huanwo renquan tongzhi fanpu" 還我人權 同志反撲 [Give me back human rights homosexuals react]. *LHB*, August 19, 1997.

Lu, Sheldon H. *Chinese Modernity and Global Biopolitics: Studies in Literature and Visual Culture*. Honolulu: University of Hawai'i Press, 2007.

Luciano, Dana, and Mel Y. Chen. "Has the Queer Ever Been Human?" *GLQ: A Journal of Lesbian and Gay Studies* 21, nos. 2–3 (2015): 183–207.

Luibhéid, Eithne, and Lionel Cantú Jr., eds. *Queer Migrations: Sexuality, U.S. Citizenship, and Border Crossing*. Minneapolis: University of Minnesota Press, 2005.

Luibhéid, Eithne, and Karma R. Chávez, eds. *Queer and Trans Migration: Dynamics of Illegalization, Detention, and Deportation*. Urbana: University of Illinois Press, 2020.

Lupke, Christopher. *The Sinophone Cinema of Hou Hsiao-hsien: Culture, Style, Voice, and Motion*. Amherst, NY: Cambria, 2016.

Ma, Jinping. "Remoulding the Chinese Mind: Mental Hygiene Promotion in Republican Shanghai." PhD dissertation, University of Warwick, 2019.

Ma, Sheng-mei. *Sinophone-Anglophone Cultural Duet*. New York: Palgrave Macmillan, 2017.

Macias-González, Victor M. "The Transnational Homophile Movement and the Development of Domesticity in Mexico City's Homosexual Community." *Gender and History* 26, no. 3 (2014): 519–554.

Mackintosh, Jonathan D. *Homosexuality and Manliness in Postwar Japan.* London: Routledge, 2010.

MacMillan, Kurt. "'Forms So Attenuated That They Merge into Normality Itself': Alexander Lipschütz, Gregorio Marañón, and Theories of Intersexuality in Chile, Circa 1930." In *A Global History of Sexual Science, 1880–1960,* edited by Veronika Fuechtner, Douglas E. Haynes, and Ryan M. Jones, 330–352. Oakland: University of California Press, 2018.

Madsen, Deborah L., and Andrea Riemenschnitter, eds. *Diasporic Histories: Cultural Archives of Chinese Transnationalism.* Hong Kong: Hong Kong University Press, 2009.

Man, Simeon. *Soldiering Through Empire: Race and the Making of the Decolonizing Pacific.* Berkeley: University of California Press, 2018.

Manalansan, Martin F. *Global Divas: Filipino Gay Men in Diaspora.* Durham: Duke University Press, 2003.

——. "In the Shadows of Stonewall: Examining Gay Transnational Politics and the Diasporic Dilemma." *GLQ: A Journal of Lesbian and Gay Studies* 2, no. 4 (1995): 425–438.

Mancini, Elena. *Magnus Hirschfeld and the Quest for Sexual Freedom: A History of the First International Sexual Freedom Movement.* New York: Palgrave Macmillan, 2010.

Manion, Jen. *Female Husbands: A Trans History.* Cambridge: Cambridge University Press, 2020.

Marshall, Thomas Humphrey. "Citizenship and Social Class." In *The Citizenship Debates: A Reader,* edited by Gershon Shafir, 93–112. Minneapolis: University of Minnesota Press, 1998.

Martin, Fran. *Backward Glances: Contemporary Chinese Cultures and the Female Homoerotic Imaginary.* Durham: Duke University Press, 2010.

——. *Situating Sexualities: Queer Representation in Taiwanese Fiction, Film, and Public Culture.* Hong Kong: Hong Kong University Press, 2003.

——. "Transnational Queer Sinophone Cultures." In *Routledge Handbook of Sexuality Studies in East Asia,* edited by Mark McLelland and Vera Mackie, 35–48. London: Routledge, 2014.

Martin, Fran, and Josephine Ho, eds. "Trans/Asia, Trans/Gender." *Inter-Asia Cultural Studies* 7, no. 2 (2006): 185–318.

Martin, Fran, Peter Jackson, Mark McLelland, and Audrey Yue, eds. *AsiaPacifiQueer: Rethinking Genders and Sexualities.* Urbana: University of Illinois Press, 2008.

Mashaal, Maurice. *Bourbaki: A Secret Society of Mathematicians.* Translated by Anna Pierrehumbert. Providence, RI: American Mathematical Society, 2006.

Massad, Joseph. *Desiring Arabs.* Chicago: University of Chicago Press, 2007.

——. "Re-Orienting Desire: The Gay International and the Arab World." *Public Culture* 14, no. 2 (2002): 361–385.

Massumi, Brian. *Politics of Affect.* Cambridge: Polity, 2015.

Matignon, Jean-Jacques. "Les eunuques du Palais Impérial à Pékin." *Bulletins de la Société d'anthropologie de Paris* 7, no. 4 (1896): 325–336.

Matsumura, Wendy. *The Limits of Okinawa: Japanese Capitalism, Living Labor, and Theorizations of Community.* Durham: Duke University Press, 2015.

McCabe, Susan. "To Be and to Have: The Rise of Queer Historicism." *GLQ: A Journal of Lesbian and Gay Studies* 11, no. 1 (2005): 119–134.

McGrath, Jason. *Postsocialist Modernity: Chinese Cinema, Literature, and Criticism in the Market Age*. Stanford: Stanford University Press, 2008.

McKeown, Adam. "Chinese Emigration in Global Context, 1850–1940." *Journal of Global History* 5, no. 1 (2010): 95–124.

——. "Conceptualizing Chinese Diasporas, 1842 to 1949." *Journal of Asian Studies* 58, no. 2 (1999): 306–331.

McLelland, Mark. *Queer Japan from the Pacific War to the Internet Age*. Lanham, MD: Rowman and Littlefield 2005.

McMahon, Keith. "The Pornographic Doctrine of a Loyalist Ming Novel: Social Decline and Sexual Disorder in *Preposterous Words* (Guwangyan)." In *Sexuality in China: Histories of Power and Pleasure*, edited by Howard Chiang, 50–75. Seattle: University of Washington Press, 2018.

Mead, Margaret. *Sex and Temperament in Three Primitive Societies*. New York: Morrow, 1935.

Meeker, Martin. *Contacts Desired: Gay and Lesbian Communications and Community, 1940s–1970s*. Chicago: University of Chicago Press, 2005.

Meijer, M. J. "Homosexual Offences in Ch'Ing Law." *T'oung Pao* 71, no. 1 (1985): 109–133.

Meisner, Maurice. *Mao's China and After: A History of the People's Republic*. 3rd ed. New York: Free, 1999.

Mendoza, Victor Román. *Metroimperial Intimacies: Fantasy, Racial-Sexual Governance, and the Philippines in U.S. Imperialism, 1899–1913*. Durham: Duke University Press, 2015.

Meng Yue. *Shanghai and the Edges of Empire*. Minneapolis: University of Minnesota Press, 2006.

Merewhether, Charles. *The Archive*. Cambridge, MA: MIT Press, 2006.

Meyerowitz, Joanne. "A History of 'Gender.'" *American Historical Review* 113, no. 5 (2008): 1346–1356.

——. *How Sex Changed: A History of Transsexuality in the United States*. Cambridge, MA: Harvard University Press, 2002.

——. "Louise Lawrence." In *Encyclopedia of Lesbian, Gay, Bisexual, and Transgender History in America*, edited by Marc Stein, 151–152. New York: Charles Scribner's Sons, 2004.

——, ed. *Not June Cleaver: Women and Gender in Postwar America, 1945–1960*. Philadelphia: Temple University Press, 1994.

——. "Sex Research at the Borders of Gender: Transvestites, Transsexuals, and Alfred C. Kinsey." *Bulletin of the History of Medicine* 75 (2001): 72–90.

Micale, Mark S. "On the 'Disappearance' of Hysteria: A Study in the Clinical Deconstruction of a Diagnosis." *Isis* 84, no. 3 (1993): 496–529.

Mignolo, Walter D. *The Darker Side of the Renaissance: Literacy, Territoriality, and Colonization*. Ann Arbor: University of Michigan Press, 1995.

——. *The Darker Side of Western Modernity: Global Futures, Decolonial Options*. Durham: Duke University Press, 2011.

Miller, Neil. *Out in the World: Gay and Lesbian Life from Buenos Aires to Bangkok*. London: Penguin, 1992.

Miller, Paul Allen. "The Classical Roots of Poststructuralism: Lacan, Derrida, and Foucault." *International Journal of the Classical Tradition* 5, no. 2 (1998): 204–225.

———. *Postmodern Spiritual Practices: The Construction of the Subject and the Reception of Plato in Lacan, Derrida, and Foucault*. Columbus: Ohio State University Press, 2007.

Minton, Henry L. *Departing from Deviance: A History of Homosexual Rights and Emancipatory Science in America*. Chicago: University of Chicago Press, 2002.

Mirandé, Alfredo. *Behind the Mask: Gender Hybridity in a Zapotec Community*. Tucson: University of Arizona Press, 2017.

Mitsuhashi Junko 三橋順子. "'Sei tenkan' no shakaishi (1): Nihon ni okeru 'sei tenkan' gainen no keisei to sono jittai, 1950–60 nendai o chūshin ni" '性転換'の社会史 (1)—日本における' 性転換'概念の形成とその実態、1950–60年代を中心に [A social history of "sex change" (1): The emergence and reality of the "sex change concept" in Japan, 1950–1960]. In *Sengo Nihon josō dōseiai kenkyū* 戦後日本女装'同性愛研究 [Research in postwar Japanese transvestism and homosexuality], edited by 矢島正見 Yajima Masami, 397–435. Tokyo: Chuo University Press, 2006.

Mittler, Barbara. *A Newspaper for China? Power, Identity, and Change in Shanghai's News Media, 1872–1912*. Cambridge, MA: Harvard East Asia Monographs, 2004.

Mizoguchi Yuzo. *Ribenren shiyezhong de zhongguoxue* 日本人視野中的中國學 [China as method]. Translated by Li Suping 李甦平, Gong Ying 龔穎, and Xu Tao 徐滔. 1989; Beijing: Chinese People's University Press, 1996.

Money, John. "Hermaphroditism, Gender, and Precocity in Hyperadrenocorticism." *Bulletin of the Johns Hopkins Hospital* 96 (1955): 253–264.

Morache, Georges. *Pékin et ses habitants: Étude d'hygiene*. Paris: J.-B. Baillière, 1869.

Morgensen, Scott Lauria. "Settler Homonationalism: Theorizing Settler Colonialism Within Queer Modernities." *GLQ: A Journal of Lesbian and Gay Studies* 16, nos. 1–2 (2010): 105–131.

———. *Spaces Between Us: Queer Settler Colonialism and Indigenous Decolonization*. Minneapolis: University of Minnesota Press, 2011.

Morris, Rosalind C. "Three Sexes and Four Sexualities: Redressing the Discourses on Gender and Sexuality in Contemporary Thailand." *positions: east asia cultures critique* 2, no. 1 (1994): 15–43.

Mortimer-Sandilands, Catriona, and Bruce Erickson, eds. *Queer Ecologies: Sex, Nature, Politics, Desire*. Bloomington: Indiana University Press, 2010.

Moscucci, Ornella. *The Science of Woman: Gynaecology and Gender in England, 1800–1929*. Cambridge: Cambridge University Press, 1990.

Moses, Claire Goldberg. "'What's in a Name?' On Writing the History of Feminism." *Feminist Studies* 38, no. 3 (2012): 757–779.

Mungello, David E. *Western Queers in China: Flight to the Land of Oz*. Lanham: Rowman and Littlefield, 2012.

Muñoz, José Esteban. *Cruising Utopia: The Then and There of Queer Futurity*. New York: New York University Press, 2009.

———. *Disidentifications: Queers of Color and the Performance of Politics*. Minneapolis: University of Minnesota Press, 1999.

———. "Thinking Beyond Antirelationality and Antiutopianism in Queer Critique." *PMLA* 121, no. 3 (2006): 825–826.

Munsterhjelm, Mark. *Living Dead in the Pacific: Contested Sovereignty and Racism in Genetic Research on Taiwanese Aborigines*. Vancouver: University of British Columbia Press, 2014.

Murray, Stephen O., and Will Roscoe. *Islamic Homosexualities: Culture, History, and Literature.* New York: New York University Press, 1997.

Mushkat, Roda. *One Country, Two International Legal Personalities: The Case of Hong Kong.* Hong Kong: Hong Kong University Press, 1997.

Najmabadi, Afsaneh. "Beyond the Americas: Are Gender and Sexuality Useful Categories of Analysis?" *Journal of Women's History* 18, no. 1 (2006): 11–21.

——. "Mapping Transformations of Sex, Gender, and Sexuality in Modern Iran." *Social Analysis* 49, no. 2 (2005): 54–77.

——. *Professing Selves: Transsexuality and Same-Sex Desire in Contemporary Iran.* Durham: Duke University Press, 2014.

——. "Transing and Transpassing Across Sex-Gender Walls in Iran." *WSQ: Women's Studies Quarterly* 36, nos. 3–4 (2008): 23–42.

——. *Women with Mustaches and Men Without Beards: Gender and Sexual Anxieties of Iranian Modernity.* Berkeley: University of California Press, 2005.

"Nan biannü de guojun dabing Xie Jianshun guoqu de shenghuo yu shengli biantai" 男變女 的國軍大兵謝尖順過去的生活與生理變態 [The life history and physical pathology of the Male-to-Female KMT Soldier Xie Jianshun]. *Kung Sheung Daily News*, September 2, 1953.

Nandy, Ashis. *The Intimate Enemy: Loss and Recovery of Self Under Colonialism.* New York: Oxford University Press, 1984.

"Nanxing yanjiu" 男性研究 [Men's studies]. *Liangxing pingdeng jiaoyu jikan* 兩性平等教育季刊 [Equality of two sexes education quarterly], no. 12 (2000): 1–142.

Needham, Joseph. *The Grand Titration: Science and Society in East and West.* London: Allen and Unwin, 1969.

Newton, Esther. "The Mythic Mannish Lesbian: Radclyffe Hall and the New Woman." *Signs: Journal of Women in Culture and Society* 9, no. 4 (1984): 557–575.

Ng, Fiona. "Interview: Love in the Time of Tiananmen." *IndieWire.* www.indiewire.com /2002/07/interview-love-in-the-time-of-tiananmen-stanley-kwans-lan-yu-80279/.

Ngai, Jimmy. "A Dialogue with Wong Kar-wai: Cutting Between Time and Two Cities." In *Wong Kar-wai*, edited by Jean-Marc Lalanne, David Martinez, Ackbar Abbas, and Jimmy Ngai, 83–117. Paris: Dis Voir, 1997.

Ngo, Tak-Wing, and Hong-zen Wang, eds. *Politics of Difference in Taiwan.* London: Routledge, 2011.

Novak, David, and Matt Sakakeeny, eds. *Keywords in Sound.* Durham: Duke University Press, 2015.

Nyong'o, Tavia. *The Amalgamation Waltz: Race, Performance, and the Ruses of Memory.* Minneapolis: University of Minnesota Press, 2009.

Omatsu, Glenn, ed. "Salute to the 60s and 70s: Legacy of the San Francisco State Strike." *Amerasia Journal* 15, no. 1 (1989): i–352.

Ong, Aihwa. "Cultural Citizenship as Subject-Making." *Current Anthropology* 37, no. 5 (1996): 737–762.

——. *Flexible Citizenship: The Cultural Logics of Transnationality.* Durham: Duke University Press, 1999.

Oosterhuis, Harry. *Stepchildren of Nature: Krafft-Ebing, Psychiatry, and the Making of Sexual Identity.* Chicago: University of Chicago Press, 2000.

Oswin, Natalie. *Global City Futures: Desire and Development in Singapore*. Athens: University of Georgia Press, 2019.

Oudshoorn, Nelly. *Beyond the Natural Body: An Archaeology of Sex Hormones*. London: Routledge, 1994.

Palmie, Stephen. "Creolization and Its Discontents." *Annual Review of Anthropology* 35 (2006): 433–456.

Palumbo-Liu, David. *Asian/American: Historical Crossings of a Racial Frontier*. Stanford: Stanford University Press, 1999.

Pan Guangdan 潘光旦. "TaoLiu dusha'an de shehui zeren" 陶劉妬殺案的社會責任 [The social responsibility of the Tao-Liu jealousy murder case]. *HN* 1, no. 2 (1932): 25–26.

——. "TaoLiu dusha'an de xinli beijin" 陶劉妬殺案的心裡背景 [The psychological background of the Tao-Liu jealousy murder case]. *HN* 1, no. 1 (1932): 4–5.

——. "Wudu you'ou de tongxing jiansha'an" 無獨有偶的同性姦殺案 [Not a singular case of homosexual love murder]. *HN* 1, no. 11 (1932): 205.

——. "Zailun TaoLiu an de diaocha buzu" 再論陶劉案的調查不足 [Revisiting the insufficient investigation into the Tao-Liu case]. *HN* 1, no. 26 (1932): 504–505.

——. "Zaiti TaoLiu dusha'an" 再提陶劉妬殺案 [Revisiting the Tao-Liu jealousy murder case]. *HN* 1, no. 5 (1932): 82–83.

Pan Shaw-yu 潘少瑜. "Shishang wuzui: *Ziluolan* banyuekan de luoji meixue, zhengzhi yishi yu wenhua xiangxiang" 時尚無罪:《紫羅蘭》半月刊的邏輯美學、政治意識與文化想像 [Fashion is no crime: The aesthetics of editorship, political awareness and cultural imaginary of the semi-monthly *Ziluolan*]. *Chung Cheng Chinese Studies* 中正漢學研究, no. 22 (2013): 271–302.

Patton, Cindy, and Benigno Sánchez-Eppler, eds. *Queer Diasporas*. Durham: Duke University Press, 2000.

Pecic, Zoran Lee. *New Queer Sinophone Cinema: Local Histories, Transnational Connections*. New York: Palgrave Macmillan, 2016.

Peletz, Michael G. *Gender Pluralism: Southeast Asia Since Early Modern Times*. London: Routledge, 2009.

Peng, Hsiao-yen, and Ella Raidel, eds. *The Politics of Memory in Sinophone Cinemas and Image Culture: Altering Archives*. London: Routledge, 2018.

Penrose, Walter. "Hidden in History: Female Homoeroticism and Women of a 'Third Nature' in the South Asian Past." *Journal of the History of Sexuality* 10, no. 1 (2001): 3–39.

Peraino, Judith. *Listening to the Sirens: Musical Technologies of Queer Identity from Homer to Hedwig*. Berkeley: University of California Press, 2006.

Perdue, Peter C. *China Marches West: The Qing Conquest of Central Eurasia*. Cambridge, MA: Belknap Press of Harvard University Press, 2005.

Petersen, Carole J. "Sexual Orientation and Gender Identity in Hong Kong: A Case for the Strategic Use of Human Rights Treaties at the International Reporting Process." *Asian-Pacific Law and Policy Journal* 14, no. 2 (2012): 28–83.

Pflugfelder, Gregory M. *Cartographies of Desire: Male-Male Sexuality in Japanese Discourse*. Berkeley: University of California Press, 1999.

——. "'S' Is for Sister: Schoolgirl Intimacy and 'Same-Sex Love' in Early Twentieth-Century Japan." In *Gendering Modern Japanese History*, edited by Barbara Molony and Kathleen Uno, 133–190. Cambridge, MA: Harvard University Asia Center, 2005.

Phillips, Robert. "'And I Am Also Gay': Illiberal Pragmatics, Neoliberal Homonormativity and LGBT Activism in Singapore." *Anthropologica* 56, no. 1 (2014): 45–51.

Phillips, Steven E. *Between Assimilation and Independence: The Taiwanese Encounter Nationalist China, 1945–1950.* Stanford: Stanford University Press, 2003.

Piaget, Jean. *Structuralism.* New York: Harper and Row, 1970.

Pickowicz, Paul G. "Huang Jianxin and the Notion of Postsocialism." In *New Chinese Cinemas: Forms, Identities, Politics,* edited by Nick Browne, Paul G. Pickowicz, Vivian Sobchack, and Esther Yau, 57–87. Cambridge: Cambridge University Press, 1994.

Plummer, Ken. "Speaking Its Name: Inventing a Gay and Lesbian Studies." In *Modern Homosexualities: Fragments of Lesbian and Gay Experience,* edited by Ken Plummer, 3–28. London: Routledge, 1992.

Po, Ronald. *The Blue Frontier: Maritime Vision and Power in the Qing Empire.* Cambridge: Cambridge University Press, 2018.

Pomeroy, Wardell. *Dr. Kinsey and the Institute for Sex Research.* New York: Harper and Row, 1972.

Potts, Jason, and Daniel Stout, eds. *Theory Aside.* Durham: Duke University Press, 2014.

Povinelli, Elizabeth A. *Geontologies: A Requiem to Late Liberalism.* Durham: Duke University Press, 2016.

Povinelli, Elizabeth A., and George Chauncey. "Thinking Sexuality Transnationally: An Introduction." *GLQ: A Journal of Lesbian and Gay Studies* 5, no. 4 (1999): 439–450.

Pratt, Mary Louise. "Arts of the Contact Zone." *Profession* (1991): 33–40.

Price, Richard. "The Concept of Creolization." In *The Cambridge World History of Slavery,* vol. 3, *AD 1420–AD 1804,* edited by David Eltis and Stanley L. Engerman, 513–537. Cambridge: Cambridge University Press, 2011.

——. "*Créolisation,* Creolization, and *Créolité.*" *Small Axe* 21, no. 1 (2017): 211–219.

Prosser, Jay. *Second Skins: The Body Narratives of Transsexuality.* New York: Columbia University Press, 1998.

——. "'Some Primitive Thing Conceived in a Turbulent Age of Transition': The Transsexual Emerging from *The Well.*" In *Palatable Poison: Critical Perspectives on* The Well of Loneliness, edited by Laura Doan and Jay Prosser, 129–144. New York: Columbia University Press, 2001.

Pu Shui 蒲水. "Jiujiu guoji shangde mingyu ba" 救救國際上的名譽吧 [Save the international reputation]. *WXZB* 8, no. 353 (1929): 77–78.

Puar, Jasbir. "Rethinking Homonationalism." *International Journal of Middle Eastern Studies* 45 (2013): 336–339.

——. *The Right to Maim: Debility, Capacity, Disability.* Durham: Duke University Press, 2017.

——. *Terrorist Assemblages: Homonationalism in Queer Times.* Durham: Duke University Press, 2007.

Qi Fan 豈凡. "Mei Lanfang yangming haiwai zhiyi kaocha" 梅蘭芳揚名海外之一考察 [An investigation into Mei Lanfang's reputation abroad]. *WXZB* 8, no. 353 (1929): 72–76.

——. "Nübiannan yu nübannan" 女變男與女扮男 [Woman becoming man and woman dressing up as man]. *Renyan zhoukan* 人言週刊 [Gossip weekly] 2, no. 9 (1935): 171.

"Qiankun hunyuan yiti cixiong jingneng liangquan" 乾坤混元一體 雌雄竟能兩全 [Male and female hybridized into one: Maleness and femaleness can functionally coexist]. *LHB,* September 25, 1956.

Qin Fuzhen 秦富珍. "Tongwanjie 9 yue 2 ri dengchang" 同玩節 9月2日登場 [Taipei LGBT civil rights movement festival starts on September 2]. *LHB*, August 28, 2000.

"Qishi niannian you jinnia renyao duo: Nanban nüzhuang guairenyao" 奇事年年有 今年人妖多： 男扮女裝怪人妖 [Strange things happen annually, numerous human prodigies witnessed this year: Male cross-dressing weird human prodigy]. *Zhongwai Chunqiu* 中外春秋 [Sino-Foreign annals], no. 51 (September 17, 1947).

Qiu Yuan 秋原 (possibly Hu Qiuyuan 胡秋原), trans. "Tongxinglian'ai lun" 同性戀愛論 [On same-sex romantic love]. *Xin nüxing* 新女性 [New woman] 4, no. 4 (1929): 513–534; and no. 5 (1929): 605–628.

Rado, Sandor. "A Critical Examination of the Concept of Bisexuality." *Psychosomatic Medicine* 2, no. 4 (1940): 459–467.

Rancière, Jacques. *The Names of History: On the Poetics of Knowledge*. Translated by Hassan Melehy. Minneapolis: University of Minnesota Press, 1994.

Rawski, Evelyn. "Reenvisioning the Qing: The Significance of the Qing Period in Chinese History." *Journal of Asian Studies* 55, no. 4 (1996): 829–850.

Reddy, Gayatri. *With Respect to Sex: Negotiating Hijra Identity in South India*. Chicago: University of Chicago Press, 2005.

Reed, Christopher. *Gutenberg in Shanghai: Chinese Print Capitalism, 1876–1937*. Vancouver: University of British Columbia Press, 2004.

Rees v UK (1986) 9 EHRR 56.

Reid, Anthony, and Kristine Alilunas Rodgers, eds. *Sojourners and Settlers: Histories of Southeast Asia and the Chinese*. Honolulu: University of Hawai'i Press, 1996.

"Renyao" 人妖 [Human prodigy]. *HN* 3, no. 4 (1934): 62–63.

"Renyao" 人妖 [Human prodigy]. *Shenzhou huabao* 神州畫報 [Shenzhou pictorials] (1910).

"Renyao" 人妖 [Human prodigy]. *Tuhua ribao* 圖畫日報 [Pictorial daily], no. 166 (1909): 12.

"Renyaoan fusheng xuanpan" 人妖案複審宣判 [The appeal of the human prodigy case was ruled]. *ZLWB*, October 22, 1951.

"'Renyao' beibu zhi qianyin houguo" 「人妖」 被捕之前因後果 [The reasons and consequences of the arrest of "renyao"]. *XSH*, no. 83 (September 11, 1947).

"Renyao fuchuxian: Zhuangnan ban nüzhuang" 人妖復出現 壯男扮女裝 [Human prodigy reappears: A strong man dressed as a woman]. *MSRB*, July 20, 1957.

"Renyao helai" 人妖何來 [Where does renyao come from]. *Yanbao fuzhang* 燕報附張 [Yanbao supplement], January 10, 1910.

"Renyao jiedi Taibei: Gaoyuan zuowenxun" 人妖解抵台北 高院昨間訊 [The human prodigy arrived in Taipei and was interrogated by the high court yesterday]. *LHB*, September 23, 1951.

"Renyao jieshou tijian: Chunyang haobu shenyin" 人妖接受體檢 純陽毫不滲陰 [Human prodigy found completely male after medical exam]. *MSRB*, September 26, 1956.

"Renyao nüyou quishi nanren" 人妖女友 卻是男人 [Human prodigy's girlfriend is a man]. *MSRB*, September 26, 1956.

"Renyao 'Shen Wuye' beibu!: Yilishabo gongyu puohuo mimi yinku" 人妖 「沈五爺」 被捕 ！：依利莎伯公寓破獲秘密淫窟 [Human prodigy Shen Wuye arrested! Elizabeth Apartment discovered to hide a lust cave]. *XSH*, no. 67 (May 2, 1947).

"Renyao tan" 人妖談 [Discussions on renyao]. *Yanbao fuzhang* 燕報附張 [Yanbao supplement], no. 16 (January 21, 1910).

"Renyao yiyu Yunlin: Laofu mata buxiao" 人妖移玉雲林 老父罵他不孝 [Human prodigy relocated to Yunlin: Father calls him unfilial]. *MSRB*, September 27, 1956.

"Renyao Zeng Qiuhuang" 人妖曾秋煌 [Human prodigy Zeng Qiuhuang]. *MSRB*, May 26, 1951.

"Renyao Zeng Qiuhuang an gaoyuan shengxun zhongjie" 人妖曾秋煌案 高院審訊終結 [The Investigation of the case of the human prodigy Zeng Qiuhuang by the high court concluded]. *ZLWB*, October 18, 1951.

"Renyao Zeng Qiuhuang beitiqi gongsu" 人妖曾秋煌 被提起公訴 [Charges filed against the human prodigy Zeng Qiuhuang]. *LHB*, August 26, 1957.

"Renyao Zeng Qiuhuang beitiqi gongsu" 人妖曾秋煌 被提起公訴 [Charges filed against the human prodigy Zeng Qiuhuang]. *MSRB*, August 26, 1957.

"Renyao Zeng Qiuhuang nanweile kanshou" 人妖曾秋皇 難為了看守 [The human prodigy Zeng Qiuhuang gave the guard a hard time]. *LHB*, October 18, 1951.

"Renyao Zeng Qiuhuang wushi Zeng Chaodong mingri fenbie shousheng" 「人妖」曾秋皇 「舞師」曾朝東 明日分別受審 [The "human prodigy" Zeng Qiuhuang and the "Dance Teacher" Zeng Chaodong to be investigated individually tomorrow]. *LHB*, October 17, 1951.

"Renyao zhaqi'an zuofupan Zeng Qiuhuang gaichuxing yinian" 人妖詐欺案咋覆判 曾秋煌改處刑一年 [The case of human prodigy reheard yesterday: Zeng Qiuhuang resentenced to one year]. *LHB*, October 23, 1951.

"Renyao zuoerduo tiechuang suiyue chang" 人妖作惡多 鐵窗歲月長 [Human prodigy receives a long sentence for wrongdoing]. *MSRB*, September 1, 1957.

Rich, Adrienne. "Compulsory Heterosexuality and Lesbian Existence." *Signs: Journal of Women and Culture in Society* 5, no. 4 (1980): 631–660.

Riechert, James. *In the Company of Men: Representations of Male-Male Sexuality in Meiji Literature.* Stanford: Stanford University Press, 2006.

Ritchie, Jason. "Pinkwashing, Homonationalism, and Israel-Palestine: The Conceits of Queer Theory and the Politics of the Ordinary." *Antipode: A Radical Journal of Geography* 47, no. 3 (2015): 616–634.

Robcis, Camille. "'China in Our Heads': Althusser, Maoism, and Structuralism." *Social Text* 30, no. 1 (2012): 51–69.

——. *The Law of Kinship: Anthropology, Psychoanalysis, and the Family in France.* Ithaca: Cornell University Press, 2013.

Robertson, Jennifer. *Takarazuku: Sexual Politics and Popular Culture in Modern Japan.* Berkeley: University of California Press, 1998.

Rodgers, Daniel T. *Age of Fracture.* Cambridge, MA: Belknap Press of Harvard University Press, 2011.

Rofel, Lisa. *Desiring China: Experiments in Neoliberalism, Sexuality, and Public Culture.* Durham: Duke University Press, 2007.

Rogan, Tim. *The Moral Economists: R. H. Tawney, Karl Polanyi, E. P. Thompson, and the Critique of Capitalism.* Princeton: Princeton University Press, 2017.

Rogaski, Ruth. *Hygienic Modernity: Meanings of Health and Disease in Treaty-Port China.* Berkeley: University of California Press, 2004.

Rojas, Carlos. *Homesickness: Culture, Contagion, and National Reform in Modern China.* Cambridge, MA: Harvard University Press, 2015.

——. "Queer Utopias in Wong Kar-wai's *Happy Together*." In *A Companion to Wong Kar-wai*, edited by Martha P. Nochimson, 508–521. Malden, MA: Wiley-Blackwell, 2016.

——. "Writing the Body." In *Transgender China*, edited by Howard Chiang, 199–223. New York: Palgrave Macmillan, 2012.

Romesburg, Don, ed. *The Routledge History of Queer America*. London: Routledge, 2018.

Roscoe, Will. *Changing Ones: Third and Fourth Genders in Native North America*. New York: St. Martin's, 1998.

——. *The Zuni Man-Woman*. Albuquerque: University of New Mexico Press, 1991.

Ross, Kristin. *May '68 and Its Afterlives*. Chicago: University of Chicago Press, 2002.

Rothwell, Matthew D. *Transpacific Revolutions: The Chinese Revolution in Latin America*. London: Routledge, 2012.

Roudometof, Victor. *Glocalization: A Critical Introduction*. London: Routledge, 2016.

Rowen, Ian. "Inside Taiwan's Sunflower Movement: Twenty-Four Days in a Student-Occupied Parliament, and the Future of the Region." *Journal of Asian Studies* 74, no. 1 (2015): 5–21.

Rupp, Leila J. "The Persistence of Transnational Organizing: The Case of the Homophile Movement." *American Historical Review* 116, no. 4 (2011): 1014–1039.

——. "Toward a Global History of Same-Sex Sexuality." *Journal of the History of Sexuality* 10, no. 2 (2001): 287–302.

Sakai, Naoki. "Modernity and Its Critique: The Problem of Universalism and Particularism." *South Atlantic Quarterly* 87, no. 3 (1988): 475–504.

Salamon, Gayle. *Assuming a Body: Transgender and Rhetorics of Materiality*. New York: Columbia University Press, 2010.

——. "Transfeminism and the Future of Gender." In *Women's Studies on the Edge*, edited by Joan Wallach Scott, 115–136. Durham: Duke University Press, 2008.

Sang, Tze-Lan D. *The Emerging Lesbian: Female Same-Sex Desire in Modern China*. Chicago: University of Chicago Press, 2003.

Sankar, Andrea. "Sisters and Brothers, Lovers and Enemies: Marriage Resistance in Southern Kwangtung." *Journal of Homosexuality* 11 (1986): 69–82.

Schäfer, Dagmar, and Marcu Popplow. "Technology and Innovation within Expanding Webs of Exchange." In *The Cambridge World History*, vol. 5, *Expanding Webs of Exchange and Conflict, 500 CE—1500 CE*, edited by Benjamin Z. Kedar, 309–338. Cambridge: Cambridge University Press, 2015.

Scherpe, Jens M. "Changing One's Legal Gender in Europe—The 'W' Case in Comparative Perspective." *Hong Kong Law Journal* 41, no. 1 (2011): 109–123.

Scott, Joan W. "The Evidence of Experience." *Critical Inquiry* 17, no. 4 (1991): 773–797.

——. *Gender and the Politics of History*. New York: Columbia University Press, 1988.

Scull, Andrew. *Hysteria: The Biography*. Oxford: Oxford University Press, 2009.

Sears, Clare. *Arresting Dress: Cross-Dressing, Law, and Fascination in Nineteenth-Century San Francisco*. Durham: Duke University Press, 2015.

Sedgwick, Eve Kosofsky. *Between Men: English Literature and Male Homosocial Desire*. New York: Columbia University Press, 1985.

——. *Epistemology of the Closet*. Berkeley: University of California Press, 1990.

———. *Tendencies.* Durham: Duke University Press, 1993.

———. *Touching Feeling: Affect, Pedagogy, Performativity.* Durham: Duke University Press, 2003.

Sengoopta, Chandak. *The Most Secret Quintessence of Life: Sex, Glands, and Hormones, 1850–1950.* Chicago: University of Chicago Press, 2006.

———. *Otto Weininger: Sex, Science, and Self in Imperial Vienna.* Chicago: University of Chicago Press, 2000.

Serlin, David Harley. "Christine Jorgensen and the Cold War Closet." *Radical History Review* 62 (1995): 137–165.

Seymour, Nicole. *Strange Natures: Futurity, Empathy, and the Queer Ecological Imagination.* Urbana: University of Illinois Press, 2013.

Shah, Nayan. "Between 'Oriental Depravity' and 'Natural Degenerates': Spatial Borderlands and the Making of Ordinary Americans." *American Quarterly* 57, no. 3 (2005): 703–725.

Shah, Shanah. *The Making of a Gay Muslim: Religion, Sexuality and Identity in Malaysia and Britain.* New York: Palgrave Macmillan, 2018.

Shah, Svati P. "Queering Critiques of Neoliberalism in India: Urbanism and Inequality in the Era of Transnational 'LGBTQ' Rights." *Antipode* 47, no. 3 (2015): 635–651.

Shao Bingru 邵冰如. "Taiwan caihongguo yaoban menggongyuan" 台灣彩虹國 要辦夢公園 [Taiwan's rainbow nation organizes dream park]. *LHB*, June 19, 1997.

———. "Tongzhi jinye jiti sanbu" 同志今夜 集體散步 [Gay and lesbians take it to the streets together this evening]. *LHB*, August 9, 1997.

Sheffield and Horsham v UK (1998) 27 EHRR 163.

Shen Changlu 沈長祿. "Tongxinglian tuanti panhuo zunzhong" 同性戀團體 盼獲尊重 [Homosexual groups seeking respect]. *LHB*, February 8, 1996.

Shen Xiaoxiang 沈孝祥. "Tongxing cansha'an Tao Sijin chusixing tantao" 同性慘殺案陶思瑾 處死刑探討 [Discussing the death penalty of Tao Sijin in a homosexual murder case]. *Shiyejie zhuankan* 實業界專刊 [Industry column] 3 (1932): 17–19.

Shernuk, Kyle. "A Queerness of Relation: The Plight of the 'Ethnic Minority' in Chan Koon-Chung's *Bare Life.*" In *Keywords in Queer Sinophone Studies*, edited by Howard Chiang and Alvin K. Wong, 80–102. London: Routledge, 2020.

Shih, Shu-mei. "Against Diaspora: The Sinophone as Places of Cultural Production." In *Global Chinese Literature: Critical Essays*, edited by Jing Tsu and Davd Der-wei Wang, 29–48. Leiden: Brill, 2010.

———. "The Concept of the Sinophone." *PMLA* 126, no. 3 (2011): 709–718.

———. *Fanlisan: Huayuyuxi yanjiulun* 反離散: 華語語系研究論 [Against diaspora: Discourses on Sinophone studies]. Taipei: Linking, 2017.

———. "Forward: The Sinophone as History and the Sinophone as Theory." *Journal of Chinese Cinemas* 6, no. 1 (2012): 5–7.

———, ed. "Globalisation: Taiwan's (In)Significance." *Postcolonial Studies* 6, no. 2 (2003): 143–249.

———. "Globalisation and the (In)Significance of Taiwan." *Postcolonial Studies* 6, no. 2 (2003): 143–153.

———. "Global Literature and the Technologies of Recognition." *PMLA* 119, no. 1 (2004): 16–30.

——. "Introduction: What Is Sinophone Studies?" In *Sinophone Studies: A Critical Reader*, edited by Shu-mei Shih, Chien-hsin Tsai, and Brian Bernards, 1–16. New York: Columbia University Press, 2013.

——. "Is the *Post-* in Postsocialism the *Post-* in Posthumanism?" *Social Text* 110 (2012): 27–50.

——. *The Lure of the Modern: Writing Modernism in Semicolonial China, 1917–1937*. Berkeley: University of California Press, 2001.

——. "On the Conjunctive Method." In *Queer Sinophone Cultures*, edited by Howard Chiang and Ari Larissa Heinrich, 223–225. London: Routledge: 2013.

——. *Visuality and Identity: Sinophone Articulations Across the Pacific*. Berkeley: University of California Press, 2007.

Shih, Shu-mei, and Ping-hui Liao, eds. *Comparatizing Taiwan*. London: Routledge, 2015.

Shih, Shu-mei 史書美, Chia-Ling Mei 梅家玲, Chaoyang Liao 廖朝陽, and Dung-Sheng Chen 陳東升, eds. *Zhishi Taiwan: Taiwan lilun de kenengxing* 知識臺灣: 臺灣理論的可能性 [Knowledge Taiwan: The possibility of Taiwanese theory]. Taipei: Rye Field, 2016.

Shih, Shu-mei, Chien-hsin Tsai, and Brian Bernards, eds. *Sinophone Studies: A Critical Reader*. New York: Columbia University Press, 2013.

"Shishi xianping: renyao" 時事閒評: 人妖 [Current affairs: renyao]. *Xinshijie xiaoshuo shebao* 新世界小說社報 [New world fiction house magazine], no. 7 (1906): 1.

Shohat, Ella. "Notes on the 'Post-Colonial.'" *Social Text*, nos. 31–32 (1992): 99–113.

Showalter, Elaine. *The Female Malady: Women, Madness, and English Culture, 1830–1980*. New York: Pantheon, 1985.

Shu Kei. "Farewell to My Concubine: A Letter to Chen Kaige." *Cinemaya* 20 (1993): 18–20.

Shukin, Nicole. *Animal Capital: Rendering Life in Biopolitical Time*. Minneapolis: University of Minnesota Press, 2009.

Siegel, Marc. "The Intimate Spaces of Wong Kar-wai." In *At Full Speed: Hong Kong Cinema in a Borderless World*, edited by Esther C. M. Yau, 277–294. Minneapolis: University of Minnesota Press, 2001.

Silvo, Teri. "Chinese Opera, Global Cinema, and the Ontology of the Person: Chen Kaige's *Farewell My Concubine*." In *Between Opera and Cinema*, edited by Jeongwon Joe and Rose Theresa, 177–197. New York: Routledge, 2002.

Sim, F. L. "Alice Mitchell Adjudged Insane." *Memphis Medical Monthly* 12, no. 8 (August 1892): 377–428.

Sinnott, Megan. *Toms and Dees: Transgender Identity and Female Same-Sex Relationships in Thailand*. Honolulu: University of Hawai'i Press, 2004.

Sircar, Oishik, and Dipika Jain, eds. *New Intimacies, Old Desire: Caw, Culture and Queer Politics in Neoliberal Times*. New Delhi: Zubaan, 2017.

Skidmore, Emily. "Constructing the 'Good Transsexual': Christine Jorgensen, Whiteness, and Heteronormativity in the Mid-Twentieth Century Press." *Feminist Studies* 37, no. 2 (2011): 270–300.

——. *True Sex: The Lives of Trans Men at the Turn of the Twentieth Century*. New York: New York University Press, 2017.

Skinner, G. William. "Creolized Chinese Societies in Southeast Asia." In *Sojourners and Settlers: Histories of Southeast Asia and the Chinese*, edited by Anthony Reid and Kristine Alilunas Rodgers, 51–93. Sydney: Allen and Unwin, 1996.

Smallwood, Stephanie E. "The Politics of the Archive and History's Accountability to the Enslaved." *History of the Present* 6, no. 2 (2016): 117–132.

Smith, Andrea. *Conquest: Sexual Violence and American Indian Genocide*. Durham: Duke University Press, 2015.

Smith, Peter H. "Mexico Since 1946: Dynamics of an Authoritarian Regime." In *Mexico Since Independence*, edited by Leslie Bethell, 321–396. Cambridge: Cambridge University Press, 1991.

Smith, Roger. *Being Human: Historical Knowledge and the Creation of Human Nature*. New York: Columbia University Press, 2007.

Smith-Rosenberg, Carroll. *Disorderly Conduct: Visions of Gender in Victorian America*. New York: Knopf, 1985.

——. "The Hysterical Woman: Sex Roles and Role Conflict in Nineteenth Century America." *Social Research* 39, no. 4 (1972): 652–678.

Snediker, Michael D. *Queer Optimism: Lyric Personhood and Other Felicitous Persuasions*. Minneapolis: University of Minnesota Press, 2009.

Snorton, C. Riley. *Black on Both Sides: A Racial History of Trans Identity*. Minneapolis: University of Minnesota Press, 2017.

Snow, C. P. *The Two Cultures*. 1959; Cambridge: University of Cambridge Press, 2001.

So, Richard Jean. *Transpacific Community: America, China, and the Rise and Fall of a Cultural Network*. New York: Columbia University Press, 2016.

"Soldado Chino Convertido en Mujer." *El Siglo de Torreón*, August 22, 1953.

"Soldier May Become Woman." *Singapore Free Press Straits*, August 22, 1953.

Sommer, Matthew. "Confusion in the Archive: Qing Dynasty Sodomy Cases from the Ba County Court." Paper presented at the Queer Asia as Historical Critique conference, University of Warwick, May 25, 2013.

——. *Sex, Law, and Society in Late Imperial China*. Stanford: Stanford University Press, 2002.

Spivak, Gayatri Chakravorty. *Death of a Discipline*. New York: Columbia University Press, 2003.

——. *Other Asias*. Malden, MA: Blackwell, 2008.

——. "Subaltern Studies: Deconstructing Historiography." In *Selected Subaltern Studies*, edited by Ranajit Guha and Gayatri Chakravorty Spivak, 3–32. New York: Oxford University Press, 1988.

——. "Woman in Difference: Mahashweta Devi's 'Douloti the Bountiful.'" *Cultural Critique*, no. 14 (1989–1990): 105–128.

Stallings, L. H. *Funk the Erotic: Transaesthetics and Black Sexual Cultures*. Urbana: University of Illinois Press, 2015.

Steakley, James D. *The Homosexual Emancipation Movement in Germany*. New York: Arno, 1975.

Steedman, Carolyn. *Dust*. Manchester: Manchester University Press, 2001.

——. "The Space of Memory: In an Archive." *History of the Human Sciences* 11 (1998): 65–83.

Stein, Marc. *City of Sisterly and Brotherly Loves: Lesbian and Gay Philadelphia, 1945–1972*. Chicago: University of Chicago Press, 2000.

——. *Rethinking the Gay and Lesbian Movement*. London: Routledge, 2012.

——. *The Stonewall Riots: A Documentary History*. New York: New York University Press, 2019.

Stella, Francesca, Yvette Taylor, Tracey Reynolds, and Antoine Rogers, eds. *Sexuality, Citizenship and Belonging: Trans-National and Intersectional Perspectives*. London: Routledge, 2016.

Stent, G. Carter. "Chinese Eunuchs." *Journal of the North China Branch of the Royal Asiatic Society* 11 (1877): 143–184.

Sterne, Jonathan ed. *The Sound Studies Reader*. London: Routledge, 2012.

Stewart, Charles, ed. *Creolization: History, Ethnography, Theory*. Walnut Creek, CA: Left Coast, 2007.

——. "Creolization, Hybridity, Syncretism, Mixture." *Portuguese Studies* 27, no. 1 (2011): 48–55.

Stockard, Janice E. *Daughters of the Canton Delta: Marriage Patterns and Economic Strategies in South China, 1860–1930*. Stanford: Stanford University Press, 1989.

Stoler, Ann Laura. *Along the Archival Grain: Epistemic Anxieties and Colonial Common Sense*. Princeton: Princeton University Press, 2009.

——. *Carnal Knowledge and Imperial Power: Race and the Intimate in Colonial Rule*. Berkeley: University of California Press, 2002.

——. "Colonial Archives and the Arts of Governance." *Archival Science* 2 (2002): 87–109.

——. *Duress: Imperial Durabilities in Our Times*. Durham: Duke University Press, 2016.

——, ed. *Haunted by Empire: Geographies of Intimacy in North American History*. Durham: Duke University Press, 2006.

Stoler, Ann Laura, Carole McGranahan, and Peter C. Perdue, eds. *Imperial Formations*. Santa Fe, NM: School for Advanced Research Press, 2007.

Stryker, Susan. "De/Colonizing Transgender Studies of China." In *Transgender China*, edited by Howard Chiang, 287–292. New York: Palgrave Macmillan, 2012.

——. "My Words to Victor Frankenstein Above the Village of Chamounix: Performing Transgender Rage." *GLQ: A Journal of Lesbian and Gay Studies* 1, no. 3 (1994): 237–254.

——. "Stonewall in the Middle: Reperiodizing Queer History." Keynote presented at the 2019 Queer History Conference, San Francisco, California, June 17, 2019.

——. *Transgender History*. Berkeley: Seal, 2008.

——. *Transgender History*. 2nd ed. New York: Seal, 2017.

——. "Transgender History, Homonormativity, and Disciplinarity." *Radical History Review*, no. 100 (2008): 145–157.

——. "The Transgender Issue: An Introduction." *GLQ: A Journal of Lesbian and Gay Studies* 4, no. 2 (1998): 145–158.

——. "Transgender Studies: Queer Theory's Evil Twin." *GLQ: A Journal of Lesbian and Gay Studies* 10, no. 2 (2004): 212–215.

Stryker, Susan, and Aren Aizura. "Introduction: Transgender Studies 2.0." In *Transgender Studies Reader 2*, edited by Susan Stryker and Aren Aizura, 1–12. New York: Routledge, 2013.

Stryker, Susan, and Talia M. Bettcher, eds. "Trans/Feminisms." *TSQ: Transgender Studies Quarterly* 3, nos. 1–2 (2016): 1–329.

Stryker, Susan, Paisley Currah, and Lisa Jean Moore. "Introduction: Trans-, Trans, or Transgender?" *WSQ: Women's Studies Quarterly* 36, nos. 3–4 (2008): 11–22.

Su Chao-pin and John Woo, dir. *Reign of Assassins* 劍雨. Hong Kong: Media Asia and Beijing: Beijing Galloping Horse Group, 2010.

Su Lin 蘇林. "Yang Huinan *Ai yu xinyang* guanhuai fojiao tongzhi tuanti" 楊惠南《愛與信仰》關懷佛教同志團體 [Yang Huinan's *Love and Belief* attends to Buddhist gay and lesbian groups]. *LHB*, January 30, 2005.

Sueyoshi, Amy. "Queer Asian American Historiography." In *The Oxford Handbook of Asian American History*, 267–278. New York: Oxford University Press, 2016.

——. *Queer Compulsions: Race, Nation, and Sexuality in the Affairs of Yone Noguchi*. Honolulu: University of Hawai'i Press, 2012.

Sullivan, Nikki. "Transmogrification: (Un)becoming Other(s)." In *The Transgender Studies Reader*, edited by Susan Stryker and Stephen Whittle, 553–563. London: Routledge, 2006.

Sullivan, Nikki, and Samantha Murray, eds. *Somatechnics: Queering the Technologisation of Bodies*. Farnham, Surrey, UK: Ashgate, 2009.

Sun Yaoting 孫耀庭. "Wozai mingguo zuo taijian" 我在民國作太監 [Being a eunuch in the Republican period]. *ZJWX* 57, no. 2 (1990): 113–133.

——. "Wozai mingguo zuo taijian" 我在民國作太監 [Being a eunuch in the Republican period]. *ZJWX* 57, no. 3 (1990): 115–134.

Suran, Justin David. "Coming Out Against the War: Antimilitarism and the Politicization of Homosexuality in the Era of Vietnam." *American Quarterly* 53, no. 3 (2001): 452–488.

Sutton, Katie. "Sexological Cases and the Prehistory of Transgender Identity Politics in Interwar Germany." In *Case Studies and the Dissemination of Knowledge*, edited by Joy Damousi, Birgit Lang, and Katie Sutton, 85–103. London: Routledge, 2015.

"Suzu wenhua yishutuanti fangwen youhaoguojia" 速組文化藝術團體 訪問友好國家 [Formation of culture and arts group for visiting friendly countries]. *LHB*, May 27, 1956.

Taiwan Tongzhi Hotline Association. *Renshi tongzhi shouce* 認識同志手冊 [A handbook on tongzhi]. Taipei: Taipei City Government Department of Civil Affairs, 2003.

——. *Renshi tongzhi shouce* 認識同志手冊 [A handbook on tongzhi]. Taipei: Taipei City Government Department of Civil Affairs, 2004.

"Taizhongshi renyao chuxian: Xunluojing mangqing ruju" 台中市人妖出現 巡邏警忙請入局 [Human prodigy appears in Taizhong City again: Police took him to the station]. *MSRB*, September 25, 1956.

Takezawa, Yasuko, and Gary Y. Okihiro, eds. *Trans-Pacific Japanese American Studies*. Honolulu: University of Hawai'i Press, 2016.

Tan, Chris K. K. "A 'Great Affective Divide': How Gay Singaporeans Overcome Their Double Burden." *Anthropological Forum: A Journal of Social Anthropology and Comparative Sociology* 26, no. 1 (2016): 17–36.

Tan, E. K. "A Queer Journey Home in *Solos*: Rethinking Kinship in Sinophone Singapore." In *Queer Sinophone Cultures*, edited by Howard Chiang and Ari Larissa Heinrich, 130–146. London: Routledge, 2013.

——. *Rethinking Chineseness: Translational Sinophone Identities in the Nanyang Literary World*. Amherst, NY: Cambria, 2013.

Tan, Jia. "Beijing Meets Hawai'i: Reflections on *Ku'er*, Indigeneity, and Queer Theory." *GLQ: A Journal of Lesbian and Gay Studies* 23, no. 1 (2017): 137–150.

Tang, Denise Tse-Shang. *Conditional Spaces: Hong Kong Lesbian Desires and Everyday Life*. Hong Kong: Hong Kong University Press, 2011.

Tang, Denise Tse-Shang, Diana Khor, and Yi-Chien Chen. "Legal Recognition of Same-Sex Partnerships: A Comparative Study of Hong Kong, Taiwan, and Japan." *Sociological Review* 68, no. 1 (2020): 192–208.

Tang, Shawna. *Postcolonial Lesbian Identities in Singapore*. London: Routledge, 2018.

Tarling, Nicolas. *Orientalism and the Operatic World*. Lanham: Rowman and Littlefield, 2015.

Taylor, Jami K., and Donald P. Haider-Markel. *Transgender Rights and Politics: Groups, Issue Framing, and Policy Adoption*. Ann Arbor: University of Michigan Press, 2014.

Terman, Lewis M., and Catharine Cox Miles. *Sex and Personality: Studies in Masculinity and Femininity*. New York: McGraw-Hill, 1936.

Terry, Jennifer. *An American Obsession: Science, Medicine, and Homosexuality in Modern Society*. Chicago: University of Chicago Press, 1999.

Tessier, Max. "Farewell to My Concubine: Art Over Politics." *Cinemaya* 20 (1993): 16–18.

Thompson, E. P. *The Making of the English Working Class*. London: Victor Gollancz, 1963.

——. "The Moral Economy of the English Crowd in the Eighteenth Century." *Past and Present*, no. 50 (1971): 76–136.

Thompson, Janet (Louise Lawrence). "Transvestism: An Empirical Study." *IJS* 4, no. 4 (1951): 216–219.

Tian, Min. "Male Dan: The Paradox of Sex, Acting, and Perception of Female Impersonation in Traditional Chinese Theatre." *Asia Theatre Journal* 17, no. 1 (2000): 78–97.

——. *Mei Lanfang and the Twentieth-Century International Stage: Chinese Theatre Placed and Displaced*. New York: Palgrave Macmillan, 2012.

"Tianzhongzhen faxian zhenxing yinyangren" 田中鎮發現 真性陰陽人 [Tianzhong Township discovers a true hermaphrodite]. *MSRB*, April 16, 1955.

Tortorici, Zeb. *Sins Against Nature: Sex and Archives in Colonial New Spain*. Durham: Duke University Press, 2018.

Traub, Valerie. *Thinking Sex with the Early Moderns*. Philadelphia: University of Pennsylvania Press, 2015.

Treat, John Whittier. "The Rise and Fall of Homonationalism in Singapore." *positions: asia critique* 23, no. 2 (2015): 349–365.

Trouillot, Michel-Rolph. "Culture on the Edges: Caribbean Creolization in Historical Context." In *From the Margins: Historical Anthropology and Its Futures*, edited by Brian Ketih Axel, 189–210. Durham: Duke University Press, 2002.

Truman, Sarah E., and David Ben Shannon. "Queer Sonic Cultures: An Affective Walking-Composing Project." *Capacious: Journal for Emerging Affective Inquiry* 1, no. 3 (2018): 58–77.

Trumbach, Randolph. "The Birth of the Queen: Sodomy and the Emergence of Gender Equality in Modern Culture, 1660–1750." In *Hidden from History: Reclaiming the Gay and Lesbian Past*, edited by Martin Duberman, Martha Vicinus, and George Chauncey, 129–140. New York: New American Library, 1989.

Tsai, Chien-hsin. *A Passage to China: Literature, Loyalism, and Colonial Taiwan*. Cambridge, MA: Harvard University Asia Center, 2017.

Tsai, Henry Shi-shan. *The Eunuchs in the Ming Dynasty*. Albany: State University of New York Press, 1996.

Tseng, Hsiu-ping 曾秀萍. *Guchen, Niezi, Taibeiren: Bai Xianyong tongzhi xiaoshuolun* 孤臣‧孽子‧台北人：白先勇同志小說論 [Alienated courtiers, impious sons, and Taipei ren: Essays on Pai Hsien-yung's tongzhi fictions]. Taipei: Elite, 2003.

Tsu, Jing. *Sound and Script in Chinese Diaspora.* Cambridge, MA: Harvard University Press, 2010.

Tsu, Jing, and Benjamin A. Elman, eds. *Science and Technology in Modern China, 1880s–1940s.* Leiden: Brill, 2014.

Tsu, Jing, and David Der-wei Wang, eds. *Global Chinese Literature: Critical Essays.* Leiden: Brill, 2010.

——. "Introduction: Global Chinese Literature." In *Global Chinese Literature: Critical Essays,* edited by Jing Tsu and David Der-wei Wang, 1–14. Leiden: Brill, 2010.

Tsui Hark, dir. *Flying Swords of Dragon Gate* 龍門飛甲. Hong Kong: Distribution Workshop, 2011.

Tu, Wei-ming. "Cultural China: The Periphery as Center." *Daedalus* 120, no. 2 (1991): 1–32.

Tuisi Zhaizhu 退思齋主. "Renyao" 人妖 [Human prodigy]. *Libailiu* 禮拜六 [Saturday], no. 191 (1922): 23–24.

Valentine, David. *Imagine Transgender: An Ethnography of a Category.* Durham: Duke University Press, 2007.

van Rij, Jan. *Madame Butterfly: Japaonisme, Puccini, and the Search for the Real Cho-Cho-San.* Berkeley: Stone Bridge, 2001.

Veracini, Lorenzo. *Settler Colonialism: A Theoretical Overview.* New York: Palgrave Macmillan, 2010.

Vincent, J. Keith. *Two-Timing Modernity: Homosocial Narrative in Modern Japanese Fiction.* Cambridge, MA: Harvard University Press, 2012.

Vitiello, Giovanni. *The Libertine's Friend: Homosexuality and Masculinity in Late Imperial China.* Chicago: University of Chicago Press, 2011.

Volpp, Leti. "The Culture of Citizenship." *Theoretical Inquiries in Law* 8, no. 2 (2007): 571–602.

W v Registrar of Marriages [2010] 6 HKC 359.

W v Registrar of Marriages [2012] 1 HKC 88.

W v Registrar of Marriages [2013] HKCFA 39.

Wadler, Joyce. "The True Story of M. Butterfly: The Spy Who Fell in Love with a Shadow." *New York Times,* August 15, 1993.

Wan, Marco. "Doing Things with the Past: A Critique of the Use of History by Hong Kong's Court of First Instance in *W v Registrar of Marriages.*" *Hong Kong Law Journal* 41, no. 1 (2011): 125–138.

——. "What's So Unusual About W?" *Hong Kong Law Journal* 41, no. 1 (2011): 5–6.

Wang, Chih-ming. *Transpacific Articulations: Student Migration and the Remaking of Asian America.* Honolulu: University of Hawai'i Press, 2013.

Wang, David Der-wei. "'Gen' de zhengzhi, 'shi' de shixue: Huayu lunshu yu Zhongguo wenxue" 「根」的政治，「勢」的詩學：華語論述與中國文學 [The politics of "root," the poetics of "propensity": Sinophone discourse and Chinese literature]. *Zhongguo xiandai wenxue* 中國現代文學 [Modern Chinese literature] 24 (2013): 1–18.

——. *The Monster That Is History: History, Violence, and Fictional Writing in Twentieth-Century China.* Berkeley: University of California Press, 2004.

Wang, David Der-wei 王德威, Chia-cian Ko 高嘉謙, and Kam Loon Woo 胡金倫, eds. *Huayi-feng: Huayuyuxi wenxue duben* 華夷風: 華語語系文學讀本 [Sinophone/Xenophone: Contemporary Sinophone literature reader]. Taipei: Linking, 2016.

Wang, David Der-Wei, and Shu-mei Shih. "'Huayu yuxi yu Taiwan' zhuti luntan" 「華語語系與台灣」主題論壇 [Forum on Sinophone Taiwan]. *Zhongguo xiandai wenxue* 中國現代文學 [Modern Chinese literature], no. 32 (2017): 75–94.

Wang Erh-min 王爾敏. "Zhongguo jindai zhishi pujihua chuanbo zhi tushuo xingshi—Dianshizhai huabaoli" 中國近代知識普及化傳播之圖說形式——點石齋畫報例 [The illustrated form of news for the diffusion of the modern world knowledge in nineteenth-century China: The Tien-Shih-Chai pictorial newspaper, 1884–1900]. *Bulletin of the Institute of Modern History Academia Sinica* 19 (1990): 135–172.

Wang, Gungwu. *China and the Chinese Overseas.* Singapore: Times Academic, 1991.

——. "Chineseness: The Dilemmas of Place and Practice." In *Cosmopolitan Capitalists: Hong Kong and the Chinese Diaspora,* edited by Gary G. Hamilton, 118–134. Seattle: University of Washington Press, 1999.

——. *The Chinese Overseas: From Earthbound China to the Quest for Autonomy.* Cambridge, MA: Harvard University Press, 2000.

Wang Hui. *The End of Revolution: China and the Limits of Modernity.* London: Verso, 2009,

——. "The Idea of Asia and Its Ambiguities." *Journal of Asian Studies* 69, no. 4 (2010): 985–989.

——. "Scientific Worldview, Culture Debates, and the Reclassification of Knowledge in Twentieth-Century China." *boundary 2* 35 (2008): 125–155.

Wang, Ling-chi. "The Structure of Dual Domination: Toward a Paradigm for the Study of the Chinese Diaspora in the United States." *Amerasia Journal* 21, no. 1 (1995): 149–169.

Wang Ping, Ni Jiazhen, et al. "Xingbie zhengzhi yu tongzhi yundong" 性別政治與同志運動 [Gender politics and lesbian/gay movement]. In *Huaren tongzhi xin duben* 華人同志新讀本 [A new reader on Chinese *tongzhi*], edited by Lu Jianxiong 盧劍雄, 87–90. Hong Kong: Huasheng shudian, 1999.

Wang, Wen-Ji. "*West Wind Monthly* and the Popular Mental Hygiene Discourse in Republican China." *Taiwanese Journal for Studies of Science, Technology and Medicine* 13 (2011): 15–88.

Wang, Wen-Ji, and Hsuan-Ying Huang. "Mental Health." In *The Making of the Human Sciences in China: Historical and Conceptual Foundations,* edited by Howard Chiang, 460–488. Leiden: Brill, 2019.

Wang, Xiaojue. *Modernity with a Cold War Face: Reimagining the Nation in Chinese Literature Across the 1949 Divide.* Cambridge, MA: Harvard University Press, 2013.

Wang Zhihong 王志弘. "Taibei Xingongyuan de qingyu dilixue: Kongjian zaixian yu nan tongxinglian rentong" 台北新公園的情慾地理學: 空間在線與男同性戀認同 [Erotic geographies of Taipei New Park: Spatial representations of gay identity]. *Taiwan: A Radical Quarterly in Social Sciences* 22 (1996): 195–218.

Warner, Michael. *The Trouble with Normal: Sex, Politics, and the Ethics of Queer Life.* New York: Free, 1999.

Wat, Eric C. *The Making of a Gay Asian Community: An Oral History of Pre-AIDS Los Angeles.* Lanham, MD: Rowman and Littlefield, 2002.

Wei, Jingsheng. *The Courage to Stand Alone: Letters from Prison and Other Writings*. New York: Viking, 1997.

Weiss, Gail. *Body Images: Embodiment as Intercorporeality*. London: Routledge, 1998.

Wesling, Meg. "Neocolonialism, Queer Kinship, and Diaspora: Contesting the Romance of the Family in Shani Mootoo's *Cereus Blooms at Night* and Edwidge Danticat's *Breath, Eyes, Memory*." *Textual Practice* 25, no. 4 (2011): 649–670.

White, Hayden V. "The Burden of History." *History and Theory* 5, no. 2 (1966): 111–134.

——. *Metahistory: The Historical Imagination in Nineteenth-Century Europe*. Baltimore: Johns Hopkins University Press, 1973.

——. "The Value of Narrativity in the Representation of Reality." *Critical Inquiry* 7, no. 1 (1980): 5–27.

Whiteley, Sheila, ed. *Queering the Popular Pitch*. London: Routledge, 2006.

Wiener, Martin J. "The Idea of 'Colonial Legacy' and the Historiography of Empire." *Journal of the Historical Society* 13, no. 1 (2013): 1–32.

Wikan, Unni. "Man Becomes Woman: Transsexualism in Oman As a Key to Gender Roles." *Man* 12 (1977): 304–319.

Williams, Walter L. *The Spirit and the Flesh: Sexual Diversity in American Indian Culture*. Boston: Beacon, 1986.

Winichakul, Thongchai. *Siam Mapped: A History of the Geo-Body of a Nation*. Honolulu: University of Hawai'i Press, 1994.

Winter, Sam. "Transgender Science: How Might It Shape the Way We Think About Transgender Rights?" *Hong Kong Law Journal* 41, no. 1 (2011): 139–153.

Wisenthal, Jonathan, Sherrill Grace, Melinda Boyd, Brian McIlroy, and Vera Micznik, eds. *A Vision of the Orient: Texts, Intertexts, and Context of Madame Butterfly*. Toronto: University of Toronto Press, 2006.

Wittgenstein, Ludwig. *Philosophical Investigations*. Oxford: Blackwell, 1997.

Wolff, Charlotte. *Magnus Hirschfeld: A Portrait of a Pioneer in Sexology*. London: Quartet, 1986.

Wolin, Richard. *The Wind from the East: French Intellectuals, the Cultural Revolution, and the Legacy of the 1960s*. Princeton: Princeton University Press, 2010.

Wong, Alvin K. "Postcoloniality Beyond China-Centrism: Queer Sinophone Transnationalism in Hong Kong Cinema." In *Keywords in Queer Sinophone Studies*, edited by Howard Chiang and Alvin K. Wong, 62–79. London: Routledge, 2020.

——. "Queering the Quality of Desire: Perverse Use-Value in Transnational Chinese Cultures." *Culture, Theory and Critique* 58, no. 2 (2017): 209–225.

——. "Queer Sinophone Studies as Anti-Capitalist Critique: Mapping Queer Kinship in the Works of Chen Ran and Wong Bik-wan." In *Queer Sinophone Cultures*, edited by Howard Chiang and Ari Larissa Heinrich, 109–129. London: Routledge, 2013.

——. "Queer Vernacularism: Minor Transnationalism Across Hong Kong and Singapore." *Cultural Dynamics* 32, nos. 1–2 (2020): 49–67.

——. "Transgenderism as a Heuristic Device: On the Cross-Historical and Transnational Adaptations of the *Legend of the White Snake*." In *Transgender China*, edited by Howard Chiang, 127–158. New York: Palgrave Macmillan, 2012.

Wong, Jin, dir. *Royal Tramp* 鹿鼎記. Hong Kong: Golden Harvest, 1992.

Wong Kar-wai, dir. *Happy Together*. Hong Kong: Jet Tone, 1997.

Wong, Lily. *Transpacific Attachments: Sex Work, Media Networks, and Affective Histories of Chineseness*. New York: Columbia University Press, 2018.

Wu, Chao-Jung. "Performing Hybridity: The Music and Visual Politics of Male Cross-Dressing Performance in Taiwan." In *Perverse Taiwan*, edited by Howard Chiang and Yin Wang, 131–160. London: Routledge, 2016.

——. "Performing Transgender Desire: Male Cross-Dressing Shows in Taiwan." In *Transgender China*, edited by Howard Chiang, 225–262. New York: Palgrave Macmillan, 2012.

Wu, Chia-rong. *Supernatural Sinophone Taiwan and Beyond*. Amehrst, NY: Cambria, 2016.

Wu, Chien-heng. "'Tiger's Leap Into the Past': Comparative Temporality and the Politics of Redemption in the Orphan of Asia." In *Comparatizing Taiwan*, edited by Shu-mei Shih and Ping-hui Liao, 33–58. London: Routledge, 2015.

Wu, Cuncun. *Homoerotic Sensibilities in Late Imperial China*. London: Routledge, 2012.

Wu, Cynthia. *Sticky Rice: A Politics of Intraracial Desire*. Philadelphia: Temple University Press, 2018.

Wu, Judy Tze-Chun. *Doctor Mom Chung of the Fair-Haired Bastards: The Life of a Wartime Celebrity*. Berkeley: University of California Press, 2005.

Wu Youru 吳有如 et al., ed. *Qingmuo fushihui:* Dianshizhai huabao *jingxuanji* 清末浮世繪：《點石齋畫報》精選集 [Late Qing Lithographs: Best collections of *Dianshizhai huabao*]. Taipei: Yuanliu, 2008.

Wu, Zhouliu. *Orphan of Asia*. Translated by Ioannis Mentzas. New York: Columbia University Press, 2006.

Xi Liu 細柳. "Xiandai renyao Shen Junru: Shanghai zhongshengxiang" 現代人妖沈俊如：上海眾生相 [Modern human prodigy Shen Junru: Public appearance in Shanghai]. *Yisiqi huabao* 一四七畫報 [One four seven pictorial] 12 (1947): 4–5.

Xi Yuan 西源. "Dadao danjiao de daibiaoren Mei Lanfang" 打倒旦角的代表人梅蘭芳 [Defeating Mei Lanfang, the representative dan]. *WXZB* 8, no. 353 (1929): 62–65.

Xie Peijuan 謝佩娟. "Taibei Xingongyuan tongzhi yundong: Qingyu zhuti de shehui shijian" 台北新公園同志運動：情慾主體的社會實踐 [Gay movement in Taipei New Park: The social practices of sexual subjectivity]. MA thesis, National Taiwan University, 1999.

"Xin Zhonghua minguo xingfa" 新中華民國刑法 [New penal code for the Republic of China]. *Zhonghua minguo xingfa xinjiu quanwen duizhao biao* 中華民國刑法新舊全文對照表 [Comparison chart of the old and new Republican penal codes]. Beiping: n.p., 1935.

Xu Xiangyun 徐湘芸, Wang Ruoying 王若穎, and Luo Wenyu 羅文妤. "Kuabuguo de 'lan': Xing/bie shehui zhong yincang de kuaxingbie zhe" 跨不過的「欄」——性／別社會中隱藏的跨性別者 [The border that cannot be crossed: The hidden transgender individuals in sexed/gendered society]. *Zhengda daxue bao* 政大大學報 [NCCU news], no. 1681 (June 21, 2018). https://unews.nccu.edu.tw/unews/跨不過的「欄」-性%EF%BC%8F別社會中隱藏的跨性別者/.

Yan, Yunxiang. *Private Life Under Socialism: Love, Intimacy, and Family Change in a Chinese Village, 1949–1999*. Stanford: Stanford University Press, 2003.

Yang, Chia-Ling. "Challenges to LGBTI Inclusive Education and Queer Activism in Taiwan." In *Queer Social Movements and Outreach Work in Schools: A Global Perspective*, edited by Dennis A. Francis, Jón Ingvar Kjaran, and Jukka Lehtonen, 52–92. Cham: Palgrave Macmillan, 2020.

Yang, Dominic Meng-Hsuan. *The Great Exodus from China: Trauma, Memory, and Identity in Modern Taiwan*. Cambridge: Cambridge University Press, 2020.

Yang Huinan 楊惠南. "Tongxin fanxing: Dangdai Taiwan fojiao tongzhi pingquan yundong" 童心梵行: 當代台灣佛教同志平權運動 [Childish heart, brahma behaviour: Contemporary Taiwanese Buddhist gay and lesbian equality movement]. *Dangdai* 當代 [Contemporary] 173 (2002): 30–51.

Yang, Jiao, dir. *Super Eunuch* 超能太監. Beijing: Seven Entertainment, Huayi Brothers, and Beijing Skylimit and Culture Media, 2016.

——, dir. *Super Eunuch 2: Golden Right Hand* 超能太監 2: 黃金右手. Beijing: Seven Entertainment, Huayi Brothers, and Beijing Skylimit and Culture Media, 2016.

Yang Jinyan 楊金嚴. "Taibei gongyuan gengming jiangli liangkuai beiwen" 台北公園更名 將立兩塊碑文 [Taipei Park renamed with two epitaphs]. *LHB*, March 16, 1995.

Yang Ruisong 楊瑞松. *Bingfu, huanghuo yu shuishi: "Xifang" shiye de zhongguo xingxiang yu jindai Zhongguo guozu lunshu xiangxiang* 病夫, 黃禍與睡獅: 「西方」視野的中國形象與近代中國國族論述想像 [Sick man, yellow peril, and sleeping lion: The images of China from the Western perspectives and the discourses and imagination of Chinese national identity]. Taipei: Chengchi University Press, 2010.

Yang Zhengguang 楊爭光. *Zhongguo zuihou yige taijian* 中國最後一個太監 [The last eunuch in China]. Beijing: Qunzhong chubanshe, 1991.

Yau Ching 游靜, ed. *As Normal as Possible: Negotiating Sexuality and Gender in Mainland China and Hong Kong*. Hong Kong: Hong Kong University Press, 2010.

——. *Lingqi luzao* 另起爐灶 [Starting another stove]. Hong Kong: Youth Literary Bookstore, 1996.

Ye, Shana. "The Love That Does Not Speak Its Name: Affect and Transnational Production of 'Queer China.'" PhD diss., University of Minnesota, 2017.

——. "A Reparative Return to 'Queer Socialism': Male Same-Sex Desire in the Cultural Revolution." In *Sexuality in China: Histories of Power and Pleasure*, edited by Howard Chiang, 142–162. Seattle: University of Washington Press, 2018.

Yee, Karen L. M. "*W v Registrar of Marriages*: From Transsexual Marriage to Same-Sex Marriage?" *Hong Kong Law Journal* 40, no. 3 (2010): 549–562.

Yeh, Jonathan Te-hsuan 葉德宣. "Cong jiating shouxun dao jingju wenxun: *Niezi* zhong fuxi guo/jia de shenti guixun dijing" 從家庭授勳到警局問訊:《孽子》中父系國／家的身體規訓地景 [From Familial decoration to police interrogation: Bodily discipline by the patrilineal nation/family in *Crystal Boys*]. *Chung-Wai Literary Monthly* 中外文學 30, no. 2 (2001): 124–154.

——. "Liangzhong luying/yin de fangfa: *Yongyuan de yinxueyan* he *Niezi*" 兩種露營/淫的方法: 永遠的《尹雪豔》和《孽子》 [Go camping: Gender crossing in *Yongyuan de yinxuanya* and *Niezi*]. *Chung-Wai Literary Monthly* 中外文學 26, no. 12 (1998): 67–89.

——. "Yinhun busan de jiating zhuyi chimei: due quanyi *Niezi* zhuwen de lunshu fenxi" 陰魂不散的家庭主義魑魅: 對詮釋《孽子》諸文的論述分析 [The haunting spectre of familialism: A discursive analysis of interpretations of *Niezi*]. *Chung-Wai Literary Monthly* 中外文學 24, no. 7 (1995): 66–88.

Yen, Ching-hwang. *A Social History of the Chinese in Singapore and Malaya, 1800–1911*. Singapore: Oxford University Press, 1986.

Ying Yi 影憶. "Fanchang shehui de chanwu" 反常社會的產物 [An abnormal product of society]. *WXZB* 8, no. 353 (1929): 66–72.

"Yinyang guaiqi renyao zhuangshen bangui xingqiang" 陰陽怪氣人妖 裝神扮鬼行搶 [Enigmatic human prodigy assumes supernatural status for robbery]. *MSRB*, August 7, 1957.

"Yinyangren Zeng Qiuhuang chuxing sannian jiuyue" 陰陽人曾秋皇 處刑三年九月 [The yinyang person Zeng Qiuhuang received a three-year-and-nine-month sentence]. *ZGSB*, September 14, 1957.

"Yiyiwang dajin quanan jiangyisong fayuan" 已一網打盡 全案將移送法院 [Completely under control: The entire case is now being delivered to the court for investigation]. *ZGSB*, November 14, 1955.

Yoneyama, Lisa. *Cold War Ruins: Transpacific Critiques of American Justice and Japanese War Crimes.* Durham: Duke University Press, 2016.

Young, Iris Marion. *Justice and the Politics of Difference.* Princeton: Princeton University Press, 1990.

——. "Polity and Group Difference: A Critique of the Ideal of Universal Citizenship." *Ethics* 99, no. 2 (1989): 250–274.

Yu Ke 雨殼. "Nanban nüzhuang de Mei Lanfang" 男扮女裝的梅蘭芳 [Female impersonating Mei Lanfang]. *WXZB* 8, no. 353 (1929): 82–84.

Yu, Ting-Fai. "Queer Migration Across the Sinophone World: Queer Chinese Malaysian Students' Educational Mobility to Taiwan." *Journal of Ethnic and Migration Studies.* www .tandfonline.com/doi/full/10.1080/1369183X.2020.1750946.

Yue, Audrey. "Queer Asian Cinema and Media Studies: From Hybridity to Critical Regionality." *Cinema Journal* 53, no. 2 (2014): 145–151.

——. "The Sinophone Cinema of Wong Kar-wai." In *A Companion to Wong Kar-wai*, edited by Martha P. Nochimson, 232–249. Malden, MA: Wiley-Blackwell, 2016.

——. "Trans-Singapore: Some Notes Toward Queer Asia as Method." *Inter-Asia Cultural Studies* 18, no. 1 (2017): 10–24.

Yue, Audrey, and Olivia Khoo. "From Diasporic Cinemas to Sinophone Cinemas: An Introduction." *Journal of Chinese Cinemas* 6, no. 1 (2012): 9–13.

——, eds. *Sinophone Cinemas.* New York: Palgrave Macmillan, 2014.

Yue, Audrey, and Helen Hok-Sze Leung. "Notes Towards the Queer Asian City: Singapore and Hong Kong." *Urban Studies* 54, no. 3 (2017): 747–764.

Yue, Audrey, and Jun Zubillaga-Pow, eds. *Queer Singapore: Illiberal Citizenship and Mediated Cultures.* Hong Kong: Hong Kong University Press, 2012.

"Yuejing yu chunü mo: Tao Sijin shengli shang yanjiu" 月經與處女膜：陶思瑾生理上研究 [Menstruation and the hymen: on Tao Sijin's physiology]. *Shibao* 時報 [Eastern times], June 9, 1932.

Yuxuan Aiji 魚玄阿璣 et al. "Taibei Tongwanjie zhuanti" 台北同玩節專題 [Feature articles on the Taipei lesbian and gay festival]. *Nü pengyou* 女朋友 [Girlfriend], no. 33 (2000): 6–23.

Zeitlin, Judith. *Historian of the Strange: Pu Songling and the Chinese Classical Tale.* Stanford: Stanford University Press, 1993.

"Zeng Qiuhuang yijie Yuanlin" 曾秋皇 移解員林 [Zeng Qiuhuang released in Yuanlin]. *LHB*, September 26, 1956.

Zhang, Everett Yuehong. *The Impotence Epidemic: Men's Medicine and Sexual Desire in Contemporary China*. Durham: Duke University Press, 2015.

——. "Rethinking Sexual Repression in Maoist China: Ideology, Structure, and the Ownership of the Body." *Body and Society* 11, no. 3 (2005): 1–25.

Zhang, Qing Fei. "Transgender Representation by the People's Daily Since 1949." *Sexuality and Culture: An Interdisciplinary Quarterly* 18, no. 1 (2014): 180–195.

Zhang, Qingfei. "Representation of Homoeroticism by the *People's Daily* Since 1949." *Sexuality and Culture* 18, no. 4 (2014): 1010–1024.

Zhang Renhao 張仁豪. "Renshi tongxinglian Taibei Tongwanjie zhoumuo dengchang" 認識同性戀 台北同玩節周末登場 [Getting to know homosexuality Taipei LGBT Civil Rights Movement Festival begins this weekend]. *LHB*, September 2, 2000.

——. "Tongxinglian jianian huahui biekai shengmian" 同性戀嘉年華會 別開生面 [Homosexual carnival breathes new life]. *LHB*, September 3, 2000.

Zhao, Dingxin. *The Power of Tiananmen: State-Society Relations and the 1989 Beijing Student Movement*. Chicago: University of Chicago Press, 2001.

Zheng Sheng 正聲, trans. "Zhongxinglun" 中性論 [The intermediate sex]. *Funü zazhi* 婦女雜誌 [Ladies journal] 6, no. 8 (1920): 1–14.

"Zhi renyao" 誌人妖 [Documenting renyao]. *Shishi baoguan wushen quannian huabao* 時事報館戊申全年畫報 [Current affairs annual pictorial] 30 (1909): *juan* 10.

Zhi Shui 止水. "Guanyu Tao Sijin Liu Mengying de guangan" 關於陶思瑾劉夢瑩的觀感 [A perspective on Tao Sijin and Liu Mengying]. *Doubao* 斗報 2, no. 8 (1932): 7–10.

Zhou Shoujuan 周瘦鵑. "Diandao xingbie zhi guainü qinan" 顛倒性別之怪女奇男 [Odd women and strange men of sexual inversion]. *Ziluolan* 紫羅蘭 [Violet] 4, no. 5 (1929): 1–6.

Zhu Rutong 朱汝曈. *Zhongguo xiandai wenxue liupai mantan* 中國現代文學流派漫談 [Modern Chinese literary schools]. Taipei: Showwe, 2010.

"Zhuoyao rongyi jingyaonan Zeng Qiuhuang nanyu anpai" 捉妖容易禁妖難 曾秋煌難於安排 [The prodigy is easy to catch but hard to keep: The difficulty of allocating Zeng Qiuhuang]. *LHB*, August 8, 1957.

Zondek, Bernhard. "Mass Excretion of Oestrogenic Hormone in the Urine of the Stallion." *Nature* 133 (1934): 209–210.

Zou, John. "Cross-Dressed Nation: Mei Lanfang and the Clothing of Modern Chinese Men." In *Embodied Modernities: Corporeality, Representation, and Chinese Cultures*, edited by Fran Martin and Ari Larissa Heinrich, 79–97. Honolulu: University of Hawai'i Press, 2006.

Zubillaga-Pow, Jun. "The Negative Dialectics of Homonationalism, or Singapore English Newspapers and Queer World-Making." In *Queer Singapore: Illiberal Citizenship and Mediated Cultures*, edited by Audrey Yue and Jun Zubillaga-Pow, 149–159. Hong Kong: Hong Kong University Press, 2012.

Index

human rights, 77, 160, 164, 182–184, 186, 193–194, 197, 202–204, 220, 289
humanhood, 11, 104, 119, 134
humanities, 14, 92; medical, 10–11, 138
Hu Shi, 110
Hung, Celina, 172
Hwang, David Henry, 157, 163–164, 274
hybridity, 112, 172, 279, 291
Hyderabad, 35–36
hysteric, 54, 56

identity (identitarian), 4, 6–7, 19, 20, 37, 43, 56–57, 71 73, 80–81, 84, 114, 129–130, 139–140, 144, 150–151, 153–155, 157–158, 162–163, 170, 174, 187–188, 195, 200, 204, 207, 211, 220, 225, 228
Ihlenfeld, Charles, 22, 230
impersonation, 31, 107, 110, 120, 123, 133, 143
incest, 98, 131
India, 6, 8, 33, 99, 103
Indian Ocean, 172
Indiana University, 26, 32
indigeneity, 74–76, 172
Indochina War, 79
inhumanism, 5, 9, 97–98, 100, 112, 114, 116, 119, 124, 135, 158, 170, 212
injection, 13, 23, 60–63
insanity plea, 44, 47, 54–56
inscription, 12, 167, 173, 212, 222
Institute of Sexual Science, 13
intercorporeal governance, 137–138, 156, 170
International Gay and Lesbian Human Rights Commission (OutRight Action International), 183
International Journal of Sexology, 33–34
intersectionality, 70, 76
Intersex, Transgender and Transsexual people Care Association, 205, 291

intersexuality, 26, 59, 61, 98, 108, 120, 129, 131, 183, 186, 205, 266–267, 291
Iran, 22, 42, 44, 56–57
isomerism, 13, 134–135
Israel, 8, 221
Italy, 36
Ittila'at, 45–46, 48

Jamaica, 39
Japan, 6, 35–37, 55, 68, 79, 82, 84, 100–102, 123, 135, 159, 163, 203, 210
Jin Yong, 145, 168
jingshen bing (psychiatric disorder), 53
jingshen shuairuo (deterioration of the mental condition), 52–54
Johannesburg, 37
Johns Hopkins University, 35, 37, 39
Johnson, Barbara, 167
Jorgensen, Christine, 30–31, 39, 58–59, 63, 128, 210, 267
Ju Guangzao, 124, 266
Juan, Gerardo, 37

Kang, Wenqing, 108–109
kathoey, 6
Kelliher, Diarmaid, 73
Kinsey, Alfred, 26, 29–30, 32–33
Kinsey Institute, 32
Kinsey reports, 22
Kinsey scale, 24, 61, 226
Kondo, Dorine, 157
Korean War, 79
Krafft-Ebing, Richard v., 25, 56, 226
Kristeva, Julia, 160
kuaxingbie (transgender), 185–186
ku'er (queer), 68, 173, 175, 204, 241, 291
Kwan, Stanley, 76–80

Lacan, Jacques, 139, 162, 275
Lahijan, 42, 44–45
Lai Shi, China's Last Eunuch, 141–144, 165

Pacific, 1–2, 9, 11–14, 58, 66, 68, 79, 93, 98, 164, 171–172, 174–175, 190, 211, 221

Padidarnazar, Mahin, 42–49, 52, 54–58, 63, 210, 232

Pai Hsien-yung, 111, 185

Palmie, Stephan, 172

Pan Guangdan, 56

Paris, 2, 159–161, 163, 169

Patel, Geeta, 69

Peking opera, 108–109, 121, 143–144, 160

Penang, 160

Pennsylvania State University, 35

People's Republic of China (PRC), 10, 13, 67–68, 71–77, 79–81, 86, 92, 100, 165, 168, 190–191, 196–197, 200, 202–203, 206–207, 248, 268

People's Voice Daily, 124, 129, 131

Peranakans, 172

performativity, 14, 223

Philippines, 37, 84, 250

physics, 32

Pillay, A. P., 33

pinkwashing, 8, 220

Pingtung County, 176–178

Pingtung District Court, 178

Portugal, 67

postcolonialism, 8–11, 69, 74–75, 79, 82–86, 92, 99, 101–103, 112, 127, 136–137, 172–174, 176, 187, 190, 200, 203, 206, 212, 257, 268, 279, 288

postsocialism, 71, 75–77, 79–80, 82, 247–248, 262

Pots Weekly, 183

power, 1, 4, 6–7, 11, 24, 65, 70, 73, 75–76, 92, 98–99, 101–102, 108, 118, 138–139, 144–145, 147–150, 155, 157, 159, 161, 164–165, 168, 172, 174, 189–190, 194, 198–200, 218, 244, 291

The Precious Sunflower Scripture, 144, 146

Prince, Virginia, 31

procreation, 171, 191–193, 196–197

prostitution, 98, 105, 108–109, 111, 116, 124, 126–127, 143, 159, 291

psychoanalysis, 26, 32, 56, 158, 227. *See also* Sigmund Freud

psychology, 23, 26, 37, 45, 47, 51–56, 107, 111, 120, 123, 192, 223

psychotherapy, 26

Pu Songling, 106

Puar, Jasbir, 8, 221, 289

Puccini, Giacomo, 158–159, 164, 274

Qianlong, 68

Qing dynasty, 68, 99, 106–107, 112, 135, 140–141, 143, 149, 155, 165, 168, 233, 241, 270, 276

qingyi (the virtuous lady), 128

Queer History Conference (QHC19), 1–2, 4, 7, 13, 93, 215

Queer'n Class (Gender/Sexuality Rights Association Taiwan), 183

race, 6, 49, 159, 162, 215, 216, 220

racism, 11, 169, 216, 288

Rancière, Jacques, 14

Reading (Pennsylvania), 33

Red House, 81

Red Rose, White Rose, 78

Rees v UK, 193–194

regionalism, 2, 7–8, 42, 56, 61, 63, 67, 69, 83, 103, 140, 152, 156–157, 161, 171, 173–175, 200–201, 203, 215, 239

Registrar of Marriages, 188, 190. *See also W v Registrar of Marriages*

Reign of Assassins, 148, 150–157, 165

renyao (human prodigy), 6, 10, 12, 97–137, 143, 170, 209, 212, 219, 256–257, 260

Republic of China, 73–74, 100, 102, 111, 133, 135, 205, 233–234 residual, 13, 187, 190–191, 197, 288

resistance, 2–3, 6, 11, 64, 66, 71, 73, 75, 84, 166, 172, 182, 200, 203, 205, 232, 253

rhetoric, 8, 11–12, 14, 54, 60, 77, 135, 155, 160, 168, 212

Ribeiro, Robert, 191, 193–194, 196–198

Rich, Adrienne, 21, 23–24

riots, 2, 64–65, 70, 160, 238

Rojas, Carlos, 86

Ross, Kristin, 160

Royal Tramp, 168

Rupp, Leila J., 42

sadism, 55–56

St. Louis, 39, 51

Sakai, Naoki, 82

Salamon, Gayle, 159

San Francisco, 1–2, 33, 65, 216

San Francisco State University, 1

Sang Chong, 108, 114

Sartre, Jean-Paul, 160

Schönberg, Claude-Michel, 159

science, 14, 23, 27–30, 32, 56–57, 61, 114, 118–120, 123–124, 165, 168, 194–195, 200, 223, 226, 229, 264; human, 274; medical, 98; metaphor, 13, 15; military, 149; quantitative, 13, 23; sexual, 11, 13, 22–24, 32–33, 39, 56, 114, 123, 226, 264; social, 92, 224;

scientism, 110, 261

Sears, Clare, 20

Sedgwick, Eve Kosofsky, 4–5, 42, 109, 154, 209, 242, 260

Sekandari, Pari, 47

separatism, 42–43, 61, 109

set theory, 60

sex change operation, 30–31, 36, 39, 199

Sex Change Operation Technical Management Standard, 209

Sex Orientation Scale (SOS), 22, 24–27, 30–31, 33, 35, 37, 41, 58, 61, 226, 230

sex reassignment, 10, 27, 35, 58–60, 129, 188, 199, 231, 237, 267, 290

sexology, 10, 13, 22–28, 32–34, 39, 41, 56–57, 61–62, 120–121, 123–124, 223, 226–228, 239, 249

Sexology, 39

sexual assault, 177

sexual inversion, 56–57, 121

shang feng baisu (public indecency), 133

Shanghai Life and Health Society, 56

Shanxi, 108

Sheffield and Horsham v UK, 194–195

Shelby County Criminal Court, 44

Shen Junru, 124, 265–266

shenjing shuairuo (neurasthenia), 52

Shih, Shu-mei, 10, 67–69, 74–75, 83, 87, 100–101, 145, 200, 219, 241

Sichuan, 124, 197

Sick Man of Asia, 140

Sikhs, 8

Singapore, 8, 58, 84, 171, 202, 220–221, 236, 250, 268, 281, 290

Sino-British Joint Declaration, 1

Sinocentrism, 66, 70, 164

Sinology, 91–92, 100–101, 254

Sinophilia, 160

Sinophone, 1, 9–14, 63–93, 98–100, 110–111, 128, 130, 134–135, 137–144, 147, 149, 152–153, 155–158, 164–177, 186, 190, 204–207, 211–212, 221–222, 231, 239, 241–242, 246, 248, 250, 252–253, 256–257, 261, 273, 275–276

Sinophone Studies, 68

Sinosphere, 200

The Smiling, Proud Wanderer, 145

Snediker, Michael, 171

socialism, 10, 71–72, 75, 77, 80, 91, 101, 176, 205, 248

sociology, 23, 32

titration, 12–13, 97, 99, 104, 118–119, 135, 170, 212, 256–257

Tokyo, 2, 36,

tomboy, 50, 244

Tong-Kwan Light House Presbyterian Church, 182

tongxing lian'ai (homosexuality), 54, 111, 262

tongzhi (comrade or LGBTQ), 70–73, 76–77, 81, 92, 111, 133, 173–176, 180–187, 204–205, 207, 243, 245, 262, 279–280, 282–283, 285–286, 291

Tongzhi Assistance Association, 182

Tongzhi Citizen Action Front, 182

Tongzhi Hotline Association, 176, 183–184, 186, 286

Tongzhi Spatial Action Front, 182

Toronto, 2

trans*, 20, 22, 58

transgender, 2, 4–14, 19–25, 28–33, 36, 41–43, 57–63, 66, 72, 93, 97–98, 100, 104, 109–110, 112, 118–119, 124, 135, 137–140, 144, 147, 153, 156–160, 162, 164, 167, 169–171, 173–176, 181, 183–190, 196, 198–201, 204–212, 215, 218–220, 222–223, 225, 237, 255, 257, 268, 270, 276, 285, 287–292

Transgender History, 6

transitivity, 20–21, 42–43, 61, 109, 172

transmogrification, 140–141, 143–145, 151–153, 163–165, 168

transnationalism, 8–9, 77, 83–84, 89, 239, 293. *See also* minor transnationalism

transness, 4–6, 9–13, 21–23, 42–43, 58, 61, 63, 65, 98, 118–119, 130, 135, 139, 156, 170, 172–174, 187, 189–190, 200, 204, 207, 209–212, 220–222, 237, 257

transphobia, 3, 5, 7, 9, 22, 91, 109, 170, 174, 190, 200–203, 207–209, 288

The Transsexual Phenomenon, 24, 33, 35, 229

transsexualism, 24, 26–28, 30–33, 35, 37, 41, 140, 192, 203, 226, 231, 270

Transsexualism and Sex Reassignment, 35

transtopia, 4–13, 19–24, 42–43, 57–58, 60, 62–63, 65, 98–99, 119, 130, 135, 137, 139, 141, 153, 164, 170, 172, 174–175, 187, 200, 204, 207–212, 218, 220, 222, 237

Transvestia, 31, 35

transvestism, 24–31, 33–35, 37, 116, 121, 123, 157, 159, 183, 186, 226, 229

Trouillot, Michel-Rolph, 172

True Sex, 6

Tsai, Henry, 148

TSQ, 6

Tsu, Jing, 67, 138

Tsui Hark, 138, 141, 145–149

Tsutsumi Taeko, 36

Tu, Wei-ming, 69

Turnabout, 35

two-spirit, 6, 219

Umbrella Movement, 13, 217

United Daily News, 124–125, 127, 129, 131

United Nations, 100

United States, 6, 8, 22, 32, 36–37, 39, 42, 56–59, 69, 83–84, 135, 202, 215, 228, 237, 256, 259, 267, 269, 277, 289

University of Minnesota, 39

University of Pennsylvania, 35

University of the Philippines, 37

Ushuaia, 88

utopia, 4, 24, 88, 161, 164, 171, 218

Valentine, David, 5

Vancouver, 2

GPSR Authorized Representative: Easy Access System Europe, Mustamäe tee
50, 10621 Tallinn, Estonia, gpsr.requests@easproject.com